Telecommunications Industry in India

Telecommunications Industry in India

State, Business and Labour in a Global Economy

Dilip Subramanian

Routledge
Taylor & Francis Group

LONDON AND NEW YORK

First published 2018
by Routledge
4 Park Square, Milton Park, Abingdon, Oxon OX14 4RN
605 Third Avenue, New York, NY 10017

First issued in paperback 2023

Routledge is an imprint of the Taylor & Francis Group, an informa business

Publisher's Note
The publisher has gone to great lengths to ensure the quality of
this reprint but points out that some imperfections in the
original copies may be apparent.

Print edition not for sale in South Asia (India, Sri Lanka, Nepal,
Bangladesh, Pakistan or Bhutan).

British Library Cataloguing in Publication Data
A catalogue record for this book is available from the British Library

Library of Congress Cataloging in Publication Data
A catalog record for this book has been requested

ISBN-13: 978-1-138-55253-1 (hbk)
ISBN-13: 978-1-03-265303-7 (pbk)
ISBN-13: 978-1-315-14822-9 (ebk)

DOI: 10.4324/9781315148229

Typeset in AGaramond
by Tulika Pint Communication Services, New Delhi 110 049

SOCIAL
SCIENCE
PRESS

Contents

Tables

Acknowledgements

L ike many academic books, this one too has its immediate roots in a doctoral dissertation I began in the late 1990s at the Ecole des Hautes Etudes en Sciences Sociales in Paris. But its antecedents go back much earlier, to the end of the 1970s in fact when I first became interested quite fortuitously in industrial labour. Totally uninspired both by the fare on offer and the teaching ethos in my undergraduate history course, I had dropped out of college early and after various twists and turns had ended up being hired as a 'research' assistant of sorts at a catholic left-oriented Non Governmental Organization (NGO) in Bangalore. It was here that I first enthusiastically absorbed the gospel of the proletariat's triumphant onward march to the terminus of revolution. However simplistic and dogmatic this version of marxism may have been, the vision of history it conjured up to my impressionable mind proved far more stirring, ennobling and action-filled than all that I had been taught hitherto.

My convictions were further strengthened after visiting the radical independent union leader Shankar Guha Niyogi (assassinated in 1991 by an unidentified hit man in the pay of local employers) at his base in the Chhattisgarh region. Niyogi's courage, integrity and commitment, not to mention his success in rapidly building a powerful organization among mine workers did not fail to leave a profound impression on me. This faith in the working classes' ability to shape the course of history–reinforced by my exchanges with local communist party militants–I carried over intact when I later became a journalist for a brief while in a regional English language newspaper in Bangalore where I episodically covered labour issues.

During the time I lived in the city two major strikes erupted, and I was fortunate to have followed both of them in their immediacy. Retrospectively, it was these two events that could be said to have influenced my subsequent decision to come to Europe and pursue the study of labour seriously. Both strikes were unprecedented in the history of the Bangalore labour movement, though not for the same reasons. The first strike was staged in the autumn of 1979 at a large modern private firm, MICO. The demands raised by workers were novel, revolving as they did exclusively around questions of work intensification, machine manning levels, and labour productivity. In the process, the conflict threw into full relief the distance that existed between a new and well-qualified workforce and a traditional union leadership whose experience of tackling traditional bread-and-butter grievances left it incapable of articulating and defending the strikers' positions. Once the strike ended, I wrote a longish piece (*sans* a single footnote, I must confess) in the journal, *Economic and Political Weekly* analysing the principal issues at stake. While I had heard about Harry Braverman's theses on the labour process, applying his findings to my own work would come only many years later when I actually got down to reading his pathbreaking book.

The second strike I witnessed broke out exactly a year later and involved the public sector on this occasion. Although the demands focussed on securing higher wages, this struggle too broke fresh ground by bringing together for the first time on a common platform unions and workers in all the five central government enterprises located in the city. Christened the 'parity strike', it turned out to be the longest and costliest conflict in the history of the public sector in India. The MICO strike had ended in a partial victory for the workers, this one, however, ended in a crushing defeat.

From the 1960s onwards, a large number of modern private engineering firms had struck roots in Bangalore. Nevertheless, the big state-owned firms continued to dominate the scene and imaginations.

The daily flow of buses marked HMT, HAL or ITI transporting workers to and from the factories provided a constant reminder of the numerical importance of these firms' workforces in the labouring landscape of the city and their contribution to its overall economy. This factor was no doubt what persuaded me to go out and study the conflict, especially once no quick end seemed in sight. So for much of the 77 days that it lasted, armed with an antiquated tape recorder I went and talked to a number of workers living in my neighbourhood about their experiences of the strike. I also conducted several interviews with the managements and union leadership of the five companies. In the end, the constraints inherent in commercial journalism saw to it that very little of the oral and archival material I had gathered got used satisfactorily.

Hopes of putting this material to more productive ends once I arrived in Europe in 1984 also collapsed when for a variety of reasons I was obliged to surrender my ambitions of returning to academics. Only in the mid-1990s was I finally able to translate my plans into reality. The study of the parity strike and the institutional arrangements underpinning the industrial relations system in the public sector constituted the basis of my masters degree dissertation. At the same time, it served as a springboard for my doctoral research in more than just a formal procedural sense. The detailed exploration of the strike, by unveiling and illuminating various aspects of the functioning of state-run undertakings, was what helped me to frame the central problematic of this book, namely the distinctive nature of the production regime of a public company. This monograph on ITI can therefore be seen at once as a continuation or extension of my earlier work and as marking a closure of my engagement with the public sector in Bangalore.

* * *

As with all intellectual undertakings, the making of this one too would not have been possible without incurring countless debts to various individuals and institutions. This book owes much to the guidance and stimulus of my dissertation supervisor Alain Dewerpe who has followed from the beginning my academic engagement with industrial labour in Bangalore with interest. His availability and readiness in responding to my many requests proved extremely reassuring.

In India, my greatest debt is of course to the management of ITI for having granted me permission to undertake this study. I would in particular like to thank the following executives at the personnel department of the main Bangalore factory as well as the corporate office for their assistance: S.K. Chatterjee, Shankar Prasad, Gnani Rao, U.V. Paradkar, C. Vasudevan and R. Venkatraman.

Several management officials, workers and union leaders gave generously of their time and shared their knowledge of the company with me in discussions and interviews. I cannot overemphasize my gratitude to them for their cooperation, and especially to Michael Fernandes, Vadiraj Hatwar, Irudayaraj, M.V. Srinivasa Rao, S.K. Rammanna and B.K. Sharma.

Jonathan Parry, Rayaprolu Nagaraj and Janaki Nair took the trouble to read large portions of the manuscript. To say that I have benefited immensely from their critical questions, valuable insights and helpful suggestions would be a colossal understatement. My intellectual debt to these three scholars will also be evident from the numerous references to their work scattered throughout this book. Other helpful readers were Bernard D'Mello, Chitra Joshi, Gérard Heuzé, Sushil Khanna, Evelyne Ribert, Bagaram Tulpule and an annonymous reviewer whose constructive comments I wish to thank.

My gratitude to Sabyasachi Bhattacharya for having travelled all the way to Paris in order to sit on my dissertation committee is only equalled by my debt to him for his assistance and encouragement in bringing out this book. Patrick Fridenson presided over the dissertation committee with his customary talent and his encyclopaedic knowledge and advice stood me in good stead. The other exaniners—Didier Demazière, Gérard Heuzé and Danièle Linhart—asked precisely the right hard questions, though I am unsure whether I have succeeded in fully answering all of them. The monthly seminars on managerial and labour practices organized by Yves Cohen at EHESS Paris, not only provided an unending source of inspiration and helped to sharpen my questions. It also brought me into contact with a much-needed intellectual community. Among the participants of the seminar, I wish in particular to acknowledge the assistance extended by Cedric Lomba, Pierre Fournier, Séverin Muller and Nicolas Hatzfeld.

I must express my thanks to Balaji Parthasarathy for having shared some of the material from his research with me. Grants from the Ecole des Hautes Etudes en Sciences Sociales and the Fondation de France, via the Association Histoire des Télécommunications et des Techniques de l'Information, partially supported the fieldwork on which this research is based. I am grateful to the library staff at the Centre for Indian and South Asian Studies in Paris, the Institute for Public Enterprises in Hyderabad, the Indian Institute of Management in Bangalore, the Indira Gandhi Institute for Research and Development in Bombay, and the Bureau of Public Enterprises in Delhi.

For responding graciously to my myriad and frequent demands over the years, I would like to thank Kimman Balakrishnan, Jérome Créel, Eudes Delafon, Denise Leulliette, Evelyne Ribert and Sujata Sriram. During the course of my fieldwork in India, I enjoyed the hospitality of family and friends at various places. In Bangalore, Janaki Nair and Madhava Prasad provided a home away from home as did Ayisha Abraham and Jitu Mayor as well as Manjunath and his family. In Delhi, I was always warmly welcomed by Dom, Kimman and Geetha Sunderam. My parents in Hyderabad, and my sister Sujata in Bombay took care to lighten the anxieties of field work. I am indebted to them for their encouragement. Duarte Barretto was responsible for getting me interested in labour during those formative years in Bangalore, Ivo Rodrigues did much to keep that interest alive and but for Dominique Cresson the eventful journey to Paris might never have materialised.

In an era of small marketable books and of mainstream publishers who believe that the 'public sector is past history' and 'labour does not sell', my publisher Esha Béteille deserves a special mention for having had the courage to accept a big book. Meenakshi Chawla possessed all the qualities that any writer could expect from a copy editor: meticulous, understanding and prompt.

This book which became an extra member of our household for many long years is dedicated to my wife Sophie and my daughter Doriane. To them I owe a special debt for their forbearance, understanding and unstinting support.

Introduction

For all but a small number of Indian public sector enterprises, the introduction of orthodox economic reforms in 1991 marked a watershed in their development. After ruling over the 'commanding heights' of the national economy for over four decades, they were expelled from these positions virtually overnight. In the case of companies which commanded monopolistic privileges, the transition from regulatory planning to economic liberalism signalled the end of their exclusive market power. For those which already faced limited amounts of competition from private Indian firms, they now also had to measure their forces against the might of foreign players authorised to penetrate the domestic market.

Unalerted to the shift in official policy orientations, state-owned undertakings were totally unprepared to cope with this abrupt and massive transformation of the business environment. The refusal of policy makers to allow for even a minimal adjustment phase which would have given these companies some breathing space to adopt steps enabling them to better withstand competition only served to accentuate their woes. Predictably, many of them sustained huge financial losses in the aftermath of economic liberalization, the loss of traditional captive markets translating into a severe decline in their activities which in turn hindered them from generating much needed investments to modernize their technological base and production infrastructure and rapidly downsize, all measures indispensable for their survival. In sum, public sector companies found themselves trapped in a vicious cycle where a demand crunch combined with a resource crunch to precipitate a crisis of unprecedented magnitude.

Much the same predicament characterizes Indian Telephone Industries (ITI), the company which is the object of this book. Independent India's first state-run enterprise, it was founded in 1948 in Bangalore. The company manufactures a wide range of telecommunications equipment over which it effectively enjoyed a monopoly until the advent of deregulation in 1991 (though some of the product segments in which it operated were thrown open to competition from 1984 itself). In the pre-reforms era, it supplied practically all its output to the Post & Telegraphs department (later rechristened Department of Telecommunications, or DoT), its principal customer as well as parent authority. In addition to the factory in Bangalore, ITI also controls five other production units in different parts of the country. While the compass of this book embraces these units as well, its focal point essentially bears on developments at Bangalore, the oldest and most important plant.

Employing essentially a male, semi-skilled workforce in 1991, ITI counted 32,215 non-officers and officers on its pay rolls, including 17,692 in Bangalore. A decade later, this number had shrunk by 30 per cent to touch 22,691 employees, a vivid illustration of the downturn in the company's fortunes. Badly destabilized by the decision of the DoT to diversify its supplier network and purchase equipment from multinational corporations such as Alcatel, Ericsson and Lucent, the company has seen both turnover and profits plummet. After suffering losses for three consecutive years during the mid-1990s, it has again been haemorrhaging cash from 2002 onwards. While it has endeavoured to cut costs, among other things by implementing an early retirement programme to shed manpower deemed surplus, these efforts have failed to deliver the expected results for a variety of structural reasons.

At the same time, the coming of deregulation has not coincided with a change in the company's status. Unlike certain other public undertakings which have undergone privatization, ITI still remains under state control via the DoT. The gains of state ownership undoubtedly outstrip the costs. But for the protective cover of what has been described as 'state paternalism' through the operation of soft budget constraints, it is very likely that the company would have collapsed by now.[1] Nevertheless, state ownership also signifies the continued absence of operational autonomy for the management with all strategic decision-making powers concentrated in the hands of DoT officials.

It is because the government owns a majority share holding in ITI that plans formulated by the management to close the loss-making unit of Rae Bareli, for instance, located in the parliamentary constituency of Sonia Gandhi, have never materialized. In other words, in the aftermath of economic reforms ITI has come to typify the hybrid status acquired by the Indian public sector, exposed to the high winds of competition and caught between the contradictory pressures and logics of bureaucratic imperatives and market forces, but denied the full benefits of either state regulation or market coordination.

The different phases in this evolution from a cyclically stable, strongly regulated, and protectionist configuration to an unstable, delicensed and market sensitive environment forms the backbone of this book. In tracing this evolution and its implications for ITI, I will be ranging over events that span a period of almost six decades, from the birth of the company till the present day with the reforms acting as a temporal divider. Like for most public sector companies, for ITI too there was unmistakeably a 'before' and an 'after' 1991, the two epochs polarizing to varying degrees workers and managers' recollection of events past and present. Any history of ITI must therefore be framed, in part at least, in terms of a rupture, the old rules of action no longer serving as a viable navigational mechanism to orient the company's decisions, even as we remain attentive to the underlying situational continuities that characterized the two periods. Many of the organizational problems which would plague the company following deregulation had their roots in fact in the earlier years and were already visible then. By superimposing new sets of constraints on older ones, competition by establishing a new operational framework merely exacerbated these problems. The entry of domestic and foreign private players with markedly different corporate cultures and modes of functioning, not to speak of their far superior access to technological and material resources, especially in the case of transnational

[1] Janos Kornai, 'The Soft Budget Constraint', *Kyklos*, Vol. 39, 1986, pp. 3–30.

corporations, has placed tremendous strain on the entire structure of ITI as it struggles to come to terms with the rollback of its monopoly power.

Paradoxically, while ITI's condition has slipped from bad to worse, the telecommunications sector overall has marched from strength to strength. The number of telephone lines per 100 habitants or telephone density which remained in single digits even as late as 1990 has jumped to 51 two decades later.[2] This achievement is only clouded by the fact that practically all the handsets and the infrastructural equipment required to operate the network are imported even as an empty order book at ITI condemns workers to idleness.

Two rather contrasting dynamics have structured the development of the telecommunications sector since Independence. Although policy makers deeming the provision of telephone services and the manufacture of telecommunications equipment as 'strategic' reserved both these segments exclusively for state investment, their subsequent actions flatly contradicted these ambitions. Because telephones were regarded essentially as a status symbol rather than a utility, both P&T and ITI were starved of adequate budgetary resources resulting in turn in interminable waiting lists for fresh connections and abysmal customer services, not to mention considerable loss of potential revenue for the state. From the early 1980s onwards, the situation gradually underwent a change once it was realized that telecommunications was a stimulus of economic prosperity. The onrush of liberalization which has seen private capital spearhead the growth of the industry has further confirmed this trend.

This said, the play of events in the post-reforms period has proved much kinder to Bharat Sanchar Nigam Limited (BSNL) and Mahanagar Telephone Nigam Limited (MTNL), the two erstwhile service arms of DoT, than it has to ITI. While the deregulation, first, of equipment manufacture and, then, of basic telephone services eliminated the monopolistic privileges of public enterprises in general, BSNL and MTNL have, for diverse reasons, coped far more successfully with the rigours of competition. If private companies, essentially foreign-based, have been able to establish a near complete stranglehold over the field of equipment production, the likelihood of a similar scenario materializing with respect

---

[2] Telecom Regulatory Authority Of India, Press Release No. 15/2010, 29 March 2010 (www. trai. gov.in).

to the provision of telephone services seems uncertain given that the two public firms continue to maintain a relatively firm foothold.

Thus, in the present context where the roles have been reversed and the stewardship of the national economy firmly thrust upon private enterprise, to choose to write a book charting the fortunes of a public sector company can appear as anachronistic. The consecration of a pro-market reform agenda has done more than just bury the paradigm of state-sponsored industrial development pursued by the country's ruling elites since 1947. One of the principal consequences of the turn to market liberalization has been to seal the triumph of the 'Delhi Consensus'. In so doing, it has furnished the advocates of this mantra within the bureaucracy, media and academia with the ideological legitimacy to dismiss the entire mechanism of regulatory planning as an abject failure. According to its detractors, since the country had made little tangible progress in the four odd decades after colonial rule ended in reducing poverty, improving the wealth and living conditions of its citizens, and, more generally, arriving at the standards and structures of a 'modern' nation, the institutional and normative complex established by policy makers to realize this transformative mission was flawed at its very heart.

This blanket indictment of state intervention embodied in neo-liberal strictures has, predictably enough, found an easy target in the public sector. After all, it had been assigned a vanguard role by political leaders and bureaucrats in accomplishing a wide range of development objectives. Few of these objectives were realized, however, it is once again argued, a premise which has served to justify the discredit heaped on state-owned undertakings. Public sector bashing had already become fashionable in official circles ever since Indira Gandhi returned to power in 1980.[3] Nevertheless, it required the advent of a deregulated business environment in the aftermath of economic reforms, and the attendant marginalization of state-run companies, for scholarly criticisms in particular to gain in

[3] Launching a ferocious assault on the failings of the public sector, the likes of which had never been witnessed in the past, the Sixth Plan, for instance, blamed the public sector's poor rates of return on investment and weak resource generating capacity as an important reason why the 'resource base of the Indian fiscal system (had) . . . considerably eroded . . .' *The Sixth Five Year Plan Report*, New Delhi, 1980, p. 237. See also *The Times of India*, 20 September 1980, and *The Hindu*, 12 May 1981, for the disparaging remarks made respectively by Indira Gandhi and the then Finance Minister R. Venkatraman, with respect to the performance of state-controlled undertakings.

vehemence. Eyesores from a past that needed to be effaced at the earliest, these companies came to symbolize a great deal of what had apparently gone wrong with the Indian economy during the pre-reforms era.

In the words of the noted economist Jagdish Bhagwati, the 'spreading stain of inefficient public enterprises' renders them beyond redemption.[4] Instead of continuing to pour good money after bad, the government would therefore be better advised to get rid of them by privatising them. Equally harsh in her judgement, Isher Ahluwalia writes that 'as for the expectation that the public sector would . . . make additional resources available for development, the disillusionment has been phenomenal'.[5] For these and other neo-liberal economists, the dismal performance of the public sector ranks high on the list of reasons as to why India in contradistinction to the achievements of Northeast Asian countries remained afflicted for several decades by low gross national product growth, the celebrated 'Hindu rate of economic growth'.

A weighty corpus of academic literature contends that state-owned undertakings far from fulfilling their original function of serving as catalysts of accelerated industrial development have not only been a terrible drain on the exchequer. Their purportedly dismal return on investments is also held up as one of the principal causes of the failure of the Indian state to mobilize adequate resources for improving facilities in vital areas such as education, public health care, and infrastructure provision. Invariably sheltered from the rigours of both domestic and foreign competition, public sector managements could afford to run their companies without taking into consideration either cost or quality

[4] Jagdish Bhagwati, *India in Transition. Freeing the Economy*, Oxford, 1993, p. 17, 64–71 (cit. p. 17).

[5] Isher J. Ahluwalia, 'New Economic Policies, Enterprises and Privatization in India', in R. Cassen and V. Joshi (eds.), *India: The Future of Economic Reform*, New Delhi, 1996, pp. 232–59 (cit. p. 240). For other critical evaluations of the public sector's performance, see, *inter alia*, I.J. Ahluwalia, *Industrial Growth in India: Stagnation Since the Mid-sixties*, New Delhi, 1985, especially chap. 5; I.J. Ahluwalia and I.M.D. Little (eds.), *India's Economic Reforms and Development. Essays for Manmohan Singh*, New Delhi, 1998; V. Joshi and I.M.D. Little, *India: Macroeconomics and Political Economy 1964-1991*, Washington D.C., 1994, especially chaps. 12 and 13; *idem, India's Economic Reforms, 1991–2001*, Oxford, 1996, pp. 3–7, 171–94; Rakesh Mohan, 'Public Sector Reforms and Issues in Privatization', in C. Oman (ed.), *Policy Reform in India*, Paris, 1996, pp. 55–97; Baldev Raj Nayar, *The Political Economy of India's Public Sector. Policy and Performance*, London, 1990.

factors. Unsuccessful in providing technological leadership to Indian industry at large, the profitability levels of these enterprises are also adjudged considerably lower than those of private firms. These shortcomings were compounded by direct state ownership which resulted in ill-advised and frequent political interference in the internal affairs of public enterprises. By contributing to the politicization of the spatial location of plants, the choice of technology, and employment and pricing policies, state intervention, so the argument ran, had translated into cost overruns, overmanning, the utilization of obsolescent or inappropriate equipment and so forth, and consequently impeded their efficient development.

Moreover, because public undertakings oversaw the 'commanding heights' of the organized industrial sector, low productivity and other inefficiencies in their functioning are seen as having generated bottlenecks in the operations of the private sector as well. The latter was deprived of important productive inputs such as steel, electricity, finance, and transport, because of which the pace of industrial growth slowed down altogether. The chronic dysfunctioning of the public sector thus accounted for both macro and micro-level deficiencies of the Indian economy, and contributed in no small measure to stoking the fires that ignited the fiscal crisis of 1991.

A repudiation of the neo-liberal critique as baseless would be absurd. That the overall performance of the public sector has failed to live up to expectations, and that mismanagement of resources and inefficiencies of all kinds have plagued the functioning of several individual companies, are points on which all scholars concur. The numerous enquiries conducted by official bodies into the workings of state-owned enterprises have revealed the extent to which government policy regulations, political and bureaucratic interference, as well as managerial shortcomings have combined to take a steep toll on the health of these companies.[6]

But is the overall picture as black and mediocre as its detractors portray

---

[6] State-owned enterprises tend to be a convenient target for scholars, and the public in general, to take pot shots at because their functioning receives wide exposure given the nature of their ownership ties. Organizational inefficiencies, laid bare by countless fact-finding bodies, are therefore readily available for critics to dissect. This is in sharp contrast to the private sector where the strict codes of secrecy, normally observed by top management with regard to operational issues, means that problems become visible only in moments of crisis.

it to be? R. Nagaraj, for one, has argued that when analysing the results of the public sector it is necessary to distinguish between administrative departments, departmental undertakings which are owned and run directly by public authorities, such as electricity boards, road transport corporations, public works departments, and railways, and finally, non-departmental enterprises where the central or state governments control equity in excess of 51 per cent. Once this break-down is established, the arguments of the neo-liberal school tend to lose some of their force.

For as Nagaraj has demonstrated in a series of rigorously researched essays, notwithstanding received wisdom, the question of the public sector failing to generate sufficient surpluses in order to finance public investment, especially during the crucial decade of the 1980s, has more to do with the growing expenditure of, and subsidies granted to, administrative departments than the declining performance of non-departmental enterprises. On the contrary, even after excluding the contribution of public sector financial houses and the petroleum industry, state undertakings were successful in posting a sharp increase in profitability throughout the 1980s. What is more, the stronger results reflected improvements in operational efficiencies, notably more optimal allocation and handling of resources, combined with higher production and capacity utilization rates.[7] Nagaraj's findings thus cast considerable doubt on the validity of some of the key theses posited by the neo-liberal school.

The neo-liberal charge against the public sector intersects with a second and more potent criticism, levelled this time at state ownership of industry. From this perspective, state control is viewed as economically irrational or undesirable under all circumstances because it invariably leads to malfunctioning organizations and wasted resources. Such a proposition is grounded not in analytical fact but in ideological doctrine. There is no reason to suppose why private ownership is innately and exclusively

[7] R. Nagaraj, 'Further Evidence and towards an Explanation and Issues', *Economic and Political Weekly*, Vol. XXV, No. 41, 13 October 1990, pp. 2313–32 (hereafter *EPW*); *idem*, 'Public Sector Performance in Eighties; Some Tentative Findings', *EPW*, Vol. XXVI, No. 50, 14 December 1991, pp. 2877–83; *idem*, 'Macroeconomic Impact of Public Sector Enterprises: Some Further Evidence', *EPW*, Vol. XXVIII, Nos. 3–4, 16–23 January 1993, pp. 105–09. Joshi and Little acknowledge that it is the government administration that has been responsible for the deterioration of public finances. But according to them, the improvement in the savings of public enterprises in the 1980s did not stem from an improvement in profitability. *Macroeconomics and Political Economy*, pp. 20–1, 322–9.

blessed with all the competences indispensable to the efficient conduct of a business enterprise.[8] If ever supplementary evidence of the fallibility of private management was required it has been provided in full by such spectacular corporate debacles as Enron, WorldCom and Global Crossing. What conditions organizational efficiency is not so much ownership structure as the 'Washington/Delhi consensus' would like us to believe, but market structure, i.e., the nature and degree of competition which prevails in a given sector of industry. After all, private monopolies and/ or oligopolies have been no less immune to bankruptcy owing to poor management than have public monopolies, though it must be said that the tax payer has more often than not prevented the latter from going under.

The starting postulate that *dirigisme* makes bad economic sense also perhaps explains why neo-liberal economists have striven to present the failure of policy elites to transform India into an industrial powerhouse in absolute as opposed to relative terms. But it is clear that this failure was only a relative one. Given the limited investment capabilities of Indian big business on the eve of Independence, direct state intervention in the capital accumulation process was a *sine qua non* for creating a modern industrial infrastructure designed to lessen India's dependence on developed countries for capital goods. In this task of transforming a backward and underdeveloped economy, the heaviest burden by far was borne by the public sector. That the state alone commanded the means to mobilize the massive resources required for this purpose was recognized from the outset by the capitalist class, a number of whose most eminent representatives were signatories to the famous Bombay Plan of 1944.[9]

In view of its distributive failures and irrationalities, the market, by itself, was 'not perceived as sufficient to meet the aspirations of a latecomer to industrialization'.[10] As Sudipta Kaviraj has remarked, the Nehruvian

---

[8] On this point, see Bruce Greenwald and J. E. Stiglitz, 'Externalities in Economies with Imperfect Information and Incomplete Markets', *Quarterly Journal of Economics*, May 1986, Vol. 101, No. 2, pp. 229–64.

[9] For a discussion of the Bombay Plan, see notably Vivek Chibber, *Locked in Place. State Building and Late Industrialization in India*, New Delhi, 2003, pp. 88–98; and Aditya Mukherjee, 'Indian Capitalist Class and Congress on National Planning and Public Sector 1930–1947', in K.N. Pannikar (ed.), *National and Left Movements in India*, New Delhi, 1980, pp. 45–79.

[10] Deepak Nayyar, 'Economic Development and Political Democracy. Interaction

developmental projet was an 'internally consistent project which sought to pursue the rather discordant objectives of capitalist growth and social equity [in] the particularly unpropitious conditions of recent decolonisation'.[11] True, one could find much to fault with about the way priorities were determined, resources allocated, and technology and locational choices made, the combined effect of which, doubtless, was to significantly push up costs and squander scarce investment resources. But it is impossible to escape the fact that without concerted public action, the twin objectives of widening and deepening the industrial base, and narrowing the technology gap separating India and the advanced economies without weakening national sovereignty would never have been realized.

Regardless of the reality of the performance of public enterprises in the pre-reforms period, what is indisputable today is that they no longer occupy the dominant place they once did in the national economy. The goal fixed by state officials when orchestrating the transition to market-driven capitalism has thus been attained. A wave of corporate-friendly measures adopted by successive post-reform governments has resulted in steadily expanding the frontiers of the private sector to a point where its share of total gross capital formation exceeds that of the public sector. To seize the full measure of this policy reorientation, it is worth recalling that in 1990–91 the private sector's share of total gross capital formation stood at 17.2 per cent as compared to 38.8 per cent for the public sector. In 2004–05, the former's contribution had risen to almost 29 per cent while that of the public sector had shrunk to 25.3 per cent.[12]

This trend is also bound to persist in the years to come given that political leaders and bureaucrats have firmly established the private sector as the principal vehicle of economic growth. Nevertheless, the importance of public enterprises remains unsurpassed on the employment front. Although deregulation has caused job losses, the public sector still employs twice as many people with permanent jobs as does the private

of Economics and Politics in Independent India', *EPW*, Vol. XXXIII, No. 49, 5 December 1998, pp. 3121–31 (cit. p. 3123).

[11] Sudipta Kaviraj, 'The Modern State in India', in M. Doornbos and S. Kaviraj (eds.), *Dynamics of State Formation–India and Europe Compared*, New Delhi, 1997, pp. 225–50 (cit. p. 236).

[12] Source: Reserve Bank of India. (*http://www.rbi.org.in/scripts/PublicationsView. aspx?id=8563*; site accessed on 22 January 2009.)

sector.[13] Trade union opposition in slowing down the pace of privatizations in India must not be minimized. A more crucial reason why the disinvestment programme has made so little headway, much to the chagrin of the neo-liberal camp, however, has to do with the realization on the part of all governments that their legitimacy and chances of electoral success rests, at least in some measure, in preserving public sector jobs given the complete absence of a social security net.

Irredeemable in neo-liberal eyes, and increasingly marginalized in the wake of the demise of *dirigisme*, the current turn of events thus neither bodes well for the long-run prospects of the public sector, nor is conducive to persuading scholars to take it up for study.[14] This is not to imply that it was a hotly-disputed topic of research in the past. As academic fashions went, state-owned enterprises even during their heyday stood relatively low on the hierarchy of priorities. The total indifference exhibited by historians and sociologists/social anthropologists bears out this point:[15] practitioners from neither discipline have ever considered it worth their while to explore the internal workings of these enterprises in any depth.[16]

[13] ibid. In 2004–05, employment levels in the private sector stood at 8.45 million people as against 18.01 million in the public sector. However, the period from 1991–92 to 2004–05 saw the number of jobs in the latter drop by 6.2 per cent.

[14] A sampling of a few titles devoted to Indian industry in 2008 eloquently reflects current intellectual and publishing preferences and priorities. See, for example, Jagdish Bhagwati and Charles Calomiris (eds.), *Sustaining India's Growth Miracle*, New York, 2008; Harish Damodaran, *India's New Capitalists: Caste, Business and Industry in a Modern Nation*, New York, 2008; Amar Nayak, *Multinationals in India: FDI and Complementation Strategy in a Developing Country*, New York, 2008; William Nobrega and Ashish Sinha, *Riding the Indian Tiger: Understanding India—The World's Fastest Growing Market*, New Jersey, 2008.

[15] Dwijendra Tripathi writes that despite its 'undeniable importance', the public sector has 'remained almost unnoticed by historians'. Unfortunately, even in his own admirable summary of the evolution of Indian business from colonial times the public sector goes by and large 'unnoticed'. There is not even a single reference to ITI, for instance. *The Oxford History of Indian Business*, New Delhi, 2004, p. 5 (cit.), 313–19.

[16] As far as sociologists and social anthropologists are concerned, Jonathan Parry's pathbreaking series of essays on state-owned Bhilai Steel Plant constitute virtually the sole exception to this remark. See, *inter alia*, 'Lords of Labour: Working and Shirking in Bhilai', in J. Parry et al (eds.), *The Worlds of Indian Industrial Labour*, New Delhi, 1999, pp. 107–40; 'Two Cheers for Reservation: The Satnamis and the Steel Plant', in R. Guha and J. Parry, (eds.) *Institutions and Inequalities: Essays for André Béteille*, New Delhi, 1999, pp. 128–69; and '"Sociological Marxism" in Central India: Polanyi, Gramsci and the Case of the Unions', in C. Hann and K. Hart (eds.) *Market and Society. The*

The absence of publicly accessible sources and archival material could probably explain business and labour historians' absorption with the colonial period, and its corollary, the failure of the public sector to arouse their interest. Nevertheless, one consequence of the continued emphasis on those trusted staples of historiography (cotton, jute, mining, plantations, banking, etc.) is that the most modern and capital intensive sectors of industry, the principal engines of growth which arose after Independence, have been entirely shunned.[17]

In the case of sociology, the first generation of scholars can take much of the credit for the pioneering studies conducted into the lives and experiences of modern factory workers, practically all of whom, though, were employed in the private sector. More recent sociological research on wage earners has tended to address either the new information economy or the unorganized sector. If the spectacular growth of the information technology industry in the post-1991 era accounts for the attention it is receiving, in the case of the informal sector the reason probably has to do with its earlier neglect. But if such enquiry is to be at the expense of research on the public sector, and more generally large scale industry, on the (politically correct?) grounds that workers here represent a 'labour aristocracy', then our understanding of Indian labour as a whole will be poorer if only because it will obscure the circular flow of exchanges binding the informal and the formal sectors.

With the human sciences turning its back on the public sector, most of our knowledge of its functioning has been derived in the main from economists whose work predictably reflects the presuppositions of their discipline. While these macro and micro-level analyses shed valuable light on the financial performance of state firms, levels of capacity utilization, transfer of technology agreements and so forth, the social organization of these companies merits absolutely no attention.[18] Besides, these

Great Transformation Today, Cambridge, 2009, pp. 175–202. Although public sector workers feature in Mark Holmström's study of the Bangalore labour force, they do not occupy centre stage. *South Indian Factory Workers. Their Life and their World*, Cambridge, 1976.

[17] For a stock taking exercise of the development and state of labour research in India, see Sabyasachi Bhattacharya, 'Introduction', in R.P. Behal and M. van der Linden (eds.), *Coolies, Capital and Colonialism: Studies in Indian Labour History*, (*International Review of Social History*), Vol. 51, Supplement 14, December 2006, pp. 7–19.

[18] A good example of the industrial economic approach, highly reliant on various

analyses often tend to concentrate on specific aspects of a company's operations with the result that even from the economic standpoint we lack comprehensive studies framing the entire picture. So this historical monograph on Indian Telephone Industries constitutes the first full-length study of a state-owned firm. To understand the dynamics of the process of industrialization in the post-Independence period until the onrush of liberalization, to take stock of both the successes and failures, it is essential, I believe, to study the public sector.[19] As I have already mentioned above, empowered to function as the industrial arm of the state, it played a strategic role in overseeing the transformation of the country from a backward, predominantly agrarian society to one boasting of a relatively modern and diversified economy. To belittle this achievement would amount to travestying history.

Moreover, Bangalore's renaissance as the icon of India's burgeoning information technology revolution should not obscure the fact that it was (and still is) an important centre of the traditional 'bricks-and-mortar' economy at the forefront of which stood quite a few large public enterprises besides ITI. If the city has come to be indelibly associated the world over with call centres and software programming, it also remains home to thousands of blue collar workers whose worlds could not be further removed from those peopling the 'virtual' economy. To rescue their past and present from the 'enormous condescension of posterity', to borrow E.P. Thompson's memorable phrase, is also one reason for this book.[20]

The significance of the public sector cannot, however, be captured exclusively through the calculus of the economy. It did more than just provide the wherewithal to ensure India had the means to build infrastructural facilities and produce a wide range of capital and other goods. It also paved the way for the emergence of a modern labour force

---

formal models for its explanatory effect and from where all traces of the social have been expunged can be found in Subir Gokarn et al. (eds.), *The Structure of Indian Industry*, New Delhi, 2004. Nichols also alerts us to economists' disinterest in training their lens on the impact of specific management activities on firm behaviour and performance. Theo Nichols, *The British Worker Question: A New Look at Workers and Productivity in Manufacturing*, London, 1986, p. 21, 37.

[19] See also the recent essay by Ramachandra Guha on the intellectual gains to be had for historians by actively engaging with contemporary post–1947 themes. 'The Challenge of Contemporary History', *EPW*, Vol. 43, Nos. 26–27, 28 June 2008, pp. 192–200.

[20] E.P. Thompson, *The Making of the English Working Class*, New York, 1963, p. 12.

defined by decent wages, generous welfare benefits, good working conditions, union representation, and the respect of all statutory rights specific to workers. Whether or not state firms could have afforded the economic costs of such benevolence had they been constrained to evolve in a competitive environment, though, remains a moot point.[21] Treating its employees equitably and humanely served to propagate the message that the public sector contributed just as much to the economic advancement of the nation as to its social uplift, and therefore was legitimately entitled to rule over the 'commanding heights' of the Indian economy. In other words, the responsibility of state-sector firms was not just to produce public goods, but also a new kind of worker, guaranteed of material well-being and security, and, consequently, better able to serve the nation.

To the extent that these workers occupied the most desired positions on the blue collar job market we are justified in categorising them as a 'labour aristocracy'. Ever since it was first formulated by Engels and subsequently theorized by Lenin, this term has invariably been employed in a disparaging and denunciatory sense, regardless of the socio-historical context, to connote class collaborative and economistic behaviour.[22] Because the self-interests of the best-paid sections of the labour force lead them first and foremost to defend and advance their own status entitlements, they have supposedly become, on the one hand, politically conservative or quiescent and, on the other, totally alienated from the rest of the working classes whose life worlds they evidently do not share.

The Indian variant of the argument both diverges and draws inspiration from the Leninist thesis. First, it holds to the view that the

---

[21] Marxist narratives, reframing the original Leninist analysis, attribute the ability of employers to 'bribe', to use Lenin's own words, their workforces by distributing high salaries and other extra-wage advantages essentially to the exercise of monopoly power and the 'super profits' this situation generates. They overlook other causal variables, however, such as labour productivity levels and the capital intensity of production which tend to be equally important in explaining specific forms of capital-labour relations. V.I. Lenin, *Imperialism: The Highest Stage of Capitalism. A Popular Outline*, London, 1996, pp. 6–9; Ernst Mandel, *Late Capitalism*, London, 1975, chap. 3; Paul Sweezy and Paul Baran, *Monopoly Capital*, New York, 1966.

[22] Karl Marx and Frederick Engels, *Selected Correspondence*, Moscow, 1982, p. 103, 130 and *passim*. A more contemporary interpretation of the labour aristocracy thesis can be found in John Foster, *Class Struggle and the Industrial Revolution. Early Industrial Capitalism in Three English Towns*, London, 1974, pp. 203–04, 223–4 and *passim*.

boundaries distinguishing the lower ranks of the middle class and the upper ranks of the working class, are either rapidly dissolving or have altogether dissolved.[23] As a result, the latter, by virtue of their incomes, life-styles and aspirations, are 'now overwhelmingly "middle class"'.[24] Second, these accounts certainly eschew both Lenin's polemical tone and his damning indictment branding this 'stratum of bourgeoisified workers' as 'the labour lieutenants of the capitalist class'.[25] Nevertheless, they contend that comfortably ensconced in the 'citadel'[26] of permanent employment, the labour aristocrats have seldom been inclined to manifest any signs of solidarity with their weaker brethren.[27] To talk of a unified working class bound by shared ties of mutuality and class dispositions is therefore meaningless.

What is more, the refusal on the part of worker elites and their representative organs, resolutely wedded to reformist doctrines and bureaucratic unionism (reliance on grievance procedures, routine collective bargaining, and internal labour markets) to forge a solidary movement with the labouring poor is believed to have proved no less detrimental for one than for the other. Struggles waged in isolation were invariably doomed to defeat—if this bitter lesson needed no repetition for informal sector workers, it was one that organized labour was also painfully learning, powerless in the face of the fierce ongoing offensive launched by employers with the complicity of state authorities to realize their objectives of labour flexibility.[28]

---

[23] André Béteille, 'Hierarchical and Competitive Inequality', in *idem, Equality and Universality. Essays in Social and Political Theory*, New Delhi, 2002, pp. 181–203; Jan Breman, 'A Dualistic Labour System? A Critique of the "Informal Sector" Concept', *EPW*, Vol. XI, No. 50, 11 December 1976, pp. 1939–44; *idem*, 'The Formal Sector: An Introductory Review', in Parry et al., *The Worlds of Indian Industrial Labour*, pp. 1–41; Holmström, *South Indian Workers*, pp. 137–8; Jonathan Parry, 'The "Embourgeoisement" of a "Proletarian Vanguard"?', Draft Paper. I am deeply grateful to the author for permitting me to cite from this paper.

[24] Parry, 'Proletarian Vanguard?'.

[25] Lenin, *Imperialism*, p. 9.

[26] The much-used citadel metaphor, of course, comes from Holmström, *South Indian Factory Workers*.

[27] Arvind Das, 'Epilogue', in Jan Breman and Arvind Das, *Down and Out. Labouring Under Global Capitalism*, New Delhi, 2000, p. 153. One is tempted to ask how often university professors, including those specializing in labour studies, actively take up the cause of their less advantaged colleagues, especially in matters such as tenure.

[28] Jan Breman, *The Making and Unmaking of an Industrial Working Class. Sliding*

Referring to the core workforce at the state-owned Bhilai steel plant Jonathan Parry writes that it has become '*so* "aristocratic" that it makes no sense to see [it] as proletarian with significant interests in common with those locally known as the "labour class"'.[29] The growing appeal exerted by reactionary ideologies be it Hindutva or anti-Dalitism over this upper stratum of the working class is likely to have further reinforced its image as a politically retrograde force. But militant Hindu nationalism has won followers even among the urban Dalit working poor (and tribals).[30] So worldviews and the actions they produce cannot be reduced to an exclusively materialistic referential. Nor is it possible to apprehend the content of working class politics, or any class politics for that matter via a mechanical linkage to wage differentials. One could also argue that each segment of the working class is always an aristocracy in the eyes of those ranked below it in the social ladder, its relative privileges and entitlements avidly coveted by non-beneficiaries.[31]

Down the Labour Hierarchy in Ahmedabad, India, New Delhi, 2004, pp. 284–5. Unwilling perhaps to cast the object of his enquiry in a negative light, the author, however, cannot decide whether textile mill hands in their glory days formed or not a privileged minority. On the one hand, he produces considerable evidence to demonstrate that households 'living on a mill wage could afford to take a more relaxed approach to the cares of daily life' compared to their less fortunate neighbours (p. 124); on the other, he claims that the 'income enjoyed by mill workers in *no way* testified to an aristocratic lifestyle' (p. 247, emphasis added). Elsewhere, he advances the specious argument that the 'rigorous discipline' (p. 119) enforced on these workers freed them from the qualifier labour aristocracy without explaining the correlation between the absence of disciplinary constraints and the formation of such an aristocracy.

[29] Parry, 'Proletarian Vanguard?'. Emphasis in original. John Harris too concurs with the view that the distinction between 'permanent wage workers in large enterprises and the working poor *may be* a very important one with serious political ramifications'. He refrains, though, from spelling out the implications of these 'ramifications'. 'The Working Poor and the Labour Aristocracy in a South Indian City: A Descriptive and Analytical Account', *Modern Asian Studies*, Vol. 20, No. 2, 1986, pp. 231–83 (cit. p. 235; emphasis in original).

[30] Vijay Prashad, *Untouchable Freedom: A Social History of a Dalit Community*, New Delhi, 2001, p. x, xi, xiii-v and *passim*. On the involvement of tribal communities in the 2002 Gujarat riots see, *inter alia* Asghar Ali Engineer, 'Gujarat Riots in the Light of the History of Communal Violence', *EPW*, Vol. 37 No. 50, 14 December 2002, pp. 5047–54; Lobo Lancy, 'Adivasis, Hindutva and Post-Godhra Riots in Gujarat', *EPW*, Vol. 37, No. 48, 30 November 2002, pp. 4844–9.

[31] Based on their personal experiences, Richard Hoggart and Robert Roberts' perceptive analyses of working class communities have allowed us to understand just

In much the same vein, whatever the truth underlying the 'embourgeoisement thesis' we must not lose sight of the relational dimension structuring class. The manner in which groups perceive each other both within and across class boundaries is instrumental in framing a sense of collective identity. As John Goldthorpe and David Lockwood have noted in their well known study of the British working class, any discussion of the notion of embourgeoisement must distinguish between its three strands: economic, normative and relational.[32] Hence it is one thing to conclude that the behaviour and self-representation of public sector workers defined them as middle class; it is quite another to posit that the other middle classes' self-representation extended to including the former group, let alone to accepting them on equal terms. To claim that the mappings of the 'middle' middle classes and the upper middle classes would have found no place for the public sector workers hardly amounts to an extravagant proposition, but one is inclined to think that even the lower middle classes, especially its white collar government bureaucracy fringes, held an identical perspective. This, I believe, has to do with the traditional disdain for manual labour informing Indian society. True, state enterprises mobilized a vast phalanx of white collar employees. Nevertheless, they had to rub shoulders daily with their blue collar counterparts and their workday was ruled by the factory clock—two differentiating elements which might have contributed to lowering their status in the eyes of the lower middle classes.

Stating this is not to imply the labour aristocracy thesis, at least its Indian *avatar*, is devoid of explanatory value. In the Indian context, it is undeniable that state legislation and policy initiatives have had the effect of polarizing the labour force into two strata defined by sharply contradictory interests: on the one side, a large toiling mass employed

---

how important, and varied, expressions of status distinctions were for families in setting themselves apart from their neighbours. Hoggart, *The Uses of Literacy. Aspects of Working Class Life with Special Reference to Publications and Entertainments*, Harmondsworth, 1992, pp. 60–90; *idem, 33 Newport Street. Autobiographie d'un intellectuel issu des classes populaires anglaises*, Paris, 1991, pp. 40–1, 55 and *passim*; Roberts, *The Classic Slum. Salford Life in the First Quarter of the Century*, Harmondsworth, 1971, pp. 13–25.

[32] Among the several criticisms levelled by the two authors at the embourgeoisement thesis in the context of the British working class, one of them pertains precisely to the absence of evidence to show that workers are treated as social equals by the middle classes. John Goldthorpe and David Lockwood, *The Affluent Worker in the Class Structure*, Cambridge, 1972, p. 25.

pre-eminently in the informal sector and characterized by significant differences in wages, hours and conditions of work, job security, labour rights, union coverage and so forth; on the other, a small privileged enclave holding well remunerated permanent jobs essentially, but not exclusively, in large public enterprises. The importance of job security in moulding working class status and political attitudes should not be minimized.[33] Virtual lifelong tenure, by conjuring the spectre of joblessness, long regarded universally as the defining attribute of a proletarian condition, is arguably the factor that has contributed most to constituting public sector personnel as a group with distinct interests of its own.

Acquiring a foothold in state firms may in some instances have been facilitated by the possession of the right educational credentials and skill sets. But other criterion as diverse as clientelisme, luck, corruption, entitlements for sons-of-the-soil and the like could often weigh just as heavily. In other words, the structural division of the working class could not be legitimized by invoking meritocratic principles anchored in objectively quantifiable norms to validate individual competencies. Moreover, it will not do to measure the gains of an established position in state enterprises in purely monetary terms, namely the size of the pay packet plus fringe benefits, though neither of these are in any way negligible. (By the early 1990s, workers at the Bangalore plant of ITI earned a monthly wage ranging from Rs 9,000 to Rs 12,000.) In a country where government employment symbolized the greatest imaginable good, substantial supplementary economic and symbolic benefits also accrued to public sector workers in the larger social sphere. Not only were young workers in a position to leverage their status to command higher dowries on the matrimonial market than most of their counterparts in the private sector, so were middle-aged workers when it came to finding brides for their male offspring, even when unemployed.[34]

---

[33] Robert Castel has drawn attention to how in the post-1945 West a combination of state and employer regulation began guaranteeing a measure of employment security. Such contractual provisions by rendering wage labour more reliable and stable, also turned it in to a relatively attractive means of gaining one's livelihood. *Les métamorphoses de la question sociale*, Paris, 1995, pp. 523–41.

[34] Although some of my informants were convinced that being employed in the public sector earned them greater consideration and respect than private sector workers and even businessmen when dealing with city functionaries and the police, others worried about the declining prestige associated with their positions in the wake of economic liberalization.

A secure state enterprise job also signified more than a job. It signified the dignity of a career extending into the future, a working life whose potentialities could be charted in the form of 'a line leading somewhere [and] not just a list of things that happened' to an individual.[35] This process of 'life-narrative thinking' where it became possible to plan strategically, to realistically orient one's expectations to a future point in time was enabled just as much by the stability derived from public sector employment as by the perspective of mobility.[36] Institutional arrangements, such as internal labour markets revolving around the principle of automatic seniority-based promotions assured workers of steady upward progression. Knowing exactly where they were going to stand on the occupational hierarchy in five or ten years' time and how much they were likely to earn meant they could envisage such crucial decisions as when to buy a house, what kind of education they could offer their children or when they could arrange their marriages. Some of the more fortunate workers could even expect to realize their life-long ambition of retiring from the factory as low ranking officers, even if the title's symbolic distinction outstripped its real rewards. So if as Richard Sennett remarks, the 'idea of being able to plan defined the realm of individual agency and power', there was no doubt that the labour aristocracy was well endowed on both counts.[37] Job security and mobility opportunities, the two catalysing forces allowing entitlements to be converted into material gratifications and fulfilments, mutually reinforced expressions of agency and power.

This said, direct state intervention in the labour market resulting in the creation of a special class of beneficiaries in those sectors of the economy under its control was by no means something specific to India. Public sector workers the world over represent a labour aristocracy, if only because they tend to 'own' their jobs for life either through the sanction of legislation or custom, though it is clear there is an appreciable difference of degree between the two situations.[38] What, however,

---

[35] Mark Holmström, *Industry and Inequality. The Social Anthropology of Indian Labour*, Cambridge, 1984, p. 258.

[36] Richard Sennett, *The Culture of the New Capitalism*, New Haven, 2006, p. 24.

[37] ibid, p. 23.

[38] In France, for instance, legally enshrined rights, known as *statuts* safeguard the job security of all categories of public sector employees. See, *inter alia*, Jocelyne Barreau et al (eds.), *Une irrésistible modernisation des entreprises de service public?*, Rennes, 2000;

distinguishes the Indian scenario from that prevailing in the developed economies in particular is not only the fact that these pockets of privilege concern no more than a tiny fraction of the country's total industrial work force, estimated at just under 11 per cent in 2004–05.[39] It is also the tremendous disparities, both material and social, that characterize the positions of those situated at the top-most reaches of the labour hierarchy and the immense majority concentrated at the bottom, an upshot of the chronic failure of the official machinery to ensure the implementation of basic employment laws. The inability of the state to guarantee a daily minimum wage in most cases even as it showers public sector employees with a panoply of advantages is what has served to reinforce the accusatory charge inherent in the notion of labour aristocracy.

Following from the above, because these advantages were not the fruit of resolute struggle, but stemmed from an act of unilateral concession by the Nehruvian developmental state, the best organized sections of the working class had no incentive to demand if not similar largesse, at least a minimal legally enforceable social safety net for all those sections of the labour force denied this protection. Indeed, Parry's comments with regard to Bhilai that the 'privileges of the labour aristocracy have cost unorganized sector labour dear' applies to the country at large.[40] As he rightly claims, an important reason why 'most are now left out in the cold with only limited access to risibly deficient … government [welfare] provisions' is due to the fact that the 'labour elite has never had to fight for [these provisions] on behalf of all workers'.[41] This contrasts with the

---

Jean-Noel Retière, 'L'industrie des tabacs dans la deuxième moitié du XIXème siècle. Un patronage d'État', in M.Mansfield, R.Salais, N.Whiteside (eds.), *Aux sources du chômage 1880–1914. Une comparaison interdisciplinaire entre la France et la Grande-Bretagne*, Paris, 1995, pp. 111–39; Pierre-Eric Tixier, Nelly Mauchamp (eds.), *EDF-GDF: une entreprise publique en mutation*, Paris, 2000. Frederick Cooper's superb study of Kenyan dockers chronicles a similar process of state activism in the creation of a permanent labour force. *On the African Waterfront. Urban Disorder and the Transformation of Work in Colonial Mombasa*, New Haven, 1987, pp. 3–4, 7–11, 142–62.

[39] Official statistics reveal that even as the size of the total industrial work force registered an increase between 1999–2000 and 2004–05, organized sector's share declined significantly from 14.44 per cent to 10.61 per cent during the same period. 'Definitional and Statistical Issues', Task Force Report, National Commission for Enterprises in the Unorganized Sector, New Delhi, 2008, p. 69 (Table 4.2).

[40] Parry, 'Proletarian Vanguard?'.

[41] ibid.

West where the gains yielded by the protest actions of the labour aristocracy in favour of mandatory social insurance and unemployment benefits, the bedrock of basic citizenship rights, diffused right through the ranks of the working class.[42]

Lastly, the Indian situation stands out on account of the near total absence of mobility opportunities for sizeable groups of workers vainly hammering at the gates of the citadel seeking entry. It is not so much a glass ceiling as an iron wall that separates the world of legally binding standard work arrangements from non-standard ones. If reservations have opened a small window of opportunity for the Scheduled Castes and Scheduled Tribes, for members of other communities who have been excluded from tenured positions in the public sector second chances rarely come, especially if they lack access to powerful political patrons, kinship connections or cash to bribe officials.

The primacy accorded to the Indian state in spearheading the overall process of industrial development then has had signal implications for both working class formation and politics in the post-1947 period. Even as official policy gave rise to a strata of modern, affluent workers, it laid the basis for an enduring and profound division within the labour force which if anything has widened rather than shrunk over time. Already differentiated by all manner of primordial loyalties, the structural segmentation of the working class attendant upon the dualization of Indian industry into an organized and unorganized sector even as it has further deepened the existing fault lines has made the prospects of finding common ground for collective action more elusive. That such a development could only have served the interests of the ruling elites is to state a truism. Indeed, with the possible exception of the 1974 railway strike, the six decades following Independence have passed without labour being in a position to mount a serious concerted challenge to the ruling classes' domination, thus bearing warrant to the effectiveness of the measures pursued by policy-making actors.

Of equal significance, by curtailing the reach of labour laws to virtually

---

[42] Belying the standard representation of public sector unions as self-seeking, parochial organizations, union representatives at ITI's Bangalore factory consistently fought to obtain secure jobs for casual workers and proved successful on numerous instances. Thus between 1975–78 alone, the company absorbed on its permanent rolls 646 casual labourers. Minutes management–union meeting, ITI Bangalore, 18 November 1978.

the same group that also enjoyed a raft of additional entitlements, the state has not only directly contributed to generating and perpetuating a situation of widespread inequality. It has also appeared to endorse the principles of selective as opposed to universal justice where what is granted to a minority is denied to the majority. While one can hardly fault official redistributive measures for improving the living standards of public sector workers and their families, the norms of democratic rule call for fair and equitable treatment for all sections of the workforce.[43]

One final point on this question is in order. The cleavage of the labour force into two groups whose material conditions, consumption habits, and worldviews bear little resemblance supposed the precedence of sectional identities over a common class identity.[44] Yet even if the labour aristocracy sought to self-consciously assert a distinct social identity, we must be wary of exaggerating the impermeability of the boundaries separating it from the others. Failing to do so we run the risk of obscuring the constant flow of connections that marked the everyday lives of these groups in much the same way that too sharp a demarcation of manufacturing activities in the formal and informal sector can prevent us from grasping the organic links knitting the two. For despite the segmented nature of the job market, the different categories of workers were crosscut by broader social relations, as certain studies have shown.[45] Backed by the findings of his research on a Coimbatore slum, John Harris writes that the labour elite, workers in small workshops, poor traders, petty producers and casual workers all participated in many of the same political and social activities in the community.[46]

Not only did the elite strata often share residential space in neighbourhoods with other working people, company-built townships housed only a fraction of the total public sector workforce, disproving

---

[43] On this point see Barbara Harris White and Nandini Gooptu, 'Mapping India's World of Unorganised Labour', in L. Panitch and C. Leys (eds.), *Working Classes: Global Realities, Socialist Register 2001*, London, pp. 89–118.

[44] Parry, however, defends the position that the opposition between the labour aristocracy and the informal sector workforce is an opposition foregrounded in class, i.e., the middle class versus the proletariat. 'Proletarian Vanguard?'

[45] Breman, *The Making and Unmaking of an Industrial Working Class*, p. 126; Harris, 'The Working Poor and the Labour Aristocracy'; Holmström, *Industry and Inequality*, pp. 278–9.

[46] Harris, 'The Working Poor and the Labour Aristocracy'.

the idea that they lived in discrete worlds, at the level of individual families considerable interaction could and did exist.[47] Many public sector employees' families contained members who worked in the informal sector, high rentals in the big urban centres obliging the latter to turn to their better-paid relatives. Many of them also accommodated for relatively long periods kinfolk from rural areas who had come to the city seeking jobs or to study. Thus the composition of labour aristocracy households tended to be anything but homogenous, consolidating wage earners drawn from both the organized and the unorganized sectors as well as the jobless.[48] Likewise, while some among the labour elite may have severed all ties with their ancestral homes, others continued to send occasional remittances to needy dependents.

It is this network of social obligations and sentiments enmeshing organized sector workers that forms the premise of Mark Holmström's 'levelling down' argument. According to him, their pay is 'spread thin' among many dependents.[49] Although the individual worker in a state enterprise may well earn ten or twenty times more than his counterpart in a small non-unionized workshop down the road, the differentials in household incomes of organized and unorganized sector workers are generally much smaller. This is because of 'the moral pressure on well-paid workers to feed and accommodate relatives who earn little or nothing'.[50] In other words, formal sector households whose structures could but did not always coincide with those of the joint family, operated as sites for the redistribution of resources to support jobless, under-employed or poorly paid family members.

[47] Interestingly, Sandbrook and Cohen advance a fairly identical set of arguments to dispute the view that unionized urban African workers belong to a privileged group. Among other things, they claim that the relative advantage of higher income is offset by the larger size of the dependent urban household and the higher cost of living in towns. Richard Sandbrook and Robin Cohen, 'Workers and Progressive Change in Underdeveloped Countries', in *idem* (eds.), *The Development of an African Working Class: Studies in Class Formation and Action*, Toronto, 1975, p. 3.

[48] The households surveyed by Parry in one Bhilai colony while including young rural kin, however, had no members working in the informal sector. 'Proletarian Vanguard?' Heather Joshi concurs with this viewpoint in her study of the Bombay informal sector, but admits her findings are tentative. 'The Informal Urban Economy and its Boundaries', *EPW*, Vol. XV, No. 13, 29 March 1980, pp. 638–44.

[49] Holmström, *Industry and Inequality*, p. 10, 268–74 (cit. p. 10).

[50] ibid, p. 270.

Evidence contradicting this conclusion can, no doubt, be marshalled, but for the moment they are patchy. What is more, in a social configuration as 'traditional' as India where the strength of normative values inculcating the importance of family duties requires no repeating, the assumption that some degree of interdependency existed between the better-off and the more deprived kinfolk within the working class is hardly untenable. Thus overall, while the term labour aristocracy is helpful to understanding the dynamics of working class formation and politics in the post-Independence period, we must be careful not to overestimate its explanatory punch. The need to exercise caution is all the more important given its strong judgemental overtones, its polemical core often being undistinguishable from its analytical core. The term can certainly shed light on several dimensions of workers' actions, but not all.

Tarring the public sector workforce with the labour aristocratic brush should also not obscure an important detail concerning its overall composition. A fairly significant proportion of those hired to operate these temples of modern India belonged to the traditionally most disadvantaged social groups in the country, namely the Scheduled Castes and Scheduled Tribes. Possessing little or no educational capital, if they were fortunate not to be entirely excluded from the process of industrial development this was wholly because of the mandatory and relatively well-implemented job reservation programme instituted by the government—a programme whose ambit did not extend to the private sector but only to the public sector. Whether these SC-ST beneficiaries too went the way of the rest of the public sector workforce, morphing into a 'creamy layer' cut off from their informal sector caste fellows, is however, a development we must not overrule.

This purposive endeavour to better the life chances of the socially and economically backward sections of the population went hand in hand with another equally laudable nation-building project: the industrialization of economically backward regions of the country. Both the needs of long term economic strategy and ideological legitimation in a poor country made a redistributive programme indispensable.[51] Towards

---

[51] For unspecified reasons Kaviraj has chosen to qualify such a redistributive programme as 'abstract'. There was, however, nothing abstract about establishing factories in undeveloped regions so as to provide jobs for the local population. Sudipta Kaviraj, 'A Critique of the Passive Revolution', *EPW*, Vol. 23, Nos. 45–47, November 1988, pp. 2429–44 (cit. p. 2433).

this end, the locational decisions orienting the spatial expansion of state-run enterprises were dictated less by efficiency rationale than by the ambition of reducing existing regional imbalances and generating employment. While the planning process *per se* may have been detached from the 'squabbles and conflicts of politics' as Partha Chatterjee claims, this was hardly the case with respect to resource allocation priorities in the implantation of new public sector factories.[52] If planning sought to imprint a 'rational' and orderly format in determining priorities in the face of diverse contending claims, the immediacy of politics, on the other hand, tended to impose a more 'irrational' and messy logic. The employment-generating potential large state units offered constituted a highly effective source of patronage dispensation for politicians. Consequentially, party politics and considerations of electoral advantage often bulked large in the spatial distribution of these units compromising their operating efficiency and financial viability. But these 'costs' have to be counterpoised to the 'benefits' derived from siting new plants in greenfield areas by way of the measure of prosperity they undoubtedly brought to inhabitants. The developmental mission handed to the public sector, which as Chatterjee justly underlines, had come to be 'identified as the embodiment of the general' then also contained a strong social and distributive justice dimension.[53]

In the context of a post-colonial democratic state like the Indian one which 'acquired its representativeness by directing a programme of economic development on behalf of the nation', industrial growth had to usher in socially just outcomes.[54] Rendering this imperative all the more urgent was the 'dominant argument of nationalism against colonial rule, [namely] that the latter was impeding the further development of India'.[55] The legitimacy of the ruling bloc, in particular that of one of its components, the bureaucracy, therefore rested a great deal on its ability to deliver on its promise of social amelioration.[56] Failing this, the

---

[52] Partha Chatterjee, *The Nation and its Fragments. Colonial and Postcolonial Histories*, Princeton, 1993, pp. 201–11 (cit. p. 202).

[53] ibid, p. 219.

[54] ibid, p. 203.

[55] ibid.

[56] Given the centrality of the post-independent Indian state in the management of economic demands, scholars have identified the bureaucracy as a crucial player in the ruling coalition alongside industrial and agrarian capital. Pranab Bardhan, *The Political*

fundamental objective of the developmental state of advancing capital accumulation through the institution of centralized planning risked being jeopardized. To overlook or downplay all these elements as neo-liberal economists are wont to do would be sanctioned ignorance. Indeed, the well-known business historian Dwijendra Tripathi believes the failure of public enterprises as business enterprises has tended to camouflage the wide ranging indirect benefits they have yielded to the country.[57]

This dual aspect of the public sector's mission brings me to a fundamental methodological concern, one that I have hopefully addressed through the overall architecture of the book and the range of themes it embraces. When I set out to write this book, my intention was not to focus just on the state and the management, or just on the union and workers. Instead, it was to fashion a narrative which would integrate all four groups by treating each group as symmetrically as possible. Labour history and industrial sociology, and not just in India, have typically given pride of place to the life experiences of wage earners, the direct producers of wealth. This has had the effect, especially in the case of historians, of flattening the diversity of managerial strategies and practices and reducing them exclusively to the issues of labour recruitment and labour control. (Not the least of the paradoxes is that by stressing the control or coercive dimension, these analyses inscribe an overarching 'capital logic' to the social relations of production where workers are denied the possibilities of agency.)

If an important component of their action, managers, however, do

---

Economy of Development in India, New Delhi, 1984, pp. 51–3; Kaviraj, 'Critique of the Passive Revolution'. What is more, the demise of the discredited *dirigiste* framework can hardly be said to have eroded the bureaucracy's influence in shaping and implementing policy. If anything the exposure of the upper echelons to neo-liberal ideologies via their involvement in various transnational institutions transformed them from as early as the 1980s onwards into fervent champions of orthodox market reforms. Senior officials 'well regarded by the Indian business community' in fact headed some of the high level committees set up by Indira Gandhi after her electoral triumph in 1980 to study how the private sector could wrest control of the commanding heights of industry from the public sector. Atul Kohli, 'Politics of Economic Growth in India, 1980–2005', *EPW*, Vol. 41, No. 13, 1 April 2006, pp. 1251–9 (cit. p. 1256). See also Ajit Singh and Jayati Ghosh, 'Import Liberalization and the New Industrial Strategy. An Analysis of their Impact on Output and Employment', *EPW*, Vol. 23, Nos. 45–47, November 1988, pp. 2313–42.

[57] Tripathi, *The Oxford History of Indian Business*, p. 317.

much more than merely extract effort from those under their command. Their tasks range from raising capital for investment and allocation purposes and making technology choices to coordinating production flows, to determining appropriate organizational structures and finding the right supply sources through to developing new products and devising means of marketing and selling these products, not to mention lobbying public authorities to protect or further the company's interests. The upshot of an ideological division of labour within academic disciplines, mapping all these variegated facets of managerial activities has devolved to business history and organizational theory. But in investing managers, and especially top managers alone with agency, this bias being exemplified in Alfred Chandler's celebrated studies on the emergence of the modern business corporation, these narratives have wiped workers, unions, labour processes, industrial relations all clean off the slate.[58]

Thus in different ways, though the end result has been identical, the accounts produced on the one hand by labour history and industrial sociology, and on the other by business history and organizational theory have tended to yield a rather distorted and one-sided image of the business firm where valorizing one of the two principal social categories has entailed the disappearance or the caricaturing of the other. It was a dissatisfaction with both the labour-centric and the management-centric perspective, and a desire to correct the imbalances inherent in each perspective that has prompted me to pay just as much attention to the strategies deployed by state and management in all spheres of corporate activity as to the strategies guiding the actions of the union and workers, and their mutually constitutive interplay, even while recognizing the unequal access of each party to the resources constitutive of their actions. The focus on the role played by the state also allows me to avoid one of the pitfalls inherent in monographical studies where the firm is typically viewed as a hermetic entity, abstracted from the larger environment in which it is embedded, and whose dynamics imposes constraints on the behaviour of all parties as well as affords possibilities.

Hence, only under these conditions where the analysis takes into

---

[58] Alfred D. Chandler Jr., *The Visible Hand. The Managerial Revolution in American Business,* Cambridge (Mass.), 1977; and *idem, Strategy and Structure. Chapters in the History of the Industrial Enterprise*, Cambridge (Mass.), 1991. A similar academic division of sorts can be observed between economic analysis and management research.

consideration the multiplicity of actors and treats their practices on a symmetrical basis, but without occluding the asymmetry of their positions, the source of power and domination, can we imagine a genuine social history of the business firm, conceived as an organizational system constituted by specific sets of social relations and reproduced by specific patterns of social interaction between all the participating groups.[59] The symmetrical but critical history that I have sought to pursue also offers the methodological advantage of envisioning the firm as the institutional locale where the research interests of business history, labour history and the history of technology intersect. For it is within the boundaries of the enterprise that the transformation of labour power into workplace performance, the transformation of technology into production facilities, and the transformation of organizational concepts into organization occurs.[60]

A central theme of this monograph revolves around the specific character of the production regime prevailing in a state-controlled enterprise (be it in India or elsewhere), and the strategies and interrelations linking the four principal actors—state, management, union and workers—the two elements, system and actors, being obviously imbricated and shaping each other. For want of a more apposite term, I have chosen to designate this system of production as a bureaucratic production regime.[61] A caveat is in order here. A bureaucratic regime of production must not be confused with a bureaucratic organizational design. Following Weber, we can state that all large scale organizations

[59] This reading of the history of a firm as an analytical construction sensitive to both symmetries and asymmetries in its treatment of actors owes to Yves Cohen, *Organiser à l'aube du taylorisme. La pratique d'Ernest Mattern chez Peugeot 1906–1919*, Besançon, 2001, pp. 187–8.

[60] Thomas Welskopp, 'Class Structures and the Firm: The Interplay of Workplace and Industrial Relations in Large Capitalist Enterprises', in P. Robertson (ed.), *Authority and Control in Modern Industry: Theoretical and Empirical Perspectives*, London, 1999, pp. 73–119.

[61] The notion of a production or factory regime is derived from Michael Burawoy. It offers the conceptual advantage of uniting two elements often considered separately: on the one hand, the organization of work, and on the other, the institutions or apparatuses regulating production relations, such as collective bargaining, grievance procedures and the internal labour market. In his study, Burawoy identifies different types of factory regimes, distinguishing between capitalist and state socialist ones. *The Politics of Production. Factory Regimes Under Capitalism and Socialism*, London, 1990, p. 8, 12, and chap. 4.

in particular are by definition bureaucratic in character. By this we mean they rely on a technology of control and coordination informed by a system of abstract, calculable, universally applied rules in order to achieve a wide array of objectives. Rules serve to establish a hierarchy of offices, determine standards for recruitment and career advancement, specify routines for job execution and the people qualified to excute them, dictate behaviour, etc.[62] Adherence to such a framework of rules is a defining trait of large corporations. However, by no means are all bureaucratic organizations governed by a bureaucratic system of production.

From the theoretical literature available on the subject of state enterprises, the exclusive output of economists from both the classical and the neo-institutionalist school, we can state that a bureaucratic factory regime reposes upon a triple foundation: state ownership, soft budget constraints, and monopoly market power. Having identified these three attributes, it is possible to develop a tentative model which summarily hypothesizes how each of these attributes conditions at once the workings of public companies and the dispositions of state officials, managers and employees. I argue that it is the combination of all three factors, rather than any one of them treated in isolation that imbues the bureaucratic regime of production with its distinctive culture. My book shall therefore concentrate on studying the implications of a bureaucratic regime in defining the practices of the main protagonists, relating questions such as the form state intervention assumes in a public firm, the way managerial responsibilities are exercised, or the particular nature of shopfloor social relations to the overall system of production undergirding the functioning of the company.

We all know that public enterprises, in particular the bigger-sized ones, share several technological, organizational and institutional features in common with large private corporations. Both employ high levels of fixed capital, utilize standardized techniques of mass production, depend

---

[62] Max Weber, *Economy and Society. An Outline of Interpretive Sociology*, (Guenther Roth and Claus Wittich, eds.), Berkeley, 1978, Vol. 1, pp. 217–26; Vol. 2, pp. 956–58. The sea change in business conditions experienced since the 1980s by firms the world over has, however, thrown into question the validity of the bureaucratic corporate form as the most appropriate cross-national organizational paradigm. For an analysis see Paul DiMaggio, 'Introduction: Making Sense of the Contemporary Firm and Prefiguring its Future', in *idem* (ed.), *The Twenty-First Century Firm. Changing Economic Organization in International Perspective*, Princeton, 2001, pp. 3–30.

on professional managers to run their operations, deploy taylorized labour processes, mobilize bureaucratic procedures to coordinate their activities, dominate the product markets in which they operate, recognize the importance of unions as a means of controlling their workforces, regulate conflict through various collective mechanisms and so forth.

The question then is what sets them apart, what complex of variables helps to endow the production systems of publicly owned companies with their distinctive character. Can one assert, for instance, that public firms in general can afford to tolerate both higher levels of organizational slack and for longer periods than private firms. Or are better able to distribute generous welfare benefits to its employees without extracting countervailing concessions in the guise of heavier work loads. To answer these questions it is imperative to uncover the structural differences between the two. Posing the problem in this fashion also attenuates the temptation to idealize the capitalist enterprise and see it as a paragon of economic rationality and industrial discipline. The private firm is no more naturally inclined to efficiency than is the public firm to inefficiency. The performance of one or the other is the result of a confluence of factors where ownership patterns, budgetary constraints, and market forces conjointly exert a determining influence.

Let us now see how the model works by examining the impact of each of these structural determinants as it is presented in the academic literature on the overall functioning of public enterprises. State ownership as opposed to private ownership implies by definition a difference in the mode of appropriating and redistributing surplus value. Whereas in a private enterprise the surplus extracted from the direct producer is siphoned away by private capital, in a public enterprise this function is discharged centrally by the state which then determines its mode of reallocation as well as the circuits through which this process is achieved. Direct state intervention in the cycle of surplus appropriation and redistribution means that the use value of the goods produced by the public sector often prevails over their exchange value since an essential mission of these companies is to attend to social needs by developing the basic economic infrastructural framework.

Under these circumstances, cost considerations and profitability, it is contended, often tend to take a back seat to social and political objectives which are exploited in different ways to their own benefit by politicians, bureaucrats, management, unions and workers alike. Or to put it slightly differently, given the obligation of public companies to provide social goods, achieving annual objectives, defined either in physical or monetary terms, rather than meeting stringent financial criteria of efficiency, becomes the yardstick by which their performance is often judged, a tendency reinforced by the type of budgetary constraints they are subjected to.

State sector enterprises operate under soft budget constraints as opposed to hard budget ones which weigh on private companies. The survival of the latter hinges exclusively on their continued ability to record profits. State undertakings, however, are not threatened with the risk of bankruptcy even when they tend to be chronic loss makers because they can count on the exchequer to bail them out through various forms of financial assistance (additional credit, tax reductions, subsidies, grants, etc.).[63] Nor are such injections of aid which reflect social and political pressures to keep the firm alive contingent on repayment obligations. Political accountability then prevails over financial accountability.[64]

Moreover, expectations of external monetary support are strongly built into the behaviour of managers.[65] Since the administrative prices adopted to govern commercial transactions between state authorities and public companies seldom succeed in restricting expenditures because they tend to be fixed on the basis of negotiations between the two sides, they are automatically adjusted to absorb cost increases. At the same time, by removing the spectre of liquidation from the horizon of public enterprises, soft budget constraints places them in a paternalistic relationship with the state where their existence is framed not in economic terms but in political ones.[66] This has tremendous implications for managements whose autonomy is usurped by administrative bureaucracies invested with the authority not just to nominate key personnel but, more crucially,

[63] An elaboration of the concept of the soft budget constraint is available in Janos Kornai, *Economics of Shortage*, Amsterdam, 1980, p. 28, 303–19.

[64] Pranab Bardhan and John Roemer, 'Market Socialism: A Case for Rejuvenation', *Journal of Economic Perspectives*, Vol. 6, No. 3, Summer 1992, pp.101–16. See also Pranab Bardhan, 'On Tackling the Soft Budget Constraint in Market Socialism', in P. Bardhan and J. Roemer (eds.), *Market Socialism. The Current Debate*, Oxford, 1994, pp. 145–55.

[65] Kornai, 'Soft Budget Constraint'.

[66] Kornai, *Economics of Shortage*, pp. 562–8. See also Michael Burawoy and Janos Luckacs, *The Radiant Past. Ideology and Reality in Hungary's Road to Capitalism*, Chicago, 1992, p. 63.

to formulate all long term strategic objectives ranging from resource allocations and technological choices to product portfolios and industrial relations. With virtually all the rules of action established outside the firm, thereby depriving managements of most of their command prerogatives, projecting and preserving the legitimacy of their authority *vis-à-vis* employees and their representatives becomes problematic.

But from the standpoint of state authorities too, the loss of managerial autonomy is not without adverse consequences. It discourages personal initiative and fosters a culture of unaccountability. Excluded as they are from the process of corporate policy formulation, executives can neither be expected to display much commitment to or enthusiasm for these policies nor can they be held in any way responsible for their failure. Ultimately, it is not so much managements' operational competencies as the broader parameter of choices embraced by state authorities that determines the overall performance of public enterprises.

Both state appropriation of surplus value and soft budget constraints then define and illuminate in their own ways certain distinctive features of a bureaucratic production regime. Still, they do not shed light on all aspects of its functioning. To get a more complete picture we must integrate another shaping influence, namely competition. Monopolistic or oligopolistic market positions are hardly exclusive to public companies. Thus by itself the argument of lack of competition is of limited explanatory utility. However, when merged with state ownership and soft budgetary constraints, the role played by market forces in configuring the bureaucratic system is crucial. So it is only by bringing together all three elements within a common analytical framework that we succeed in fully grasping the specific character of this production regime.

The mutually reinforcing effect of these elements is supposed to have one very significant implication for a bureaucratic factory regime. It practically eliminates all secular pressures for change. If one can argue that all organizations are governed by inertia, this tendency strikes much deeper roots in public companies.[67] Incentives for technological innovations, cost economies, improving product quality, intensifying labour productivity, enforcing disciplinary controls are all conspicuous by their absence. The impetus for organizational reform can only

---

[67] Thomas K. McCraw 'Introduction', in *idem* (ed.), *The Essential Alfred Chandler: Essays Toward a Historical Theory of Big Business*, Boston, 1988, pp. 1–21.

materialize in moments of political crisis when state authorities threaten to scrap or harden soft budgetary constraints.

The foregoing discussion then broadly resumes the principal theses set out in economic theory with respect to the key institutional determinants underpinning the functioning of public enterprises. The next step consists in moving from a formalization of these general propositions to their operationalization in empirical research by putting to the test this ideal-typical model of what I have termed the bureaucratic factory regime. How heuristically useful is it in accounting for ground realities without glossing over or downplaying findings that sit uncomfortably with the hypotheses formulated by the model? Are we justified in positing a causal connection, and to what degree, between this system of production and ITI's actual performance? If not, in which case the neo-liberal critique of the public sector stands further invalidated, what are the reasons that permit us to do so? Answering these questions will be the primary task of this book.

A monograph by definition tends to greater exhaustivity in its treatment of the object than say a multi-sectoral or industry-wide study. In consequence, this book will not directly engage with the larger macro-level debate, involving neo-liberal commentators and their critics, about the aggregate contributions of state-owned enterprises to the process of capital formation. Nevertheless, it does aim to further this debate by examining the extent of the fit between the 'big picture' and the detail. To what degree did a company like ITI conform to the neo-liberal stereotype of the low productive, overstaffed, and socially wasteful public enterprise capable only of turning out high cost-poor quality goods? Or, on the contrary did it represent an exception to the 'rule' and stand out as a byword for efficiency and responsible cost-conscious management practices? And if this is the case, to what set of variables then can we attribute these results. Only through a micro-macro confrontation of this kind which allows us to evaluate the pertinence of the broader conclusions posited about the public sector through the eyehole of an individual firm will we be in a position to arrive at a better and more nuanced understanding of the performance of state-owned enterprises.

The need to train our analytical lens more sharply at the functioning of individual public companies is also dictated by the distinctive nature of the market structure in which they often tended to operate. ITI, for instance, ranked among the best performing public sector companies until the launch of economic reforms. Profits rose consistently ever since its foundation with the result that it could exhibit a relatively satisfactory rate of return on investments These figures, of course, represent an important index of the company's strength and vitality. However, in a market context where ITI not only long enjoyed a monopolistic position, but was assured of a steadily expanding volume of demand for its products, which, moreover, were purchased by P&T on the basis of a cost-plus pricing arrangement, financial data can tell us only a part of the story. Profit levels cannot adequately convey whether or not the management optimally utilized its resources and manufacturing capacities, achieved the required quality standards, or effectively deployed its workforce. To properly grasp these issues, a more fine grained and complete account of the company's operations is required, and this can be obtained only through an exploration of the concrete realities of its functioning.

Let me add that this task of augmenting our knowledge of the public sector is rendered all the more urgent by the current economic and political context. The break with state interventionist strategies as embodied in the Nehru-Mahalanobis model of planned industrial development, poses a fundamental threat to the existence of the public sector. At a time when state-owned enterprises are taking the axe to their workforces as part of their cost-cutting drive aimed at survival, the list of questions—the precise nature of state intervention, managerial and worker practices, working conditions, the role of the unions, forms of collective protest, provision of social benefits, etc.—for which satisfactory answers are unavailable is unfortunately still too long given the dearth of company–specific enquiries. We have miles to go before the 'hegemony of the monograph' becomes a reality either in the field of Indian business studies or labour studies.[68]

SOURCES

A few words are in order on the kind of source material I have relied on in writing this monograph. I have not utilized any public archives because they contained no material of interest, so most of the manuscript sources

---

[68] Donald Reid, 'Reflections on Labor History and Language', in L. Berlanstein (ed.), *Rethinking Labour History: Essays on Discourse and Class Analysis*, Urbana-Chicago, 1993, pp. 39–54 (cit. p. 51).

I consulted were company files. The majority of the documents to which I gained access came from the personnel department both at the Bangalore factory of ITI and the corporate office, located a few kilometres away, as well as from one product division, telephones. In the telephone division, I have drawn on material from the following departments: R&D, methods, production planning, and production. I was also able to consult certain files, pertaining essentially to incentive schemes, maintained by the central office of the Industrial Engineering Department at the Bangalore plant. Access to the records maintained by DoT would have undeniably enriched my research. However, I was refused permission, nor did I enjoy much greater success in interviewing officials from the parent authority.

The fact that I was able to consult a fairly extensive range of sources at ITI may give the impression that a methodically organized, carefully preserved system of corporate archives existed. Nothing could be further from the truth. Besides having no tradition of allowing outsiders to scrutinize its records, ITI like the majority of Indian firms is totally lacking in historical consciousness. It perceives no interest in maintaining documentary evidence of past events reflecting its development. No resources whatsoever are devoted to record keeping, and even a complete set of the in-house magazine is unavailable for other periods barring the 1990s.[69] Thus, the company has strictly speaking no archives at all as materialized spatially in a specific site.

Leaving aside files classified as strategically important, and definitions of importance of course varied from one incoming executive to the other, the normal practice followed by each department consists of consigning all documents older than a couple of years to what is euphemistically called 'stores', a dusty, dank, cobweb enveloped room from where they are periodically cleared and sent to the 'burning yard' for destroying in order to make room for a fresh lot of files that have outlived their utility. To my utter dismay and chagrin, one such mass incineration followed the relocation of the personnel department at the Bangalore plant from one wing of the administration building to another.

---

[69] Poorly maintained and under-funded, the library at the Bangalore plant is of a piece with the rest of the factory in the post-reforms era. In fact, an internal note bemoaned the absence of new journals or books since absolutely no expenditure had been incurred on the library. 'This has posed considerable problem for R&D engineers to get updated with the latest advances in technologies.' Ref. R/GMR/41, 3 August 1998.

Moreover, the lack of financial resources coupled with the insensitivity to the company's past means that preserving records on microfilms as a space-saving measure has never been considered. In addition, I had to contend with the 'negative' effects, from the standpoint of the historian, of the application of ISO 9000 norms. The convention's emphasis on good housekeeping and 'zero paper' has accelerated the process of elimination of old records, their preservation being ideologically cathected not just to connote physical disorder, but, more significantly, a resistance to 'change' and clinging on to old ways of doing things.

But fortunately not all the old archives had disappeared into the maw of the incinerator. Luck, persistence and cooperation from a number of employees enabled me to track down a number of valuable sources. Given the culture of indulgence that defines the functioning of public sector companies, once both employees and middle-level managers, my principal interlocutors, had become accustomed to my presence, I was free to put my head into shelves and cupboards to see if they contained anything I could put to use. I was also considerably aided by the fact that lower ranking employees in the personnel department, disregarding their superiors' instructions, had occasionally preserved old files on certain issues with an eye to protecting their own interests. Indiscriminately destroying all old records, they understood, could only complicate their own task the day they were required by senior officials to hunt information on some aspect of past policy decisions.

Let me also add that my status as a 'foreign'-based research scholar, in command over the 'language of command' were resources that served me well.[70] The prestige attached to studying at a first-world academic institution meant that unlike young students from local universities whose paths sometimes crossed mine inside the factory, I was never obliged to bow and scrape for information, or sent running from pillar to post. So with the exception of certain confidential documents such as minutes of board meetings, where the sources physically existed I was able on most occasions to access them.

The archival sources mobilized for the purpose of this book are extremely diverse in nature and can be regrouped under five broad

---

[70] Bernard Cohn, 'The Command of Language and the Language of Command', in *idem, Colonialism and its Forms of Knowledge. The British in India*, Princeton, 1996, pp. 16–56.

categories: documents relating to employment relations; production and technology issues; commercial and financial subjects; correspondence with the supervisory ministry and other official bodies; and publicity and informational material. A non-exhaustive list of these documents would include annual reports, individual personnel files, management and union circulars, collective bargaining agreements, minutes of management-union meetings, minutes of management meetings, minutes of management-P&T meetings, audit reports, reports of consultants, project reports, departmental notes and memorandums, factory standing orders, process sheets, notes to the board of directors, replies to official surveys, disciplinary enquiry proceedings, letters and petitions addressed by workers to management, product brochures, etc.

One type of manuscript sources of extreme value and importance were the personnel files of employees. In effect, the multi-variate statistical analysis I conducted, the results of which are presented in chapter 7, is based on a study of 1129 capsule biographies of employees who joined the Bangalore plant between 1948 and the mid-1990s. An examination of these records enables us to reconstitute the social background of an individual and follow his/her work career at every stage until retirement. These sources contain two types of information which can be broadly classified as sociological and professional in content. The sociological data is consigned in the main in the job application form. The documents shedding light on an employee's professional career, even though sharing in common certain formal features, namely correspondence exchanged between the company and the individual, are extremely diverse in character (official notifications relating to a range of issues—warnings, punishments, promotion decisions and transfers—personal requests of all kinds, and so forth). Scrutinizing the personnel files thus supplies a wealth of material not only on individual itineraries prior to joining ITI, but also on all the events, big and small, that helped to fashion the course of a work career.

I have merged these manuscript sources with direct non-participant observation during the course of my plant visits, and oral material in the form of personal-open ended interviews. A total of 220 hours of tape recorded interviews were conducted with top and middle management officials, union representatives, technicians, and blue and white collar employees. Those who spoke to me included both retired personnel and people still in company employment. If management officials were interviewed only in English, workers expressed themselves in the main in Kannada and Tamil. Some pseudonyms have been used to preserve individual privacy.

The recourse to oral history proved invaluable in illuminating from a different, more personal, angle the official version of events embodied in the written documents, even as it enabled one to hear in their own voices actors' perceptions of these events. Its utility in helping to fill the lacunae contained in the archival sources cannot be overemphasized. At the same time, oral accounts can help to serve as an useful safeguard against the reificatory tendencies always inherent when conceptualizing massive and anonymous social process such as industrialization and proletarianization. By integrating the lived experiences of actors into the narrative, it is perhaps possible to escape an interpretation of industrial development or factory work as overarching phenomenon which tend to single-mindedly impose their logic on the behaviour and practices of individuals and groups, leaving them with no other option but to 'submit' or 'resist'.

* * *

In organizing this monograph, I have by and large preferred a thematic order to a chronological one. Chapters one to five cover the strategies of the Indian state, the supervisory ministry and the management. Chapter one which treats the pre-reforms era examines the nature of the relationship between P&T and ITI within a market structure defined by monopoly-monopsony ties and vertical integration. It also analyses the policy orientations of the state towards the telecommunications sector.

Having framed the overall context, I move next to the question of politics as refracted in the historical evolution of the company's technology base from its inception in 1948 until the launch of economic reforms in 1991, and its geographical expansion. Starting with the manufacture of one type of electro-mechanical switching equipment, strowger, ITI progressed to a more sophisticated electro-mechanical system, crossbar, in the late 1960s, before making the leap to electronic exchanges during the mid-1980s. I ask how these technology choices were made and who made them. What consequences did such decisions have for the company and the national telecommunications network? How successful was ITI's own R&D department in developing effective proprietary technology? How did locating three of the six operating units of ITI in the state of

Uttar Pradesh impinge on the fortunes of the company? These and other question form the subject matter of Chapter two.

The following chapter probes various facets of the company's operations in order to answer the question of how efficiently the management discharged its responsibilities. Focussing in detail on the organization of the production process, the nodal point from which the interconnections between a whole range of issues (material flows, delivery discipline, cash administration, inventory control, machine and labour productivity, incentive schemes and the like) can be considered helps in turn to shed valuable light on managerial and worker practices. I argue that the chronic dysfunctioning of ITI stemmed as much from official regulations and inefficiencies on the part of P&T as from the management's own shortcomings, all three elements having a mutually reinforcing effect.

The next two chapters are devoted to the post-reforms period. Chapter four investigates the disastrous impact of deregulation on ITI. A combination of cut throat competition, lack of orders from its principal customer, falling prices and inappropriate technology provoked a deepening financial crisis which after erupting first in the mid-1990s saw the company again posting losses from 2002 onwards. Chapter five explores the response of the company to the threats posed by a radically transformed market environment. To cut costs and improve its competitive position, the management implemented various measures, one among them being a voluntary retirement scheme. None of these initiatives, however, yielded the solicited dividends because of worker resistance, poor implementation, lack of 'will', and inadequate organizational and financial resources.

Chapters six to nine engage from different angles with the strategies and actions of workers and their elected representatives. Chapter six revolves around an ethnographic account of work in the printed circuit board assembly shop. The need to enlarge the palette of resources traditionally available to historians in order to better interpret social phenomenon within the context of their production has prompted me to accord an important place to ethnography in this book. So in addition to describing the labour process underpinning the assembly of printed boards, I elaborate on the ways operatives carried out their tasks, the variations in individual practices, their motivations for working in the absence of managerial pressure, and relations between different members of the work group. Despite the standardized nature of the product and its low economic value, we shall see that operatives allocated to this task dispose a significant degree of autonomy in their daily activities.

Chapter seven is structured in two parts. Part one is given over to a sociological survey of workers at ITI's Bangalore plant. The largest of its kind to be conducted of organized sector employees in the country, the survey delineates both transformations and regularities in the composition and attributes of the labour force. For this purpose I have harnessed the procedures of a conventional sociological tool, multi-variate analysis, to historical ends by integrating an inter-generational perspective. It is important to note that unlike certain other public sector enterprises (Bhilai, Rourkela, etc.) where the numbers of cheap, short term workers have been increasingly growing at the expense of regular employees, in ITI we witness no such phenomenon. Questions related to unionism as it took root and developed at the Bangalore factory make up the second half of the chapter. A deep seated tradition of independent plant-level unionism marched in step with a culture of internal leadership. Both these factors imparted a distinctive character to the union's relations with the management on the one hand, and with the rank-and-file on the other.

The last two chapters deal with the theme of class and non-class identities. Chapter eight looks at the various forms of protest activity staged by workers and the union to secure higher monetary benefits, better promotion opportunities and shopfloor rights. Spontaneous rank-and-file discontent provided the impulse for several of these protests which were levelled as much at the company and the state as at the union. Chapter nine tracks the expression of more particularistic solidarities, defined along linguistic and caste lines. It will study the contest for domination of the factory public sphere opposing Kannada speaking workers against their Tamil counterparts as well as the antagonisms racking relations between caste Hindu and Scheduled Caste employees. Beacons of modernity erected to usher in a nationally self-conscious worker shorn of all traditional attachments, the Nehruvian vision exalting the public sector was more often than not betrayed by conflicts between contending primordial loyalties, each group intent on garnering what it deemed to be its rightful share of the fruits of industrialization.

chapter one

Construction of a Monopoly

I n line with the objectives of the ruling elites seeking to establish a 'mixed' economy regime, the first Industrial Policy Resolution, issued in April 1948, identified six industrial sectors deemed to be of national importance. In these sectors, the Indian state reserved for itself the exclusive right to start new ventures if it so wished. One of these was the production of telecommunications equipment.[1] Accordingly, in July 1948, the government founded ITI, making it the first public sector unit to be established after Independence. Protected from internal competition following the government's decision to exclude the private sector, ITI would also be protected from foreign competition, owing to the stringent restrictions enforced on imports. In other words, tariff barriers would supplement politico-legal measures to entrench its monopoly.

Organized at first as a departmental production unit of the Department of Post and Telegraph (P&T) which was itself attached to

---

[1] The other sectors were coal, iron and steel, aircraft manufacture, shipbuilding and minerals. Full state ownership was to be imposed, though, only on the railways, ordnance and atomic energy. The Second Industrial Policy Resolution, formulated in 1956, substantially increased the number of industries reserved exclusively for the state to 17.

the Ministry of Communications, ITI was incorporated as an independent enterprise under the Companies Act two years later with an initial authorized share capital of Rs 25 million. This would be raised subsequently to Rs 40 million of which the government of India owned 89.7 per cent, the Mysore state government 7.8 per cent, and the English company and ITI's first technology partner, Automatic Telephone and Electric Company (ATE), 2.5 per cent.[2]

Contrary to any outward impression, the transition from a department under the control of P&T to a full-fledged commercial company, while marking a formal change in ITI's status, did not bring about any transformation in the relations between the two organizations. It continued to remain under the administrative authority of P&T whose representatives sat on the ITI board of directors to whom the management was now officially responsible. Moreover, what distinguished ITI from practically all the other public sector enterprises, with the exception of companies producing defence equipment and fertilizers, was that P&T was not merely its parent body. It was also its sole customer. This would have significant implications for the functioning of the company throughout its existence.

The objective of setting up ITI had been to fabricate the equipment P&T needed to equip the national telecommunications network with. Inversely, ITI was the sole supplier of equipment to the state carrier.[3] This relationship of a monopsony-monopoly type in which the two sides were entwined thus gave their dealings a unique character, generating a sense of mutual dependency and symbiosis. It would take the onset of deregulation four odd decades later for these bonds to begin disintegrating. But while overall the power ratio may have favoured P&T, we must be cautious not to overemphasize this point. As the exclusive supplier of equipment, ITI too possessed adequate resources to ensure

[2] Estimates Committee, *11th Report on the Ministry of Transport & Communications— Indian Telephone Industries Ltd.*, New Delhi, 1958, p. 17. (Hereafter EC Report 1958.) ATE increased its shareholding later to 3.5 per cent, while that of the government of Mysore decreased marginally to 6.3 per cent. The shares held by ATE would be transferred back to the central government in 1977 consonant with the terms of its agreement. Annual Report 1971–72, p. 6.

[3] However, infrastructural equipment such as transmission cables would be produced by another state-owned enterprise, Hindustan Cables. Established in 1952, it would not report to P&T, unlike ITI and Hindustan Teleprinters (HTL) which was set up by the government in 1960 to manufacture teleprinters and accessories.

its own interests were not compromised. While it was, no doubt, unable to make its voice heard on issues of strategic importance, on operational questions at least, it could leverage its monopoly position. It could, therefore, not only extract concessions from the parent concern but also negotiate a definition of the situation that did not operate entirely to its disadvantage. The very fact that P&T had no choice on several occasions but to downgrade its quality norms and accept sub-standard equipment that the company produced itself demonstrated that the scales of power did not systematically tilt in the direction of the tutelary authority.

This cosy arrangement offered, at least on paper, appreciable benefits for both P&T and ITI. The latter was assured of a buyer for the totality of its output, as well as an unbroken even growing demand given the continuous expansion of the national network, thereby allowing it to operate in conditions of relative stability. If anything, lacking sufficient capacity, or failing to utilize it optimally, the company often struggled to meet P&T's requirements, obliging the latter to go in for imports with World Bank-backed financial assistance.[4] A practice of advance payments whereby ITI received, during the first half of the financial year, 50 per cent of the value of the total annual budgeted production also reduced the obligation to obtain working capital from external commercial sources.[5]

In addition, the cost-plus pricing system devised by P&T to govern its commercial transactions with ITI guaranteed the company healthy profits regardless of its production expenses. While this arrangement had the merit of encouraging supplier transparency with regard to production costs because the supplier was assured of generating profits, it also contributed to waste and, more generally, to low levels of cost consciousness and efficiency. The report submitted by the high-power Committee on Telecommunications (also known as the Sarin Committee) to the government in December 1981, in fact, categorically declared

---

[4] Between July 1976 and June 1984, for instance, P&T imported 50,000 lines of automatic switching equipment, and 24,000 lines of electronic trunk automatic exchange equipment, in addition to a variety of transmission systems. DoT, *Forty Years of Telecommunications*, New Delhi, nd (1987), p. 163; Committee on Public Undertakings (1981–82), *Indian Telephone Industries Ltd.—Research & Development and New Projects*, 38th Report, Seventh Lok Sabha, New Delhi, 1982, pp. 19–20. (Hereafter COPU 1982.)

[5] Advance payments would drop to 35 per cent in 1986, and fluctuate thereafter between 35 and 75 per cent.

that the 'present system of pricing should be given up as this has an imperceptible but growing deleterious effect on . . . efficiency . . .'[6] Initially, profit margins on equipment sales to P&T were fixed at 7.5 per cent before being hiked to 10 per cent in 1961, the figure staying more or less flat thereafter until 1986 when the ministry introduced a new pricing policy.[7] Not surprisingly therefore, the first time that ITI recorded losses in its history was in 1994–95 after deregulation had blown away its monopoly privileges. To cite a former ITI executive,

P&T only checked how we arrived at our costs. Its cost check units would verify prices of all components. But there was no auditor to determine whether and by how much we could reduce our costs.[8]

From the standpoint of P&T, full ownership of a captive industrial arm represented no negligible advantage either. Even the feeble moves initiated by ITI management to lessen its dependence on the state carrier by diversifying its revenue base, encountered strong opposition from the latter. Above all else, ownership of ITI paved the way for vertical integration, albeit of a bureaucratic variety. Since the company catered exclusively to its demands, P&T could make sure that the entire output was closely calibrated to, and technically fully in conformity with the requirements of the national network. In turn, ITI's familiarity with the workings of the network meant that it could respond easily to its parent's exigencies, thus bringing down transaction costs. Then, it enabled P&T to pool its resources with those of ITI, as well as coordinate and monitor their deployment more effectively. This point is well illustrated by the indigenous development of a fairly wide array of transmission equipment, owing to which the country could largely dispense with foreign technological inputs during the initial years. Next, a vertically integrated

[6] *Concluding Report of the Committee on Telecommunications*, New Delhi, Ministry of Communications, 7 December 1981 (mimeo), p. 82. None of the eight reports submitted by the eight-member committee, whose members included future Prime Minister Manmohan Singh, were made public.

[7] A new agreement signed between P&T and ITI in 1972 not only allowed a 10 per cent profit on interest charges paid by ITI, but hiked the profit margin on spare parts from 10 to 30 per cent. Ref. No. 57–34/70-NA, 10 June 1972. The Committee on Telecommunications would, however, later write that the high mark-up for spares was unjustified.

[8] Interview with L.G. Varadharajan, ex-General Manager, Telephone Division, ITI Bangalore, February 1999.

configuration provided P&T with a great deal of flexibility. The manufacture of transmission equipment again serves as a good example. Indigenously conceived designs lacked the sophistication of foreign ones, and P&T engineers frequently revised specifications, based on field reports of product performance, which in turn often imposed a stop-go rhythm on the ITI manufacturing schedules.[9] Such customer-induced interruptions of production flows would in all probability have been resisted by independent suppliers, but ITI, as a captive unit of P&T, had no choice but to bow to the wishes of its owner and principal buyer. Indeed, a former chairman of the company, who had spent his entire career with P&T before coming to ITI, accused the parent authority of treating ITI as its 'personal workshop'.

They (P&T officials) would ask ITI to make anything they had difficulty in making or were importing. For example, they found it difficult to import the clocks with telephone exchanges which measures conversation time. They asked ITI to manufacture it . . . The utilization of manufacturing resources was entrusted to P&T rather than ITI . . . *The demand from P&T was such that it would distort any sensible production planning.* You have to have production runs which are economical, but it was not so.[10]

Finally, backward integration by P&T facilitated, to some extent, the circulation of information. Systems engineering for strowger automatic exchanges, for instance, a task vested in the hands of ITI until P&T's own research cell, the Technical Research Centre, took it over in the early 1970s, called for the smooth exchange of information in both directions.[11] Based on the data furnished by P&T on the total number

[9] When a changing technology poses product redesign problems, specifying contractually the full range of contingencies may be prohibitively costly if not infeasible. Integration, on the other hand, permits an adaptive and sequential decision process to be utilized. Oliver Williamson, 'The Vertical Integration of Production: Market Failure Considerations', *The American Economic Review*, Vol. 61, No. 2, May 1971, pp. 112–23.

[10] Interview with C.S.S. Rao, ex-Chairman and Managing Director ITI, 9 August 1996. Emphasis added. (Interviewed by Balaji Parthasarathy.)

[11] As George Smith has remarked in his study, the integration of equipment producer Western Electric into the Bell system in the wake of the former's acquisition by AT&T was considerably facilitated by the close coordination and the sharing of information on business and technical problems in the engineering of exchanges between the two organizations. He goes on to write: 'The organizational genius of the Bell telephone system as it reached maturity in the early twentieth century was its highly integrated vertical structure'. *The Anatomy of a Business Strategy. Bell, Western Electric and the Origins*

of exchanges required for a given geographical area as well as estimates of traffic volumes, ITI had to actually design the exchanges, determining the exact number of switches and the types of switches needed, the number of racks, and so forth. Known as a trunking diagram, this blueprint would then be submitted to P&T, and only after it had given its approval could production commence. Communication lapses could either lead to production shortfalls or the supply of wrong kinds of equipment, and as a result, delay the commissioning of new exchanges. Errors in communication could therefore prove to be costly and had to be kept to a strict minimum.

Were the two key features of the market that we have identified, monopsony-monopoly relations and vertical integration, particular to India? The answer is no.[12] Identical conditions prevailed in the telecommunications sector in the USA, Canada and Italy. Prior to its dismantling in 1984, AT&T, for example, depended totally on its industrial affiliate Western Electric to turn out the full gamut of equipment the private American monopoly needed for the provision of economical services. At the same time, much like ITI, Western's monopolistic advantages were tightly interrelated to the fact that it could not accept work from any other customer barring the US defence forces, and even here, parent AT&T often voiced strong objections.[13] Across the border, Bell Canada operated in roughly the same manner, buying most of its equipment from subsidiary Northern Telecom.

Though the pattern in the other developed countries diverged somewhat from that of North America, it must not be forgotten that there too in the high noon of *dirigisme*, national telecommunications agencies by virtue of their monopolistic positions inevitably ended up

of the American Telephone Industry, Baltimore, 1985, pp. 127–33, 153 (citation). On AT&T's ties with Western see also Stephen B. Adams and Orville R. Butler, *Manufacturing the Future. A History of Western Electric*, Cambridge, 1999.

   [12] For an overall analysis of the telecommunications market structure in developed countries see Christiano Antonelli, *La diffusion des télécommunications de pointe dans les pays en développement*, Paris, 1991, pp. 65–9; Anne Marie Delaunay-Maculan, *Histoire comparée de stratégies de développement des télécommunications*, Paris, 1997, p. 22, 24–5, 46–7; OECD, *Les télécommunications. Perspectives d'évolution et stratégies des pouvoirs publics*, Paris, 1983, pp. 38–9, 43–4; Gerald Santucci, *L'industrie mondiale des télécommunications*, Paris, 1984, pp. 8–10.

   [13] Adams and Butler, *Manufacturing the Future*, pp. 148–50, 155–60.

being monopsonists. Second, even if vertical relations of a formal, institutional kind did not exist, national carriers generally tended to restrict the purchase of equipment to a small and select network of suppliers who usually shared the orders between them on a non-competitive basis.[14] In turn, the latter, capitalizing on their long-standing relations with the telecommunications carriers, acquired an intimate knowledge and experience of the structure and functioning of the network and so could easily adhere to the specifications, hence managing to considerably reduce transaction costs for their main customers. As Mark Granovetter asserts, it 'takes some kind of "shock" to jolt the organisational buying out of a pattern of placing repeat orders with a favoured supplier or to extend the constrained set of feasible suppliers'.[15]

If the protectionist policies followed by domestic carriers, plus the oligopolistic nature of the telecommunications manufacturing industry, partly accounted for the privileged commercial linkages that united buyers and suppliers, other factors also militated in favour of such a development. The technical complexity and scale of the equipment, the relatively high level of investments involved, the need for new switching gear to be compatible with the existing exchanges, supplemented by the fact that the equipment would be inducted into public networks counting large numbers of end users, and therefore constituted 'public goods', all of this rendered essential very close cooperation between service providers and equipment vendors. Such cooperation would be further reinforced by the creation of joint research teams as each country sought to come up with its own electronic switching systems.[16]

---

[14] The British Post Office's needs were catered to by a cartel of three equipment makers (GTC, Plessey, and STC-ITT) designated as the 'ring'. Geoffrey Owen, *From Empire to Europe. The Decline and Revival of British Industry Since the Second World War*, London, 1999, pp. 284–5. I am grateful to the author for the reference. In France, telecommunications operator PTT sourced the bulk of its equipment from three firms: ITT, CIT, and Ericsson. Laurence Bancel-Charensol, *La déréglementation des télécommunications dans les grands pays industriels*, Paris, 1996, pp. 98–9. The vendor base of the German Bundespost was even narrower, Siemens, and, to a lesser extent, Lorenz-ITT equipping the entire network. Delaunay-Maculan, *Histoire comparée de stratégies*, p. 40.

[15] Mark Granovetter, 'Economic Action and Social Structure: The Problem of Embeddedness', *The American Journal of Sociology*, Vol. 91, No. 3, November 1985, pp. 481–510 (cit. p. 496).

[16] On the crucial role played by state telecommunications agencies in promoting R&D in the developed countries, see Robert J. Chapuis and Amos Joel Jr., *100 years of*

CONSTRAINTS OF BACKWARD INTEGRATION

A system of bureaucratic backward integration did not, however, yield only advantages to P&T and ITI. It also had obvious disadvantages which probably penalized ITI far more heavily than it did the parent administration, and accounted for many of the chronic inefficiencies visible in the functioning of the company. The greatest cause for complaint by P&T was with respect to product quality standards. On paper, the speedier information flows arising from vertical relations, by strengthening ITI's problem-solving capabilities, should also have benefited P&T. But judging from the company's dismal quality record, as we shall study, this does not appear to have been the case. If, following from Albert Hirschman, integration can be considered as an arrangement for institutionalizing and routinizing voice which in turn is able to convey more information to organizations than 'exit', transforming 'voice' into corrective action is by no means guaranteed in all circumstances.[17] Indeed, it was precisely the lack of responsiveness displayed by ITI, and, its corollary, the reluctance and/or inability of P&T to take its industrial arm to task, which exposed most acutely the limitations of this bureaucratically integrated vertical structure. In view of their total domination of the domestic market, neither protagonist had much incentive to resolve the operational deficiencies that beset their respective organizations and improve the overall performance of the telecommunications network. Steps in this direction would only be forthcoming from the mid-1980s onwards when the rigours of competition shook, in a small way, both P&T and ITI out of their inertia.

Telephone Switching. Electronics, Computers and Telephone Switching (1960–1985), Amsterdam, 1990 (Vol. 2), pp. 59–62, 320–2; Louis-Joseph Libois, *Genèse et croissance des télécommunications*, Paris, 1983, pp. 142–3, 149–50, 158–71; OECD, *Les équipements de télécommunication: Transformations des marchés et des structures des échanges*, Paris, 1991, pp. 17–18. For a similar discussion with regard to developing countries, see Delaunay-Maculan, *Histoire comparée de stratégies*, chap. 6; and Bo Göransson, 'Third World Challengers on the International Market for Telecommunications Equipment: A Study of Brazil, India and South Korea', in C. Brundenius and B. Göransson (eds.), *New Technologies and Global Restructuring. The Third World at a Crossroads*, London, 1993, pp. 224–50.

[17] Albert O. Hirschman, 'Exit, Voice and Loyalty: Further Reflections and a Survey of Recent Contributions', in *idem, Essays in Trespassing. Economics to Politics and Beyond*, Cambridge, 1981, pp. 213–35.

Insofar as ITI was concerned, the very fact that the parent ministry treated it as its 'personal workshop' spoke volumes for its lack of autonomy. As one executive pointed out, P&T 'did not allow ITI the discipline required to run a manufacturing unit'.[18] What this essentially implied was that the company was deprived of the possibility of economies of scale in its operations. Indeed, the fact that it had to constantly adjust its production planning to cater to the demands of the state carrier defeated the very logic of mass production. Production runs for equipment such as telephones tended to be extremely short given the nature of P&T orders. If frequent product and tool changeover together with the snags involved in restarting production added up to a considerable loss of time, small unit volumes discouraged investments in capital-intensive processes and the search for more efficient manufacturing methods. Likewise, P&T's insistence on different types of phones (ordinary subscriber and multi-line instruments) being fabricated simultaneously augmented the management's coordination difficulties. It had to monitor the flow of a wide variety and quantity of parts and sub-assemblies, most of which were non-interchangeable, for the different product lines.

Initially P&T wanted separate colour coil cords, blue for blue phones, etc. This created lots of problems in terms of ordering, procuring, stocking and feeding specific colour cords in correct quantities to each line. There were also variations in colour from batch to batch and P&T used to object if the colour of the cord did not match the instrument. We were able to later convince it to standardize all coil cords to black colour.[19]

The dual status of P&T, simultaneously parent concern and principal customer of ITI, afforded the state carrier the legitimacy to cast an iron hand over all strategic and operational issues, to treat the company as a 'subordinate office' of the ministry, depriving the management of much of its autonomy.[20] Inheriting as it did the colonial bureaucratic legacy

[18] Interview with C.S.S. Rao.

[19] Interview with S.K. Ramanna, ex-General Manager, Telephone Division, ITI Bangalore, March–April 1999.

[20] *Report of the Economic Administration Reforms Commission on Government and Public Enterprises*, New Delhi, Government of India, 1983, p. 33. As various official committees set up to investigate the workings of public sector companies have underlined, the erosion of managerial autonomy was a generalized phenomenon affecting undertakings across the country to different degrees. See, *inter alia*, *Report of the Administrative Reforms Commission Study Team on Public Sector Undertakings*, New Delhi,

where suspicion and interventionism defined the norms of conduct adopted by the rulers towards the ruled, P&T's style of action *vis-à-vis* its industrial affiliate naturally placed heavy emphasis on both these elements.[21] As the principal buyer and user of ITI's products, P&T believed it occupied the vantage position to determine the public sector company's objectives, and implacably exercised its impressive arsenal of ownership powers to ensure these objectives were translated into results.

It prescribed basic policies of operations, strategies of growth, allocation of resources, and the course of industrial relations. It also played the role of both 'price maker' and 'quality maker', establishing the profit margins it was willing to pay ITI, and the product quality norms it believed the company should achieve. If capacity expansion and the location of new units were invariably political decisions brokered at the highest level of the government, technology choices, investment options, product mix, annual production targets, and appointment of top executives were all issues where the tutelary authority had the final, or often, the only say. Above the modest sum of Rs 1 million, the management could incur no capital expenditure on projects without securing the prior permission of the board. The board itself could sanction capital expenditure to the extent of Rs 4 million beyond which it had to submit all proposals to the government for approval. In the industrial relations area, not only did all wage agreements and employment conditions have to be authorized by P&T, but the latter also frequently dictated the timing as well as the overall terms and content of the collective bargaining process.

These formalized control procedures would subsequently be duplicated at a further level, that of the Bureau of Public Enterprises, the regulatory organ set up by the government in the mid-1960s to monitor the workings of state-owned companies. Only in the recruitment of the workforce did the management have a free hand. So, while entrusted with the managerial functions of governance and administration, virtually

---

Government of India, 1967, pp. 16–17; *Report of the Committee to Review Policy for Public Enterprises*, New Delhi, Government of India, 1986, pp. 5–11; COPU, 1988–89, *Accountability and Autonomy of Public Undertakings*, 50th Report, Eight Lok Sabha, New Delhi, 1989. (Hereafter COPU 1989.)

[21] A good overall presentation of the relationship between the administrative ministries and public sector companies can be found in S. Laxmi Narain, *Principles and Practice of Public Enterprise Management*, New Delhi, 1980.

the entire framework of rules upon which ITI executives relied to guide their actions tended to be formulated outside the enterprise.[22] Moreover, to the extent that the equipment vendor had no power to fix prices, the overriding trait of a monopoly, and set quality standards only by default as a quality 'spoiler', it was at best, a toothless monopoly.

To ensure that the management complied with its instructions, P&T dispatched its own officials on deputation to occupy all the key positions in the company. In addition, it reserved the top post of ITI chairman for the Secretary, Ministry of Communications, who normally belonged to the P&T administrative corps and also headed it. This was symbolic in that it marked the subordination of the equipment maker to the interests of the tutelary body. This latter practice would be discontinued in the late 1970s when the functions of the managing director of ITI were merged with those of the chairman, giving the company an 'independent' full time chairman.[23]

P&T PERSONNEL POLICIES RESENTED BY ITI MANAGERS

The parent body's practice of nominating its people to all the top administrative, financial, production, and research jobs caused much chagrin among the directly recruited ITI executives who found their promotion opportunities blocked.[24] Though the restructuring of the Bangalore plant into four separate divisions in the early 1970s, each

[22] Fayol defined governance as the act of piloting the enterprise towards its objective by optimally utilising the resources available, while administration consisted of drawing up the overall plan of action, constituting the workforce, or what he called the social corps, coordinating the efforts of all, and harmonizing their actions. Henri Fayol, 'General and Industrial Management', in *The Development of Management Science*, Vol. 1, London, 1993, pp. 7–8.

[23] In 1958 itself, a parliamentary committee had recommended the appointment of a chairman who had 'severed his connections with the administration'. But it would take the government nearly two decades to implement this measure. EC Report 1958, p. 11.

[24] As early as in 1953, an American scholar wrote that the 'most important operating problem of the new Government of India plants has been the development of effective top management. This means at minimum that each enterprise must develop a strong managerial group of its own with more authority, responsibility, continuity, and self confidence than an enterprise is likely to develop if run as a branch of a ministry'. George Baldwin, *Industrial Growth in South India. Case Studies in Economic Development*, Glencoe (Illinois), 1959, pp. 321–2.

devoted to a particular product line (strowger, crossbar, transmission, and telephones) afforded additional possibilities to the 'insiders' to move up the hierarchy, deputationists retained charge of certain divisions as well as the all-important post of general manager production. The deputationists by and large performed their jobs proficiently by the admission of career ITI executives themselves, but the latter also believed there was sufficient skill and experience available internally for the company not to have to rely on 'outside' expertise. P&T's practice of parachuting its own personnel into top company positions also affected the balance of power between the supervisory ministry and ITI in another manner. Since the deputationists provided P&T with the informational base required to monitor the company's operations, it was not reliant on the specialized expertise that local managers commanded, on their definition of the situation as it were, especially at critical moments. As such, they were deprived of a valuable strategic resource, the use of which could have helped to strengthen their hands when dealing with the tutelary body.[25]

At the same time, reframing the colour bar principle of the colonial epoch where no coloured person could exercise authority over a white person, the parent ministry made sure no deputationist reported to a locally recruited official: they were systematically placed one grade above the 'insiders', once again underlining the subordinate status of the company. The P&T personnel also enjoyed a number of material advantages, including higher salaries, special allowances, and accommodation in the ITI township. What further irked ITI executives was that the ultimate loyalties of the deputationists, right from the managing director downwards, lay not with the company, but with P&T. At the most, they spent three or four years working in ITI before returning to the parent body within whose ranks they continued to pursue their career trajectories.

---

[25] It was the monopoly over specialized knowledge exercised by salaried managers in big US industrial corporations that made them independent from the control of owners and sealed the triumph of managerial capitalism. Alfred D. Chandler Jr., 'The United States: Seedbed of Managerial Capitalism', in A.D. Chandler and H. Daems (eds.), *Managerial Hierarchies. Comparative Perspectives on the Rise of the Modern Industrial Enterprise*, Cambridge (Mass.), 1981, pp. 13–14. See also Max Weber who notes that even the absolute monarch is powerless when faced with the specialized technical knowledge of the bureaucratic expert. *Economy and Society*, Vol. 2, pp. 993–4.

Though it would be unfair to contend that these 'birds of passage' were inclined to sacrifice the company's interests to those of P&T, there is no doubt that they were not entirely committed to the future growth of the company. Their own long term personal interests also invariably led them to support the cause of the tutelary authority, notwithstanding personality clashes between the deputationists and their ministerial counterparts. They were thus far removed from the ideal of the 'organization man'. Further, P&T's policy of replacing the deputationists at relatively short intervals gave rise to a situation of quasi-permanent instability at the top. To be sure, this accentuated the lack of accountability that was an inherent aspect of the functioning of public sector enterprises: officials felt they could not be held responsible for measures initiated by their predecessors. As one former career ITI executive commented, the deputationists

refused to point out to P&T what was wrong in its system . . .They tried to always cover up P&T and expose ITI as wrong doers . . . They were not interested in putting forward the company's point of view effectively, what problems the company was facing. As a result, there were no solutions to the overall problems which kept recurring. ITI blamed P&T and vice versa.[26]

According to another 'insider', the deputationists viewed their stints in ITI as

a platform for greater glories, or to get experience in industry, or to try out certain experiences before returning to the Ministry, though the majority sought to play safe and only ensure that production was higher than what their predecessor(s) had achieved.[27]

Hence, the mutual dependency characteristic of relations between P&T and ITI did not in any way imply that these relations were harmonious or consensual. Even though overt conflict never broke out, interactions between the two sides carried a permanent undercurrent

---

[26] Interview with L.G. Varadharajan.

[27] Interview with M.V. Srinivasa Rao, ex-Executive Director, ITI Bangalore, February–March 1999. Highly critical of the attitude of the deputationists, one author writes: 'His (the deputationist's) stake in the enterprise is to the extent of not earning a bad name and bad reports from higher-ups...(and) he is happy as long as there is no accusation against him of mis-management or mis-handling of labour relations, etc.' S.K. Jain, 'Role of Trade Unions in Public Sector Enterprises', *Lok Udyog* , Vol. VII, Nos. 7 & 8, October–November 1974, p. 19.

of tension. Retired ITI executives especially expressed considerable resentment at the scope of P&T's ownership prerogatives which resulted in drastically curtailing the management's sphere of action and autonomy. A former head of the flagship Bangalore factory described the relationship between P&T and ITI as one of 'love-hate,' and where trust was lacking.

It was never a business relationship . . . We were the production arm of P&T; we were only an implementing agency . . . Lots of initiative that ITI could have taken was curbed by P&T . . . So even if we felt that things could be bettered, rather than argue with P&T we would get on with the job respecting existing specifications . . . P&T also lacked trust in ITI. This was reflected even in attitude of P&T personnel who had previously worked in ITI and then went back to the ministry.[28]

A bureaucracy in the weberian sense of the term being rigidly structured as a hierarchical pyramid with explicit regulations governing its internal and external interactions, P&T was also guilty of imposing its own bureaucratic style of functioning on ITI.[29] A blend of excessive attention to procedural detail, adherence to an infinite range of rules, dilatoriness, and the concentration of decision-making powers and competence at the apex, the diffusion of this bureaucratic culture was further facilitated by the deputationists monopolizing all the command levers in their hands.

The factory general manager would take most decisions, and all others would only execute instructions. There was no question of challenging the rationale behind the decision or even of taking initiative. Everything was driven by the rule book.[30]

Of course, the process of laying down explicit and highly formalized regulations capable of almost limitless extension, was a dynamic common

---

[28] Interview with Srinivasa Rao.

[29] According to Bhagwati and Desai, the civil service background of the deputationists meant that they 'inevitably tended to act with bureaucratic caution and unimaginativeness rather than in bold and inventive ways'. Jagdish Bhagwati and Padma Desai, *India, Planning for Industrialization. Industrialization and Trade Policies Since 1951*, New Delhi, 1979, p. 165. A point of view that is endorsed by Bagaram Tulpule who briefly ran the state-owned Durgapur steel plant. 'Management and Workers in Public Sector', *EPW*, Vol. XI, No. 22, 22 May 1976, pp. M49–57.

[30] Interview with Srinivasa Rao.

to all large companies, public or private.[31] However, bureaucratization not only struck deeper roots in the public sector on account of the pressures of 'political contingency' attendant on direct state ownership; ministerial interventions and the multiplication of official watchdog bodies to whom the managements were periodically obliged to report also played their part.[32] It was also perhaps more entrenched in ITI than in some of the other public sector enterprises because, compared with other administrative ministries, P&T, exploiting its dual role as owner and customer, maintained a much tighter grip over the company. Drawing attention to the progressive elimination of entry barriers to the telecommunications equipment manufacturing segment, a management note to the ITI board in 1986 recognized that the existing culture was far too bureaucratic and the company needed to 'become more competitive and change over to a new culture which would put emphasis on innovativeness and creativity'.[33] Certain measures initiated by the personnel department, for instance, had to be approved and countersigned by no less than seven different executives.[34]

Finally in 1978, in line with the government's moves to encourage all public sector companies to build their own managerial cadre and realizing the negative effect the presence of the deputationists was having on morale, ITI's first full time Chairman and Managing Director, C.S.S. Rao, decided to put an end to this practice.[35] Rao himself had personally resolved the dilemma of divided loyalties by choosing to quit P&T to become a regular employee of the ITI. He now named a career ITI executive to oversee all production operations at the main Bangalore plant. In parallel, nine senior P&T officials were transferred back to the

[31] Richard Edwards, *Contested Terrain. The Transformation of the Workplace in the Twentieth Century*, New York, 1979, chap. 8; Charles Perrow, 'A Society of Organizations', *Theory and Society*, Vol. 20, No. 6, December 1991, pp. 725–62.

[32] Political contingency is defined as the diversity of economic and political demands that are brought to bear upon state-owned enterprises and corporations by governments, ministries, political parties, public user bodies, private sector interest groups and so forth. Eric Batstone et al, *Consent and Efficiency. Labour Relations and Management Strategy in the State Enterprise*, Oxford, 1984, pp. 10–11.

[33] Note to ITI Board, 220th Meeting, Item No. B15, July 1986.

[34] Ref. ADP 020, 13 July 1998.

[35] The proportion of deputationists dropped from 6.2 per cent of the total managerial strength in all public sector enterprises in March 1966 to 1.7 per cent in January 1981. *Public Enterprises Survey* 1980–81, New Delhi, BPE, Vol. I, p. 259.

administrative ministry to make room for internal talent, while others were given the option of either permanently working for ITI or going back to P&T within a specified time frame. As Rao pointed out,

ITI had the expertise and there was a genuine feeling that they were not given the same opportunity as P&T . . . It caused a lot of heartburn . . . A man 20 years younger would come (from P&T) and order around.[36]

MOVES TO RATIONALIZE ITI FAIL

However, P&T stuck to its policy of regularly shuffling the chairman and managing director, sometimes within barely two years, with the result that the company continued to suffer from a lack of continuity at the top. Over a period of two decades, starting from 1978, as many as eight chairmen presided over the fortunes of ITI.[37] More significantly, until the mid-1990s at least, the tutelary authority clung on to its prerogative of handpicking one of its officials for the top job. A non-P&T functionary became chairman of ITI for the very first time in 1985, and the incumbent K.P.P. Nambiar owed this distinction largely to his personal equation with the then Prime Minister Rajiv Gandhi. This personal rapport also served to explain why Nambiar, an electronics engineer reputed for his dynamism and having experience of both the private and the public sector, was successful in overcoming fierce hostility from P&T towards his efforts to win a greater degree of freedom for the management by pushing through a reorganization of the ITI board of directors.

Hitherto, government representatives had dominated the eight-member board with four members, including two from the supervisory ministry, all of whom were part-time directors. The management was represented only by the managing director, and later the chairman and managing director.[38] Taking a cue from other state-owned companies

---

[36] Interview with C.S.S. Rao. There were still 34 deputationists on the company's rolls in July 1979. *Public Enterprises Survey* 1978–79, New Delhi, BPE, p. 239.

[37] Turnover was hardly lower in other public sector plants: between 1957–71, the Durgapur steel plant saw six general managers come and go. Bagaram Tulpule, 'Managing Durgapur: Experiences of a Trade-unionist' (Part I), *EPW*, Vol. XI, No. 52, 25 December 1976, pp. 1993–2003.

[38] By the early 1970s, the board had been enlarged to ten members. While the management now had three representatives, the administrative ministry had four, besides having the power to count on the support of the remaining members.

such as BEL and BHEL, Nambiar now sought to transform what he called a 'free lunch board virtually ruled by P&T' into a professional one, comprising in the main full time directors, by changing its composition.[39] Though it would require almost two years before the new configuration fully materialized, the heads of the three largest production units (Bangalore, Rae Bareli, and Mankapur) were brought in together with the finance and R&D chiefs, thus ensuring a majority for the management. But in subsequent years, the heads of the Rae Bareli and Mankapur plants would not sit on the board.

Nambiar was also the architect of a more radical proposal to sever all ownership links between ITI and P&T. Already in the past, there had been a move to transfer the control of ITI from the Ministry of Communications to the Ministry of Industries on the grounds that the company would grow at a faster pace and in new directions as well as be in a position to exercise greater decision-making powers if it were attached to an administrative ministry which was not also its principal customer.[40] However, both P&T and the Communications Ministry had persuaded the government that the existing arrangement was best suited to the interests of all sides. Nambiar now challenged this view, arguing instead that ITI stood to gain far more if the Department of Electronics took the company under its wing. On this occasion too, the Communications Ministry managed to outmanoeuvre Nambiar, although it also had to abandon its own ambitions of restructuring ITI.

In effect, in November 1981, the Committee on Telecommunications, which had been set up by the government with the objective of improving the performance of the telecommunications system in the country, had drawn up a plan to bifurcate ITI into two geographically distinct and

[39] Interview with K.P.P. Nambiar, ex-Chairman and Managing Director ITI, 23 July 1996. (Interviewed by Balaji Parthasarathy.) In 1989, the government accepted a recommendation made by the parliamentary committee on public undertakings to restrict the number of administrative ministry representatives on the ITI board to just one. But P&T often continued to nominate two members. COPU 1989, pp. 16–17.

[40] This was, for instance, the case with Hindustan Cables; though it made transmission cables, and though the Ministry of Communications, which was its principal customer, wanted for this reason the company to report directly to it, the latter remained under the authority of the Ministry of Industries. *Concluding Report of the Committee on Telecommunications*, p. 16.

independent companies.[41] The plan called for regrouping the two plants located in the south (Bangalore and Palakkad) into one company, while the three existing northern plants (Rae Bareli, Naini, and Srinagar) would form the second. In recommending the division of ITI, the committee was motivated primarily by the desire to create a more streamlined and efficient organization, capable of better response to the demands of P&T in terms of both quantity and quality.

With a workforce of nearly 27,000 employees, distributed in five different sites across the country, the company had become far too large and dispersed, the committee opined (Table 1.1). It therefore concluded that the top management was unable to provide the necessary focus and direction at a time when the government actively envisaged the introduction of new electronic switching technologies as well as the expansion of the company. As it stated,

The size of the operations and the geographical positioning of the units is such that coordination, control and management by a centralised agency cannot be effective resulting in delays, shortfalls in production and loss of efficiency . . . (F)or . . . factory organizations manufacturing a variety of equipment there is an optimum size beyond which the viability and overall performance get affected. At present ITI has a large complex at Bangalore . . . The Corporate Office has to devote much of its attention to this complex. But greater attention and control is equally needed now at other places to handle the major production units which are coming up.[42]

Rationalization, though, was not without its drawbacks. Apart from the likely increase in overall staff levels, the economies derived from the sharing of common resources in areas such as R&D, marketing and quality control would certainly have to be sacrificed. With equipment having to come from several independent units, problems of coordinating deliveries to customers could also arise as could ensuring balanced supplies. Still, the committee believed these disadvantages were more than outweighed by the advantages.

If units are medium sized and viable, problems can be more clearly identified, they can be managed better and higher operational efficiency can be achieved.[43]

[41] *Fifth Interim Report of the Committee on Telecommunications*, New Delhi, Ministry of Communications, November 1981, pp. 36–8.

[42] ibid, pp. 36–7.

[43] ibid, pp. 37–8.

Table 1.1: Workforce Strength at Seven Units of ITI

Year	Bangalore	Sri-nagar	Naini	Rae Bareli	Manka-pur	Pala-kkad	EC Unit (B'lore)	Total*
1970	13,869	14						13,883
1971	14,342	37						14,379
1972	14,816	38	410					15,264
1973	15,873	48	635					16,556
1974	16,571	64	1674					18,309
1975	17,078	85	2672	188		25		20,048
1976	17,825	82	3326	805		84		22,122
1977	18,353	89	3901	1409		108		23,860
1978	19,055	102	3939	1948		109		25,153
1979	19,378	107	4120	2308		108		26,021
1980	19,496	120	4402	2659		122		26,799
1981	18,618	121	4449	2761		153		26,102
1982	18,375	138	4434	2985		186		26,118
1983	18,165	147	4580	3353	111	213		26,569
1984	18,245	163	4577	4121	211	229		27,546
1985	18,075	181	4595	5658	393	273		29,175
1986	18,061	180	4576	6246	998	367		30,428
1987	18,011	236	4573	6182	1402	596		31,000
1988	17,306	240	4635	6160	1777	804		32,447
1989	16,813	241	4637	6216	1812	820		32,368
1990	16,494	240	4676	6314	2063	832		32,298
1991	15,920	238	4731	6241	2436	877		32,215
1992	14,039	145	4713	6185	2473	889		30,230
1993	13,409	234	4676	6160	2530	911	481	29,730
1994	12,527	158	4666	6113	2503	903	466	28,633
1995	11,423	155	4680	6048	2481	892	452	27,477
1996	10,358	151	4618	6004	2455	869	428	26,272
1997	9556	160	4523	5935	2411	840	496	25,915
1998	8880	191	4436	5879	2395	813	493	24,553
1999	8250	194	4374	5821	2399	815	633	23,945
2000	7897	194	4358	5788	2355	812	686	23,567
2001	7222	201	4273	5715	2289	798	708	22,691
2002	5685	194	4136	5633	2302	775	658	21,518
2003	4545	184	3899	5475	2264	744	591	19,679

Note: *From 1992 figure includes corporate office and regional sales and marketing offices.

Source: ITI Personnel Department.

In the end the ministry decided against implementing the plan for unknown reasons. According to the management, its argument that dividing ITI would considerably weaken the northern plants, as they would no longer benefit from the resources controlled by the mother unit in Bangalore, had succeeded in convincing P&T, but we have no means of verifying this contention.[44] Following the launch of the new electronic switching factory at Mankapur in 1983, P&T again toyed with the idea of dismantling ITI, but this time into three separate structures. While the Rae Bareli, Naini and Srinagar units would comprise one entity, a second would unite Mankapur and Palakkad, which shared the same technology base, leaving Bangalore to operate as a stand alone organization. This proposal too met with the same fate as its predecessor.[45]

GOVERNMENT ACCORDS LOW PRIORITY TO TELECOMMUNICATIONS SECTOR

Despite being in the position of a monopoly service provider, the telephone arm of P&T, as opposed to the postal and telegraph arm, remained a perennially fund-starved monopoly. This was for two reasons: first, smaller than the latter, the telephone division was nonetheless the principal revenue earner of P&T, but most of its profits went to subsidize the loss-making activities of the post and telegraph services.[46] This situation would only end in 1985 when the government separated post and telegraphs from telephones, and created an autonomous structure, the Department of Telecommunications, to take charge of the national telephone network.[47]

---

[44] Interviews with M.S. Jayasimha, ex-Executive Director (R&D), ITI Bangalore, February–March 1999; and Srinivasa Rao.

[45] Minutes of ITI Apex Level Negotiating Forum Meeting, 16 October 1984; ITI Employees Union, Bangalore, Circular No. 19/87, 22 May 1987.

[46] Krishnalal Shridharani, *Story of the Indian Telegraphs: A Century of Progress*, New Delhi, 1953, pp. 85–6.

[47] In France too, only after the telecommunications department won a self managing role in the 1970s did its subordination to the interests of the postal services cease and the development of the national network take off in a big way. Claude Giraud, *Bureaucratie et changement. Le cas de l'administration des télécommunications: "Du 22 à Asnières" à la télématique*, Paris, 1987, pp. 49–54.

Second, since policy makers viewed telecommunications as a luxury item catering exclusively to urban markets and not as a developmental priority, they completely neglected this sector. As one official document put it, telecommunications 'is a consumer item particularly of the rich. At best, it deserves the same priority as five star hotels'.[48] Indeed, a widely circulated joke amongst ITI executives held that only the health care department ranked below P&T in the government's hierarchy of priorities. Not until the mid-1980s would the government appreciate the potential of telephone density as a dynamo of economic progress. Despite the overall growth in investments, telecommunications' share in successive plan outlays from 1951 to 1985 showed but minimal increases, averaging around two per cent of the total (Table 1.2). The story was much the same with respect to its share of gross domestic investment which averaged roughly 1.3 per cent.[49] Far from approving P&T's demands for higher allocations, the government, in fact, systematically scaled down its financial requirements, and also prohibited it from resorting to public borrowings.[50]

As a result, the state carrier had to depend exclusively on a combination of direct budgetary support and internal resource generation to fund the expansion of the national network.[51] While it managed to mobilize fairly substantial surpluses, these were still woefully insufficient to satisfy the spiralling demand for new telephone connections. One report would categorically declare that the 'main problem . . . has been the allocation of inadequate resources for telecommunication development'.[52] Even compared to other developing countries such as Brazil, South Korea or

[48] Cited in R. Balashankar, *Golden Era of Indian Telecommunications 1947–1997*, New Delhi, 1998, p. 30.

[49] DoT, *Forty Years of Telecommunications*, pp. 48–9.

[50] For the Fourth Plan, for instance, as against an estimated requirement of Rs 8460 million, P&T was only granted a sum of Rs 4662.5 million, forcing it to lower its target of new telephone connections. Estimates Committee (1972–73), *41st Report on Ministry of Communications (Telephones)*, New Delhi, 1973, p. 11, 17, 29. (Hereafter EC Report 1973.) Only from the late 1980s onwards was the Department of Telecommunications, via its subsidiary MTNL, authorized to raise money on the capital market.

[51] Between 1951–85, P&T generated a sum of Rs 21,380 million by way of internal resources which represented 43.8 per cent of the total plan outlay for the telecommunications sector. DoT, *Forty Years of Telecommunications*, p. 48.

[52] *Eight Five Year Plan for Telecommunication Services* (1992–97), New Delhi, Government of India, 1997, p. 18.

Table 1.2: Financing of Telecommunications Investments

Five Year Plan	Telecom Investment (Rs. millions)	Telecom % Total Plan Outlay	Budgetary Support % Telecom Investment	Internal Resources % Telecom Investment	Borrowings % Telecom Investment
First Plan (1951–56)	470	2.40	79	21	0
Second Plan (1956-61)	660	1.41	68	32	0
Third Plan (1961–66)	1640	1.91	61	39	0
Annual Plans (1966–69)	1590	2.40	na	na	0
Fourth Plan (1969–74)	4150	2.63	28	72	0
Fifth Plan (1974–78)	7810	2.73	0	100	0
Annual Plans (1978–80)	5190	2.26	na	na	0
Sixth Plan (1980–85)	27,220	2.48	33	67	0
Seventh Plan (1985–90)	81,230	3.6	14	66	20
Annual Plan (1990–92)	30,400	na	1	84	15
Eight Plan (1992–97)	251,100	na	0	75	25
Ninth Plan (1997–2002)	464,420	na	0	100	0

Source: Department of Telecommunications; Annual Report (various years); *Forty Years of Telecommunications.*

Sri Lanka, the ratio of telecommunications investment to gross fixed capital formation, it added, was 'poor in our case'.[53]

Other problems included the lack of advance planning given the considerable lead time necessary for establishing new production facilities,

[53] ibid.

deflated forecasts, inadequate realization of the benefits of new technologies, and slow and complex procedures. The cumulative effect of all these constraints provoked a chain reaction where an overstretched and under-equipped grid became synonymous with the provision of extremely unsatisfactory services to subscribers, as reflected in the long wait lists, low teledensities, and high fault rates, which in turn led to a substantial loss of potential revenue for P&T. In 1950, the number of telephone main lines per 100 inhabitants stood at 0.05. Three-and-a-half decades later, the figure had barely crept up to 0.386 (compared to a worldwide telephone density of roughly 7). Echoing this economy of shortages, the official waiting list skyrocketed from 22,000 lines in 1955 to 295,000 lines a decade later to 637,000 lines in 1975.[54] Delays of a year or more before subscribers obtained new connections were frequent even in the principal urban centres.

The low priority given to telecommunications had important consequences for ITI which, like its parent organization, constantly suffered from a paucity of resources. While the company never failed to post profits until the early 1990s, these were far from adequate for it to independently finance its development. Consequently, it was both under-capitalized all along, and faced a crisis of under-capacity for several years. The government's general indifference to the growth prospects of the telecommunications sector was evident in its reluctance to augment its stake in the company whose share capital stayed flat for a number of years, first, at Rs 40 million, and, then, at Rs 250 million. Even subsequently, the figure would only climb up to Rs 1000 million. The narrow equity base would contribute greatly to ITI's financial difficulties in the aftermath of deregulation in 1991.

Direct government funding from the plan outlays also remained quite low initially. Despite the widening gap between P&T's demand requirements and ITI's equipment supply capabilities, the company received a total of only Rs 191.7 million by way of investment assistance for its growth during the first four plans (1951–74). By the end of the Third Plan (1966), it was turning out barely 100,000 exchange lines

[54] *Indian Telecommunication Statistics*, New Delhi, 1985, p. 4, 75. Demand for new lines sharply declined after 1975 once P&T made it compulsory for all potential subscribers to pay an advance deposit. Still, in 1980 the waiting list contained close to 330,000 names.

and an equal number of telephones annually.[55] Although the main
Bangalore plant witnessed a steady expansion of its production facilities,
it was not until 1969 that the government gave permission for the setting
up of a second factory at Naini in Uttar Pradesh. A third unit came up a
few years later, in 1973, at Rae Bareli, also in Uttar Pradesh. From this
point onwards the government started injecting larger sums in a hurried
bid to increase production capacity and reduce the waiting list for new
connections. From Rs 528.5 million in the Fifth Plan (1974–78), outlays
earmarked for ITI more than doubled to Rs 1367.3 million in the Sixth
Plan (1980–85), before jumping to Rs 3350 million in the Seventh Plan
(1985–90). But as the Committee on Telecommunications would declare
in its report in 1981,

The creation of additional capacities for production has been *too little* and *too
late*, and has taken unduly long time to implement.[56]

In the first year of the Sixth Plan, for instance, ITI's total value of
production stood at Rs 945.5 million, or less than half of P&T's annual
estimated needs of Rs 2720 million. According to the committee, to
fulfil the targets laid down in the plan, ITI would have to turn out 1.83
million local exchange switching lines over a period of five years, but it
boasted a potential capacity of only 1.15 million lines, and this figure
assumed the launch of two new factories.[57] To compensate for the
shortfall, the government therefore intended to go in for higher imports,
setting aside the amount of Rs 6770 million for this purpose.[58] This
represented a massive hike over the Fourth Plan (1969–74) where the

[55] *The Third Five Year Plan Report*, New Delhi, Planning Commission, 1961,
p. 567.

[56] *Fifth Interim Report*, p. 3. Emphasis added. For a good all-round discussion of the
factors responsible for the below-par performance of the national network as well as
P&T/DoT's inability to satisfy consumer demand see also Ghayur Alam, 'Performance
of Imported Technology in LDCs. The Case of the Telephone Industry in India', New
Delhi, 1981 (mimeo).

[57] The production targets laid down in the Sixth Plan were in fact substantially
lower than the demand forecasts for switching equipment calculated by the
Telecommunications Capacity Planning Committee in 1973. According to it, the country
required at least 3.9 million lines during the Plan period. *Report of the Technical Team
for Switching System Selection*, New Delhi, P&T, December 1975 (mimeo), p. 10.
(Hereafter Switching System Selection Report.)

[58] *Fifth Interim Report*, p. 4, 51–52.

value of telecommunications equipment imports did not exceed Rs 113.20 million.[59]

Furthermore, because P&T itself was handicapped by severe financial constraints, it proved to be equally tight-fisted towards its manufacturing arm. Indeed, top officials would openly declare one year that ITI was capable of 'greater achievements' but for the resource crunch faced by the parent administration.[60] Attempts were made to substitute the cost-plus arrangement with a fixed price contract which, by yielding higher profits, would have enabled the company 'to accumulate sufficient reserves', but P&T turned down the proposal.[61] On another occasion the management complained about the state carrier's inability to pay the company on account of fund restrictions. This in turn impinged on production and put a 'great strain on the cash resources' of ITI, obliging it to secure short-term commercial loans of Rs 150 million.[62] Similarly, in December 1983, after noting that a downward revision in production volumes both for the current and the following year would, besides hurting its own cash flow position, have a 'serious impact on ITI's credibility with suppliers and its performance as a production unit', the management wanted that

a permanent solution to this problem should be found as the country appears to require the equipment that ITI would produce, and ITI could also not diversify and export as the production lines are oriented towards the requirement of Indian P&T (sic).[63]

This statement amply illustrated the severe constraints inherent in this form of bureaucratic vertical integration where P&T was simultaneously unable and unwilling to encourage the future expansion of ITI. Handicapped by the lack of adequate resources, P&T equally apprehended the ensuing likely loss of authority and control if it allowed ITI to diversify its revenue and customer base. Company executives also singled out the contradiction between, on the one hand, the government mandating sizeable capital expenditures to start new factories with the

---

[59] EC Report 1973, p. 29.

[60] Annual Report 1962–63, p. 7.

[61] Annual Report 1964–65, p. 12.

[62] Annual Report 1983–84, p. 5.

[63] Ref. K/B3/1/82 (199), Minute No. 4179 of Board of Directors, 21 December 1983.

objective of augmenting telecommunications equipment output levels, and, on the other, P&T struggling to obtain the requisite budgetary support to purchase this equipment. But though the parent administration promised to explore the possibility of raising funds directly from the market, no permanent solution to the question of resource shortfalls would be forthcoming.

chapter two

History and Politics of Technological Change

The story of the development of the telecommunications equipment sector during the colonial epoch is of a piece with the rest of the capital and intermediate goods industry in the country at this time. Shortages occasioned by the onset of World War II reduced the reliance of the telephone and telegraph network on imports, coming in the main from the UK, and provided the impetus to begin producing certain kinds of equipment indigenously. Workshops had been established in different parts of the country, including key centres like Calcutta and Bombay, for repairs and maintenance. Controlled by the P&T whose monopoly over the provision of telephone and telegraph services across the nation was definitively sealed by the early 1940s, the activities of these entities were now considerably expanded. In addition to turning out certain types of telephone and telegraph equipment—manual trunk exchanges and manual switchboards were, for instance, successfully made for the first time in India—they also displayed considerable initiative by designing and manufacturing some of the machinery needed for this purpose.[1]

[1] DoT, *Forty Years of Telecommunications*, p. 117.

Yet, notwithstanding their achievements, the overall output of the workshops was not only small in scale and variety, but confined exclusively to low-value, technologically unsophisticated products. Automatic switching exchanges, open wire carrier transmission systems and other high value-high technology equipment continued to be imported in totality from the UK. Obviously because industrialization had occurred along a very narrow front, even the production of relatively low technology items, like transmission cables, which could easily have been undertaken indigenously was not done.

In addition to the P&T workshops, a private British firm called Telephone Manufacturers of India (TMI) was also involved in the production of telecommunications equipment. Founded sometime before the end of World War II, it seems to have been financially linked to the Liverpool-based ATE, ITI's future technology partner.[2] TMI controlled two small facilities in India. The first, situated in Dehra Dun, employed no more than 150 people who assembled telephones as well as manufactured parts for telephones and exchanges.[3] The second unit was established in Calcutta to cater to the communication needs of big private business houses, and focussed on importing private automatic exchanges and private automatic branch exchanges which it then installed and serviced.[4] However, whatever hopes TMI may have entertained of strengthening its operations in India were dashed by the advent of Independence and the decision of the Indian government to entrust the manufacture of telecommunications equipment exclusively to domestic state-owned enterprises.

Consequently, by the end of 1948, the firm had shut down both its units. Not only would ITI inherit the bulk of its machine stock; more vitally, it would recruit a number of skilled and experienced workmen from the Dehra Dun factory, appointing them as supervisors and chargehands to oversee key manufacturing areas such as the tool room, the automatic machines shop, the plating section, and the relay machine

[2] Our information on TMI, based largely on oral sources, is rather patchy.

[3] Interview with S. Mukherjee, ex-Superintendent automatic machines shop, ITI Bangalore, 8 February 1999; D Subramanyam, ex-Works Manager, ITI Bangalore, 1 April 1999.

[4] L. G. Varadharajan, 'Production of Telecommunication Equipment in India in Public and Private Sectors', (mimeo), nd.

shop.[5] Likewise, the two British managers who headed TMI would be dispatched by ATE to ITI as part of the agreement to provide foreign technical personnel to run the plant until such time as local staff had been trained to replace them.

Thus, at the time of Independence, the telecommunications sector, like most branches of the engineering industry, was characterized by an extremely modest manufacturing base, capable of producing at best a narrow range of low technology equipment. While small pockets of skills were available which ITI could and did tap, these resources were more than offset by the absence of any real technical or production expertise in the fabrication of modern telecommunications equipment. The company would therefore be obliged to build from scratch, and rely on a combination of state investment and specialized foreign technological assistance to lay down the foundations of a telecommunications network and industry deserving of their name.

Notwithstanding the official post-independent discourse emphasizing the making of an economically self-reliant India, and the restrictions imposed on foreign investments, from the outset, policy officials (and the world of business) realized that the foundations of the modern industrial infrastructure they planned to establish would have to perforce rest on massive infusions of imported technology.[6] The tremendous acceleration of the technological revolution ever since the inter war years,

---

[5] One such worker was S. Mukherjee. An SSLC graduate, he had entered TMI as an unpaid apprentice in 1944 at the age of 17, rising to the post of chargehand by the time the Dehra Dun factory folded up four years later. He was then hired by P&T's Calcutta workshop to run the automatic machines section. Contacted by ITI in the middle of 1949, he promptly agreed to work for the new company, only to discover when the appointment letter arrived that the salary on offer was much lower than what he was actually taking home. ITI management responded positively to his demand for better terms, but the new offer still left Mukherjee unsatisfied. Then, the ITI Assistant Works Manager, who knew Mukherjee from TMI and was well aware of his skill and qualities, convinced the management to match Mukherjee's current salary. In September 1949, he finally joined ITI. Appointed as chargehand in the automatic machines shop, he remained there until his retirement in 1985.

[6] Even as the big Indian business houses took over the old European managing agencies at the time of Independence, they simultaneously entered into technical collaborations with transnational corporations. Rajat K. Ray, *Industrialization in India. Growth and Conflict in the Private Corporate Sector 1914–47*, New Delhi, 1982, pp. 275–6, 362–4.

prompting Eric Hobsbawm to speak of a 'technological earthquake', had transformed the gap separating the developed and the developing countries into a yawning gulf.[7] Indeed, the absence of a dynamic capital and intermediate goods sector was synonymous with the absence of a strong technology base; India counted just two industrial research institutes at the time of Independence. The Second Five Year Plan (1956–61) clearly underscored the contradiction between the ambitious growth objectives outlined by the government and the insufficient number of technicians available in the country to realize these projects.[8]

In December 1947, P&T sent a technical officer to Europe to contact leading telephone equipment manufacturers for discussions on a technology tie-up.[9] Of the four offers that the officer received, only two were considered seriously by the government. One of these was from a Swiss company whose name remains unknown, while the other came from ATE, the pioneering manufacturer of automatic switching equipment in the UK. Subsequently, a proposal was also made by the transnational ITT which declared its willingness to provide technical assistance for the production of radio and wireless equipment in addition to telephone equipment. In the end, the government selected the English firm ATE entering into a 15 year-long agreement with it in May 1948.

Thus ATE equipped India's first automatic exchange at Simla in 1914 with the step-by-step strowger system, and won similar orders for other cities both from the government and the Bombay Telephone Company.[10] By the mid-1920s it had supplied close to 15,000 lines to India. The fact that several public exchanges in the country had already installed strowger exchanges would, no doubt, play a decisive part in the Indian

---

[7] E.J. Hobsbawm, *Age of Extremes. The Short Twentieth Century 1914–1991*, London, 1996, p. 265. See also David Landes, *The Unbound Prometheus. Technological Change and Industrial Development in Western Europe from 1750 to the Present*, Cambridge, 1993, pp. 517–22.

[8] *The Second Five Year Plan Report* (1956–61), New Delhi, Planning Commission, 1956, pp. 165–7, 402–03.

[9] All the material on the selection of a technology partner for ITI comes from EC Report 1958, pp. 2–3.

[10] A private British firm licensed to install and operate exchanges in some of the major Indian cities, the Bombay Telephone Company's assets would be purchased by the government in 1943 and transferred to P&T. Shridharani, *Story of the Indian Telegraphs*, pp. 88–104, 158–60.

government's decision to collaborate with ATE.[11] In addition, the company offered to sell its know-how on far more attractive terms than the other two candidates. While the Swiss firm demanded licence fees and royalty payments of Rs 14.6 million, as well as an engagement committing the government to purchase equipment from it, and ITT Rs 13.3 million, ATE asked for a sum of Rs 8.7 million.[12]

Once the government had settled the question of a technology partner for ITI, it proceeded to finalize the location of the new company. Certain sections within the administrative ministry apparently wished to see it come up in the proximity of P&T's own workshops either at Calcutta or Jabalpur. However, the government did not favour this solution, and announced that ITI would be established in Bangalore. Strategic considerations partly dictated the government's decision. Having already fought one war against neighbouring Pakistan, one of its major concerns was to situate the new capital goods industries at a safe distance from the border between the two countries.[13]

The other reason that lay behind the choice of Bangalore was the commitment given by the Government of Mysore to help set up ITI. In particular, it promised to provide free land, and acquired a huge tract of land, covering 368 acres, seven miles away from the main city. Apart from accessibility to a water tank, the site had the added advantage of being situated next to a railway station, with a siding extended all the way into the factory. The aid extended by the Mysore government to ITI must be seen as a continuation of the policy of state-sponsored industrialization that the former had vigorously pursued even prior to

---

[11] Patented by Almon Strowger in the US in May 1891, the strowger electro-mechanical switch marked the birth of automatic telephonic switching. Known also by its generic name of the 'step-by-step' system, the switch responded to pulses emitted by the rotary telephone dial. Robust, simple to operate, of proven reliability, and relatively inexpensive to manufacture, the exceptional longevity of the strowger technology can be measured from the fact that it remained operational in certain countries for over 50 years.

[12] The total cost of the technology purchased from ATE would ultimately work out much higher to Rs 11.21 million, of which Rs 5.37 million comprised the actual royalties, while the remainder went into taxes ITI had to pay on behalf of the English company. The percentage of technology costs to the overall project costs is unknown. COPU (1972–73), *Indian Telephone Industries Ltd.*, 34th Report, Fifth Lok Sabha, New Delhi, April 1973, p. 4. (Hereafter COPU 1973.)

[13] Baldwin, *Industrial Growth in South India*, p. 153.

Independence, winning for itself a reputation as the foremost standard-bearer of industrial development amongst the princely states.[14]

Prior to the creation of ITI, Bangalore was already home to another state-owned company, Hindustan Aircraft, later rechristened HAL, founded in 1940 by Walchand Hirachand and nationalized two years later. In the 1950s, two other public sector companies would also come to be located here: HMT, specializing in the fabrication of machine tools, and BEL producing electronic components. The identity of the city as the 'citadel of the giant public enterprise' would be stamped even more strongly on its geography in 1965.[15] That year the central government commissioned a fifth public sector enterprise, BEML, by spinning off HAL's rail coach and heavy earthmoving equipment divisions into an independent entity. The five undertakings totally dominated the industrial landscape of Bangalore in terms of capital investments, turnover and manpower. With close to 80,000 people on their rolls in 1980–81, they accounted for almost a quarter of the total workforce employed in the manufacturing and repair sectors in the city.[16] The spatial concentration would also encourage the managements of these companies to strive for a closer coordination of their actions, especially in the industrial relations field where they successfully forged a multi-plant organizational and wage-bargaining platform. This collective response would in turn serve as the catalyst for the trade unions' own unity-building drive.

ITI TAKES DIRECT TECHNOLOGY TRANSFER ROUTE

The technical assistance agreement negotiated between the government and ATE constituted a full package, encompassing manufacturing know-how, product design and consultancy services. ATE directly transplanted to ITI its systems, production processes, and products. Technical

---

[14] ibid, p. 39. An official report also attributed the emergence of a relatively broad manufacturing base in Mysore to the 'bold industrial policy' of the princely authorities. Kasturbai Lalbhai, *Report on State-aided Industries in Mysore*, New Delhi, Government of India, 1951.

[15] E.A. Ramaswamy, *Worker Consciousness and Trade Union Response*, New Delhi, 1988, p. 128.

[16] According to the 1981 census, a total of 362,394 people held manufacturing and repair jobs in Bangalore urban district. *Census of India 1981*, Series 9 Karnataka, General Economic Tables Part III A&B (i) and (ii).

personnel from the English firm had the task of supervising the detailed lay-out of the new factory and overseeing its running until such time as local managers had acquired sufficient competence and experience to assume operational responsibilities. Between 1948–57, the year when the management of ITI passed over completely into Indian hands, ATE sent 23 people, underlining the importance of the personal mechanism in the transmission of industrial technology.[17] They occupied various posts in the company, including the key ones of works manager and chief inspector, besides heading the administration and recruitment department, most of the production shops, and the training school. The reputation which ITI would subsequently gain for strong systems discipline, though by the 1970s much of it would be observed only in the breach, was a decisive contribution made by the foreign technicians who prescribed methodical procedures to regulate all aspects of the factory's activities. The transfer of know-how was thus confined not solely to technical expertise, but also extended to practical expertise pertaining to the overall organization of work.[18]

Everything was written down. The procedure for incoming materials, for instance, specified how it should be received, stored, inspected, by whom, what procedures were to be followed for rejection and acceptance, movement to stores, etc. Over 300 such procedure orders were drawn up . . .[19]

Adds another senior ITI executive:

The systems we inherited from the British were very good, fool proof . . . They were far superior to ISO 9000 . . . Everything was properly documented, standardized and structured . . . We inherited the British manufacturing culture . . . but it got diluted over time because with the exit of old timers.[20]

---

[17] Edwin Mansfield, 'International Technology Transfer: Forms, Resource Requirements and Policies', *American Economic Review*, Vol. 65, No. 2, May 1975, pp. 372–6; Nathan Rosenberg, 'Economic Development and the Transfer of Technology: Some Historical Perspectives', in *idem, Perspectives on Technology*, Cambridge, 1976, pp. 151–72.

[18] Claude Durand, 'De la planification socialiste à la transition: les pays de l'Est', in *idem (ed.), La coopération technologique internationale, Les transferts de technologie,* Brussels, 1994, pp. 225–43.

[19] Interview with S.K. Ramanna.

[20] Interview with K. Nagaraj, ex-Deputy General Manager telephone division R&D, ITI Bangalore, March-May 1999.

A small group of ITI engineers also received training at ATE's Liverpool plant for periods ranging from three to six months. To spare it the cost of having to send them all the way from India, ITI had recruited most of these engineers in the UK itself where they had been working for other firms or had just completed their studies.

By integrally importing all the process and design elements associated with a specific manufacturing technology, ITI then followed the direct technology transfer path. In other words, it embraced what some authors have termed an 'imitative' or 'dependent' strategy.[21] More significantly, the monopolistic privileges enjoyed by ITI signified that recourse to an imitative strategy carried no competitive disadvantages with it. There were no rival firms looking to either improve on the technology employed by ITI or to underprice it. Thus if the absence of sufficiently-trained technical resources tended to foreclose the indirect technology transfer route, other causalities ensured that alternative strategies, even though less attractive, could be gainfully exploited.

Fairly modest in scale, the original ground plan envisaged that ITI would turn out 25,000 exchange lines annually and an equal number of telephones with a workforce not exceeding 5,000 people. But the plant was conceived as a fully integrated and self-contained structure, capable of fabricating internally all the parts and sub-assemblies needed for automatic switching exchanges and telephones. Whether the rationale behind integration derived from the absence of supplier industries, and hence the impossibility of building strong subcontracting relationships, or was dictated by the search for economies of scale remains unknown. Production commenced some time during the first half of 1949 in two makeshift army hangars while the company waited for the factory buildings to come up. Output during the early years consisted of telephones, later followed by strowger selectors and relays, assembled from knocked-down kits shipped by ATE. By 1952 the construction of

[21] Christopher Freeman and Luc Soete, *The Economics of Industrial Innovation*, London, 1997, pp. 275–81. Of the three most common types of technology transfer— material, design and capacity—identified in the literature on the subject, in the case of material and design transfers, the recipient is a passive consumer of knowledge developed by others. Melvin Kranzberg, 'The Technical Elements in International Technology Transfer: Historical Perspectives', in J.R. McIntyre and D.S. Papp (ed.), *The Political Economy Of International Technology Transfer*, New York, 1986, pp. 31–45.

all the factory buildings was over, and the company started progressively feeding the assembly shops with components manufactured in-house.

SPATIAL ORGANIZATION OF THE FACTORY

Initially, the plant comprised a total of eight buildings, in addition to the administrative offices. The form of spatial organization adopted by ITI which expressed itself as much in the geographical location of the plant as in the design of its workplaces and its extensive physical spread, diverged sharply from the way the cotton and jute mills of the first industrial revolution had traditionally ordered the environment in big Indian cities. These alternative patterns of spatio-territorial relations revealed that the factors differentiating the branches of the first industrial revolution from those of the second to which ITI belonged were not restricted to questions of capital intensity, technology, production processes, and the management of the workforce; they also had a spatial dimension.[22] Cotton mills invariably settled in the very heart of the city, in close proximity of residential neighbourhoods, boasted a highly visible presence, and, despite their walls, were physically more permeable to the exterior.[23] In contrast, by locating themselves on the outskirts of the city, on sites 'without history'[24] or, more appropriately, without an official and collective history, plants like ITI tended to be more 'anonymous'. The inside-outside cleavage between the factory and its surrounding environment was thus radically asserted.

[22] For a discussion of the dynamic relationship between factory design and industrial organization see, *inter alia*, Robert Lewis, 'Redesigning the Workplace. The North American Factory in the Interwar Period', *Technology and Culture*, Vol. 42, No. 4, October 2001, pp. 665–84; Daniel Nelson, *Managers and Workers. Origins of the New Factory System in the United States 1880–1920*, Madison, 1975, pp. 11–15, 22–3; Michèle Perrot, 'De la manufacture à l'usine en miettes', *Le Mouvement Social*, No. 125, October-December 1983, pp. 3–12. A more general analysis of how the conception and ordering of industrial space is integral to managerial practices is provided in Cohen, *Organiser à l'aube du taylorisme*, p. 364, 370.

[23] According to Morris, who relies on various reports, people poured in and out of the Bombay textile mills at all hours of the day. Some of the owners had also granted concessions to tea shops and barbers to ply their business inside the mill compounds. Morris David Morris, *The Emergence of an Industrial Labor Force in India. A Study of the Bombay Cotton Mills, 1854–1947*, Berkeley, 1965, pp. 113–15.

[24] Gérard Noiriel, *Les ouvriers dans la société française, XIX-XXème siècle*, Paris, 1986, p. 167.

A comparison of the spatial orientations embraced by the older industries and the 'new modern factory' also brought to the fore two opposing conceptions of factory layout which were attendant upon both technical exigencies and production needs.[25] The design features of cotton mills corresponded to an organizational type that could be called 'compact', with the bulk of their machinery and fixtures concentrated under one roof, even though they could sometimes be distributed vertically between floors of a multi-storey building rather than on a single horizontal plane. In comparison, like many engineering firms, ITI fitted the model of a 'dispersed' factory.[26]

In view of the company's multiple product line, and the enormous variety of parts these products required, it was more rational to organize its manufacturing activity by spreading it across different buildings situated within the same site, each devoted to a specific product or sub-assembly, but tightly integrated into a whole.[27] But extensive though the productive arena was, ITI owed its huge size more to the reproductive arena. For in line with other public sector enterprises, the company had provided housing facilities for a section of the workforce. The centrepiece of the welfare programme sponsored by ITI, it was the construction of this sprawling township, covering roughly 250 acres of land, which left the strongest imprint on the territory as well as the public imagination.

Last but not least, the architectural differences between the traditional and the modern branches of industry extended to the design of the factory buildings itself. Whereas the old mill structure mainly utilized brick and mortar, ITI, which like most engineering firms had opted for the standard saw-tooth roof and vertical glass-covered plane, could take advantage of the availability of new building materials such as reinforced concrete, high tensile steel, glass and corrugated iron. Besides affording greater

[25] The term, of course, comes from Nelson, *Managers and Workers*.

[26] I have adapted the notion from French historian Odette Hardy-Nemery who has characterized the spatial distribution of the giant Denain steel plant as an *usine deployée*. 'Une nébuleuse en expansion au XIX et XXe siècles. L'espace de l'usine sidérurgique de Denain', *Le Mouvement Social*, No. 125, October-December 1983, pp. 57–78.

[27] Following the post-First World War refashioning of the internal geography of the Lorraine steel mills, they became a closed and circular space whose unity was defined by the interdependence between its parts. Gérard Noiriel, 'Espace de production et luttes sociales. L'exemple des usines sidérurgiques Lorraines (1880–1930)', *Le Mouvement Social*, No. 125, October-December 1983, pp. 25–56.

flexibility in construction as well as ensuring better lighting and ventilation, these new materials had the effect of giving the manufacturing premises a lighter, less monumental appearance compared to the textile mills.

However, by choosing to build the administrative office, where all the senior ITI executives sat, out of thick granite blocks and to give it greater elevation than the factory buildings, the company clearly sought to emphasize the 'symbolism of managerial authority' through the imposing character of the building.[28] A high wall also separated the administration or 'stone' building, as ITI personnel referred to it, from the production units, in order to both ensure the protection of top officials in the event of labour protests, and to spatially demarcate white collar work from blue collar. Moreover, it was the administration building, the material embodiment of management, which stood exposed to the public view, directly visible from afar to all observers, while the factory buildings remained completely hidden in the background.

Such a representation of the company was destined to convey an unambiguous message to the outside world: it informed them of who held power internally and where it physically resided. As Michelle Perrot has alerted us, spatial organization is at once a technical arrangement and a symbol of social relationships.[29] But not everybody enjoyed equal treatment within the 'stone' building. A board on the door of the lift servicing the first and second floors announced that it was reserved for officers, and carpeting was installed only on the staircase leading from the first to the second floor where the offices of the highest-ranking managers were located. Similarly, there were separate toilets for officers and non-officers.

The factory itself was divided into two rows of four buildings, each measuring 120 feet by 180 feet. Undergirding this spatial organization

---

[28] Noëlle Gérome, 'Les espaces symboliques des usines—organisations et subversions. Pratiques de la seconde moitié du XXème siècle', in *Historiens et Géographes*, No. 350, October 1995, pp. 275–88. On the use of architectural grandeur as a means of symbolic domination of the workforce see also Tamara Hareven, *Family Time and Industrial Time. The Relationship Between the Family and Work in a New England Community*, Cambridge, 1982, pp. 12–13.

[29] Michèle Perrot, 'The Three Ages of Industrial Discipline', in John Merriman (ed.), *Consciousness and Class experience in Nineteenth century Europe*, New York, 1979, pp. 149–68.

was a product-centred layout which in terms of the flow of material held both advantages and disadvantages. In each building, only one type of job or product was executed. Both the machine shop and the assembly shop were housed under one roof and on the same level, with assembly generally occupying a larger surface area. By physically uniting these two activities the management intended to better coordinate the movement of parts from the machine to the assembly shop. Since they were placed under the authority of the same shop superintendent, the possibility of mutual recriminations in case of production bottlenecks was also reduced. Machines were grouped together by family or class of work. The scale of operations was not big enough to accommodate a linear or sequential arrangement where the dividends from machine specialization could have been exploited. On the other hand, a traditional layout simplified the job of tool setting and change-over.

However, the main drawback with the overall layout devised by ATE was that it did not permit the rational circulation of material. On the contrary, the flow of parts and sub-assemblies kept criss-crossing. To give just one example, once the machining work on strowger switches was completed the metal parts were taken to an adjacent building for plating, before being brought back to be assembled. The switches then had to be transported a distance of about 250 metres to a building standing diagonally opposite for the final stage of the operation where they were mounted on racks. The goal of progressively integrating the product as it moved from one workspace to the next that engineering firms generally strive to achieve was thus defeated by the internal geography of the plant. Only after the introduction of the more advanced crossbar technology in the early 1960s, would the ITI management learn the techniques of process layout which considerably facilitated the flow of work and minimized the handling of work-in-progress.

In the layout provided by the Belgians (suppliers of the crossbar technology) there was a continuous linear movement from start to finish . . . there was a clear logic unlike in strowger . . .[30]

Because of financial constraints, there was also an acute shortage of space. So the company was compelled to utilize the same facilities that had been originally conceived to sustain a production capacity of 25,000

---

[30] Interview with Srinivasa Rao.

lines of strowger equipment annually, to now turn out close to 125,000 lines.

RELAY ADJUSTERS PROTEST AGAINST WORKING CONDITIONS

Two key operations underlying the manufacturing of strowger exchanges were relay adjustment and rack wiring. Relays were one of the two main sub-assemblies, the other being selectors, required for mounting an exchange equipment rack. The strowger automatic relay consisted of an energized coil wound around an iron core and then screwed to a yoke to which were fitted a set of contact springs and an armature comprising a lever and 30 odd parts. The adjustment of the relay was a painstaking job.

It was a minute and precise task that required patience and dexterity. But an even more indispensable quality was sharp vision: adjusting and positioning the thin springs exerted an enormous strain on operatives' eyesight.[31] Consequently, though adjustment ranked one or two grades above other assembly jobs on the skill ladder, and though it offered more promising promotion prospects, it attracted very few candidates. This in turn meant that few exit opportunities were available to those who were posted here, earning for the section the reputation of being a 'well with no steps to come out'.[32] As Krishnan, who worked as a relay adjuster from the start of his factory career in 1963 until the closure of shop nearly two and a half decades later, commented:

For the first three months after we were sent here, my friends and I fought to try and leave this section, but we got no transfers. Senior workers told us that we would die here in adjustment.[33]

The harsh reputation burdening the section was exacerbated by the sanctions imposed during the early years on operatives who failed to maintain efficiency levels in excess of 75 per cent. They were either

---

[31] Thompson and Bannon write that the life of the relay adjuster at ATE's Liverpool plant was short since the job was reserved for young workers. In return for earning high bonuses, the adjusters sacrificed their eyesight. Paul Thompson and Eddie Bannon, *Working the System. The Shop Floor and New Technology,* London, 1985, pp. 26–7.

[32] Interview with Surappa, 9 January 1998.

[33] Interview with D. Krishnan, 3 November 2001.

demoted to a lower category, or, in the case of learners, forced to quit the factory at the end of their trial period. Yet these measures to extract effort did not always succeed, and workers often reacted to the management's refusal to shift them to easier jobs by restricting output. In fact, along with rack wiring and selector adjustment, company officials tended to consider relay adjustment as one of the 'troublesome' strowger shops. The relay adjusters could exercise substantial leverage over the production process: their performance determined in part whether or not bottlenecks arose in rack wiring due to inadequate supplies.

But not everybody was dissuaded, at least initially, by the strenuous working conditions prevailing in relay adjustment. Tempted by the prospect of obtaining quick promotions and higher salaries, some workers disregarded their colleagues' warnings against joining this department. One of them was Surappa, a young 20-year-old Telegu speaking operative.

The first day, the charge hand asked if I was suffering from headaches because job was very minute. But he said if individual efficiency was maintained we would get promotions quickly compared to other departments . . . I got two promotions within 11 months of entering the factory. I was getting Rs 95 after one year compared to Rs 75 for operatives in the same category. Later I spoilt my eyes, but despite complaints to the doctor it was very difficult to get transfers because nobody wanted to come to relay adjustment.[34]

Similarly, we learn from a company note of 25 operatives having voluntarily opted to work in relay adjustment in 1983. However, no sooner had they taken up their new posts than many of them expressed a desire to return to their former departments. The company rejected their applications. But it acknowledged that these workers had not 'shown any liking, interest, and enthusiasm in their job (sic)', and their efficiencies were extremely low despite having been censured orally and in writing.[35] Nevertheless, in response to pressure from the shop floor and the union, factory officials announced the creation of a committee to investigate the issue of providing alternative jobs to workers, especially those aged above 40 years, and who had been employed in this shop for over eight years. Echoing the adjusters' anxieties, the union had repeatedly insisted that the nature of work here was such that it impaired workers' visual abilities over time. It had also wanted an eye specialist to not only examine

[34] Interview with Surappa.
[35] Personnel department files, 22 November 1983.

the adjusters, but, more importantly, to submit a report on the potential vision-related hazards associated with these jobs. Nothing seems to have materialized from its demands.[36]

Then, in August 1981 the entire relay adjustment workforce signed a petition requesting to be shifted to 'any other department', and submitted it to both the management and the union.[37] Despite undergoing periodical medical checkups, job rotation alone could 'prevent the fading away of our eye vision (sic)', declared the mass petition.[38] But the adjusters' hopes of seeing their grievances even partially satisfied were dashed by the contradictory findings of the four-member committee consisting of two management and two union representatives.[39] The committee's inconclusive report allowed the company to promptly dismiss the transfer demands of the adjusters as baseless. Outsourcing these jobs, as the union had suggested, was not a viable solution either as it would have 'serious repercussions' on the rest of the workforce.[40] The ready acceptance of overtime work by the adjusters also apparently persuaded shop managers to treat their protests less seriously. These workers would need to wait for the strowger production line to be completely phased out in 1989–90 before emerging from the 'stepless well'.

DETAILED DIVISION OF LABOUR AND SOLIDARITIES IN RACK WIRING SHOP

Rack wiring, was the last stage in the strowger fabrication chain. One former executive likened the department to a 'hydra-headed monster' given that the output of the other three strowger shops fed the output of this one shop.[41] In a nutshell, the work here entailed attaching to a rack all the equipment utilized in a public exchange, and then wiring it to form a complete exchange unit, after which the rack was directly shipped to the customer for installation. Responsible for turning out the final product, the rack wiring department occupied a critical position in the

---

[36] Minutes of management-union meeting, 26 September 1961 and 25 April 1966.
[37] Personnel department files, 26 August 1981.
[38] ibid.
[39] Personnel department files, 22 May 1984; 9 June 1984.
[40] Minutes of management-union meeting, 27 November 1985.
[41] Interview with Srinivasa Rao.

production process, a fact which both its workforce and factory management were acutely conscious of.

Constructed of steel, a rack measured in general 10.6 ft in height and 4.6 ft in breadth and contained different kinds of equipment such as call meters, contact banks and relay sets. Mounting and wiring a rack was an extremely time-consuming operation, incorporating no less than 10 different tasks and passing through four different stages. Under normal conditions this task took close to two months to accomplish for a team of three workers. The fastidious nature of wiring work in particular can be gauged from the fact that certain equipment contained as many as 600 wires that needed to be connected and soldered. The multiplicity of operations involved in putting together a rack had two consequences in terms of the workforce.

First, of all the strowger departments rack wiring was by far the biggest, employing nearly 400 men and women. But here as in the other assembly areas like telephones, relay and coil winding where female workers could be found, their overall numbers were not only exceedingly small, but kept progressively shrinking. The weak female numerical presence went hand in hand with their relegation at the bottom of the skill hierarchy. Although a few women had risen to the post of inspector in the telephone division and later the transmission division, the overwhelming majority held low qualified jobs. In rack wiring, women were discriminated against in terms of career advancement opportunities in part for their alleged inability to climb ladders since they wore saris.

Chowdhury, the rack wiring department head, would jokingly say they should wear pants in response to complaints from women workers that there were promotion vacancies in rack wiring but these were not filled by women.[42]

Thwarted from working on sub-assemblies situated in the upper sections of the rack, women were therefore forced to take up extremely monotonous and demanding jobs such as wiring bank multiples or relay sets.

Claiming that they were acting in deference to the requests of female operatives who were apparently opposed to entering into physical contact with their male colleagues, shop officials also maintained a strict sexual separation. No such segregation, however, prevailed in telephone and relay assembly, giving rise to doubts that rack wiring line managers were

[42] ibid.

perhaps guilty of over interpreting the wishes of female workers to suit the sexual behavioural norms that accorded with their own patriarchal preoccupations. Even in the case of tasks allotted to both sexes like bank multiples, women were placed in one row and men in another row facing them at a distance of four to six feet. But going by the accounts of both executives and workers, these spatial barriers appear to have neither dissuaded male operatives from flirting with their female co-workers, nor come in the way of more intimate relationships between certain employees. Rack wiring, in fact, celebrated a much higher number of intra-department marriages than the other shops: eight or ten of the 40 odd women employed in rack wiring had found their husbands here.

The large number of operations a rack underwent, and the equally vast palette of specialized knowledge and techniques mobilized for this purpose, also meant that this department encapsulated all seven of the skill categories across which the entire factory workforce was distributed. An extensive and intricate sub-division of labour characterized the nature of work here. Though all the jobs could be classified under four broad headings—assembly, wiring, repair and testing—and virtually all of these depended on workers' ability to read circuit drawings and blueprints, one job description manual listed as many as 24 specific job titles, each of which was finely graded according to skill. Scrutinizing the various job categories showed that the most skilled employees were the generalists, those possessing the all-round knowledge essential to performing a wide variety of jobs. This was in distinct contrast to the least skilled employees, the specialists, whose limited competences could only be channelled into repetitive, standardized tasks.

Paradoxically, the high degree of functional stratification defining the organization of work in rack wiring does not appear to have had a negative impact on the cohesiveness of the workgroup.

The team work and team spirit was tremendous in rack wiring. There was a very good group dynamism brought about by the leadership, Chowdhury, the shop superintendent, and his main foreman, Rajan. If the workers had to stay back in March (to complete the orders by the end of the financial year), all would do so, pool money to get food from outside, sit together and eat.[43]

---

[43] Interview with A.V. Krishnamurthy, ex-Additional General Manager, ITI Bangalore, 24 May 1999.

Envied by the rest of the factory for the sense of mutuality workers in this department had succeeded in forging, they also enjoyed a reputation for combativeness unrivalled by the other strowger employees. Aware that racks, the plant's end product, were its principal revenue earner, and that production stoppages could retard the delivery of equipment, rack wiring workers did not hesitate to press the advantage gained from controlling a strategic position in the production chain.[44] Both shop officials and the factory management therefore went to considerable lengths to preserve a harmonious industrial relations climate by responding favourably to employee demands. Time standards for most operations in rack wiring were thought to be set quite loosely as much in order to enable workers to maximize incentive earnings as to assure the company of stable output.

Workers here also received higher wages because rack wiring jobs tended to be graded higher than similar jobs elsewhere in the factory. In terms of mobility as well, they benefited from faster promotions compared with the rest of the workforce. All these factors not only contributed to shaping the self-image of rack wiring workers as an elite group, but also fostered considerable rivalry between them and employees from the other strowger shops, besides provoking charges of favouritism and leniency from certain official quarters.

Chowdhury was very popular with his workers because his human relations was excellent . . . He was very sympathetic to workers' problems. If workers required a bus for some social function, he would directly ring up transport officer rather than go through personnel. But in terms of managerial efficiency, *he was not tough enough.* He would not force the issue.[45]

Adds Michael Fernandes, the ITI union president and a former officer himself:

There was always a sense of competition between rack wiring and other shops in terms of meeting targets, earning incentive . . . Chowdhury had various

---

[44] Crozier and Friedberg point out that it is not so much the existence of common grievances or a set of shared goals that allows workers to structure themselves effectively into groups as their collective capacity to exploit a strategic situation together with their level of interaction. Michel Crozier and Erhard Friedberg, *L'acteur et le systeme. Les contraintes de l'action collective*, Paris, 1981, pp. 51–3, 215–16.

[45] Interview with Srinivasa Rao. Emphasis added.

methods, some straight, others crooked, to motivate workers, make them feel proud of their work, and get more overtime and incentive for them.[46]

However, Fernandes acknowledged that the solidarity and combativeness exhibited by the rack wiring workers presented occasional difficulties for the union as well which struggled to balance the sectional claims of the former with the collective interests of the entire workforce.

If there was an all-ITI issue like incentive rates, job evaluation results or work practices, rack wiring workers would claim their own pound of flesh and the union had to yield to this pressure. Not only were they very united but they were also a very big and vocal group of about 300 workers.[47]

If the privileged treatment rack wiring workers received at the hands of the management represented an important element in helping to build a distinct and vigorous group identity, the homogenous composition of the workforce played a conspicuous part as well. In other assembly shops, sharp cleavages set apart the adjusters from the rest of the operatives. Adjusters, often ranked one or two grades higher, tended to view themselves as a skilled elite and were therefore, reluctant to support or join with the other trade groups. Rack wiring suffered from no such divisions. The overwhelming majority of employees here were wiremen with common interests and obligations, this despite both the individual nature of the job and the considerable variations from one job to another. Shared occupational ties made the framing of demands as well the coordination of action a relatively smoother task as it provided workers with a common idiom. Furthermore, the traditional barriers separating machine shop operatives from assembly operatives, which often acted as a powerful brake on worker unity in various departments, was irrelevant in rack wiring. Mounting and cabling an exchange rack were purely assembly tasks.

TRANSITION TO THE NEW CROSSBAR TECHNOLOGY

In absolute contrast with the ATE tie-up which had proceeded without a hitch from start to finish, the transfer of technology negotiated with

---

[46] Interview with Michael Fernandes, President ITI Employees Union, Bangalore, June 2000.

[47] ibid.

Bell Telephone Manufacturing (BTM) for the next generation of automatic switching equipment, crossbar systems, turned out to be a fiasco from the very outset. This was as much related to the incompatibility of the choice of technology with local needs as to inefficiencies on the part of the technology provider, which lacking adequate resources, could not fulfil its contractual obligations. The crossbar agreement, in fact, represented a textbook case of all that went wrong in the diffusion of know-how from a developed to a developing country. This injudicious decision would also inflict unprecedented damage on an already chronically dysfunctional telecommunications network, the effects of which would be felt for almost two decades.

In view of the various technical limitations inherent in the strowger system, from the late 1950s onwards, P&T had begun exploring the possibilities of securing a replacement technology designed to help modernize the national network, and facilitate the introduction of national subscriber trunk dialling. In April 1963, an expert body, the Telephone System Switching Committee made up essentially of officials from the state carrier recommended the introduction of the crossbar switch.[48] Capable of interworking satisfactorily with strowger, the new technology would equip all new public exchanges installed in the country as well as existing exchanges at the time of their expansion.

A year later, acting on the committee's recommendations, the government announced that out of seven companies it had chosen BTM, the Belgian subsidiary of International Standard Electric Company (ISEC), itself a part of the giant ITT corporation, to provide the manufacturing technology.[49]

What must be underlined here is that at no stage of the technology selection process did P&T attempt to consult ITI. No executives from

---

[48] While the concept of a crossbar switch emerged even before the end of World War I, the first major exchange incorporating this technology would not be introduced before 1938 in the US. Another decade of experimentation would be required before the technology fully stabilized. Though an electro-mechanical system like strowger, the crossbar represented a far superior technology. It lowered operating costs; it reduced equipment size; calls could be routed and completed faster; maintenance posed lesser problems than strowger; finally, crossbar offered a far more extensive range of features such as call transfer, calling number identification and detailed call billing. On the flip side, this technology was uneconomical for low-density areas.

[49] In addition to BTM, Ericsson and Nippon EC also responded to the government tender.

the company figured on the committee which first prescribed the type of switching system the country should adopt, and then evaluate the offers made by the potential foreign collaborators. Questioned subsequently on this particular point by a parliamentary fact finding team, ITI Chairman C.S.S. Rao replied:

The selection of the equipment was by the user, that is the P&T . . . ITI was informed . . . by the Government . . . that (it) was designated as the Company to manufacture the said equipment . . . No representative from ITI . . . appears to have gone to the Ministry *because ITI is only a manufacturer.* Particularly in the team for system selection, ITI has no representative.[50]

Rao's statement unambiguously captured the nature of the relations between the parent ministry and ITI. The subordinate position attendant upon the company since it was 'only a manufacturer' signified that it had no say whatsoever in the formulation of corporate strategy. Its role was confined to executing the accord P&T had concluded, though this would hardly deter the government from seeking compensation later from the company for having produced defective crossbar equipment.[51] A decision as vital as the choice of a technology partner was also an important symbolic marker, for it afforded P&T an opportunity to reaffirm its ownership prerogatives and authority far more decisively than the routine exercise of bureaucratic power. It laid bare the unequal nature of the relationship between the supervisory ministry and its industrial arm in a way that their day to day transactions and mutual dependency tended to somewhat obscure.

The ITI engineers actually preferred the Ericsson exchange; though costlier than the Pentaconta system supplied by BTM, it was supposedly more sophisticated and sturdier, and boasted of a better call handling capacity. Indeed, study teams appointed by P&T in the early 1970s, after evaluating the working of various exchanges, would arrive at a definite consensus on the superiority of Ericsson over the BTM system.[52] By then, however, it was too late.

---

[50] ITI Corporate Office files, nd. Emphasis added. However, according to one source which fails to give additional details the managing director and general manager of ITI were associated in the Switching Committee's negotiations with the foreign firms. Annual Report,1962–63, p. 7.

[51] COPU 1973, p. 23.

[52] *Switching System Selection Report*, p. 85. See also pp. 70–2.

To present the choice of a particular technology within a framework of pure economic calculus is simplistic. As Robert Thomas has reminded us, technology decisions are rarely a straightforward and rational affair, if only because they are mediated by the exercise of power. Other factors such as the personal and professional interests of different organizational groups also intervene to influence the selection process. In other words, apart from technical and economic criteria, technologies are also adopted for their political and symbolic value.[53] Nevertheless, it would seem that only financial considerations convinced the P&T and the government to accept BTM's offer. Starved for orders and hence in considerable financial trouble, the Belgian firm is thought to have quoted the lowest price in order to win the tender. As per the terms of the licensing agreement which would last for seven years, the royalties charged by BTM were capped at $100,000 annually for a period of five years. This ultimately worked out to a total of Rs 1.35 million.[54]

At the same time, parent ISEC promised to pump in large sums of money into ITI. Apart from providing a loan of $1 million to facilitate the purchase of machinery and equipment, it purchased equity worth $1.25 million, giving it a stake of 12.7 per cent in the public sector company.[55] To finance the expansion of the factory so that it could take up the production of the new exchanges, ITI's paid-up share capital was raised from Rs 40 million to Rs 45.4 million.[56] The company estimated it would incur a capital expenditure of Rs 12.7 million on the project with the bulk of the amount going into plant, machinery and equipment (Rs 9.4 million), followed by the construction of new buildings (Rs 2.8 million).[57] The crossbar technical collaboration, like the previous strowger one, was a complete package, integrating all facets of product know-how; ITI was therefore once again embarking on the direct technology transfer route, though on this occasion it would turn out to be a very rocky one.

[53] R.J. Thomas, *What Machines Can't Do: Politics and Technology in the Industrial Enterprise*, Berkeley, 1994, pp. 5–6, 82–4, 227–9. Much the same point is emphasized by David Noble, 'Social Choice in Machine Design: The Case of Automatically Controlled Machine Tools', in A. Zimbalist (ed.), *Case Studies on the Labour Process*, New York, 1979, pp.18–50.

[54] COPU 1973, p. 15.

[55] ibid, p. 14. Of the equity amount, ISEC capitalized its know-how at $500,000, while paying the remaining $750,000 in cash.

[56] Annual Report 1964–65, pp. 6–7.

[57] Annual Report 1963–64, p. 4.

Right from its inception, the Pentaconta project ran into very serious difficulties. A new 9,400 line crossbar exchange in Bombay, equipment for which came directly from BTM, failed very shortly after it was commissioned by P&T in November 1967, provoking embarrassment and shock for the state carrier. In view of the abysmally low teledensities in India—only 0.1 connections per 100 population existed in 1971— phones tended to be used more far frequently, especially during peak hours, than in advanced countries. Since the Pentaconta had been conceived to operate in countries where phone usage rates were lower, its traffic handling capacity was accordingly restricted.[58] The high phone usage rates characteristic of the Indian telecommunications network therefore saturated or overloaded the Pentaconta system resulting in a large number of failed calls. Monthly fault rates per 100 lines at the Janpath I exchange in Delhi, for instance, ranged between 19 to 25 per cent as against the norm of 1 to 3 per cent fixed by P&T.

If P&T had taken care to inform its Belgian collaborator in advance of the specific traffic conditions prevailing in India, the latter could possibly have adapted the circuitry layout to better cater to local conditions. But the state carrier failed to anticipate the problem because, as it publicly admitted, its engineers were familiar only with the functioning of strowger and possessed no knowledge of the crossbar technology and its limits. On its part, BTM whose selection had been justified, to some extent, by P&T both on the grounds of its 'vast experience in the manufacture of varied types of telecommunication equipment' in many parts of the world, and its expertise in harmonizing crossbar exchanges with strowger, had neglected to make allowances for the differences in telephone usage habits between the advanced and the developing countries.[59]

The efficiency of the Pentaconta system was further eroded by mechanical complications. Several components gave trouble and the absence of an airconditioned atmosphere coupled with the neglect of

[58] Göransson has argued that telecommunications equipment technologies developed by the industrialized countries are, as a rule, inappropriate for the requirements of industrializing countries given the differences in traffic density, climatic conditions and capital-labour ratios. 'Third World Challengers on the International Market'.

[59] COPU 1974–75, *Action taken by Government on Recommendations contained in 34th Report of Committee of Public Undertakings, Fifth Lok Sabha*, 57th Report, Fifth Lok Sabha, New Delhi, 1975, p. 6. (Hereafter COPU 1975.)

dust control measures only led to more breakdowns. To remedy all these defects, in June 1974, the government launched the Indian Crossbar Project. Spearheaded by a team of 200 engineers drawn from TRC and ITI, their mandate was to redesign the imported crossbar technology so that it functioned more reliably under Indian conditions. Mass production of the revamped system would subsequently be taken up by ITI's Rae Bareli factory. But to actually fabricate the equipment, P&T and ITI were constrained to enter into a fresh collaboration with BTM, in spite of their less than happy experience dealing with it, since ITI lacked the necessary process technology.

Crippled by technical deficiencies, the Pentaconta technology transfer agreement was also plagued by cost overruns and severe delays in the fabrication of equipment by ITI. Because of various problems, the company would never be able to meet the target originally envisaged of manufacturing 100,000 exchange lines annually in a single shift at the Bangalore plant. Its total capacity would first be scaled down to 80,000 lines and then to 60,000 lines.[60] Moreover, this goal was achieved only in March 1972 as against the stated objective of reaching full capacity utilization by July 1967 within 36 months of the crossbar line going on stream. But notwithstanding the shortfall in production, expenditures had shot by up by roughly 60 per cent to Rs 20.14 million. With 1432 people employed on the project, the size of the workforce also considerably exceeded initial projections, even as efficiencies stood much below what was planned.[61] In the end, ITI would fail to satisfy the demand

---

[60] 'Report of the Working Group on the Study of Phasing out the Electromechanical Switching Equipments from the Telecommunication Network', New Delhi, P&T, July 1984 (mimeo), p. 23.

[61] Targets and Actual Achievements in ITI's Crossbar Project

Parameters	Targets July 1967	Actuals March 1972
Project cost	Rs 12.7 mn	Rs 20.14 mn
Production	100,000 lines	80,000 lines
Personnel	1339	1432
Operating efficiency	100 per cent	a) 60.87 per cent b) 50.72 per cent

Notes: a) efficiency of assembly division; b) efficiency of machine shops.
Source: COPU 1973.

requirements of P&T for crossbar equipment to the extent of 234,000 lines during the course of the Fourth Plan (1969–74).

The responsibility for this disastrous outcome lay in part with P&T which had delayed finalizing its technical specifications as well as its equipment requirements. Consequently, BTM was neither able to deliver on schedule the entire documentation, nor the knocked-down kits and testing equipment, nor send its technicians to instruct local personnel in assembling the imported machinery.[62] At the same time, the Belgian firm was guilty of grave planning lapses having neglected to supply the necessary stock of machines. As ITI executives would find out to their surprise, the total manufacturing capacity installed would not allow for the production of 100,000 lines as programmed, but only 50,000 lines. Admitting to 'some incorrect calculation' on its part, BTM agreed to make good the shortfall by providing 12 additional machines, including certain upgraded versions, free of cost.[63] Yet even after the arrival of the new machines, the effective installed capacity only reached 65,000 lines.

However, it took ITI over two years to become aware of this problem, and though BTM again agreed to furnish nine more machines free, these would be received only in 1972. Thus between the time when the shortages first came to light and when the issue was finally resolved, almost five years had lapsed, explaining, to a great extent, the reasons for the implementational delays in the project. Furthermore, since P&T had omitted to include a penalty clause in the agreement, compensation could neither be claimed from the Belgian firm for late supplies, nor for the ensuing loss of production. The government would subsequently try to cover up this grave oversight by claiming that foreign technology suppliers generally refused to accept penalty clauses.[64]

The incorrect assessment of ITI's machinery requirements by BTM may well have stemmed from a genuine error as one senior crossbar manager claimed.[65] Other executives, though, accused the Belgian firm

---

[62] Even as late as August 1970, or six years after the inception of the project, ITI had still not received time standards for many machine and assembly operations. ibid, p. 39.

[63] ibid, p. 35.

[64] COPU 1975, p. 74.

[65] Interview with S.K. Ramanna. Assistant Works Manager of the crossbar division from 1964–71, before being removed overnight when labour troubles erupted, Ramanna also stated that the BTM executive who was responsible for the error later suffered a nervous breakdown.

of attempting to cut costs by 'under-sourcing ITI and P&T in all areas' after having quoted the lowest price in order to win the crossbar tender.[66] Some also believed that the dual constraints of requiring to deliver exchange equipment to P&T and establishing production facilities at Bangalore exerted enormous pressure on BTM's resources.[67] The fact that it did not have all the elements of the technology under its own control may have exacerbated its difficulties. Since several features of the Pentaconta switch had been designed by other European subsidiaries of parent concern ITT, more often than not, BTM struggled to directly furnish solutions to the problems confronting P&T and ITI engineers. The same also applied to machinery and assorted components: it could supply these to its Indian clients only after having first procured them from sister ITT companies and subcontractors.[68]

The ITI officials also complained that, in contrast to the earlier collaboration with ATE, the staff sent by BTM to provide training was, by and large, not well qualified. Moreover, owing to the delays, machines and tools would often be unavailable when the experts arrived so that they remained idle during long periods of their stay. Finally, cooperation between the two sides appears to have been strained by the language barrier and the attitudes of certain BTM personnel. None of the local managers spoke Flemish, while the foreign technicians were not always fluent in English.

The practice of the Belgians in man-management was quite erratic. They had a superiority complex, and felt that locals were there only to learn from them.[69]

Insufficient machinery was not the only obstacle impeding the continuity of production at ITI. Company officials would also have to deal with the vexatious question of accidents. Between 1969–73, as many

---

[66] Interview with Srinivasa Rao.

[67] Interview with Y. Munnuswamy, ex-Works Manager, ITI Bangalore, January-February 1999.

[68] Transnational ITT has sometimes been compared to the Austro-Hungarian empire. Attempts made by the parent company to promote greater coordination between the various European affiliates, especially in terms of harnessing their research activities, invariably foundered on the opposition of 'nationalist' unit heads. Chapuis and Joel, *Electronics, Computers and Telephone Switching*, p. 226; Robert Sobel, *Histoire d'un empire. ITT*, Montreal, 1984, p. 22.

[69] Interview with Srinivasa Rao.

as 15 accidents occurred in the crossbar machine shop. All of them concerned power press operatives who sustained very serious hand injuries, often permanently losing one or two fingers. Unlike strowger presses which could not be run without closing the safety guard, most crossbar presses were 'open-throated'. Moreover, in the initial batch, the machines were all feet operated with the hands remaining free. Some of the injuries may well have been caused by negligence on the part of operatives who in order to gain time did not bother using the tongs to extract the components. But as certain executives themselves recognized, no training had been given either to supervisory personnel or to workers handling these machines.

It was a criminal neglect on the part of Bell Tel and ITI executives. Once the first accident took place, ITI should have insisted that machines be changed or training provided, instead of remaining focussed on production. But there was a compulsion to give output.[70]

The accidents ceased after the company and workers began exercising greater vigilance, and after the installation of new machines, fitted with double levers to ensure both hands were occupied.

The inability of ITI to achieve production targets, however, had no adverse impact on its finances. On the contrary, from 1965–66 to 1968–69, the company's crossbar revenues exceeded the original projections by Rs 31.2 million, and profits by Rs 2.81 million. If it was able to post these figures in spite of low levels of labour efficiency and capacity utilization, the key to the 'mystery' lay in the cost-plus pricing arrangement which guaranteed the company profits regardless of its efficiency. Declaring that ITI's financial results had in reality 'proved to be an extra burden for the exchequer' and should not be read as a 'true index of its efficiency', a parliamentary fact-finding committee would deliver a harsh indictment of the way the company had handled certain aspects of the collaboration agreement:

. . . at a time when the country is seriously short of telephone equipment and the waiting list runs into several years in metropolitan towns . . . (t)he Committee are greatly dissatisfied with the lack of urgency with which the various manufacturing problems encountered have been tackled in ITI . . .[71]

---

[70] ibid.
[71] COPU 1973, p. 57, 41.

As one high-ranking executive acknowledged, the company lacked the capacity to absorb the crossbar know-how.

Nobody from top management connected with production had seen the BTM factory before the contract was signed. Initially, nobody was sent from ITI machine shop to Bell Tel for training, although this was a crucial area . . . Only after three or four years did we send somebody, and that too for a far too limited duration.[72]

RIVALRIES BETWEEN CROSSBAR AND STROWGER DIVISION PERSONNEL

By no means, were ITI's worries limited to the production front only. It also had its hands full coping with social difficulties as the introduction of the crossbar technology had a profoundly disruptive effect on the inner fabric of the Bangalore plant and would durably transform both the nature of labour-management relations and intra-worker relations. Nor would the management be free from the tensions generated by the technological and social changes that were reconfiguring the factory. The launch of the new project would provoke strong antagonisms between the crossbar and strowger divisions, and these cleavages, shored up by an explosive mixture of issues—mobility, status and linguistic differences—would reproduce themselves just as much within the upper echelons of the company as the lower.

Officials and employees working in strowger would not only lose the dominant position they had commanded within the factory by virtue of being the most important division and the company's principal revenue earner. They would also come to be viewed as the 'old' division, both demographically and in terms of the technology deployed. The resentment arising from this collective sense of devaluation would be accentuated by the privileged treatment crossbar workers received at the hands of the management, as well as the superior attitudes of crossbar executives and workers *vis-à-vis* their strowger counterparts.

There was an attempt by some crossbar officers to drive a wedge between crossbar and the other divisions by saying that since it was a new product it was a higher technology project . . . A separate entrance was made for crossbar, and people from strowger were not allowed to enter even at middle management level. If

---

[72] Interview with Srinivasa Rao.

strowger officers visited, crossbar managers would ask why we were wasting time there. The attitude of crossbar bosses percolated to the workers.[73]

These viewpoints were corroborated by a strowger official who had been transferred to crossbar:

The sentiment that crossbar was the better division was consciously encouraged by the management among workers here. Management felt that crossbar would be an island of efficiency . . . It also initially wanted to put up sign boards saying unauthorized personnel would not be allowed into certain shops. Under pressure, it was forced to change the board to read that entry into some shops would be restricted . . . The factory general manager used to spend more time on crossbar since this was a new project, whereas strowger heads would only receive criticism if they failed to meet targets.[74]

Denying the charges of arrogant behaviour, a senior crossbar manager claimed that

officers and workers who could not come to crossbar from strowger thought we were snobs and exclusive because we used to move around a lot with Belgian experts. We never wasted time going around to the other divisions . . . We had no time . . . We would meet colleagues from strowger and transmission only in the canteen . . . There was also some jealousy among strowger officers since crossbar managers were sent abroad for training in some cases.[75]

Irked by the showcasing of the crossbar as the technological icon of ITI, strowger executives retaliated by refusing to cooperate with their colleagues in the new division. Urgently needed tools and components which had to come from the strowger tool room and plating shop since separate facilities had not been systematically set up in all areas for crossbar in a bid to reduce costs, tended to be supplied after considerable delay. This in turn affected the timely commissioning of the new crossbar exchanges.

. . . whatever was required for crossbar was treated as secondary by the strowger division people. So while we had supplied P&T with about 167,000 lines of exchange equipment, the iron work supplied was hardly for 32,000 lines because this item had to be provided by strowger shops. So equipment could not be erected.[76]

---

[73] Interview with A.V. Krishnamurthy.
[74] Interview with Srinivasa Rao.
[75] Interview with S.K. Ramanna.
[76] Interview with L.G. Varadharajan.

In addition to the technology base, another key feature differentiating strowger from crossbar was the age and education levels of their respective workforces. Operatives in the crossbar division were generally much younger and better qualified than their colleagues in strowger, and hence tended to display a greater degree of combativeness as well—a detail overlooked by the management. In effect, when setting up the new product line the company had recruited large numbers of new workers. Top management had been won over by crossbar executives' arguments that the complex and sophisticated nature of the technology necessitated a younger and more skilled workforce, amenable both to discipline and high effort norms.

In principle, strowger operatives with good service records could apply to join the new division. Yet, despite being eligible their applications were sometimes rejected creating a strong sense of resentment. For these workers just as much as for those recruited to the new division, the sense of distinctiveness attached to operating a modern technology exercised an undeniable appeal. In the words of Irudayaraj who joined crossbar as a 18-year old learner,

I am definitely proud of saying that crossbar workers were much tougher than strowger. We were young and willing to do all kinds of work allotted by the supervisor . . . We got good training in crossbar. Work was also much more difficult here . . . So if you have worked in cross bar, you can work anywhere else . . . Because it was designed by Belgians, procedures were very systematic here. If you had any work problems, the moment you told the supervisor it would be solved . . . (the) shop clerk would sit on the shop floor . . .[77]

A problem inherent in oral recollections of the past such as this, and the others cited above is that they invariably carry the imprint of other times and experiences, especially the present. While it is by no means certain that assembly and machine shop jobs in crossbar uniformly demanded much greater levels of effort than those performed in the other divisions, assertions such as this or others to the effect that their training and skills gave crossbar workers the confidence to work in all areas of the factory were as much intended to highlight the masculine logic inherent in their labour as to valorize past trajectories. Self-esteem derived from the belief that other workers were incapable of achieving what crossbar workers

[77] Interview with Irudayaraj, 8–12 May 1999.

could achieve, 'the manly confrontation with the task'.[78] Yet Irudayaraj's testimony is revealing in so far as it makes clear that the 'pride in belonging to a new project . . . in want(ing) to be different from the other divisions' was not restricted to crossbar officers alone; these sentiments were also shared by workers.[79]

Moreover, despite the incidence of accidents in the crossbar machine shop, the overall environment and working conditions were a definite improvement on those prevailing in strowger. Three new and spacious factory buildings, each measuring 3000 square metres had been erected at a cost of roughly Rs 2 million. The adoption of more efficient layout techniques meant that the shop floor was less congested and untidy. Wiring jobs which had been traditionally performed standing up were now done sitting down, though the smaller size of the crossbar frame also partly facilitated this. The company had also devoted greater attention to the question of workers' comfort. Specially designed stools and workbenches eliminated the need for workers to bend down when assembling relays. Tools were disposed within close reach of the worker so that 'even without looking if he put out his hand he could pick them up'.[80] Whereas strowger operatives had to be satisfied with ordinary screwdrivers to carry out wiring tasks, their counterparts in crossbar were supplied with compressed air or pneumatic guns which considerably eased the discomfort caused in using screwdrivers.

The flow of work was organized in a more orderly fashion as well. Workers were provided with standardized bins for specific sub-assemblies. All the components required for assembling a relay, for example, were placed in the bin, and once the worker had finished the job, he put the relay back in the bin which was then sent to the next stage. Apart from simplifying the work of the stores keeper, operative, supervisor and inspector, this system allowed for better control as problems like shortage of parts could be immediately identified. Collection centres were also set up directly on the shop floor to feed workers with material, thus cutting down on unnecessary movement and loss of time.

But the fundamental reason why workers sought to join crossbar was

---

[78] Paul Willis, 'Shop Floor Culture, Masculinity and the Wage Form', in J. Clarke et al, *Working Class Culture. Studies in History and Theory*, London, 1979, p. 196.

[79] Interview with S.K. Ramanna.

[80] ibid.

that it offered far brighter career prospects than strowger. Jobs in crossbar, particularly those situated at the bottom of the hierarchy, had generally been classified one or two categories above those in strowger. Some jobs such as final inspection, certain machining operations, involving the utilization of multi-stage tools, and wiring operations certainly called for much higher levels of skill and/or effort. One report, after stating that at practically every stage of the production chain the new technology mobilized greater knowledge and competences than strowger, wrote that even very experienced strowger operatives when transferred to the new division could not cope with their new responsibilities and had to 'return to their original trade'.[81]

Counter balancing this claim was the much greater emphasis on semi-automated and automated techniques, interchangeable parts, and material and process standardization characteristic of crossbar. A crossbar switch, for instance, contained only around 1300 parts compared to the 9000 odd parts that could be found in strowger.[82] This increased reliance on mechanization definitely enabled ITI to modernize its production technology which in turn yielded productivity gains. But they also just as clearly resulted in simplifying work methods in a number of areas to a point where it would not be incorrect to speak of a reduction in skills. This is partly borne out by an internal study classifying 67.5 per cent of the 2774 workers employed in the crossbar division in April 1985 as unskilled; of the remainder, 15 per cent held semi-skilled positions, and 15.75 per cent skilled positions.[83]

Yet, following the introduction of a job evaluation scheme in 1971, the company decided to upgrade the crossbar jobs, no doubt, influenced by the fact that it was a new and more advanced technology. Pressure from the workforce also partly dictated this decision. 'Because they were younger and hot blooded, workers insisted that their jobs be of a higher order than strowger', commented Michael Fernandes, the union head.[84] Ranked above their counterparts in strowger, crossbar operatives also enjoyed the benefit of faster promotions together with the material and status distinctions it bestowed.

[81] *Switching System Selection Report*, p. 13.

[82] Interview with L.G. Varadharajan.

[83] ITI Corporate P&A, 'Change of Technology, Retraining, Deployment: A Case Study in Indian Telephone Industries', nd.

[84] Interview with Michael Fernandes, April-May 1999.

One strowger worker told me: 'Sir my youngest brother who has joined in crossbar is already in a higher category than me, and his wife makes fun of my wife.'[85]

Another official added:

. . . over time, a feeling developed among strowger personnel that the crossbar workforce was being pampered, while strowger was being neglected.[86]

The deleterious effects of these discriminatory company policies on industrial relations would soon become evident. In June 1971, strowger division workers spontaneously downed tools insisting their jobs be re-evaluated. Only after these protests would top officials wake up to the need of assuaging the tremendous bitterness and discontent that had accumulated among these workers. To defuse the highly volatile situation, it promised to promote all low-ranking strowger operatives by one grade. As an executive put it, the management had no choice but to restore equity in its dealings with different sections of the workforce for it was impossible to 'maintain two standards in the same house'.[87]

According to an official report, many of the 'organizational problems' that had developed had done so because of 'mixing up production (of strowger and crossbar) at the same site (sic)', glossing over the fact that these problems had largely been of the company's own making.[88] The labour unrest persisted, though its locus now shifted to crossbar. Standing the management's initial assumptions on its head that a new and young workforce would show greater docility, especially in contrast to the older strowger employees, crossbar operatives in certain shops staged repeated go-slows during the 1970s. It was partly on account of these protests that the company was forced to relax the manning standards it had initially attempted to strictly implement, and hire more employees in order to obtain higher volumes of output.

A problem of an even greater magnitude confronting ITI during this same period was linguistic conflict. For besides age and qualifications, a third element of differentiation in the composition of the strowger and the crossbar workforce was language. Whereas strowger comprised in the main of Tamil speakers, quite a few of whom were migrants from the

[85] Interview with L.G. Varadharajan.
[86] Interview with Srinivasa Rao.
[87] ibid.
[88] *Switching System Selection Report*, p. 13.

neighbouring state of Tamil Nadu, the overwhelming majority of crossbar workers were local Kannada speakers. For several reasons that we shall discuss at length in a later chapter, the company had consciously opted to privilege workers of Kannada origin when recruiting personnel for crossbar. The en masse arrival of these new workers which intersected with the emergence in the late 1960s of a nativist political movement in Bangalore, virulently opposed to everything Tamil, would ignite an intense clash of linguistic identities inside ITI. A climate of fear and violence soon proceeded to grip both the factory and the township only abating from the mid-1970s onwards.

THE ERA OF ELECTRONIC SWITCHING TECHNOLOGY

As with electro-mechanical systems, the government decided that foreign collaboration was indispensable for the manufacture of electronic switching equipment too. Such a course of action had been strongly recommended by the various committees appointed by P&T from the mid-1970s onwards to examine how best the transition to electronic switching could be handled. These expert bodies had arrived at the conclusion that indigenous initiatives to design and fabricate electronic switching systems (ESS) were inevitably doomed to failure: neither the infrastructure to develop high-quality professional grade components nor the process expertise to mass produce the equipment existed in the country.[89]

Representing a fundamentally radical change, since nothing less than the adoption of a 'new technological paradigm' was at stake, ITI's transition from electro-mechanical to electronic systems turned out to be just as controversial and complicated as the strowger to crossbar transition.[90] In June 1980, a ground plan submitted by the company to

[89] Sunil Mani, 'Technology Acquisition and Development. Case of Telecom Switching Equipment', *EPW*, Vol. XXIV, 25 November 1989, pp. M181–M192; Alam, 'Performance of Imported Technology in LDCs'. However, according to the head of the P&T research team, indigenous attempts to build an electronic switch were defeated by the presence of a strong import lobby within the national carrier and by transnational corporations. G.B. Meemamsi, *The C-DOT Story. Quest, Inquest, Conquest*, Noida, 1993, pp. 16–17.

[90] Eric Brousseau et al, 'Des changements majeurs dans l'offre de services de télécommunications', in *idem* (eds.), *Mutations des Télécommunications, des Industries et des Marchés*, Paris, 1996, pp. 11–80.

P&T recommended the establishment of two separate factories by 1983–84, with a capacity of 500,000 lines each, to fabricate local electronic exchanges. Besides calling for the new units to be placed under its control, the company stressed the importance of situating one of them at least in Bangalore in order to absorb the surplus labour resulting from the progressive scaling down of strowger output. However, the Ministry of Communications, which in principle as ITI's parent ministry, was supposed to defend its interests, would formulate a radically different proposal. In a policy paper presented in December 1980 to the high-power Cabinet Committee on Economic Affairs, chaired by the prime minister, the Communications Ministry wrote that the first ESS factory 'should be under a Corporate entity separate from ITI', while a decision concerning the second would be taken later.[91] To worsen matters, the paper added that the question of whether ITI would even be allocated the second plant remained unresolved.

These recommendations would be endorsed in part by the Sarin Committee which was headed by the secretary, Ministry of Communications but included representatives from other official agencies as well. In one of its reports, it agreed that the first ESS plant should not come under ITI's purview, but felt the second plant must be a part of the company, though built on a new site in Bangalore. This was probably with a view to ensuring the emergence of a more efficient and disciplined work culture.[92] As the report pointed out, apart from facilitating the redeployment of part of the excess strowger manpower,

. . . considerable R&D and production capabilities exist in the ITI Bangalore and will be available to the new unit, thus importantly helping in stepping up production in a relatively short period.[93]

The Sarin Committee disagreed with the Communication Ministry on another point as well: it wanted no delays in launching the second factory, underscoring the chronic shortfall in the availability of switching equipment.

---

[91] COPU, *Indian Telephone Industries Ltd. Research & Development and New Projects*, 38th Report, Seventh Lok Sabha, New Delhi, 1982, pp. 17–18. (Hereafter COPU 1982.)

[92] *Fifth Interim Report of the Committee on Telecommunications*, p. 15.

[93] ibid.

In the end, none of the proposals drawn up by the different committees would be fully taken into account by Indira Gandhi's Congress-I government. In the second half of 1982, it announced the creation of one new electronic switching plant which would come under the control of ITI. But instead of Bangalore it selected Mankapur in the state of Uttar Pradesh as the site. The plant would make large local exchanges with technology being sourced from the French state-owned transnational CIT-Alcatel whose E10B system was identified as appropriate to Indian usage patterns once P&T had found its newer E10S system too expensive.

Even though Alcatel had not responded to the global tender issued by the government, the bilateral agreement signed between the Indian and French authorities in May 1982 conclusively settled matters in its favour. The French offered to provide financial assistance to the tune of FFr 1 billion (roughly Rs 5 billion) covering all aspects of the transfer of technology tie-up (royalty fees, machinery, equipment, training and R&D).[94] In addition to helping set up the Mankapur plant, Alcatel would also supply know-how to fabricate trunk automatic switching equipment at ITI's existing Palakkad plant. Notwithstanding the attractive aid package tied to the Alcatel collaboration, two foreign scholars have argued that it was not the most beneficial of deals for India either from the economic or the technological standpoint.[95] Among other things, the government is thought to have paid an extremely high price for the E10B system despite it being a less exploited or proven technology in foreign markets compared to a similar exchange developed by Ericsson.[96]

[94] Half the FFr 1 billion credit was to take the form of a soft loan (at 1.5 per cent), and the rest as commercial credit (at 9 per cent). Claes Brundenius and Bo Göransson, 'Technology Policies in Developing Countries—The Case of Telecommunications in Brazil and India', *vierteljahresberichte*, No. 3, March 1986, pp. 43–64. It was also rumoured that the Alcatel deal was part of a bigger and more crucial commercial transaction involving the purchase of Mirage fighter planes by India.

[95] ibid.

[96] By the end of the 1980s, 71 countries had adopted Ericsson's AXE switch, and of the total 22.9 million lines installed worldwide, 90 per cent were in foreign markets. In comparison, the E10B was in use in 57 countries, and though more lines had been installed worldwide (25.4 million), foreign markets accounted for only 22 per cent of the total. D.K. Sangal, 'India made Wise Choice in E10-B', *Telematics India*, Vol. 5, No. II, February 1989, p. 3. Cited in Mani, 'Technology Acquisition and Development'.

POLITICAL EXPEDIENCY GUIDES GEOGRAPHICAL
EXPANSION OF ITI

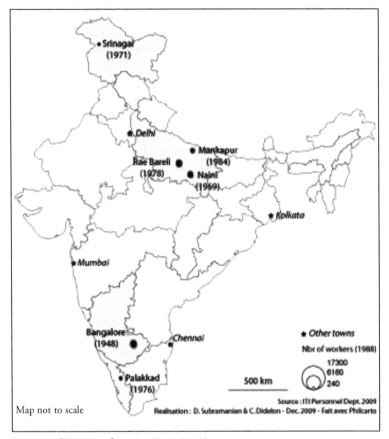

Location of ITI Manufacturing Units (1988)

In the wake of the launch of the new ESS factory in Mankapur, ITI now
managed six production facilities in different parts of the country. In
addition to the main Bangalore unit, one was situated in Srinagar
(Kashmir), another in Palakkad (Kerala), and the remaining three in UP.
Of the six plants, the Srinagar plant was by far the smallest and had been
built in 1971 to fulfil essentially a political purpose as in the case of the
other diversifications.

It was to show that public sector was investing in a so-called backward state. It was all mere *tamasha*. Labour here was not skilled at all.[97]

Supplying telephone cords to start with before being upgraded to assemble phones, the plant experienced problems of sub-standard quality. Output levels also never reached the installed capacity of 200,000 telephones annually, and began to seriously decline from 1989–90 onwards due to the political disturbances affecting the state. By 1993–94, production had dropped to a record low of 25,000 instruments, while losses had accumulated to around Rs 140 million.[98] Threats of violence levelled at certain groups of employees also obliged the company to expatriate over a third of the 240 permanent employees working here to its other units. Still, the Srinagar factory continued to stay in operation, for the 'unit has to be run purely for country's political reasons', even though it 'is not a commercially feasible proportion for ITI (sic)'.[99]

Established in 1976 to fabricate electronic PABXs, the Palakkad plant was also a fairly small operation to start with: until the mid-1980s, less than 400 employees figured on its rolls. But from this point onwards, the workforce would double. Following the expansion of the factory, at a cost of Rs 564 million, to undertake the production of digital trunk exchanges with Alcatel know-how, employment climbed to a maximum of 911 people in 1992–93.[100]

Three of the six units belonging to ITI were implanted in one and the same state, UP. The reason for this geographical over-representation was neither favourable economic conditions by way of access to resources and markets, nor strategic considerations, but short-term political compulsions. The fact that it was the 'home' state of Indira Gandhi as well as other influential Congress politicians served to explain the rationale behind the locational choices of the government. Given the strong employment generating potential public sector enterprise companies commanded, both directly in terms of providing factory jobs and

---

[97] Interview with L.G. Varadharjan.

[98] Note to ITI Board, 284th Meeting, Item B2, November 1995.

[99] Note to ITI Board, 269th Meeting, Item B3, December 1993. Since the unit was being kept open for political imperatives, the company, in view of its difficult financial situation following deregulation, wanted the government to fully compensate it for the losses incurred. But only a small portion of this amount was reimbursed.

[100] COPU (1996–97), *Indian Telephone Industries Ltd.*, 10th Report, Eleventh Lok Sabha, New Delhi, 1997, p. 16. (Hereafter COPU 1997.)

indirectly in terms of stimulating a range of feeder services, bringing the units of ITI to the state was, for these politicians, an important means of consolidating and nurturing their electoral base by ensuring voter loyalty. As Gérard Heuzé has rightly observed, the location of any new state-owned company represented high stakes for the political class.[101] In 1990–91, when they were running at their peak strength, the three ITI factories established in UP jointly employed 13,408 people out of a total workforce of 32,215.[102]

The first of the UP units to come up was the Naini transmission and telephone factory, and it was situated in the Allahabad parliamentary constituency of the then Communications Minister H.N. Bahuguna. It also marked the first major geographical expansion of the company outside Bangalore. Sanctioned by the government in October 1969, the transmission division went on stream two years later at a cost of Rs 34 million with technology developed indigenously by P&T and ITI engineers. With Bangalore proving incapable of single-handedly satisfying the needs of P&T, in August 1970, the government also authorized the launch of a second division to manufacture telephones, investing Rs 75.9 million for this purpose.[103] While the creation of the Naini unit definitely eased the overall supply constraints with respect to telecommunications equipment, it affected the main Bangalore plant rather severely. Since it had to divert part of its output to Naini until operations there could get underway fully, Bangalore was saddled with idle assembly capacity for fairly long periods.[104]

[101] Gérard Heuzé, 'Marché du travail, données communautaires et stratégies individuelles: un exemple dans l'Inde contemporaine', *Sociologie du travail*, No. 2, 1990, pp. 155–72. See also Sudip Chaudhuri, 'Public Enterprises and Private Purposes', *EPW*, Vol. XXIX, No. 22, 28 May 1994, pp. 1338–47; and Keshabananda Das, 'Politics of Industrial Location: Indian Federalism and Development Decisions', *EPW*, Vol. XXXII, No. 51, 20–26 December 1997, pp. 3268–74. The last study in particular clearly shows how political compulsions ride roughshod over guidelines on locational decisions stressing criteria such as availability of raw material, proximity to markets, access to transport facilities, etc.

[102] Of the three, Rae Bareli had the biggest workforce (6241), followed by Naini (4731), and Mankapur (2436). (*Source*: ITI Corporate Office.)

[103] Report of the Comptroller and Auditor General of India, Indian Telephone Industries Ltd., Union Government No. 12 (Commercial) of 1992, p. 4. (Hereafter CAG Report 1992.)

[104] Interview with U.D.N. Rao, ex-ITI Chairman, 18 July 1996. (Interviewed by Balaji Parthasarathy.)

The second ITI plant in UP would be situated in Rae Bareli, the parliamentary constituency of Indira Gandhi. Prospective sites in Kerala and Madhya Pradesh had also been inspected, but the government opted once again in favour of UP.[105] Although the choice of the switching system to be manufactured was to be finalized later on the basis of the proposals submitted by an expert body, it was commonly expected that the Rae Bareli factory would adopt the Pentaconta crossbar technology.[106] However, with the Pentaconta performing poorly, the government, acting on P&T's recommendations, decided in 1974 that it would produce 100,000 lines of strowger equipment annually as a stopgap measure so that the plan targets could be partly achieved.

The plant was scheduled to commence operations from May 1978. But even five years after that, the plant was producing only about 81,000 lines instead of the programmed 100,000 lines.[107] The company attributed its inability to install the full manufacturing capacity, and the attendant shortfall in output, essentially to the difficulties involved in developing infrastructural facilities in a greenfield area. As one ITI chairman explained to a parliamentary committee,

infrastructural facility includes electrical, sewerage . . . In that area nothing was there. Everything had to be developed and created by ITI . . .[108]

When questioned as to why this location had been selected 'when nothing was available there', the chairman replied that the 'site was recommended by the Ministry (of Communications) and ITI was not involved in decision making in this regard'.[109] Being a greenfield area dominated by an exclusively agricultural workforce, the management also struggled to recruit adequate numbers of skilled workers, and instructions specifying that it employ as many local people as possible further tied its hands. In the absence of adequate infrastructure and trained personnel, quality standards inevitably suffered.

[105] Project Report for Strowger Switching Equipment Factory at Rae Bareli, November 1973.

[106] Note from N.V. Shenoi, Secretary, Ministry of Communications to the Cabinet, Ref. No. 1.F.(11)/69, 20 October 1973.

[107] CAG Report 1992, p. 4.

[108] COPU 1997, p. 13.

[109] ibid.

... things got so bad at one stage that two to three months of equipment were rejected by P&T . . . So people had to be sent from Bangalore to train Rae Bareli staff and Rae Bareli staff also came to Bangalore.[110]

In 1980, the government incurred a much bigger investment of Rs 645 million at the Rae Bareli plant, expanding it so that it could undertake the manufacture of the locally designed Indian Crossbar Project (ICP) exchanges. Production began in 1982–83. But despite manpower exceeding requirements, at no point of time in the next decade or so did the factory ever succeed in reaching the peak annual capacity of 100,000 lines.[111]

The decision to allocate to Rae Bareli the ICP technology which would be declared obsolete by 1994–95 flew totally in the face of reason and prevented the most optimal utilization of both the company's resources and public investments. Firstly, it would have been far more logical for the main Bangalore plant to make the ICP switch since it was already turning out Pentaconta exchanges, and therefore possessed the necessary infrastructure and expertise. Secondly, and more significantly, fabricating ICP equipment in Bangalore would also have made more sense as the Rae Bareli unit could then have embraced digital technology. For it must not be forgotten that at about the same time as the ICP division was going on stream, P&T and the government were finalizing plans to launch the first ESS factory. One could well argue that had the authorities decided to produce the Alcatel-designed E10B system at Rae Bareli, the necessity of establishing a totally new unit at Mankapur for this purpose would not have arisen at all, thus saving the exchequer considerable expenditure.

Nambiar when he was chairman (of ITI) protested to the Ministry (of Communications) that setting up the crossbar plant in Rae Bareli was a wrong choice since electronic exchanges were then coming on stream world over.[112]

Thus, instead of making the leap to electronic switching, the Rae Bareli unit would find itself stuck in the electro-mechanical era with a product mix comprising one totally outdated technology, strowger, and the other, ICP, with the disadvantage of being neither an advanced nor a proven technology. Much of the difficulties the unit would subsequently wrestle

---

[110] Interview with Srinivasa Rao.
[111] CAG Report 1992, p. 5, 22.
[112] Interview with Srinivasa Rao.

with, of over manning and lack of orders, would stem from these ill-advised technology choices imposed upon it by P&T.

Like Rae Bareli, Mankapur, which fell within the constituency of a Congress member of parliament with close links to Indira Gandhi, was a greenfield area. Like Rae Bareli, the setting up of a modern factory here would be handicapped by the absence of adequate infrastructural facilities.[113] The most immediate consequence of siting the plant in a remote location was cost overruns with the project finally costing 20 per cent more than the original projections. (Investment estimates for establishing the plant at Bangalore had worked out to be much lower, at Rs 1490 million.)[114] The high social costs incurred on the project can be measured from the fact that over a fifth of the total investments would go towards the development of infrastructural facilities.[115]

Second, although the principal objective of locating the plant in a backward area was to encourage economic growth, notably by providing employment opportunities, these benefits seem to have been available only to a limited extent to the local population. Because of the paucity of trained employees, a sizeable proportion of jobs actually went to outsiders. Moreover, even outsiders, especially supervisory and management personnel, were extremely reluctant to come and work in a place where all material comforts were lacking. A number of skilled jobs therefore remained vacant for long periods.

It was impossible to induce soft ware engineers to go to a god-forsaken place like Mankapur . . . Nothing was available there, not even a glass of water . . . The suggestion to give lower technology jobs and alternative projects to Mankapur instead of high technology electronic exchanges was vetoed by Indira Gandhi.[116]

Third, as a result of all these factors, the project would suffer from delays. Production was originally scheduled to get underway in December 1984

---

[113] For want of 'physical amenities and accommodation' both in Mankapur as well as the adjoining city of Faisalabad 'to lodge the French team', ITI would be obliged to base the headquarters of the project several hundred kilometres away in Lucknow. Note to the ITI Board of Directors, Item B24, July 1983.

[114] CAG Report 1992, p. 6.

[115] ibid. Initially, infrastructural costs had been fixed at Rs 274.40 million, but following the cost overruns the figure rose to Rs 475.90 million. See also COPU 1997, pp. 17–18.

[116] Interview with Srinivasa Rao.

and the full capacity of 500,000 lines achieved 60 months (or 5 years) later. But this target would only be reached after 92 months (or 7 years and 8 months) in 1991–92.[117] Over time, the Mankapur unit would become the most profitable of the company's six units. Yet, from the perspective of the flagship Bangalore plant, no other expansion measure decided by the government with respect to ITI would have more adverse effects than the one to locate the first ESS factory in Mankapur.

At the same time, the locational choices pushed through by the government foregrounded squarely the contradiction between the goals of planned industrial development and social equity and the logic of industrial operations. On the one hand, regardless of short-term political considerations, the authorities could hardly be faulted for having wanted to site the new units of ITI in greenfield areas with a view to generating jobs for and improving living standards of the local population. The economic and social disparities between the different regions of the country could only be narrowed down by promoting such purposive measures. On the other, they triggered an inflation in project costs as well as delays in implementation and bringing the plants to peak capacity.[118] Both capital and labour productivity, and in turn, the rate of return on investments, hinged on the optimal allocation and utilization of all available resources. Since this was not the case, the operating efficiency of the units inevitably declined, while their capital-output ratio increased.

Equally importantly, the proliferation of spatially extended plants led to a fragmentation of ITI's manufacturing capacity and prevented it from exploiting economies of scale in its operations. Doubtless, one explanation why ITI products were overpriced lay in scale dis-economies. Production volumes in none of the company's factories were high enough to allow the benefits of mass production to be translated into higher productivity.

---

[117] CAG Report 1992, pp. 6–7.

[118] Stating that all 'economy boils down to the economy of time', Sukhamoy Chakravarty observes that India's experience in the completion of projects has been 'highly unsatisfactory'. *Development Planning. The Indian Experience,* New Delhi, 1987, pp. 57–8. A viewpoint corroborated by a study which showed that out of the 290 medium and large public sector projects, sponsored by the central government as on March 1987, 186 suffered from cost inflation and 162 from delays. Sebastian Morris, 'Cost and Time Overruns in Public Sector Projects', *EPW,* Vol. XXV, No. 47, 24 November 1990, pp. M154–68.

As one official pointed out, output levels for many of the products turned out by ITI were 'too small for a big company and too big for a small company'.[119] Criticizing the decision to manufacture local electronic exchanges in Mankapur and trunk exchanges in Palakkad, the Department of Programme Implementation, attached to the Planning Commission, wrote that it raised transport costs, affected skill development and neutralized potential scale gains.[120]

Top officials of ITI also did not adopt any concerted measures to forge a cohesive corporate culture, in sharp contrast to another public sector multi-unit enterprise like BHEL. Until the late 1980s, a systematic policy of transferring middle and senior managers from one unit to the other did not exist, nor were any incentives provided to encourage staff movement. Executives from the main Bangalore plant stubbornly refused to be relocated at the northern factories, arguing they could not cope with the intense climatic variations, linguistic barriers, and other 'cultural' differences, not to speak of the absence of material comforts in greenfield sites such as Rae Bareli and Mankapur. With interaction restricted to formal high-level meetings, and directed along rigidly demarcated official channels, cooperation between the various units of the company then left much to be desired.

In a segment such as telephones, for example, there was no exchange of best practices or other information between the Naini and Bangalore units. As a result, cost-reduction efforts at the former are thought to have got underway much later than at the Bangalore unit.[121] As a company note pointed out, 'plants within ITI must trust each other, before outside customers can trust ITI'.[122] The consequences of the management's failure to take seriously the task of building strong inter-unit operational linkages and communication flows would become sharply evident at the time of the company's restructuring into business groups in the mid 1990s. For among the reasons why the business group

---

[119] Interview with Srinivasa Rao.

[120] Sunil Mani, 'Technology Import and Skill Development in a Micro-electronics based Industry: The Case of India's Electronic Switching Systems', in A.K. Bagchi (ed.), *New Technology and the Workers' Response, Micro Electronics, Labour and Society*, New Delhi, 1995, pp. 98–122.

[121] Interview with B.K. Sharma, Deputy General Manager Telephone Division, ITI Bangalore, May 1999.

[122] Ref. CM/13.1A, 30 January 1997.

experiment aborted were coordination difficulties as well as restrictions on the movement of inventory from one unit to another as individual plant managements strove to defend their interests against those of the enterprise.

DELAYS IN INTRODUCING DIGITAL TECHNOLOGY IN BANGALORE

In their respective recommendations, both ITI and the Sarin Committee, the latter even at the cost of disagreeing with the Communications Ministry, had strongly urged that at least one digital switching factory should be based in Bangalore. This consensus was based on the awareness of the need to rapidly upgrade the technological capability of the main Bangalore plant. For ever since the early 1980s, it had become evident that the older electro-mechanical systems would be progressively phased out. In 1984, a working group appointed by the P&T Board would categorically state in its report that ITI should stop manufacturing both strowger and crossbar switching equipment in Bangalore by 1990, though the closure of the crossbar division would actually occur two years ahead of this time limit.[123] Steps to introduce new product lines therefore had to be taken quite urgently failing which a large section of the workforce risked being made redundant.

The government, however, selected Mankapur as the site of the first ESS unit.[124] In itself, this policy option would not have proved so damaging to the interests of the Bangalore unit and the company as a whole, had it been backed up by the immediate launch of a second ESS plant in Bangalore. In fact, the cabinet had given its blessings to such a plan in June 1983 with know-how again to be sourced from Alcatel, and the factory was supposed to reach full production capacity by 1990. But due to 'inexplicable delays' it would finally never see the light of day.[125] It was this more than anything else that caused tremendous difficulties for the company. For it would not be able to synchronize the phasing

---

[123] *Study of Phasing out Electromechanical Equipments*, pp. 37–40, 62.

[124] The government itself was divided on this question as can be seen from the fact that Indira Gandhi divested the then Communications Minister C.M. Stephen of his portfolio. Stephen had strongly urged that the first ESS factory should come up in Bangalore.

[125] *Report of the Expert Committee*, chap. 11, p. 1.

out of the obsolete electro-mechanical technologies at the main Bangalore plant with the introduction of new digital technology which in turn frustrated its attempts to redeploy an estimated 6000 surplus workers.[126]

At the same time, the failure to establish the second ESS plant in Bangalore retrospectively underscored even more strongly the irrationality of the government's decision to site the first ESS plant in Mankapur. For even as workers at the Bangalore plant were idling, the company was recruiting fresh hands at Mankapur, and by 1991 when both the strowger and crossbar divisions had been shut down, the latter plant already had 2436 employees on its rolls. As K.P.P. Nambiar, the ITI chairman who ran the company during these crucial years of transition to electronic switching, bluntly put it, locating the first ESS plant in Mankapur was a 'disaster for ITI'.[127]

To the extent that ITI was constrained to carry sizeable quantities of excess labour, its profitability was certainly affected. However, it cannot be denied that, compared with electro-mechanical exchanges, the manufacture of electronic exchanges was a far more capital-intensive operation. The elimination of practically all machining tasks, accompanied by the introduction of printed circuit boards and integrated circuits, plus greater recourse to automated testing techniques, all meant that the labour requirements of the new digital systems were two to three time lower than those of strowger and crossbar. 'The once labour intensive switching industry (had) . . . become a capital intensive industry'[128]— this is substantiated by the massive reductions in staff strength experienced by big equipment makers globally all through the 1970s and the early 1980s.[129]

---

[126] CAG Report 1992, p. 21. It is extremely difficult to accurately evaluate the extent of overstaffing at the Bangalore plant. The figure varies from 4000 to 9000. The figure here has been cited by the government audit report.

[127] Interview with K.P.P. Nambiar.

[128] Chapuis and Joël, *Electronics, Computers and Telephone Switching*, p. 565. Labour requirements at the Plessey plant in Liverpool, as documented by Thompson and Bannon, were 40–60 per cent lower for the semi-electronic TXE exchanges than the corresponding figure for the old electro-mechanical exchanges. In turn, the digital System X exchange eliminated 90 per cent of the labour used for TXE. *Working the System*, p. 12, 73.

[129] Between 1973–83, the number of employees in the telecommunications manufacturing industry in the US fell from 140,000 to 124,900; in France from 66,000 to 52,749; and in Germany from 77,590 to 58,580. Santucci, *L'industrie mondiale des télécommunications*, p. 5.

Further, the poor qualifications of the ITI workforce were bound to have hindered optimal redeployment. In 1985, barely 5 per cent of the roughly 2800 employees in the Bangalore crossbar division had any training pertaining to electronics or electrical engineering.[130] Likewise, no more than 500 of the approximately 4150 employees on the strowger division's rolls in 1990 possessed formal technical qualifications of any sort.[131] So even if the second ESS plant had come up, the company would have been hard pressed to find jobs for all the surplus workers. But the problem would unquestionably have been of a much lower magnitude.

Most of the 'inexplicable delays' that brought about the abandonment of the second ESS factory project at Bangalore had to do with events that occurred within the telecommunications sector during the second half of the 1980s. In February 1984, the Congress-I government, headed by Rajiv Gandhi, created an autonomous research body, the Centre for Development of Telematic Services (C-DoT) with a mandate to indigenously develop state-of-the-art digital technology. This was piloted by a dynamic Indian telecommunications specialist living in the US, Satyen Pitroda who enjoyed the confidence and support of Rajiv Gandhi. C-DoT, which began operating in August 1984, announced a very ambitious '36 months, 36 crores' objective.[132] It promised to deliver a large electronic switch with a capacity of 40,000 lines that would be one if not two generations ahead of the E10B within three years and at a cost of Rs 360 million. This represented a fraction of the $500 million to $1 billion that major transnational corporations had incurred by way of R&D expenditures on building their respective digital systems.[133] C-DoT had played an extremely positive role in extending the reach of

---

[130] ITI Corporate P&A, 'Change of Technology, Retraining, Deployment: A Case Study in Indian Telephone Industries', nd.

[131] Minutes of management-union meeting, 8 March 1990. Of the 16,813 people employed at the Bangalore plant in March 1989, 7178 did not even have a high school degree, what to speak of technical qualifications. (*Source*: ITI Personnel Department.)

[132] See Pitroda's account of how he was able to convert the country's political leadership to the view that telecommunications far from being an irrelevant luxury gadget could serve as an indispensable vehicle in piloting economic growth and wealth creation. Satyen Pitroda, 'Development, Democracy, and the Village Telephone', *Harvard Business Review*, Vol. 71, No. 6, 1993, pp. 66–79.

[133] Meemamsi claims that from 1985–89 C-DoT spent only $40 million in research. *The C-DOT Story*, pp. 118–19.

the national network, especially by connecting rural areas. But as one of its key executives himself later admitted, the '36 months, 36 crores' objective was 'over ambitious'.[134]

Capitalizing on the delays in establishing the second ESS factory, C-DoT now recommended to the government, that ITI should adopt the indigenous switch it was in the process of designing, rather than the Alcatel system. The research body had no doubt come up rapidly with a 128-line public automatic branch exchange (PABX), followed by a 128-line rural automatic exchange (RAX), its most acclaimed achievement. These two small exchanges had also been licensed for production to private and public sector firms, including ITI. Private vendors, in the wake of deregulation, had been allowed to operate in certain segments of the telecommunications equipment market. At the insistence of C-DoT officials who arguably felt that discipline and quality standards could be better assured with a smaller workforce groomed in a 'new culture', ITI in fact launched a new plant dedicated exclusively to C-DoT technology.[135] Known as the Electronic City unit and located in the south of Bangalore, some 20 kms away from the mother factory, at its peak in the mid-1990s, it would employ close to 700 people.

As the 36-month deadline drew closer, C-DoT was nowhere close to making a breakthrough on its primary mission, the 40,000-line Main Automatic Exchange (MAX). Disregarding this lapse, in the latter half of 1987, the prime minister's office decided that the second electronic switching factory in Bangalore should only go in for indigenous systems. Warnings of the threat of under-employment at the main Bangalore plant were issued from various quarters.[136] The political leadership disregarded this information, apparently convinced by the assurances of top C-DoT executives that delays would not in any way compromise their efforts. But as ITI would discover to its profound dismay, the first MAX would not be ready before August 1989, and this possessed a maximum capacity of just 1400 lines. While a bigger 10,000 line switch was developed in 1991, the 40,000 line switch (MAX-XL) would come out only in 1995 by which time it was much too late to realistically consider adopting this

---

[134] ibid, p. 22, 36–7.

[135] ibid, pp. 58–9.

[136] *Report of the Expert Committee for Assessment & Evaluation of the Centre for Development of Telematics,* New Delhi, Government of India, March 1990.

technology. So with C-DoT failing to deliver its large switch on time, whatever hopes ITI might still have nurtured of establishing the second ESS factory in Bangalore now vanished for good. The company thus paid a high price for the vacillations surrounding technology selection, and lost over three years waiting to make the cross-over from electro-mechanical to electronic systems at the main Bangalore plant.[137]

In 1990, ITI re-opened negotiations with Alcatel to acquire an upgraded version of its digital exchange, the OCB-283. With the Rajiv Gandhi government having been ousted from power by then, C-DoT had 'lost its political patronage and direct access to the Prime Minister'.[138] So the way was again clear for ITI to import foreign technology. Despite the apprehensions of the Bangalore union that this new system too would be diverted to Mankapur, it was finally inducted at the mother factory.[139]

---

[137] C-DoT's failure to deliver its large digital switch on time appears far less dramatic when viewed against the backdrop of the difficulties experienced by telecommunications administrations and equipment suppliers in advanced countries in embracing electronic technology. For example, ITT's inability to successfully adapt its System 12 to the constraints of the US market, even after a delay of two years and spending $150 million, was partly responsible for the giant corporation's decision to sell off its telecommunications activities. Chapuis and Joël, *Electronics, Computers and Telephone Switching*, p. 570. Likewise, Adams and Butler point to the planning failures of Western Electric in the US, a consequence of it having misread the speed of the transition from electro-mechanical to electronic systems. *Manufacturing the Future*, pp. 190–3. See also Gareth Locksley, *The EEC Telecommunications Industry. Competition, Concentration and Competitiveness*, Brussels,1983, p. 84, 119, for an analysis of Siemen's botched attempts to make the switch to electronic technology.

[138] Meemamsi, *The C-DOT Story*, p. 71. The C-DoT top management, and the organization as a whole, would pay a high price for its delays in designing a large switch. Acting on the findings of an enquiry committee, the subsequent National Front government would remove all the top directors of C-DoT. Corruption charges would also be brought against Satyen Pitroda forcing him to return to the US. The controversy dragged on for several months, and left C-DoT thoroughly destabilized. It led to a large number of engineers quitting the organization, profoundly disturbed by what they believed, not totally unjustly, was a witchhunt organized by the new government against Pitroda. For details see Meemamsi, *The C-DOT Story*, pp. 71–105; *High Level Expert Committee for the Assessment & Evaluation of Centre for Development of Telematics: Dissenting Note of Four Members*, New Delhi, Government of India, March 1990.

[139] To ensure the Bangalore plant secured the OCB 283 project, the union actively lobbied parliamentary representatives from Karnataka to exercise pressure on the government, and a petition to this effect was signed by all the MPs and submitted to the prime minister. See ITI Employees Union, Bangalore, Circular No. 43/91, 4 December 1991; Circular No. 51/91, 24 December 1991.

But the OCB project would only furnish a partial solution to the question of excess labour, facilitating the redeployment of no more than 1000–2000 workers.[140] As company officials pointed out, 'being a sophisticated line, it is least manpower oriented . . . So, surplus manpower continues with us'.[141]

Measures to effectively re-allocate surplus employees were also thwarted by a combination of shop floor resistance and union non-cooperation. Constraints on the management's authority to distribute manpower were not new, and dated back to the institution of a seniority based promotion scheme in the late 1970s. But in the present context of widespread redundancies, the question of optimal utilization of the labour force became a far more pressing one. Factory managers therefore insisted on making both intra and inter-unit employee transfers compulsory so that they could exercise greater flexibility. For not only was the possibility of transfers from one unit of ITI to another virtually ruled out, given the 'benevolent' character of the industrial relations regime, even within the same unit there were obstacles to the movement of personnel 'from surplus areas to deficit areas', obliging shop managers to occasionally outsource work.[142] In the present context, it was lower level union officials who were instrumental in slowing down the pace of re-deployment by adopting a 'contrary stand' to the top leadership, but the latter 'is not able to sort out their differences'.[143] Fears of earning less incentive and having to work in shifts in case of transfers apparently motivated the resistance of the lower echelons. Nor did their attitudes change over time. As late as July 1996, during a visit by the chairman to the Bangalore factory, workers, officers, leaders of the union and the officers association alike, were unanimous in informing him that the biggest difficulty confronting the factory was that

some divisions had adequate manpower but not enough orders, resulting in idling of men and machinery, while other divisions had enough orders, but not requisite hands to execute orders (sic).[144]

---

[140] While the union claimed that the new project would employ 2000 workers, the company said the requirements did not exceed 1000.

[141] COPU 1997, p. 43.

[142] Minutes of 11th meeting of Joint Committee of Management and Unions of all ITI units, 30 December 1993.

[143] Personnel Department note, nd (1993).

[144] Ref. EDRS/Nt, 25 July 1996.

Unfortunately for ITI, whatever success it may have achieved in re-adjusting the crossbar and strowger workforces would also turn out to be shortlived. Contracting demand for its digital exchanges in the face of cut-throat competition from transnational corporations would make the problem of redundancies resurface from the late 1990s onwards.

LIMITED ACHIEVEMENTS OF ITI R&D

By this time, ITI's own efforts to develop electronic switching technology in-house had been well and truly buried. An earlier foray in this area, an integrated local-cum-trunk digital exchange, which was basically a large EPABX, had proved technologically inferior to and costlier than comparable C-DoT products, despite the company allocating substantially more funds overall for research than C-DoT. Subsequently, while waiting for C-DoT to deliver its large digital switch, ITI's engineers had begun working on a comparable configuration. Having built the bulk of the hardware, the company claimed that the switch, baptised XD-90, was scheduled to go into production by June 1993. Yet eighteen months later, far from commencement of production, the entire project itself had been jettisoned.

The main reason why XD-90 remained stillborn had to do with the reluctance of the then Chairman B.B. Chadha to commit the necessary resources and people. A finance professional, Chadha's first priority was to cut costs, given the company's mounting financial troubles in the aftermath of deregulation. Further, he is thought to have entertained little faith in ITI R&D's ability to commercialize the switch now that DoT could select from a wide spectrum of foreign systems. Analysing retrospectively the company's failure to make headway in electronic switching, one senior executive, voicing a widely-held view, argued that

there was no avenue in switching for us since R&D on electronic exchanges was monopolized by TRC (Technical Research Centre, P&T's research cell) . . . ITI had no mandate to go into electronic switching in a big way. The company also lacked funds since lots of money is required to develop a switch . . .[145]

More generally, the aborted XD-90 experience was illustrative of the difficulties experienced by ITI R&D in bringing its projects to fruition,

---

[145] Interview with M.S. Jayasimha.

and raised questions about the effectiveness of its activities. Of the 185 research projects taken up from 1975–76 to 1989–90, only 17 were completed, and of these, not a single one went into production.[146] The company attributed this dismal conversion rate to a combination of factors: technology imports, want of orders from P&T/DoT, unsatisfactory performance, lack of infrastructure, and long lead times. The fact that none of the research projects managed to cross the trial phase was all the more striking when contrasted with the ample financial and material resources disposed by R&D. Over a 15-year period between 1976–77 and 1990–91, investments in research as a percentage of sales averaged 6.6 per cent, though a deceleration was distinctly visible towards the end.[147]

This was an impressive figure by any standards. A former research director confirmed that

top management was always supportive of R&D; whatever we wanted we got by way of capital requirements (new equipment, instruments, etc.), though working capital was more difficult to secure. R&D was the company's showcase.[148]

Being the 'company's showcase' yielded other material and symbolic privileges as well. R&D officers generally benefited from faster promotions. They also made frequent trips abroad. In the words of one line manager:

R&D was considered as the blue eyed boys . . . they would go around the world whereas production people would go to KR Puram (the area where ITI was located) to get what was required to run the show for the day . . . (R&D) got considerable budgetary allocation on a discretionary basis compared to production where

---

[146] CAG Report 1992, p. 31.

[147] While one official committee had recommended that at least 5 per cent of ITI's revenues should be devoted to research, investments in this domain reached almost 7.8 per cent during the decade 1976–77 to 1985–86, before declining to 4.3 per cent for the period 1986–87 to 1990–91. Annual Report, various years. In comparison, research expenditures of transnational corporations fluctuated on average between 5 to 8 per cent of their sales during the 1960s and 1970s, before rising to around 10 per cent from the mid-1980s onwards. Delaunay-Maculan, *Histoire comparée de stratégies*, p. 83, 145. Another estimate showed the average research intensities for 10 major equipment firms increasing from 8.4 per cent in 1987 to 10.3 per cent in 1999. Jean-Paul Goulvestre, *Economie des télécoms*, Paris, 1997, pp. 88–9; Eurostaf, *Les équipementiers télécoms*, Paris, 2000, (Vol. I), p. 64.

[148] Interview with M.S. Jayasimha.

everything had to be accounted for . . . When it (R&D) wanted to develop micro-circuits in the 1990s, it was given any amount of money (sic).[149]

All these factors served to denote the superior status of R&D over production, and in so doing reinforced the traditional rivalry that marked the relations between these two functional groups.

Table 2.1: R&D Expenditures: ITI Bangalore (Rs million)

Product	1980–81	1981–82	1982–83	1983–84	1984–85
Transmission	11.41	9.85	33.1	36.72	25.36
Electronic switch	6.81	5.22	7.35	23.4	19.8
Electro-mech. switch	4.21	4.77	4.9	6.44	7.95
Telephones	0.75	0.78	3.51	4.26	4.47
Total	23.18	20.62	48.86	70.82	57.58

Note: Figures for 1982–83 to 1984–85 are estimates.
Source: ITI.

But despite commanding considerable resources, and enjoying the backing and confidence of top management, ITI R&D's record was extremely modest. True, a relatively high degree of self-reliance had been achieved in the transmission segment where in collaboration with P&T engineers its research personnel had successfully designed and brought out a wide array of equipment. In fact, the main thrust of the company's research activities had all along targeted this area, a detail borne out by the data we dispose for R&D spending levels at the Bangalore plant (see Table 2.1). Yet, from the early 1980s onwards even with respect to transmission equipment, ITI had begun turning towards foreign suppliers for technologically sophisticated products. The ITI R&D could also boast of having catered to most of the army's telecommunication requirements, albeit with some help from foreign sourced technology.

Counterbalancing these achievements was the fact that ITI realized no more than 30 to 40 per cent of its overall revenues from in-house designed products. By the mid-1990s, this figure would have declined to just 20 per cent.[150] In the crucial switching equipment area, the

---

[149] Interview with Srinivasa Rao.
[150] COPU 1997, pp. 48–9.

mainstay of its business, it was never able to shake off its dependence on external sources for technological inputs. The successful launch in the late 1980s of an electronic push button telephone, equipped with the moving coil receiver which would become the industry standard, must be measured against R&D's earlier failure to come up with a good quality rotary instrument, necessitating recourse to foreign expertise even in a low-technology category such as this.

When the collaboration was signed with the Italian company FACE, DoT asked us whether we were not ashamed of going in for a foreign accord after 30 odd years of working on telephones. There was lot of heart burning in ITI over this issue.[151]

In ITI's defence, it could perhaps be argued that its limited R&D achievements owed in part to resources and energies being often tied up in rendering imported technology compatible with local usage conditions. The Pentaconta fiasco aside, in the case of strowger too, the circuit design architecture needed to be adapted in-house so as to allow for the manufacture of exchanges of up to 10,000 lines. At the same time, the complete monopoly exercised by P&T's own research wing, the Technical Research Centre (TRC), over development work in electronic switching technology until the early 1980s prevented ITI engineers from building up much-needed expertise and skills in this critical domain.[152] Company officials' claims that a number of projects had fallen victim to the rivalries in which TRC and ITI were permanently locked, must also not be discounted.

. . . there always used to be a tussle between TRC and ITI transmission R&D . . . over who would take credit for developing a project . . . TRC people would be jealous that top ITI R&D officials were frequently travelling abroad, whereas they would struggle to get one foreign trip in a life time. So they would retaliate by not approving (ITI) projects where there was a minor deficiency.[153]

---

[151] Interview with Srinivasa Rao. Like the BTM crossbar tie-up, the FACE project too would be caught in a tangle of complications and delays, though with less serious consequences for P&T as well as ITI, and never quite got off the ground.

[152] Since most innovative activity is firm-specific and cumulative in nature, tacit knowledge obtained through experience is crucial. Therefore, even though firms can buy in technology and skills, 'what they have been able to do in the past strongly conditions what they can hope to do in the future.' Keith Pavitt, 'Some Foundations for a Theory of the Large Innovating Firm', in G. Dosi et al (ed.), *Technology and Enterprise in a Historical Perspective*, Oxford, 1992, pp. 212–28 (cit. p. 213).

[153] Interview with M.S. Jayasimha.

Despite the bold assurances of Chairman I.K. Gupta in the early 1970s that the company had deep enough pockets to fund its research activities in case P&T was unwilling to do so, as with all of ITI's ambitions, the scale and scope of its R&D programme too was conditioned by the parent authority's liberality in allocating money. A study of the exchange of correspondence between the two sides during the 1980s vividly revealed the wrangling and tensions that the question of R&D expenditures generated. We find TRC regularly complaining about the disproportionately heavy overheads charged by ITI, and the need therefore to fix limits,[154] or blocking payments on the grounds that the sums reclaimed by it 'appear to be very much on the higher side'.[155] They also refused to reimburse the full amount either because the company had breached operating procedures by undertaking projects without obtaining the prior approval of TRC—projects which the latter claimed it planned to directly pursue—or because the expenditure was unjustified.[156]

Another means by which the parent authority sought to keep in check ITI's research ambitions consisted of imposing extremely stringent specifications on the products it developed. For it must not be forgotten that the responsibility for framing the technical norms which governed the evaluation and validation of equipment by P&T, prior to induction into the national network, was vested in TRC's hands.[157] Hence, while ITI often struggled to secure 'type' approval for its designs, TRC's own projects, or those undertaken with its blessings, faced no such difficulties.

The relationship between TRC and ITI soured only because ITI took the initiative in getting designs other than TRC's . . . Naturally, TRC was jealous so they asked BEL to take up development and manufacture (of transmission equipment) . . . They would give BEL concessions which they would not give us. This is the sort of in-house conflict that was going on.[158]

---

[154] Ref. 8/156/79-TRC-Vol.V, 3 December 1983; Ref. No. 8–158/83-TRC-Vol.1, 21 January 1984.

[155] Ref. No. 73–10/84-TRC, 10 October 1984 and 10 December 1984.

[156] Ref. E/PD/86, 25 April 1983; Ref. E/PD/R&D REIM, 6 April 1984; Note, 5 September 1987.

[157] The conflict of interests this situation created, where TRC both designed equipment and drew up equipment specifications, was only resolved in 1987. A separate body was established, the Telecommunications Engineering Centre, charged specifically with determining technical specifications, and evaluating new products and systems.

[158] Interview with C.S.S. Rao.

However, it cannot be denied that internal inefficiencies were also to blame for ITI's inability to build strong technological capabilities. Like the rest of the company's operations, R&D too was afflicted by the same problems of organizational inertia, red tape and indiscipline. According to one executive, the research department at the main Bangalore plant had grown so big that it had become 'unmanageable'.[159] Shirking was widespread; for the rest of the factory, the acronym R&D had come to stand for 'roaming and disappearing'. Divided into two entities, transmission R&D and switching R&D, which also encompassed telephones, the department already counted 1469 employees on its rolls in 1978. By the eve of deregulation in 1991, the figure had risen further to 1649 employees, after which it would start contracting.[160] Of this number, no more than a quarter were engaged in genuine 'research' tasks; the rest either performed a variety of auxiliary jobs (documentation, field trials, vendor development, etc.) or worked in the manufacturing and testing facilities controlled by R&D where designs were converted into product prototypes, fabricated and tested.

The sheer size of the department coupled with the absence of competitive pressures also entailed a lack of focus and direction. As one former research chief stated,

...the government said 'you do research' and we did research. The government was very happy to have research done here. We were very happy because the profits were there . . . Research was a hobby rather than a business . . . We were doing national projects in ITI when the government was not giving us the money for them. *We were wasting the future.* We were not doing research on switches or transmission systems. We did not do very purposeful recruiting.[161]

Resources were often squandered. Investments allocated to establish a semi-conductor manufacturing facility yielded few returns because 'commercially it was not a viable project'.[162] At the same time, a number of potentially strategic projects, such as the design of application-specific integrated circuits for electronic telephones which the semi-conductor

[159] Interview with Srinivasa Rao.

[160] The larger of the two wings, switching R&D, employed 832 people in 1978, and transmission R&D, 637.

[161] Interview with Sira G. Rao, ex-Director ITI Bangalore, 5 August 1996. Emphasis added. (Interviewed by Balaji Parthasarathy.)

[162] Interview with M.S. Jayasimha.

plant could have legitimately pursued, fizzled out due to inertia and delays. Nor were any determined measures adopted by R&D to shorten development lead times to accelerate the process of new product introduction. Often, delays at every stage of development resulted in cycle times stretching from two to six or seven years. This in turn made a product technologically obsolete by the time it was ready to be commercialized.

Moreover, the lethargy and time overruns characteristic of the conception of new equipment so constrained R&D at times that it had the contrariwise effect of inducing it to take shortcuts with extremely negative consequences for the company. An internal document, dissecting the weakness of the department, remarked that it was 'continually ignoring meticulous field trials and customer validation'.[163] So new designs tended to be produced and commercialized well ahead of the completion of the full development cycle. This was attributed as much to the non-availability of funds to fabricate adequate quantities of prototypes for field trials as to the undue haste exhibited by R&D and the rest of company, intent on marketing the product as quickly as possible. The result of these premature launches was 'large scale failures' and 'huge after–sales service costs' by way of repair and replacement of equipment. Such after sales costs, the document added, were 'one or two orders of magnitude larger than the extra R&D cost that would have been incurred in conducting meticulous trials'.[164]

Further adding to these difficulties were the antagonisms and poor cooperation that bedevilled relations between R&D and production, the upshot of which was to affect the performance of in-house designed equipment.

[The] R&D thought its duty was only to make a one-off sample, see that it works, and then consider that its job was over, whereas production is a continuous process . . .[165]

No less accusatory, another line manager stated that,

[The] R&D does not interact with production when preparing a new model. We have told them to share information with us so that they don't design a

---

[163] Note from Director R&D, ITI Bangalore to Director Bangalore Complex, 25 April 1994.
[164] ibid.
[165] Interview with Srinivasa Rao.

model which is very difficult to produce and then requires modifications later
. . . They come with a model and regardless of our objections would not be
willing to change it . . .[166]

The manner in which R&D transferred manufacturing information to
shop officials with respect to newly completed projects also attracted
criticism. The information was often passed on to shop officials verbally,
thereby resulting in research personnel getting caught up on an 'ad hoc
basis in production functions and [being] accountable for production'.[167]
A proposal to improve communication flows between R&D and the
shop floor by creating an intermediary agency was put forward some
time in the late 1970s. Apparently fearful of the emergence of a 'parallel
power centre', R&D executives, however, convinced top management
to drop the plan.[168] Justifying his opposition to the proposed
arrangement, a former research head at the Bangalore plant claimed it
would not have permitted R&D to concentrate more effectively on
research.

Eighty per cent of our research efforts was not original R&D; what we were
doing like most other companies was engineering, that is manufacturing similar
products to competitors, but using our own components. All original research
is done in universities or exclusively R&D labs, but not in the R&D lab of a
manufacturing unit . . . In electronics, you need to keep development, engineering
and production under the same umbrella . . . If you separate these three processes,
it leads to unnecessary duplication of efforts and increases costs.[169]

Only in 1998, or almost two decades after it was first mooted, would
this initiative to restructure the activities of the R&D department be
implemented following the creation of a 'core' R&D cell.

SUBCONTRACTORS HURT BY SHIFT TO ELECTRONIC TECHNOLOGY

The transition from electro-mechanical to electronic systems would also
impose tremendous hardship upon ITI's subcontractors. Totally

---

[166] Interview with R. Yuvakumar, Assistant General Manager, ITI Bangalore, 13–16 April 1999.
[167] Note from Director R&D.
[168] Interview with Srinivasa Rao.
[169] Interview with M.S. Jayasimha.

dependent on the public sector enterprise which guaranteed the purchase of their entire output over fairly long periods, the subcontracting firms would soon be confronted with near-empty order books following the introduction of digital exchanges. If some of the bigger and more dynamic entrepreneurs, especially in Bangalore, managed to subsequently secure other customers, a number of other subcontractors were forced to close down.

The first steps taken by ITI to promote the growth of an ancillary network dated back to the early 1980s. A decade later, there were over 90 firms supplying the company with an extensive array of components, sub-assemblies and spares, for strowger and crossbar exchanges as well as for telephones where in some cases, they even made the entire instrument.[170] While more than half the ancillaries were located in Bangalore, others emerged around the Naini and Rae Bareli units.[171]

To what extent outsourcing was a deliberate strategy, aimed at improving operating efficiencies and reducing costs, or whether it was merely the upshot of the management imitating the example of other public sector firms, besides complying with government directives to generate employment, remains open to debate. Underlining the fact that the main Bangalore plant had already grown to massive proportions with 14,000 employees on its rolls, resulting in communication difficulties and 'lack of proper control and supervision', top executives definitely saw subcontracting as a safety valve.[172] It offered a convenient means of containing further increases in the size of the workforce while simultaneously enabling ITI to augment much-needed production capacity in certain areas. Much the same point was emphasized in a subsequent document outlining the company's expansion plans.[173] No

---

[170] The company outsourced 1500 types of piece-parts, components, and sub-assemblies, according to a former ITI chairman. C.S.S. Rao, 'Ancillary Development in ITI', *Lok Udyog*, Vol. XIII, No. 12, March 1980, pp. 9–13.

[171] In 1981–82, out of the 93 ancillaries working for ITI and employing a total of 3605 people, 49 were located in Bangalore (2525 people), 32 in Naini (950 people), and 12 in Rae Bareli (130). A decade later, this figure stood at 105, with 46 located in Bangalore, 30 in Naini, 26 in Rae Bareli, and 3 in Srinagar. *Public Enterprises Survey*, 1984–85, BPE, p. 302 (Vol. 1); ITI Corporate Office.

[172] Letter from ITI chairman to division heads, Ref. CM-27.8, 15 July 1971. See also minutes of management-union meeting Bangalore plant, 2 November 1974;

[173] Brief for the Task Force VI, Telecommunications and Electronic Industry, November 1972.

precise data is available to determine whether or not these twin objectives of boosting capacity without fresh recruitments were achieved. But the company appears to have had greater success in satisfying P&T's incessant demand for spare parts, besides realizing substantial margins on their sales to the parent administration, given the ancillaries' much lower overheads. For instance, switch board plugs turned out at a cost of Rs 20 by the ancillaries were sold to P&T at Rs 33.[174] However, contrary to conventional wisdom, a former ITI chairman claimed that in several instances, the prices charged by ancillaries tended to be less economical than in-house manufacture.[175] According to him, the poor quality of bought-out components was also one of the factors hurting the reputation of ITI products. This was certainly true: as early as in 1958, the management had qualified its 'experience of subcontracting' as not being 'a happy one . . . as it involves lowering of standards'.[176] But on the questions of production costs, the evidence at our disposal suggests otherwise. Labour charges, for example, incurred on assembling a telephone in-house stood at Rs 9.79 as against Rs 2.80 externally.[177]

Yet, the public sector enterprise never strove to step up the scale of its outsourcing operations. As Balaji Parthasarathy has put it, ITI's relationship with its ancillaries was 'static, in terms of technology and products and it maintained an arms-length distance', with them.[178] The company's substantial workforce, no doubt, impeded it from fully exploiting this option. Indeed, beyond a certain point, subcontracting may well have proved counterproductive as ITI operatives would have found themselves without sufficient work, and it was precisely on this

[174] Interview with L.G. Varadharajan.

[175] Rao, 'Ancillary Development in ITI'. The author, however, refrains from providing evidence to back his claim, nor does he advance any reasons to explain why markets happened to be costlier than hierarchies.

[176] EC Report 1961, p. 44. See also P&T Board memo of 1983–84, 15 February 1984; Minutes of 19th Telecommunications Quality Assurance Circle, 19 December 1988. But by encouraging price-based competition and refusing to disqualify unrealistically low bids, especially in a context where input costs were known to all parties, ITI also contributed to further undermining the quality of sub-contracted products.

[177] Telephone Division note, Ref. PPC-T/18, 23 April 1986. (Hereafter Tel. Divn.)

[178] Balaji Parthasarathy, 'Globalization and Agglomeration in Newly Industrializing Countries: The State and the Information Technology Industry in Bangalore, India', Unpublished Phd dissertation, Berkeley, University of California, 2000, p. 266.

issue that the union concentrated its objections. On more than one occasion, it protested that externalization was being pursued at the expense of company personnel who remained idle.[179] Workers once even prevented a lorry loaded with components for delivery to an ancillary firm from leaving the factory; this action, though, was provoked more by the fear of losing soft high-earning incentive jobs than any possible ill-effects of idleness.[180] Subsequently, audit authorities also censured the Bangalore telephone division management for trying to expand output through subcontracting instead of optimally utilizing internal capacity and labour resources.[181] As a former head of the division conceded, line officials were inclined to 'take the soft option' and depend on subcontracting, rather than exercise their authority to extract higher effort from the workforce.[182]

In some cases, production was done in parallel both internally and outside . . . Costs were rising but nobody was worried about it . . . If questions were raised as to why subcontracting was being resorted to when internal capacity was available, officers would say that without subcontracting targets cannot be met.[183]

That outsourcing never constituted an integral element of the company's production strategy can be deduced from the following figure: at no point of time did sales by the ancillaries ever exceed beyond 5.3 per cent of ITI's total revenues. This level was reached in 1979–80. Thereafter, the volume of sales continued to steadily decline, and by 1990–91, it had sunk to 1.4 per cent of the company's revenues before falling even further to 0.22 per cent by the mid 1990s.[184] The principal reason for this decline was the arrival of electronic switching technology. Far less labour intensive than the older strowger and crossbar exchanges, the new digital systems involved the assembly of several critical components (resistors, capacitors, integrated circuits, etc.) which could only be manufactured in large volumes with automated process equipment and necessitated stringent quality control measures. Small and

[179] Minutes of union-management meeting Bangalore plant, 21 July 1975; 12 May 1980; 14–15 February 1983; 23 August 1988.
[180] Minutes of union-management meeting Bangalore plant, 17 August 1977.
[181] Tel. Divn. note 27 January 1990.
[182] Interview with R. Yuvakumar.
[183] ibid.
[184] Data provided by ITI corporate office.

undercapitalized, the ancillaries were totally lacking in resources to invest both in such machinery as well as in the equipment required for assembly work, not to speak of hiring qualified personnel. Moreover, even assuming the ancillaries had been able to afford these investments, ITI was now hardly in a position to outsource any part of the production of digital exchanges, saddled as it was with excess labour. In fact, in an effort to keep the workforce occupied, it even decided to start making spares and components for electro-mechanical exchanges in-house.

To conclude, the transition from one generation of production technology to the next proved anything but a smooth process for ITI. On the contrary, difficulties occasioned by the import of know-how unsuited to local conditions, tensions generated by the efforts to adjust the company's social organization to its technical apparatus, and delays in the introduction of new technology all posed severe challenges to the management's ability to successfully undertake the modernization of the company's technology base. The introduction of the crossbar system in particular furnished an especially strong illustration of the argument that organizations are composed of interdependent technical and social systems. Hence evolutions in one sphere generally occasion adaptation and/or disruption in the other.

The manner in which the company chose to implement this technology had ramifications that extended well beyond the technical sphere, and resulted in a fundamental reordering of the prevailing pattern of social relations within the enterprise. It was thus less new technology *per se* than managerial decisions with respect to recruitment, job classification and promotions attendant to the induction of technology that was the driving force behind organizational change. Indeed, the unintended social consequences concomitant to the adoption of crossbar proved just as problematic for factory executives to resolve as the various technical deficiencies that beset the system.

A couple of other points need to be stressed as well. First, the process of technology selection dramatically underscored the heteronomy of ITI management in determining long-term corporate growth policies. The state and P&T/DoT played a pivotal role as they forcefully exercised their political and administrative prerogatives to determine the strategic options the public sector company would embrace. In certain instances, P&T, as the customer and final user of the product, felt that it was more competent than ITI to evaluate which technology best suited the requirements of the network. But as the crossbar deal eloquently demonstrated, its lack of expertise could lead to very costly errors. In other instances, as in the choice of technology to be adopted for the jinxed second ESS factory at Bangalore, it was the government which directly intervened and imposed its preference, based on political considerations. The wrong or ill-conceived technology choices made by P&T and the government thus gave rise to a vicious cycle: instead of remedying the situation, these decisions aggravated the poor functioning of the telecommunications network and further strained equipment supplies, leaving the authorities sometimes with no alternative but to resort to imports in order to satisfy the burgeoning demand for telephone connections.

Second, company executives were excluded from the process of strategy formulation in another crucial area: the expansion of production facilities and resource allocation. All the locational decisions touching upon the creation of the different units were not only taken by the government, but they obeyed political compulsions rather than economic ones. In turn, this bureaucratic and political interference in the affairs of ITI, which had tremendously negative consequences all around, by depriving management of its autonomy also freed it from being accountable for the performance of the company. State ownership even as it subjected the functioning of public enterprises to intense scrutiny from various official agencies thus had the paradoxical effect of discouraging managerial accountability.

While the overall policy of siting new plants in greenfield areas with a view to promoting the development of backward regions was a perfectly laudable and justified objective, the rationale underlying certain decisions, notably the establishment of the first digital switching factory at Mankapur, was hard to understand. If ITI suffered heavily on account of such choices, the price the economy as a whole was required to pay was no less substantial by way of increased capital expenditures and time overruns. Inefficiencies in the allocation of fresh investment resources also had a supplementary effect: existing productive capacities created at a high cost were squandered given that new plants came up at the expense of older ones whose capacity remained under utilized. In other words, the expansion of ITI underlined the fundamental contradictions between the principles of a civic order of worth, resting on the equitable distribution of scarce national investments, that the government wished to promote, and those of an industrial order of worth, stressing the efficient use of those investments so as to ensure the profitable long-term growth of the enterprise.[185]

Third, government policies aimed at reserving the telecommunications equipment sector for state-owned enterprises were no doubt successful in building a relatively solid domestic manufacturing base. This goal was, however, achieved paradoxically through repetitive imports of technology via licensing agreements. Self-reliance in the production of equipment, though even here the need for periodic imports to offset shortages was not completely eliminated, therefore went in hand with a high degree of dependency on foreign know-how. As Ashok Desai has justly remarked, confronted with the technological weakness of Indian industry, the government has always opted in favour of dependence rather than stagnation with respect to state-owned enterprises.[186]

Despite the official rhetoric on the importance of developing indigenous capability, neither the research structures of P&T nor ITI proved capable of acquiring the design capacities indispensable to replacing imported technologies. Even in the case of low-tech products such as telephones where ITI boasted considerable development and manufacturing experience, specialized foreign assistance had to be secured. For a variety of reasons ranging from bureaucratic procedures to inadequate emphasis on local skill development and import substitution measures to lack of focus, P&T and ITI could not adapt technology purchases from abroad effectively enough to local conditions to make them yield breakthroughs in the form of a continuous stream of improvements both in product characteristics and in production methods.[187]

---

[185] The terms civic and industrial order of worth are borrowed from Luc Boltanksi and Laurent Thévenot, *De la justification. Les économies de la grandeur*, Paris, 1991.

[186] Ashok Desai, 'Technological Performance in Indian Industry. The Influence of Market Structures and Policies', in *idem* (ed.), *Technology Absorption in Indian Industry*, New Delhi, 1988, pp. 1–29.

[187] A voluminous literature exists on the causes of India's technological lag. If all sides attack government policies, some blame the highly regulated economic framework within which industry had to operate until 1991, while others, on the contrary, attack excessive imports which they see as undercutting domestic R&D activities. Both the 'right' and the 'left' critiques are presented in Dipayan Datta Chaudhuri, 'Technological Capability in Indian Electronics Industry under Economic Liberalism', *EPW*, Vol. XXX, No. 7–8, 18–25 February 1995, pp. M13–18.

In effect, in the Indian context, technology absorption more often than not had a restrictive connotation. It suggested, at best, efforts to tailor blue prints and processes in response to local environment constraints, and/or integrate indigenous raw material and components, as opposed to a coherent and purposive long-term research programme geared to releasing new products and new processes by innovating upon imported know-how. In other words, the assimilation or unbundling of foreign technology generally did not extend beyond incremental improvements. Only after the founding of C-DoT in the mid-1980s, and its success in developing small and medium electronic switching systems, was the telecommunications sector able to experience a degree of self reliance. This would, however, not last very long. The unrestricted entry of transnational corporations into the Indian market following deregulation in 1991, together with insufficient official support for C-DoT's research activities, would once again place the state and domestic companies in a position of dependency *vis-à-vis* foreign technology suppliers.

chapter three

The Burden of Monopoly and State Regulation

One of the features of factory life that scholars studying questions of state-sponsored industrialization and labour practices in the former Soviet bloc often highlight is the phenomenon of 'end-year rush-work' or 'arrhythmia'.[1] The term describes a pattern of industrial production where state-owned enterprises mobilize all the resources at their disposal during the last ten days of the month, the last month or last quarter of the year, resulting in a dramatic intensification of worktime and effort, in a desperate bid to fulfil the targets laid down in the plan directives. A direct upshot of the economy of shortages, material and labour that characterized the socialist system, factory managers and the

---

[1] See, *inter alia*, Mihaly Laki 'End-Year Rush-Work in Hungarian Industry and Foreign Trade', *Acta Oeconomica*, Vol. 1–2, 25, 1980, pp. 37–65; Collectif URGENSE, 'Un taylorisme arythmique dans les économies planifiées du centre', *Critiques de l'économie politique*, No. 19, April-June 1982, pp. 99–146; Joseph Berliner, 'A Problem in Soviet Business', in *idem, Soviet Industry from Stalin to Gorbachev. Essays on Management and Innovation*, Ithaca, 1988, pp. 47–60; Donald A. Filtzer, *Soviet Workers and Late Stalinism: Labour and the Restoration of the Stalinist System After World War II*, Cambridge, 2002, pp. 214–16.

labour force designated these periods of feverish activity as *sturmovcina* in Russian or *hajra* in Hungarian, both terms signifying literally 'storming' in English.

A similar phenomenon of end-year rush-work could also be observed in ITI. Indeed, management officials' inability to synchronize and co-ordinate the volume of production flows uniformly throughout the year was perhaps the single biggest difficulty facing the company on the manufacturing front, and one which proved practically impossible to resolve. This in turn had serious repercussions on equipment delivery schedules, product quality standards, billing procedures, and finally, cash flow. Given the interrelated nature of factory operations, deficiencies in one area automatically triggered off a chain reaction impairing the performance of the organization as a whole. As in the case of the socialist regime enterprises, almost half of ITI's entire annual output came out during the final three months of the financial year from January to end March, due to the 'hurricane efforts' made to meet targets.[2] The month of March alone sometimes accounted for 25 per cent of the total.

In the case of big orders, it was also not rare for work to spill over into April, although to comply with statutory requirements, the records formally showed the orders as having been completed by the end of the financial year.[3] Pointing out that the massive numbers of telephone instruments delivered by ITI during the last quarter exerted a considerable strain on the resources of its inspection and testing wing, which was not equipped to handle such large quantities, P&T complained that for the year 1983–84 it had received a mere 40 per cent of the order up to December.[4] Statistical data for the years 1986–87 to 1994–95 tell much the same story. Despite some improvement during the last two years, on average barely 30 per cent of the total annual production was undertaken during the first two quarters of the year (April to September), approximately 23 per cent during the third quarter, and the balance

---

[2] Minutes of management-union meeting, 4 April 1979. A similar phenomenon is observed by Jonathan Parry at state-owned Bhilai steel plant. 'Lords of Labour', p. 125.

[3] Ref. ADP 020, 13 July 1998.

[4] Minutes of 27th Production Coordination Committee meeting, 3 February 1984. (Hereafter PCC.) See also Minutes of 9th PCC Meeting, 13 February 1978, where P&T claimed that it experienced great difficulties in providing exchange lines to various regions because supplies had not been evenly spread throughout the year.

during the final quarter.[5] A senior manager at the Bangalore telephone division claimed that in the ten years since he assumed production responsibilities, output had never been constant throughout the year even on a single occasion.

If things go off smoothly during the first half of the year, some problem will invariably crop up during the second half. Or it is the other way around . . . And once there is a break in production, restarting is quite a misery . . . it takes two to three weeks to build capacity again.[6]

According to an audit enquiry, even a 10 per cent improvement in output during the first nine months would improve ITI's cash flow position, and yield savings of Rs 30 million annually by way of lower interest charges.[7] For in view of the fact that the company earned a substantial portion of its turnover only at the year-end, it found itself invariably starved of funds at the start of the financial year, and so had to depend on high-cost short-term borrowings to cover its working capital requirements.[8] Yet, notwithstanding both the repeated injunctions of top management and the changed market environment engendered by the economic reforms of 1991 where the company's worsening financial condition made it all the more imperative that it operate at greater levels

[5] Production in percentage to total

Year	April-Sept	Oct-Dec	Jan-March
1986–87	31.5	23.3	45.2
1987–88	34.8	25.8	39.4
1988–89	30.4	19.3	50.3
1989–90	26.3	23.4	50.3
1990–91	29.4	21.1	49.6
1991–92	27.1	20.4	52.5
1992–93	25.5	21.5	53
1993–94	36.5	24.6	38.9
1994–95	33.1	25.3	41.6

(*Source:* COPU, *Indian Telephone Industries Ltd.*, 10th Report, Eleventh Lok Sabha, New Delhi, 1997, p. 24.) (Hereafter COPU 1997.)

[6] Interview with B.K. Sharma, 6 December 2001.
[7] CAG Report 1992, p. 18.
[8] Interest charges on these borrowings varied between 15 and 18 per cent, according to an audit report. Ref. No. 1/85–86/BG/86–87/150, 23 September 1986.

of efficiency, the goal of uniform production remained stubbornly beyond its reach.[9] Nor did threats by DoT that its quality wing would not inspect more telephone instruments during the last quarter of the year than the total production during the first three quarters succeed in acting as a catalyst.[10] Illustrative of the depth of organizational inertia, even when the company faced a demand crunch from the second half of the 1990s onwards, and hence needed to promptly execute the available orders before it could hope to obtain more work from its parent authority, little urgency was shown during the initial months.

Doubtless, one explanation for end-year rush-work was the negligent professional ethics and laxity of discipline prevailing within the company.

If questions were asked about why workers were idling, shop floor officers would reply that when the need arose from December onwards they would work very hard.[11]

An outgrowth of its monopoly status, the absence of accountability that pervaded all spheres of public sector functioning meant that nobody was taken to task for this loss of production time. Output was also affected by the high levels of absenteeism commonly registered during the first quarter of the financial year. Between 1967–68 and 1971–72, absenteeism at the Bangalore plant jumped from 8.35 to 12.3 per cent, and despite the decline between 1973–78 when it averaged around 8.1 per cent, the figure again climbed up to approximately 12 per cent for much of the 1990s (unfortunately, data for the 1980s is limited to only a few years).[12] As one ITI chairman candidly recognized,

In the initial period say in May, June or July when the schools and colleges are closed there is high absenteeism. They (employees) go out and after the close of the year there is some slackness also. I am not denying it . . . *in the public sector that is the culture which has been developed.* As a commercial organization this may not be reasonable (sic).[13]

---

[9] Just how intractable this problem proved to be is borne out by the fact that already in the mid-1970s, top management had defined as one of its principal objectives levelling 'the peaks that usually occur at the end of the year'. Annual Report 1974–75, p. 5.

[10] Tel. Divn. memo, nd.

[11] Interview with Y. Munnuswamy.

[12] COPU 1973, p. 65; ITI Personnel Department statistics.

[13] COPU 1997, pp. 24–5. Emphasis added. See also Minutes of 9th PCC meeting, 13 February 1978.

But the principal reason why the problem of end-year rush-work stubbornly persisted at ITI lay in material scarcities. The shortage syndrome would emerge as a recurring explanation for a number of the other difficulties experienced by the company as well, such as target slippages, late deliveries, quality deterioration, low machine and labour utilization rates, and even indiscipline. Just as the economist Janos Kornai has demonstrated with regard to state-owned enterprises in the Soviet bloc command economies, many of the dysfunctional features of shop floor organization that beset ITI stemmed from the supply-side or resource constraints.[14]

Mired in red tape, the company's long drawn out procurement procedures played no small part in slowing down the flow of goods and leading to a substantial increase in the overall manufacturing cycle time. A study of manufacturing operations at the Bangalore plant, conducted by consultancy firm PricewaterhouseCoopers (PwC) in the year 2000, indicated that material procurement orders passed through no less than fifteen stages and the cycle time for processing purchase requirements and placing orders could take from two to four months. Not surprisingly then, less than one-fifth of material deliveries were made in the required month.[15] Stock control policies were also badly wanting in rigour. Already in 1955 an audit officer observed that records 'had not been properly maintained' and 'were very haphazard'.[16] Neither surpluses nor shortfalls were being accurately recorded. Conditions do not appear to have changed very much two decades later. A memo issued by the telephone division in 1977 stated that in the absence of effective supervision and clear-cut instructions, inventories for various components stood dangerously low. This had 'come as a surprise to all and the production line affected, practically coming to a standstill . . . (sic)'.[17]

More than the incidents themselves, what is revealing is that they cropped up just after the company had brought in a team of consultants from the Administrative Staff College, Hyderabad, in the early 1970s to review its procurement procedures. Critical of the 'way in which purchase is functioning . . . causing considerable problems in production', the

---

[14] Kornai, *Economics of Shortage*, p. 5, 27–40.
[15] Ref. DB/COM/2000–2001, 27 June 2000.
[16] Cited in EC Report 1958, p. 78.
[17] Ref. PPC-T/4, 17 March 1977.

report effectively highlighted several deficiencies, such as 'organizational inflexibilities', 'adherence to elaborate procedural formalities', and 'ad hoc decisions . . . without adequate preplanning', before going on to propose a number of changes.[18] Judging by the above cases of stock-outs it is doubtful whether any of the recommendations of the consultants were implemented in earnest. Retarded computerization due to cash constraints also meant that stock control was an extremely tedious and error-prone process as well. These failings were compounded by the constant tug-of-war between the stores department and the manufacturing shops.

Shop people would complain that stores had not issued material. Stores would say that material had been laid out, but shop had not taken delivery on time. Shop then would say that fork lifts were not available or that labourers were absent to transport material.

GOVERNMENT REGULATIONS RESULT IN MATERIAL SHORTAGES

It was factors external to ITI's functioning, however, that were essentially responsible for input deficits. The chief among these were the tight import regulations laid down by the Indian government in the mid-1950s. The proliferation of bureaucratic procedures which governed the delivery of licences to import raw material and semi-finished goods placed severe checks on the operational efficiency not just of ITI, but all Indian companies in general. In the words of a former ITI chairman,

. . . Instead of concentrating on technology, manufacture and things like that, most of the time we had to go to Delhi, get import licences, clearances. It was a most unproductive activity.[19]

One senior manager adds:

There was a lot of suspicion among bureaucrats when we wanted to import material. They would not believe us that local producers either did not exist or

---

[18] COPU 1973, p. 108.

[19] Interview with U.D.N. Rao. One is reminded here of Berliner's insightful remark that the energy spent by the Soviet manager on obtaining materials is spent by the American manager on selling and advertising. 'Managerial Incentives and Decision-Making. A Comparison of the United States and the Soviet Union', in *Soviet Industry from Stalin to Gorbachev*, pp. 61–96.

were incapable of meeting our requirements. The pressure to indigenize was constant.[20]

Moreover, because of the deteriorating balance of payments position in the country from the early 1960s onwards, ITI was not granted sufficient foreign exchange to be able to import all of its requirements because it did not qualify as a 'priority' industry.[21] Even basic inputs such as steel sections were therefore either unavailable or in short supply, with the result that bottlenecks on the shop floor were inevitable and frequent occurrences, notwithstanding the progressive reduction in import content for many products. Indeed between 1966–67 and 1970–71, the company cited difficulties in procuring foreign-sourced supplies as one of the main causes for target under-fulfilment at the strowger and transmission divisions in Bangalore.[22] But other divisions suffered as well. As one government document underlined, the target for new telephone connections during the Fourth Plan (1969–74) had to be scaled back from 760,000 to 700,000 instruments on account of delivery delays by ITI. These delays were caused by the shortage of critical imported raw materials and components.[23] A loan provided by the International Development Agency in 1970, earmarked exclusively for foreign purchases, would have helped overcome some of the financial obstacles, but import controls remained a constant irritant.

In parallel, the government's import substitution strategies turned out to be a deep thorn in the sides of public and private companies alike. Apart from contributing to an increase in overall manufacturing costs and a decline in product quality standards, these measures, which left Indian firms with no choice but to rely on local vendors for a wide range of supplies, also tended to disrupt the flow of output by creating material shortfalls. In response to questions from a task force committee examining the performance of telephone instruments, the ITI management pointed out that imports of carbon steel and stainless steel required to produce piece parts for the rotary Tamura dials were prohibited. But domestic sources had not only failed to deliver the material on time; their samples

---

[20] Interview with L.G. Varadharajan.
[21] COPU 1973, pp. 59–60.
[22] Annual Reports; COPU 1973, pp. 6–7, 12.
[23] *The Fourth Plan: Mid-Term Appraisal. A Summary*, New Delhi, 1972, pp. 96–7.

were of much inferior quality.[24] Supplies of products or materials not conforming to specifications often led to further delays, as they had to be reworked by the company before they could be utilized. Local vendors were inclined as well to turn down orders for spares and components when quantities were small or non-standard.

To give another instance of the adverse impact of official policy, an internal note dated September 1986 stated that production for the previous month of the 677 telephone model at the Bangalore factory had been badly affected because the company had not received the adequate number of micro-switches from two indigenous manufacturers.[25] In February 1989, the telephone division again suffered from acute supply shortages, on this occasion, of moulding powder. Although production had almost come to a halt, the authorities turned down the company's request to make temporary imports on an emergency basis. The authorities' refusal was on the grounds that ITI had failed to show that domestic firms were not capable of meeting its requirements.[26] The signing of exclusive long range contracts with certain vendors also proved at times to be clearly detrimental. An audit enquiry revealed that speech integrated circuits made by public sector company BEL, the sole indigenous source for this component, had been delivered late and were of poor quality.[27] The erratic flow of inputs in turn retarded the supply of the end product: even a 10 per cent shortfall in components needed for assembling printed circuit boards, the heart of all telecommunications equipment, could cause delays of at least 20 days in handing over the item to the customer.[28] Import substitution thus exacted a high price on the efficiency of ITI.

Policy directions designed to encourage self-reliance sometimes also ended up having the contrary effect as in the case of the ferrite core project.[29] An input central to the manufacture of transmission equipment,

---

[24] Tel. Divn. note, 3 April 1987. See also COPU 1973, p. 8.

[25] Tel. Divn. note, 2 September 1986.

[26] Letter Tel. Divn. to Directorate General of Trade and Development, 7 February 1989. A subsequent note dated 10 August 1989 said that the DGTD had agreed to invite ITI and the suppliers to a meeting and in case the results proved inconclusive the regulatory body would allow ITI to go in for imports.

[27] Audit Enquiry No. 4 of resident audit officer, Ref. RAP III/ITI/93–94/15, 12 April 1993.

[28] Ref. DB/COM/2000–2001, 27 June 2000.

[29] Alam, 'Performance of Imported Technology in LDCs'; Shiv Visvanathan,

ITI was purchasing its entire annual requirements of ferrite cores, estimated at 10 tons and valued at Rs 5.5 million, from foreign suppliers.[30] Shortages of transmission equipment, it must be noted, had limited the installation of new switching lines. To reduce its dependency on imports, the company therefore recommended as early as 1963 constructing a plant with foreign technological assistance to indigenously produce ferrite cores. The government, however, vetoed the proposal on the grounds that state-owned research body, National Physical Laboratory (NPL), possessed the resources to make available this technology to ITI. Ultimately, NPL failed to transfer the know-how obliging ITI to continue importing large quantities of the material.[31]

In addition to the regulatory regime, P&T's bureaucratic and erratic style of working could also be faulted for material shortages. The creation in 1974, after the disastrous experience of the crossbar project, of a joint body, the Production Coordination Committee, brought together officials from P&T and ITI twice a year to review a broad spectrum of production-related issues. It had proved to be a relatively effective trouble shooting mechanism, yet problems persisted.

First, the telecommunications carrier often neglected to communicate the details of its annual equipment requirements to ITI at the start of the financial year.[32] There were also instances when it failed to place orders on time. With normal cycle times for the execution of major orders ranging from 18 to 24 months, and for standard equipment from 6 to 18 months, delays in the placement of orders were bound to spark a chain reaction throughout the system, holding up material purchases which in turn led to tardy equipment deliveries, and ultimately, slowed down the commissioning of new exchanges.[33]

Organizing for Science. The Making of an Industrial Research Laboratory, New Delhi, 1985, pp. 215–25.

[30] COPU 1973, p. 123.

[31] Visvanathan has pinned the onus of NPL's inability to hand over the technology on time essentially on the uncooperative attitude adopted by ITI. The company was apparently reluctant to accept the research laboratory's process for ferrite cores in the light of its past unsatisfactory experience of utilizing NPL processes for the manufacture of silver mica capacitors. *Organizing for Science*, pp. 217–20.

[32] Minutes of 29th PCC meeting, 29 November 1984; Minutes of 15th PCC Meeting, 16 November 1979.

[33] COPU 1973, p. 76.

Second, P&T engineers introduced frequent design changes and revised material specifications at very short notice, with a view to improving the quality and reliability of the equipment. Both factors led to disruptions in the manufacturing cycle as ITI could neither effectively plan its input requirements, nor make arrangements to procure raw material and other components sufficiently in advance, especially in view of the long lead times necessary for imports. The parent authority, for instance, announced that printed circuit cards fabricated out of composite epoxy, should be utilized, instead of the glass epoxy cards, but then it abruptly decided to go back to glass epoxy a few months later. Predictably, production of electronic push button telephones declined for a few months as the management struggled to secure inputs on time.[34] It is worth citing in this connection the comments of a parliamentary committee.

. . . ITI should impress upon the P&T . . . the necessity of intimating actually the firm requirements (of P&T) *sufficiently in advance and of not making changes in them frequently* . . . this should be possible by undertaking proper planning in the P&T . . . it is important to point out that for economical working, schedules once fixed should not be frequently altered since such changes result not only in decreased productivity, but also in loss of work-flow and inefficient use of manpower and machines.[35]

Subsequently, one ITI chairman called for a 'roll-on' three-year order book so that the company could stabilize production schedules, and benefit from the flexibility afforded by a sufficient volume of orders.[36] But the administrative ministry does not appear to have given this proposal much consideration.

NEGATIVE EFFECTS OF RECOURSE TO OVERTIME WORKING

The fallout from end-year rush-work would impact negatively on more than one area of the company's functioning. But by far the most immediate and important consequence was the inordinate expenditure

[34] Interview with B.K. Sharma.
[35] EC Report 1958, p. 30. Emphasis added.
[36] Minutes of 31st PCC meeting, 12 December 1985.

ITI was forced to incur on overtime.[37] To compensate for the shortfall in output during the preceding months, the management had no other alternative but to offer the workforce higher wages in return for working longer hours during the final quarter of the financial year. Questioned by a study team 'alarmed to notice the huge amount' paid out in the form of overtime, company executives defended their actions by underlining the importance of retaining the 'good will in the Indian and international markets by fulfilling the promises and work-loads well in time (sic)'.[38] It added that it could not cope with the large number of orders the company received by operating only during regular factory hours.

The extended workday, however, came at a heavy price. From Rs 11.03 million in 1971–72, overtime payments skyrocketed to Rs 30.67 million in 1974–75. Thereafter the amounts would show a relative decrease, but in 1979–80, the last full year of overtime working, ITI still paid out Rs 19.63 million. Overall, for the period 1971–72 to 1981–82, overtime expenditure at the flagship Bangalore plant amounted to a massive Rs 179.25 million.[39] Hence, while the strategy of using overtime, as opposed to recruiting additional personnel, as a means of boosting production may have been economically viable in the 1960s, the option had clearly become an extremely onerous burden a decade later, as both P&T and ITI executives came to recognize.

A letter from the ITI chairman to all divisional heads of the Bangalore plant in January 1973 stated that the minister of communications in person had expressed concern about the high levels of overtime payments and wanted it to be brought down. Orders were therefore issued to ensure that overtime was 'allowed only in sections where it is inescapable' and 'severely restricted in non-productive sections'.[40] Towards this end only

[37] A similar point is made with respect to Hungarian firms by Laki, 'End-Year Rush-Work'; and Istvan Kemeny, 'La chaine dans une usine hongroise', *Actes de la recherche en sciences sociales*, No. 24, November 1978, pp. 62–77.

[38] *A Study of Management Styles and Practices, Personnel Policies and Implementation of Labour Laws and Trade Unionism in Indian Telephone Industries Bangalore 1971–75*, New Delhi, Ministry of Labour (Implementation and Evaluation Division), nd, p. 32.

[39] Replies to Ministry of Labour questionnaire, 1976; Note to the Board, 184th meeting, Item B8, December 1981. Under the Factories Act of 1948, overtime payment is calculated on the basis of twice the rate of basic pay plus normal allowances such as Dearness Allowance, House Rent Allowance, etc. For details of overtime expenditures at the Bangalore plant see table on overtime and incentive expenditures, foot note 187.

[40] Ref. CM/13.1/A, 23 January 1973.

middle management and above were authorized to grant overtime, since supervisors and foremen were suspected, not wrongly, of yielding too easily to worker pressure. The instructions, however, do not appear to have been fully carried out. For another letter written by the chairman in July 1976, while observing the 'drastic reduction in overtime working in production areas', mentions that in some non-production areas 'sizeable overtime is still being booked'.[41]

Besides contributing to the augmentation of manpower costs, the indiscriminate and widespread recourse to overtime working also brought in its wake two other difficulties.[42] First, it was blunting the effectiveness of the different incentive schemes devised by the company to improve labour productivity. An internal document had categorically declared that the advantages of securing higher output through incentive formulas outweighed those obtained through overtime, since the former by definition tended to be more cost-optimal than overtime. It went on to add that 'working on incentive . . . rather than on overtime basis makes for better discipline in general (sic)'.[43] These comments followed a review of the existing incentive scheme which concluded that the rates offered 'did not appear to stimulate the operators to increase production substantially' since overtime fetched much more money.[44]

The second problem was that overtime, or more precisely the struggle to appropriate the monetary benefits attached to it, was developing into a source of growing tension within the factory. On the one hand, sections of the workforce were restricting production during regular hours in order to compel shop officials to grant overtime. This was especially true of the crossbar division, where, according to the company, despite relaxing time standards, labour efficiency remained below 50 per cent, compared with over 90 per cent in strowger and telephone, due to the 'deliberate attempt on the part of all or few workers to work slow'.[45] To cite another

---

[41] Ref. CM/13.1/IV, 5 July 1976.

[42] Because of the high number of overtime hours worked, ITI also frequently contravened factory regulations, limiting the duration of overtime to 50 hours per employee every three months. The company therefore had to request the labour department for a waiver at regular intervals, generally citing the exigencies of military production to justify the breach of rules.

[43] Note to the Board committee, November 1975.

[44] Personnel Department note, 24 March 1972.

[45] Minutes of management-union meeting, 26 October 1973.

note, 'even when material is available, the tendency is to accumulate work during the normal time to justify OT (overtime)'.[46] Fully aware of the pressures weighing upon the upper echelons of the company to achieve the annual goals set by P&T, workers were also encouraged to persist with these tactics by the management's diffidence in taking disciplinary action, fearful that such an action might lead to 'go-slows' and further disrupt output.

On the other, verbal clashes between line authorities and irate employees, resentful at not having been granted overtime, were breaking out with increasing frequency. In some cases, shop managers, especially in the crossbar division, even received threats from 'rogue' workers, whose poor records in principle rendered them ineligible for overtime working. The tactic apparently proved quite effective, for by the management's own admission, these workers were generally given a few hours' overtime.

A concept of social OT developed. If departments where workers held back production got 4 hours OT, other departments which were more efficient got 2 hours OT whether it was required or not, in order to keep workers happy.[47]

Reports of supervisors and foremen demanding bribes or favouring certain workers were not uncommon either, nor were complaints from newcomers and juniors of discrimination. In one instance, we find the management sanctioning a machine shop boss in the transmission division for misconduct after he had 'booked' overtime for two operators. This was notwithstanding their low productivity levels, and specific instructions from his superiors that only efficient workers be 'privileged' for OT. Justifying his decision, the foreman, quite correctly, stressed the importance of 'getting good production, maintaining peace in the shop' and ensuring 'good co-ordination between the Officers and Operators'.[48]

Overtime working had a downside for the workforce too. True, it represented a financial windfall: the bigger pay-packets that employees took home during these years assured their security by enabling a number of them to realize their life ambitions of acquiring property or becoming home owners. But these gains did not come for free. The longer workday,

[46] Personnel Department note, 2 March 1971.

[47] Interview with Srinivasa Rao. Tulpule writes that overtime at the Durgapur Steel Plant in West Bengal had grown to the proportions of a racket. 'Managing Durgapur', Part II *EPW*, Vol. 12, Nos. 1–2, 8 January 1977, pp. 21–32.

[48] Worker Personnel File No.1984, 13 July 1973.

stretching in some cases to 16 hours, was bound to have taken a toll on workers' health, in particular the older ones; many of them acknowledged returning home exhausted. Overtime working is also alleged to have aggravated the problem of alcoholism with employees drinking more in order to compensate for the physical strain.[49] In fact, one executive described overtime as a 'phenomenon of mutual exploitation' where employees sought to extract increasing sums of money from the company in return for which the management demanded higher levels of effort.[50]

At the same time, an examination of the security department sources raises serious questions about just how productive workers were during overtime. Instructed to maintain a check over the activities of employees in the chemical laboratory, a security officer submitted this report which is worth citing in full:

On 8–9–80, eleven employees on OT from 4.45 to 8.30 pm. At 6.50 pm, seven employees left workspot and went to canteen and returned at 7.45 pm, but do not go inside the department. They stood outside talking and smoking till 8.05 pm. The remaining employees except one sitting and reading books and magazines. *Only one employee is actually working.* At 8.20 pm department was closed.

On 9–9–80, thirteen employees on OT. At 6.50 pm, six employees left workspot and went to canteen and returned at 7.45 pm. One employee punched out and left at 7.15 pm. *The remaining were smoking, reading books and talking to their in-charge.* At 8.30 pm, only nine employees present at punching machine, but on verification all thirteen employees cards were punched out.

On 10–9–80, twelve employees on OT. One punched out at 5.30 pm and left. At 6.50 pm, seven employees left workspot and went to canteen and returned at 7.45 pm. *After returning they were smoking and wasting time in their Department.* Punching clock out of order that day, so no one punched their cards.[51]

Drinking in the evening and at night also appears to have been an established feature of overtime working. There are regular references to

[49] According to Uma Ramaswami, it was health factors which accounted in part for the unions' opposition to overtime in the Coimbatore textile mills. *Work, Union and Community. Industrial Man in South India*, Delhi, 1983, p. 26. On the negative effects of overtime on the quality of workers' social life see also Goldthorpe and Lockwood, *The Affluent Worker*, pp. 61–4, 157–8.
[50] Interview with Srinivasa Rao.
[51] Ref. SY/FD/10, 15 September 1980. Emphasis added.

security personnel foiling workers' attempts to smuggle alcohol into the factory or finding them in an inebriated state.[52] In one such instance, after mentioning that a worker in the telephone division was in 'deep slumber . . . and smelling of alcohol' when a security guard entered the shop, the report states:

it is strange . . . how the Supervisory staff have allowed him to sleep fully drunk while performing overtime and came to know the truth only when Security pointed out.[53]

On another occasion, three workers, including the shop supervisor, in the heat treatment department were caught drinking country liquor during the night shift. These incidents revealed how drinking, by dissolving the boundaries separating workers from foremen and supervisors many of whom had risen from the ranks, reactivated certain complicities that already existed between the two groups.[54]

While we must be careful not to overly generalize on the basis of these documents, two points clearly stand out. First, workers were not inclined to exert themselves during overtime, to a large extent because only junior-level shop floor executives were on duty to supervise work. This is corroborated by workers themselves:

During night shift without supervisor's notice, some workers would take a few hours rest during OT in the cloak room using packing material for sleeping purposes. Other workers would keep guard to warn them if security came. Officers were not present during OT, but sometimes there would be surprise checks . . . No targets were fixed for OT. So some fast workers would do the entire production during day shift, then claim OT and roam about or sleep then.[55]

---

[52] After a helper in one shop, returning to the factory following the dinner break, had been caught with two quarter bottles of whisky and one quarter bottle of brandy in his possession, a security report remarked that the alcohol may not have been intended for his own consumption, '. . . because it may not be possible to consume all the 3 bottles of different brands during the short span of time . . . Nathan (the helper) has innocently brought the liquor bottles to oblige others, since there is a fear of intimidation if he does not oblige superiors in his department (sic)'. Ref. SY/FD/10, 2 April 1979.

[53] Ref. SY/FD/10, 17 December 1977.

[54] Ref. SY/FD/10, case No. 84/76–77, 19 February 1977.

[55] Interview with C. Sahadevan, May 1999. Workers sleeping during the 'graveyard' shift and making arrangements to be woken up if discovery was likely were routine industrial practices. See, for instance, Melville Dalton, *Men Who Manage. Fusions of Feeling and Theory in Administration*, New York, 1959, p. 80.

If shirking followed from lax supervision, it also owed to the fact that the company was often not in a position to accurately assess productivity levels. As an internal memo unambiguously declared, barring a few departments where the final product could be easily counted, it was not possible to estimate the quantity of output turned out during overtime.[56] Second, shirking went hand in hand with fraudulent time keeping, a practice to which workers resorted to normally with the complicity of their superiors. As the above-cited case of the employees in the chemical laboratory evidenced, 'proxy punching' during overtime working, whereby workers asked colleagues to punch their attendance cards and then slipped out of the plant, was not uncommon. Although an official circular warned offenders of the risk of dismissal, it is doubtful whether this threat brought the malpractice to an end.[57]

What is surprising is that despite all these alarm signals, throughout the 1970s the company made no attempt to root out the 'overtime disease'.[58] Instead, it preferred to adopt an attitude that could best be described as one of resigned tolerance, no doubt out of apprehension that if it abolished overtime, output levels would drop and P&T would take it to task. Ultimately, it required the suppression of an industrial dispute launched by the workers in 1980–81, before top management could steel itself to act. Capitalizing on the effects of both the prolonged work stoppage as well as the harsher industrial relations climate that prevailed after the factory reopened on employees' morale and their capacity for further resistance, the company announced the elimination of overtime working in all but a few essential service departments.

Paradoxically, its task was facilitated by the tacit support this measure enjoyed within the ranks of the union leadership as well. For, as one top executive rightly remarked, the fight to obtain overtime was disturbing the harmonious working of the union too. In the departments where line managers awarded overtime, union officials promptly claimed credit for the move, whereas in the other departments which were deprived of this opportunity, representatives not only came in for sharp criticism from the rank-and-file, but found themselves under growing pressure to

---

[56] Personnel Department note, 16 October 1970.

[57] Circular No. 888, 8 April 1963.

[58] Interview with C.R. Datta Gupta, ex-Executive Director, ITI Bangalore, March–April 1999.

secure similar benefits.[59] This in turn gave rise to jealousies and recriminations among different sections of the union bureaucracy, forcing the top leadership to expend both time and energy to sort out the differences. Consequently, the end of overtime working does not appear to have drawn even a symbolic shout of protest from the union.

FAILURE TO RESPECT DELIVERY SCHEDULES PROVES COSTLY

To what extent did ITI succeed in attaining its output goals now that the life-belt of overtime working had been discarded? Although we do not dispose precise quantitative data on the question, and our sources for the 1980s remain incomplete, the picture that emerges is one of slippages occurring on and off. Between 1986–87 and 1991–92, the company was able to fulfil its sales objectives on only one occasion while shortfalls ranged from roughly 4 per cent to a high of 32 per cent.[60] Over-ambitious targets fixed by the marketing department were no doubt partly responsible for this performance. But several instances of 'inordinate delays' in supplying a gamut of equipment moved the audit authorities to fire a string of adverse remarks at factory officials for their failure to develop an efficient marketing structure capable of '. . . schedul(ing) production to ensure customer satisfaction and improv(ing) control over order management'.[61]

With respect to crossbar switches alone, the shortfalls in selector frames for the Pentaconta exchanges manufactured at the Bangalore plant between 1984–85 and 1987–88, fluctuated between 4 per cent and 58

---

[59] ibid.
[60] ITI Sales Performance (1986–87 to 1991–92)

Year	1986–87	1987–88	1988–89	1989–90	1990–91	1991–92
Target (Rs. Mn)	4586.6	5681	9134.3	10974.4	12707.8	9217.8
Actuals (Rs. Mn)	4407	5084.8	6251.8	9587.5	9784.6	10847
Shortfall (%)	–3.99	–10.5	–31.6	–12.6	–23	+17.7

Source: CAG Report 1992, p. 39.

[61] ibid, pp. 42–3.

per cent.[62] In a letter sent to the ITI chairman in August 1986, the Ministry of Communications wrote that production shortfalls at the Rae Bareli plant for strowger and crossbar equipment, and at the Bangalore plant with respect to crossbar and telephones 'has caused concern . . . (and) cannot but be taken serious notice of . . .'.[63] Other customers such as the army were also affected by delivery slippages. Unsuccessful in meeting its commitments on even a single occasion over a span of seven years from June 1985 and March 1992, the defence production department at the Bangalore plant had accumulated a supply backlog to the tune of roughly Rs 4000 million.[64]

That poor delivery performance was inflicting considerable damage on ITI's reputation was clearly recognized by the ITI Chairman B.B. Chadha who declared that the time had come '. . . to convey a message to the customer that we are changing in our approach to meet delivery schedules (sic)'.[65] That the company also enjoyed little success in changing its approach is testified to by a letter addressed to all unit heads in April 2000 by ITI's Executive Director (Operations), following an important conference organized by DoT and presided over by the communications minister in person. He stated that during the conference, where close to 600 delegates were present, including participants from several public sector enterprises, ITI had to suffer

. . . great humiliation which cannot be described in words. When asked by the Minister for the reasons for shortfall in meeting targets, all DoT field heads said this was because ITI had not supplied equipments in time. *No other PSU (public sector undertaking) came under attack.* The Minister also said that the good opinion that he had about the company was short lived due to the enormous complaints from field units (sic).[66]

Earlier, in a tender for electronic push button telephones, DoT placed the company in fourteenth position out of eighteen contenders in overall delivery ratings, prompting the marketing chief to write that 'it is a

[62] ibid, p. 64. Kornai writes: 'In a resource-constrained economy, the normal backlog of unfulfilled orders considerably surpasses the minimum level justified by organizational factors'. *Economics of Shortage*, p. 119.

[63] Ref. D.O. No. U.58013/8/86-FAC, 12 August 1986.

[64] CAG Report 1992, pp. 43–4.

[65] Ref. D.O. No. CM/UH/0010, 21 April 1993.

[66] Ref. EDRO-1–2, 11 April 2000. Emphasis added.

matter of concern that our rating is 14 when compared with other suppliers'.[67]

However, the strongest evidence of lax delivery discipline is provided by the substantial penalties frequently imposed upon ITI by way of liquidated damages by its principal customer. For the period 1987–88 to 1993–94 alone, it paid as penalties a colossal sum of approximately Rs 1553 million, or around 0.5 per cent of its total turnover.[68] More alarmingly, even in the aftermath of the financial crisis into which the company sank from the mid-1990s onwards, top management showed itself incapable of adopting the necessary corrective measures to stem the cash outflows. As ITI Chairman Motial remarked, the company could ill afford, on the one hand, to complain of inadequate orders and declining prices, and on the other, continue squandering its scarce cash resources, especially following DoT's decision to hike the penalty from 5 to 12 per cent of the total equipment value. But, as on previous occasions, neither the vow taken by all unit heads 'that during the current year on the new orders no LD (liquidated damages) will be paid', nor the management committee constituted to address the question, served their purpose.[69] For 2000–01, liquidated damages amounted to roughly Rs 250 million, despite the fact that

. . . orders were available with sufficient lead time for production, and, by and large, inventories were also available at the disposal of the Plants.[70]

Guilty of not supplying equipment on time, the company was also guilty of not supplying equipment, in particular strowger and crossbar switches, in sequential order.[71] In other words, it failed to conform to the 'package' disciplines stipulated by P&T in the purchase contracts.

[67] Ref. EDRM/23, 10 June 1998.

[68] COPU 1997, p. 36; Annual Reports. P&T was not the only customer to impose liquidated damages. Between 1983–84 and 1989–90, the Indian army charged ITI a sum of Rs 6.87 million for late supplies. CAG Report 1992, p. 45.

[69] Ref. D.O. No. CM/27.4, 25 July 2000.

[70] Ref. D.O. No. CM/27.4, 8 May 2001. Subsequently, as part of its effort to assist the company, DoT reimbursed a substantial portion of the liquidated damages paid by ITI. COPU, *Action Taken by Government on Recommendations Contained in 10th Report (11th Lok Sabha)*, 6th Report, Twelfth Lok Sabha, New Delhi, 1999, pp. 39–40.

[71] Minutes of 1st PCC meeting, 1 February 1974; Minutes of 34th PCC meeting, 21 May 1987. P&T complained that even on those instances when the company certified a package as complete, certain items remained undelivered.

Concretely what this meant was that ITI tended to dispatch parts of the exchange equipment such as power and supply panels before it did the iron frames or racks which normally had to be delivered first, for without this basic element the rest of the exchange could not be assembled. Although, a supply schedule chart existed, a legacy of the systems discipline handed down by ATE, the procedure specifying the order in which material had to be delivered to the end-user had lapsed over time. Reacting to complaints from the supervisory ministry, the ITI board of directors admitted that

(i)t was necessary to find out a fault-free method to solve this problem so that both the image of ITI and that of DoT would not be impaired and certain self-discipline has to be self-imposed.[72]

With P&T withholding 10 per cent of payments as penalty for non-adherence to package disciplines, the price the company was forced to pay for its deficiencies proved anything but negligible. As a memo from the head of finance in the mid-1990s noted, at a time when the company lacked funds to even meet 'its bare minimum needs including wage bill', customers had not been billed a sum of Rs 60 million on account of non-sequential supply of goods and non-completion of the package.[73]

In addition to material deficits arising from the byzantine control systems integral to the licence *raj*, three other factors contributed to production slippages and, its logical corollary, ITI's mediocre delivery record. The first was shortcomings on the part of the management, related in particular to the functioning of the shipping department. Delays in dispatching equipment to customers were commonplace, and the phenomenon of end-year rush-work, which considerably intensified the workload of employees in the shipping section, only worsened matters. According to a senior executive, once the product reached the shipping department, it normally took between two days to four weeks for it to leave the plant; but in March the waiting time could stretch on occasions to two or even three months.[74] As Chairman Motial admitted,

. . . whatever production we achieve during the last quarter, the entire production

---

[72] Cited in CAG Report, (1986–87), Indian Telephone Industries Ltd., 1987, p. 8. (Hereafter CAG Report 1987.)

[73] Ref. CRT-36, 23 September 1996.

[74] Interview with Srinivasa Rao.

cannot be passed by the inspection wing and, as such, large quantities of finished goods are left over at the year-end.[75]

The findings of an external consultant added:

Adhering to time schedule does not seem to be a matter of priority in doing anything. Manifestations of this are observed in many places, starting from coming to work and going all the way up to time taken to clear important/urgent papers. One apparent fallout of this behaviour is slipping of delivery schedules.[76]

What is more, as with other dysfunctional aspects of ITI's internal coordination, in this area as well we are confronted with the all-too familiar pattern of the problem recurring, despite top executives announcing a raft of preventive measures, thus epitomizing its structurally embedded character.

While one obvious consequence of the delays in the shipment of equipment was the payment of liquidated damages, the other, and equally damaging, was the locking up of scarce and expensive working capital resources, given the constraints on internal fund generation, in finished goods inventory. Between 1986–87 and 1995–96, the value of finished goods inventory averaged 1.36 months of sales, thus exceeding the stipulated norms by almost three times.[77] Shipments were further hampered by bottlenecks in the packing of equipment. A special task group report stated that telephone instruments were not collected and packed

. . . even after a lapse of several days, weeks and even months. On any given day the number of telephones waiting for collection by packing is of the order of 10,000 on average and value of more than Rs 1 crore (Rs 10 million), while the number of telephones available in stores is of the order of 20,000.[78]

The report cited insufficient number of packing staff, non-cooperative attitude of helpers and packers, and union interference as major impediments to the effective working of the department. Dispatches were further retarded by shortages of wood and packing cases as well as

---

[75] COPU 1997, p. 46.

[76] Brief Report highlighting salient issues brought out during visit to various units and the corporate head quarters, ITI, nd. Emphasis added.

[77] CAG Report 1992, p. 28; COPU 1997, p. 46.

[78] Special Task Group Report No. 155, ITI Bangalore Telephone Division, 24 September 1988.

other packing material. This was hardly surprising considering the company utilized close to 544 different types of packing boxes. After standardization, the number reached slightly more manageable proportions of 218.[79]

Some of these problems could perhaps have been checked, if not eliminated, had top management acted decisively to persuade shop officials to look beyond the confines of their individual departments, motivating them to assume responsibility not only for production schedules, but also for shipping equipment out promptly in the interests of the company. Indeed, one document singled out the 'lack of macro-perspective' as a key organizational drawback. ITI managers, it argued, were 'good in their micro-sectional work'.[80] But their 'ability to relate what they do on a day-to-day basis with organizational growth and profitability is poor', because most of the deputy general managers who headed these sections 'have literally grown on the same chair (sic)'.[81] The report went on to state that no appreciation of the financial consequences of managerial inefficiencies could be 'found in the operating behaviour of the organization'.[82]

Identifying the strengths and weaknesses of the company, another note categorically declared that 'inter departmental, divisional and unit co-operation is much below the desired level'.[83] Suggestions to concentrate all activities, such as material planning, stock control and purchase, assembly and testing, and shipping, in one building in order to both curtail employee movement and improve 'personal interaction' were never translated into action.[84] The barriers to cooperation were heightened by the

'we' versus 'they' culture. Whether it is a section, a division, or an unit, a typical outlook is to make it appear that 'we' have done better than 'them'. This vitiates smooth working in the organization and obviously comes in the way of free flow of needed information.[85]

---

[79] Annual Report, 1975–76, p. 11.
[80] Brief Report highlighting salient issues.
[81] ibid.
[82] ibid.
[83] Corporate Office note, 14 December 1996.
[84] Personnel Department note, 5 October 1998.
[85] Brief Report highlighting salient issues.

But if we follow Melville Dalton, vertical clique formation of this kind is a development intrinsic to industrial organizations partly because of the formal division of labour which 'provokes a given group to magnify the importance of its function in the system and to ignore and minimize that of others'. Job identity, he adds, forces personnel into defensive action to get their share of credit and honours.[86]

Apart from deficiencies internal to its operations, slippages also stemmed from ITI accepting unrealistic delivery schedules. In fact, one note claimed that officials in many cases made commitments 'knowing fully well' they could not be respected.[87] Such infeasible promises could perhaps be faulted on the eagerness of the marketing department to conclude orders for the company in the context of eroding demand for its products. But it is also quite possible that the pressure exercised by its principal customer compelled the management to agree to unrealistic delivery schedules.

There is enough evidence on hand to suggest that DoT often tended to impose extremely short deadlines, especially with respect to terminal equipment, and then proceeded to systematically penalize its manufacturing arm when it failed to comply with the scheduled dates, thus further depressing telephone prices. Given the weak order-book position in which ITI found itself, top management faced a cruel dilemma. It could either incur a loss by turning down orders attached to delivery conditions impossible to fulfil resulting in capacity under-utilization; or accept the levy of liquidated damages, the cost of which would be lower than keeping capacity idle.[88] Changes in material specifications, introduced by DoT often at very short notice, also tended to disrupt production runs, and ended up slowing down equipment delivery. For instance, ITI suffered losses amounting to roughly Rs 7.1 million on an order for 650,000 electronic phones. After suddenly deciding to revise technical norms for printed circuit cards, insisting that a 40 micron-thick card be utilized instead of a 5-micron card, ministry officials then arbitrarily slashed prices in response to late deliveries.[89]

---

[86] Dalton, *Men Who Manage*, pp. 53–4.

[87] Ref. EDRO/1, 28 January 1997.

[88] See Audit Enquiry No. 9, 8 January 1991; Tel Divn. letter to resident audit officer, Ref. AGMT/114/A.E.No.8/L.D/TF, 18 April 1999.

[89] Ref. No. RAP-II/ITI/99–2000/277, 19 January 2000; Tel Divn. letter to resident audit officer, 28 April 2000.

Quality lapses associated with both product design and the manufacturing process were the final explanation for shortfalls and late deliveries. In 1986, following a large number of complaints from users, DoT halted further purchases of the Plan 103 telephone virtually overnight. Production was suspended for almost a year until the parent administration gave its approval to the design improvements the company's research engineers had come up with. But the delay obliged ITI to pay liquidated damages to the tune of Rs 6.3 million.[90] On another occasion, DoT discontinued all testing of telephones at the Bangalore plant after three consecutive batches had been rejected for major faults. An internal memo declared that 19,000 sets were therefore awaiting clearance, and the scarcity of trolleys, needed to stock the instruments, made further assemblies impossible. Under these conditions, fulfilling the production goals 'looks grim although material . . . is available'.[91] While even the most efficiently run company is not invulnerable to supply bottlenecks arresting the pace of manufacturing at some point of time or the other, in the case of ITI, it was the enduring, even systemic, nature of the problem, stemming from a combination of draconian official policies, erratic functioning of the parent administration, and internal mismanagement, that captured attention, and because of which there could be no easy or immediate solution.

For the tutelary authority too, the costs of ITI's inability to deliver equipment on time, or in a sequential pattern, turned out to be quite onerous. New exchanges were often commissioned behind schedule. A test check conducted by the audit authorities of 51 projects, executed by P&T/DoT between 1981–82 and 1986–87 in six different states, cited 22 cases of 'abnormal delays', ranging from four to 76 months, in the supply of exchange equipment.[92] The delays impacted on the performance of the entire system, as it hindered efforts to reduce the load of the

[90] Tel. Divn. letter to resident audit officer, Ref. AGM(T)/114-Insp. Report 1988–89, 30 August 1990.

[91] Tel. Divn. notes, 30 October 1993 and 30 November 1993.

[92] CAG Report, Union Government (Post & Telecommunications), 1988. The states concerned were Andhra Pradesh, Bihar, Orissa, Punjab, Rajasthan and Uttar Pradesh. See also CAG Report 1992, pp. 40–3. But lest we forget, delays in the installation of new equipment also often stemmed from gross inefficiencies in the functioning of P&T, as the audit reports amply illustrate. See, for instance, CAG Report (1990–91), No. 7, Post & Telecommunications, 1992, pp. 98–117, 122–8, and 152–4.

network, increased maintenance requirements (which P&T was not able to satisfactorily assure), and slowed down the pace of installation of new telephone connections. This in turn translated into potential revenue losses for P&T, because of which ITI too suffered.

In other words, inefficiencies in the operations of ITI had extremely negative consequences for the telecommunications service provider as well as its manufacturing wing. Both found themselves trapped in a vicious cycle, vindicating Michel Crozier's thesis that the equilibrium of a bureaucratic organization rests on the existence of a series of relatively stable vicious cycles.[93] Attributing the steep shortfall in its commissioning programme essentially to non-sequential equipment supplies, a P&T board member warned the management that the 'problem is sufficiently grave as to threaten the growth plans both of P&T and of ITI'. He went on to add that it would be extremely difficult to convince the Planning Commission to allocate sufficient resources for the telecommunications sector unless there was 'a very substantial improvement' in capacity generation for carrying long distance communication, and in the number of new subscriber lines installed.[94]

What is more, the failure of ITI to ensure reliable deliveries could only have strengthened the hands of the 'import lobby', purported by ITI executives to exist within P&T with the blessings of the World Bank, in favour of foreign equipment. Starting from the early 1960s, the World Bank channelled loans and credits, through different agencies, totalling about $802 million to P&T essentially for the purpose of importing telecommunications equipment.[95] With demand for telephones and telecommunications facilities growing at a much faster pace than the accretion of manufacturing capacity in the country, imports were, no doubt, indispensable. But in view of the company's disappointing performance, ITI management could neither have opposed these measures, nor sought to influence their content, even if it had wanted to.

[93] Michel Crozier, *Le phénomène bureaucratique. Essai sur les tendances bureaucratiques des systèmes d'organisation modernes et sur leurs relations en France avec le système social et culturel*, Paris, 1985, p. 237.

[94] CAG Report 1987, p. 8.

[95] DoT, *Forty Years of Telecommunications*, pp. 162–4. Between 1962–78, the World Bank provided long term loans worth $1.7 billion to the telecommunications sector as a whole, in addition to directly financing projects to the tune of $6.2 billion across the world. OECD, *Les télécommunications*, p. 61.

HOARDING RESULTS IN HIGH INVENTORIES

Paradoxically, despite the repeated material shortages, inventory holdings continued to remain extremely high. Indeed, a parliamentary committee expressed surprise that 'while on the one hand ITI are carrying excessive inventories, on the other labour remains idle for want of materials'.[96] With material costs accounting for almost two-thirds of public sector enterprises' overall operating expenditures, it was obvious that large inventories translated into large amounts of capital, often borrowed at substantial costs, being frozen. The short-term loans, bearing high interest charges of 15 per cent, that ITI was constrained to obtain in order to meet its working capital requirements during the early and mid-1980s were the 'direct consequence of excessive inventory holdings'.[97] So, even minor reductions in inventory levels could fetch important savings particularly in an economic environment defined by resource constraints. But for much of the 1980s and 1990s, total inventories as a percentage of ITI's sales averaged nearly 58 per cent as against the norm of 50 per cent that it had fixed. Subsequently, the figure declined to 42.4 per cent, reflecting perhaps the efforts undertaken by the management to implement the recommendations submitted by consultancy firm PwC.[98] Another objective consisting of scaling raw material inventories to three months of the company's productions needs also remained unattainable throughout the decade of the 1990s.[99]

What placed severe limits on the scale of the inventory reduction programme was the lack of adequate financial resources. Despite requests over a three year period from the telephone division at the Bangalore plant for computerized networking facilities, which by connecting different departments (purchase, stores, material planning, sales, shipping

[96] COPU 1973, p. 60; EC Report 1958, p. 39.

[97] CAG Report 1987, p. 20.

[98] Annual Report (various years). Notwithstanding the recommendations of a parliamentary team urging greater material standardization with a view to achieving lower inventory holdings, in 1980 the stores of the Bangalore plant still contained 129,000 types of raw material and components. COPU 1973, p. 109; Annual Report, 1974–75; Replies to Expert Committee of Public Undertakings on Materials Management, November 1980. Subsequently, Pricewaterhouse claimed that the rationalization of raw materials and stores inventories would yield cost savings of Rs 15 million annually. Ref. DB/COM/2000–2001, 27 June 2000.

[99] Annual Report (various years).

and billing) would make available information on time for stock procurement and control, the company had still not sanctioned the sum of Rs 1.3 million demanded for this purpose. Pointing out that the telephone division alone did not possess such online information systems, and that staff attrition due to voluntary retirements accentuated the problems stemming from material planning and management, divisional officials spoke of a 'vicious cycle' where, on the one hand, top executives kept reiterating the necessity of scaling down inventory levels, but on the other 'failed to provide optimum infrastructure'.[100]

Once again, a combination of slack managerial practices, omissions by DoT, and the regulatory regime, all contributed to ITI constantly carrying stocks far in excess of its requirements. Because of the restrictions imposed by the government on imports and foreign exchange, company executives strove for the 'safety factor'.[101] In other words, when purchasing from foreign vendors, they often tended to over-order, hoarding stocks as insurance against the risk of potential material scarcities obstructing output flows. As the management stated, procurement uncertainties together with frequent changes in official policy meant that it was 'necessary to keep a much bigger stock of imported raw materials than is done by the manufacturers in the Western countries'.[102] Thus, even when the company possessed sufficient raw material stocks to satisfy its production requirements for the full year, it continued to place orders on suppliers.[103]

Understandable from a managerial perspective, such stratagems,

---

[100] Tel. Divn. note, 28 September 1996. Another note, dated 28 July 1998, stated that in the event of finances not being available for networking facilities, permission for the purchase of at least 12 computers should be granted, since, barring a few exceptions, all the existing computers 'are...no more than junk and practically is of no use (sic)'.

[101] Berliner, *Factory and Managers*, pp. 76, 88–99. As he and other specialists of command economies have noted, the uncertainties and inefficiencies of the procurement system was one reason why Soviet bloc managers systematically inflated their material requirements and resorted to hoarding in order to anticipate interruptions in the flow of supplies. See also, Kornai, *Economics of Shortage*, pp. 100–03.

[102] Estimates Committee, *Action Taken by Government on Recommendations Contained in the 11th Report of the Estimates Committee (Second Lok Sabha) on the Ministry of Transport and Communications (Department of Communications), Indian Telephone Industries Ltd.*, 105th Report, Second Lok Sabha, New Delhi, 1961, p. 15. (Hereafter EC Report 1961.)

[103] EC Report 1958, p. 39.

though, were thoroughly injudicious from a commercial angle, and not merely because they had the effect of freezing valuable capital resources. In the telecommunications industry where technological innovation constantly reconfigured product characteristics, a direct consequence of hoarding was that a portion of the inventory became obsolete in the course of such transformations, leaving the company with no choice but to write off fairly large amounts of money. Indeed, this was precisely the predicament in which the ITI management would find itself.

By the early 1970s, the value of supplies either no longer required for production or used very sparingly had risen to almost Rs 22 million, while write-offs amounted to Rs 3.74 million.[104] The price of stock-piling would prove even steeper over time. In the mid-1990s, ITI had no choice but to write off technologically outdated components worth Rs 406 million.[105] More significantly, with the company carrying unused and dormant inventory estimated at a gigantic Rs 2278 million in March 2000, the likelihood of further and costlier write-offs was perhaps even stronger in the future.[106] Under these circumstances it was not surprising that, together with liquidated damages payments, top management traced the other major cause of wasteful expenditure to 'the tendency to purchase items in excess of requirement, especially for products likely to become obsolete with the change of technology'.[107]

If end-year rush-work invariably resulted in delivery delays, it also quite logically led to delays in customer billing and collection of payments which in turn had significant repercussions on the company's cash flow stream. An internal evaluation, conducted into certain aspects of the working of the Bangalore telephone division in 1988, pointed out that the time taken for converting finished goods into cash varied from a

---

[104] Even the disposal of obsolete material as scrap did not always turn out to be a financially gainful exercise for the company. A surprise check conducted on auction sales of dormant stock found that one lot which had been sold for the 'meagre sum' of Rs 5000 actually consisted of 'costly unused items' worth Rs 200,000, and included material which were in scarce supply at the crossbar division. Following this incident, the management decided to create a committee which would inspect all scrapped items before they were auctioned. Tel. Divn. note, 6 July 1976.

[105] Criticizing the company's inventory handling policies, a parliamentary enquiry later ordered it to adopt 'suitable measures . . . in order to avoid recurrence of such incidents'. COPU 1997, p. 46, cit. p. 66.

[106] Minutes of CoM Meeting, 3 May 2000.

[107] Corporate Office note, 11 December 1997.

minimum of 22 days to a maximum of 188 days. The report went on to state that shortages of packing materials and labourers, spatial constraints in the central shipping department, tardiness in forwarding dispatch documents to the billing department, and DoT red tape in clearing sales documents, all conspired to create delays at each stage of the transaction.[108] According to another study, undertaken by consultant PwC in 2000, the time lag between shipping and billing at the Bangalore plant stretched on average from one to two months.[109]

At the same time, outstanding payments as a percentage of sales for the entire company showed a steep upward trend, jumping from 34.8 per cent in 1980–81 to an astonishing 91.5 per cent in 1986–87, or over nine months of its annual turnover, before declining to 72.9 in 1994–95.[110] The costs of failing to realize these debts promptly would turn out to be no less negligible. For with cash inflows blocked, the management had no other option but to finance its working capital requirements through external borrowings on the market. Indeed, if the company suffered from chronic liquidity shortages, the cause lay first and foremost in excessive inventories and the massive volume of unpaid bills.

Already in 1958, an official enquiry had judged 'particularly unbusinesslike' the top management's decision to borrow Rs 12.7 million, on which it had to pay interest of Rs 500,000, because it had neglected to collect payments on time from its principal customer.[111] This was a trivial amount in comparison to the estimated annual loss of Rs 253.7 million incurred subsequently by the company by way of interest charges over a five year period from 1981–82 to 1985–86.[112] As the finance chief observed, interest charges could be sharply pruned 'if liquidity improves through better recovery of dues'.[113] Threats from the corporate office to withhold financial assistance to the Bangalore plant had prompted all divisions to constitute teams, comprising marketing, purchase, production and finance personnel, with the objective of

---

[108] Special Task Group Report No. 159, Tel. Divn., 5 October 1994.

[109] Ref. DB/COM/2000–2001, 27 June 2000.

[110] Annual Report (various years). Overall, for the two odd decades from 1980–81 to 2002–03, outstandings averaged a sizeable 65.4 per cent of ITI's turnover.

[111] EC Report 1958, p. 20.

[112] CAG Report 1987, p. 10.

[113] Ref. CO/DRF/008, 25 June 1998.

speeding up cash collection. But it is doubtful whether these initiatives persisted beyond the short term.[114]

To be sure, the volume of outstanding payments would not have grown to mountainous heights had ITI's principal customer displayed greater financial discipline and speedily settled its bills. Of the total Rs 14,131 million owed to the company at the end of the financial year 2002–03, DoT alone accounted for as much as 85.2 per cent.[115] In principle, the department was committed to pay ITI in full within 20 days of having received the invoice.[116] But this was seldom the case, and given the imbalance in the power ratio, the company wielded no leverage to pressure the parent administration into respecting its engagement. This also probably explained why the management never really sought to include a clause in the pricing agreement levying interest charges in case of delayed settlement of bills, as suggested by one committee.[117]

The uphill task faced by company officials in prising open DoT's purse strings can be evidenced from the following letter addressed by the head of the Bangalore telephone division to the Chief General Manager, Assam Telecom Circle, which we cite in some detail.

I take this liberty to write to you out of *utter frustration to our fruitless efforts* to realise payments against the supplies already made to your circle . . . It can be seen that the bills are more than one & half years old. So far we have sent *four representatives in the course of last Nine months* who have personally followed table to table to receive payments . . . Initially our officers were given with standard reply that bills have not been received or inspection documents are not available . . . then they were sent back with the assurance that every thing has been cleared and payment will be realised shortly, which finally never materialised. Off late we have been given with another reason that funds are not available although the bills are quite old. We were asked to follow up for the release of funds from Delhi . . . Since we feel there is a lack of eagerness at the appropriate level to clear payments which are long outstanding, I am left with no other alternative but to seek your personal intervention in this matter . . . I

---

[114] Ref. GMF/055, 26 July 1996. Ref. GMF/103, 25 April 1997.

[115] Government agencies headed ITI's list of debtors, contributing to nearly 95 per cent of its unsettled dues. The outstandings amount includes both 'good' and 'doubtful' debts. Annual Report 2002–03, p. 90.

[116] EC Report 1961, p. 9.

[117] Extracts from Comprehensive Appraisal of Working of ITI Bangalore, CAG Report 1987–88. (Hereafter CAG Report 1987–88.)

am looking forward that you may give suitable instructions to clear the bills . . . without any further delay or harassment to us (sic).[118]

Our sources do not tell us whether this appeal proved persuasive enough to compel the DoT hierarchy to finally agree to clear its debts. But the decentralization policy subsequently pursued by the state carrier seems to have placed additional hurdles in the company's path. As the management claimed, it now had to

follow across length and breadth of the country and there is invariably a delay by DoT clearing . . . bills (sic).[119]

However, to accuse DoT alone of being responsible for ITI's cash flow constraints would be unfair. If anything, the former's dilatory tactics were, to a good measure, fostered and reinforced by the latter's own inefficiencies.[120] For as the tutelary authority rightly pointed out, delays in payment essentially occurred because of end-year rush-work, its personnel being hard pressed to cope with the sudden increase in workload caused by the huge mass of bills sent out by ITI. To remedy the problem, DoT, quite naturally, suggested spreading production evenly throughout the year which in turn would usher greater regularity in billing procedures.[121]

Two other interconnected factors served to retard payments even further. The first of these was the highly bureaucratic invoicing system employed by ITI. Not only did multiple copies of the same bill have to be made, but each shipment had to include a bill, and since equipments were shipped out in several batches, the paperwork soon attained colossal proportions. Thus, between 1984–86, the strowger division in Bangalore submitted no less than 31,500 bills, and transmission, 7803 bills.[122] The upshot of this paper avalanche was that follow-up, traceability, and verifications by both ITI and DoT became an enormously protracted and complicated process. Negligent work practices by ITI's shipping staff was the second factor holding up payments. In addition to the

---

[118] Ref. AGMT/31, 27 October 1995. Emphasis added.

[119] Tel. Divn. note, nd (1996).

[120] See EC Report 1958, p. 20.

[121] CAG Report 1992, p. 46; COPU, *Action Taken by Government on Recommendations Contained in 10th Report (11th Lok Sabha)*, 6th Report, Twelfth Lok Sabha, New Delhi, 1999, pp. 18–19. (Hereafter COPU 1999.)

[122] CAG Report 1987, p. 12.

delays involved in billing customers, clerical errors of all kinds were common. This led to DoT returning 40 per cent of the bills submitted by the strowger division between 1984–86.[123]

LOW LEVELS OF MACHINE, LABOUR AND CAPACITY UTILIZATION

What incidence did material shortages, and other deficiencies such as poor machine maintenance, indiscipline, and so forth, have on machine and labour utilization rates at ITI? Gaps in our sources, partly due to the management's method of collecting information, allows us to only provide periodic snapshots.[124] Thus between 1964–65 and 1971–72, machine utilization at the all-important automatic machine shop in the Bangalore plant averaged 73.5 per cent, though there was a clear drop in efficiency towards the end.[125] With respect to five other machines shops, the figure stood slightly lower at 68.2 per cent.[126] Among the factors responsible for machine 'idle time', or non-utilization, machine repairs ranked first while absenteeism came next.[127] Subsequently, utilization rates declined to 65.4 per cent for all three divisions of the Bangalore plant (strowger and telephone, transmission and, crossbar).[128]

The objective of 75 to 80 per cent utilization, set by top management,

---

[123] ibid, p. 13.

[124] Not only have the records for certain years disappeared, but our sources are also incomplete because (a) the data assembled by the company up to 1972 pertains only to those machine shops operating on individual worker incentive schemes; (b) machine utilization cards were maintained for barely 27 per cent of the total machine stock. In addition, as an internal document noted, there was no uniform policy of filling up these cards. Hence, '. . . the machine utilization figures obtained may not reflect the exact utilization as idle time of smaller duration are not being included at least in some sections (sic)'. Draft Report on Capacity Utilization at ITI, nd.

[125] COPU 1973, p. 61. Utilization rates dropped from approximately 80.8 per cent in 1964–65 to 69.3 per cent in 1971–72. For the financial year 1970–71, data pertains only to the months of July to March.

[126] ibid, pp. 62–3. The shops concerned were moulding, miscellaneous machines, selectors, telephone, and relays. The data covers the period 1967–68 to 1971–72.

[127] Between 1964–65 and 1971–72, machine breakdowns represented on average roughly 35.6 per cent of idle time, absenteeism 32 per cent, power and material shortages 19.2 per cent, and tool set up 13.4 per cent. COPU 1973, p. 61.

[128] Replies to Ministry of Labour Questionnaire on Industrial Relations and Implementation of Labour Laws, 1976.

thus never appears to have been reached. However, machine utilization at ITI could never be as high as in certain other engineering industries, not to speak of process industries. This was as much because of the 'large amount of product mix' together with the relatively short production runs, which demanded frequent tooling changes, as 'the continuous changes in the pattern of production, and other difficulties with regard to procurement of materials etc. from time to time (sic)'.[129] The optimal performance of the machine stock was also severely compromised by the fact that it had seen better times, much of it being over ten years old.

One consequence of the antiquated plant was that machine breakdowns constantly plagued factory operations. Although the management had pegged machine downtime norms, on account of repairs, at 5 per cent of the total machine hours available, it struggled to fulfil this goal.[130] The non-availability of spare parts aside, restricting breakdowns to tolerable proportions posed severe problems because a number of machines had outlived their life-span, therefore necessitating extensive overhauling. An imported Timble & Wright capstan lathe, for instance, which had a normal life span of seven years, remained in operation at the ITI Bangalore telephone division for as long as 40 years. The question of obsolete machinery was, for certain, beyond the management's control. With machinery imports severely restricted and the government and P&T unwilling to invest the sums required to enable the company to modernize its manufacturing infrastructure, shop officials had no alternative but to exploit as best as they could their existing resources even at the cost of overworking them.

However, the failure to ensure effective machine maintenance at regular intervals aggravated conditions. Although preventive maintenance implied perforce additional expenditure, as an internal document observed, in the long run, it would pay for itself both by making available

[129] ibid, p. 63.

[130] From 5.3 per cent in 1971–72, the figure climbed sharply to 7.3 per cent a few years later, and despite contracting to 5.8 per cent in 1979–80, it again rose to 8.3 in 1981–82. Replies submitted by ITI to COPU on Productivity in Public Undertakings, February 1983, p. 28. Depending on contextual circumstances, definitions of repair can vary sharply and tend to reflect the way employers arbitrate between opposing criteria such as the need to maintain output levels, preserve quality standards and ensure the safety of both workers and machinery. Nicolas Dodier, *Les hommes et les machines. La conscience collective dans les sociétés technicisées*, Paris, 1995, p. 78.

optimum machine hours for continuous production and prolonging the life of the machinery, contributing in turn, to higher production and productivity.[131] But concretely applying this advice appears to have been beyond the company's reach. The pressure exerted by shop authorities on the maintenance department to postpone repair schedules, so that output levels did not fall, succeeded in creating precisely the opposite effect. Greater machine wear and tear resulted in longer and costlier breakdowns, thus increasing the time lost in production stoppages. The safety valve that overtime working constituted compensated for some of this loss, but in doing so, top management got an additional reason to neglect preventive maintenance and that further perpetuated the vicious cycle. According to a retired executive, who felt that the company's efforts were essentially geared to what he termed 'fire fighting',

once production departments had gained the upper hand, maintenance department's authority . . . suffered. Before it would forcibly shut down machines for preventive maintenance regardless of the impact on production . . . Moreover, when the number of machines increased, but plant mechanical staff remained stationary, it became difficult to ensure preventive maintenance.[132]

The contradictions sustaining the rival logics of volume and prevention were, of course, constitutive of the functioning of mass production systems. Regardless of whether the power balance favoured operation or maintenance personnel, friction invariably clouded their relations, be it in a private or a publicly-owned plant.[133] Nevertheless, even as the deleterious effects of prioritizing output over regular maintenance had become increasingly evident, ITI officials persisted with this strategy.

An internal study, conducted by the industrial engineering department in November 1979, sheds light on another reason for sub-optimal

[131] 'Manufacture of Telecommunications Equipments in a Developing Country', ITI, nd (mimeo), p. 100.

[132] Interview with Srinivasa Rao. But fire-fighting, as opposed to preventive maintenance, can also serve the interests of maintenance workers. It furnishes them with the opportunity to deploy the tricks of their trade, and thus valorize their skills and position, as well as conserve their bargaining power, both of which they would lose in case machine breakdowns became a rare or predictable occurrence. Erhard Friedberg, *Le pouvoir et la règle. Dynamiques de l'action organisée,* Paris, 1997, pp. 287–8.

[133] It is, however, instructive comparing ITI's indifferent attitude to preventive maintenance with the scientific approach adopted by the TISCO management. S.B. Datta, *Capital Accumulation and Workers' Struggle in Indian Industrialization: The Case of Tata Iron and Steel Company, 1910–1970,* Stockholm, 1986, pp. 81–2.

machine utilization: absenteeism and indiscipline. The study focussed on the workings of the power press section in the strowger selector machine shop, literally the backbone of the entire department since the 38 power presses and three shearing machines installed here turned out the basic piece parts required by all the other groups for further machining as well as assembly operations. But utilization rates for these machines were 'as low as a dismal 20 per cent'.[134] The figure stood even lower at 14.6 per cent with respect to the shearing machines or 'guillotines' whose functioning was critical to the section's efficiency since they fed the presses with cut metal strips which were then machined.

. . . though the cut strips were available near the guillotines, they were not moved by helpers to power presses in time . . . this was due to the . . . slackened pace of work which is traceable to inadequacy of control over them (sic).[135]

Workers were either absent from the factory, missing from the workspot, leaving early for lunch and returning late, or taking coffee and tea breaks. Together these four factors accounted for approximately 56 per cent of all idle time in the section. The study ended by urging upon the management the 'need to exercise better control over operatives . . .'.[136] With the transition from electro-mechanical to electronic switching technologies from the mid-1980s onwards, the need to achieve optimal machine utilization would, however, progressively decline in importance. Greater reliance on electronic components, procured from external sources, coincided with a sharp fall in the volume of machining processes. Henceforth what the company would be preoccupied about was in eliminating the 'eyesore' represented by the large numbers of 'machines lying unused in the machine shop because they had ceased to be useful'.[137]

An analysis of the evidence that we dispose on labour utilization, primarily for the 1980s and 1990s, does not present a more efficient picture of the company's operations. First, and most importantly, ITI was having to forego a significant portion of the production time for which it was paying on account of absenteeism as well as idle time arising from a cluster of factors such as irregular raw material and component

[134] Activity Sampling Study on Power Presses—Strowger Selector Machine Shop, 28 January 1980.
[135] ibid.
[136] ibid.
[137] Tel. Divn. note, Ref. FMT.62/136, 9 October 1993.

supplies, machine cleaning and change of jobs, welfare activities, lack of work, and so forth.[138] The extent of its loss can be gauged from the fact that between 1986–87 and 1997–98, production hours as a percentage of the aggregate paid-for man hours averaged only 68.8 per cent at the main Bangalore plant.[139] In other words, nearly a third of the total man hours was going unutilized.[140] The figures were even higher during the mid-1990s when the company, reeling under the impact of the deregulation of the telecommunications equipment sector, experienced an acute demand crisis. Explaining why some of these years saw barely half the purchased man hours being devoted to purposeful productive activity, Chairman Motial told a parliamentary committee,

. . . we have . . . surplus manpower; that manpower is paid whereas we do not have the production.[141]

Second, although there was absolutely no dearth of orders during the pre-economic reforms era, the data brings to the fore the difficulties encountered by the company notably in extracting work from its personnel.[142] Stabilizing employees' job activities and regulating intensity are the central functions of effort controls which entail the entire array of administrative arrangements elaborated by managements. It is in these two functions that the coercive component inherent in effort controls emerges to the fore.[143] The enforcement mechanisms deployed at ITI,

---

[138] It is worth attention that a considerable proportion of idle time went totally unaccounted for. Between 1986–87 and 1990–91, for instance, close to half the total idle time could not be attributed to a definite cause. This underscored not merely the laxity of time-keeping operations, but, more generally, the absence of cost consciousness that defined the management's overall style of functioning. CAG Report 1992 p. 25.

[139] All statistical data in this and the following paragraphs provided by the industrial engineering department at ITI Bangalore.

[140] Evidence for the other units of ITI is restricted to the years 1986–87 to 1991–92, so a comparison with the situation at Bangalore is not possible. But exploiting production time optimally appears to have been equally problematic in these plants. At Mankapur, for instance, 34 per cent of the aggregate man hours on average was not utilized during this six-year period, at Naini 27 per cent, and at Rae Bareli 21 per cent. CAG Report 1992, p. 24.

[141] COPU 1997, p. 45.

[142] For the period 1978–79 to 1990–91, idle time as a percentage of production hours (i.e., net of absenteeism) averaged no less than 12.3 per cent.

[143] William Baldamus, *Efficiency and Effort. An Analysis of Industrial Administration*, London, 1967, pp. 36–7, 39–47.

however, apparently retained little of their original coercive force. Otherwise, it is unlikely that a considerable portion of the work day would have been lost on account of machine cleaning and welfare and sports activities as was currently the case, indicative of the management's inability to both restrict these facilities and check possible employee abuse by ensuring that supervisory personnel diligently executed their tasks. Remarking that 'idle time recorded against cleaning of machines, want of shop orders, mechanical and electrical breakdowns, setting up of tools and try outs…appears to be excessive', the Telecommunications Commission, in a strongly-worded letter to the ITI chairman in 1998, arrived at the 'inescapable conclusion that there has been a management failure'.[144]

Another essential indicator of an industrial organization's efficiency is capacity utilization. Evaluating ITI's performance on the basis of this evidence, though, can land us on shaky ground. This was because licensed capacity not only often failed to correspond to installed capacity; even the latter figure could not be fully relied upon. Writing to the statutory audit in 1988, the management admitted its ignorance as to how the figure of 275,000 telephone instruments that it had declared to be the installed capacity at ITI Bangalore had been calculated. 'We are trying to find out basis for reckoning this figure (sic).'[145] Similarly, it argued that the 'large and varying product mix from year to year' of the strowger and transmission divisions in Bangalore ruled out a precise assessment of their capacities.[146] Measuring decreases or increases in physical production in terms of value of output was not a viable option either since equipment prices were revised upwards at regular intervals. Hence, higher turnover did not *per se* signify higher levels of capacity utilization.

Determining the extent of capacity utilization was also rendered problematic by the absence of a detailed breakdown of physical production quantities according to in-house manufacture, equipment assembled from knock-down sets, and components and sub-assemblies turned out by ancillary units. Given the non-availability of such

---

[144] IED files, 30 December 1998.

[145] Ref. No. RAP/ITI/CA-I/87–88/165, 26 December 1987. An earlier estimate had pegged annual installed capacity at 250,000 instruments. COPU 1973, p. 156.

[146] COPU 1973, p. 4. See also *Annual Report on the Working of Industrial and Commercial Undertakings of the Central Government*, 1972–73, BPE, Vol. 1, p. 236.

information, higher overall production capacity could well have been achieved through subcontracting while in-house capacity remained under utilized. After noting that between 1985–86 and 1991–92 the telephone division's production exceeded the rated capacity by 11 per cent to 66 per cent, despite sub-optimal utilization of machines, an audit report contended that the management had either under assessed capacity, or was farming out the manufacture of components at the cost of keeping internal capacity idle.[147] There is no means of ascertaining whether or not outsourcing resulted in internal capacity remaining idle. But the company acknowledged that the assistance extended by the ancillaries explained why telephone production volumes on certain occasions stood in excess of rated capacity.[148]

Viewed against this backdrop, the evidence, once again fragmentary, presented must necessarily be treated with circumspection. Thus between 1966–67 and 1974–75, capacity utilization at the Bangalore telephone division ranged from roughly 84 per cent to 99 per cent. In the case of strowger, during the years 1966–67 to 1971–72, barring a few exceptions, capacity was under utilized for almost all the sub-assemblies (relays and relay sets, selectors, multiple racks, etc.).[149] Analysing the information for the following years is rendered impossible by the discrepancies in the method of compiling the data by the company.[150] As far as the crossbar division was concerned, the fiasco caused by the import of technology incompatible with Indian conditions meant that between 1965–68 capacity utilization for different components and sub-assemblies never rose above 41 per cent, and in some areas even sank to zero per cent.[151] Thereafter, leaving aside a couple of years, the division appears to have

[147] CAG Report 1992, p. 19. During the same period, telephone production at the Naini unit was also higher than the rated capacity. Having farmed out the manufacture of transmitters, ringers and dials, the management claimed it was able to siphon this freed capacity towards the production of additional instruments. ibid, p. 16.

[148] Tel Divn. letter to resident audit officer, Ref. AGM(T)/114-Insp. Report 1990–91, 27 October 1992.

[149] COPU 1973, pp. 157–8. The figure varied from roughly 58 to 98 per cent with respect to 3000 type relays, 64 to 99 per cent for relay sets, and 65 to 90 per cent for MAX small exchanges.

[150] The data at our disposal for the period 1975–76 to 1986–87 amalgamates both the Bangalore and Rae Bareli plants, but while taking into account output at Rae Bareli from the start capacity utilization is assessed only in 1984–85.

[151] COPU 1973, p. 171.

worked continually at full capacity.[152] Nevertheless, as early as in 1983, the management admitted to a steady decrease in capacity utilization levels for the company as a whole, attributing this to the prevalence of obsolete machinery.[153]

INDUSTRIAL ENGINEERING NORMS CONTESTED BY SHOP FLOOR

The foregoing discussion of machine and labour utilization rates as well as capacity utilization brings us to the role of the industrial engineering department (IED) and its effectiveness in setting manning norms and time standards. Quite strong during the early years, the department owed much of its influence to its first head, S. Ramalingam. One of the select group of engineers trained by ATE at its Liverpool plant, he also ranked second to the works manager in the factory hierarchy in terms of seniority, and so was in a position to make sure production shops enforced the directives issued by his department. But once he left the company, and once the drive for output volumes became top management's exclusive priority from the mid-1960s onwards, industrial engineering, as with maintenance and quality control, saw its authority steadily undermined by line officials.

If the restructuring of the Bangalore plant's operations into separate divisions in the early 1970s further eroded industrial engineering's power, it was the divisionalization of the department itself in 1981 which definitely sealed its decline, obliged as it now was to report directly to production. Henceforth 'many of its decisions were only of a recommendatory nature, and divisional managers had the last word', particularly on the issue of manpower allocation and deployment.[154] IED also had no powers to conduct time study operations without the express authorization of the divisional heads. As one IED executive sadly remarked, whereas in the past the prestige attached to the department attracted a number of competent candidates, subsequently only 'unwanted or inefficient people were posted here'.[155]

---

[152] Draft Report on Capacity Utilization, nd.
[153] Replies submitted to COPU on Productivity, p. 21.
[154] Interview with S.K. Ramanna.
[155] Interview with S. Satish, Deputy General Manager IED, 25 May 1999.

Whether the loss of autonomy suffered by industrial engineering resulted in over manning is a question we cannot answer, just as it is not possible to determine the extent of surplus staff. Rough estimates provided by executives tend to place the figure at about 20 per cent with respect to officers, and between 10–15 per cent in the case of workers. As one former chief of the Bangalore plant stated, 'to meet production targets when we were behind we had two choices, over manning or overtime'.[156]

An official report published in 1958 refers to staff increases, especially in the administrative departments being on the 'high side'.[157] However, the only accurate evidence we dispose on the question pertains to the crossbar division at the Bangalore plant during the early 1970s. As against the initial projection of 15 officers and 1235 direct and indirect workers needed to turn out 100,000 lines annually, in March 1972 the division already carried on its rolls 31 officers and 1401 workers, even though production was only of the order of 80,000 lines.[158] In other words, the company had employed 432 employees in excess of the norms. Voicing harsh criticism of this action, a parliamentary report felt such instances of over manning were

indicative of the laxity with which the appointments of staff are made in the beginning which militates against disciplined hard work and thereby vitiate the atmosphere in Public Undertakings for achieving optimum production results.[159]

Although its first technology partner ATE had provided time standards for all the operations, ITI management opted to introduce its own norms. The timings set by the UK company for skilled jobs especially were considered to be beyond the reach of Indian operatives.[160] Since ITI

---

[156] Interview with Srinivasa Rao.

[157] EC Report 1958, p. 54.

[158] COPU 1973, p. 51.

[159] ibid, p. 52. An assessment made by the Bureau of Public Enterprises in 1978 showed that 46 out of 163 public sector enterprises were overmanned to varying degrees. Productivity studies undertaken in certain firms also revealed staff requirements in excess of 10 to 15 per cent. COPU (1983–84), *Productivity in Public Undertakings*, 97th Report, Seventh Lok Sabha, New Delhi, 1984, p. 44. (Hereafter COPU 1984.)

[160] Interview with Y. Munnuswamy. On the difficulties in transposing economic indicators such as worker productivity from one national context to the other without falling into the trap of constructs such as 'national character','mentalities', 'cultural traits' see Alain Cottereau, 'Problèmes de conceptualization comparative de l'industrialization: L'exemple des ouvriers de la chaussure en France et en Grande

workers were paid on the basis of day rates, which would later be converted to monthly wages, and not according to piece rates, the primary objective in carrying out time and motion studies was less to determine compensation levels than to help in the implementation of incentive schemes for which base efficiencies needed to be fixed. Beginning on an experimental footing in the mid-1950s, standardization proved to be a fairly long drawn-out process, for although jobs in the majority of production departments were measured by the mid-1960s, the task was not fully completed until 1983.

Establishing and enforcing time norms brought challenges from all quarters to the authority of industrial engineering. On the one hand, workers and their representatives exerted constant pressure on shop officials to relax timings for various jobs, when they did not seek to directly obstruct industrial engineering personnel from carrying out their duties. A study to calculate tool setting rates on press operations in different divisions had to be partially abandoned because

. . . we could not even make an attempt to observe on higher tonnage presses (80 ton and above), especially in Crossbar Division due to strong resistance from the setters pleading on the score that time standards for setting on these machines could not be established precisely . . .[161]

According to the telephone division head,

no timings as fixed initially by IED are accepted by workers. They say this element has not been taken into account, that element not taken into account. So we will have to take all this in to consideration and arbitrarily increase time rates by 2 to 5 per cent. That is how timings have been decided all these years.[162]

The IED's hands were also tied by the terms of incentive agreements which stipulated that job timings could be changed only during the first year of the life of the agreement. The government's indigenization policy, prohibiting the replacement of imported machinery, constituted a supplementary obstacle. Because locally manufactured power presses were heavier, and so more strenuous to operate, timings had to be augmented

Bretagne', in Susanna Magri et Christian Topalov (eds), *Villes ouvrières, 1890–1950*, Paris, 1990, pp. 41–82.

[161] Industrial Engineering Department Report, 1981.

[162] Interview with B.K. Sharma.

for several jobs.[163] Yet, paradoxically, a World Bank report delivered a rather positive appreciation. It noted that time rates for operations such as press work, drilling, coil winding, relay adjustment were 'realistic and not unduly inflated'.[164] The only reservations expressed concerned certain kinds of wiring work where because of obsolete methods norms were thought to be slack.

On the other, industrial engineering had to counter both the apathy of supervisory personnel and active resistance from shop officials. Supervisors conniving with the men and women under their control to manipulate timings is a well established phenomenon in all industrial settings. Without such transactions and adjustments securing the everyday consensus on the shop floor essential to getting the job done could end up being a relatively intractable exercise.[165] In the case of ITI foremen and supervisors, inadequate exposure to industrial engineering techniques partly explained their reluctance to enforce tight time rates.[166] But production imperatives also often prompted them to back workers' claims to relax standards—a stratagem which enabled foremen to achieve two goals at one stroke. They could be sure of reaching the volume targets fixed for individual sections and escaping censure even as they kept workers contented by assuring them of higher incentive rewards.

Officers when questioned about low production would say workers were unhappy about job timings. So top management would ask IED to reconsider the timings . . . No scientific studies were conducted in some areas like strowger rack wiring. The shop superintendent here would say so many hours were required, and it would be given.[167]

Initiatives by industrial engineers to amend standards on the rare

[163] Interview with Srinivasa Rao.

[164] ITI Factories Appraisal, World Bank Technical Supervision Mission Report, June-July 1981, p. 40.

[165] Based on his own shop floor experiences, Burawoy contends that foremen typically sided with operators in their hostility to time study men, but operators remained suspicious of the former's motives. Michael Burawoy, *Manufacturing Consent. Changes in the Labor Process under Monopoly Capitalism*, Chicago, 1979, p. 62. See also R.P. Dore, *British Factory–Japanese Factory: The Origins of National Diversity in Industrial Relations*, Berkeley, 1973, pp. 86–7.

[166] See also COPU 1984, pp. 6–7, highlighting the 'insufficient penetration of industrial engineering approach and productivity consciousness among executives and staff of other departments' in public sector firms.

[167] Interview with Y. Munnuswamy.

instances when processes underwent a change, or when new products were launched, also often aborted due to the uncooperative attitude of line managers. If hostility to work studies from the workforce and the union was predictable, the fact that certain executives shared rather similar attitudes may come as a relative surprise. But it serves to underline the overall premise that the management, rather than constituting an undifferentiated bloc united vertically as well as horizontally, is instead composed of different functional groups, each of whom are engaged in the pursuit of specialized sets of interests and which for this reason could enter into conflict. As Dalton has reminded us, corporate organizations must be seen 'not as a chiselled entity, but as a shifting set of contained and ongoing counter phases of action'.[168]

Following the introduction of an internal switching main telephone in 1980, IED claimed that shop management was refusing to make available the facilities required to undertake the time study, and this was proving to be a 'frustrating experience' for its personnel who even 'after waiting nearly one hour daily' could not proceed with their job.[169] Arguing that the production department's estimates for certain assembly operations were not backed by a detailed analysis, the note added that the 'right to study a new model should rest' with industrial engineering 'and cannot be surrendered as it is bound to have tremendous repercussions . . .'[170]

In their reply, shop authorities first pointed out that no radical differences existed between the new and old models, and though timings were presumed to be slack workers' incentive earnings remained modest. They then drew attention to the fact that with only four months left before the financial year ended 'any adverse reaction by labour would seriously affect our production and our commitment to P&T . . . particularly as an indication was given that the new rates would be substantially lower'.[171] It therefore wanted the work study to be postponed until April when the division would have fulfilled its targets, a decision which appears to have secured the approval of top management.

The conflicting priorities of industrial engineering and line

[168] Dalton, *Men Who Manage*, p. 4.
[169] Ref. IED/O&M/70, 28 November 1980.
[170] ibid.
[171] Tel. Divn. note, 5 December 1980.

management, central to the latter's concern being the preservation of industrial peace even at the expense of productivity so as to guarantee the continuity of production, emerged equally sharply in the course of a second incident. In November 1984, IED called for the re-study of an operation connected with the assembly of a ringer in the 677 model telephone after a metal component had been replaced with a moulded part. But according to shop officials, regardless of the change in material, the effort demanded was identical. They also disapproved of IED's proposal to reduce the norms by as much as 60 per cent, stating that when 'production is going on smoothly it is not at all justifiable in disturbing the present rates'. [172] In a later note, the shop head wrote that although the union was willing to 'settle for a compromise', IED's insistence on drastically cutting timings had made it a 'prestige issue' and this was likely to disrupt output.[173] In the end, it required the intervention of the head of the Bangalore plant for the deadlock to be broken.

Justifying his department's stand, the industrial engineering chief claimed that whereas the job should take no more than 93.61 hours for 1000 ringers, the new rate had been pegged at 121 hours. This was entirely due to the opposition of workers who had made it

. . . impossible to conduct a proper time study. When this is brought to the notice of the Shop Management, they expressed their inability to do anything and demanded that IED may demonstrate how to do. As a very special case, this job was demonstrated by IED officers and this was resented by the operators. *Instead of helping IED to do a free and fair time study to arrive at a realistic rate in the interest of production and productivity, the shop management, methods etc. are posing more problem than helping IED . . . * (sic).[174]

Complaining that routine problems were being brought to the 'notice of higher management who are put to lot of pressure and embarrassment to arrive at a compromise which is neither realistic nor scientific', the note went on to add

. . . IED is not allowed to function properly resulting in unscientific rate fixing and attendant bad effect on production and productivity.[175]

---

[172] Tel. Divn. note, 8 November 1984.
[173] Tel. Divn. note, 17 November 1984.
[174] Ref. IED/0&M/40, 29 December 1984. Emphasis added.
[175] ibid.

Hemmed in from both top and bottom, the combination of opposition from the rank-and-file and its representatives and resistance from line management placed IED in a position where it had often no choice but to agree to a dilution of time standards. As long as the company enjoyed monopoly access to the domestic market, it could conveniently ignore the consequences of such a policy, notably on the cost of its products. But once competition arrived, it had no choice but to address the matter. Thus at the Bangalore telephone division, process improvements brought about an appreciable reduction in time standards for the assembly of transducers from 170 hours for 1000 transducers to 141.7 hours over a period of nine years. To utilize labour more optimally, certain assembly jobs were transferred to the machine shop which in turn resulted in a tightening of assembly time standards. Work cycles were also intensified. In the past, workers in the moulding department enjoyed a brief break of 40 seconds between each machine operation. Demanding that this time be employed productively, the management now introduced an additional operation. When workers initially refused, it threatened to take disciplinary action, whereas in the past it would have probably displayed a greater readiness to temper opposition by softening its stand. Still, divisional executives had to agree to pay moulding operators additional incentives.

INCENTIVE SCHEMES UNSUCCESSFUL IN BOOSTING LABOUR EFFICIENCY

Together with the determining of manpower requirements and time standards, another sphere of factory activity where industrial engineering deployed its competence, and one which occupied a considerable portion of its time, concerned the formulation of incentive plans. In principle, this mode of payment by results simultaneously fulfils two functions: it permits the stabilization of effort levels as well as leads to an increased intensity of effort.[176] But few employers are fortunate enough to boast such optimal achievements on an enduring basis.[177] Further, regardless

---

[176] Baldamus, *Efficiency and Effort*, p. 43.

[177] Since incentives are estimated to 'bite' with maximum effect on no more than 33 to 50 per cent of all jobs in a factory, a large gap always exists between physical possibilities and actual achievement. William F. Whyte, *Money and Motivation. An Analysis of Incentives in Industry*, Westport, 1977, pp. 28–9.

of their performance, incentive plans invariably give rise to all sorts of conflicts between workers and the management, and unions and the management.[178] Evidently, ITI proved no exception to the rule. Notwithstanding the considerable material resources and energies expended in implementing the different incentive schemes, none of them lived up to the expectations invested by company officials. Poorly conceived to start with, the efficient functioning of these schemes received a further hammer blow from slack managerial oversight, worker disinterest and malpractices of all manner.

Steps to draw up an incentive arrangement at ITI dated back to 1956; they were related to the management's plans to substantially expand production of both switching lines and telephones. Although ATE provided the inspiration, contrary to the practice followed by the UK-firm where only operatives physically engaged on the job were rewarded, in ITI both direct and auxiliary workers such as feeders, tool setters, charge hands, inspectors, and so forth, received the benefits in a proportion of 70 to 30 per cent. If indirect workers were not motivated in this way, shop officials feared they 'will not feel interested to supply goods and service to the other shops' on time, and thus hold up production.[179]

Unlike Frederick Taylor's famous differential piece rate formula, allegedly prone to causing 'nervous breakdowns' among its beneficiaries, ITI management claimed that its own scheme was free from such stress-inducing elements on workers' health for the simple reason that even those who failed to reach production targets were guaranteed a minimum income.[180] Yet the first scheme which lasted for three years (1958–61) did not enjoy much success on the shop floor because 'it required lots of

[178] E.A. Ramaswamy, for instance, notes that the incentive system introduced in a Coimbatore-based textile factory satisfied neither the employer nor the workforce. *Power and Justice: The State in Industrial Relations*, New Delhi, 1990, pp. 70–1. Similarly, at another Bangalore-based public sector plant, HMT Machine Tools, the existing incentive arrangement contributed much to 'workplace friction and little to productivity'. J. Mohan Rao, 'Capital, Labour and the Indian State', in Juliet Schor and Jong-Il You (eds.), *Capital, the State and Labour. A Global Perspective*, Aldershot-Brookfield, 1995, pp. 238–81 (cit. p. 245).

[179] IED note, nd.

[180] IED note, nd. A systematic account of Taylor's differential piece rate system is available in Daniel Nelson, *Frederick W. Taylor and the Rise of Scientific Management*, Madison, 1980, pp. 37–46.

mathematical calculations, and so workers did not understand how it would fully benefit them'.[181] The amounts they were gaining were also perceived as not being commensurate to the effort put in, a factor which would have significant consequences for labour efficiency, as we shall shortly see.

However, far from simplifying the design of the schemes, the refinements progressively incorporated by the IED only succeeding in rendering them more complicated. Evaluating a slab system of payments, composed of three differential hourly base rates, which was implemented in 1965 ostensibly in order to 'enthuse workers to achieve higher incentive payments with a corresponding increase in output', an internal document was forced to acknowledge that this had 'made the scheme more cumbersome for the operators to comprehend and calculate their likely incentive amount'.[182] Ironically, even the very architects of the incentive plan, industrial engineering, were finding it hugely problematic to administer these plans, so unwieldy had they become.

Practically operating the scheme was a colossal task . . . There were no computers then so all the calculations had to be done manually. So you can imagine the clerical effort and paper work involved.[183]

In addition to these constraints, the effective working of the incentive schemes in ITI was also impeded by the emergence of several other difficulties. By far the most pressing of these concerned the unbroken decline in labour efficiency.[184] This general downward trend in labour efficiency could neither be arrested by the introduction of a new incentive scheme in 1965, nor top management's decision, three years later when drawing up a fresh scheme, to grant 'more liberal' rates to direct workers.[185] Industrial engineering believed the problem had less to do with the amounts on offer than with workers' aversion to expending greater effort; instead of trying to reach the top of the payment scale,

---

[181] Interview with A.V. Krishnamurthy.

[182] Note to ITI Board Committee, November 1975.

[183] Interview with C.R. Datta Gupta.

[184] Between 1963–64 and 1972–73, efficiencies dropped from close to 110.4 per cent to 91 per cent, while incentive payments, albeit certain yearly variations, climbed from Rs 1.93 million in 1964–65 to Rs 2.67 million in 1972–73. COPU 1973, pp. 9–10, 162–9.

[185] IED note, 7 August 1968.

they preferred to work less and take home less incentive. As efficiencies continued to fall after 1969, notwithstanding the increased incentives, IED's viewpoint appears to have been vindicated.[186]

As we have already mentioned, a fundamental reason for the relative ineffectiveness of the incentive plans arose from the terms of the effort bargain. Workers could derive higher monetary benefits at a lower cost from overtime working as opposed to incentives. Between 1971–72 and 1980–81, overtime expenditures totalled almost 60 per cent more than the amounts distributed by way of incentives.[187] Barring 1980–81 when a major strike broke out at the Bangalore plant precisely during those months—December to March—when overtime was integral to production, in only one other year did incentive payments exceed those incurred on overtime, and that too marginally. But this was not the only explanation why 'the motivational element of the incentive has been eroded'.[188]

In response to queries from a parliamentary investigation team in the early 1970s, company officials explained the waning interest in terms of the broadening gap between workers' wages and incentive earnings, with

[186] IED note, 27 March 1968.

[187] Overtime and Incentive Expenditures (Rs. million):

Year	OT	Incentives
1971–72	11.03	2.52
1972–73	16.70	2.67
1973–74	14.88	2.96
1974–75	30.67	2.99
1975–76	25.07	4.93
1976–77	10.09	**10.36**
1977–78	19.70	11.08
1978–79	26.20	11.48
1979–80	19.63	12.95
1980–81	4.58	**9.45**
Total	178.55	71.39

Figures in bold indicate years when incentive payments exceeded those of overtime. *Source:* Replies to Ministry of Labour questionnaire, 1976; Note to the Board, 184th meeting, Item B8, December 1981; IED statistics.

[188] COPU 1975, p. 3.

the latter not growing at the same pace as wages. In effect, the two wage settlements negotiated in 1969 and, especially, in 1972 had allowed employees to realize important gains. To overcome all these obstacles in the way of greater production volumes, the company once again pushed up incentive rates in 1976 by as much as 50 to 60 per cent for operatives in the lowest categories. Despite the additional cost, the fresh plan was forecast to secure higher levels of output of the order of at least 10 per cent as well as generate economies in overtime expenditures.[189] Such optimism does not appear to have been misplaced at least in the short term. From 92.4 per cent in 1974–75, labour efficiency at the Bangalore plant jumped to around 110 per cent in the space of two years, before reaching 122 per cent in 1980–81.[190]

Unfortunately, our sources shed little light on the question of labour efficiency for the later periods.[191] But what does emerge fairly clearly is the workers' continued disinterest in earning incentives given their high wages. One company document pegged at 20 to 30 per cent the total number of individuals employed in the different ITI units who took home no incentives.[192] Likewise, 15 per cent of the operatives at the Bangalore telephone division failed to appear on the list of incentive beneficiaries for the period April 2000 to August 2001.[193] With average monthly incentive gains in this division amounting to less than 5 per cent of workers' basic pay, it is hardly surprising that quite a few of them considered foregoing incentive payments altogether as a more worthwhile alternative.[194]

It is also important to note that for the purpose of distributing incentives, ITI had established extremely modest base efficiency levels.

[189] The company was expected to incur an additional expenditure of Rs 4.5 million, over the Rs 3 million it spent in the last year of the old plan. Ref. K/SFC-1, 9 December 1975.

[190] IED statistics.

[191] The government audit observed that labour efficiency levels between 1983–84 to 1985–86, as reported by the Bangalore telephone division, bore no correlation with those concerning capacity utilization, machine utilization, and labour utilization. Letter from resident audit party to Tel. Divn., 20 July 1987.

[192] Minutes of 11th Meeting of Joint Committee of Management and Unions of all ITI units, 30 December 1993.

[193] IED telephone division efficiency statement, 19 October 2001.

[194] In comparison, incentive earnings represented on average 15 per cent of workers' salaries in 1986. IED note, 6 December 1986.

Whereas the ILO standards stipulated minimum efficiencies of 80 per cent, and in the private sector the equivalent figure was 90 to 100 per cent, in the schemes introduced from 1983 onwards at the public sector undertaking workers needed to only achieve efficiencies of 50 to 60 per cent to start earning incentives. Given its monopoly access to the domestic market, ITI could no doubt afford to adopt such a tactic without any risk to its competitive or financial position. At the same time, since there were neither rewards for good performance nor penalties for poor performance, company officials were hardly motivated to augment labour productivity by imposing stricter norms.

So, viewed against the backdrop of the low efficiency thresholds prevailing in the company, the decision of certain sections of the ITI workforce to forego incentives meant that they were working at barely 50 per cent efficiencies, and in some cases at even lower levels. In other words, although paid to work 170 hours a month, they were turning out no more than 85 hours of output, vividly underlining the management's chronic inability to enforce strong effort norms. As one document bluntly put it, '. . . *in certain cases one can get incentives for doing work, and wage for doing nothing*'.[195] Scathing in its criticism of the way incentive plans in the public sector had evolved, a parliamentary report observed that incentives 'appear to have degenerated into additional wage, having been linked to production even below the threshold level . . . one could very well say that these schemes are not based on payments for additional work (sic)'.[196]

Declining or low labour efficiencies aside, the numerous malpractices which had over time infiltrated the entire fabric of the incentive plans also severely compromised ITI management's prospects of reaping the benefits of higher productivity and output. Because of the way the plans were designed, they offered considerable opportunities for abuse which the supervisory personnel responsible for maintaining the time records did not fail to exploit in tandem with the rank-and-file. Most of the irregularities sprang from the manipulation of time 'bookings' under various heads with respect to the completion of work tasks, as foremen and supervisors sought to conceal their own inefficiencies, or to ensure

[195] Brief Report highlighting salient issues. Emphasis added.
[196] COPU 1984, p. 44.

optimal incentive benefits for workers in their shops. To quote a former IED head:

The foreman has to be very honest . . . If a worker has sat idle for 30 minutes on account of tool setting or material delays, the foreman should write 30 minutes and not one hour in the delivery tickets. But it is very difficult to control this . . . I don't know if workers were sharing money gained this way with foremen and supervisors, but often foremen would be negligent in booking time.[197]

Whereas the procedures called for individual job cards to be punched at the start and finish of each job, more often than not foremen filled out the cards by hand, claiming that the clocks were not functioning. 'It was easy to make the clocks go out of order.'[198]

Another easy and common way of falsifying records consisted of allotting time to what were known as 'charge-to-payable' operations. These were jobs such as packing, jobbing, shearing, soldering, repairs, and so forth, for which no time measurement studies had been conducted because the nature of the work did not permit standardization. According to the management, from the late 1970s onwards there had been a steady increase both in the volume of 'charge-to-payable bookings' and employee incentive earnings without a commensurate increase in output.[199] Malpractices in time reckoning also had the effect of boosting labour efficiencies to exaggeratedly high levels. After 18 departments had posted efficiencies of 150 per cent in 1979–80, IED observed that 'consistently high efficiency . . . raises doubts about correctness of time booking and quantity accounted for . . . and necessitates thorough check-up of documents and bookings'.[200]

It was to put a stop to all these abuses that the company decided to introduce a fresh scheme in June 1983 which it hoped would pave the

[197] Interview with C.R. Datta Gupta.

[198] Interview with S. Satish.

[199] Minutes management-union meeting, 29 January 1983. Distorting time keeping records, by entering excessive claims for work stoppages, was also not an uncommon practice among operatives at Hawthorne, the legendary American telecommunications equipment producer, site of Elton Mayo's pioneering experiments in industrial sociology. F. J. Roethlisberger and William Dickson, *Management and the Worker. An Account of a Research Program Conducted by the Western Electric Company, Hawthorne Works, Chicago,* Cambridge (Mass.), 1950, pp. 432–3, 445.

[200] IED note, 26 September 1980.

way for more 'realistic time bookings and efficiencies'.[201] In parallel, industrial engineering proceeded to establish time standards for several operations which had previously gone unmeasured, and so sharply reduced the scope for supervisory personnel to allot time under the 'charge-to-payable' head. However, whether or not the new incentive formula succeeded in eliminating the problem of pilferage is unclear. For among the fraudulent practices that shop officials had to contend with was the tendency among operatives working in the second or afternoon shift to steal components made by their co-workers in the morning shift which they then added to their own output. Already when devising the very first incentive plan, the management had expressed fears of workers making off with 'work-in-progress to show more production than what had actually been produced'.[202] Indeed, one report after mentioning that an operative had walked away with 120 metal brackets that had been kept for inspection, added that stores and the finishing department were regularly complaining of shortfalls between the output registered on the job cards and the quantities sent for inspection.[203] Company executives therefore wanted the work-in-progress stores be kept firmly locked at all times.

But similar precautionary measures were not, or could not be, envisaged with respect to the production of first shift workers. Pilferages, therefore, not only represented a constant source of tension on the shop floor, they also explained in part the paradox of individual output outweighing the total shop output on a certain number of occasions, though this anomaly could also be attributed to the 'fudging' of job cards by workers in collusion with inspectors and shop planners. Moreover, since stock verification was not carried out daily, contrary to the procedures, shop managers were rarely in a position to detect such cases of fraud on time and so avoid having to pay incentive.

Predictably enough, the union and workers responded with less enthusiasm to the jettisoning of the previous scheme. In the crossbar plating shop, output remained low for a number of months following the introduction of the new plan, employees being sorely disappointed with their meagre incentive earnings. On another occasion, we find the

---

[201] Ref. IED/O&M/68, 1 January 1985.
[202] IED note, nd.
[203] IED, 16 March 1963.

union accusing IED and shop officials of having 'trampled all the established norms while implementing incentives' after earnings showed an appreciable decrease in three machine shops.[204] Responding to the union's protests IED, however, attributed the lower incentive gains not so much to the application of tighter time standards, as to employee misuse in the past which had resulted in efficiency figures being inflated.

WORKER ACTIONS DENT EFFECTIVENESS OF INCENTIVES

The final set of constraints impinging on the effective functioning of the incentive plans related to worker actions. Two broad types of actions can be distinguished: categorial demands for improved incentive coverage, and attempts to protect incentive earnings. By far the most insistent of the groups pressing for higher incentives were the inspectors. Though classified as indirect staff together with supervisors, shop clerks and shop planners, inspectors received lower benefits than these three groups. Management officials justified this disparity on dual grounds. First, inspection staff were not directly connected with shop production activities, sharing no responsibilities, for instance, in co-ordinating the flow of inputs or outputs. Second, accurate standards could not be fixed to measure their performance. Moreover, unlike the other auxiliary shop personnel, inspectors formed a far more sizeable group, numbering over 1450 in 1978. So increasing their earnings would be a substantial cost for ITI.

Challenging the company's stand, in December 1977 inspectors in the crossbar division submitted a petition requesting equal treatment with the other three groups. Initially well disposed to the inspectors' claims, as it 'will motivate the . . . staff and speedy clearance of equipments at Inspection stage is anticipated', top management, however, finally decided otherwise.[205] It was no doubt aware that a positive answer on its part would trigger off a spate of similar demands from other departments such as methods, central planning, and plant maintenance.[206] But there

[204] Ref. IED/O&M/17, 7 June 1986.

[205] IED note, 15 March 1978.

[206] Demands for a readjustment of incentive earnings had already been raised by operatives in the transmission and switching R&D prototype machine shops as well as the strowger methods improvement cell. IED note, 17 April 1979.

was another more important reason for turning down the inspectors' demands. Senior executives apprehended, and quite rightly so as later events would prove, a deterioration in product quality in case inspectors were grouped with the other shop auxiliary personnel since their incentive payments would be directly dependent on the physical quantities produced by operatives. Consequently, inspectors would tend to be less strict in controlling defective parts so as to maximize their earnings by ensuring high output volumes.

Four years later inspectors renewed their appeal. This time the union also extended its support, less because it was convinced of the merits of the case, than with the objective of safeguarding the interests of operatives. For given the power inspectors disposed to reject or clear workers' output, the union feared that in case their demand went unmet they were likely to retaliate by creating trouble for operatives and denting the workers' incentive earnings.[207] The management, however, stayed firm on the position it had adopted in the past.[208] Yet, by 1986 inspectors had succeeded in winning their demand, and were placed in the same incentive group as the other auxiliary shop personnel. Our sources do not inform us of the reasons why the company changed its mind. But the consequences of its decision on product quality would be experienced soon enough.

A letter sent by the head of the Bangalore plant to divisional managers and IED in April 1987, or less than a year after the new incentive scheme came into effect, categorically stated that including the inspection department with the other indirect shop staff had 'resulted in non-conformity with quality standards at various stages, and rejections had become very high at the customer-inspection level'.[209] As officials had correctly anticipated, inspectors were progressively sacrificing quality levels at the anvil of higher incentive gains. An audit conducted shortly afterwards remarked that the existing scheme 'provides an attitude for increased incentive earnings at the cost of quality'.[210]

[207] Minutes management-union meeting Tel. Divn., 14 February 1983.

[208] IED note, 21 February 1984.

[209] Ref. EDB/36, 24 April 1987; Minutes management-union meeting, 18 July 1987.

[210] 25 January 1988 (IED files).

Malpractices associating inspectors and operatives only compounded the problem. In an anonymous letter addressed to the company, one operative bitterly protested against

certain Inspectors in Relay Adjustment (who) . . . are demanding <u>bribe</u> up to Rs. 50/- and above from each operators, to pass the relays . . . please save the operators from the clutches of Inspectors, and punish the culprits (sic).[211]

A security report confirmed that a group of ten inspectors and ten adjusters in this department had arrived at an understanding whereby the former cleared about 100 relays daily so as to enable operatives to reach the incentive ceiling of Rs 350 every month. 'As gratification for showing leniency while passing . . .' each inspector was collecting as much as Rs 500 monthly from the workers.[212] Pointing out that this had resulted in the 'large-scale failure' of relays during assembly and 'huge quantities of rejected relays' were lying dormant in the department, the report wanted IED to conduct surprise checks of the output passed by the inspectors.[213] Whether or not abuses of this nature were a generalized phenomenon affecting several departments is something we cannot answer, but lax inspection controls were a major contributory factor to ITI's dismal quality record.

In addition to the demand for higher incentives, workers also fought hard to conserve their existing incentive benefits, opposing any management measure that could lead to decreased earnings. Challenges from the shop floor, in fact, grew in intensity precisely at a time when the Bangalore factory was witnessing rapid technological evolution with the phasing out of the strowger and crossbar switches from the mid-1980s onwards, and when the company desperately needed flexibility in redeploying manpower as well as in ensuring adequate capacity utilization. But its plans were often foiled by workers.

In a discussion with the union in July 1987, after declaring that low

---

[211] Security Department files, January 1986. Emphasis as in original. Factory operatives were not the only victims of inspectors' rapacity. In a letter to ITI management, one ancillary owner complained that whereas inspection staff were typically in the habit of taking bribes of Rs 100 to 150 every month, an inspector in the plating department was now demanding Rs 200 on every batch of material supplied. Security Department files, 22 July 1981.

[212] Security Department note, 25 January 1986.

[213] ibid.

workloads in the strowger and crossbar divisions were translating into financial losses, top management protested that, despite the large number of surplus staff, workers here were resisting both the introduction of higher productivity measures and transfers to other production areas on the grounds that it would erode their incentive benefits.[214] Another document added that operatives were neither willing to work as a team 'when change is contemplated in product or process', nor to accept new assignments 'because of fear of loss of incentive earning opportunity'.[215] According to the security chief, workers even showed reluctance to rectify faults as it would mean losing incentive. In case officers exerted pressure,

workers say that quantum of work done by them should be boosted in the job card so that they can get incentive.[216]

Moreover, the price the company was frequently required to pay to secure the union and workers' consent to its measures took the form of 'incentive protection'. This meant paying operatives, who were assigned new jobs, incentive benefits equivalent to what they were earning in their earlier position until such time as they picked up the required skills of their new jobs. Such protection normally covered a period of three to six months, though extensions of up to one year were not uncommon especially with regard to new products whose technical specifications had not yet been 'frozen' or stabilized, and time standards fixed. But even this delay was considered insufficient in some instances, prompting the head of the Bangalore plant to write that the provision for incentive protection was being misused.

In the light of all these difficulties, it is not surprising that in July 1987, ITI management called for a thorough review of the existing incentive scheme, declaring that it had resulted in 'under utilization of capacity, deterioration in quality, resistance to launch new products/ projects', and that the 'Company's overall interest is affected'.[217] The following year, a four-man management committee came up with a proposal binding incentive payments to the shipment of the product to the customer, or in other words 'only when there is a return for the

[214] Minutes of management-union meeting, 18 July 1987.
[215] IED note, 26 November 1987.
[216] Ref. SY/RM/90–91, 26 November 1990.
[217] Note from Executive Director Bangalore Complex, July 1987.

company'. [218] As one document put it, 'the philosophy of final dispatch must be built up in the operator who now thinks only of his individual component or sub assembly'.[219] However, the demand squeeze provoked by deregulation obliged the company to altogether abandon the idea of reforming the mode of incentive payments. It was not until 1999 that the plan was again revived, and a fresh proposal submitted to the union at the Bangalore plant. The company also informed unions in all ITI plants of its intention to adjust upwards by 20–25 per cent the base efficiencies above which workers were entitled to earn incentives.[220] Yet, none of these points were actively pursued, neither during the wage negotiations, concluded in 2001, nor subsequently, thus raising serious doubts about just how determined the management was to realize its goals.

LOW QUALITY PRODUCTS IMPACT ON FUNCTIONING OF TELECOMMUNICATIONS NETWORK

In addition to the long delays in obtaining new connections, the growing waiting list, and extremely low telephone densities, the other defining trait of the Indian telecommunications network, prior to the reforms initiated by the Rajiv Gandhi government in the mid-1980s, was the abysmal quality of services. Erratic connections, disconnections, mishandled calls were all common occurrences. To make a successful local call, 2.5 attempts were required on an average.[221] The success rate for subscriber trunk dialling or automatic trunk calls was a paltry 20 per cent in 1985–86, while over a quarter of ordinary trunk calls failed to go through.[222] An explanation for the deficient functioning of the network resided, no doubt, in the shortcomings of P&T/DoT. The low levels of

---

[218] Incentive Scheme proposal, nd (1999); Corporate Office note, Ref. CPA/ADR-A/18, 29 September 1988.

[219] Incentive Scheme proposal, nd (1999).

[220] Management letter to union, 15 June 1999.

[221] *Fifth Interim Report of the Committe on Telecommunications*, p. 6. The figure tended to be much higher in reality, for in the big cities a small proportion of subscribers received the majority of all calls. In 1984–85, the number of faults per 100 telephones stood at 33.2 per month and the monthly average duration of the faults at 9.5 hours. DoT Annual Report, 1984–85.

[222] DoT, *Forty Years of Telecommunications*, p. 71.

qualification of its employees, inadequate training, extremely high absenteeism,[223] and careless work practices all severely tested its ability to provide reliable and efficient service.[224]

But the flawed and unreliable equipment supplied by ITI to its principal customer also contributed in good measure to the below-par performance of the telephone system. Like most mass production organizations, ITI interpreted quality control in a restricted manner, relying on testing-focussed procedures at each stage of the product cycle. This was before the concept of in-process self-inspection and total quality control, first conceived by Japanese firms, became watchwords in manufacturing, as indeed in other industries too. Specialist inspectors were entrusted with the task of ensuring that piece parts, sub-assemblies and final assemblies satisfied the prescribed norms as did raw materials and purchased components.

Generally speaking, the quality-through-inspection system contained three major drawbacks. First, because operatives did not directly share the responsibility for quality, defects quite often got passed on from one stage of the production process to the next, thereby tending to generate a multiplier effect. Even allowing for the existence of rigorous controls, inspection found it virtually impossible to guarantee zero errors. Second, and following from the above, rework was an integral feature of the system. Depending upon employers' success in inculcating concepts such as 'get it right the first time every time', the time and effort expended in correcting faults identified by inspection varied from one firm to another, but few could pretend to having totally eliminated rework. Third, the efficacy of the system was further undermined by the fact that the inspection process tended to slow down the pace of production and was expensive to operate, since it rested on the backs of a vast army of

---

[223] Absenteeism among telephone operators in particular sometimes exceeded 50 to 55 per cent, while nearly half the line maintenance personnel were thought to be illiterate. EC Report 1973, p. 63; Bella Mody, 'State Consolidation through Liberalization of Telecommunications', *Journal of Communications*, Vol. 45, No. 4, 1995, pp. 107–24.

[224] Even when measured by the yardstick of developing countries, productivity levels at the state carrier were highly unsatisfactory. In 1985 the number of main lines handled per employee was just 8.4, before rising to 28 a decade later, as against an average of 59 lines per employee for lower income Asia-Pacific countries. DoT Annual Report, 1984–85; *Asia-Pacific Telecommunication Indicators 2000*, Geneva, ITU, 2000, p. 65.

inspection staff. As far as ITI was concerned, the number of inspectors employed by the Bangalore plant had already shot up to 1461, out of a total of 10,821 operatives, by the late 1970s, or a ratio of roughly 1 inspector for every 7 workers.[225] Although controls by inspectors were reinforced by a further series of checks, conducted by both ITI and P&T/ DoT personnel, none of these measures yielded tangible benefits to users of telecommunication services in the country by way of making available to them superior quality products.

Even prior to the start of the liberalization process, P&T officials had repeatedly given vent to their unhappiness about the unreliability of the equipment turned out by its manufacturing arm. In early 1984, the parent concern directly submitted a note to the ITI board of directors in order to draw attention to the need to 'bring about improvements on highest priority'.[226] The note was particularly harsh in its criticism of the performance of indigenous products, notably transmission systems and telephones.

It is known that the production techniques, production processes and quality assurance schemes in regard to these equipment based on indigenous designs are not good enough to produce equipment to the quality required in a telecom network (sic).[227]

Earlier, a senior P&T executive had sought to

. . . impress upon the ITI that if adequate precautions are taken to supply the P&T with instruments of high quality, then the incidence of faults occurring on the instruments working in the field will also be automatically low . . . (and) require less maintenance effort . . . (sic).[228]

Between March 1979–81, rejection rates for telephone instruments averaged respectively 12.2 per cent and 20.9 per cent at the Bangalore and Naini units. The performance of the switching and, to a lesser extent,

---

[225] IED statistics. Approximately the same ratio obtained at the Hawthorne plant: at the peak of the economic boom in 1929, the inspection department employed about 5200 employees out of a total factory strength of 40,000. Joseph M. Juran, 'Early SQC Historical Supplement', *Quality Progress*, September 1997, pp. 73–81. I am grateful to Denis Bayart for the reference.

[226] P&T Board Memo of 1983–84, 15 February 1984.

[227] ibid.

[228] Ref. No 3–10/82-PHM, 20–22 September 1982.

transmission equipment was no more promising.[229] A report submitted by a World Bank consultant pointed out that it was not unusual for new subscribers to call in P&T repairmen three times within the first six months of getting a connection to attend to faulty instruments. But he attributed this as much to rough handling in the service carrier's warehouses and 'low standard installation work' as to poor quality control by ITI.[230]

Indeed, it was concerns about the 'telephone system . . . seem(ing) to have deteriorated steadily' that led to the constitution of a parliamentary fact finding committee with the express objective of reviewing the quality of ITI products.[231] In the committee's report, published in 1982, P&T claimed that defective telephone instruments accounted for 15 to 20 per cent of the faults in the telecommunications network, and switching equipment for another 10 per cent. The statistics would probably have painted an even more unfavourable picture had P&T inspection personnel insisted that the equipment comply with all the technical specifications. But as the secretary, Ministry of Communications, openly conceded, 'under compelling circumstances' the tutelary authority had no choice but to relax certain quality parameters and accept 'sub-standard supplies, knowing fully well that the telephone system would not give satisfactory service'.[232] Otherwise,

[229] Rejection Rates (percentages)

Equipment	1979–80	1980–81	1981–82
Telephones (B'lore)	11.57	12.82	na
Telephones (Naini)	24.2	17.7	na
Strowger (B'lore)	6.5	28.7	11.5
Transmiss'n (B'lore)	11.4	0.3	12
Crossbar (B'lore)			
i) Selector Frames	21.9	21.9	24.7
ii) Junction	35	29.4	27.8
iii) Register	42	37	25.4

Source: COPU 1982, p. 3.

[230] Review of Factory Operations, World Bank Technical Supervision Mission (Sixth, Seventh and Eight Telecommunications Projects), June-July 1981, Attachment 2, p. 3.
[231] COPU 1982, p. 27.
[232] ibid, p. 3.

applicants waiting for telephones will not get their connections, we (P&T) will not be able to fulfil our plan targets, our revenues will not start coming . . .[233]

In the wake of the parliamentary investigation, the supervisory ministry formulated a new approach to quality which it wished to see ITI embracing. As it correctly pointed out 'inspection is only *defect detection* (and) cannot ensure consistent quality or reliability of the telecom equipment What is required is *defect prevention*'.[234] In other words, P&T wanted the company to work towards building quality into the production system from the outset by instituting rigorous process controls, thereby enabling both sides to be less reliant on large numbers of inspectors to spot faults. The weight placed on 'quality assurance' over 'quality control' by the parent body was also significant. The latter was based on the notion that quality was a specialized function, targeting in the main the inspection and quality control departments, but not the rest of the organization. Quality assurance, on the other hand, as pioneered by the Japanese companies Nissan and Toyota, was a systematic activity, developed all the way from top management to the shop floor and covering practically all functional areas, directed at achieving the quality goals demanded by the customer.[235]

But if P&T officials had banked on ITI drawing inspiration from this total, all inclusive conception of quality, they were sorely disappointed. Rejections for telephones at the Bangalore plant continued to run well in excess of the prescribed norm of 2.5 per cent. Averaging 13.5 per cent from December 1985 to December 1986, the figure while declining slightly to 13.2 per cent between February and November 1988, reached as high as 18 per cent between April and October 1987.[236] Complaining to the Telecommunications Board about the performance of the 677 model which equipped most of the national network, the general manager of the Andhra Pradesh Circle claimed that close to half the total number of faults detected by, or brought to the attention of the

---

[233] ibid, p. 2.

[234] P&T Board Memo of 1983–84. Emphasis added.

[235] Izumi Nonaka, 'The Development of Company-Wide Quality Control and Quality Circles at the Toyota Motor Corporation and Nissan Motor Co. Ltd.', in S. Haruhito et al (eds.), *Fordism Transformed. The Development of Production Methods* in *the Automobile Industry*, Oxford, 1995, pp. 139–59.

[236] Minutes of Quality Assurance meeting, 24 April 1986; 14 August 1986; 13 February 1987; 3 May 1988; 28 July 1988; 3 January 1989.

circle, were located in the telephone instrument. According to him, faults occur due to manufacturer's inefficiency, bringing bad name to our field staff. Therefore, unless the quality of the instruments is improved, it may demoralize the field staff . . .[237]

Earlier, P&T had warned ITI that it had issued clear instructions to all circles not to accept 677 multi-line telephones 'unless the reliability problems are solved to the satisfaction of the customer'.[238] These problems, though, persisted since neither the Bangalore nor the Naini factory had taken any concerted measures to analyse and integrate the results of the fault data compiled by the P&T quality department.[239] Not surprisingly, the company found itself ranked in the lowest category in the new three-tier quality rating system drawn up by its biggest customer in 1991 to evaluate telephone manufacturers. In a letter addressed to the ITI chairman, the head of DoT's quality assurance wing justified this decision on the grounds that the department was receiving a large number of 'feedback complaints regarding mal-functioning of ITI made push-button phones'.[240]

The low quality characteristics of ITI products derived generally from material and process-oriented failures, though design errors were also not uncommon.[241] Whether or not the material faults evolved in the main from the government's import substitution policies and/or ITI's lack of production expertise, both of which were intertwined, is a question we are unable to answer. But in quite a few instances, faults could clearly

---

[237] Ref. D.O. No. TA/XM/42-Genl/86–87, 19 January 1987.

[238] Minutes of QA Meeting, 21 November 1986.

[239] Quality Status Report on External Plant, DoT Quality Assurance Wing, Bangalore, 10 March 1985, p. 4.

[240] Ref. No. 21–23/94-QA, 1 December 1991. Defects were not exclusive to the telephones manufactured by ITI. Between 15 to 20 per cent of the electronic push button instruments installed in the national network were failing every year. Meeting DoT-electronic push button manufacturers, 7 October 1993.

[241] From an analysis of field complaints over a two-year period with regard to strowger and the Pentaconta crossbar switching equipment, material defects accounted for 43 of the 66 cases listed, process defects, including poor workmanship, for eleven cases, design defects for six cases, design and material defects for two cases, material and process defects for one case, while the remaining three cases could have been either due to process or material defects. Status Report on Strowger Equipments, QSR-002; Status Report on Crossbar Equipments, QSR-003, P&T Quality Assurance Wing, Bangalore, April 1982.

be traced back to sub-standard domestically sourced raw materials and purchased components. To give but one example, a persistent problem the company encountered when utilizing indigenous flux cored solder was 'dry' or 'lump' soldering which entailed large scale rejections of printed circuit cards.[242] As the Ministry of Communications itself readily admitted,

(t)he quality of telephone instruments has suffered partly due to *the pressure on ITI from other Government agencies to use indigenous components* and raw materials which are not of the required quality ... The main handicap in making products of an acceptable quality is the absence of a good indigenous components base.[243]

The slow pace of technology induction due to the tight restrictions placed on acquiring foreign know-how as well as machinery also meant that ITI continued to depend on outdated manufacturing processes and machines. 'We had to virtually reinvent the wheel, do everything ourselves.'[244] Assembly techniques and testing facilities were badly in need of modernization. A foreign technical team from the World Bank visiting ITI in 1981 described telephone and dial assembly lines at the Bangalore and Naini plants as

excessively labour intensive and are prone to faulty production due to their primitive nature and reliance on operators' skills and attentions.[245]

Commenting on the wide variations in results during final testing at the Srinagar plant depending upon the way the material was handed, another World Bank report wrote that until 'urgent action' was taken to replace the 'completely obsolescent and unreliable equipment ... the quality of telephones assembled in this plant must be suspect ...'[246] For want of mechanized cutting and forming machines, components were generally hand formed and manually inserted into printed circuit boards. Apart from being time consuming, such work methods contributed to inferior

[242] Tel. Divn. note, 3 April 1987.

[243] COPU 1983, pp. 5–6. Emphasis added. Recourse to locally-sourced supplies, contend Brundenius and Goransson, had entailed making compromises, detrimental to quality and efficiency, not only in the design of equipment, but at all levels of the telecommunications system: production, installation and maintenance. 'Technology Policies in Developing Countries'.

[244] Interview with M.S. Jayasimha.

[245] Review of Factory Operations, p. 2.

[246] ibid, 1981, pp. 4–5.

quality by increasing the risk of bad joints due to contamination of the leads. The tool rooms, wrote one survey, 'are reasonably well equipped, although much of their plant is overdue for replacement'.[247] As a retired research engineer remarked, ITI lagged far behind European and Japanese telecommunications equipment manufacturers which relied heavily on automated and semi-automated processes to deliver high volume, economical and dependable products.

We were working in a closed environment, doing day-to-day routine work, so there was no time to improve process technology. We very badly needed foreign collaboration.[248]

To conclude from the above that ITI's dismal quality record was entirely the making of state policy interventions and technological deficiencies would, however, hardly be justified. A number of internally-induced factors, situated in the main in managerial inefficiencies, played an equally important part. The most immediate one was again end-year rush-work. With the bulk of the factory's annual output being generated during the final three months, quality was inevitably the prime casualty of the 'the lopsided production schedules' in the desperate race by the company to try and meet its physical objectives.[249] Testing and inspection procedures which were never adhered to very rigorously even at the best of times tended to become even more slack during this phase of feverish activity. As the secretary, Ministry of Communications, declared, although the parent authority had advised ITI to 'deliver your products more or less evenly throughout the year so that proper attention can be given to the quality of the product even by your own internal quality control, so that our quality control acceptance testing does not have to give relaxation', the management had been unsuccessful in introducing a 'new ethos' in the work culture of the factory.[250]

What we must now stress is that end-year rush-work only exacerbated

---

[247] ITI Factories Appraisal, p. 38.

[248] Interview with K. Nagaraj. Speaking in 1982, or prior to the introduction of electronic exchanges, the secretary, Ministry of Communications, felt that '…if you take into account the latest (technological) developments in advanced countries, we are lagging far behind and we have not yet reached a stage that obtained in advanced countries like USA and Japan even 10 years back'. COPU 1982, p. 16.

[249] Quality Status Report on External Plant, p. 4.

[250] COPU 1982, p. 2, 6.

the problem of poor quality. It was at best a secondary determinant; even had the company's endeavours to regulate production in a more balanced fashion fetched dividends it is doubtful whether the ultimate result would have been a substantial improvement in product performance. For the root cause of sub-standard quality lay in the absolute precedence the logic of quantity and volume enjoyed over the logic of quality in the management's hierarchy of priorities. From the early 1960s onwards, senior ITI executives channelled all their energies and resources in the direction of higher physical output so that they could satisfy the burgeoning demand requirements of a badly under-equipped network. As against P&T's annual requirements of 300,000 telephones annually, ITI was able to supply barely 200,000 sets, and the resulting 'extreme shortage . . . in the country has created considerable unrest about our telephone system'.[251]

Under constant pressure from P&T/DoT to maintain unbroken production flows, a task already fraught with difficulties on account of the endemic material shortages, the imperatives of quality constituted a supplementary constraint, and an unwelcome one at that too, as it often tended to disrupt the tempo and flow of work. Hence, company officials were only too willing to sacrifice customer concerns about quality at the anvil of higher output. In the words of one retired executive,

(w)e failed to recognize consumer complaints. The management's reaction was that P&T inspectors complain all the time, so no attention was paid to P&T's objections.[252]

In the context of the monopoly positions both P&T and ITI commanded for over three decades, the price to be paid for such a policy was also negligible. Moreover, it is also quite probable that management equated satisfying predetermined standards of precision and performance with increased operating costs.[253]

---

[251] EC Report 1973, pp. 31, 35. Although the number of new telephone connections provided by P&T had risen by almost 200 per cent in the decade from 1960 to 1970, the official waiting list for new connections had also progressed at virtually the same pace (195 per cent). In comparison, the growth in telephone production at the Bangalore plant of ITI had only been of the order of 142 per cent. P&T and ITI Annual Reports.

[252] Interview with Srinivasa Rao.

[253] Manufacture of Telecommunications Equipment in a Developing Country, ITI, nd, p. 83.

That quality was not the overriding preoccupation of ITI top management was amply evidenced by the fact that 'a well defined and documented quality assurance programme' simply did not exist until almost the early 1990s.[254] More significantly, one World Bank report cited a line official candidly declaring that quality control had no authority to halt production even if faulty components were being produced.[255] The subordination of quality to the exigencies of production was also doubly reflected in the subordinate status accorded to quality control in the organizational structure. Since the chief quality manager in each division reported to the divisional head, production was in a position to easily override quality directives, or insist on standards being relaxed as and when it suited its requirements.[256]

In deciding to harness the concerns of quality to the demands of production, ITI was not acting inconsistently with the logic of mass production where economies of scale were contingent upon high and stable volume flows. Nor was it behaving very differently from other big organizations, all of whom, believing that quality and quantity were incompatible virtues, had made identical strategic choices at one point of time or the other in their histories, as various scholars have shown. According to quality guru Joseph Juran, throughout the 1920s the top priority of line managers at Western Electric's celebrated Hawthorne Works was not to attain product quality but to meet output schedules.[257] Similarly, James Womack et al speak of the 'move the metal' mentality that characterized the mass production auto industry: regardless of defects

[254] ITI Factories-Appraisal, p. 42.

[255] Review of Factory Operations, Seventh Telecommunications Project (World Bank), October 1979, Attachment 2a, p. 72. Womack et al claim that any operative at Toyota was authorized to stop the assembly line the moment defects were observed. James P. Womack et al, *The Machine that Changed the World*, New York, 1990, p. 57, 79–80.

[256] In his account of the engine factory where he worked as an operative, Burawoy, after writing that quality control came under the responsibility of production, observes that the latter invariably defeated quality when it came to bargaining over a piece that inspection claimed had failed to meet specifications. *Manufacturing Consent*, pp. 56–7, 126, 227. Interestingly, in Soviet firms the inspection department was placed outside the scope of authority of the works manager precisely to safeguard its independence. David Granick, *The Red Executive. A Study of the Organization Man in Russian Industry*, London, 1960, p. 274.

[257] Juran, 'Early SQC Historical Supplement'.

circulating from one manufacturing stage to another, assembly lines were kept running in order to guarantee high yields.[258]

The indifferent attitude of the company's upper echelons to quality percolated downwards throughout the organization, and came to be shared by supervisors, inspection staff and workers alike. Notwithstanding the steady growth in the size of the inspection department, there was a drastic slackening in inspection controls which, combined with shoddy workmanship, gravely undermined quality. The P&T officials repeatedly voiced their dissatisfaction with lax testing by ITI personnel at all stages of the manufacturing cycle, holding this factor to be responsible for many of the faults identified in telephone instruments and switching equipment. To cite only one such instance, no less than 10 per cent of the defects noticed in one rotary telephone model were blamed on the 'lack of proper testing'.[259] Complaints about slipshod inspection practices could also be heard from within the company. A memo from a quality manager at the Bangalore plant mentioned that a third of the 100 push button telephones supplied to a private customer, Neyvelli Lignite, carried minor or major flaws because inspectors had neglected to carry out stage checks.[260] Acknowledging that inspectors and quality audit staff were 'not doing a thorough job', the head of the Bangalore telephone division believed that the problem of time indiscipline did not concern operatives alone; a number of inspectors were also taking advantage of managerial neglect to leave the factory on the sly after the lunch break.[261]

But lest we forget, top management itself had indirectly contributed to the decline in work ethics by agreeing to concede inspectors' demands for direct incentive. As documented earlier, this extremely imprudent measure, which made their incentive payments dependent on the physical output of operatives, opened the way for slack quality controls. In fairness to inspection personnel, it must be said that the reasons for inspection

---

[258] Womack et al, *Machine that Changed the World*, pp. 55–7. See also Patrick Fridenson, 'Fordism and Quality: The French Case, 1919–93', in *Fordism Transformed*, pp. 160–83; and Timothy R. Whisler, *The British Motor Industry 1945–1994. A Case Study in Industrial Decline*, Oxford, 1998, p. 340.

[259] Ref. COR/QS/005, 15 November 1996. See also Status Reports on Strowger Equipments, QSR-002 and Crossbar Equipments, QSR-003; and Minutes of QA meeting, 29 January 1991.

[260] Note ITI Bangalore telephone division, DGM/CQA/43, 20 May 1987.

[261] Interview with B.K. Sharma.

deficiencies could also be traced back to insufficient training and, more crucially, to the outdated testing procedures and infrastructure utilized by ITI. In the opinion of a World Bank committee, inspection methods in general were 'not suitable for a factory of the size and complexity of ITI'.[262] Recommendations to modernize testing systems also remained on the whole unimplemented, partly due to a lack of resources. Only in 1986–87, following the tie-up with the Italian company, Face, would ITI succeed in securing relatively sophisticated testing facilities for telephone production. But a decade later much of this equipment had again become obsolete, and with the company engulfed by a deepening financial crisis from the mid-1990s onwards the question of replacing it just did not arise. [263]

As in the case of lax inspection controls, poor standards of workmanship were also both an important cause and a symptom of the overall deterioration in product performance. An internal assessment of the quality of ITI telephones, undertaken in 1977 at the Bangalore plant, after stressing the necessity of dust-free conditions for the manufacture of certain critical sub-assemblies so as to minimize defects, noted that 'all the components' required for assembling these two products 'had dust accumulated on them and they are being used . . . even without cleaning'.[264] Certain parts were not being cleaned after soldering, nor were workers utilizing any of the gauges provided to check the functioning of the sub-assemblies, thereby contributing to a further lowering of quality levels. Likewise, human errors accounted for a significant share of the defects, as much as 80 per cent of the total going by the management's

---

[262] ITI Factories Appraisal, p. 43, 49. Inappropriate inspection techniques partly explained why defects missed by in-process inspection, but revealed subsequently by quality audit checks, were of the order of 5 per cent or double the established norms. Whereas big foreign factories had adopted statistical sampling plans long ago, ITI continued to conduct fixed percentage checks, a technique widely held to be both inconclusive and uneconomical.

[263] On at least two occasions the finance department rejected proposals submitted by telephone division officials in Bangalore to purchase new testing sets. Tel. Divn. notes, 14 October 1998; undated (2001).

[264] Report of Committee for Assessing Quality of ITI Telephone Instruments, p. 1. But as the company itself recognized, the dust-free room with forced draught ventilation that had been built for receiver manufacture 'is very ineffective and noisy and pushes up dust'.

estimates, in the assembly of printed circuit boards.[265] However, as company officials themselves conceded, a proportion of these mistakes were unavoidable. The presence of an aging labour force meant that many operatives no longer possessed the sharp vision and/or the nimble fingers required to manipulate and insert the minute components on the printed cards with precision.[266] Moreover, accustomed to handling electro-mechanical components that were larger in size, they experienced considerable difficulties in switching over to smaller electronic components, especially at an advanced stage of their working lives.

The failure to respect operating procedures was a supplementary reason for faults. In order to ensure the optimal performance of components like transducers, transmitters and receivers, these had to be assembled in a totally dust-proof environment. The company had provided air conditioning facilities only to find workers repeatedly keeping 'many windows and doors . . . open allowing dust to enter'.[267] Workers defended their actions on health grounds, arguing that air conditioning aggravated the respiratory ailments afflicting a number of them. Line managers also complained that, notwithstanding instructions to the contrary, operatives continued to violate 'process discipline' by either not wearing the special rubber footwear they had been provided with to keep the dust out, or wearing it even outside the transducer assembly department.[268] Thus,

operators can be seen wearing rubber *chappals* to cloak rooms, canteens and even on wet roads. Rubber *chappal* soles having large cavities are thus carrying more dust and mud lumps than normal shoes (sic).[269]

Frustrated by these every-day acts of 'resistance', the management finally abandoned its attempts to enforce these procedures, arguing that the design improvements it had incorporated in transducer production had

---

[265] The three most common kinds of worker-related faults identified were missing components, wrong assemblies (for example, a diode inserted in the place of a capacitor, or a 100 ohm resistor in the place of a 1k ohm resistor), and improper soldering.

[266] In 1987, 5193 employees, or 28.7 per cent of the total workforce at the Bangalore plant, were aged between 46 to 55 years. Personnel Department Statistics. Subsequently, when I conducted my field observation in 2001 in the printed circuit card section of the Bangalore telephone division (see chapter 6), the youngest of the 20 operatives working here was aged 50 years.

[267] Tel. Divn. note, Ref. E/PD/144, 22 March 1996.

[268] Tel. Divn. note, 8 October 1994.

[269] Tel. Divn. note, Ref. FMT66/189, 2 March 1994.

dispensed with the need for a dust-controlled work environment.[270] But an internal document underlined the company's implication as well in the errors committed by operatives. Adequate information and guidance was not given when launching the production of a new printed circuit card. Suggestions made by workers tended to be ignored. Nor did requests for the provision of good quality tools, jigs and card carriers receive consideration.[271] Similarly, poor housekeeping by the management further pushed up rejection rates. Quality meetings constantly referred to DoT officials raising objections to the 'continuing bad upkeep and handling of telephones' which were scratched and dusty.[272]

If poor workmanship translated into poor quality equipment, it also generated, by all accounts, fairly high levels of wastage. Scrap allowance norms theoretically varied between 2 to 10 per cent depending upon the type of raw material utilized, and 1 to 2 per cent with respect to certain components.[273] Even though precise data is unavailable with us, the massive numbers of shop orders that remained pending spoke for the limited success the management enjoyed in restricting waste to the above limits. Factory regulations prescribed that all shop orders be closed within a period of six months. Moreover, for a given item no more than two shop orders were supposed to run concomitantly so as to assure accountability for the material used. However, these procedures were progressively diluted. Whenever scrap levels exceeded the norm stipulated in a given shop order resulting in lower output, a fresh shop order would be issued and material drawn on that to make good the shortfall, which in turn necessitated releasing a new shop order, with the process repeating itself until the production of a new component or sub-assembly got underway. Consequently, a number of shop orders did not materialize fully. In 1988, the statutory audit, after observing the continuing 'large

[270] Interview with B.K. Sharma.

[271] Tel. Divn. note, 15 September 2001.

[272] Minutes of ITI-DoT quality meeting, 27 October 1989, 13 July 1990; Ref. DGM(CQA)/38, 12 December 1988. On the importance of housekeeping and maintaining cleanliness in the workplace, both of which serve as markers of orderly production techniques and efficient management of workers see Cohen, *Organiser à l'aube du taylorisme*, pp. 163–4; and Michelle Perrot, 'Travailler et produire: Claude-Lucien Bergery et les débuts du management en France', in *Melanges d'Histoire sociale offerts à Jean Maitron*, Paris, 1976, pp. 177–90.

[273] Replies to Expert Committee on Public Undertakings on Material Management, November 1980.

delays' in closing a number of shop orders, wrote categorically that in many instances

. . . there were huge differences between the expected quantity of output and actual quantity delivered against such shop orders . . .[274]

An enquiry into five shop orders at the telephone division revealed an average shortfall of 48.5 per cent between the quantity ordered and the quantity delivered. Or, to put it slightly differently, roughly half the material handed over to the shop tended to be scrapped. In the case of crossbar (six shop orders), the figure stood even higher at 67.7 per cent; on three shop orders at the strowger and transmission divisions, waste averaged respectively 22.5 per cent and 70.8 per cent.[275]

ITI PRODUCTS FACE COMPETITIVE DISADVANTAGE

What effect did the regulatory framework and managerial inefficiencies have on the cost of ITI products? If the price of telecommunications equipment did not unduly preoccupy the management up to the early 1980s, with the advent of competition it would be impossible to ignore the issue. At a meeting held in 1988, the telecommunications secretary wanted the company to review the pricing of its telephone instruments which 'is rather higher' than that supplied by private domestic firms.[276] Other government customers such as the railways, state electricity boards and Doordarshan had also complained about the high cost of PAXs, PABXs and multi-line phones manufactured by the company when compared with that of imported equipment.[277]

For want of information we are not in a position to compare the competitivity of ITI-made products during the pre-deregulation era with those manufactured by transnational corporations. But it would be safe to assume the existence of a substantial price differential, as the subsequent opening of the telecommunications equipment segment so brutally exposed. Even allowing for lower labour costs, which we cannot take for granted in view of over manning and the generous social benefits afforded

[274] CAG Report 1987–88.
[275] CAG Report 1992, p. 65.
[276] Minutes of Performance Review Meeting, 6 March 1988.
[277] Ref. EDB/6, 24 April 1986.

Table 3.1: ITI Sales and Profits (1951–52 to 2002–03)

(all figures in millions of rupees)

Year	Sales	Profit (after tax)	Year	Sales	Profit (after tax)
1951–52	15.96	0.178*	1977–78	921.6	58
1952–53	19.12	0.457*	1978–79	929.3	45.5
1953–54	29.19	0.236	1979–80	1099.7	64.2
1954–55	30.24	1.07*	1980–81	853.9	19.3
1955–56	25.89	2.59*	1981–82	1572.6	104.3
1956–57	27.44	2.35	1982–83	1820.5	156.5
1957–58	30.84	1.10	1983–84	2121.1	125.1
1958–59	33.44	1.19	1984–85	2369.3	155.1
1959–60	35.84	1.41	1985–86	2995.3	126.6
1960–61	42.36	1.85	1986–87	4407	274.9
1961–62	56.40	2.49	1987–88	5084.8	167.8
1962–63	77.28	4	1988–89	6251.8	275.7
1963–64	93.04	5.93	1989–90	9587.5	294.8
1964–65	103.17	5.78	1990–91	9784.6	360.7
1965–66	125.22	7.43	1991–92	10,847	572.3
1966–67	160.15	13.19	1992–93	14,8395	858.9
1967–68	203.3	15.32	1993–94	15,272.5	843.5
1968–69	212.5	15.29	1994–95	10,366.2	(–819.1)
1969–70	213.8	14.98	1995–96	7826.2	(–2839.6)
1970–71	259.5	18.59	1996–97	10,212.1	(–509)
1971–72	335.1	24.31	1997–98	12,630.5	152.6
1972–73	419	22.39	1998–99	15,390.9	271.0
1973–74	498.3	31.8	1999–2000	20,851.8	457.9
1974–75	635.1	36	2000–01	21,442	275.5
1975–76	753.7	37.1	2001–02	23,170	220
1976–77	880.9	53.8	2002–03	17,950	(–3750)

Note: * before tax; figures within brackets show losses.
Source: ITI Annual Reports.

Sales-Profit (1970–71 to 2002–03)

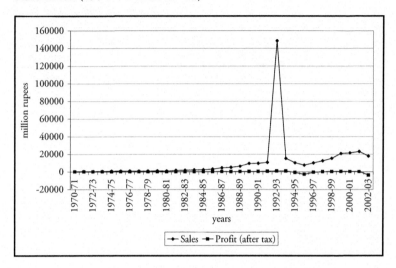

to ITI employees, a number of variables placed ITI at a huge cost disadvantage *vis-à-vis* its foreign rivals: lower physical output per worker, outdated processes and machinery, highly labour intensive work practices, high levels of vertical integration, high manufacturing and operating costs, and sub-optimal capacity utilization. To round off this red list, we need also mention government and DoT policies, not to speak of managerial shortcomings in various areas together with the near-total absence of cost-consciousness that characterized the functioning of the company during the monopoly years. The combined effect of all these structural constraints on the efficiency of the company need hardly be underestimated. According to a foreign consultant, the selling price of approximately $40 quoted by P&T for a telephone in the late 1970s was equivalent to the cost of a comparable instrument manufactured in Australia. Labour costs there, though, were approximately eight times higher than those prevailing in India, revealing in the bargain the low levels of productivity prevailing in ITI.[278]

To take the case of policy-induced pressures on production costs, by pushing up the prices of locally-sourced raw materials import substitution strategies also invariably caused finished goods to be more expensive,

---

[278] ITI Factories Appraisal, p. 37.

creating a vicious cycle in the process.[279] Indeed, the higher unit prices of electronic telephone instruments manufactured by ITI arose from its total dependence on an indigenous producer of certain kinds of transistors and diodes which leveraged its monopolistic position to sell these components at prices three to four times in excess of those quoted by foreign firms.[280] A similar issue of opportunistic overcharging plagued the supplies of another critical item, moulding powder.

However, as top executives themselves acknowledged, internal operational inefficiencies also played no small role in inflating the cost of ITI products. After officials from the company's sales offices had expressed concern on several occasions about ITI equipment struggling to find a ready market as they were overpriced, the management, diagnosing the likely causes of high costs, cited several elements.[281] One of them was obsolete processes: the company had neither moved quickly enough in embracing improvements in manufacturing practices, nor in substituting cheaper raw materials. In fact, in the mid-1960s, alongside a conventional methods department, a methods improvement cell had been set up with a view to updating manufacturing processes. The experiment, however, left almost no impact on production techniques. A casualty of departmental rivalries, the cell was rapidly absorbed by methods and reduced to executing routine tasks.[282] A second reason advanced by the management for high costs concerned the failure to sufficiently enlarge its vendor base for some imported and indigenous supplies. Finally, high levels of wastage and lax time standards were incriminated for the negative influence they exercised on pricing. Since timings had been 'fixed long back with reference to old type of equipment' and processes 'some of the hours which we have been claiming on our products are found to be excessive'.[283]

To this bill of shortcomings, two other elements could be added: poorly conceived suggestion schemes, and the absence of a rigorous cost

---

[279] In practice not only infant industries, but elderly incompetents were afforded protection from foreign competition, thus giving rise to a high cost industrial structure which could not operate except in a sheltered domestic market. Ahluwalia, *Industrial Growth in India*, pp. 112–26.

[280] Replies to Task Committee on Indigenization, nd.

[281] Ref. EDB/6, 24 April 1986.

[282] Interview with Srinivasa Rao.

[283] Ref. EDB/6, 24 April 1986.

accounting system.[284] By failing to offer attractive enough rewards, the various suggestion schemes, ever since their inception in 1949, generated an extremely lacklustre response from workers, insufficiently motivated to place their fund of technical practical knowledge 'freely' at the company's disposal.[285] Consequently, the company cut itself off from a potentially invaluable wellspring of ideas which, conjoined with its own endeavours to make ITI products more competitive, could have enabled the company to reap tremendous benefits. In fact, the issue of inadequate compensation, and the need to enhance it, had been recognized by the management as early as in 1961.[286] But as one retired official bluntly stated, there was no incentive to develop an effective suggestion scheme since there was no urgency to compress costs, at least during the monopoly years.[287]

The data available is extremely lacunary, but between 1971–72 and 1974–75 the number of suggestions received dropped from 149 to 102.[288] After questioning both workers and officers, a government fact-finding team attributed this unsatisfactory situation to two possible reasons: ignorance of the existence of the plan, and delays in implementing suggestions and distributing rewards. Employee indifference waxed even stronger a decade or so later. For the year 1988–89, for instance, the Bangalore unit registered barely 42 contributions, of which 11 were accepted, while the size of the rewards handed out was even lower than the sum paid in the early 1970s.[289] In the aftermath of deregulation, top

[284] The introduction of suggestion schemes within taylorist work organizations exposes one of the pretentions of scientific management as an ideology, namely that regardless of their efforts it is not possible for employers to completely dispossess workers of their knowledge of production processes.

[285] On the efficacy of suggestion plans in promoting productivity improvements and cost reductions see, *inter alia*, Michael Cusumano, *The Japanese Automobile Industry. Technology and Management at Nissan and Toyota*, Cambridge (Mass.), 1991, p. 357; Pascale Quincy Lefebvre, 'Le système social Michelin de 1945 à 1973 ou l'epuisement d'un modèle', in A. Gueslin (ed.), *Michelin, les hommes du pneu. Les ouvriers Michelin à Clermont de 1940 à 1980*, Paris, 1999, p. 113, 132; Nicolas Hatzfeld, *Gens d'usine. 50 ans d'histoire à Peugeot-Sochaux*, Paris, 2002, pp. 98–102, 317–19.

[286] EC Report 1961, p. 23.

[287] Interview with Srinivasa Rao.

[288] A Study of Management Styles, p. 71. See also Annual Reports, 1971–72 and 1972–73.

[289] Personnel Department note, 30 September 1989, The overall savings realized by the plant amounted to Rs 54,495 against which rewards of Rs 2175 were handed out.

management admitted that low monetary rewards explained why the number of suggestions trickling in every year was totally disproportionate to the size of the organization. It therefore suggested increasing the sums distributed. But the increases proposed were apparently not substantial enough to convince employees to participate more actively in the scheme. For according to a circular dated June 1999, notwithstanding 'employees' potential', the company had received very few suggestions over the last two years.[290]

At the same time, ITI products were invariably overpriced because, in the absence of a well-defined cost accounting system, managers did not possess the means to precisely calculate input costs.[291] According to one official report, the costing practices followed by the company 'does not provide for an effective control on the cost of the product and affects the profitability of the undertaking'.[292] Subsequently, an ITI chairman would express surprise at the inability of unit heads to accurately determine product costs, 'making it difficult to give proper quotations while going in for tender bidding'.[293] By far the most serious flaw in internal procedures was that while standard costs were computed for each product, actual costs were not compiled under this head, thereby rendering impossible comparisons with standard costs. Moreover, even standard costs were not an entirely reliable indicator for controlling expenditures.[294] At the same time, as the company itself admitted, data on cost variations, obtained upon completion of the shop order, was often collected with a delay of two to three months, and hence tended to be 'of limited use for control or corrective purpose'.[295]

Strongly advised by one parliamentary body in the early 1970s to put its 'costing system on a sound footing', top management, however, made no attempt to do so even after an interval of a decade and a half.[296] For

[290] Personnel Dept. Circular No. 4241, 29 June 1999.

[291] Interestingly, state-owned British Motor Corporation suffered from much the same handicap in the late 1960s. Whisler, *British Motor Industry*, p. 56, 75, 89.

[292] COPU 1973, p. 85. See also CAG Report (Commercial), Part VI, Comprehensive Appraisal of the Working of Indian Telephone Industries Ltd., 1970, pp. 41–5.

[293] Corporate Office note, 22 September 1997.

[294] Not only did the management fail to systematically integrate variations in material prices, but cost breakdowns for each component (raw materials, labour and overheads) were available only at the first stage of production, the manufacture of components.

[295] Replies submitted to COPU on Productivity, p. 34.

[296] COPU 1973, p. 85. The Third Plan had already highlighted the failure of public

we find an audit report, examining the functioning of the flagship Bangalore plant in 1988, uncovering much the same and other defects.[297] As the report noted, the prevalence of higher actual costs as compared with standard costs, and the growing gap between the two, was indicative of the 'absolute lack of cost control measures'.[298] Such organizational slack, one is tempted to argue, was only in the order of things. Given that the cost-plus pricing formula concluded with its parent authority assured the company of systematically making profits, manifesting a sense of cost-consciousness was in no way incumbent upon ITI management. Neatly resuming the situation, a former director of the Bangalore plant declared:

> ITI was never put to the test in respect of costs. That was a basic issue . . . The cost-plus system protected inefficiencies in ITI. Extra labour, extra overheads would all be absorbed by P&T. ITI was not bothered because P&T paid all our costs; P&T was not bothered because it could go on increasing tariffs . . . So we continued to work in the same old way for many years.[299]

In conclusion, emphasizing the organizational dysfunctions of ITI should not be interpreted to read as an endorsement of a Darwinist 'survival of the fittest' type theory of industrial evolution. As Steven Tolliday and Jonathan Zeitlin have noted, empirical research on business failure casts doubts that the surviving firms are in any way the most efficient or profitable. Unsuccessful firms, the two authors believe, are eliminated not so much on the basis of objective judgements about past performance as on subjective assessments of future prospects.[300] Having said this, an explanation of the unsatisfactory performance of ITI must

---

enterprises to employ cost accounting and other management tools on a systematic basis. *Third Plan*, p. 269.

[297] CAG Report 1987–88.

[298] ibid. The variation between standard and actual costs over this four-year period at the main Bangalore plant, while averaging 4.2 per cent, rose from 1.4 per cent in 1983–84 to 8.8 per cent in 1986–87. Buttressing this lack of cost consciousness was the isolation of the finance function from the organizational mainstream in public sector enterprises. Hiten Bhaya, 'Public Sector: Colossus with Feet of Clay?' *EPW*, Vol. XVIII, No. 22, 28 May 1983, pp. M50–M66.

[299] Interview with Srinivasa Rao.

[300] S.Tolliday and J. Zeitlin, 'Employers and Industrial Relations Between Theory and History', in *idem* (eds.), *The Power to Manage. Employers and Industrial Relations in Comparative Historical Perspective*, London, 1991, pp. 1–31.

take into account the interplay between the overall policy environment, market structure, and managerial shortcomings. For certain, a number of the operational difficulties that confronted the company owed as much to the bureaucratic logic prescribing the workings of the regulatory regime as to the omissions of the parent ministry. Nevertheless, it cannot be denied that the disruptive impact of policy-induced inefficiencies often tended to be exacerbated by the failures of top management.

Furthermore, even allowing for the fact that the line separating managerial shortcomings *per se* from policy-induced constraints in explaining several of the blockages weighing down upon the effective functioning of state-owned enterprises is often quite indistinguishable, allowing key personnel to generally escape censure, ITI officials had to assume entire responsibility for several of the deficiencies that progressively cropped up. This was particularly true in areas such as the implementation of incentive and suggestion schemes, establishing time standards, enforcing quality controls, and the exercise of discipline where the management could deploy its command prerogatives with unrestricted discretion. So while recognizing the extent to which government intervention in corporate strategy formulation deprived ITI executives of a large chunk of autonomy and operational flexibility, we must also not ignore that heteronomy can operate as a convenient cover to minimize or mask managerial negligence.

The exclusive market power enjoyed by ITI for three and a half decades, together with the cost-plus pricing system, furnished a fertile terrain where what one ITI chairman called a 'culture of monopoly' could easily strike deep roots. A pervasive sense of complacency developed from top to bottom where, on the one hand, change was either shunned or resisted, and, on the other, work ethics were allowed to steadily decline, even as a strict adherence to procedural formalities continued to be stressed. The point that must be emphasized is that in the absence of competition, and with P&T/DoT unwilling to impose sanctions, the price the company was required to pay for end-year rush-work, delivery delays or poor fund realization, was minimal in the years preceding the opening up of the telecommunications equipment segment. Therefore there was little incentive for it to take any remedial measures. Even subsequently, the financial lifejacket that soft-budget constraints provided greatly reduced the urgency for action.

Moreover, the total absence of reward mechanisms sustained and reinforced the growth of the 'culture of monopoly'. Just as public sector top managers were almost never sanctioned for their errors, they were also rarely rewarded financially for their achievements. Or as one author put it, 'proving merit is as impossible as proving incompetence'.[301] Unlike Soviet-era managers who received handsome bonuses for fulfilling, or over-fulfilling production targets, the government never considered it worth while to introduce a comparable system in India to stimulate the public sector executive cadre. So in a corporate structure where individual merit obtained no material compensation, the incentive, correspondingly, to explore and find new, more efficient and productive organizational avenues simply did not exist.

[301] Bhaya, 'Colossus with Feet of Clay?' p. M51.

chapter four

The Advent of Competition
A Fallout of Global Telecommunications Deregulation

The launch of economic reforms in July 1991 emphasizing the adoption of a pro-business cum pro-market developmental strategy clearly represented a watershed in the trajectory of the post-colonial state.[1] At the same time, it must not be forgotten that from the early 1980s itself competitive pressures had begun to rock certain branches of Indian industry.[2] One such segment was the manufacture of telecommunications equipment which witnessed the elimination of some, but not all, entry barriers. Thus the loss of ITI's monopoly position

---

[1] On the conceptual distinction between a business-oriented model of economic growth as opposed to a market-oriented one see Atul Kohli, 'Politics of Economic Growth in India, 1980–2005', *EPW*, Vol. 41, Nos. 13 and 14, 1 and 8 April 2006, pp. 1251–9 and 1361–70.

[2] The former Reserve Bank of India governor, I.G. Patel, for one, dates the starting point of India's liberalization process to the New Economic Policy initiated by the Rajiv Gandhi government in 1985. *Economic Reforms and Global Change*, New Delhi, 1998. However, others argue that the package of measures launched in the early 1990s was 'very different from the incrementalist approach' to reforms adopted during the mid-1980s. Montek Singh Ahluwalia, 'India's Economic Reforms', in R. Cassen and V. Joshi (eds.), *India: The Future of Economic Reform*, New Delhi, 1996, pp.13–29 (citation p. 15).

predated the dramatic transformations inaugurated by the new liberalized industrial policy of 1991. These macro-level policy interventions radically altered market conditions and therefore had manifold consequences on the corporate sphere of action. No longer guaranteed of a stable and lucrative outlet for its products, not only would ITI perforce have to lock horns with a raft of big and small private firms, its interactions with the DoT would also undergo a sea change.

The coming of competition set into motion a chain of events and policy moves that would blow apart the mutually exclusive relationship the industrial arm and its parent administration and principal customer had enjoyed for over three decades. With the stakes transformed for each side the terms of the alliance were fundamentally reshaped, and the bonds of reciprocal dependency that had united both sides in the past giving way to unequal dependency. Top ITI managers were persuaded that 'hawks in the DoT were intent on teaching us a lesson' now that the state carrier had the choice of turning to private firms for equipment supplies.[3] Having failed to adopt a 'customer friendly attitude *vis-à-vis* DoT' in the past, these executives believed that the public sector company would now pay a high price in the changed business scenario.[4] Future events did not prove them wrong.

For analytical purposes, it is convenient to break down the sequence of developments into three interlocking phases. The first extended from 1984–91 during which only a portion of ITI's activity was exposed to competitive pressures. The second phase ran from 1991–97 when the full blast of competition hit the firm and it recorded losses for three consecutive years. The final phase, stretching from 1997–2003, saw an ephemeral recovery in the company's fortunes before it plunged again into a new and deeper financial crisis. The fall-out from deregulation was therefore experienced relatively progressively, and even during the second phase, ITI continued to post profits until 1994–95. This was true for certain years even after 1997. Separating events in this manner presents the advantage of overcoming the pitfalls inherent in scholarship of reifying a process whose outcome was by no means predetermined. For if a long-term perspective, by threading together the disparate set of developments into a coherent unbroken strand, enables us to synthesize the entire period

---

[3] Interview with Srinivasa Rao.
[4] ibid.

as one characterized by an irremediable decline in the company's market position, this is essentially an *ex post* construction, and it is crucial to avoid interpreting the decline as something inevitable or linear.

This is all the more necessary since the front-line actors themselves, managers and workers, are unlikely to have perceived ITI's predicament in this manner, viewing its difficulties more as a series of short-term crises, each unlinked to the other, rather than as a continuous chain. Such a periodization also enables us to distinguish the influence exercised by various factors on the company's performance during the different phases. For in addition to policy orientations and administrative interface, another factor that would prove decisive in determining the health of ITI in the post-liberalization era was technology. The company's acute dependence on external sources for its technology needs had serious consequences on its capacity to mount an effective challenge to the domination of transnational corporations. The rapid evolution from wired to wireless communication would also leave it totally unprepared to respond to the new demands of DoT.

* * *

As analysts have noted, the commitment of the Rajiv Gandhi-led Congress (I) government (1984–89) to liberalizing the economy, while initially strong progressively weakened over time with the mounting political difficulties faced by the government and the decline in the electoral fortunes of the ruling party.[5] One area, however, where official policies did leave an enduring imprint was telecommunications. The changes introduced during these years were by far the most significant in the history of post-independent India until the reform wave of the 1990s, and radically recast the contours of the telecommunications sector. 'For the first time consumer interest became a top priority' even as telecommunications were made accessible to greater numbers, especially in small cities and rural areas, with the help of technology developed indigenously by C-DoT. As mentioned in chapter two, the research

---

[5] Joshi and Little, *India: Macroeconomics and Political Economy 1964–1991*, 1994, pp. 62–4; Atul Kohli, 'The Politics of Economic Liberalization in India', in E. Suleiman and J. Waterbury (eds.), *The Political Economy of Public Sector Reform and Privatization*, Boulder, 1990, pp. 364–88.

organization, headed by Satyen Pitroda, itself owed its birth exclusively to the patronage extended by Rajiv Gandhi.[6]

A certain number of institutional transformations also characterized this period.[7] Indeed, the organizational framework within which the P&T had operated since the colonial epoch was for the first time subjected to overhaul. The bifurcation of P&T and the setting up of a separate department DoT, with control over all telecommunication functions in January 1985, as well as the creation of two new corporate entities Videsh Sanchar Nigam Limited (VSNL) and Mahanagar Telephones Nigam Limited (MTNL), to mention only a couple of key initiatives, would lay the foundations for the second wave of institutional reforms in the mid-1990s. Finally, as part of the drive to liberalize industry, the Rajiv Gandhi government decided in March 1984 to open up the manufacture of customer premises equipment (telephones, fax machines, modems, PBXs, PABXs) to private sector companies. For ITI, it signalled the first breach in the monopoly hold that it had exercised over the domestic telecommunications equipment market since its inception in 1948. Intersecting with similar endeavours in the US, Britain and Japan,[8] it is tempting to interpret this convergence in telecommunications deregulation as a good illustration of what has been described as 'policy bandwagoning' or emulation.[9] Since states tend to frame similar general

---

[6] Balashankar, *Golden Era of Indian Telecommunications*, p. 32.

[7] For details see M. B. Athreya, 'India's Telecommunications Policy: A Paradigm Shift', *Telecommunications Policy*, Vol. 20, No. 1, January-February 1996, pp. 11–22; Rekha Jain, 'A Review of the Indian Telecom Sector', in S. Morris (ed.), *India Infrastructure Report 2001*, New Delhi, 2001, pp. 189–210.

[8] The monopoly exercised by AT&T over the US market for nearly nine decades formally ended on 31 December 1983. In Britain, the first licence to a private service provider (Mercury) was granted in February 1982, followed by the Thatcher administration privatizing British Telecom in November 1984. In Japan, the change in NTT's status from a public monopoly to a corporation occurred in April 1985. Chantal Ammi, *La concurrence dans les télécoms*, Paris, 1998, pp. 26–50; Bancel-Charensol, *La déréglementation des télécommunications*.

[9] John Ikenberry, 'The International Spread of Privatization Policies: Inducements, Learning and "Policy Bandwagoning"', in *Political Economy of Public Sector Reform*, pp. 88–110. 'Bandwagoning', in fact, can also be understood as a good example of what has come to be known as coercive isomorphism where powerful nation states and/or transnational organizations exert pressures for homegeneity on weaker states. See Witold J. Henisz et al., 'The Worldwide Diffusion of Market-Oriented Infrastructure Reform, 1977–1999', *American Sociological Review*, Vol. 70, No. 6, December 2005, pp. 871–97.

goals, governing elites monitoring political change abroad may seek to emulate successful policy innovations in anticipation of similar economic and political rewards.

TELEPHONE BUSINESS OF ITI HIT BY LOW DEMAND

From the perspective of the DoT, the decision of the Rajiv Gandhi government to inject a dose of competition into one sphere of telecommunications manufacturing was very much a step in the right direction. It promised to provide at least a partial solution to some of the problems that the department had been facing and trying, unsuccessfully, to overcome for a number of years. The most intractable of these, of course, was the huge pent-up demand for telephone connections. By 1985, the waiting list for new connections had climbed to about 842,000, while the average waiting period stood at 2.67 years compared to 1.5 years in 1980.[10] Further, because of insufficient capital investments, demand for telephones, as reflected in waitlist figures, was growing at a faster pace than the number of new lines installed.[11]

With the deregulation of the subscriber equipment segment in 1984, some of these bottlenecks would disappear. The inflow of private investment created much-needed additional capacity in the area of telephone manufacturing. Between March 1984 and April 1988, as many as 49 letters of indent and industrial licences were issued for the fabrication of electronic push button instruments in both the private and joint sectors.[12] The industry would, in fact, soon be saddled with high levels

[10] Mani, 'Technology Acquisition and Development'. That the registered waitlist does not indicate the full potential demand for basic services is well known. There are also significant variations over the national average with regard to the waiting period. Depending on the geographical area and the application category, the actual delay before obtaining a phone could take as long as 5 or 6 years or even more.

[11] Between 1978–95, the growth rate in the waiting list for new connections increased at a higher rate of 15.38 per cent annually compared with the growth rate of direct exchange lines which increased only by 10.62 per cent. Sunil Mani, 'Deregulation and Reforms in India's Telecommunications Industry', in M. Kagami and M. Tsuji (ed.), *Privatization, Deregulation and Economic Efficiency. A Comparative Analysis of Asia, Europe and the Americas,* Cheltenham, 2000, pp. 187–205.

[12] CFCE, 'Le secteur des télécommunications en Inde', Paris, 1995 (mimeo). Though some of the licences, no doubt, remained dormant, there were still 33 private firms producing push button phones in 1994, testifying to the emergence of a large manufacturing base.

of excess capacity. As against an installed capacity of 8 million sets in March 1994, annual off-take would stay relatively flat at 1.8 million sets, despite the needs of the DoT and customer demand.[13]

At the same time, the low levels of technological sophistication that characterized electronic telephone manufacturing, translating into a low degree of product differentiation, explained why this sector would experience conditions of cut-throat competition. The only means available to firms for gaining market share rapidly was by slashing rates. Between 1986–2002, prices of telephone sets would drop by a vertiginous 81.6 per cent.[14] If this free fall in prices obviously suited DoT's interests which could now purchase telephones at a fraction of the costs it had paid earlier, their effects would prove disastrous for ITI, severely undermining the profitability of its telephone activities. Extremely high overheads meant that the company's products were invariably overpriced and on a number of tenders it only managed to recover material costs. In a few cases, even this limited objective would prove to be beyond the company's reach. Likewise, there would also be instances of private players failing to make deliveries after having won the tender, because the prices they had quoted were unrealistically low.

The competitive disadvantage prevailing between private sector firms and ITI became evident soon enough when DoT floated a tender in September 1986 for 300,000 telephones. In this tender, Tata Keltron, with a tie-up with Siemens, quoted Rs 780 and Swede India, whose technology was sourced from Ericsson, Rs 812. The rate quoted by ITI Bangalore for the same model was Rs 850.[15] In a subsequent tender, the public sector company succeeded in lowering its prices considerably, but its efforts were still not good enough.[16] Commenting on the new market climate, a note to the ITI Board stated that the new entrants could take advantage of 'modern and highly productive processes and technology' to reduce their manufacturing costs. Furthermore, despite resorting to price cuts, these firms' margins remained relatively unaffected 'because

---

[13] ibid.

[14] In April 1986, the sales price of an ITI-made push button set stood at Rs 1033.33. By 2002–03, phone prices had dropped to Rs 190.

[15] ITI Bangalore telephone division note, 1 September 1986.

[16] ibid, 13 September 1989. Whereas BPL and Tata Keltron quoted respectively Rs 635 and Rs 681, ITI's lowest offer was Rs 718.

their expenditure is contained to incurring basic necessities only'; in other words, they provided no social benefits whatsoever, and the government had given them tax incentives.[17]

What must be stressed here is that the decision of the authorities to deregulate the terminal equipment segment, without having ensured that ITI had adopted the necessary measures to enable it to withstand the 'free' play of market forces, would place the company at an acute competitive disadvantage.[18] The supervisory ministry had made no attempts to enquire beforehand into the difficulties that the altered business conditions was bound to create for ITI. It was thus neither alerted to nor prepared for the fact that its monopoly was going to be eliminated. The comments made by a parliamentary committee with reference to the post-1991 reforms are equally applicable to the preceding phase of reforms:

Even if the removal of certain kinds of protection to PSUs (public sector undertakings) was inescapable, it would have been more expedient had it been done in a methodical and phased manner instead of doing it in one go. Before throwing the floodgates open . . . an environment should have been created for the public sector to face such a challenge . . .[19]

Moreover, the elimination of entry barriers coincided with a major technological transformation at the telephone division of ITI Bangalore, namely the phasing out rotary or electro-mechanical telephones and the introduction of electronic push button instruments. Consequently, the management's energies and attention were focussed as much on resolving the numerous problems caused by the technology change as in coping with the new market context. The phasing out of electro-mechanical telephones would make redundant nearly 150 direct operators, all of whom would have to be redeployed elsewhere.

---

[17] Note to the ITI Board, 234th meeting, Item B18, August 1987.

[18] Policy-induced changes in the mid-1980s, especially with regard to import deregulation, also affected the performance of other profitable state-owned enterprises such as BHEL, EIL and HMT, according to Vijay Kelkar and Rajiv Kumar. 'Industrial Growth in the Eighties. Emerging Policy Issues', *EPW*, Vol. XXV, No. 4, 27 January 1990, pp. 209–22. See also Singh and Ghosh, 'Import Liberalization and the New Industrial Strategy'.

[19] COPU (1997–98), *Sickness in Public Undertakings*, 11th Report, Eleventh Lok Sabha, New Delhi, 1997, p. 67.

The telephone division was initially protected from the full shock of deregulation by the cushion provided by one area of its activity: the manufacture of multi-line instruments, also known as Plan or 'Boss-Secretary' phones. Technologically outdated and labour intensive, these electro-mechanical rotary dial-fitted phones were a money spinner for ITI which subcontracted their manufacture.[20] But by 1989–90 with electronic exchanges being increasingly inducted into the national network, demand for the older instruments had virtually dried up. While an electronic push button version designed in-house shortly replaced the electro-mechanical model, the switchover proved to be financially ruinous. Whereas the company had fixed a production target of 200,000 sets for the first year, it received firm orders from DoT for barely 6000 sets. To make matters even worse, the department priced it at Rs 2087 per set and that did not even cover the raw material costs of Rs 2578, not to mention the actual production costs, estimated at Rs 3296.[21] The following year production ceased, technological change being cited as the main reason for the resounding failure. Subsequently, the management came in for criticism from audit officials for having developed the model without undertaking any market survey or feasibility study.

Events took a near-identical turn with respect to the manufacture of standard instruments as well. An empty order book obliged the company to agree to supply 300,000 electronic push button phones to DoT in February 1990, despite the fact that it would result in massive losses of Rs 54.84 million. Whereas the department had unilaterally fixed a price of Rs 630, production costs stood at Rs 1199.90 for one model and Rs 915.94 for another.[22] Replying to an audit enquiry, the management justified its decision on the ground that labour would have remained idle and capacity unutilized had it rejected the order, thus leading to even greater losses. As it pointed out categorically:

[20] Between 1985–86 and 1988–89, the telephone division recorded a growth in turnover from Rs 310.20 million to Rs 556 million, while profits increased from Rs 24.7 million to Rs 61.6 million. Audit Inspection Reports of ITI Bangalore telephone division, 1988 and 1989. (Hereafter Audit Report.)

[21] Audit Report No. 3, 1996. The total loss incurred by ITI amounted to Rs 6.46 million, excluding write offs in inventory and work-in-progress to the tune of Rs 12.87 million.

[22] Audit Enquiry No. 7, 7 January 1991.

Our main customer DoT is forcing lower rates on instruments and the company has to accept such uneconomical orders so as to stay in the field and also to utilize the infrastructure available and recover as much revenues as possible...[23]

In another instance, the company was confronted with the painful choice of turning down an order that the DoT had placed at the last minute and under-utilizing capacity or accepting it and paying liquidated damages since it would not have succeeded in supplying the phones on schedule for various reasons. It eventually opted for the latter alternative and paid a penalty of Rs 3.75 million.[24]

For the year 1990–91, as against a target of 500,000 instruments, the telephone division at the Bangalore plant supplied only 346,389 sets due to the shortfall in orders from DoT and its subsidiaries. Prospects of the situation improving also looked bleak. As an audit inspection report warned, 'unless the Division obtains sufficient orders or plans for diversification there will be enormous under utilization of capacity and consequent loss'.[25] So by the time the Congress (I) government initiated economic reforms in July 1991, ITI's telephone activities were clearly in trouble. Turnover which had already registered a fall in the previous year declined further in 1990–91, and for the first time in its history the division posted a loss of Rs 35.82 million.[26] Henceforth, it would continuously be in the red.

Overall, however, ITI's activities continued to remain profitable in the pre-reforms period. Between 1984–85 and 1990–91, despite showing sharp year-to-year swings, profit before tax averaged an impressive annual growth of roughly 35 per cent, and turnover 25.5 per cent (Table 4.1). Offsetting this sanguine picture were the declining profitability rates of the flagship Bangalore and Rae Bareli plants which manufactured in the main strowger and crossbar exchanges, two obsolete technologies, and the company's growing dependence on its Mankapur unit for the bulk of its profits (Table 4.2). For the year 1990–91 alone, the Mankapur unit, where the new E10B electronic switches were made, accounted for two-thirds of the total profits.

---

[23] Letter Tel. Divn. to resident audit officer, Ref. AGMT/II4-Insp. Report 1990–91, 27 October 1992.

[24] Letter Tel. Divn. to resident audit officer, Ref. AGMT/II4/AE8/L.D./TF, 18 April 1999.

[25] Audit Enquiry No. 8, 8 January 1991, p. 7.

[26] Audit Report, 1991.

Table 4.1: ITI Financial Results 1984–85 to 1990–91

Year	Sales (Rs mn)	Per cent growth	Profit before Tax (Rs mn)	Per cent growth	Profit before Tax (% Sales)	Value Added (% Sales)
1984–85	2369.3	11.7	186.7	–0.4	7.9	67.9
1985–86	2995.3	26.4	181.6	–2.7	6.1	62.6
1986–87	4407	47.1	407.4	124.3	9.2	59.8
1987–88	5084.8	15.4	239.5	–41.2	4.7	61
1988–89	6251.8	22.9	391.8	63.6	6.3	65
1989–90	9587.5	53.3	461.5	17.8	4.8	51.7
1990–91	9784.6	2	835.4	81	8.5	53.1
Average		*25.5*		*34.6*	*6.8*	*60.1*

Note: Profit before tax does not include prior period adjustments.
Source: ITI Annual Report, various years.

Table 4.2: Profit Before Tax at ITI Manufacturing Units (Rs million)

Unit	1986–87	1987–88	1988–89	1989–90	1990–91
Bangalore*	198.5 (48.7%)	196.2 (81.9%)	188.3 (48.1%)	27 (5.8%)	36.1 (4.3%)
Rae Bareli	28.9 (7.1%)	134 (55.9%)	148 (38.8%)	78 (16.9%)	74.5 (8.9%)
Naini	153.3 (37.6%)	109.9 (45.9%)	88.1 (22.5%)	37.5 (8.1%)	98 (11.7%)
Mankapur	7.8 (1.9%)	*–191.5*	8.2 (2.1%)	189.1 (41%)	551.6 (66%)
Palakkad	14.4 (3.5%)	*–19.9*	*–50*	123.2 (26.7%)	*–8.5*
EC Unit	—	—	*–0.9*	14.4 (3.1%)	99.9 (11.9%)
Srinagar	8.1 (2%)	10.7 (4.5%)	8.4 (2.1%)	*–10.2*	*–17*
Installation & Maintenance	*–3.7*	0.1	1.7 (0.4%)	2.5 (0.5%)	0.8
Total	407.3	239.5	391.8	461.5	835.4

Notes: Profit before tax does not include prior period adjustments.
Percentage figures in brackets indicate share of total profits.
Losses indicated in italics.
*Includes Corporate Office.
Source: CAG Report 1992, p. 13.

PARTIAL DISINVESTMENT BY GOVERNMENT PLACES ITI IN DOUBLE-BIND

The launch of the reform programme in 1991 ended what remained of ITI's monopoly. The deregulation of the customer premises equipment segment aside, the public sector company had also faced other kinds of competition from 1988 onwards. This was for certain types of transmission equipment as well as small and medium range electronic exchanges once the C-DoT designed Rural Automatic Exchange (RAX) became available. Now, in line with the government policy objectives to introduce greater cost discipline in Indian industry and integrate the domestic economy more closely with the global economy by removing most entry barriers, Indian and foreign private companies were authorized to invest in all areas of the telecommunications equipment market.[27] Over the next few years leading transnational vendors such as AT&T, Alcatel, Ericsson, Fujitsu, NEC and Siemens would establish production facilities in India in partnership with domestic capital.

What the entry of private Indian and foreign capital effectively signified for ITI was that its main lines of business, switching and transmission equipment manufacture, would from here onwards also be exposed to competition.[28] The company would have to adjust to a radically altered market context where it could no longer depend on guaranteed orders and guaranteed prices. The cost-plus pricing arrangement which had governed its dealings with its parent authority since the start would give way to an open tendering system as the basis for equipment procurement, and the company would have to supply products in line with the prices quoted by its competitors. In the pre-reforms period, ITI had suffered mainly from inadequate resources. Now in the post-reforms era, it would face the double disadvantage of having to cope with both resource and demand problems.[29]

---

[27] The only segment closed to foreign players was small exchanges with capacities below 10,000 lines; their production was reserved for domestic firms, including ITI, using indigenously developed C-DoT technology.

[28] In 1989–90, switching accounted for roughly 64 per cent of its total revenue, and transmission, 26.2 per cent, whereas terminal equipment, though the most visible product in its portfolio, contributed only 9 per cent. (ITI Annual Report, 1989–90).

[29] According to Kornai, with the classical capitalist firm demand constraint is binding; with the traditional socialist firm it is the resource constraint. In the post-reforms era,

In parallel, the government which had announced that economic liberalization would include a review of the 'existing portfolio of public investments with greater realism', proceeded to reduce its shareholding in ITI.[30] This decision was partly justified on the ground that public trading of state-owned companies' shares would make their managements more sensitive to commercial profitability.[31] Between March 1992 and March 1995, the government therefore offloaded 22.98 per cent of equity in four tranches with the initial sale of just under 20 per cent netting the exchequer approximately Rs 175 million.[32] The bulk of the shares were picked up by financial institutions, banks and mutual funds, and though ITI employees were also later allowed to acquire a stake, their holding stood at an insignificant 1.12 per cent. Valued at Rs 59 at the time of their sale to employees in July 1995, ITI share prices would collapse to a record low of Rs 4 eighteen months later when the company reported to the Board of Industrial Finance and Reconstruction (BIFR) after running up losses for the second consecutive year.

From the perspective of the ITI management, the partial disinvestment by the government, which only succeeded in creating a 'new hybrid corporate creature', meant that the company was in no position to free itself from the pervasive web of controls entangling the functioning of state-owned enterprises.[33] The political contingencies flowing from state ownership that made the formulation and implementation of strategy in public enterprises a far more complex and uncertain process than in the

---

ITI combined features of both these pure types of firms. Kornai, *Economics of Shortage*, p. 27 (Vol. A).

[30] Statement on Industrial Policy, Government of India, July 1991. On the twists and turns of the disinvestment programme see, *inter alia*, T.G. Arun and F.I. Nixson, 'The Disinvestment of Public Sector Enterprises: The Indian Experience', *Oxford Development Studies*, Vol. 28, No. 1, February 2000, pp. 19–31; Sunil Mani, 'Economic Liberalization and the Industrial Sector', *EPW*, Vol. XXX, No. 21, 27 May 1995, pp. M38–M50; Mohan, 'Public Sector Reforms and Issues in Privatization'.

[31] This assumption can only be qualified as naive, considering how limited the dilution of government equity would eventually prove to be.

[32] *Economic Survey* 1996–97, New Delhi, Government of India, p. 121; Annual Report 1991–92.

[33] D.N. Ghosh, 'Incoherent Privatization. Indian Style', *EPW*, Vol. XXVI, No. 21, 25 May 1991, pp. 1313–16.

private sector, would continue to impinge upon managerial autonomy. The ultimate decision-making locus on all policy matters and long term corporate goals would remain the DoT and the Ministry of Communications with strategic choices being determined not so much on the basis of the commercial interests of the company as on those of the parent organization. The flexibility that was so indispensable for efficiently running a business enterprise and conducting commercial transactions would thus continue to be denied to ITI executives, 'asked to meet the new competitive conditions with their hands tied behind their backs'.[34] In other words, the government's market-oriented reform programme had failed to remove the constraints under which public enterprises operated, while eliminating, virtually at a single stroke, the advantages they enjoyed, thereby accentuating their difficulties.[35]

What is more, the blow caused by the sudden shift from regulatory planning to economic liberalism could have been somewhat softened had the authorities mobilized the proceeds of disinvestment to strengthen the competitive position of companies such as ITI by modernizing infrastructure and upgrading technology. Recommendations along these lines had, in fact, been made by different bodies, including the Disinvestment Commission. Instead, the government preferred to utilize the revenues generated by disinvestment to reduce the budgetary deficit with the result that ITI and other public sector enterprises were left without adequate resources.[36]

Although the government was finally persuaded in the wake of the

[34] Joshi and Little, *India's Economic Reforms, 1991–2001*, p. 178. See also the observations of the Disinvestment Commission which called for a revamping of the 'multi-dimensional accountability' to which public enterprises were subjected, besides granting greater autonomy to managements. *Disinvestment Commission Report I*, Part B, New Delhi, February 1997, pp. 29–46.

[35] Stating this is not to argue in favour of privatization on the grounds that accountability and autonomy are incompatible, as certain neo-liberal economists have done. It is only intended to underscore the fact that liberalization ended up creating anything but a level playing ground for state-owned undertakings. For details see COPU, *Sickness in Public Undertakings*.

[36] *Disinvestment Commission Report I*, Part B. Raja Chelliah has described as a 'totally wrong policy', the transfer of funds from disinvestment to reduce the fiscal deficit. 'Economic Reform Strategy for the Next Decade', *EPW*, Vol. XXXIV, No. 36, 4 September 1999, pp. 2582–7.

reforms, and more than a decade after the issue first arose, to institute a system of performance contracts or Memorandum of Understanding (MoU) with a view to delegating greater authority and operational flexibility to public sector managements, this measure had anything but the desired results.[37] On the contrary, it may have even become an added bureaucratic burden for managements. Just how ineffective and ritualized an instrument the MoU actually proved to be can be gauged from two aspects of its working. First, not even one of the MoUs negotiated between DoT and ITI from 1991–92 to 1996–97 was signed on time. While in theory the document had to be finalized before the start of the financial year so that each side was fully aware of what was expected of it in terms of objectives and commitments, delays in signing ranged anywhere from three to nine months.[38]

Second, as the then ITI Chairman S.S. Motial informed a parliamentary committee, DoT was conspicuous by its failure to fulfil its obligations.[39] Despite formally committing itself in the MoU on a number of crucial issues such as budget outlays, placement of orders, reimbursement of voluntary retirement scheme payments, clearing long-standing debts, or 'freezing' equipment specifications on time, the department was found wanting time and again. Frustrated by the tutelary authority's indifferent, even cynical, attitude, ITI, in fact, refused to sign the MoU for the year 1996–97 for almost nine months, stating point blank that it had no relevance when one side chose to systematically disregard its commitments.[40]

---

[37] An idea imported from France by the Arjun Sengupta Committee in 1984, under the MoU system the performance of state-owned enterprises is evaluated with reference to a wide range of targets. Adopted on an experimental basis in 1987, it was only after the 1991 economic reforms that MoUs became standard practice. For two contrasting assessments, see K.R.S. Murthy, 'MOU: More Memorandum than Understanding', *EPW*, Vol. XXV, No. 21, 26 May 1990 pp. M59–M69; and Prajapati Trivedi, 'Lack of Understanding on Memorandum of Understanding', *EPW*, Vol. XXV, No. 47, 24 November 1990, pp. M175–M182.

[38] COPU 1997, p. 58.

[39] A major drawback of the MoU system was not merely the absence of credible sanctions against managements which failed to meet their commitments, but also against administrative ministries reneging on their obligations.

[40] COPU 1997, p. 58.

TRANSNATIONAL AND PRIVATE FIRMS RESORT TO PREDATORY PRICING STRATEGIES

It would not be long before ITI experienced first hand the repercussions of the opening of the switching segment to transnational equipment manufacturers. In April 1994, DoT issued a tender for 1.7 million large exchange lines. Of the eight bidders, the lowest rate of Rs 4291 per line was quoted by Alcatel-Modi whereas ITI ranked seventh with a bid of Rs 5993. The ITI employees union in Bangalore immediately accused the French company and its local partner of resorting to dumping, adding that it was selling its OCB-283 switches at prices that failed to even cover raw material costs.[41] To back its charges, the union pointed out that the rates proposed by the public sector company were in fact based on the raw material prices it had paid to Alcatel and its approved vendors, given that the French company had provided ITI with the same OCB-283 switching technology, as we saw in chapter two.[42] Interestingly, the Disinvestment Commission and at least one parliamentary committee would also come to the conclusion that the rates quoted in the tender were far too low, but not DoT.[43] It alone claimed that no evidence of dumping existed because the equipments were manufactured locally, before admitting in the same breath that 'some of the competitors may be making conscious loss (sic)'.[44]

[41] Memorandums submitted by ITI Employees Union, Bangalore to the Union Minister of Commerce (7 August 1998); to the Parliamentary Standing Committee on Communications (9 October 1998); and the Union Minister of Communications (26 December 1998).

[42] According to the union, which certainly relied on the management for its information, ITI's raw material costs per line worked out to approximately Rs 5500, of which it directly paid Alcatel Rs 4400, and the remainder to Alcatel–approved vendors. Since the OCB-283 switch was a brand new technology in 1994, ITI had to source all its components from the French company. This was notwithstanding the fact that the latter, having floated its own joint venture in India, had gone from being a technology partner to a market rival, and therefore extended very limited credit facilities to ITI.

[43] The Disinvestment Commission observed that to 'penetrate the potentially large Indian market, multinational players seem to have quoted unrealistically low prices in tenders floated by DoT'. *Report II, ITI Ltd.*, Part B, April 1997, p. 81. See also Standing Committee on Communications (1996–97), Demands for Grants, 11th Report, Eleventh Lok Sabha, 1997, p. 33.

[44] COPU 1997, p. 51. After the tender, four transnational corporations, Alcatel, Ericsson, Fujitsu and Siemens, allegedly joined hands to demand from DoT an upward

Despite the union's protests against what it called 'the bogus or phoney competition', ITI had no alternative but to supply equipment to the state carrier at the prices quoted by the lowest bidder.[45] The union claimed that the tender prices imposed by DoT would cause losses worth Rs 4200 million to the company. But the consequences of turning down the order were likely to have been greater. For one thing, there was the risk of the parent authority reconsidering its new preferential purchase policy of reserving 35 per cent of all equipment orders for the two public sector manufacturers, ITI and HTL.[46] For another, there was the certainty of production capacity and manpower remaining idle. Already, union representatives in one switching division at the Bangalore plant had complained to the management that employees lacked work and this 'results in idleness and idleness is the main cause for indiscipline which can even pollute the industrial climate and harmony (sic)'.[47]

How credible were the union's allegations that foreign vendors had resorted to predatory pricing practices so as to establish their domination over the market from the outset? With DoT having revised its rules, whereby the company that put in the lowest bid was guaranteed half the tender quantity with the balance being divided among the other participants, it was obviously in the interests of bidders to scale down prices. More importantly, since the early 1980s the leading telecommunications equipment companies were coming under increasing pressure to expand the scope of their operations for a couple of inter-linked reasons.[48] Demand for fixed-line switching equipment in most

---

revision of prices or a five year order with a cost escalation clause after two years. *Business Line*, 23 August 1995.

[45] Memorandum to the Union Minister of Commerce.

[46] The reserve quota of 35 per cent was initially divided between ITI and HTL in the ratio of 25:10. Where ITI was the sole public sector manufacturer of a product, as in the case of electronic push button telephones, the reserve quota was fixed at 30 per cent. The disinvestment of HTL in 2004 would lead to the elimination of reservations in its favour. ITI's share would also be revised upwards later.

[47] Letter from ITI union to management, 19 February 1993.

[48] For a detailed discussion of this question see Annemarie Roobeek, 'Telecommunications: An Industry in Transition', in H.W. de Jong (ed.), *The Structure of European Industry*, Dordrecht, 1988, pp. 297–328; A. Roobeek and J. Broeders, 'Telecommunications: Global Restructuring at Full Speed', in H.W. de Jong (ed.), *The Structure of European Industry*, Dordrecht, 1993, pp. 273–306; Bertrand Quélin, 'Dynamique concurrentielle et globalization: la concentration de l'industrie des equipements de télécommunication', in *Mutations des Télécommunications*, pp. 431–55.

developed countries was peaking.[49] Then, there was the need to recover the enormous R&D expenditures that equipment suppliers had sustained in designing and developing digital exchanges.[50] At the same time, technological obsolescence and, its corollary, shorter product life-cycles rendered this task both more complicated and urgent.[51] Viewed against this backdrop, it is more than plausible that as part of their entry strategy into the Indian market, which offered a relatively high growth potential, foreign equipment companies had deliberately quoted extremely low prices. An OECD study noted in unmistakable terms that dumping of telecommunications equipment was a standard practice throughout the 1980s, partly because of the diverse forms of assistance transnational corporations received from their respective governments.[52]

The ITI union's allegations against the foreign vendors appear to have been borne out to some extent by the second round of tenders floated by DoT in April 1996. In this tender for 1.3 million switches, ITI ranked

[49] Between 1989–95, the market for public switching systems, the biggest segment of the overall telecommunications equipment market, registered negative growth of –0.5 per cent in EC countries, –0.4 per cent in North America, and –2.2 per cent in Japan. In comparison, the rest of the world posted a growth of 6.7 per cent. Observatoire mondial des systèmes de communication (OMSYC), *Key Figures and Indicators for the World Telecommunications Market 1998–99*, Paris, 1998, p. 60. Overall, although developed countries still accounted for over two-thirds of all telecommunications equipment sales, between 1992 and 2000 these markets registered an average growth of only 4 per cent as against 10 per cent for Asia (excluding Japan). Goulvestre, *Economie des télécoms*, pp. 93, 69–70.

[50] In the mid-1980s, a worldwide market share of at least 8 per cent was estimated as indispensable for telecommunications manufacturers in order to remain profitable. By the early 1990s, this threshold figure would double owing to the additional expenditure required to upgrade digital systems as well as incorporate new features. Roobeek and Broeders, 'Telecommunications: Global Restructuring at Full Speed'; OCDE, *L'industrie des télécommunications. Les défis des mutations structurelles*, Paris, 1988, pp. 79–80.

[51] Technological advances paradoxically coincided with a progressive reduction in the life of switching equipment, considering that strowger systems had a life span of 35 years compared with 20 years for crossbar systems, and just 5 to 8 years for digital systems.

[52] Antonelli, *La diffusion des télécommunications de pointe*, p. 69, 72. He argues that while developing countries benefit initially from dumping by way of lower equipment prices, they face the risks of a technology 'lock-in' over the long run. Customers may have no choice but to depend on the same supplier, often paying a much higher price for new equipment, because inducting rival switching systems into the network can create problems of compatibility.

sixth whereas Alcatel-Modi again emerged as the lowest bidder. However, the rate quoted by the French company represented a massive 70 per cent increase over the previous tender two years ago. Although DoT had wanted additional features to be included in the equipment on this occasion, leading to a higher software content, these changes could not totally justify the hike in bid prices. The sudden mark-up promptly gave rise to suspicions of a possible cartel formation by certain big foreign players.[53] However, after considerable bargaining, DoT succeeded in bringing down the price from Rs 7299 per line to Rs 5650.[54] Once again, ITI was forced to supply equipment at this rate. But on at least one future instance, the top management declined to execute an order for large digital switches, for fear that the uneconomical prices fixed by the tutelary authority would augment the company's losses.[55] Describing the competition faced by ITI as being 'unhealthy', Chairman Motial would claim that prices in the case of five or six major products were 'unreasonable'.[56] A note from the company's marketing department added that material costs for certain products were 'more than the prices given by customer or almost equal to the selling price'.[57]

The effects of the price squeeze were compounded by a demand squeeze. Orders for certain types of transmission equipment had sharply tapered down.[58] Problems of a similar nature also cropped up with respect to the C-DoT designed switches for which ITI ranked amongst the biggest suppliers. With demand for both RAX and MAX-L switches remaining stagnant, competition was particularly intense in this segment. Burdened with excess capacity, private licensees had launched a merciless price war in an effort to obtain orders and liquidate their inventories, slashing

---

[53] *The Economic Times*, 6 April 1996 (hereafter *ET*); *The Hindu*, 4 September 1997. It is also possible that transnational firms significantly increased their prices because of lack of competitive pressure from domestic manufacturers of C-DoT exchanges, handicapped by insufficient orders from DoT.

[54] Memorandum to the Union Minister of Commerce.

[55] COPU 1997, p. 9. Unremunerative prices had also pushed HTL in 1996–97 to refuse orders resulting in a big shortfall in its production of digital switching equipment. Standing Committee on Communications (1997–98), 15th Report, Eleventh Lok Sabha, New Delhi, 1997, p. 8.

[56] COPU 1997, p. 50.

[57] Ref. EDRM/1, 7 November 1994.

[58] COPU 1997, pp. 21, 61–2.

rates by even 50 to 60 per cent in some cases.[59] An official report would later state that contracts were awarded to the 'lowest bidder irrespective of the fact whether the prices quoted by the tenderer are feasible or not'.[60] But there were limits some times even to cut-throat competition. In one tender for 1000–2000 line medium range switches, the prices arbitrarily fixed by DoT were so unattractive that all the bidders backed out. The only exception was ITI which being a captive unit of DoT had no choice but to fulfil the order. No less alarmingly for the company, at the same time as competitors were eating into its market share, they were also raiding it for a vital resource, its research personnel. As we shall study in the next chapter, a large number of ITI engineers quit to join transnational corporations attracted by the extravagant pay packets and perks that the latter dangled before them. The ensuing brain drain would gravely endanger ITI's research capabilities.

If the situation was critical for ITI's switching business, it was disastrous for its subscriber equipment business. Sinking steadily deeper into the red, between 1991–92 and 1994–95 the Bangalore telephone division recorded annual losses averaging 90.5 per cent of its turnover.[61] Physical production of telephone instruments also fell far short of the targeted volumes, resulting in capacity under-utilization. Over a four year period from 1993–94 to 1996–97, the division would work on average, at just 68 per cent capacity.[62] Explaining the reasons for this dismal performance to a parliamentary delegation, the management blamed shortages of orders and unremunerative prices. If competitive pressures were, no doubt, driving telephone manufacturers to slash rates, the decision of the Telecommunications Commission in September 1992 to decentralize

---

[59] The total commissioned capacity for the manufacture of C-DoT switching equipment stood at 2.4 million lines annually. But despite the massive expansion of the telecommunications network, orders for C-DoT switches are estimated to have stayed flat at 940,000 lines annually from 1992–93 to 1994–95. CFCE, 'Le secteur des télécommunications en Inde', See also *Business Line*, 12 November 1994.

[60] COPU 1997, p. 67. Private firms guilty of frequently defaulting on their tender commitments were also not blacklisted by DoT, giving rise to suspicions of financial impropriety.

[61] Audit Report (various years). To take just the year 1991–92, while turnover stood at Rs 224.9 million, losses totalled Rs 222 million.

[62] Public Enterprises Survey, BPE (various years). After falling from 346,389 sets in 1990–91 to 295,000 sets in 1992–93, telephone production climbed up to 313,631 sets two years later. Audit Report (various years).

the purchase of electronic push button phones only contributed to accelerate this trend. With the heads of all telecommunications circles authorized to directly procure instruments from approved vendors, circles now began vying with each other to obtain the lowest price. In a tender for 1.5 million instruments launched in January 1993, for example, ITI together with BPL had quoted the lowest bid of Rs 580 per phone. But DoT arbitrarily reduced the rate to Rs 531, and successfully enforced it on both companies.[63]

Attempts made by the telephone division to diversify its product portfolio also ran into difficulties. Faced with the problem of surplus manpower, lack of orders and declining profitability of electronic phones, the management had initiated a number of new projects. One such venture with a high growth potential was the fabrication of miniature relays. An extensively used component both in switching equipment and telephones, ITI's entire requirement of relays, which stood at around 2.5 million annually, was imported. Its hopes of fabricating these relays in-house were rapidly dashed when the research team working on this project quit the company to join private sector firms.

Plans to manufacture RAXs had to be abandoned as well for want of orders from DoT. In addition to spending around Rs 15.7 million in creating additional manufacturing facilities, the telephone division had invested heavily on raw material to the extent of Rs 100 million.[64] But of the 409 exchanges manufactured over a two-year period, it managed to sell only 173 to DoT, and that too at a loss, since it was forced to supply them at the rates quoted by private suppliers. The unsold systems were later broken up and some of the components transferred to other ITI units. Still, the division would be burdened with inventory worth Rs 50 million. Justifying its decision to expand into this area, the management contended that given the new market environment it was compelled to take some risks in developing and fabricating new products in anticipation of orders, before adding:

it has become necessary to assess the new products by its contribution to the reduction in fixed costs than by its profitability.[65]

---

[63] *Communication Today*, October 1993. See also audit enquiry No.RAP/ITI/S.A/T/62–63, 3 July 1996.

[64] Audit Report, year ended 1994.

[65] Letter to resident senior audit officer, 17 October 1995.

The explanation, however, failed to satisfy the government statutory audit. It pointed out that apart from the telephone division, the Electronic City plant and the Rae Bareli factory were also making these exchanges and with an equal lack of success because of inadequate orders.[66]

In the end, the only diversification project to yield dividends was the manufacture of data cards. Since 1991–92 the telephone division had supplied over 9000 such cards to DoT and MTNL, and in the absence of competition it was able to realize extremely high margins. As against material costs of approximately Rs 6000 for a 64 kilobyte card, the data card was priced slightly in excess of Rs 20,000.[67] Following the entry in the late 1990s of private firms, ITI sought to preserve its control via a voluntary reduction in prices to Rs 14,000, arguing that it had made 'enough profit on this card' for the last four to six years.[68] Further, even the scaled down prices fetched substantial profit margins.

LACK OF SUPPORT FROM DOT INCREASES PROBLEMS FOR ITI

It is necessary at this juncture to evaluate the attitude adopted by the DoT towards ITI during the initial years of deregulation. Like the equipment manufacturer, the state carrier's position had undergone important changes in the aftermath of economic reforms, but with far less disastrous consequences. The DoT had effectively seen the monopoly power it enjoyed since colonial times as a provider of basic telephone services come to an end. In September 1994, the government authorized private companies to enter the market for basic telephony and value added services. Cellular mobile services were also thrown open to competition, but DoT refused to surrender control of its two most lucrative activities, national and international long-distance communications.[69]

---

[66] Letter from resident senior audit officer, 31 January 1996. The decision of the Bangalore telephone division to go in for RAX production ruffled feathers within the company as well. ITI's Electronic City unit, specialized in C-DoT products, was apparently 'refusing to give necessary technical assistance and training in inspection and testing areas for C-DoT systems' to telephone division personnel. Tel. Divn. note, Ref. DGMT/5, 2 March 1994.

[67] Tel. Divn. note, Ref. LTG-402/DIC, 11 January 1999.

[68] Tel. Divn. note, Ref. LTG-402/DIC, 4 May 1998.

[69] Both activities were subsequently deregulated. Private operators were licensed to

The National Telecommunication Policy, announced in May 1994, emphasized the importance of private sector participation in order to accelerate the expansion of the telecommunications network. However, government hopes of attracting substantial volumes of private investment were dashed by a combination of factors, including delays in establishing a regulatory authority, terms of the interconnection fees charged by DoT, and so forth. Even the remedial measures brought in by the New Telecom Policy in 1999 to give a new impetus to the liberalization process did not succeed in reversing the trend.[70] A year later private firms had rolled out basic telephony services in only three states (Maharashtra, Andhra Pradesh and Madhya Pradesh), and that too, on a very limited scale. A robust competitive environment struck roots only in cellular telephony, though even here not until the very end of the 1990s did private operators start cutting a fairly deep swathe. Thus, notwithstanding an evolving landscape, DoT's stranglehold over the provision of telecommunications services went virtually unchallenged during the first decade of economic reforms.

This was in stark contrast to the situation faced by ITI. Yet between 1992–96, apart from reserving a 35 per cent preferential share on equipment orders for ITI and HTL, a measure which in reality turned out to be a poisoned gift since it compelled both companies to manufacture at a loss, no other form of assistance was extended by the supervisory ministry to its industrial affiliate. The parent administration's reluctance to spare the organizational resources needed to make ITI more competitive was also in contradiction with its official pronouncements defending the necessity of developing a strong public sector manufacturing base which would serve as a countervailing force to opportunistic actions by private firms and transnational corporations. Although the top management and the unions had insisted on the importance of drawing up a suitable strategy so as to 'get the best of

---

provide national long distance services from August 2000, while VSNL, the international services arm of DoT, was privatized and acquired by the Tatas in 2002.

[70] For information on the telecommunications liberalization process and the implementational problems associated with it see, *inter alia*, T.H. Chowdary, 'Telecommunications in India', in E. Noam (ed.), *Telecommunications in Western Asia and the Middle East*, Oxford, 1997, pp. 20–37. (I am grateful to the author for the reference.); Rafiq Dossani (ed.), *Telecommunications Reform in India*, New Delhi, 2003; Jain, 'A Review of the Indian Telecom Sector'.

existing resources', none of the measures mooted by them to ensure better capacity utilization found favour with ministry officials.[71] The situation, they contended, could not be viewed solely from the 'corporate angle of ITI', and the overall requirements of the country also had to be kept in mind.[72] One could hardly find fault with this line of reasoning, especially in the context of a shortage economy. But it is arguable whether the twin goals of rapidly absorbing the penury of telephone connections and revitalizing ITI were as incompatible as DoT wished or liked to think.

Plans developed by the company to integrate downwards by providing basic telephone services once the government had deregulated this sector in the mid-1990s were also foiled by the state carrier (see chapter five). Other measures enforced by the latter placed ITI at an even greater competitive disadvantage. Thus in August 1992, DoT suddenly discontinued the system of advance payments.[73] The bulk of this amount was used to finance ITI's working capital requirements which tended to always be on the high side because of poor cash management and high inventories. Now, following the decision to cancel advances, it had no choice but to borrow from commercial lending institutions, leading to a steep escalation in interest payments which in turn dented its profitability.[74]

A question we must ask here is whether top ITI executives lacked the requisite foresight. Did their failure to anticipate, or react with sufficient speed, to the roll back of the company's monopoly translate into a failure to adopt the corrective measures indispensable to its survival in the transformed competitive structure. Stating this is to imply, first of all, that the lifting of entry barriers in 1984 in one segment, terminal

[71] ITI corporate office files, 20 October 1993.

[72] COPU 1997, p. 53. See also *ET*, 5 May 1995, for the comments of the chairman Telecommunications Commission that DoT could not let itself be 'tied to the apron strings of ITI'.

[73] The company had regularly received 35 per cent, later increased to 45 per cent, of the value of the order in advance whenever its principal customer placed an order.

[74] Between 1992–93 and 1996–97, borrowings increased by nearly 8.6 per cent while the interest burden went up by a staggering 72.5 per cent. Annual Report (various years). Debt equity ratios which had always exceeded the stipulated 1:1 norm also showed a corresponding rise. From 1.24:1 in 1993–94, the ratio climbed sharply to 5.54:1 in 1996–97, before falling to 2.93:1 the following year. Extract of Government Audit Report, 1987.

equipments, was going to culminate in the elimination of barriers in all segments of telecommunication manufacture seven years later. With the benefit of hindsight it is, no doubt, possible to view one event as the logical outcome of the other. Yet at the time there was nothing inevitable or automatic about this process. Second, even if we assume that ITI's destiny was, for all practical purposes, sealed in the mid-1980s itself, it is worth recalling that the attention of the management during this period was rivetted on resolving the problems caused by the delays in inducting the new digital switching technology at both the flagship Bangalore factory and Rae Bareli (see chapter two).

Third, as we have seen, ITI chairmen were not only all handpicked by DoT; they had no freedom to boot in determining the strategic options the company needed to pursue. To cite one executive, 'management always felt that it was the ministry's job to decide policy'.[75] An evidence of the belief of the tutelary agency that ITI's problems in the wake of deregulation were, above all, financial was its choice of ITI directors. During the crucial years between 1992–96, all of its incumbent directors were drawn from the field of finance, persons who lacked the indepth understanding of technological issues to run a technology-driven enterprise. On the other hand, ITI executives were convinced that the company's interests would have been best served by a telecommunications specialist at the helm. Lastly, and to further worsen matters, ITI was left 'headless' for relatively long stretches at critical periods during the mid-1980s and 1990s, as the parent ministry delayed appointing a chairman. For instance, for a fifteen month period between June 1995 and September 1996, when ITI was in desperate financial straits and its turnaround contingent on the management's ability to take strong and decisive measures, the top slot was occupied by an acting chairman.[76] Perhaps this act of omission, more than anything else, best reflected the DoT's total lack of concern for the difficulties faced by the company. A parliamentary committee was subsequently moved to describe ITI as a

[75] Interview with Srinivasa Rao.

[76] Management vacuum at the top levels of public sector companies was a very common occurrence. At any point of time nearly 70 to 80 posts of chairman and full time directors remained vacant, notes Prahlad Basu. 'Government Failure Overshadows Management Failure. Strategic Issues of Management of Public Enterprises', *EPW*, Vol. XXV, No. 21, 26 May 1990, pp. M50 M58.

'typical example' of a public sector undertaking victim of 'the apathetic attitude of the Government'.[77] In its opinion,

. . . the company could have been prevented from the (crisis) situation in which it finds itself today, had the necessary and timely assistance been forthcoming from the Ministry.[78]

Another aspect of DoT and government policy worth attention, and one which handicapped ITI as well as private domestic firms, is that in sharp contrast to China, little encouragement was offered to indigenous equipment manufacturers.[79] Though state officials had listed the creation of a strong domestic manufacturing base as one of its goals in both the National Telecommunications Plan (1994) and the New Telecommunications Policy (1999), attempts to give a real substance to this objective were non-existent. Under pressure from DoT which had declared that it would purchase equipment only from 'local' manufacturers and disallow imports of finished products, though this policy would not apply to later entrants, foreign companies had, for certain, been obliged to install their operations in the country.[80] But, contrary to the government's expectations, manufacturing activity in these units was by and large limited to assembling imported SKD kits.[81]

Suggestions from ITI calling upon the state carrier to give weightage to local value addition when placing orders also did not elicit a positive response.[82] Nor were incentives granted subsequently to private service providers to promote the purchase of locally made equipment for their networks. This was a serious policy shortcoming, especially in a market context where domestic equipment suppliers unlike transnational

---

[77] COPU 1997, p. 67.

[78] ibid.

[79] The head of HFCL, a leading private sector equipment vendor, would, in fact, urge the government to 'learn from Chinese experience where domestic manufacturing industry flourished . . . because of the encouragement by the Chinese government . . .' *ET*, 6 February 1999.

[80] Dossani argues that limited internal demand was the main reason why India was less successful than China in attracting foreign investment in telecommunications manufacturing. 'Introduction', in *Telecommunications Reform in India*, pp. 1–24.

[81] However, even in domestically assembled or manufactured switches, the import content was estimated to be as high as 45 to 50 per cent.

[82] In the 1994 Telecommunications Plan, the utilization of indigenously manufactured equipment, by private firms bidding for the provision of basic telephone services, attracted a weightage of merely 3 per cent.

corporations lacked the resources to offer vendor financing for their products through facilities such as easy credit terms or deferred payments. Finally, the cause of local manufacture would be further weakened by the prevailing duty structure. For in the wake of the reduction of basic customs duties on various types of telecommunications equipment in the year 2000, imports of finished equipment became much cheaper.

Whether or not ITI was being discriminated against by DoT and the Ministry of Communications because of its inability as a public enterprise to pay kickbacks to officials, as the unions more than once alleged, is, of course, something we cannot answer. What we do know for certain is that, first, the years 1992–96 were the years when the Ministry of Communications was headed by Sukh Ram. Second, perhaps in order to demonstrate the ministry's commitment to the new 'open doors' doctrine, a deliberate bias against all forms of indigenous technology defined official policy in this period—even private manufacturers of C-DoT equipment received few orders, as we have already seen—though much the same trend persisted later too. Third, during this first heady flush of economic liberalization, the dealings of the Ministry and the DoT with respect to equipment purchases were stained in irregularities. The subsequent court convictions of Sukh Ram and a senior department official sentencing them to prison terms of respectively three and two years for defrauding the exchequer exposed the magnitude of the 'Dial M for Money' scam.[83] Lastly, it would require the defeat of the Congress (I) government in the 1996 general elections, and the departure of Sukh Ram, before DoT could be persuaded to take a more helpful stance *vis-à-vis* its industrial affiliate. But by then irreparable damage had been inflicted on its competitive position.

Having said this, we cannot overlook the fact that the tutelary body faced significant constraints of its own, notably the need to address the problems evolving from the tremendous unsatisfied demand for new telephone connections. Over the years the registered waiting list had grown increasingly longer, and by 1990, it counted almost 1.7 million

---

[83] For details of the Sukh Ram affair see Rishab Ghosh, 'Indian ex-Minister for Telecom raided; Harris Corp jv in trouble', *The Indian Technomist*, 19 August 1996 (http:// dxm.org/techonomist/news/ 19aug96.html); *The Hindu*, 5 July 2002. See also Comptroller and Auditor General Report, Union Government Post & Telecommunications (6 of 1997), 1995–96, paras 8–8.1.6, for rampant irregularities in equipment procurement by DoT.

applicants.[84] Viewed against this backdrop, it is quite plausible that DoT considered the rapid installation of new lines at the lowest cost as its foremost priority, rather than extending assistance to ITI. Indeed, the state carrier could boast of an impressive record in the wake of liberalization, exceeding the objectives set for it during the course of the Eight Plan (1992–97) as well as the Ninth Plan (1997–2002). More telephone connections were added in the decade 1990–2000 than in the preceding four decades since Independence.[85] Teledensity levels rose over six-fold during this period.[86] Furthermore, the expansion of the network was financed entirely by DoT through internal revenue generation, supplemented, to some extent, by external borrowings.[87] Hence, the failure of ministry officials to adopt effective measures to redress ITI's fortunes could perhaps be interpreted in part as the upshot of the choice, understandable and partly justifiable, to channel DoT's organizational capabilities and financial muscle into extending the reach of telecommunication infrastructural facilities in the country.

By the mid-1990s, ITI's relations with its supervisory ministry had reached their nadir. In May 1995, the DoT secretary and chairman Telecommunications Commission would declare point blank that ITI management should meet the challenge of deregulation on its own without any government or 'artificial support'.[88] The timing of this remark was interesting. It came at a moment when it had already become starkly evident that the public sector company would collapse without government support. The first signs of an impending financial crash came in 1993–94 when both value of production and profit after tax registered a marginal fall in growth. Then, in 1994–95, for the first time

---

[84] *The India Infrastructure Report. Policy Imperatives for Growth and Welfare*, Vol. II, Sector Reports, New Delhi, 1996, p. 102.

[85] In 1989, the country possessed barely 4.6 million fixed line telephones; by 2000, the number had skyrocketed to 26.5 million, an achievement only overshadowed by the fact that the waitlist still contained over 2.7 million potential subscribers. *Infrastructure*, New Delhi, February 2003, p. 254.

[86] From 0.55 lines per 100 inhabitants in 1989, teledensity shot up to 3.6 lines in 2001. *Economic Survey of India 2002–03*, New Delhi, p. 188. Sharp variations, however, continued to characterize urban and rural areas.

[87] The task of single-handedly financing the development of the network was, however, considerably facilitated by DoT's continued monopoly over the two most profitable segments of the market: national and international long distance calls.

[88] *ET*, 5 May 1995.

in its history, ITI declared losses of Rs 853.2 million as turnover plummeted by nearly 32 per cent over the previous year (Table 4.3). The results for the next two years would be no better. Turnover for 1995–96 slumped by a further 24.5 per cent, reducing it to less than what it was in 1989–90, while losses rose more than three-fold to almost Rs 2677 million.

Table 4.3: ITI Financial Results 1991–92 to 1996–97

Year	Sales (Rs. mn)	% growth	Profit before Tax (Rs. mn)	% growth	Profit before Tax % Sales	Value Added % Sales
1991–92	10,847	10.8	967.2	15.8	8.9	57.6
1992–93	14,839.5	36.8	1746.5	80.6	11.7	50.8
1993–94	15,272.5	2.9	2053.8	17.6	13.4	51.3
1994–95	10,366.2	(32.1)	*–853.2*	(58.4)	—	40.9
1995–96	7826.2	(24.5)	*–2676.9*	(213.7)	—	35.8
1996–97	10,212.1	30.5	*–645.7*	(75.9)	—	39
Average						*45.9*

Notes: Profit before tax does not include prior period adjustments.
        Figures in brackets indicate negative growth. Losses indicated in italics.
Source: ITI Annual Report, various years.

At the same time, value added as a percentage of revenue, which had fluctuated between 51 and 65 per cent through the previous decade, fell sharply to 35.8 per cent in 1995–96. The bulk of the losses were accounted for by the Bangalore, Rae Bareli and Naini units, the three biggest and technologically least-advanced of the six units that the company controlled (Table 4.4).

Indeed, from this point onwards these units would be continually in the red. ITI's share of national telecommunications equipment production also registered a decline from 27.22 per cent in 1991–92 to 13.38 per cent in 1994–95, as did its share of DoT's total equipment purchases.[89]

---

[89] Parthasarathy, *Globalization and Agglomeration in Newly Industrializing Countries*, p. 283. DoT realized barely 46 per cent of its overall equipment purchases from ITI in 1996–97, down from 73 per cent in 1993–94. Memorandum to Parliamentary Standing Committee from ITI Employees Union, Bangalore.

Table 4.4: Profit Before Tax at ITI Units 1993–94 to 1996–97 (Rs. million)

Unit	1993–94	1994–95	1995–96	1996–97
B'lore*	*–386*	*–939.3*	*–1108.90*	*–687.6*
Rae Bareli	*–37.1*	*–244.4*	*–489.3*	*–295.7*
Naini	231.4	*–281*	*–739.3*	*–496*
Mankapur	1197.9	500.3	4.3	704.3
Palakkad	332.9	*–52.9*	*–285.1*	384.2
EC Unit	502.6	205.4	*–183.6*	*–165.5*
Srinagar	*–32.4*	*–28.8*	*–29.4*	*–47.9*
Installation & Maintenance**	1.4	17.9	34.9	*–57.1*
Regional Offices	*–47.2*	*–3.7*	*–43.3*	15.6

Notes: Profit before tax includes prior period adjustments.
Losses indicated in italics.
*Includes Corporate Office. **Installation and Maintenance would be later renamed Network Systems Unit (NSU).
Source: ITI Annual Report, various years.

But, paradoxically, the company's dependence on the latter increased, reflecting its lack of success in diversifying its revenue base: over 90 per cent of its revenues came from the parent organization which only served to compound its difficulties.

In addition to shrinking demand, the management claimed that the company had suffered a decline in prices to the extent of Rs 4000 million.[90] The price erosion was steepest with respect to C-DoT equipment (Table 4.5). For a 5000-line MAX exchange, for instance, prices had tumbled by about 60 per cent between November 1992 and May 1995, and by 42 per cent, for small RAXs. Transmission products were hit equally hard to a point where sales value melted by half.[91] If technological innovations partly explained this downward push, the driving factor was undoubtedly competitive pressures, especially for C-DoT products, where DoT's bias against domestically designed exchanges caused a severe market slump.

[90] Letter from ITI chairman to unit and division heads, 29 May 1995.
[91] Prices for certain Multiple Access Rural Radio systems crashed by almost 67 per cent, whereas in the case of microwave equipment, it fluctuated between 26 per cent to 62.5 per cent.

Table 4.5 : ITI Product Revenues & Equipment Prices 1993–94 to 1996–97

Product Category	1993–94	1994–95	1995–96	1996–97
Switching Revenues (Rs mn)	9056.3	5810 *(–35.8%)*	5317.3 *(–8.5%)*	6888.4 (29.5%)
Switching Prices				
i) C-DoT RAX	Rs 485,000		Rs 280,000	
ii) C-DoT MAX (2000 line exch.)	Rs 14.16 mn		Rs 6.93 mn	Rs 5.67 mn
iii) C-DoT MAX (5000 line exch.)	Rs 31.47 mn		Rs 12.46 mn	Rs 11.27 mn
iv) Digital Local Exch.	Rs 8000 (per line)		Rs 7298 (per line)	
Transmission Revenues (Rs mn)	4619.6	3375.2 *(–26.9%)*	1651.9 *(–51%)*	1808.9 (9.5%)
Transmission Prices				
i) MARR	(VHF) Rs 333,000	(VHF) Rs 256,000	(UHF) Rs 530,000	(UHF) Rs 177,000
ii) VSAT	Rs 2.62 mn	Rs 1.13 mn		Rs 1.99 mn
iii) OLTE + MUX	Rs 174,00		Rs 97,000	Rs 94,000
iv) 13 GHz MW			Rs 1.11 mn	Rs 829,000
v) 6 GHz MW		Rs 1.01 mn		Rs 612,000
Telephone Revenues (Rs mn)	936.1	657.7 *(–29.7%)*	571.4 *(–13.1%)*	903.7 (58.1%)
Telephone Prices	Rs 531	Rs 410	Rs 361	Rs 351
Services Revenues (Rs mn)	156.3	233.2 (49.2%)	266.6 (14.3%)	562.6 (111%)

Notes: Figures in brackets indicate percentage growth and/or decline; negative growth indicated in italics.

Source: Annual Reports, various years; ITI corporate office.

GOVERNMENT VETOES AID PACKAGE TO REVIVE ITI

If the decline in ITI's fortunes can, to some extent, be attributed to the short-sighted policies pursued by the Congress (I) government which turned a blind eye to the financial improprieties committed by Sukh Ram and other DoT officials during these years, its recovery, fragile and temporary though it was, owed just as much to the assistance extended by the department. Addressing the unions, the ITI chairman would speak of a 'total change' in the DoT's attitude towards and relationship with the company, adding that it was now willing to give orders and support.[92] While this statement was not without exaggeration, the arrival of the United Front government in June 1996, and the appointment of a new Communications Minister, did signal a shift in DoT's policies towards its manufacturing wing. Already in 1995–96 it had agreed to both resume advance payments of up to 50 per cent (later hiked to 75 per cent) when placing orders on ITI, and augment the company's share of the reserve quota for switching equipment from 25 to 30 per cent. It also agreed to provide government guarantees for bonds floated by ITI.

More crucially, it injected approximately Rs 1870 million into the company's coffers between 1996–98, thus helping the latter tide over the immediate effects of its financial crisis. None of this amount, however, consisted of 'fresh' capital. The DoT was either refunding or waiving the huge penalties it had arbitrarily levied in the past by way of liquidated damages, settling long-standing financial and pricing wrangles, or only fulfilling some of its obligations specified in the MoUs such as partially reimbursing ITI for voluntary retirement payments, or compensating it for the losses incurred in operating the Srinagar unit.[93] Nor did this cash relief come anywhere close to meeting the demands raised by top management.

Towards the end of 1996 itself, the company had requested DoT and the government to provide a comprehensive investment package spread over a period of five years and totalling nearly Rs 11,000 million with the objective of ensuring that the company's turnaround rested on as solid a foundation as possible.[94] But in early 1999, after a delay of nearly two years, the aid package was rejected out of hand, partly on the ground

[92] Minutes of 20th Joint Management Committee Meeting, 14 May 1997.

[93] COPU 1997, pp. 4–8; Letter from Telecommunications Commission to ITI, 30 December 1997; and DoT letter to ITI, Ref. No.115–32/95-MMD (Vol.II), 31 March 1998. Between 1991–92 and 1993–94 alone, ITI was required to pay liquidated damages to the extent of approximately Rs 1060 million.

[94] The proposal included a demand for a soft loan worth Rs 1500 million for the purpose of meeting working capital requirements and upgrading the company's technology base, as well as an annual grant of Rs 1400 million for five years to enable it to absorb its high social overheads. Standing Committee on Communications (1996–97), Demand for Grants, 2nd Report, Eleventh Lok Sabha, 1996, pp. 16–18. See also *ET*, 22 December 1996.

that the company's financial position had improved.[95] In the overall context of liberalization and an environment wherein the reduction of the public sector deficit was a key government priority, even though the resultant bottlenecks in infrastructure threatened to severely jeopardize future economic growth, the chances of the government agreeing to grant the substantial sums that the management had requested were always weak. Yet the final decision not to extend any financial assistance whatsoever effectively condemned ITI's prospects of a viable, long term recovery.

Left to fend for itself, the company would now be locked in a vicious cycle. On the one hand, it was unable to generate adequate internal surpluses because of its lack of competitivity which in turn was related to its high fixed cost structure, especially escalating manpower costs, and the absence of proprietary technology. On the other, in order to tackle these fundamental problems, and strengthen its market power in the bargain, it required considerable resources. As the next chapter will discuss, since the early 1990s the management had taken a series of measures to turn around ITI. These included hiring a consultancy firm to restructure operations, reducing material costs as well as the size of the workforce, bringing down overheads and tightening discipline. Besides these, product quality was improved and the interest burden lowered due to better cash management. But these measures were insufficient to guarantee its ability to withstand the pressures of competition given the structural nature of its problems. Thus, not surprisingly, after a brief phase of recovery between 1997–98 and 2001–2002 where turnover, but not profit, recorded relatively strong growth, at least initially, the company resumed its downhill journey.

The company's predicament might perhaps have been less distressing had it possessed proprietary technology. However, as one study revealed, the share of own-technology products in its business mix stood at barely 8 per cent, as against 83 per cent for transfer of technology products, while the remainder came from services.[96] In the all-important switching

---

[95] Standing Committee on Communications (1998–99), 13th Report, Twelfth Lok Sabha, 1999, p. 34. Responding to DoT's veto, the parliamentary body would, in fact, urge it to re-examine ITI's request for a special financial package in the form of equity or soft loan so as to accelerate the company's turnaround.

[96] PwC Recommendations on Strategy Formulation, Options Generation and Selection, September 2000, p. 12. The company itself claimed that it derived 20 per cent of its turnover from products of in-house design. COPU 1997, p. 49.

sector, which normally accounted for one-third of all equipment investments made in the national network, it had always relied on external sources, acquiring know-how from both foreign companies such as Alcatel, and indigenously from C-DoT. One consequence of the failure to build local innovation capability was that it found itself stuck in a relatively low value addition activity, manufacturing. As top management acknowledged, profitability was affected because 'home-grown technologies are not in the majority'.[97] Burdened with a huge infrastructure for assembly and testing, its manufacturing business offered extremely low net margins, and the steady erosion in equipment prices hardly helped matters. Underlining the 'intense competition' the public sector company faced from the plants of transnational corporations located in Southeast Asian markets coupled with the threat of cheap Chinese imports flooding the domestic market in the wake of the WTO accords, in a document submitted to the government, the management clearly stated that in the long run, its production operations 'may not be sustainable'.[98]

What must be noted is that the price squeeze experienced by ITI was not an isolated phenomenon. Vendors the world over were coming under pressure to cut rates from service providers who themselves faced severe competition. Alcatel, for instance, suffered a 20 to 30 per cent fall in rates annually, despite overhauling its product portfolio from year to year.[99] It was largely in response to this trend that transnational corporations were increasingly outsourcing their production activities and moving towards high value-added segments of the business such as software development and customer management.[100] For obvious reasons,

---

[97] DO No. DB/Cor.Cors., 9 July 2001.

[98] ITI Revival Plan, 24 September 2003.

[99] Telecommunications manufacturers were, in reality, caught in a pincer movement. Apart from the demand for cheaper equipment from service operators, they also had to cope with volatile raw material markets, notably for semi-conductors where prices were subjected to strong cyclical fluctuations. A combination of these upstream and downstream factors explained why the average operating margins of equipment vendors slipped from 17.8 per cent in 1997 to 15.5 per cent in 1999. Eurostaf, *Les équipementiers télécoms*, pp. 26–9, 80 (Vol. 1).

[100] Intent on concentrating its financial resources exclusively on R&D, by the late 1990s, Ericsson had hived off most of its production facilities to contract manufacturers. In 2000, Nortel turned over seven of its plants to Solectron, a leading global contract manufacturer, while Motorola had fixed a target of outsourcing 50 per cent of its production by 2002. Eurostaf, *Les équipementiers télécoms*, pp. 48–9, 67–9.

ITI could not embark upon a similar strategy. Neither could it try and diversify its customer base by taking advantage of the rollback of DoT's monopoly to approach private telecommunications service providers since it lacked proprietary technology.[101] As a consultant's report highlighted:

There are no high value addition businesses with good future potential. This is a gap in ITI's portfolio.[102]

Such a high degree of dependence on external sources for technology also presented other greater dangers. As a major supplier of C-DoT equipment, the company suffered from inadequate demand following the swing in DoT's procurement policies towards foreign technology where as the trade unions noted, perhaps not unjustly, the opportunities for negotiating kickbacks were far more promising. Despite its economic superiority, the share of C-DoT switches in the total number of lines commissioned would drop from about 44.7 per cent in 1993–94 to 30.5 per cent in 1996–97 with the trend worsening subsequently.[103] The state carrier would initially justify its decision against selecting indigenous technology on the ground that that these switches could not support integrated services digital network (ISDN) facilities, notwithstanding the minuscule number of subscribers using this facility. But the bias in DoT's policies continued even after C-DoT had upgraded its equipment. As a result, ITI would be forced to close down its Electronic City unit dedicated to the manufacture of C-DoT exchanges and one of

---

[101] Whether or not private operators would have sourced their equipment requirements from ITI in case it had the right products is another question. Despite the outstanding track record of C-DoT switches and their low costs, not even one private firm was using these indigenously developed exchanges, notes Ashok Jhunjhunwala. 'Looking beyond NTP 99', in *India Infrastructure Report 2001*, pp. 210–16. Parthasarathy has, however, argued that the failure of the National Telecommunications Policy (1994) to provide the right incentives for private basic service operators to speedily roll out their network limited the development of the domestic market for equipment manufacturers. *Globalization and Agglomeration in Newly Industrializing Countries,* pp. 290, 301–2.

[102] PwC Recommendations, p. 9.

[103] Sunil Mani, 'Deregulation, Entry of MNCs, Public Technology Procurement and Innovation Capability in India's Telecommunications Equipment Industry', Institute for New Technologies Discussion Paper Series (Maastricht), April 2003, p. 32. Subsequently, from a high of 610,490 lines in 2000–01, the number of C-DoT lines supplied to BSNL-MTNL would plummet to 90,230 in 2002–03 (*Source*: C-DoT).

its best performing plants.[104] Production volumes at the plant had reached a record high of 804,000 lines of switching equipment in 2000–01. But the following year, the figure sank to 473,300 lines on account of 'sluggish market conditions', and in 2002–03, it would receive virtually no orders for C-DoT equipment.[105] The Rae Bareli unit which also made C-DoT exchanges faced a similar situation of a near-empty order book. In a letter sent to the communications minister in July 2002, the union complained that during the current financial year the factory had not received a 'single work order, so manpower and raw material are becoming idle (sic)'.[106]

More crucially, it would be C-DoT's inability to come up with a mobile switch that would be the principal source of ITI's difficulties in the coming years, exposing in the process the perilous situation that the company's lack of proprietary technology had placed it in. In the restructuring plan drawn up in 2000 for ITI by consultancy firm PwC, its key strategic recommendations took for granted continued and strong growth in fixed telephony. Although this assessment did not turn out to be wholly incorrect, it completely failed to anticipate the explosion in demand for mobile telecommunications, revealing the extent to which PwC had misread consumer trends in the telecommunications market.[107] Whereas fixed line connections averaged an annual growth of 21.56 per cent between 1997–2002, the corresponding figure for mobile lines, though starting from a very low base, was a staggering 80 per cent, and the rate of growth was expected to be even higher in the coming years.[108] In the absence of a detailed technology foresight exercise for the

---

[104] ITI Revival Plan.

[105] Annual Report, 2001–02, p. 16.

[106] Letter from ITI Karamchari Sangha Rae Bareli to the minister of state for communications, 12 July 2002.

[107] Based on its market analysis, PwC had forecast a 'strong revenue growth of 25 per cent per annum' for ITI from 1999–2000 over the next five years, and a 'significant increase' in profit before tax which was set to grow eight fold. Barely two years later, a severe demand crunch engulfed the public sector company and it began haemorrhaging increasingly bigger amounts of cash. PwC Recommendations, p. 9.

[108] *Draft Tenth Five Year Plan*, New Delhi, 2002, p. 1029. The late 1990s, in fact, witnessed a shift in national telecommunications investment strategies. An increasing number of developing countries substituted mobile telephones for fixed telephony or made a direct leap to mobile telephony without deploying any fixed infrastructure. OMSYC, *The World Telecommunications Market*, Paris, 2002, p. 25.

telecommunications sector, the pace of change in the switchover from wired to wireless communication, reflected in the boom in cellular mobile telephony, caught both C-DoT and ITI totally unprepared (as also the private sector), and would have serious consequences for both organizations.

A warning was given to C-DoT that continuous slippages with regard to technology upgradation and new product development may compel DoT to review its procurement policies, fuelling reports that the government planned to close down the research centre.[109] In the case of ITI, orders for fixed or land lines, the mainstay of its business netting it annual revenues of Rs 5000 million, soon started to dry up. But it had no substitute product on hand to compensate for the shortfall. Already, the sharp decline in the price of switching equipment had obliged the management to temper its optimism and readjust downwards future projections of the contribution from this line of activity to its revenue stream in the next few years.[110] Now, an internal note entitled 'Areas of Concern: ITI Ltd.' stressed that due to insufficient orders for OCB main exchanges, plant capacity at the Mankapur unit was idling.[111] This was a particularly alarming development because this factory was by far, the most profitable of the company's seven production facilities.

So with C-DoT unable to transfer cellular technology, ITI again had to scout for foreign collaborations. Since both Bharat Sanchar Nigam Limited or BSNL (as the service arm of DoT became known in the year 2000) and MTNL were in the process of rolling out their cellular operations, the company had no option but to acquire expertise in this

[109] *Business Line*, 6 April 2001; *Hindustan Times*, 21 September 2001; *The Hindu*, 10 February 2003.

[110] ITI Revival Plan. The price of large digital switches fell from approximately Rs 7800 per line in March 1996 to Rs 4250 in February 1999, before crashing to under Rs 2000 the following year. In a tender for 2.45 million lines in 2000, for instance, Lucent (ex-AT&T) emerged as the lowest bidder with a rate of Rs 1990 per line, whereas ITI which had linked up with Alcatel on this occasion, quoted Rs 2400 and came third. Saturated markets in the developed countries plus competition from domestic manufacturers of C-DoT exchanges who were able to supply switches at a cost of Rs 2500 to 3000 per line, could explain why transnational corporations had sharply reduced prices. But Lucent's bid would again spark accusations of dumping, and denials by DoT. *Pragati*, No. 8, August 2000. Minutes of Standing Committee on Telecommunications, nd.

[111] ITI Corporate Office, nd.

and other areas. A technical collaboration agreement with Lucent provided access to Global System for Mobile (GSM) cellular technology. The partnership proved quite successful, winning three lucrative, high profile tenders floated by MTNL and BSNL between 2000–02 in the face of strong competition from transnationals such as Alcatel, Ericsson and Motorola.[112] Whereas Lucent provided the infrastructure equipment, the mobile switching centres, ITI undertook the installation and commissioning of the networks on a turnkey basis. Technical-commercial alliances were concluded in other fields as well with foreign partners.[113] However, the financial benefits yielded by these agreements were marginal, because the equipment was often not being manufactured in-house and ITI was only trading in them. To quote a company document:

for 'in' products in current scenario like GSM and WLL-CDMA (Wireless in Local Loop-Code Division Multiple Access) . . . there is little value addition, and in most of the cases the percentage of raw material costs to sales value is very high. This requires high turnover to meet the fixed overheads and operational costs in order to achieve break-even.[114]

Though the contribution of access products and mobile communications to the company's turnover, estimated at about 40 per cent in 2003–04, was already set to exceed that of switching equipment, and perhaps grow even bigger in the coming years, for the moment, their sales volumes were still inadequate to generate strong profits. It was partly to overcome this obstacle that an agreement negotiated in September 2003 between ITI and a leading Chinese equipment vendor Shenzhen Zhongxing Telephones specified that ITI would locally manufacture WLL-CDMA network equipment, as well as GSM and CDMA mobile handsets.[115] Top ITI management had recognized the

[112] The MTNL tender was for the roll-out of its cellular mobile network in Bombay and Delhi, while the BSNL tender concerned the installation of its mobile network in four states (Maharashtra, Gujarat, MP and Chattisgarh). *ET*, 5 June 2003. Lucent's subsequent decision to stop manufacturing GSM systems, however, threatened to create problems for ITI, especially with regard to equipment upgradation.

[113] A tie-up with Qualcomm, for instance, enabled ITI to secure a foothold in the field of access products. But the US company was subsequently accused by BSNL of supplying sub-standard equipment, leading ITI to press compensation charges. *Business Line*, 16 June 1999; *ET*, 24 August 1999.

[114] ITI Revival Plan.

[115] For details of the deal see *ITI News*, September 2003; *Business Line*, 1 October 2003.

necessity of demonstrating that the company 'is not a trader but a manufacturer'.[116] By making products in-house, it was better placed to both increase value addition in the context of decreasing margins in manufacturing, and convince customers such as BSNL and MTNL to grant it the status of preferred supplier. But unfortunately for ITI, a government veto would cause its plans to unravel, as we shall later see.

DEMAND AND PRICE CRUNCH PLUNGES ITI INTO DEEP FINANCIAL CRISIS

Meanwhile, the demand-cum-price squeeze hitting the company's switching activities had spread to other areas as well. A letter to the corporate office from the head of the Bangalore plant mentioned that order availability for 2001–02 at the telephone division was under 50 per cent of the established targets. For transmission equipment, the figure was still lower at 20 per cent; but for spill-over orders from the previous year, things would have been much worse. He went to add:

The foregoing position thus depicts a compelling situation of forced idleness very shortly in most of the Production Groups in the Plant unless a policy decision is taken to procure materials and load the shops in anticipation of orders and also the selling price.[117]

On the competitive front, the management estimated that falling prices had affected ITI's sales margins to the extent of Rs 2500 million for the year 2000–01 alone. At the Bangalore plant, the price erosion ranged from 5 to 35 per cent for products other than switches where the decline was steeper (Table 4.8). Despite cutting material costs considerably, the efforts of the telephone division had not succeeded in keeping pace with the constant downward push in selling prices. Between 1995–96 and 2002–03, prices of electronic push button telephones had dropped from Rs 361 to Rs 190, or by 47.4 per cent, whereas ITI's material costs, which stood at roughly Rs 241 in 1998–99, remained stuck at around Rs 210.[118] In no tender floated during this period did the company emerge either as the lowest bidder.

---

[116] ITI Revival Plan.

[117] Ref. DB/EDRO/Cors., 17 April 2001; Ref. EDRO-1-11, 25 July 2001.

[118] Replying to a parliamentary commission, DoT claimed that it was not compromising on quality by purchasing equipment at prices much lower than those

Indeed, ITI's position on the market for telephone instruments had become increasingly untenable. Terminal products comprised part of the overall equipment package delivered to DoT: purchases of higher value switching and transmission systems were tied to the supply of telephones. Hence, despite being a chronically loss-making business for several years now, the company could ill afford to phase out this line.[119] On the other hand, it did not command the infrastructural resources to try and extract whatever gains the segment had to offer. Although fixed line connections witnessed a phenomenal growth from 1992 onwards, capacity constraints at both the Bangalore and Naini plants prevented ITI from capitalizing on this boom in sharp contrast to private competitors which satisfied the bulk of DoT's demands.

Whereas the state carrier had installed 32.7 million new main lines over the course of the Eight and the Ninth Plan, ITI's share stood at no more than 9 million phones.[120] One way the company could have hoped to offset, at least partially, the effects of the uninterrupted price slump was by significantly boosting production volumes in order to exploit scale economies. But since telephones represented a wholly unprofitable activity, the question of augmenting capacity through investments in faster machines and automation just did not arise, especially in the light of the company's worsening financial health. In 2001, the terms of the reserve quota required ITI to provide DoT with 2.4 million sets annually. But its total potential manufacturing capacity stood at barely half this number. Consequently, at a time when some of the company's other divisions complained of insufficient workloads, the Bangalore and Naini telephone divisions were paradoxically turning down orders.

Struggling to operate in a highly volatile market environment, ITI would soon also have to cope with a new problem arising from changes

---

quoted by ITI. COPU 1997, p. 55. Nevertheless, to put a stop to the practice of private firms subcontracting the assembly of printed circuit boards and importing very low quality moulded parts from South East Asian markets, the state carrier intended prescribing infrastructure criteria to which all telephone manufacturers would be required to conform. Tel. Divn. note, 6 October 2001.

[119] After the company had declined to supply telephones on one occasion, arguing that the selling price offered by DoT was far too low and would result in big losses, the latter threatened to retaliate by withholding purchases of all ITI-made products and cancelling the totality of its reserve quota. Interview with B.K. Sharma.

[120] *Draft Tenth Five Year Plan*, p. 1029; Annual Report (various years).

in the institutional context. In October 2000, after considerable hesitation, the government had finally resolved to separate DoT's policy functions from its service functions, turning over its operational network to a new corporate structure, BSNL. For ITI, the corporatization of DoT would have significant consequences. Arguing that it would be subjected to additional financial liabilities, which were not applicable to DoT, and must 'act henceforth as a commercial entity', BSNL informed the company that it intended to withdraw the system of advance payments, failing which it would charge interest on the advances.[121] ITI, therefore, found itself in a situation comparable to the mid-1990s where it again needed to obtain funds at a high cost from financial institutions to meet its working capital requirements. Borrowings would increase sharply by 9.6 per cent in 2001–02 while interest payments rose by 6.2 per cent.

Table 4.6: ITI Financial Results 1997–98 to 2003–04

Year	Sales (Rs. mn)	% growth	Profit before Tax (Rs. mn)	% growth	Profit before Tax % Sales	Value Added % Sales
1997–98	12, 630.5	23.7	169.7	—	1.3	44.2
1998–99	15, 390.9	21.8	324.1	91	2.1	45
1999–2000	20, 851.8	35.5	198.4	(38.8)	0.9	47.6
2000–01	21, 442	2.8	297.9	50.1	1.4	45.7
2001–02	23, 170	8	260	(12.7)	1.1	41.6
2002–03	17, 950	(22.5)	*–3740*	—	—	32.6
2003–04	12,570	(30)	*–6840*	—	—	20.7
Average						*39.6*

Notes: Profit before tax does not include prior period adjustments.
           Figures in brackets indicate negative growth. Figures in italics indicate losses.
Source: ITI Annual Report, various years.

Soon afterwards, a profound crisis convulsed the public sector company. After four years of mediocre and seesawing profits, following its recovery in the late 1990s, it posted the biggest-ever loss in its history of Rs 3740

---

[121] Letter from ITI chairman to director Bangalore Plant, Ref. DO No. CM/27.4, 8 May 2001; Minutes of union-management apex meeting, 10–11 May 2000.

million in 2002–03 (Table 4.6). Turnover contracted by 22.5 per cent over the previous year, and the fact that it shrank further in 2003–04, even as losses grew even higher, only served to underline the durable nature of the crisis confronting ITI. Value added as a percentage of revenue which had been steadily declining for a number of years averaged barely 39.6 per cent for the period 1997–98 to 2003–04.[122] The performance of the different units reflected the gravity of the overall situation. Barring Palakkad, all the other manufacturing plants were steeped in red (Table 4.7). Even the Mankapur unit, ITI's cash cow in the past, recorded losses in 2002–03, while the three main units (Bangalore, Rae Bareli, and Naini) continued to haemorrhage ever growing amounts of money.

Table 4.7: Profit Before Tax at ITI Units 1997–98 to 2002–03 (Rs. million)

Unit	1997–98	1998–99	1999–2000	2000–01	2001–02	2002–03
B'lore	*–482.4*	*–270.2*	*–39*	*–356.8*	*–367.6*	*–1363.7*
Rae Bareli	*–302.3*	*–311.7*	*–453.6*	*–277.1*	*–897.9*	*–1079.2*
Naini	*–672.8*	*–692.2*	*–386.6*	*–98.5*	*–134*	*–800.1*
Mankapur	883.1	895.1	932	92	118.1	*–899.1*
Palakkad	792	765.5	*–47.1*	157.2	565.4	392.1
EC Unit	278	76.7	161	87.8	*–94.2*	*–191.5*
Srinagar	*–41.2*	*–50.2*	*–42*	*–26.9*	*–32.9*	*–56.5*
NSU	*–101.5*	*–30.4*	23	30.8	15.9	18
Regional Offices	38.5	64.3	126.8	161.1	200.4	193.6
Corporate Office	*–221.7*	*–122.8*	*–76.20*	528.3	791.1	59.4

Notes: Profit before tax includes prior period adjustments.
Losses indicated in italics. *NSU = Network Systems Unit.
Source: ITI Annual Report, various years.

An identical scenario applied to the company's product line (Table 4.8). With the exception of the network business, all the other activities saw their revenues fall, the worst hit being telephones. Crushed by the price squeeze, telephone sales value plummeted by over 54 per cent

[122] Value added as a percentage of revenue, after averaging 60.1 per cent for the period 1984–85 to 1990–91, had dropped to 45.9 per cent for the period 1991–92 to 1996–97.

252 Telecommunications Industry in India

between 1997–98 and 2002–03. Similarly, after a temporary recovery from 1999–2000 to 2000–01, sales of transmission equipment again resumed the earlier downward trend. An advertisement put out a couple of year earlier by the Naini unit of the company had with hyperbolic flourish compared ITI to 'a new tiger with new strengths, new stamina, and with a killer instinct'.[123] It was a mortally wounded tiger that was now obliged to declare itself potentially 'sick' and to report to the BIFR with the risk of seeing its credit worthiness and financial ratings downgraded.[124]

Table 4.8: ITI Product Revenues and Equipment Prices 1997–98 to 2002–03

Product Category	1997–98	1998–99	1999–00	2000–01	2001–02	2002–03
Switching	9084.8	12,007	14,512.1	13,360	16,839.8	11,010
Revenues (Rs mn)	(31.8%)	(32.2%)	(20.8%)	*(–7.9%)*	(26%)	(–34.6)
Switching Prices						
i) C-DoT MAX-XL			Rs 3570 (per line)	Rs 3353	Rs 3210	
ii) Digital Local Exch.	Rs 5295 (per line)	Rs 4390	Rs 1989	Rs 2739		
iii) Digital Trunk Exch.			Rs 3223 (per circuit)	Rs 2158	Rs 2825	
Transmission	2173.1	1904.7	4345.6	4635	3370.6	2990
Revenues (Rs mn)	(20.1%)	*(–12.3%)*	(128.1%)	(6.6%)	*(–27.3%)*	*(–11.3%)*
Transmission Prices						
i) STM (1 terminal)			Rs 2.83mn	Rs 1.65mn	Rs 1.8mn	
ii) STM (4 terminal)			Rs 6.03mn	Rs 3.33mn	Rs 5.06mn	
iii) C-DoT SBM (400 line)			Rs 3878 (per line)	Rs 3641	Rs 4193	
Telephone	790.3	390.2	465.8	525.3	480.9	360
Revenues (Rs mn)	*(–12.6%)*	*(–50.6%)*	(19.4%)	(12.8%)	*(–8.4%)*	*(–25.1%)*
Telephone Prices	Rs 343	Rs 300	Rs 282	Rs 265	Rs 210	Rs 190
Services Revenues (Rs mn)	582.4 (3.5%)	878.8 (50.9%)	1210.1 (37.7%)	1995.4 (64.9%)	1962.6 *(–1.6%)*	2440 (24.3%)
Defence Equipment Revenues (Rs mn)	—	210	522 (148.6%)	585.8 (12.2%)	517.7 *(–11.6%)*	280 *(–45.9%)*

Notes: Figures in brackets indicate percentage growth and/or decline; negative growth indicated in italics.

Source: Annual Reports, various years; ITI Corporate Office.

---

[123] ITI Product Portfolio Brochure, nd.

[124] *Business Line*, 5 November 2002. See also notes of management-union apex meeting, 12 November 2002.

The top management's response to the debacle was roughly along the same lines as in the mid-1990s. In March 2003, it sent the government a 'Revival Plan' detailing the various measures it intended to adopt to restructure the enterprise together with a demand for a Rs 13,390 million aid package in order to implement the plan. In the same year, ITI had already received Rs 3000 million from BSNL and MTNL by issuing redeemable preference shares to both service carriers. But, according to officials, this interim financing arrangement was insufficient given the depth of the company's haemorrhage. They warned that ITI was trapped in a vicious cycle where continued losses would lead to a cash crunch which would result in a production shortfall contributing in turn to lower sales, and ultimately feeding back into even higher losses. Hence the 'assistance sought from the government is most critical for the company's survival'.[125]

To be spread over a four year period from 2003–07, the aid package, which reiterated certain demands raised by the company in the late 1990s, consisted of three main components: an equity infusion of Rs 2000 million in order to enable ITI to shed part of its high-cost debt, and in turn bring down interest costs;[126] a soft loan of Rs 4800 million to be utilized for modernizing the manufacturing infrastructure and upgrading technology; and a grant of Rs 6410 million meant to take care of future voluntary retirement expenditure. In addition, the management wanted the government to reimburse the sums the company had paid by way of voluntary retirement and liquidated damages, imposed by DoT since the late 1990s, and which jointly amounted to roughly Rs 2400 million, as well as convert a government loan of Rs 135 million into equity. A year after it had received the revival plan, DoT claimed that it was still examining the proposals, together with the finance and law ministries, notwithstanding the fact that the crisis at ITI had taken a much sharper turn for the worse by then.

A few broad remarks can be made by way of a conclusion. A combination of factors, related to state policy decisions, the company's relations with DoT and technological developments, worked in unison

[125] ITI Revival Plan.
[126] According to the secretary DoT, ITI's inadequate equity base was its 'most important problem', because of which 'the interest burden itself is becoming unbearable'. Standing Committee on Communications, 11th Report, Eleventh Lok Sabha, p. 32.

to bring about a dramatic deterioration in ITI's performance. Far from achieving the government's stated objective of introducing greater efficiencies in public sector enterprises, deregulation only succeeded in weakening ITI by transforming a once-profitable firm into a chronic loss-maker. In the words of the former ITI Chairman and Secretary, Department of Electronics, K.P.P. Nambiar, 'under the guise of liberalization the government strangled the public sector'.[127] As with other state-owned units, no measures were initiated, prior to the launch of economic reforms, to assist the company modernize its manufacturing infrastructure and upgrade its technological capabilities. The result was that it was totally unprepared to confront the harsh mechanisms of the market.[128] Nor were ITI's interests better served by the decision of policy makers to indiscriminately expose it to competition by throwing open the domestic market to foreign companies, which were often inclined to dump equipment at throw-away prices, without taking care to provide appropriate checks and balances. The bureaucracy chose to consistently disregard the fact that Indian firms, irrespective of their efficiency, were in no position to compete on equal terms with transnational corporations, backed by their huge research departments, tremendous marketing strengths and global reach. As Stanley Kochanek has noted, prominent sections of Indian big business, citing South Korea as their model, voiced their hostility to a radical integration of the domestic economy with the global economy.[129] Unrestricted inflows of foreign investment, they feared, could inflict considerable harm on indigenous industry. But while ready to listen to, and allay, the concerns of private entrepreneurs, the authorities refused to show the same solicitude to the public sector.

The difficulties encountered by ITI also stand in distinct contradiction

---

[127] Interview with K.P.P. Nambiar.

[128] Lest it be forgotten, even a government as self-consciously neo-liberal as the Thatcher administration granted British Telecom a two-year grace period to restructure its operations before authorizing the entry of private players.

[129] Stanley Kochanek, 'Liberalisation and Business Lobbying in India', *Journal of Commonwealth and Comparative Politics*, Vol. 34, No. 3, November 1996, pp. 155–73. See also K. Williams et al., 'Accounting for Failure in the Nationalized Enterprises— Coal, Steel and Cars since 1970', *Economy and Society*, 15, 1986, pp. 167–219, who, in their study of three British state-owned firms, assert that a solution to their long term problems is wholly contingent on government action to secure and safeguard their markets in a world of unfair international competition.

to scholarship portraying the dynamic of the post-1991 reform process as 'gradualist'.[130] The pluralist nature of Indian politics associated with the need to build sufficient consensus for the new accumulation model so as to ensure continuity as well as the legitimacy of the ruling elites signified that implementational delays would be part and parcel of the shift to a more open economy. So went this line of reasoning. Terms like 'gradualism', 'reforms by stealth' or 'backdoor reforms' may well be valid in evaluating policy ramifications in spheres such as the labour market or the public distribution system where the existence of relatively vocal interest groups signalled the likelihood of collective opposition to plans to overhaul the *status quo*.[131] But they definitely failed to capture the realities of micro-level corporate experiences where the rupture with the old planned industrial regime and the ensuing pace of change tended to be far more pronounced. This was essentially because power relations at these sites favoured not managements and/or workers plus their representatives, invariably constrained to mobilize in isolation, but the state. As the example of ITI graphically illustrated, the manner in which the elimination of entry barriers was decided in many product categories owed little to concerns 'to ease the pain of transition'.[132] On the contrary, exposure to the cold winds of competition was immediate, brutal and devastating in its effects. None of the obfuscation or one-step forward-two-steps-backward approach so characteristic of official action in certain areas was visible in segments such as telecommunications manufacturing. Instead, a lethal combination of opportunistic pricing tactics, official venality and the absence of regulation served to transform the prevailing business environment into a no-holds-barred jungle. The initiatives pursued were resolutely pro-market and not pro-business in emphasis, the objective being to privilege new entrants as opposed to established producers, typically beneficiaries of a pro-business strategy.[133]

---

[130] M. S. Ahluwalia, 'Economic Reforms in India Since 1991: Has Gradualism Worked?' *Journal of Economic Perspectives*, Vol. 16, No. 3, Summer 2002, pp. 67–88; and 'Understanding India's Reform Trajectory: Past Trends and Future Challenges', *India Review*, Vol. 3, No. 4, October 2004, pp. 269–77.

[131] Rob Jenkins, *Democratic Politics and Economic Reform in India*, Cambridge, 1999, chap. 6.

[132] Ahluwalia, 'Has Gradualism Worked?' p. 86.

[133] Dani Rodrik and Arvind Subramanian, 'From "Hindu growth" to Productivity Surge: The Mystery of the Indian Growth Transition', unpublished, March 2004.

Liberalization thus certainly fulfilled its assigned function of 'shock therapy' as far as several public undertakings were concerned. But the end result of permanently red balance sheets may not quite have been what the authorities had bargained for.[134]

The omissions on the part of the government were compounded by the indifferent attitude adopted by DoT with respect to ITI, notwithstanding the continued prevalence of soft budget constraints. If the tutelary authority extended only the most minimal form of assistance during the early years of deregulation, the help it agreed to provide subsequently was grossly inadequate in view of the wide-ranging nature of the problems its manufacturing arm had to deal with. It is possible though that this step-motherly treatment was the outcome of DoT deciding to concentrate its efforts and resources on expanding the national telecommunications network, a strategy which undoubtedly took precedence over reviving ITI, given the ever-growing waiting list for telephone connections. One could also argue that because the decline in the company's fortunes occurred against the rosy backdrop of an economic upswing, the government and DoT could afford to behave with relative nonchalance. Less favourable economic circumstances would certainly have diminished the exchequer's capacity to absorb the losses of ITI (and other public sector undertakings) with equal ease, and in turn, perhaps impelled the authorities to commit themselves far more energetically to restructuring the company's operations.

At the same time, in sharp contrast to the experience of other developing countries, liberalization in India did not entail the privatization of state-owned companies. In most cases, there was only a partial denationalization by the state. The upshot of this was that in place of the earlier framework of planned industrial development, a system of dual dependency arose where public companies were subjected to both types of coordination, bureaucratic and market.[135] Vertically

---

[134] There is a paucity of case studies investigating the impact of deregulation on the workings of public sector enterprises. But from the evidence available, several companies like BEL, BEML and HMT appear to have faced a crisis of varying magnitude in the post-1991 era.

[135] This analysis draws in part on Kornai's study of the operations of state-owned enterprises in the reformed Hungarian economy after 1968 and before the collapse of state socialism. Janos Kornai, 'The Hungarian Reform Process: Visions, Hopes and Reality', *Journal of Economic Literature*, Vol. XXIV, December 1986, pp. 1687–737.

dependent on the administrative ministry, which continued to intervene in key areas of corporate strategy making, public sector managements were now also dependent horizontally on its customers, and, to a much greater degree than in the past, suppliers. Bureaucratic control meant that in addition to the lack of autonomy, top executives were accountable to multiple agencies, which in turn, strongly discouraged risk-taking and the exercise of managerial initiative. At the same time, control by market forces meant that public firms were obliged to operate just as efficiently as private firms without, however, possessing the flexibility that the latter enjoyed.

In other words, given their hybrid status, public sector enterprises derived none of the benefits associated with one or the other type of coordination mechanism, whilst having at the same time to contend with the contradictory pressures emanating from the bureaucracy and the market. They were caught between the proverbial rock and a hard place. Thus, on the one hand, by eliminating its monopoly privileges, but not the constraints flowing from state ownership, and, on the other, by imposing new market-related constraints, deregulation had an extremely destabilizing effect on the operations of ITI.

chapter five

Market Forces in Full Play
Management Gains or Losses for Labour?

The progressive elimination of all entry barriers to the telecommunications equipment manufacture segment from 1984 onwards resulted in a paradigm shift in the nature of ITI's operations. In the management's own words, prior to the transition to a competitive market structure the company was not a 'business company in any real sense. It was functioning mainly as a production agency of DoT'.[1] To evolve from a 'production agency' to a 'business company', now that the Indian state had enshrined commercial rationality as the central element of a new political and economical credo, signified that ITI, like all other state-owned enterprises, had to embrace new goals and policies, and ways of doing things. From a volume-based profit strategy, it had perforce to shift to a profit strategy centred on cost reduction which involved putting into place a reformulated as well as coherent and enduring 'productive model'.[2] The capacity of the company to survive

---

[1] Minutes of 14th management-union Joint Committee meeting, 11 August 1994.

[2] Robert Boyer and Michel Freyssenet, *Les modèles productifs*, Paris, 2000, pp. 106–8. According to them, the need to rebuild, adopt or invent a new productive model generally arises when national growth patterns, or revenue generation sources and

in the new business environment depended on the speed with which it adopted the new model. Exploring just how successfully ITI coped with negotiating the process of change from a captive manufacturing unit to a commercial organization at a time when the entire telecommunications sector was in a state of flux should enable us to assess two things: the specific character of managerial practices in the context of a crisis, and the complex pattern of relationships prevailing between different sections of the management.

The principal source of ITI's difficulties as identified by senior executives and external consultants was its high fixed cost structure. In effect, this factor served to explain why its products were over-priced, thereby severely diminishing its capacity to compete effectively on the market. Fixed costs as a percentage of turnover averaged in excess of 30 per cent. Over half this figure was accounted for by one element: manpower costs. The key to the company's ability to generate adequate profits in a context marked by sharply declining margins, therefore, revolved around its success in drastically lowering its overheads, which in turn, essentially implied cutting down its salary and benefits bill.[3] To conclude from the above that the strategic focus of top managers was riveted on the workforce, would, however, be an error. Firms generally tend to react to competition in multiplex ways, and forcing down employee costs is only one of these *pace* the interpretations of labour process theorists, often prone to conflating corporate strategy with labour control strategy.[4] So in addition to the question of labour reduction, officials at the troubled public sector enterprise devised a wide array of

---

distribution mechanisms, within which the productive models operate, become destabilized. In other words, enterprise-level profit strategies derive their viability from the degree to which they successfully mesh or cohere with macro-economic policies. In the typology established by the authors, a volume-based profit strategy is coextensive with a fordist productive model, whereas a strategy consisting of permanent cost reduction is associated with the toyotist model.

[3] Following her appointment in 2001, the new ITI Chairman Lakshmi Menon had set an objective of reducing fixed expenditure by at least 15 per cent annually. Ref. DO No. CM/27.4, 8 May 2001.

[4] On this point see Batstone et al, *Consent and Efficiency*, pp. 2–4; Stephen Wood and John Kelly, 'Taylorism, Responsible Autonomy and Management Strategy', in S. Wood (ed.), *The Degradation of Work? Skill, Deskilling and the Labour Process*, London, 1982, pp. 74–89.

measures geared to help it break out of the low efficiency-high cost-poor quality syndrome.

The previous chapter has already discussed just how fundamental an issue acquiring technological capabilities was in a business context dominated by research-intensive transnational corporations. Similarly, the company's heavy interest burden, which after manpower ranked as the second proximate cause of high overheads, automatically meant that considerable attention had to be devoted to financial issues.[5] Steps to prune material expenditure had to be taken as well. Another priority area was quality given the dismal performance standards of ITI's products. No less important was the establishment of a marketing department so as to make the company more responsive to customer needs. Reducing the cycle time needed for designing and developing new products which would be more cost effective and meet market norms for quality implied in turn a reorganization of its R&D activities. The equipment manufacturer also sought to reduce its dependence on its principal customer, DoT, by exploring new markets, particularly within the country. Lastly, the management hired a consultancy firm PwC to assist it undertake an extensive restructuring of the company's operations. To paraphrase Charles Sorensen, a key aide of Henry Ford Senior, in the wake of liberalization ITI executives were beginning to painfully learn that the telecommunications business involved the fusion of three arts: the art of buying materials, the art of production, and the art of selling.[6]

Mastering these arts ultimately proved beyond the competence of top management. For a variety of reasons, the implementation of the internal reform drive would remain fitful and half-hearted, thus jeopardizing a turn around in the company's position. More prescient on this occasion than it had been in forecasting the evolution of the mobile telephony market, the warning issued by PwC that ITI's status as a state-owned undertaking 'may be a hindrance in exploring the fullest extent of strategic and financial restructuring possible (sic)', would come

---

[5] Trimming interest costs as a percentage of sales from a high of 7 per cent to 4.5 per cent, by securing cheaper sources of credit, was another essential management objective. COPU 1997, p. 35.

[6] Charles Sorensen, *My Forty Years with Ford*, New York, 1956, cited in David Hounshell, *From the American System to Mass Production: The Development of Manufacturing Technology in the United States*, Baltimore-London, 1984, p. 22.

to be confirmed by the final outcome.[7] The very nature of the functioning of the public sector tended to sap the different decisions of much of their effectiveness with worker resistance, union opposition, management deficiencies, and government indifference all playing a consequential role. Stated otherwise, regardless of the enabling force of current conditions, facilitating in principle the exercise of managerial voluntarism in pushing through change, 'path dependency' as articulated in the sequence of past decisions and activities was, in no small measure, going to inflect the rate, pace and substance of organizational mutation.[8]

AMBIVALENT REACTION OF WORKERS TO COMPANY'S DIFFICULTIES

How did the ITI workforce perceive the crisis experienced by the company in the wake of deregulation? Employees' own reactions to and understanding of the situation took multiple, and at times, contradictory forms. Corporate discourse made it abundantly clear that ITI's ability to withstand competition could only be achieved by overcoming its internal shortcomings: low productivity, poor quality, wastages, surplus manpower, escalating labour costs etc. Stress was laid in particular on the last two elements. Not surprisingly therefore, circulars, appeals and letters targeting the workforce rang aloud with emphatic sentences urging 'attitudinal change', 'sacrifices at all levels', and a 'holiday on demand'. Employees were warned that the days when 'we (got) hardly four hours of actual work in a shift of eight hours'[9] and produced equipment 'at *any cost*' were over.[10]

These exhortations might have proved slightly more effective had they not been contradicted by the management's own actions. As one senior executive observed, on the one hand, officials constantly stressed the

---

[7] PwC Recommendations, p. 13.

[8] Zan et al stress the importance of revealing 'temporal interconnectedness', by analysing how antecedent conditions, such as ownership or human resources, impact on the extent of business strategy change. Luca Zan et al, 'Introduction', in *idem* (eds.) *Perspectives on Strategic Change*, Boston, 1993, pp. xiv–xv. See also Arthur Stinchcombe, 'Social Structure and Organizations', in James March (ed.), *Handbook of Organizations*, Chicago, 1965, pp. 142–93.

[9] ITI Personnel Department files, 29 May 1986.

[10] Letter, 1 January 1998. Emphasis in original.

severity of the company's financial crisis, but, on the other, continued granting employees bonus even during the three loss-making years in the late 1990s.[11] Periodic campaigns, branded as 'operations' by top management in a bid to instil a sense of urgency, aimed at mobilizing support for its efforts to improve efficiency also rapidly acquired a ritualistic character, illustrating the 'fallacy of programmatic change'.[12] Organizational inertia aside, both executives and non-executives knew quite well that the fate of the company rested ultimately not on any local initiatives but on government policy orientations.

So during the initial stages of deregulation, workers appear to have been relatively unconcerned by the fact that the company now had to stand up to the pressures of competition.[13] Indeed, the management complained bitterly on at least one occasion that its efforts to introduce new product lines at the Bangalore plant were being resisted by workers, and that shop floor representatives were refusing to cooperate with divisional officers in solving the issue.[14] Similarly, operatives stubbornly refused to join the quality circles the company attempted to periodically promote. While acknowledging that participation in quality circle meetings could help sharpen their technical skills, operatives stayed away because they were not compensated for the loss in incentive payments they were likely to suffer during the time spent in the meetings. Shop floor recalcitrance could also in some instances be attributed to group pressure. With several of their colleagues opposed to the idea of joining quality circles, others did not want to run the risk of being branded as management stooges in case they volunteered.

It was only after the losses posted by the company in 1994–95 had made visible the effects of economic liberalization that workers started grasping the implications of the changed market environment within

---

[11] Interview with R. Yuvakumar. Bonus payments were finally stopped in 2003.

[12] Michael Beer et al, 'Why Change Programs Don't Produce Change', *Harvard Business Review*, November-December 1990, pp. 158–66. The authors pertinently observe that company-wide change programmes, promulgated by corporate headquarters, tend to be so general and standardized in their approach and appeal that they end up neglecting day-to-day operational realities of the manufacturing units.

[13] All the information in this and the following paragraphs is based on interviews conducted with both production and non-production workers at the Bangalore plant during three field visits between 1999 and 2001.

[14] Minutes management-union meeting, 17 and 20 April 1993.

which ITI now had to operate. Doubtless ITI's status as a state-owned enterprise, and its logical corollary, the high degree of job security afforded to employees, served to assuage their worst anxieties about the future.[15] Still, the initial sentiment was one of disbelief mixed with apprehension: 'how could a company that had been profitable all along suddenly sink into the red?' There were rumours of the company eliminating certain unprofitable activities such as telephones, and leasing out the infrastructure to private entrepreneurs. With over four-fifths of non-officers at the Bangalore plant aged above 40 years in 1995, and possessing only the most rudimentary of qualifications, few entertained doubts about their ability to obtain another job with ease in case the factory was forced to close down or downsize. To quote a machine shop operative:

If the company collapses, workers won't be able to get a single paisa elsewhere. Outside you have to work hard for eight hours. That everybody knows.[16]

Whereas some of the more efficient operatives who regularly earned the highest incentives and had good attendance records believed their efforts would enable them to save their jobs even if ITI was taken over by the private sector, the majority were less confident of dealing with the pressures of heavier work loads. As a number of workers admitted, they were 'unaccustomed to hard work', a factor that was just as much explicable by their age levels as by the more leisured rhythms of work practices they were accustomed to in the public enterprise.

The example of a neighbouring electronics firm, New Government Electric Factory, owned by the Karnataka government, paying its employees half wages by way of lay-off compensation also revived apprehensions that ITI would follow suit, especially since the company's losses were mounting. 'It is already difficult to maintain our families on full wages. So how will we manage on half wages?' asked one employee. All these fears subsided once ITI's financial position started to improve in the late 1990s. Even if they were required to go on voluntary retirement, workers knew they would be leaving the company with a

---

[15] Criticizing the lack of a 'sense of belonging' of public sector workforces, one writer argues that they are indifferent to the fortunes of the company because regardless of profits or losses, they continue to receive wages, bonuses, incentives, etc. In spite of occasional threats, no one seriously believes that losing concerns will eventually close down. Bhaya, 'Colossus with Feet of Clay'.

[16] Interview with Joseph, 14 May 1999.

relatively large monetary package since ITI, a central public sector enterprise, had the capacity to pay. This was in distinct contrast to many private firms.[17]

Yet this did not preclude workers, especially old-timers who had joined before 1970, from expressing a strong sense of regret, even bitterness, as they nostalgically contrasted the present decline in ITI's fortunes with past prosperity. These sentiments were never more acutely experienced as when they encountered material and spatial embodiments of the company's decline: disused machines, silent workspaces, shut down offices, idle workers. To these present day signs of inactivity and abandon which echoed their own ageing, workers counterpoised memories of past activity, testimonies to their own youthful vigour: Indian and foreign dignitaries flocking to the factory to witness its technical prowess; the plant working round the clock during the peak production months of December to March in order to meet annual targets; the din generated by scores of lathes running at full speed at the automatic machines shop; the powerful head of personnel into whose office 'workers entered trembling', and where now stacks of dusty files stood piled, and a couple of jackfruit were left to slowly ripen. Employees also found humiliating press reports comparing ITI to a 'sinking ship' or a 'dinosaur'. Such clichés, by underlining the probable death of the company, could not but have given those who had devoted almost four decades of their life to ITI, the impression that their entire work careers had been in vain as they had ended in failure. Their loyalty to the firm had not been rewarded by its perennation. Moreover, if certain workers had ruled out blue collar jobs for their children, for others this still remained an attractive employment opportunity. Hence, notwithstanding the fact that

---

[17] A study of the Durgapur area revealed that workers in private firms received on average Rs 40,000 by way of voluntary retirement compensation, compared to the Rs 144,000 paid out to public sector workers. Ratan Khasnabis and Sudipti Banerjea, 'Political Economy of Voluntary Retirement. Study of 'Rationalised' Workers in Durgapur', *EPW*, Vol. XXXI, No. 52, 28 December 1996, pp. L64–L72. According to S.K. Goyal, the average compensation distributed to central public sector employees is estimated at Rs 130,000. 'Privatization in India', in G. Joshi (ed.), *Privatization in South Asia. Minimising Negative Social Effects through Restructuring*, New Delhi, 2000, pp. 45–104. However, other examples suggest that large private corporations were better placed to offer more attractive incentives and heavier compensation than public sector firms. M. V. Srinivasan, 'Voluntary Retirement and Workers' Welfare', *EPW*, Vol. XXXIV, No. 28, 10 July 1999, pp. 1873–6.

recruitment had, for all practical purposes, ceased since 1990, workers still clung to the hope of their children getting a job in ITI, or at least receiving training as apprentices. The likelihood of the company now not outliving their working lives must therefore have been a distressing experience for these groups as it effectively signalled the end of their hopes.[18]

However, unlike the management which invariably tended to place the burden of the company's problems on employees' shoulders, the latter showed more even-handedness, apportioning blame to both sides, in addition to the government. The vast majority of employees were qualified as 'conscientious and sincere' and willing to make sacrifices for the sake of the company if required. But workers admitted to the existence of a number of shirkers in their ranks, singling out union officials and their hangers-on as the worst offenders, followed by members of the various cultural associations and workers who represented the company in different sporting activities. All three categories were accused of misusing the various facilities granted by the company so as to avoid working. 'The only group that really works is we direct operatives,' claimed one such assembly operative. But as he and others never tired of pointing out, shop officials commanded sufficient means to make sure nobody shirked or left their work spots without permission.

Criticism of the management then focussed essentially on quotidian issues such as its inability to enforce discipline and schedule raw material flows on time and of the required quality, and its practice of farming out work to ancillary units when adequate capacity existed internally. Not surprisingly, workers suspected executives of receiving kickbacks from these units. But the management was also blamed for having failed to

---

[18] Stating this does not imply in any way that jobs at ITI were like a family inheritance and handed down from one generation to the next. Though certain authors have referred to the prevalence of such *jajamani* traits in public enterprises, including ITI, no such evidence showed up in my research. See Gérard Heuzé, *Ouvriers d'un autre monde. L'exemple des travailleurs de la mine en Inde contemporaine*, Paris, 1989, p. 101; Holmström, *South Indian Factory Workers*, pp. 3–4, 47, 139. On the suffering and sense of loss experienced by workers who are prevented from transmitting their 'heritage', be it material or social, to the next generation because of changing work conditions see Chitra Joshi, 'Hope and Despair: Textile Workers in Kanpur', in *Worlds of Indian Industrial Labour*, pp. 171–203; Stéphane Beaud and Michel Pialoux, *Retour sur la condition ouvrière. Enquête aux usines Peugeot de Sochaux-Montbéliard*, Paris, 1999, pp. 20–1, 259–78.

anticipate the new market developments with the result that it had not been able to plan an appropriate strategy. Lastly, workers resented the constant demands being made upon them to forego various benefits, arguing that top executives not merely continued to enjoy all their perks, but in certain cases, even secured new ones.

Workers' harshest invective was, however, reserved for the government and politicians. If the government's open door policies had allowed transnational corporations to enter the domestic market and indulge in dumping, venal politicians had worsened matters by favouring private companies. Consequently, as the workers saw it, the solution to ITI's troubles lay in the hands of the state. If the state chose not to intervene, it was on account of vested interests which wanted to see the public sector dismantled. Simplistic though the analysis may seem to appear on the surface, it contained more than a grain of truth.

One point worth noting about the workers' discourse is that it was devoid of all traces of anger. Even the threat to exercise their voting power against the government during elections was not articulated.[19] Whether this restraint owed to the complacency arising from the possession of a public sector job, or from a sense of powerlessness that shibboleths such as 'market forces', 'government policy' and 'globalization' evoked, remains open to conjecture. It was as though the trope of 'inevitable change' in the face of inexorable external pressures had stripped workers of their capacity for resistance.[20] As current research has shown, discursive politics 'establishing the global economy as the central horizon of institutional planning' has been integral to justifying reforms in several countries and in railroading 'new public management techniques'.[21] The

---

[19] It is worthwhile contrasting this relatively passive attitude of the workers with the vindictive stance they adopted in the aftermath of the 1980–81 strike. Holding the Congress-I government squarely responsible for the defeat of the strike, workers used their votes with great effectiveness during the 1983 Karnataka state elections. In Bangalore city, the Congress-I was routed in all twelve constituences, including the six or seven where workers in general represented a sizeable proportion of the electorate. For details see Subramanian, 'Bangalore Public Sector: The Unofficial Strike 1981', *South Indian Studies*, No. 3, January-June 1997, pp. 89–143.

[20] Peer C. Fiss and Paul M. Hirsch, 'The Discourse of Globalization: Framing and Sensemaking of an Emerging Concept', *American Sociological Review*, Vol. 70, No. 1, February 2005, pp. 29–52.

[21] André Spicer and Peter Fleming, 'Intervening in the Inevitable: Contesting Globalization in a Public Sector Organization', *Organization*, Vol. 14, No. 4, 2007,

overall reaction of ITI workers then was one of resignation as eloquently manifested by the symbolic forms of protest organized by the union against the government's liberalization measures—*jail bharo*, lunch boycott, relay hunger strikes, badge wearing, slogan shouting, one-day token strikes.

EMPLOYEES RELUCTANT TO OPT FOR VOLUNTARY RETIREMENT

Even before the launch of economic reforms, the government had already authorized public sector enterprises to offer voluntary retirement schemes (VRS) to employees as a means of shedding surplus labour. Because existing labour regulations made dismissals and layoffs an extremely cumbersome process for big companies, notably, reducing manpower by persuading labour to 'voluntarily' surrender jobs in return for monetary compensation became a convenient means of circumventing the law with the tacit accord of the authorities. In October 1988, the Bureau of Public Enterprises issued a directive along these lines, specifying the size of the compensation package as well as other conditions.[22] Managements were also informed that funds for operating the schemes would either have to come from the administrative ministries or be generated internally, as in the case of ITI where DoT promptly declared it would extend no assistance.[23] Burdened with 2700 surplus employees at the main Bangalore plant in the wake of the phasing out of the strowger and cross bar production lines, ITI seems to have toyed briefly with the idea of VR in 1987 itself, before dropping it.[24]

However, once it was exposed to the full blast of competition after the lifting of entry barriers to all segments of equipment manufacturing in 1991, top management was forced to tackle seriously the issue of manpower costs. A buyout plan was rapidly drawn up, and over the

---

pp. 517–41 (cit. p. 520). See also the important article by Paul du Gay analyzing how a narrow conception of enterprise has been leveraged to enforce restructuring strategies in public sector organizations. 'Against "Enterprise" (but not against "enterprise", for that would make no sense)', *Organization*, 2004, Vol. 11, No. 1, pp. 37–57.

[22] Office Memorandum No. 2(36)/86-BPE (WC), 5 October 1988.

[23] Letter from director Telecommunications Commission to ITI chairman, Ref. No. U.49015/2/89-FAC, 11 April 1991.

[24] Note to the Board of Directors, 232nd meeting, item no. B9, June 1987.

following decade, the size of the ITI workforce would contract by almost 35 per cent, falling from 30,280 employees in 1991–92 to 19,692 in 2002–03.[25] The initial response to VR was extremely favourable as employees, attracted by the immediate prospect of obtaining a large lump sum amount, seized this opportunity to leave the company. The only groups whom the latter sought to actively retain were the technically qualified personnel such as degree and diploma holders in electronics and electrical engineering as well as other engineering disciplines. These personnel were declared ineligible for voluntary retirement.

Thus in 1991–92, the first year of the scheme's introduction in ITI, the total number of resignations were 1593, or about 5.3 per cent of the entire workforce. Thereafter, the figure would taper away sharply (see Table 5.1) until 2001–02 when the numbers again registered an upward trend. The rise coincided with the conclusion of a new wage agreement which had the effect of ratcheting up severance payments, and the introduction of a new scheme, both of which combined to make early retirement a more attractive proposition for employees.[26] Payments under this head, consequently, climbed to Rs 561.40 million in 2001–02, or nearly three times the previous year's expenditure. Overall, between 1991–92 and 2002–03, ITI would spend Rs 2368.60 million on the 8777

[25] According to official statistics, a total of 400,000 employees had opted for VR in central public sector companies as of 31 March 2002. *Public Enterprises Survey*, New Delhi, Vol 1, 2001–02. Though not as widespread as during the decade between the early seventies and early eighties, when the switch over from electro-mechanical to electronic technologies led to *en masse* employee lay-offs in the telecommunications equipment industry in Europe and in the US, the nineties witnessed significant job losses at transnational corporations such as Alcatel, Ericsson and Motorola. Alcatel, for instance, reduced its workforce from 194,365 employees in 1992 to 116,992 in 1995, or by almost 40 per cent. An exception to this trend was Nokia which, benefiting from the strong demand for its mobile instruments, increased its workforce by 10 per cent annually on average since 1995. Eurostaf, *Les équipementiers télécoms*, p. 89, Vol. 1; p. 137, Vol. 2.

[26] Whereas the compensation package in the earlier schemes favoured older workers, the new scheme also took into consideration the interests of younger workers who had several remaining years of service until retirement. In addition to the normal terminal benefits (Provident Fund, gratuity, leave encashment etc.), ITI employees were also eligible for a free electronic push button telephone, and travel allowance for the employee and his/her family to relocate in his/her home town. Corporate Personnel Policy, Circular No. 478, 10 October 2003. The new scheme was also estimated to increase the cost of severance benefits to Rs 420 million for every 1000 employees.

employees (non-officers and officers) who accepted the 'golden handshake' with individual severance benefits averaging on aggregate Rs 270,000.

Table 5.1: Voluntary Retirement Scheme Statistics

Year	No. of VRS claimants	Total work Force	VRS claimants as % of total workforce	VRS Expenditures (Rs millions)	National Renewal Fund Repayments (Rs millions)
1991–92	1593	30,280	5.26	162.60	Nil
1992–93	311	29,730	1.05	40.90	Nil
1993–94	500	28,633	1.75	67.30	Nil
1994–95	727	27,477	2.65	114.30	Nil
1995–96	684	26,272	2.6	162.60	50
1996–97	246	25,915	0.95	145	55
1997–98	902	24,552	3.67	139.70	285
1998–99	532	23,945	2.22	155.30	100
1999–2000	333	23,567	1.41	114.10	51.10
2000–01	537	22,914	2.34	208.80	Nil
2001–02	1213	21,518	5.63	561.40	Nil
2002–03	1199	19,692	6.08	496.60	Nil
Total	*8777*		*2.96*	*2368.60*	*541.10*

Source: ITI Corporate P&A, Annual Reports.

But the fact that on average, only 3 per cent of the workforce went on VR annually, is evidence of its relative lack of success. Indeed, as early as in June 1994 itself, many officials argued that the company would be hard-pressed to achieve its objective of building a 'lean and efficient' structure through the existing voluntary retirement programme 'which is restrictive and does not seem to weed out surplus staff'.[27] To borrow Hirschman's oft-quoted terms, ITI workers opposed the company's invitation to exit with an unequivocal show of loyalty. They were clearly reluctant to trade away the long term advantages that job security and the status of public sector employment represented, for short term monetary benefits.[28] Viewed against the backdrop of both decelerating

---

[27] Minutes of 1st Meeting on Company Goals and Objectives, 9 July 1994.

[28] A useful account of the impact of VR on the lives of employees and their families

employment growth and increasing casualization in most sectors of the Indian economy, their unwillingness to demonstrate what the management termed 'entrepreneurial spirit', by seeking alternate career opportunities, was well understandable.[29] Contrary to the airy affirmations of neo-liberal economists, workers, especially those for whom retirement was not an immediate prospect, knew from their first-hand experience of labour market conditions—the famous 'scarcity consciousness' of industrial wage earners that Selig Perlman[30] has spoken about of the consequences of accepting VR: either unemployment or low paid, irregular and unprotected jobs in the informal sector.[31]

Workers also gave a couple of other reasons to justify their refusal to take the golden handshake.[32] First, many of them apprehended being

---

is available in Myrtle Barse, 'Social Implications of Voluntary Retirement Scheme. A Study of Mumbai', *EPW*, Vol. XXXVI, No. 52, 29 December 2001, pp. 4828–35.

[29] On the question of employment trends see, *inter alia*, T.C.A. Anant et al, 'Labour Markets in India: Issues and Perspectives', in J. Filipe and R. Hasan (eds.), *Labour Markets in Asia*, London, 2006, pp. 205–96 (I am grateful to R. Nagaraj for the reference.); R. Nagaraj, 'Employment and Wages in Manufacturing Industries: Trends, Hypotheses and Evidence', *EPW*, Vol. XXIX, No. 4, 22 January 1994, pp. 177–86; T.S. Papola, 'Structural Adjustment, Labour Market Flexibility and Employment', *Indian Journal of Labour Economics*, Vol. 37, No. 1, January-March 1994, pp. 3–16.

[30] Selig Perlman, *A Theory of the Labor Movement*, Philadelphia, 1979, pp. 8, 239–40.

[31] A survey of textile workers in the Bombay–Thane belt, forced to take up occupations in the unorganized sector, revealed a decline of upto 50 per cent in their earnings in the post–VR phase. Ramesh C. Datta, 'Economic Reforms, Redundancy and National Renewal Fund: Human Face or Human Mask?', ISEC, December 2001 (*http://www.rcdatta.com/ KEYNOTE.PDF*). Similar conclusions of impoverishment have also been drawn by scholars investigating the situation of retrenched mill workers in Ahmedabad. See Ernesto Noronha and R. N. Sharma, 'Displaced Workers and Withering of Welfare State', *EPW*, Vol. XXXIV, No. 23, 5 June 1999, pp. 1454–60; Jude Howell and Uma Kambhampati, 'Liberalization and Labour: The Fate of Retrenched Workers in the Cotton Textile Industry in India', *Oxford Development Studies*, Vol. 27, No. 1, February 1999, pp. 109–27. Moreover, even in developed countries, the picture does not appear to be very much different. Many of the buyout takers at the General Motors assembly plant in the US, studied by Ruth Milkman, who remained in wage employment claimed to have experienced downward mobility. *Farewell to the Factory. Auto Workers in the Late Twentieth Century*, Berkeley, 1997, pp. 123, 127–34. See also Barry Bluestone and Bennett Harrison, *The Deindustrialization of America: Plant Closings, Community Abandonment, and the Dismantling of Basic Industry*, New York, 1982, pp. 10–11, 56–7.

[32] All the material in this and the following paragraphs is drawn from interviews conducted with both production and non-production workers at the Bangalore plant during my field trip from October to December 2001.

swindled out of their compensation benefits by children, relatives or friends, or of losing it in imprudent business schemes. Workers would invariably have one or two such stories to narrate, of misfortune befalling friends or colleagues. The constant exchange and circulation of such narratives could be interpreted as playing a dissuasive function, a corpus of counter-examples designed to discourage workers tempted by the promise of immediate money that the separation package offered. Second, many were reluctant to accept VR because they saw it as resulting in a loss of identity, self-worth and, in the end, malehood. Having entered the factory in many cases even before the age of twenty, work was the central reference point of their life worlds, the constitutive element in shaping their perceptions of social realities. To quote one operative:

When we bump into some of our colleagues who have gone on VR, we really feel bad (*bejaar*) to see how they look. All the life (*kalam*) appears to have drained out of their faces. [33]

More than this, being formally unemployed, as Chitra Joshi has justly noted, meant a 'diminished patriarchal presence' in the household.[34] This sentiment is unambiguously articulated by a telephone division assembly operative in the Bangalore unit; though aged 58 years, he insisted he would carry on working until retirement:

If I am still working and earning, I feel there will be discipline and order at home. I will also get respect (*mariayadei*) both at home and outside. If I am in service outside, service inside (at home) will be good. If I ask for glass of water now, my daughters-in-law will rush to get it for me. Nobody now sits directly in front of me. They come only when I call them.[35]

Male workers also expressed fear at having to share domestic spaces once they stopped working, spaces earlier occupied by women and children during the larger part of the day, and believed they would be perceived as a burden by the rest of the household. To these anxieties were added those caused by the lack of consideration and respect that workers sensed they would generally encounter in social interactions after retirement.

---

[33] Interview with Alavandar, 13 November 2001.
[34] Joshi, 'Hope and Despair', p. 201.
[35] Interview with Govindaraju, 27 November 2001.

Neighbours and other people will think that because I am retired I know nothing, that I have nothing to do. And so if they invite me to a function or a marriage, I will certainly come because I am simply sitting at home and not working.[36]

Third, if a reason commonly advanced by workers for taking the buyout was that it enabled them to arrange the marriage of their children, the converse was equally true. In an interesting illustration of how symbolic capital is translated into economic capital, they claimed that, in view of the status associated with public sector employment, remaining in their jobs enhanced the 'value' of their male offspring on the marriage market who could expect to acquire both a good bride and an appreciable dowry. Lastly, workers apprehended the boredom, enforced idleness and isolation that would accompany VR. Industrial work was often monotonous, but it was at least a shared experience. Retired life, on the other hand, threatened to be a timeless continuum that would dissolve the separation that the factory clock had instituted, sometimes at a considerable cost to their personal lives. There would be no distinction between work time, and leisure and family time, rendering meaningless in the process the boundaries between the outside productive arena and the inner reproductive arena.[37]

An examination of the statistics on VR beneficiaries at ITI calls for two broad comments. First, roughly two-thirds of those exiting from the company were non-officers. But this figure increases to a substantial 90 per cent if we also include the two lowest officer grades, since virtually all of them had risen from the ranks.[38] So in reality, officers represented only 10 per cent of the total departures. Yet, funds allocated for this purpose were shared between non-officers and officers in a ratio of 1:3, prompting top management later to describe it as a 'big fallacy which needs to be corrected'.[39]

---

[36] ibid.

[37] Some workers are so conditioned by their factory environments, especially in extremely exacting contexts, that they even tend to organize their private life spheres and leisure activities along the same taylorized principles of clock discipline. Christophe Dejours *Travail: usure mentale. Essai de psycopathologie du travail*, Paris, 1993, p. 56.

[38] Out of a total of 8777 employees who took VR between 1991–92 and 2002–03, non-officers numbered 5742, and officers 3035, of which 1666 belonged to Grade I and 497 to Grade II. All data pertaining to VR provided by ITI Corporate P&A Department.

[39] ITI Revival Plan, 24 September 2003. According to Howell and Kambampathi,

Second, and more significantly, only 10.5 per cent of those who opted for early retirement between 1995–96 and 2002–03 were aged 50 years and below, whereas 56.4 per cent belonged to the cohort 51–55 years, and the remaining one-third were aged above 55 years.[40] In other words, it was the older employees who in the main capitalized on the golden handshake, no doubt because their working lives were drawing to a close, and the less-aged groups who chose to stick with the company because they still had several years of service left. Furthermore, these groups must have been encouraged in their decision not to accept VR by the turn-around in ITI's performance in the late 1990s following the aid package provided by DoT which signalled the intent of the government to ensure its survival.

If the *en masse* exodus of older employees helped to push down, to some measure, the aggregate age levels of the labour force, it would also create difficulties for the company. These employees were by no means the best qualified section of the labour force: a reflection of the overall qualification profile of ITI's personnel, the vast majority of buyout takers, in fact, possessed at best, a high school degree.[41] However, they were

---

who cite a ILO study, the cost of the voluntary retirement programme funded by the National Renewal Fund rose substantially due to golden handshakes awarded to managerial staff. 'Liberalization and Labour'.

[40] Information on age distribution available for the 88,670 employees who took VR in 62 central public sector enterprises until 31 May 1999 shows a similar trend. Over half the employees were aged 50 years and above, whereas nearly 44 per cent belonged to the 35–50 years age group. Goyal, 'Privatization in India', p. 73.

[41] Educational qualifications of the 4962 employees who opted for VR between 1996–97 and 2002–03.

% VRS claimants	Qualification
60.3	Upto SSLC
4.8	Upto PUC
9.6	ITI Trade Certificate
11.9	Diploma
3.3	Tech graduates
5.1	Non-tech graduates
5	Post graduates

Note: SSLC stands for Secondary School Leaving Certificate; PUC is Pre University Certificate. ITI Trade Certificate is acquired after a vocational training programme. Title holders must have at least studied upto or passed SSLC.
Source: ITI Personnel Dept.

both highly experienced and concentrated at the point of production.[42] Hence a paradoxical consequence of the early retirement programme was that the company faced a shortage of production workers.[43] The problem was particularly acute at the main Bangalore plant where the ratio of direct to indirect staff, which had been steadily rising from the 1980s onwards, stood at nearly 1:3 in the late 1990s. As an internal note stressed, maintaining uniform flows of production throughout the year depended critically on the availability of direct operatives.[44]

Similarly, with minimal investments having been made on new machinery for several years, maintenance problems assumed alarming proportions as experienced repair personnel deserted the company. The head of the telephone moulding shop, for example, confessed his inability to keep breakdown levels to below 10 per cent of the total machine hours available as against the stipulated objective of 5 per cent.[45] It was mainly to try and staunch this outflow that the personnel department declared in March 1999 that assembly and machine shop operatives together with testers and inspectors would not be authorized to avail of VR.[46] Another note called for a review of the scheme since 'employees and officers most useful to the company are leaving'.[47] Top management subsequently admitted that since severance payments had been offered uniformly to all employees in the past,

[42] Between 1991–98, 71.5 per cent of the total number of workers who exited from the company's rolls for one reason or the other did so on grounds of VR. See also an internal note, 27 September 1991, which states that out of a total of 272 employees who opted for early retirement at the Bangalore plant in September 1991, 82 per cent were operatives and 64 per cent had 26–35 years working experience.

[43] Assessing the repercussions of VR on one unit situated in Kerala, of a big public sector firm, K. P. Muraleedharan writes that the scheme turned out to be counterproductive since 75 per cent of the departing employees were the best qualified ones. 'Implementation of Voluntary Retirement Scheme: Some Issues', *Productivity*, Vol. 37, No. 2, July-September 1996, pp. 278–80. Much the same unintended consequences also bedevilled the buyout programme at State Bank of India. A. Mukund and K. Subhadra, 'The State Bank of India VRS', Hyderabad, ICMR, 2001 (mimeo).

[44] For the year 1999–2000, for instance, the plant only disposed of 1685 operatives, whereas its requirements in order to meet production targets were 2178. Note 13 November 1998; 1 April 1999.

[45] Interview with K. Damodaran, 18 March 1998.

[46] Inter Office Note, Ref.CPA/P/11 (VRS3-98–99), 17 March 1999.

[47] Personnel and Administration Department note, 5 October 1998. (Hereafter P&A Dept.)

. . . those who could have been relatively more useful to the Company also opted to avail of the scheme. Such employees did not fall in the surplus category. *On the contrary, the actual surplus did not come down appreciably.*[48]

In the end, the demand crunch that hit ITI from the year 2000 onwards provided a definitive solution to the problem of skill imbalance. Lacking work, direct operatives themselves now became surplus.

Explanations as to why the buyout scheme proved to be quite unsuccessful lead straight back to the poor response it generated at two of ITI's big northern units, Rae Bareli and Naini. Out of the total of 8777 employees who accepted the severance benefits, barely 8.7 per cent came from these two plants.[49] In fact, as the management itself recognized, outside of the main Bangalore plant which having the largest and the oldest workforce also accounted for the bulk of the resignations (81.5 per cent), employee reaction to VR in all the other units had by and large 'not been up to the mark'.[50] Company officials attributed the reluctance of employees at the Rae Bareli and Naini plants to leave the company partly to the absence of alternative employment opportunities in the region, and partly to the age levels of the labour force. Both plants had been established in the early 1970s, and therefore had a comparatively lower proportion of employees aged above 50 years—the target group

---

[48] ITI Revival Plan. Emphasis added.
[49] VR: Plant-wise Distribution Statistics

Plant	VRS claimants
B'lore	7,158
Naini	491
Rae Bareli	270
EC Plant (B'lore)	229
Palakkad	92
Srinagar	23
Mankapur	18
Others*	496

Note: *Corporate Office, Network Systems Unit, and Marketing (Regional Offices and Bangalore Complex).
Source: ITI.

[50] Standing Committee on Communications (1998–99), 1st Report, Twelfth Lok Sabha, New Delhi, 1999, p. 31. See also Record of Review meeting, Ref. ADP 020, 13 July 1998.

most attracted by the golden handshake—than the Bangalore plant. But top executives also reproached the two northern units for not adopting an aggressive enough approach.[51]

Hence in a letter addressed to the Rae Bareli and Naini managements in 2003, the corporate office spelt out the need to 'take certain strategic focussed action to counsel, convince and motivate' employees to apply for voluntary retirement.[52] More specifically, an 'aggressive campaign' was to be launched by section and department heads together with the unions and officers' associations in the direction of five groups of employees.[53] These included habitual absentees, malingerers, disciplinary cases and indebted employees; those who availed of frequent and prolonged leave on medical grounds, claimed heavy medical expenses, or were medically unfit; and unskilled, semi-skilled and indirect employees as well as those possessing minimal education qualifications. What this taxonomy revealed was that the company was intent not merely on ridding itself of the 'rogue' elements within its labour force, but also of the weakest and most deprived sections, precisely those who were in greatest need of the protective cover that only a large public sector enterprise could afford to provide.

To persuade these groups to quit, the Rae Bareli and Naini managements were instructed to adopt a mix of 'carrot and stick' methods, though the latter dominated.[54] Employees categorized as 'non-performers' were to be identified and segregated from the rest of the workforce, their wages frozen and benefits curtailed. Similar measures were advocated *vis-à-vis* surplus workers in general who would not be allocated regular jobs.[55] Alive to the possibilities of resistance from sections of the labour

---

[51] Consultancy firm PwC had stressed the importance of creating the right environment where both coercive measures and positive incentives operated to ensure the success of VRS.

[52] Letter from Additional Director P&A to General Manager Rae Bareli unit and Naini Unit, 16 May 2003.

[53] ibid.

[54] Barse cites a survey wherein 62 per cent of the workers interviewed claimed they did not accept VR voluntarily. 'Social Implications of Voluntary Retirement Scheme'.

[55] While ITI was content to propose such methods, private sector companies aggressively pursued them. At Voltas, for instance, redundant workers who refused to go on VR were paid full wages, but instructed to stay at home. M.M. Monippally, 'The Restructuring of Voltas Limited', IIM Ahmedabad, 2004 (mimeo). I am grateful to the author for the reference.

force designated as surplus or non-performers, since it 'would be seen as a precursor to rationalization' PwC's report, nevertheless, minced no words. It declared that this was a means of creating pressure on employees to 'opt for separation packages being offered'.[56]

The strategy of targeting non-performers as the prime focus of VR had been elaborated at the Bangalore plant right from 1991, though apparently without enjoying much success. An internal note mentions that 20 of the 39 employees listed as chronic absentees at the electronic switching division attended a meeting organized by the personnel department where they cited family opposition as the main reason for not accepting the severance package, though they themselves were in favour of leaving their jobs.[57] The note, therefore, proposed that an officer from the personnel department 'make house visits to motivate employees' families also'.[58] A confidential letter sent subsequently to all heads of department asked them to draw up a list of all 'delinquents who are medically unfit, inefficient, or of doubtful integrity and chronically absent'.[59] In order to 'motivate' these employees to opt for the buyout, they were to be warned that the management intended to prematurely retire them which would result in their obtaining substantially lower benefits than if they applied for VR.[60] The company claimed to have 'identified close to 1100 under committed employees' in Bangalore.[61] But its contention that the numbers were expected to increase owing to insufficient orders raises the question as to whether the principal cause of 'under commitment' in many cases was not the lack of work, rather than any inherent disposition towards shirking or absenteeism.

[56] PwC Recommendations, p. 120.

[57] Chronic absentees as defined by the management were those absenting themselves from work for 100 or more days in a year for the three preceding years. P&A Circular No. 3723, 10 July 1993. The personnel files contain letters from several employees requesting the company to withdraw their applications for VR, because 'I am only bread-winner in family and need to serve in ITI until regular retirement'. In one instance, after a worker's demand to go on VR had been accepted, we find his wife submitting a letter asking the management to reconsider its decision. Such requests were generally complied with.

[58] ITI Bangalore P&A Department, 27 August 1991.

[59] Ref. DO. No. CPA/IR/037, 4 November 1991.

[60] Rule 35(2) of the ITI Standing Orders declared that the company has the 'absolute right to retire any employee at any time after the age of 55 by giving him three months notice or on payment of three months salary instead of notice'.

[61] P&A Dept. note, 14 February 1994.

It is extremely doubtful whether any of these measures achieved their objective, given the lackadaisical and patchy manner in which the management sought to implement them. Moreover, shop officials who accorded top priority to production and related issues and apprehended potential manpower shortages do not seem to have shared the personnel department's concerns on overmanning. As a senior executive acknowledged, the fact that the Bangalore plant was carrying on its rolls over 2000 surplus employees in the year 2000 proved the relative ineffectiveness of VR. In his opinion, what was now required was a compulsory retirement scheme. Otherwise,

the lesser qualified workers and non-performers will refuse to leave the company, because they have no wish to lose their job status, and the benefits of cheap food, access to telephones and other facilities when they come to work. In some cases they are also involved in activities such as money lending and petty business inside the factory. Many of them being quite aged lack the entrepreneurial spirit as well to take the benefits of VRS and become self-employed. [62]

In addition to the weak response to VR from different sections of the workforce, top management had to resolve another problem: the paucity of funds to finance this programme. Even though the Memorandum of Understandings, signed between the DoT and the company, faithfully recorded each year the former's obligation to assist ITI in securing repayment for its voluntary retirement expenditures, the department seldom respected its engagement. As against a sum of roughly Rs 2400 million spent by the company since 1991 (see Table 5.1), it received barely Rs 541 million by way of reimbursements from the National Renewal Fund, or less than a quarter of the total.[63] Government guarantees, for certain, backed the bond issues periodically floated by ITI to raise cash for VR. But the refusal of the authorities and the tutelary agency to fully reimburse the company, notwithstanding repeated requests, placed a heavy strain on its coffers, especially in a market context

---

[62] Interview with S.K. Chatterjee, 6 July 2000.

[63] For an appraisal of the working of the National Renewal Fund whose objective was both to provide compensation funds to retrenched employees in the public and private sectors as well as to assist in their retraining and redeployment see, *inter alia*, Datta, 'Economic Reforms, Redundancy and National Renewal Fund'; Mani, 'Economic Liberalization and the Industrial Sector'; Srinivasan, 'Voluntary Retirement and Workers' Welfare'.

characterized by declining sales volumes and profit margins.[64] This point was clearly recognized by a parliamentary body which in its report urged DoT to

vigorously pursue the matter (of reimbursements) at the appropriate level so that the Company gets the necessary fiscal relief for its sustenance.[65]

To what extent the resource shortage hampered the effectiveness of the buyout plan is difficult to determine. But the company sought to ease its financial burden by deciding in October 2000 that severance benefits would henceforth be paid in equal quarterly instalments, spread over a period of three to five years with employees receiving interest on these amounts.[66] If this step served to shore up profitability levels, it could possibly have had the negative effect of reducing the attractiveness of VR for certain employees interested in earning a big one-time lump sum.[67] Indeed, in its report, PwC credited the success of early retirement schemes in public sector enterprises such as BHEL and HMT, among other things, to a policy of lump sum compensation payments, and recommended the adoption of a similar policy by ITI, irrespective of the costs.[68]

With the early retirement programme having failed then to fully achieve its goals, the optimistic forecasts established by PwC projecting a sizeable reduction in manpower costs from 20 per cent in 1999–2000 to about 7.7 per cent in 2004–05 now appeared to be beyond the company's reach. Though no study appears to have been conducted to assess the actual labour requirements of each unit, the management estimated that out of a total of nearly 19,700 employees on the company's rolls in 2003, almost 11,000 were still surplus. Plans to transfer a section of them to BSNL also aborted for different reasons. Shedding these employees through early retirement buyouts, according to the company's

---

[64] Note to Board, 280th meeting, item no. B8, May 1995 and 319th meeting, July 2000.

[65] Standing Committee on Information Technology (2002–03), Demand for Grants, 34th Report, Thirteenth Lok Sabha, 2002, p. 40. The Disinvestment Commission would come forward with an identical recommendation. Report IV, pp. 11–13.

[66] Inter office note Ref. CPA/P/11 (VRS2-00–01), 25 October 2000.

[67] Moreover, even the instalments were not being paid on time, and at least one worker told me that he was 'afraid of taking VR because I don't know if ITI is capable of paying'. Interview with Renuka Aradhya, 20 November 2001.

[68] PwC Recommendations.

calculations, would cost it a colossal sum of Rs 6410 million over a five year period, but its fixed expenditure would correspondingly decline by Rs 2250 million.[69] In the Revival Plan submitted to the DoT in 2003 outlining its restructuring strategy, the management wanted the former to put up all the money for financing VR. But the parent administration had still not answered its demand nearly a year later.

Of equally great significance, despite the reduction in the size of ITI's workforce, its salary and benefits bill paradoxically continued to show a near-unbroken upward trend from the mid-1990s onwards. Between 1995–96 and 2002–03, manpower costs shot up by nearly 32 per cent and represented on average over 22 per cent of the company's turnover as against an industry norm of 5 to 7 per cent (see Table 5.2).[70] Indeed, expenditures on this head were growing at a much faster pace than the reduction in the total number of employees and explained why ITI's fixed cost structure stood so high.[71] An internal note categorically stated that to remain competitive, the company needed to contain employee costs to under 20 per cent of turnover, and any increase would have to be matched by a higher volume of production, sales, and a reduction of wastage.[72]

One reason for this escalation between 1995–96 and 2002–03 were the two wage agreements signed by the management with the government's permission in February 1995 and February 2001. The first agreement saw employee costs rise, on an average, by 15 per cent annually.[73] The second, implemented 'primarily to motivate the workforce', led to a 26 per cent jump in the wage and benefits bill for the year 2000-01 alone, and this additional burden would place a tremendous strain on the company's finances once its situation started to worsen.[74] The raising of the retirement age in May 1998 for all central

[69] ITI Revival Plan.

[70] ITI P&A note, nd.

[71] PwC estimated that manpower accounted for 60 per cent of the company's overheads.

[72] ITI P&A note, nd.

[73] Note to ITI Board, 278th meeting, item no. C3, March 1995. The wage agreement related hikes in labour costs did not cover the increased expenditures incurred by the company annually on an ongoing basis on account of promotions, increments and DA revision.

[74] Minutes of meeting between unions and officers' associations and management, 12–13 December 2001. One could justifiably argue that given the company's financial

Table 5.2: ITI Employee Costs

Year	Number of Employees	Employee Costs (Rs mn)	Employee Cost (% Sales)
1995–96	26,272 (4.4%)*	2650.9 (17.7%)°	33.8
1996–97	25,915 (1.3%)	2679.1 (1.06%)	26.2
1997–98	24,552 (5.2%)	3216.8 (20.1%)	25.5
1998–99	23,945 (2.5%)	3312.3 (2.9%)	21.5
1999–2000	23,567 (1.6%)	3474.8 (4.9%)	16.6
2000–01	22,914 (2.8%)	3980.1 (14.5%)	18.5
2001–02	21,518 (6.1%)	4040 (1.5%)	17.4
2002–03	19,692 (8.5%)	3890 (-3.7%)	21.7

Notes: *Figure in brackets indicate decline in number of employees over the previous year;
°Figure in brackets indicate increase and/or decline in employee costs over the previous year.
Source: ITI Annual Report, various years.

public sector employees from 58 to 60 years was the second reason why ITI's salary and benefits bill went up even as the size of its workforce came down. Perhaps left with no choice but to extend to state-owned undertakings the same service conditions as those made available to central government staff, following the Fifth Pay Commission's award, this decision of the BJP-led coalition government would have extremely negative implications for the company. To cite a company document:

With the enhancement of retirement age, the main purpose of VRS to reduce surplus labour and manpower cost was frustrated. This also dealt a severe blow

plight, a wage freeze, or at best only a modest hike, was the need of the hour. But since the government had handed out generous increases to officers asking workers alone to make sacrifices would have been both unjust and politically untenable.

to the already precarious financial condition of the company as it had to incur an additional expenditure towards retirement benefits and additional two years salary for those employees who would otherwise have retired from the services.[75]

If workers welcomed this initiative as a 'gift from god', the management, in contrast, was more likely to have viewed it as a piece of devilish mischief which had the effect of inflating its salary and benefits bill, thus considerably complicating its task of restoring the company's competitive advantage.

MANAGEMENT CRACK-DOWN ON EMPLOYEE BENEFITS AND INDISCIPLINE

However, in November 2001, ITI was able to secure permission from the Bureau of Public Enterprises to roll back the retirement age once again to 58 years.[76] The fallout from such a move was hardly negligible: apart from yielding savings estimated at Rs 1400 million over a five-year period, it would bring down the size of the workforce by 2500 to 3000 employees. The company's decision to implement the measure from April 2002 onwards immediately triggered a legal offensive from the unions.[77] But all the appeals filed by workers and their representatives in Bangalore, Naini and Rae Bareli were eventually dismissed by the courts. Acting on a recommendation made by PwC, top management also contemplated further lowering the retirement age to 55 years. If implemented, it would permit the retirement of an additional 3500 to 4000 people between 2003–04 and 2007–08, and savings in excess of Rs 2500 million. But apart from warning of 'stiff internal resistance', the consultancy firm claimed that the 'lack of any precedence will pose a stiff hurdle'.[78]

Employees bore the brunt of other economy generating initiatives too. With the board urging the management to declare a financial emergency in 2003, it proceeded to partially dismantle the internal 'welfare state' by taking the axe to certain benefits. The practice of

---

[75] Corporate P&A Note, nd.

[76] Corporate personnel policy circular no. 473, 27 March 2002. Permission to reduce the retirement age to 58 years was, in fact, extended to all public sector undertakings by the government in 2001. DPE Office Memorandum, 22 August 2001.

[77] ITI Employees Union, Bangalore, circular no. 11/2002, 20 April 2002.

[78] PwC Recommendations, p. 129.

supplying uniforms was ended and all leave encashment facilities cancelled. The company also stopped the education allowance for children as it did the festival or annual advance which entitled non-officers to receive a sum of Rs 2000 yearly. Monthly payment of salaries was deferred by 10 days. All these steps were expected to realize savings of about Rs 160 to 200 million for the year 2003-04 alone, according to an internal estimate.[79] At a meeting of the heads of the different units held in April 2003, senior officials, stressing the company's mounting losses, even proposed imposing a 25 per cent reduction in basic pay for all employees coupled with a freeze on Dearness Allowance (DA) payment and annual increments.[80] Plans were formulated to suspend the system of automatic promotions as well as production incentive payments. Already when concluding the last wage agreement in 2001, ITI had declared its inability to pay arrears amounting to Rs 1600 million until its financial position improved.[81] As the PwC report indicated, such measures conveyed to the employees the severity of the company's difficulties, and could therefore, also persuade them to opt for voluntary retirement.

The attempts of the corporate personnel department to unilaterally enforce the cost-cutting drive, however, ran into opposition from the unions, especially at the Bangalore plant. Though the suspension of welfare benefits would be effective from January 2003, top management, confronted with the threat of an agitation, now gave employees assurances to the contrary.[82] What is more, it removed the head of personnel, appointing in his place an official reputed for his more moderate and consensual approach. The different proposals were eventually introduced a few months later. But the unions did succeed in at least one instance in getting their way. Following criticism from the board for having paid a performance bonus in 2002, the top management had instructed all the units to recover the amount from employees' salaries. Workers' representatives at the Bangalore and Naini factories responded by arming themselves with court orders prohibiting such recoveries, whereas at Mankapur and Rae Bareli company officials themselves backed down in

---

[79] 339th Board meeting, item no. 4, 28 and 29 October 2002; ITI Corporate P&A note, nd (August 2003).

[80] ITI Corporate P&A note, 16 April 2003.

[81] Minutes of Wage Negotiation Committee meeting, 1 and 2 February 2001; ITI Corporate P&A note, 24 June 2002.

[82] Inter Office Note, ITI/COIR/13, 3 January 2003; 22 January 2003.

the face of what they described as the 'serious industrial relations situation'.[83]

At the same time, in Bangalore, the management took advantage of the shift from a monopoly to a competitive market to re-establish its control over the labour force by cracking down on indiscipline. A survey of security department records reveals that late coming, loitering, extended tea breaks, and leaving the work spot well ahead of lunch time or shift closure, all constituted an integral part of work practices.[84] Yet the problem assumed threatening proportions only from the late 1980s onwards, so much so that the 'petty pilfering of minutes', to borrow from Marx, that had all along defined employees' attitude to worktime, became the wholesale looting of hours and days.[85] The explanation was to be found as much in inadequate workloads, following the closure of the strowger and crossbar production lines and delays in inducting digital switching technology, as in management laxity in asserting its authority.

Indiscipline now mostly took the form of unauthorized absences. Growing numbers of employees deserted the factory after the lunch break, since officials, strangely enough, only insisted on their clocking in at the start of the workday, but not clocking out at the end of the workday, though the rule officially existed in the standing orders. This loophole also encouraged the widespread violation of leave regulations with leave applications going unrecorded because employees failed to turn in their slips to security when quitting the factory premises. Such violations were particularly common in the afternoon or second shift since '(s)upervision . . . is absolutely weak and naturally employees take advantage of the situation', as a security report underlined.[86] According to the report, dated March 1996, a head count taken on three successive days at the end of the previous month revealed that out of the 471 afternoon shift

---

[83] ITI Corporate P&A note, Ref. ITI/COPA/PL-07, 4 June 2003.

[84] In his account of shop floor experiences in a Russian wood factory after the collapse of socialism, Burawoy paints much the same picture of time-keeping practices. Michael Burawoy and Pavel Krotov, 'The Soviet Transition from Socialism to Capitalism: Worker Control and Economic Bargaining in the Wood Industry', in S. Clarke et al, *What About the Workers? Workers and the Transition to Capitalism in Russia*, London, 1993, pp. 56–90.

[85] Marx, however, was referring not to the labour force, but to capitalists' stratagems of extending the work day. *Capital*, Harmondsworth, 1976 (Vol. 1), p. 352.

[86] Security Department note, Ref. SY/FD/10, 6 March 1996.

employees leaving the factory during the 'lunch' break at 7 pm, only 193 returned to work. Another report claimed that when security questioned out-going afternoon shift employees whether they had submitted their leave slips, some of them reportedly replied 'why are you people (security) interested in what we do when our own Departmental Officers themselves do not bother (sic)'.[87]

In comparison, breaches in time discipline by morning shift employees took on a more individual character, but for precisely this reason, were far more difficult to detect as the following example of Ismail will bear out. Ismail's malingering was also illustrative of how individuals, if more often than not victims of the panoply of controls large bureaucratic institutions are in a position to exercise, can also take advantage of these institutions' lack of reactive capacities to slip through its meshes at least momentarily. Having failed to report to the newly formed electronic switching division, where he had been transferred from strowger, and capitalizing on his absence having gone unnoticed, Ismail had worked not even a single day for two whole years from 1990–92. He had been 'a free bird, coming and going to and from the factory at will and not being under anyone officially at work'.[88] In certain instances, offenders were caught after anonymous letters denounced them to the security department. One such letter accused Chowdappa, a chargehand in the transmission division, of conducting his business affairs outside the factory during working hours with the complicity of both his superiors, who were duly rewarded for their silence, as well as security personnel.

He is going out <u>everyday</u> at . . . lunch break, and never returns. This is going on continuously since 2 years. He never stayed up to 4.15 PM including during peak March production period. Also seems to be adjustment with Sy. (security) Staff . . . No use of passing information to DGM (XQ) (Deputy General Manager Transmission Quality) and DYMX (Testing) (Deputy Manager Transmission).[89]

To remedy the situation, top management finally chose to act on the recommendations of the security department, and in January 1999, made it mandatory for both non-officers and officers to clock out at the end of

---

[87] Security Dept. note, Ref. SY/FD/10, 14 December 1989.
[88] Security Dept. note, Ref. SY/FD/10, 7 April 1992. Emphasis in original.
[89] Security Dept. note, July 1991.

all shifts.[90] A circular issued to employees stated that this measure would contribute to improving 'productivity, work culture and discipline', adding that in order to concentrate on quality, delivery and cost, and compete in a market where ITI no longer enjoyed a monopoly a disciplined workforce was a prerequisite.[91] What must be noted is that six long years elapsed between the time the company first envisaged this measure and its actual implementation. For on this occasion too, union opposition was a severe constraint and the management was unable to enforce its decision in a timely manner. Objecting to the fact that clocking out had not been introduced in any of the other ITI units and that, as a result, the employees of the Bangalore plant were being discriminated against, the union again resorted to legal action.[92] The issue remained deadlocked from 1993–99, and certain other outstanding demands would have to be conceded before the union could be appeased.

As part of the overall drive to enforce order more forcefully at the workplace, the management also announced its intentions of placing restrictions on the movements of union officials.[93] Partially exempted from work so that they could attend to their union charges, workers' representatives had, over time, exploited managerial laxity to the full and succeeded in completely avoiding all 'productive labour'. If ordinary employees deserted the factory on the sly, their representatives did so openly, often misusing the facilities they had been accorded for personal ends. Following the union elections in 2001, the personnel department wanted to do away with such customary practices. It instructed all departments to extract at least a couple of hours of work daily from lower-ranking representatives. But from what I was able to observe during one of my field trips in 2003, this goal proved no easier to achieve now than it had been at any time in the past. Union delegates, at all levels, continued to avail of their positions to refuse all jobs allocated to them.

[90] Though the management had been considering the introduction of punch-out from 1987 itself, the fact that it eventually took a decision only six years later speaks volumes for the force of inertia weighing down the decision-making processes within public sector enterprises.

[91] P&A Dept. circular no. 4212, 5 January 1999.

[92] Letter from ITI Bangalore Employees Union, 26 November 1993. The union had also objected to officers being exempted from clocking-out, obliging the company to amend its initial proposal and apply the rule uniformly to both non-officers and officers.

[93] Interview with Shankar Prasad, Chief Personnel Manager, ITI Bangalore, 1 December 2001.

MANAGEMENT INITIATIVES TO CUT MATERIAL COSTS DELIVER MIXED RESULTS

Next to manpower, materials ranked as the other area where ITI had to imperatively control expenditure. Material costs, as a percentage of production value, had averaged on aggregate 54 per cent over a twelve-year period from 1991–92 to 2002–03.[94] On the other hand, equipment prices continued to register a downward trend. Hence, not surprisingly, the top management pressed harder to prune material costs.[95] While we lack information for the other product lines, going by the results achieved by the telephones division at ITI Bangalore, the company met with a fair degree of success in its endeavours to come up with a cheaper telephone. Since the launch of the first fully electronic push button instrument in 1988, material costs had fallen by well over half: the cost of ITI's newest model Eyetel which was launched in the year 2000 worked out to just under Rs 200 compared to Rs 460 for the E-88 model. The figure was expected to drop even further to Rs 185 for a model due to be marketed in 2002–03.[96]

To arrive at this end result, divisional managers relied heavily on value engineering methods which by combining constant process and product improvements enabled the identification and elimination of superfluous costs. Many of the modifications concerned the heart of the telephone, the printed circuit board, and the transducer which accounted for approximately a quarter of all input costs.[97] Through a process of what could be called 'technical disintensification', the number of components were reduced and high value components substituted by low value ones without impinging on the quality of the product.[98] Changes in the overall

[94] Year-to-year comparisons reveal a certain degree of fluctuation, especially during the late 1990s, but overall the figure rose from 42.8 per cent in 1991–92 to 58.4 per cent in 1996–97 before touching 63.5 per cent in 2002–03. Annual Report (various years).

[95] In 2001, ITI chairman Lakshmi Menon fixed a 7.5 per cent target in reduction of material costs and material usage in order to boost the company's operating margins by an additional Rs 1000 million. Ref. DO No. CM/27.4, 8 May 2001.

[96] Minutes of Review on Telephone Cost Reduction, 7 May 2001.

[97] The cost of a printed circuit board declined from about Rs 43 to under Rs 35, among other things, via recourse to computer-aided design which drastically compressed the size of the board.

[98] Yves Cohen speaks of a process of 'technical intensification', the objective being

design of the instrument also resulted in a lighter telephone which in turn pushed costs further down because requirements of moulding powder, a high value item, decreased.[99] In sharp contrast to the mediocre performance of suggestion schemes in other areas of the factory, shop officials at the telephone division seemed to have enjoyed greater success as well in eliciting contributions from workers.[100]

At the same time, a centralized buying department was set up at the corporate level. Pooling together high-volume material requirements of all units like relays, integrated chips, and printed circuit cards, this department negotiated long term contracts with vendors in order to make sure the company obtained competitive prices.[101] Emphasis was also placed on building stronger ties with suppliers.[102] The corporate cell appears to have functioned quite effectively. An official note dated July 1997 wrote that long term contracts had contributed to a reduction in input costs by over Rs 15 per telephone at the Naini plant and by almost Rs 12 in Bangalore.[103] Likewise, the annual performance reports of the Bangalore telephone division mention a steady fall in material costs on account of 'bulk purchasing and bargaining for lower prices with suppliers'.[104] However, in its study of the working of the Bangalore

---

to improve product performance levels as much by reducing the number of components as by replacing low value components for high value ones. 'La technique, son contexte, et le travail: Que nous dit la conception de la 201 Peugeot?' in J.F. Belhoste et al (eds.), *Autour de l'industrie: histoire et patrimoine. Mélanges offerts à Denis Woronoff*, Paris, 2004, pp. 425–38. I therefore owe my term 'technical disintensification' to him, though I describe a somewhat reverse logic.

[99] Whereas competitors' phones weighed 350 grams, ITI's Eyetel and Dhwani models weighed respectively 480 grams and 466 grams. But its new Sandesh model was set to be no heavier than 350 grams. Tel. Divn. note, Ref. PD/M/19, 29 March 2001.

[100] Tel. Divn. files, 'Meet the Challenge' suggestion scheme, nd.

[101] Individual plant managers, however, believed they could secure better conditions given their longer experience of dealing with suppliers. Indeed, on one instance the Bangalore telephone division managed to negotiate cheaper rates than those finalized by the corporate cell much to the latter's displeasure. Tel. Divn. note, Ref. DGMT/20, 21 July 1994.

[102] Besides organizing a big vendors meeting in June 1998, a 'single window' was created in all units of the company so that 'vendors are not made to run from pillar to post' when collecting payments for supplies. Ref. CMM/7, 10 July 1997.

[103] Ref. CMM/7, 10 July 1997.

[104] Annual Performance Report 1992–93, ITI Bangalore telephone division, nd.

plant, PwC highlighted significant differences in the prices of identical components purchased by certain plants notwithstanding the centralized arrangements. According to the consultant, the failure of the units to share price information accounted for the variations.[105]

In the end, ITI's growing financial difficulties which led to inordinate delays in settling suppliers' bills caused many of these purchasing arrangements to come unstuck. As the management itself acknowledged, vendors were ready to offer the company very advantageous rates, but the 'demotivating factor is ITI's payment terms'.[106] Internal memos complained of several instances of suppliers not having received payments even after 90 days, and who were therefore losing trust in the company's purchasing officials and returning purchase orders.[107]

Moreover, the company added to its own difficulties by taking the highly unwise decision of narrowing its vendor base. Desperate to cut costs by all means, it had agreed to the demand of certain vendors to conclude exclusive contracts with them in return for substantial price concessions, even though the dangers of being dependent on a few suppliers were evident enough. Not surprisingly, these firms started withholding material supplies to ITI until they had been paid, resulting in frequent interruptions to production. Voicing alarm, one note warned that unless 'timely action is taken to rebuild confidence among indigenous suppliers' raw material supplies may 'get severely affected during 1997–98'.[108] The problem would resurface a couple of years later, affecting in particular the Bangalore telephone division; being a perennial loss-maker it tended to be allocated minimal financial resources by the finance department. Production schedules therefore badly suffered as vendors blocked deliveries of various items in response to payment delays going up from 90 to 120 days.

---

[105] Ref. DB/COM/2000–2001, 27 June 2000.

[106] Ref. TD/P-66, 24 September 2001.

[107] See, for instance, Tel. Divn. note, Ref. PDG/TEL/09, 3 March 1995.

[108] Tel. Divn. note, Ref. NP/CMR/PAYMENT, 11 March 1997. Interestingly, audit authorities claimed that because of the telephone division's dependency on a single or limited sources, material costs could not be reduced substantially. Vendors were accused of raising prices frequently, delivering sub-standard material or not supplying material on time. Letter from resident audit officer, Ref. RAP II/ITI/97-98/63, 10 June 1997.

MEASURES TO REDUCE DEPENDENCY ON DOT INEFFECTIVE

Until the late 1980s, ITI had never experienced the necessity of possessing a marketing organization worth its name.[109] While a sales department operated through the company's regional offices, the company's monopolistic position meant that its activities were limited to providing price information to potential customers and relaying their orders back to the units. But with the entry of private firms in a number of product categories, the importance of setting up a specialized entity in order to meet the threat of increased competition in the future was clearly felt. After the board had baulked at the size of the investments entailed in the top management's initial ambitious blueprint, a relatively small marketing department was launched sometime towards the end of the 1980s.[110] In addition to interacting with key customers such as DoT, railways and the defence services, marketing was assigned one key task: increasing the company's share of non-DoT business and developing the export market. Subsequently, the appointment of an outside professional to head the department gave it a higher profile. As the board noted, it was 'high time now to give the required thrust to marketing in ITI'.[111]

Unfortunately, no such thrust was forthcoming. In a note dated April 1994, the head of R&D at the Bangalore plant protested angrily at R&D having to handle all business and marketing functions because

. . . our company is poorly organised for marketing. In fact, it is not at all clear who is marketing which product. Everybody seems to be attempting to market everything, from telephones to VSATs (very small aperture terminals).[112]

---

[109] Until the 1970s, Western Electric (now Lucent), the captive manufacturing arm of AT&T, also did not consider the establishing of a strong marketing organization as vital. Adams and Butler, *Manufacturing the Future*, pp. 187–8, 196–8. Moreover, while a marketing department would be subsequently added, it was only grafted onto a 'basically unchanged structure'. Peter Temin, *The Fall of the Bell System. A Study in Prices and Politics*, Cambridge, 1988, p. 162.

[110] 230th Meeting of Board, item no. B2, April 1987. The original proposal called for setting up of a marketing division, employing as many as 380 people, and necessitating an additional expenditure of almost Rs 3 million annually.

[111] 263rd Meeting of Board, item no. A8, April 1993. See also Ref. CM/13.1A, 26 August 1993.

[112] Note 25 April 1994.

He went on to add that R&D, understandably, was doing this job on a 'part-time basis and amateurishly'. This resulted not merely in lack of adequate market research on competitors' products, but also in 'high cost and non-adherence to time schedules . . . and erosion of profitability'.[113] The necessity for a strong marketing infrastructure and orientation was reiterated a year later. But the very fact that in the restructuring plan submitted to the government in 2003, the management found it necessary to write that the company should become 'more market and customer focussed' clearly meant this was still not the case.[114] Nor would the scenario change greatly in the future. The very fact that ITI continued to struggle to pick up business from customers without ties of any kind to governmental agencies was warrant to the marketing department's failure.

Moves by ITI to reduce its dependence on DoT by expanding its domestic market long predated the economic reforms.[115] From the 1960s onwards, it had begun manufacturing equipment for the railways and the defence services. Owing to import restrictions, both these organizations also had perforce to rely on ITI. In the case of the army, it purchased the bulk of its field communication requirements from ITI, becoming over time the latter's second largest customer. An exclusive defence products division was created at the Bangalore plant which took charge of the task of setting up a digital communications network along the country's borders after the company won a highly lucrative turnkey contract in 1986 from the army.[116]

The company also proceeded to undertake turnkey jobs for both public and private sector companies, supplying, installing, and even maintaining a range of communication equipment, notably private exchanges of upto 200 lines. An extremely profitable activity in the wake of economic reforms the installation and maintenance department became the seedbed of a new autonomous division, the network systems unit, entrusted with furnishing 'total telecommunications solutions' to

<hr>

[113] ibid.

[114] ITI Revival Plan.

[115] In the 1974–75 annual report, Chairman I.K. Gupta openly declared that in the context of P&T's resource shortfall, ITI must target markets outside the government sector and overseas.

[116] Note to the Board, 222nd meeting, item no. B2, October 1986.

customers.[117] When launching this unit in 1994, senior executives had declared with rhetorical flourish that the telecommunications market now offered enormous promise. Downplaying the importance of DoT 'whose main constraint seems to be in finding the necessary resources', they identified a number of other potential clients such as electricity boards, police departments, and big public sector corporations in the oil, steel and banking industries, and announced ITI's intention of tapping all these segments.[118]

But in the end, diversification yielded extremely disappointing dividends. Plans to enter the contract development field by selling ITI's low-cost expertise to foreign firms collapsed following the talent flight of its research engineers.[119] A software security product aimed at the banking and financial sector and on which the company had pinned considerable hopes attracted little interest. Many of the other projects also either never saw the light of day or struggled to find a viable market. That ITI-made equipment and services tended as a rule to be far costlier than those proposed by its competitors certainly did not help matters. For example, during 1993–94 it lost all three tenders for small electronic private exchanges in which it participated. In one tender, the price quoted by ITI was three times that of the firm winning the tender.[120] To cite an official report:

unless the company is able to check the cost of its products (which is admittedly on the higher side) it will not be in a position to compete in the market.[121]

Top officials were aware of this problem from the mid-1980s itself. Relaying complaints from organizations such as the Indian Railways, Doordarshan and electricity boards, managers of the company's regional sales offices had drawn attention to the substantial price differentials existing between ITI products and imported equipment. One document commented:

[117] Profits from the sale of equipment to non-DoT customers were reportedly three times higher than those sold to DoT. Interview with Srinivasa Rao.

[118] Note 12 April 1994.

[119] In the early 1990s, ITI had successfully undertaken design work in product sub-systems for at least one US firm, Tell Labs.

[120] The tenders were floated by the Karnataka State Electricity Board, the Delhi Central Electric Authority and the Calcutta Police. Project Report, August 1994.

[121] COPU 1997, p. 64.

It is high time that we take this complaint seriously and make a study of what contributes to the high cost of ITI products and by what measures we can reduce costs.[122]

But as the tender losses evidenced, the initiatives taken subsequently by the management in this direction remained apparently inadequate.

The impressive growth recorded by the network systems unit, its turnover reaching Rs 1850 million in 2002–03 at a time when most of the other divisions saw a decline in performance, certainly demonstrated the potential of this line of business. This was further confirmed by the fact that turnkey contracts accounted for 45 per cent of the company's sales in 2002–03. Yet, with the exception of the orders placed by the army and the Ministry of Home Affairs for a satellite-based country-wide telecommunications network, most of the work executed by the network systems unit continued to be for DoT (or its subsidiaries, BSNL and MTNL). So far from achieving its objective of augmenting its share of non-DoT business to between 25 and 30 per cent of its turnover by 2000, ITI, if anything, grew even more reliant on its principal customer.[123] Sales to the latter after reaching over 95 per cent in 1993–94 consistently averaged around 83 per cent thereafter.[124] In the words of a parliamentary committee, '. . . this over dependence of the company on DoT is one of the major reasons for its poor performance'.[125]

Attempts to enlarge its revenue base through exports to other developing countries like Tanzania, Yemen, Surinam, and Fiji also proved unsuccessful. Notwithstanding corporate discourse enjoining the company to take greater advantage of its cheap labour and excellent infrastructure facilities, foreign sales seldom exceeded more than 2 per cent of its turnover.[126] Part of the reason for these lacklustre results can be explained by the domination of Western and Japanese transnational

---

[122] Note from Director, Bangalore Complex, Ref. EDB/6, 24 April 1986.

[123] Note 25 April 1994.

[124] Annual Report (various years). In 2002–03, DoT accounted for only 71.5 per cent of ITI's turnover, but this historic low could be explained by the lower volume of orders placed on the company. ITI's situation was no different from that of Western Electric which in 1983 realized 93 per cent of its turnover from parent AT&T. Santucci, *L'industrie mondiale des télécommunications*, p. 30.

[125] COPU 1997, p. 64. See also CAG Report 1992, pp. 33–4.

[126] The agreements signed with its foreign technology suppliers authorized ITI to export strowger and crossbar switching systems to certain East African and Middle Eastern countries.

corporations. Propelled by their marketing clout, they were able to penetrate developing markets all the more easily given that their respective governments provided soft loans and other forms of assistance to African and Asian countries to help finance the purchase of telecommunications equipment. The Indian government, however, could not afford to offer the same largesse. Part of the reason had to do with the broader context of 'export pessimism', the hallmark of the government's trade policies from the mid-1950s until the 1990s at least. As economists have noted, Indian companies received few incentives from the authorities to target foreign markets.[127]

This failure of ITI, with respect to both exports and diversification, however, was also rooted in several other factors both internal and external to its operations. By far the most important of these was the hostility of parent DoT. To quote one top manager:

> The board of directors being mostly P&T men would put a brake on the company developing non-P&T sales and exports. They would restrict the percentage of production that could be diverted to these two areas when determining the company's annual programme . . . Board would argue that there was no need for ITI to export if P&T had to import to meet shortfalls.[128]

Opposition to the company seeking alternative revenue sources was understandable at least during the pre-liberalization era. Not only was it often guilty of failing to meet production schedules, it also had minimal excess production capacity to spare either for other domestic customers or for export. With the waiting list for telephone connections stretching increasingly longer from year to year, it was quite natural that DoT wanted its captive supplier to concentrate all its resources towards satisfying the huge pent-up internal demand.

What was less comprehensible, and justifiable, though, was the parent organization maintaining its opposition to ITI diversifying into new markets even in the post-reforms period. This was well illustrated by its refusal to allow the latter to provide basic telephone services once the

---

[127] See, *inter alia*, Bhagwati and Desai, *Planning for Industrialization*, chaps. 18–19; T. N. Srinivasan, 'India's Export Performance: A Comparative Analysis', in Ahluwalia and Little (eds.), *India's Economic Reforms and Development*, pp. 197–228.

[128] Interview with Srinivasa Rao. Similar parallels can be found in the attitude of parent AT&T *vis-à-vis* Western Electric undertaking outside contracts. Adams and Butler, *Manufacturing the Future*, pp. 148–9.

government had decided in 1994 to end DoT's monopoly by opening this sector to competition.[129] Given the expertise ITI already possessed in installing and maintaining exchanges, operating basic services was a logical extension of its activities, a forward integration of its business which would considerably help strengthen its competitive position. It also opened up the possibility of solving, to a degree, two of its most pressing problems at a single stroke: overstaffing and inadequate demand. Basic services could have absorbed a section of its surplus manpower as well as functioned as an alternative outlet, especially for switching equipment, in case DoT turned out to be an unwilling customer. The supervisory ministry, however, flatly turned down the management's proposal. Authorizing ITI to develop as a service provider, it argued, made no sense since it would bring the company into competition with DoT.[130]

Nevertheless, notwithstanding the restrictions on its autonomy, the top management too had to take responsibility for the company's inability to capture new domestic and foreign markets. As an internal document observed, there was a 'lack of focus among the unit heads in providing equipment to the non-DoT sector'.[131] Another note was even more forthright stating that 'no meaningful effort' had been made to broaden the company's customer base.[132] In effect, a well-defined strategy to actively seek new customers by devoting adequate physical and financial resources to marketing as well as allied activities such as sales promotion and advertising never existed. The ineffectiveness of the marketing division even in the post-reforms period when the company was paying a high price for its dependency on DoT bears out this point. It is also difficult to argue as company executives did that the technology problems encountered by ITI blunted its export thrust.[133] As far as electronic switching went, the company had access to C-DoT know-how for small and medium-sized exchanges which it could have easily produced for

[129] On the debate on privatization of basic telephone services see Standing Committee on Communications, 13th Report, Eleventh Lok Sabha, 1997.

[130] COPU 1997, pp. 29–30, 63. Strikingly, the ITI chairman stated that he came to know of DoT's decision to bar ITI from participating in basic services only from newspaper reports.

[131] Extract of 302nd Meeting of Board of Directors, 27 May 1998.

[132] Note 14 December 1996.

[133] COPU 1973, pp. 71–2.

the export market. Moreover, the low cost of C-DoT exchanges, coupled in the case of RAXs with its robust features, notably its ability to function in demanding environmental conditions without requiring air conditioning, meant that it was a product tailor-made for exporting to less affluent developing countries particularly in Africa. Yet few concerted steps were taken to expand the volume of sales to these markets. Even towards the defence services and railways, ITI demonstrated anything but a responsive and business-like approach. Its relationship with them tended to follow in many ways the pattern of its dealings with DoT, characterized by shoddy customer relations, delayed deliveries and poor quality.

During the late 1990s, a new generation of electronic field telephones, the 5C, developed especially for the army by the telephone division at ITI Bangalore, forcefully reflected some of these problems. The demand for this product was estimated to be in the region of 5 to 10,000 phones annually over a period of five years as the army intended to phase out the earlier 5B model. Priced at Rs 5000 per phone, profit margins on the 5C were also substantially higher than those for electronic push button instruments. In fact, telephone division executives had even suggested to the top management that the company's interests would be better served by limiting the production of standard push button phones, and concentrating instead on phones for the army and airforce, head-gear sets and other such high value products.[134]

While the army wanted ITI to submit the model for quality evaluation and field tests by August 2001, telephone division officials requested a delay of eight to nine months citing a difficulty in procuring tools.[135] However, illustrative of the conflicting interests of production and marketing, the latter, determined to seize as big a slice of the market as possible, promised the army that it would be ready within four months.[136] In a note to divisional management, marketing officials urged it to 'go

---

[134] Tel. Divn. note, Ref. DGMT/5, 19 November 2001.

[135] Tel. Divn. note, Ref. TD/5C, 22 January 2001.

[136] Laurent Thévenot has convincingly argued for a treatment of the firm as a 'compromising device' between several modes of coordination, in particular the market and industrial modes, each of which engage different repertoires of evaluations and are characterized by different regimes of temporality. 'Équilibre et rationalité dans un univers complexe', *Revue économique*, Vol. 40, No. 2, mars 1989, pp. 147–97.

all out to develop (the) phone with full vigour'.[137] The need to bring out the model quickly was all the more greater since for the first time ITI faced competition with Ericsson which was marketing a similar product. Yet despite this situation of urgency where a new and more efficient competitor risked making off with a traditionally captive market, the company struggled to accelerate delivery schedules and the phone was dispatched with a delay of over two months.[138] Having submitted its prototype earlier, Ericsson was able to secure validation prior to ITI, and officials acknowledged the likelihood of ITI losing the entire order to the Swedish transnational.

Another captive market that threatened to slip out of the company's hands, again on account of its own negligence, was dedicated telephones for the railways. Supplies to the railways covered a range of products from switching and transmission microwave equipment to magneto telephones and specialized remote control signalling systems. Yet from the late 1990s onwards, ITI had ceased catering to this customer, though '(it) is more than willing to buy and margins are better and literally there is no competition'.[139] Production managers tended to fault the R&D for this situation, arguing that it had failed to systematically upgrade the older models from electro-mechanical to electronic. As shop officials saw it, research engineers were not interested in working on products they considered to be outdated when they had the choice of taking up more prestigious projects such as software development or multi-line phones.[140] Hence, because of its inability to meet the railway's needs, the marketing department claimed the company was losing business worth Rs 50 million annually.[141]

Moves to tap the non-DoT market for standard electronic push button instruments, or in other words, selling phones directly 'off-the-shelf' to consumers also ended in failure. Two models, developed in-house after

---

[137] Ref. EDRM/50, 24 January 2001.

[138] In August 2001, the army directly wrote to the ITI chairman, expressing 'serious concern about the inordinate delays' and the failure of ITI to meet its commitment to supply the phone on time. Ref. B/46013/Sigs 6/11, 30 August 2001.

[139] Ref. EDRM/9B, 11 October 2001.

[140] The marketing department would level much the same charge against R&D engineers. Ref. EDRM/9B, 11 October 2001.

[141] Ref. COR/AGM-M/25, 23 August 2001.

considerable delay, never reached the mass production stage. Complaining that the numbers turned out were 'too trivial even for small scale industry to consider', R&D, deeply unhappy at the 'unnecessary waste of (its) efforts', declared that 'no proper impetus was given for the production' of these models by shop management.[142] Subsequently, a strategic plan, drawn up in autumn 1996, for the production of telephones at both the Bangalore and Naini plants, recommended that 30 per cent of the company's total output should be reserved for the non-DoT market with the figure rising progressively over time. The plan noted that this segment was being completely neglected, though prices were significantly higher than what the DoT offered.[143] Increasing the volume of sales to the non-DoT market could then help to improve the overall profitability of ITI's telephone business.

Yet by the end of 1998, this idea had for all practical purposes been abandoned. Production managers in Bangalore complained that during 1997-98 they had manufactured 50,000 telephones for the non-DoT segment, but marketing had offloaded less than 20,000 sets and even many of these remained unsold. The marketing department, doubtless, faced an uphill task in trying to sell the product directly to customers because it had failed in its efforts to build a country-wide dealer network.[144] In turn, marketing executives took production and R&D to task for failing to provide even such basic features as mute and pause in ITI-made telephones, notwithstanding their repeated recommendations.[145] Lacking these features, customers found the instruments unattractive and were therefore unwilling to purchase them. The findings of two market research surveys, conducted at an interval of

---

[142] Tel. Divn. Note, 6 August 1996.

[143] Tel. Divn. Note, Ref. AGMT/41, 27 January 1997. See also corporate office note dated 27 October 1998 declaring 'we need to concentrate on capturing this (non-DoT) market'.

[144] Despite setting up a country-wide retail chain and investing in a costly advertising campaign, Godrej found few customers for its telephones. So it is doubtful whether ITI would have fared better even had it managed to get its own dealer network off the ground. On Godrej's marketing woes, see *Business Standard*, 17 June 1997.

[145] Marketing department note, Ref. No. 3052/010, 10 September 1996; Minutes of R&D, production and marketing meeting, 16 January 1999. What must be noted is that DoT when installing a telephone connection furnished a phone. Hence subscribers wishing to acquire a second and/or more reliable instrument invariably opted for a cordless or an expensive feature-heavy imported set.

three years, arrived at an identical, and highly unflattering, conclusion: that customers perceived ITI as manufacturing old-fashioned telephones based on obsolete technology, and that too in a very limited choice of colours.[146]

At the same time, the question of diversifying the company's revenue stream threw into relief the tensions prevailing in the relations between R&D, marketing and production, revealing the composite or heterogeneous nature of management. Given their conflicting objectives, expectations of greater synergies between these three departments feeding into improvements in product development turned out to be totally illusory. It is important to keep in view, particularly in large firms, that management rarely tends to be a single, homogenous entity pursuing a common end goal. Instead, it is constituted of different groups of individuals whose interests do not always coincide because of their differing positions and the specialization of their functions.[147] Far from behaving as a unitary, strictly rational and maximizing actor, the business enterprise, as a number of scholars have argued, must be typically understood as a political coalition, or a collection of interest groups, who through a complex process of conflict, compromise, and cooperation formulate the strategic choices to be pursued by the organization as a whole.[148]

[146] Note from corporate marketing manager, 11 May 1995; Report submitted by Appeal Advertising & Marketing Consultants, 1998.

[147] As Alvin Gouldner has rightly remarked, the tendency to conceive of management as a monolithic entity is most probably influenced by Weber's study of bureaucracy where the model was the solidary government bureaucracy in which each strata pursued identical end goals. *Patterns of Industrial Bureaucracy. A Case Study of Modern Factory Administration*, New York, 1964, pp. 20–3.

[148] For an insightful analysis of this process of negotiation between different functional groups, each possessing its own mind-set see W. Bernard Carlson, 'The Coordination of Business Organization and Technical Innovation Within the Firm. A Case-Study of the Thomson-Houston Electric Company in the 1880s', in N. Lamoreaux and D. Raff (eds.), *Coordination and Information. Historical Perspectives on the Organization of Enterprise*, Chicago, 1995, pp. 55–94. On the divisions within management, in particular the conflicting priorities of line and staff managers, see, *inter alia*, Crozier, *Le phénomène bureaucratique*, pp. 143–74; Dalton, *Men Who Manage*, chaps. 3 and 4; Sanford Jacoby, *Employing Bureaucracy. Managers, Unions and the Transformation of Work in the 20th century*, New Jersey, 2004, pp. 6–7, 122–6, and *passim*.

PLANS TO REVITALIZE R&D REMAIN STILLBORN

As we saw in the previous chapter, following liberalization private companies, both Indian and foreign, rapidly grabbed a large slice of the telecommunications equipment market. But market share was not the only thing ITI lost to its competitors; it also lost a number of its best research personnel. Its monopoly position might have resulted in both depriving its R&D department of a well-defined orientation, and blunting the motivation of its engineers. Nevertheless, over the years the company had succeeded in building a large and skilled research pool. The relatively large investments, at least by Indian standards, that it had made in R&D also meant that it had created conditions wherein its engineers could gain expertise in all areas of telecommunications. It was this expertise that private and foreign firms would now attempt to siphon away. For with the withdrawal of entry barriers to the equipment manufacture segment and the development of the information technology industry, alternative career opportunities that were also highly lucrative, opened up for the first time for ITI engineers. Many of the transnationals who were beginning to source their software from India had also established a base in Bangalore, attracted by its reputation as the Indian Silicon Valley.

Consequently, from the mid-1990s onwards, ITI experienced an unprecedented brain drain.[149] Though the exact extent of the exodus is unknown, 115 people from the switching R&D department at ITI Bangalore, or roughly half the department, resigned between July 1995 and October 1997 alone.[150] As an internal document pointed out, leading private companies and transnationals had 'lured (them) away by offers of a very high salary and other perquisites', and that it was impossible to retain these engineers in view of the restrictions placed by the government on the size of public sector remuneration packages.[151] The brain drain

---

[149] A brain drain of a much greater magnitude would also affect C-DoT, severely crippling its activities. For details, see *Business World*, 24 January 1996; *Business Line*, 8 December 1997.

[150] R&D Plan Review, 9 October 1997. Between 1988–89 and 1994–95, the number of R&D personnel at the Bangalore plant shrank by almost a quarter from 1671 to 1263, though some of the attrition was on account of voluntary retirement.

[151] Note provided to Lok Sabha on R&D activities in ITI, January 1996. The flight of skilled technical personnel from public sector undertakings due to unattractive employment conditions was not a recent phenomenon. In 1961 itself, the government appointed a commission to examine the question and suggest remedies. Bhagwati and

included the head of the Bangalore plant and switching technology expert, Sira G. Rao, who joined the private group BPL, and Dr A. Prabhakar, ITI Bangalore's R&D chief. But the overwhelming majority of the engineers who quit were from the middle ranks with an experience ranging from two to about fifteen years, and who constituted as such the mainstay of the company's R&D organization.[152]

The most immediate and threatening consequence of this talent flight was that a number of key development projects had to be either abandoned or were substantially delayed. This, in turn, would jeopardize ITI's capacity to launch new products at a time when it badly needed to do so in order to remain competitive *vis-à-vis* the private sector. The company therefore became even more dependent on external sources for technology. One such project to be crippled was the cutting-edge IPX switch, capable of adapting information streams (voice, video, data, etc.), and then routing them to appropriate network interfaces. Lack of continuity also badly affected the company's plans to develop an ISDN feature phone. All twenty of the engineers whom ITI had trained were poached by private companies eager to acquire experience in this field.

It was essentially to overcome the difficulties provoked by this exodus that top management came up with a plan in 1998 to restructure its research operations. After all, only 21 per cent of the 578 employees who presently worked at the main R&D centre in Bangalore were actually engaged in design tasks, with the others involved in areas as diverse as vendor development and component approval, prototype machine shop and pilot production, documentation and field trials. The plan therefore involved splitting the two categories of personnel: while the design engineers were to be regrouped in a stand-alone entity, named 'core' R&D, all the others would form an engineering cell, this division clearly corresponding to one between intellectual and 'physical' labour.

Core R&D would devote its resources exclusively towards developing new state-of-the-art technologies and upgrading existing ones with the

---

Desai, *Planning for Industrialization*, p. 164. More than two decades later, a parliamentary report warning of the problem of brain drain, this time among middle and top management, called for a upward revision of the salary structure. COPU, *Action taken by Government on recommendations contained in the 49th Report of the COPU on Public Undertakings*, 70th Report, Seventh Lok Sabha, New Delhi, 1983, p. 27.

[152] Of the 115 engineers who resigned from switching R&D, 77 were working in middle management grades. R&D Plan Review.

dual objective of reducing the development cycle time for new products and bringing out products that could match those of private firms in terms of quality and cost. An ambitious target of three new commercially viable launches annually was fixed, with each product to realize a turnover of at least Rs 100 million within a period of two years. As one document admitted, 'the time cycle of design and development for new products had to be reduced from years to months'.[153] Interestingly, in deciding to separate research activities from the different support or back-up facilities, the company was resuscitating practically to the last detail a proposal formulated almost two decades ago, but one it had failed to implement because of opposition from top R&D officials.

Like several of the management's other policy initiatives, this one too suffered from delays. Core R&D would be set up only in September 2000 or more than two years after it was first discussed. None of the elaborate proposals concerning the functioning of the cell would also ever see the light of day. Recognizing that it was indispensable for public sector enterprises to sufficiently reward research personnel, failing which the talent flight to private firms would continue unabated, a determining component of the plan called for offering 'excellent market commensurate pay packets' as well as introducing a separate career plan and incentive scheme.[154] But perhaps on account of the objections raised by DoT, the top management was unable to put into place the improved remuneration policies. Hence, it had to resign itself to the idea that the company might neither be able to 'attract, motivate (or) retain' competent research personnel.[155] All that it could promise by way of incentives were such meagre sops as loans for the purchase of computers for private use, monetary awards for publications in scientific journals, and a partial reimbursement of residential telephone bills.[156]

At the same time, the changes in the configuration of the company's research activity would create new complications while leaving older issues

[153] Proposal for Core R&D, nd.

[154] ibid. According to Mohan, government enterprises cannot operate in future without adequate flexibility in their compensation structures. 'Public Sector Reforms and Issues in Privatisation'.

[155] Proposal for Core R&D. In its report, PwC warned that ITI's status as a state-owned enterprise imposed severe restrictions on hiring and retaining talent, a crucial element in several emerging areas of business. PwC Strategic Recommendations.

[156] Note to the Board 318th meeting, item no. B9, April 2000.

unresolved. For one thing, it failed to tackle the imbalance between electronic and mechanical trades that had arisen in certain areas with the depletion of manpower on account of voluntary retirement and the brain drain. In 1992–93, telephone R&D employed ten electronic engineers and six mechanical engineers. Seven years later, only three electronic engineers and one mechanical engineer remained, even though the telephone division continued to require mechanical skills, especially for undertaking drawings for tool design. Yet, despite the repeated pleas made by R&D for hiring fresh mechanical engineers, top officials stuck to their stance that in the electronic era the company needed no expertise other than in electronics and software development. In the words of a long-serving research executive:

There is nobody in the top management now who has an in-depth knowledge of R&D's requirement. Senior R&D people who have worked at the grass roots level and know the problems are also unable to convince the top management to accept their point of view.[157]

Handicapped by the absence of mechanical engineers, the division's ability to come up with new models was therefore hampered. Production managers also complained that electronic engineers often refused to examine the mechanical and other aspects of the telephone when problems cropped up.

Furthermore, instead of smoothening coordination between research and the shop floor and compressing cycle times, the creation of an engineering cell tended at times to have exactly the opposite effect. In the previous dispensation, R&D was organized along product lines. Though formally attached to switching, telephone R&D nonetheless functioned autonomously as a cohesive unit integrating mechanical, electronics, and product documentation. But following the reorganization, each of these three functions were separated and its personnel merged with those working in similar areas, but on other product lines. Thus all the R&D mechanical staff in switching, transmission and telephones were pooled together, and similarly, for electronics and documentation personnel.

If this measure served to diversify the know-how and skill base of R&D personnel, it is also quite likely that in the absence of a dedicated

---

[157] Interview with K. Nagaraj.

engineering team capable of handling all aspects of product development, the process of productionizing new equipment was slowed down. Indeed, shop floor managers in the telephone divisions blamed the sluggish progress in introducing a low price telephone largely on the high transaction costs generated by the new research set up. According to them, the way R&D was now structured obliged them to deal with a greater number of people than before.

Finally, the Revival Plan submitted by the management to DoT in September 2003 with regard to the restructuring of ITI, stayed virtually silent on the role R&D would play in the future of the company. In parallel, the downgrading of the position of the R&D head envisaged in the new organizational chart underlined in no uncertain manner that research would not enjoy the same prominence and importance as it did in the past. No less significant, the document presented ITI essentially as a manufacturing unit which would acquire new technologies from outside, rather than seek to build in-house capabilities. Given these circumstances, it is questionable whether core R&D, whose achievements since its birth had in any case been minimal, would ever realize the ambitions vested in it by the management of becoming the 'predominant R&D centre in the country'.[158]

RESTRUCTURING OF COMPANY INTO BUSINESS GROUPS SHORTLIVED

The top management first embarked on the road to restructuring the company in May 1994. That year ITI Chairman B.B. Chadha, a financial executive, announced plans to reorganize the company's activities into strategic business units or groups. Unfortunately our sources shed very little light on how the business group concept first germinated in ITI. What is apparent is that it was a fashionable topic of discussion in Indian managerial circles then and this could, in some measure, have prompted Chadha to put the idea into practice in ITI as a means of revitalizing the company. Business groups as they emerged in developed countries in the 1970s, partly in response to the demand slowdown caused by the recession, reflected the predominant role marketing executives had come to acquire in defining corporate strategic goals at the expense of production staff.

[158] Proposal for Core R&D.

In practice, it meant consolidating a company's operations along specific product or business lines as opposed to a mode of administration revolving around the geographically-rooted manufacturing plant, the historical centre of gravity of the modern multi-unit integrated business enterprise.[159] All the functional departments such as manufacturing, quality, marketing, R&D, sales, finance, purchasing and administrative services were to be split along product lines and integrated vertically across the different units, and centralized in the hands of individual business group heads who would run each business as autonomous profit centres. So in the case of ITI's terminal equipment segment, for example, coordination and responsibility for all aspects of the business in the three units (Naini, Bangalore and Srinagar) where telephones were manufactured, was entrusted to an executive based at the company's Naini factory.

In sharp contrast to certain other policy objectives, the management moved quickly to put into place the new structure. Seven business groups were established, each built around one of ITI's products: switching, transmission, terminal equipment, network systems, control systems, micro-electronics and computer, and customer support.[160] Stressing the importance of change, one document identified several flaws in the company's current organizational framework: poor customer orientation, the absence of clearly defined spheres of managerial authority and accountability, and frequent problems of co-ordination between production, marketing and R&D, as a result of which the corporate office and the chairman were called upon '. . . to do everything for everyone at all times'. The document went on to add:

Production was the 'unique selling point' for the organization. This is no more the case . . . The criticality of our business has moved away from our Units which we controlled to a market place we do not control.[161]

---

[159] On this point see Chandler, *The Visible Hand,* Cambridge (Mass.), 1977, especially Introduction, and chapters 13–14. While studying the rise of the diversified, multi-divisional enterprise, Chandler's opus, however, closes with the arrival of the conglomerate in the sixties.

[160] Office Order Ref. CM/13.1A, 29 May 1994. The restructuring also coincided with the company being rechristened ITI. Top management believed the old name Indian Telephone Industries did not adequately convey the wide and diverse range of activities undertaken by the company in the telecommunications field.

[161] Note to the Board 275th meeting, item no. A3, September 1994.

The business group proposal, however, encountered strong internal opposition from at least one quarter. Criticizing the break-up of the company's research facilities on the grounds that it would prove disruptive, the head of R&D at the Bangalore plant wanted the company to hire new research personnel for the business groups rather than divert existing staff. He also complained about not having been consulted by the chairman on the actual details of the project.[162] Less than a year later, he had resigned from the company. Nor would the experiment itself last very long. By 1996, or barely two years after their creation, all the different groups had been disbanded, and the company had reverted to the former manufacturing unit-oriented style of functioning. With Chadha, the driving force behind the scheme, retiring shortly after its launch, and no full-time chairman being appointed for over a year following his departure, the business groups received neither impetus nor direction from the top management. Consequently, as with other strategic decisions, this one too was never implemented in earnest.

Even though a note explicitly stated that the effective functioning of the business groups depended on their integrating the finance department, the latter continued to operate as it had in the past, reporting directly to the head of finance rather than to the business group head.[163] This was also true for R&D, particularly at the flagship Bangalore plant where the company's research base was concentrated. With these two critical departments stubbornly remaining outside their control, business group heads, quite predictably, declared that they could not be held responsible for product development. The distinct lack of enthusiasm exhibited by key sections of top officials for the business groups, indicating once again the heterogeneous nature of management, was hardly surprising. The reorganization of the company was imposed against their wishes, and, as the protests of the Bangalore R&D chief revealed, the changes were deeply resented by a number of high ranking executives who lost power as a result.

The rivalry in the uppermost strata of the company also translated at

---

[162] Note to the Board 274th meeting, item no. A3, June 1994. Interestingly, in the early seventies, consultancy firm Mckinsey had proposed organizing all of AT&T's activities along market or business lines. But, according to Temin, there was opposition from both Bell Labs and Western Electric. *The Fall of the Bell System*, pp. 162–75.

[163] Ref. No. CRT-55, 29 March 1995.

times into rivalry between the different plants and groups. An internal memo warning of transitional problems, particularly with respect to the allocation of manufacturing facilities, turned out to be totally correct as units refused to interchange inventories, affecting production in the bargain.[164] Another cause of the swift demise of the business groups was the difficulties involved in controlling production in different geographic locations from a single site—a difficulty compounded by the weak corporate 'culture' prevailing in ITI where few efforts had been made to encourage inter-organizational cohesiveness. Finally, the functioning of the new configuration tended to conflict with that of the corporate office, eroding the latter's influence. By assuming a number of co-ordination and centralization tasks handled in the past from the centre, the business groups rendered it partly superfluous. Not surprisingly therefore, one of the first decisions taken by the new ITI Chairman, S.S. Motial was to transfer all production planning and co-ordination activities as well as marketing back to the corporate office where they were once again consolidated.[165] Henceforth, each unit would be required to concentrate exclusively on production issues.

RECOMMENDATIONS OF DISINVESTMENT COMMISSION REJECTED

In May 1996, at the same time as the business groups were being dismantled, the Department of Public Enterprises, alarmed by the losses ITI was posting for the second consecutive year, suggested that it bring in a consultancy firm 'who can give proposals for turnaround of the Company in future'.[166] The top management readily agreed to the recommendation, but stated that DoT, as the major customer and owner of the company, should select the consultant so that all aspects of ITI's operations could be examined. Given the company's financial constraints, DoT was also asked to bear the cost of the consultant's fees, estimated then at Rs 40 million.[167] Both these demands were not only dismissed outright by DoT, but the plan of hiring an consultant itself was dropped

---

[164] Office Order Ref. CM/13.1A.
[165] Ref. CM/13.1A, 16 July 1996.
[166] Note to Board 287th meeting, item no. B16, 29 May 1996.
[167] Note to Board 290th meeting, item no. B3, September 1996.

once the Public Sector Disinvestment Commission submitted its report on restructuring ITI in April 1997.[168]

In its brief report the Commission made three major recommendations. The first and most radical of these was that the company should be privatized. The government should sell the bulk of its shareholding, limiting its stake to no more than 26 per cent since ITI had been classified as a 'non-core' public sector company, as opposed to 'strategic' or 'core' companies where government participation could exceed 51 per cent.[169] Following from this, the Commission, in its second recommendation, stated that a 50 per cent stake in ITI be reserved for a strategic partner 'having the latest technology, capital and skills to develop and expand the activities' of the company.[170]

In other words, the Commission was implicitly pushing for the sale of ITI to a foreign corporation as no domestic company possessed the capabilities demanded of the strategic partner. As it argued, denationalization would eliminate the need for the government to inject the 'large capital outlays' indispensable for restructuring the company, failing which its 'future . . . in its present form is an area of concern'.[171] The Commission also made it clear that in case potential investors were unwilling to acquire the company in its totality given the contrasting performance and technology levels of the different units, ITI could be divided into two entities, one comprising the southern plants (Bangalore, Electronic City, and Palakkad), and the other the northern plants (Rae Bareli, Naini, and Mankapur). In parallel, the company's defence products division would be hived off and merged with that of another Bangalore-based public sector firm, BEL. The third recommendation called for a draconian reduction in the size of the company's workforce, from roughly

---

[168] An advisory body endowed with wide-ranging terms of reference, the Disinvestment Commission was set up by the United Front government in August 1996 for a period of three years. Headed by G.V. Ramakrishna, the Commission submitted 12 reports in all to the government, covering 59 public sector companies, but few of its recommendations were implemented.

[169] The Commission justified its decision to place ITI in the 'non-core' industrial category partly on the grounds that the initial objectives of the state in reserving these industries exclusively for the public sector had been fulfilled. Disinvestment Commission Report I.

[170] Disinvestment Commission Report II, ITI Ltd, p. 24.

[171] ibid.

25,000 to 7000 employees, prior to its divestiture, by offering voluntary retirement to the surplus staff.

Whether or not the overall objective of promoting efficiency and accountability in public sector enterprises is best achieved through privatization or competition remains a contentious and inconclusive debate.[172] An abundant mass of literature reviewing the experience of developing countries, and often sponsored by powerful transnational institutions such as the World Bank, has heralded privatization as the panacea for the ills of the public sector. But the findings of other studies have increasingly questioned the axiomatic connection between ownership change and higher efficiency.[173] They maintain that the essential determinants of improved economic performance in firms are the competitive and regulatory environments. The popular horror stories about inefficient state-owned firms draining the public treasury may have more to do with their monopoly positions than their ownership status.

Arguments in favour of rolling back the state from the economy are also invariably coloured by ideology.[174] In the Indian post-reforms context, the ideological dimensions of the issue have been clearly exposed by research showing that the performance of public sector industrial companies has not been the drag on the exchequer that pro-market economists frequently and vociferously claim to justify their demands for private ownership.[175] In the end, the government never sought to

[172] As Pranab Bardhan and John Roemer argue, neither economic theory nor history has disproved the claim that private ownership is not necessary for the successful operation of competition and markets. 'Market Socialism: A Case for Rejuvenation'. See also John Vickers and George Yarrow, 'Economic Perspectives on Privatization', *Journal of Economic Perspectives*, Vol. 5, No. 2, Spring 1991, pp. 111–32; and George Yarrow, 'Privatization in Theory and Practice', *Economic Policy*, No. 2, April 1986, pp. 323–77.

[173] Samuel Paul, 'Privatization. A Review of International Experience', *EPW*, Vol. XXIII, No. 6, 6 February 1988, pp. 273–6; Pan Yotopoulos, 'The (Rip) Tide of Privatization: Lessons from Chile', *World Development*, Vol.17, No. 5, 1989, pp. 683–702; Syed Naqvi and A.R. Kemal, 'The Privatization of Public Industrial Enterprises in Pakistan', *Pakistan Development Review*, Vol. 30, No. 2, Summer 1991, pp. 105–44.

[174] Ezra Suleiman and John Waterbury, 'Introduction: Analyzing Privatization in Industrial and Developing Countries', in *Political Economy of Public Sector Reform*, pp. 1–21.

[175] Nagaraj, 'Public Sector Performance in Eighties'; and *idem*, 'Macroeconomic Impact of Public Sector Enterprises'.

implement any of the proposals put forward by the Disinvestment Commission. With various parliamentary bodies insisting that ITI be classified as a core company given the importance of the telecommunications sector in developing the country's infrastructure and stimulating economic growth, DoT declared in 2002 that the government intended to maintain its shareholding in the company at the existing level of roughly 77 per cent.[176]

Meanwhile, in July 1999, after securing the approval of DoT, the top management revived the idea of appointing an external consultant to help it restructure the company. Out of the five firms shortlisted, only two were seriously considered, PwC and KPMG, before the former was finally selected in September 1999.[177] PwC was asked to come up with a strategic blueprint by June 2000 covering both the short and the long term. To be enforced within a year, the emphasis of the short range measures was to be on improving the performance of the Bangalore plant, notably in areas such as working capital management, inventory control and reduction in material costs, whereas the long term plan would define the future direction of the company. The total cost of the consultancy project was estimated at roughly Rs 150 million.[178]

To what extent company officials actually put into practice the proposals concerning the Bangalore plant is unclear. None of the long-term initiatives were translated into action either, largely because ITI lacked the necessary financial resources, and DoT had yet to decide whether it should extend assistance. But many of the strategic recommendations listed by PwC would be incorporated subsequently into the Revival Plan presented by the management to the government in September 2003. One such suggestion pertained to the rationalization of the company's manufacturing facilities in order to both compress fixed costs and increase profitability levels. As the Revival Plan underlined, if the different units 'had their own relevance in the pre-liberalization era', at present they could no longer sustain themselves.[179]

Thus, in addition to merging the Electronic City plant, particularly badly affected by the demand crunch, with the mother Bangalore factory,

---

[176] Standing Committee on Information Technology (2002–03).

[177] 311th Board meeting, item no. B6, 9 July 1999.

[178] 314th Board meeting, item no. B9, 27 September 1999.

[179] ITI Revival Plan.

it was proposed to close down the technologically obsolete Rae Bareli unit.[180] As far as the employees here were concerned, half of them would be transferred to the other units and the other half forced to accept a 'voluntary separation scheme' which would offer more attractive benefits than the existing severance package. News of the closure of the Rae Bareli unit was publicly announced in August 2003 by the new ITI Chairman Y.K. Pandey. But confronted by noisy protests from the Congress (I), he promptly retracted his statement. Given its location in the constituency of Indira Gandhi (and later that of Sonia Gandhi) which explained why it had been set up there in the first place, Congress (I) leaders claimed that the plant was a 'living symbol of (her) memory', and that they would never allow it to be shut down.[181] Fortunately, no such controversy jeopardized the sale in October 2003 of the VLSI-II (Very Large Scale Integration) microchip fabrication unit to the Defence Research and Development Organization for Rs 260 million.[182]

Another key proposal put forward by PwC, and endorsed by the Revival Plan, concerned the necessity of concluding a strategic alliance with BSNL. Since the telecommunications carrier purchased equipment from ITI on a preferential basis, PwC stated that a modification or withdrawal of this arrangement, the likelihood of which could not be excluded in the wake of the corporatization of DoT, would have the consequence of rendering ITI's 'operations unviable'.[183] But to convince BSNL that such an alliance would be equally beneficial for it, especially in financial terms, ITI would have to sell its products at attractive prices. This in turn would depend on its ability to bring down manufacturing

---

[180] While the sale of the EC plant building and other assets was expected to fetch Rs 500 million, winding up Rae Bareli would have yielded savings in fixed costs of Rs 690 million in 2004–05 alone.

[181] *The Times of India*, 12 August 2003. In 1988, the ITI board decided to commemorate Indira Gandhi's association with the Rae Bareli unit by commissioning a statue of hers at a cost of Rs 250,000. 240th Board meeting, item no. B12, August 1988.

[182] Launched in 1993 in collaboration with the Defence Ministry and other scientific organizations, this unit which employed 130 people was engaged essentially in defence related projects. Production facilities aside, the axe also fell on other assets such as the ITI Bangalore soccer club, disbanded in October 2003 for want of funds. Like the company itself, the club had become a pale shadow of its former glory. *The Times of India*, 15 October 2003.

[183] PwC Recommendations, p. 10.

costs. Going one step further, the Revival Plan urged BSNL to make ITI its 'preferred equipment vendor', progressively outsourcing to the latter, all its non-core activities such as installation, commissioning and maintenance. In doing so, BSNL would not only be free to concentrate on key activities such as customer management, but could expect speedier supplies and a faster response to its problems, apart from checking possible cartel formation by transnational corporations. The status of 'preferred vendor' thus represented in some respects a throwback to the monopoly era, as ITI aimed to restore to its dealings with its principal customer the stability and regularity that had been so badly ruptured by deregulation.

The importance of building a privileged relationship with its industrial arm in the post-reforms period was not lost on BSNL either. At a joint meeting in 2001, one of its officials categorically declared that:

> ... ITI, being our own PSU and largest manufacturer of telecommunications equipment, have to be kept alive and sound working condition, which is in the interest of DOT/BSNL, for that it needs support (sic).[184]

The state agency also acknowledged the cooperation extended by ITI the previous year. Of all the equipment vendors, the latter alone had agreed to provide large digital switches at the price offered by BSNL. Nevertheless, it pleaded its inability to place advance orders on ITI, as top management had requested, so as to facilitate material procurement and planning. On the other hand, having understood that stronger ties with ITI was in their own interests too, both BSNL and MTNL agreed to infuse Rs 3000 million by way of redeemable preference shares into the cash-starved company in 2003. Other recommendations put forward by PwC included leveraging the company's manufacturing infrastructure by entering the field of global contract manufacturing, and expanding its product portfolio by concentrating on high value added services such as software development.[185] But neither suggestion found a mention in the Revival Plan; company officials probably both doubted the overall

---

[184] Minutes of Quarterly Performance Review meeting, 30 June 2001.

[185] According to PwC, the market for electronic manufacturing services was expanding at a much quicker pace than that of electronic equipments. Hence ITI should either try and directly outsource work from transnational corporations such as Alcatel or Siemens, or seek orders from Solectron or Flextronics, the two leading specialist contract providers.

viability of these projects and their own capacity to successfully execute them.

In conclusion, we can safely state that the internal reform drive launched by the management in the wake of deregulation, with the objective of reinforcing ITI's market power, proved to be of only limited effectiveness.[186] Its large and unqualified workforce, low-value-generating production facilities, atrophied research capabilities, near-total dependence on a single client, and chronic financial difficulties, all meant that the state-owned telecommunications manufacturer remained trapped in a volume-based profit strategy which was hopelessly maladjusted to the radically transformed market conditions. The structural features of its operations rendered the task of forging a new productive model, centred on an alternative profit strategy emphasizing cost reduction, flexibility, and innovation, if not impossible, at least extremely arduous and daunting. Nor did the firm possess adequate financial and organizational resources to address the immense scale and scope of its inter-related problems Whatever change that occurred was not only incremental, but had been introduced essentially within the framework of the existing institutional arrangements. Finding a durable solution to the crisis signified a radical departure from the prevailing operations, strategy and institutions, a task that proved beyond the capability of ITI management.

The most important measure, voluntary retirement, encountered a poor response from the workforce with the result that the company continued to be saddled with sizeable excess manpower. Employees were clearly unwilling to trade away the long term advantages accruing from public sector employment for short term monetary gains, especially in an economic context where the choice, if it can be called that, rested between ill paid, unprotected informal sector jobs and unemployment. The relative failure of the buy-out scheme had crucial chain effects as it neutralized the efforts being made in other areas to bring down manufacturing costs, thereby severely undermining the company's ability to compete in an industry characterized by declining profit margins.

Other corporate initiatives such as material cost reduction certainly

---

[186] Interesting parallels can be found between ITI's crisis-management strategy and that of British Leyland in the 1970s and 1980s. For details, see Whisler, *British Motor Industry,* pp. 1–11.

enjoyed a greater degree of success. But here again policy-induced errors on the part of the management meant that the company could derive less than optimal advantage from its gains. Steps to establish a marketing department, reduce the company's dependence on DoT by diversifying its revenue base, and reorganize R&D, all failed to generate the expected results, essentially because company officials both delayed their implementation or never attempted to implement them in earnest. Of such magnitude was the competitive disadvantage separating ITI and its private sector rivals that only through vigorous and sustained initiatives to improve efficiency and cut costs could this gap ever have begun to be narrowed. Conflicts between different factions of management, production versus marketing, R&D against shop floor, staff versus line, which reflected their differing interests and views, also acted as an additional impediment on the company's capacity to push through a strategic redirection.

Notwithstanding the pressure to remedy the ills afflicting the company, it is possible that the assurance of supplying at least 30 per cent of DoT's total equipment requirements both accounted for as well as strengthened organizational inertia. In much the same vein as protectionist policies are thought to have encouraged French automakers all through the 1970s to retard implementing much-overdue structural changes, the system of preferential quotas quite likely functioned as a life-belt.[187] By guaranteeing to provide the company with a minimal level of resources to keep day-to-day operations going, however erratically, it facilitated the preservation of the *status quo*. The lack of urgency exhibited at the helm of the company may have been further reinforced by the realization that the authorities, while tolerating its continuing decline, could not afford to allow a state-owned enterprise of the importance and size of ITI to collapse without unleashing a major political storm. In the absence of a social security network worth its name and in a system characterized by endemic unemployment, it was doubtful whether any government would take the risk of depriving close to 20,000 employees, belonging to the best organized and most vocal sections of the workforce in the country, of their jobs. As Kornai points out, 'what is really important is the psychological

---

[187] Christophe Midler, 'Les concepts au concret. Réflexion sur les liens entre systèmes téchniques et systèmes de gestion dans l'industrie automobile', in R. Salais and L. Thévenot (eds.), *Le Travail: marchés, règles, conventions*, Paris, 1986, pp. 29–51.

effect of the (budget) constraint'.[188] This is to say that managements' actions are determined above all by the degree to which they can or cannot expect external monetary assistance under loss-making conditions.

One could also well add that ITI executives' overall approach was influenced by the understanding that they could not be held fully accountable for the company's performance, and, consequently, that their own job security was not threatened. This was because bureaucratic intervention imposed severe limitations on their autonomy. Even as the new deregulated business environment placed a premium on organizational efficiency, the management was forced to shelve the introduction of a more attractive remuneration package for research engineers as well as the closure of the Rae Bareli plant, two strategic options crucial to ITI's future vitality. This in itself revealed the degree to which the constraints of political contingency inherent in direct state-ownership neutralised the possibilities for independent decision-making and flexibility.

Finally, it must be noted that the successful restructuring of ITI, as outlined in the PwC report and the Revival Plan, was crucially tied to the support policy-making officials were willing to extend, especially now that the privatization of the company had been ruled out. Irrespective of the measures the management took, or did not take and the vigour with which it pursued them, DoT and, by extension, the government alone were in a position to ensure the long-term viability of the telecommunications vendor by eliminating the most serious of the structural weaknesses handicapping its operations. Modernizing the company's manufacturing infrastructure, inducting new technologies as well as shedding the surplus workforce through voluntary retirement required considerable resources. No other institution but the government had the reach to mobilise and pump in these investments. Without this financial inflow, a manifestation of the 'paternalistic role of the modern state', ITI was condemned to a process of inevitable decline.[189]

---

[188] Kornai, 'The Soft Budget Constraint', p. 8.
[189] ibid.

chapter six

Spheres of Practice
An Ethnography of Printed Circuit Board Assembly Work

If culture can no longer be qualified as the 'great unthought' of Indian labour studies, work, defined as a concrete activity and in its everyday materiality, continues to remain the great unexplained, despite constant references to its importance in the process of identity formation.[1] Sharing a weakness endemic to labour historiography, and, perhaps to a lesser measure, to industrial sociology in the West as well, social scientists have rarely confronted this question head on.[2] The dominant tendency

---

[1] Mohapatra, 'Situating the Renewal'.

[2] Even a collection of essays expressly attached to exploring the 'meanings of work', like the one edited by Patrick Joyce, contains just one essay by Richard Whipp (' "A Time to Every Purpose": An Essay on Time and Work', pp. 210–36) focussing on the way individual workers practically accomplish their tasks. *The Historical Meanings of Work*, Cambridge, 1989. Similarly, in another influential set of essays, practice comes out distinctly second best compared to the other dimensions of work designated in the title. S. Kaplan and C. Koepp (eds.), *Work in France. Representations, Meaning, Organization, and Practice*, Ithaca, 1986. In the case of industrial sociology, notwithstanding the discipline's long and illustrious heritage in France, it has attracted considerable criticism from no less a tutelary figure than Pierre Naville for having failed to make work its point of departure. 'Rencontre avec Pierre Naville', in M. Guillaume (ed.), *L'Etat des Sciences Sociales en France*, Paris, 1986, pp. 167–8. Similarly, closer

is to view work through the prism of the division of labour, organizational methods, health and safety standards, disciplinary mechanisms, class consciousness, leisure, the labour market, industrial relations and so forth. It is always mediated through other forces and influences, studied in relation to other issues rather than recognized as a practical activity in itself deserving of attention. On the physical, cognitive and emotional content of the tasks performed by wage earners, silence often prevails.

Corporate inhospitality towards researchers particularly in an institutional setting where industrial sociology never really flourished could partly explain why sociologists and social anthropologists in India have seldom penetrated Marx's legendary 'hidden abode of production'.[3] One can rightly bemoan the 'poverty of the fieldwork tradition in the study of labour' among sociologists, but while this predicament certainly has to do with the priority accorded to 'village studies' by the discipline, difficulties in securing *entrée* to the shop floor must not be overlooked.[4] In the case of labour historians, the reasons for their neglect of work can to a large measure be traced back to the nature of the source material they typically rely upon to fashion their narratives of workplace operations and social relations. These are in the main produced by elite groups wherein not only does the normative permeate the descriptive, but a top-down vision of work predominates. The perspective of those located on the shop floor is invariably ignored to stress instead the way employers and managers organize and direct the labour of those under their command. Other archival material, such as process sheets, are equally incapable of shedding light on the act and situation of work. While perhaps telling us what an operative should do, and how he or she should

---

home, barring the ethnography-based study undertaken by Jonathan Parry, none of the other texts featured in the inter-disciplinary anthology, *The Worlds of Indian Labour*, specifically address the theme of work practices.

[3] Karl Marx, *Capital*, Vol. I, pp. 279–80. Less explicable though is why even when sociologists manage to gain relatively unrestricted access to the shop floor, they attach little importance to what people actually do there, as in the case of N.R. Sheth's otherwise admirable study, *The Social Framework of an Indian Factory*, Bombay, 1968.

[4] Jonathan Parry, 'Introduction', in *The Worlds of Indian Labour*, pp. ix–xxxvi (cit. p. xii) Not only can the number of ethnographic enquiries devoted to industrial workers be counted on one hand, but only one of these studies is grounded in direct participant observation methods. Narendra Panjwani, 'Living with Capitalism: Class, Caste, and Paternalism among Industrial Workers in Bombay', *Contributions to Indian Sociology*, Vol. 18, No. 2, 1984, pp. 267–92.

do it (even this information is not systematically given), they can never tell us what the worker really does. Does he or she adhere to the norm and why? Why does one worker follow the norm but not his or her colleague?

The only means of satisfactorily answering all these questions is by embracing an 'ethnographic stance'.[5] To uncover the contextual meaning of actions and capture the nuances and diversity of forms underpinning the actual performance of work so essential to enabling a 'thick description', a first hand observation of individual practices is indispensable. As Olivier Schwartz rightly remarks, a fundamental *raison d'être* of ethnography is the unparalleled access it offers to the universe of non-official practices.[6] More significantly, by making visible and giving substance to workers' actions in the context of their everyday schedules, ethnography restores their agentic role in shaping the distinctive character of the workplace. The micro-regulations in which their interactions are enmeshed and which often tend to be dismissed as 'illogical' or 'obstructive' by managements, can be understood as a rational response to situational constraints and opportunities. It therefore becomes possible to treat actors, especially those located at the bottom of the occupational hierarchy, as knowledgeable and capable individuals whose social practices are endowed with a relative autonomy from external structural determinants. Far from being an expression of internalized norms and rules that are mechanically applied, their actions can come to be seen as something in whose construction they actively participate both as individuals and as a collective.

For the purpose of my ethnographic research, I chose a shop assembling printed circuit boards for electronic telephones. Since many of the written sources that I disposed pertained to the operations of the telephone division, localizing my observations of work to the same division seemed a logical step. It meant I could combine the two modes of data collection, close range observation and archival material, and mutually interrogate

---

[5] Sherry Ortner, 'Resistance and the Problem of Ethnographic Refusal', in Terence J. McDonald (ed.), *The Historic Turn in the Social Sciences*, Ann Arbor, 1996, pp. 281–304 (cit. p. 281). Ortner takes care, though, to point out that an ethnographic stance need not always be anchored in fieldwork; it can also take a textual disposition just as much as it can be an intellectual position, or a mode of construction and interpretation.

[6] Olivier Schwartz, 'L'empirisme irréductible. Postface', in Nels Anderson, *Le Hobo. Sociologie du sans-abri*, Paris, 1993, pp. 265–308.

them to try and eliminate errors of judgement and/or interpretation. Unfortunately, the possibility of doing participant observation was ruled out. So I had to be satisfied with the role of a non-participant observer. Failing to personally learn how to assemble a board carried definite drawbacks, preventing me notably from acquiring a deeper insight into workers' experience of their tasks On the other hand, non-participant observation was not entirely bereft of benefits. Not being required to work myself, I could freely circulate throughout the shop to look and listen and talk.[7] This represented a significant advantage in the specific context of board assembly activity where since everybody carried out an identical set of tasks it was less the similarities in work styles than the dissimilarities that mattered. Paying careful attention to these differences, so as to decode their underlying logic then conditioned any attempt to successfully generate a 'thick description' of production activities.

My fieldwork lasted two months in all, but with a long interruption in the middle. I first spent a couple of weeks in the board assembly shop in May-June 1999, before coming back in October 2001 for a further six weeks where I concentrated on studying the activities of one work group in particular.[8] Though this latter visit was dictated by the imperatives of my personal calendar and could hardly qualify in any way as a 'revisit', its advantages soon became evident.[9] It allowed for the incorporation of a diachronic perspective into my ethnography, to account for change by assessing at first hand the mutations that had occurred between my first and second field trips and to trace their impact on the social organization of the shop floor, mutations of which I would have been quite ignorant had I not returned. In other words, enlarging the

[7] If direct observation occupies pride of place in ethnography, and is often singled out as the hallmark of this mode of research, Schwartz alerts us also to the importance of speech and listening as indispensable sources in generating material. But at the same time he spotlights the problematic nature of discursive data because unlike observational data they can rarely be verified by the researcher. 'L'empirisme irréductible.'

[8] For various reasons, the luxury of conducting fieldwork over an extended block of time may no longer be available to the 'post-modern' ethnographer, suggests Ulf Hannerz. 'Being there . . . and there . . . and there! Reflections on Multi-site Ethnography', *Ethnography*, Vol. 4, No. 2, 2003, pp. 201–16.

[9] Identifying various modes of ethnographic revisits, Michael Burawoy defines a revisit as a comparative study of the same site undertaken at a later point in time either by the same author or by some one else. 'Revisits: An Outline of a Theory of Reflexive Ethnography', *American Sociological Review*, Vol. 68, October 2003, pp. 645–79.

temporal context of my research to embrace different moments in time enabled me somewhat to evade getting stuck in a timeless present, the bane of so much ethnographic writing. If the second visit helped to demonstrate certain continuities in the productive process and work practices, it also threw into relief the demise of certain micro-regulations that governed informal arrangements among the members of individual work groups.

What kind of reception did I receive on the shop floor? Although it was clear to everybody that I owed my *entrée* exclusively to the good offices of the management, this detail did not occasion any hostility or suspicion towards me. On the contrary, I encountered nothing but friendliness and cooperation in all my daily interactions with workers throughout the duration of my fieldwork. Flattered to some extent by the attention I bestowed upon them, having come 'all the way from Paris to study about our work', workers' attitudes also probably stemmed from the respect traditionally accorded to the world of intellect by those who, for one reason or the other, had never succeeded in penetrating this world. Despite being younger than all my informants, the age gap separating us was also not too pronounced to create an imbalance in our relations. At all times, there was no question of workers not taking me seriously.

At the same time, the culture of indulgence that defined the nature of industrial relations in the plant plus the fact that many operatives stood on the verge of retirement meant they had little to fear by talking openly to me. The risk of management reprisals was virtually non-existent. So they could afford to be extremely candid in expressing their sentiments about their work, their opinions of individual officers, and their criticisms of various aspects of shop floor organization even in front of a tape recorder. (I regretted the silencing effects of a tape recorder on only one occasion when interviewing a worker-officer who had proved to be highly vocal in our informal chats. Being an officer now, and hence stripped of union protection in case of any problem, he was understandably apprehensive about his words being recorded.) Moreover, the leisurely pace of work rhythms in a public sector enterprise like ITI greatly facilitated my task as an observer. Because they were subjected to no pressure to maximize output, workers disposed sufficient time to explain the details of their tasks and answer my innumerable questions. I was therefore able to mix quite easily, and quickly erase whatever fleeting pangs of guilt may have crossed my mind about being an intruder, of constantly interfering in their activities and disturbing them to realize my own objectives.

Rivalling the freedom I enjoyed in interrogating workers about all aspects of their occupation were the difficulties I experienced, due essentially to my personal inhibitions, with respect to social issues, notably caste and linguistic affinities. Paradoxically, workers themselves showed few scruples in raising both these themes when it came to my own identity: on several instances I found myself having to deal with pointed questions as to my origins as a Tamil-speaking Brahmin. My responses were invariably defensive. I was more than conscious of the dual drawbacks my identity markers constituted, given the charged social connotations associated with them in an environment where both anti-Tamil and anti-Brahmin sentiments waxed, the former overtly, the latter more covertly. Yet, I could not bring myself to ask the workers in turn about their caste ties, encumbered, no doubt, by the complexes arising from my self-definition as a western-educated, secularized, English speaking deracinated male, but nevertheless still a Tamil Brahmin in the eyes of my interlocutors.[10]

Linguistic loyalties represented a no less sensitive subject, though for slightly different reasons. In the light of the profound scars inscribed on the factory social order by the hostilities of the early 1970s pitting Kannada workers against their Tamil counterparts together with my own coordinates as a Tamil speaker, I had to exercise considerable caution when treading this ground. I understood this quite early on in my fieldwork when an operative to whom I had addressed a few words in Tamil brusquely informed me that he was a Kannadiga. So not only did I have to be certain of the linguistic identity of my interlocutor before talking to him in Kannada or Tamil, I also obviously could not put the same question indifferently to one or the other when discussing the issue of linguistic tensions. Nor could I do so within earshot of a Kannada

[10] An anthropologist studying his own culture possesses in his 'nativehood' an advantage over the outsider, writes M.N. Srinivas, even while recognizing that some insiders may be more, or less, 'native' than others. While always problematic, questions of defining just who is an 'insider' or 'outsider' become even more complex at a time when scholars from diaspora communities increasingly return to explore their 'original' societies. 'Studying One's Own Culture: Some Thoughts', pp. 198–214; and 'The Insider versus the Outsider', pp. 226–33, in *idem, Village, Caste, Gender and Method. Essays in Indian Social Anthropology*, New Delhi, 1996.

worker when talking to a Tamil worker and vice versa. Nevertheless, at no point of time did my linguistic and caste origins become an obstacle to interacting freely with the workers.

Highly tolerant of my presence during working hours and outside the factory as well since I interviewed a number of them at length in their homes, workers' reactions towards me, however, underwent a distinct change once production came to a halt. This was most visible during the official tea and lunch breaks. When the tea trolley arrived in the shop twice a day, I was rarely asked by the workers to join them for a cup of tea or coffee. Nor was I ever invited to accompany any of them to the canteen for lunch—though they may well have felt that given my 'status' my place was in the officers' canteen rather than in the non-officers' canteen, and that my interest in their lives was confined to their work activities.[11] It took me some time to understand this sudden swing in behaviour where from being a relative 'insider' I suddenly became a rank outsider, ignored by almost everybody. A handful of people who brought lunch from home, though, regularly offered to share their food with me.

The interpretation that I finally arrived at was that workers probably sought to underline as much the difference in our respective social positions as to preserve their integrity by clearly delimiting the sphere of work from the sphere of non-work. In the former sphere, they were willing to accept or include me partly because they had no choice: I had been introduced (thrust?) into the workgroup by shop officials. In the latter sphere, they were free to exclude me. The world of non-work formed a private space, an autonomous territory where they were masters of both their time and actions, and owed no obligations to the management or those identified with it in one way or another. While a tacit accord of sorts may well have bound us at the workplace where in return for the undivided, and unasked, attention I showered upon them, workers were ready to facilitate my task of gathering data by showing and talking to me about their tasks, this accord did not extend beyond the shop floor. Since I certainly did not belong to their world, they perhaps saw no reason to reveal more of it than what I already saw.

[11] A more or less similar experience is recounted by Nicolas Hatzfeld during the course of his fieldwork as a participant observer in a French car assembly plant. 'La pause casse-croûte. Quand les chaînes s'arretent à Peugeot-Sochaux', *Terrain*, No. 39, September 2002, pp. 33–48.

ERRORS FREQUENTLY FOUND IN MATERIAL KITS

The 'nerve centre' of the electronic push-button telephone, the printed circuit board performs two functions crucial to the operation of the instrument. First, it acts as a mechanical support for all the components fastened on the board. Next, it provides electrical interconnection paths between the components after these have been soldered. At the telephone division in the Bangalore plant of ITI, the printed circuit board manufacturing cycle was divided into three distinct stages: kitting, assembling which itself decomposed into two operations, assembly *per se* and wave soldering, and, lastly, lacquering. Each stage was handled by a specific group of workers, but the occupations shared a low degree of skill requirement, and, barring wave soldering, a high degree of labour intensity.

In the initial or preparatory phase, known as kitting, all the components that went into a board were individually bundled into kits for distribution at the following stage. A single kit contained material necessary for making 50 boards.[12] The telephone model had a board measuring between 115 and 160 square cm and housed between 50 and 70 types of components. These consisted in the main of resistors, capacitors, diodes, and transistors of various electrical values and kinds, resistors and capacitors being the most commonly utilized components. The Alpha telephone produced by ITI, for instance, integrated 20 and 12 families of resistors and capacitors respectively. Many of these were also multiple families and include between two and four 'members' each. Thus the 20 categories of resistors actually multiplied into 30 individual components. In other words, the total number of resistors in a kit for 50 boards could reach up to 1500.

Given the substantial quantities and varieties of components that needed to be kitted, a painstaking and monotonous task that called for the components to be either weighed or manually counted, depending on their size, before they were put into small plastic packets, mistakes were inevitable. These mistakes also apparently exceeded the prescribed norms judging by the volume of complaints pouring out of the printed board assembly shop. Errors tended to fall into both minor and major

---

[12] For reasons of cost as well as time efficiency, the size of each kit was doubled some time in the second half of the 1990s so as to enable operatives to assemble 50 boards instead of 25.

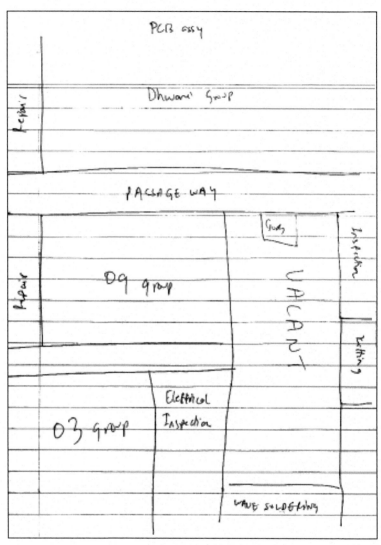

A page from the author's diary.

This sketch shows the spatial demarcation on the shop floor of the different functional groups involved in the operations of printed circuit board assembly during the course of my second field visit in 2001. The actual task of assembling the boards was undertaken by the three groups, Dhwani, 09 and 03. The legend 'Gods' refers to the photos of various Hindi divinities bedecking one section of the hangar wall.

categories. A combination of human negligence and an unreliable weighing machine often translated into shortfalls in the amount of material available in a kit. If such lapses while irksome were easily corrected, the damage caused by others could prove far more costly.

To facilitate assembly operations, a slip of paper identifying the component, its electrical value and its location on the board (the board carries a printed legend) was placed in each component packet. But as I witnessed for myself, carelessness on the part of kitting workers meant these indications were not always the epitome of accuracy. Often components of the wrong value were supplied and labels inverted which in turn directly impinged on the quality of operatives' work. In defence of kitting, it can be said that they had to cope with abrupt changes in production schedules and switch almost overnight from 'loading' one model to the next. Here is a small sample of kitting errors reproduced from my field notes:

1. 2.2 kilo ohms resistors distributed instead of 2.2 ohms;
2. labels mixed up for transistors T42 and T92 with the result they are assembled incorrectly, T42 occupying the position of T92 on the board and vice versa;
3. kit incomplete: five numbers of resistors of different values and one capacitor missing. Contrary to the rules, no slip is inserted into the kit to inform operatives of the shortfall so that they can claim the components later;
4. several Alpha components included in kit for Eyetel (a phone with a different circuitry and hence using different components).

Assembly operatives had the possibility of detecting quite a few of these errors, thus sparing themselves considerable loss of time and effort subsequently, besides reducing wastage, provided they were capable of reading the electrical value of resistors from the colour bands visible on the body of the component.[13] But as we shall discuss, for a wide range of reasons, the overwhelming majority of operatives had not learnt the colour code. Kitting faults therefore invariably mutated into assembly faults as

---

[13] Resistors are labelled using a standard colour coding scheme to indicate their value of electrical resistance and tolerance. This colour code consists of three, some times four, multi-coloured bands plus a tolerance band. Each colour corresponds to a specific value of resistance and the total value of the colour bands is the resistance of the resistor in question.

operatives 'blindly' assembled the boards which in the end failed to pass inspection.[14] Nevertheless, even repairmen critical of the assembly operatives subscribed to the consensus that better prepared kits could significantly bring down rejection rates. This fact was also not disputed by the management. Pointing out that the 'kitting centre plays a major role in creating or preventing faults', an internal note wanted workers here to be 'thoroughly trained in identifying components' since most of them lacked knowledge of the colour codification.[15] The proposal remained a pious wish.

At the same time, assembly workers reproached shop officials and the kitting section supervisor of doing nothing even when their attention was drawn to errors. Whatever steps were initiated from the mid-1990s onwards to improve standards, they appear to have progressively lapsed under the weight of organizational inertia.

When I told the kitting people to check with other groups to find if the same mistake (the supply of wrong value resistors) had not happened again, they said we were the only workers to complain and refused to investigate . . . *I am fed up of complaining to them* . . . Ten days later, the issue went up to the chief works manager because in another group 750 boards (15 kits) were rejected because of this mix-up.[16]

Nor did complaints to the union prove any more effective. Venugopalan, the union assistant secretary, admitted that kitting was full of *somberis*, the Tamil term for lazy and inefficient workers.[17] He also denounced the policy of accommodating those afflicted with disabilities and chronic ailments in this section given its light work loads, but in the same breath adds that change is impossible. Of the ten operatives listed on its rolls in 2001, four were declared to be medically unfit for any other job in the telephone division. By an ironic twist of fate, Venugopalan himself ended up working in kitting two years later. Having lost his right arm in an accident, shortly after which he failed to be re-elected in the union elections, the management decided to relocate him here on compassionate grounds.

[14] Interview with Vishwanath, 25 May 1999. Only in those cases where I conducted a 'formal' interview using a tape recorder have I cited the date.

[15] Inter office note, 13 April 1999.

[16] Interview with Irudayaraj. Emphasis added.

[17] Interview with N. Venugopalan, 9 May 1999.

Once the kits were ready and fed to the shop, phase two of the production cycle started. This consisted of the actual assembly activity characterized by a dual division of labour: one, manual: mounting the components on the board; the other largely mechanized: soldering. Prior to the mechanization of this operation, soldering the 220 odd points on a board demanded as much time as inserting the components. But with the advent of wave soldering machines, so called because the assembled board is brought into contact with the surface of a gently flowing wave of molten solder, the task could be accomplished in as little as 30 seconds. At the telephone division of ITI, where mass soldering techniques were first introduced in 1989, the time rates fixed for soldering and for the different manual operations clearly reflected the dissymmetry of effort. Whereas a rate of 21.92 hours is allowed for the soldering of 1000 boards, it took upwards of 800 hours for assembling the same number of boards.

Since soldering the components constituted an integral part of the overall board manufacturing cycle, until the late 1990s the same operatives carried out both jobs. They first mounted the components and then soldered them, taking individual responsibility for running the wave soldering machine. This arrangement suited the workers well, but shop managers expressed considerable reservations about it. Besides arguing that the time rates established for soldering were too generous, they accused workers, who had received no training whatsoever, of handling the machine roughly. The workers, managers said, not only disregarded quality norms, but also tinkered with the mechanisms in order to settle scores amongst themselves, notably by augmenting the height of the solder wave with the result that boards got regularly damaged.[18]

Rejection rates of boards due to improper soldering, it is true, ran consistently high. A complex process even after mechanization, achieving optimal soldering results rests on a combination of trial and error. The various operating parameters of the wave soldering machine had to be constantly adjusted and checked, and the equipment cleaned at regular intervals, especially if it happened to be an antiquated model as was the case with the ITI machine. These functional charges did not, however, fall within the province of assembly operatives but machine setters whose work ethics were debatable. In February 1997, the management took

---

[18] Interview with B.K. Sharma, May 1999.

advantage of a fire that broke out in the soldering room and destroyed one of the two machines in operation, to regain control of the situation. While workers' carelessness may have directly contributed to the fire, the lack of preventive maintenance, culpable housekeeping, inadequate ventilation, and poor supervision, all played their part. A new and more compartmentalized system of work organization was now imposed, clearly separating the activity of inserting components from that of soldering. Workers responsible for the former set of tasks were prohibited from operating the wave soldering machine, and two people, later raised to three, specifically appointed for soldering on a permanent basis. With this decision to carve out distinct occupational territories, the existing technical division of labour between the manual and mechanized facets of board assembly was both formalized and reinforced by a social division of labour. Following the reorganization, soldering-related defects certainly registered a steep decline. But the progressive improvement in quality standards seemed to have stemmed less from the amended work structure than from the personal engagement of the new supervisor who developed a 'regime of familiarity' with the wave soldering machine and succeeded in literally domesticating it by decoding its 'expressions' and 'temperament'.[19]

Assembly operatives' reactions to the new dispensation could best be described as ambivalent. On the one hand, they obviously appreciated the decrease in the number of soldering flaws as it meant they had fewer boards to rework or touch up. On the other, the prevalence of sharp variations in soldering performance that workers encountered individually generated a fair deal of dissatisfaction, though it was also quite possible that they felt more free to air their criticisms now that responsibility for soldering was no longer vested in their hands. Replacing the over-aged wave soldering machine used by the department would, no doubt, have helped to eliminate the recurrence of certain faults. But operatives also accused their counterparts in the soldering section of negligence.

When we were doing soldering, we would take great care because it was our cards. But now soldering is being done on a mass scale, three or four thousand cards at a time . . . The people running the machine are not very conscientious . . . If

---

[19] Laurent Thevenot, 'Le régime de familiarité. Des choses en personne', *Genèses*, No. 17, September 1994, pp. 72–101.

they are in a good mood they will accept to repair the damaged cards. Otherwise they tell us to go to hell.[20]

The criticism of the wave soldering workers must be understood within the context of the difficulties faced by the management in filling up the jobs in this section given the nature of the machine tenders' activities. After lacquering, wave soldering ranked as the least desirable occupation in the entire telephone division. Viewed as difficult, dirty and dangerous, it bore a triple stigma.[21] Kaul, the officer responsible for the section, said that when he took charge in 1998 everybody told him that he had come to a 'burning yard, a cremation *ghat*'.

The analogy was hardly exaggerated in view of the demanding work settings obtaining here. With machine temperatures ranging from 85°C to 240°C, workers had to toil under very hot conditions, especially in summer. To add to the physical discomfort, they were obliged to stand most of the time. Exposure to fumes and noxious odours represented a supplementary source of inconvenience. Both elements served as a permanent reminder of the health hazards associated with the job. Notwithstanding the management's assertions that it had made all the necessary safety arrangements, during the course of my field work in 2001 the exhaust fan functioned only fitfully and protective gear was only a pair of gloves. Workers did not even wear a special apron, let alone respirators and rubber shoes. Since the last six months, the company had also withdrawn one of the 'perks' soldering machine tenders were entitled to: a daily glass of milk by way of a health measure.

Yet, despite the section's negative image, until 1999, there were enough senior workers ready to come here of their own accord. Thereafter the number of volunteers totally dried up as voluntary retirement decimated the overall strength of the telephone division. Perfectly willing to run the wave soldering machine for their own boards, workers expressed, and continue to express, a strong aversion to being permanently posted to the 'burning yard'. Nor are shop officials in a position to override the workers' objections and impose their own wishes, since seniority rights

---

[20] Interview with Irudayaraj. Emphasis added.

[21] Machine tenders in the factory studied by Bernoux et al distinguished between 'dirty' jobs and 'rotten' jobs: the former type corresponded to physically tiring tasks, while 'rotten' jobs were physically dirty ones. Philippe Bernoux et al, *Trois ateliers d'OS*, Paris, 1973, p. 42.

govern all matters of manpower deployment. Consequently, wave soldering jobs systematically went to junior workers who lacked adequate experience, and were also apparently inefficient. They in turn bitterly denounced the inequity of the seniority norms which made no provision for rotating workers in 'dirty' occupations as well as castigated the reluctance of the union to modify the system.

When we protest to the union, it tells us to adjust mutually with other junior workers who might wish to come here. But who will come to wave soldering if they are not forced to do so?[22]

Foisting stigmatized jobs exclusively on the shoulders of junior workers was unfair, confessed John Joseph, the shop floor representative. He also pointed out that in other ITI plants fabricating telephones, the same person executed the entire chain of operations from assembling to lacquering. But recomposing the division of labour at the Bangalore plant, he claimed, would have provoked massive protests from senior workers who formed the bulk of the workforce.

The discriminatory features inherent in any framework of seniority rights stood out even more flagrantly in the case of lacquering work. Like wave soldering, these jobs too were reserved exclusively for junior workers, the management having failed in its efforts to 'break with the precedent set by the union of offering cushy jobs to seniors and tough jobs to juniors'.[23] More shockingly, however, lacquering tasks often ended up being forced onto physically handicapped workers. Thus for several years, the two operatives posted to this section were deaf and dumb. While one of them eventually opted for voluntary retirement, the other continued to toil. Possessing no formal qualifications, a never-ending series of dirty and hazardous jobs had framed their working lives, exposing in the process, the darker face of the 'philanthropic' actions of public sector enterprises, ever prompt to trumpet the employment opportunities they provide to handicapped individuals.

The third and final phase of the board manufacturing cycle, lacquering, was aimed at preventing the corrosion of contact points and copper circuits particularly in coastal regions noted for extremely high levels of atmospheric salinity. For this purpose, an insulating agent was manually

---

[22] Interview with Gururaj Rao and Manjappa (Field notes 2001).
[23] Interview with B.K. Sharma.

sprayed on both faces of the board once it had been definitively passed by inspection. In the past, the lacquering section was located in the basement of the board assembly shop. But after a fire, due possibly to insufficient ventilation, ravaged the room, the management had moved the activity to a more open site, though a methods employee felt that safety standards still left much to be desired. The spraying was carried out within a steel cubicle enclosed on three sides and equipped with a powerful exhaust to suck the fumes. To ensure that the lacquer coating on the board conformed to the required thickness, and the plastic housing protecting certain components was not disturbed, a certain degree of skill in wielding the spray gun at the right angle was indispensable.

The reason why lacquering stood even below wave soldering in the hierarchy of undesirable occupations, is easy to grasp. For one thing, it made far more strenuous demands on workers' bodies. Besides having to remain on their feet for several hours, they were required to constantly carry a spray gun weighing over half a kilo. For another, it subjected them to a much higher degree of physical discomfort both on account of the lacquering solution, a sticky substance which tends to adhere to the body, and the toxic odours released during spraying. Finally, it involved greater health risks. Yet, workers refused to wear a protective mask, arguing that it is uncomfortable. Accentuating the job's punishing character, it offered limited financial rewards. Not only were no special 'sweeteners' provided, even realizing maximal gains under the existing incentive scheme had increasingly become a uphill battle. An official admitted that workers here had to expend considerable effort, stick to their task for six or seven hours at a stretch in order to earn 'ceiling' incentive because timings are 'really tight'.[24]

VOLUNTARY RETIREMENT SAPS SHOP STRENGTH

When I first began my field work in May 1999, the printed board assembly shop counted 160 people on its rolls. Divided into eight work groups, each identified by a number, all the operatives were male and aged above 45 years. The composition of the workforce thus marked a radical break with the stereotyped image of the assembly worker as somebody both young and female. Interestingly, two posters pinned above

---

[24] Interview with I.H. Budar (Field notes 1999).

a supervisor's desk illustrated the strength of the gendered representation of electronic assembly work as essentially feminine work. Warning against the damages electric static charges can cause to equipment, both posters depicted a female operative handling a printed circuit board. But on the ITI shop floor, the only women present were a handful of inspectors and a couple of operatives in the kitting section.[25]

The board assembly workers occupied one half of a brightly illuminated but run down factory building measuring approximately 300 feet by 240 feet. They sat in pairs of rows, all facing the same direction. Repairmen, their tables easily identifiable by the heaps of haphazardly stacked boards, were aligned along the entire length of one wall. A medium-sized room adjacent to where the assembly workers sat accommodated the kitting section. The wave soldering machine stood in another room, or 'shed' as the workers called it, at the opposing end of the principal entrance. Large framed pictures of Ganesh, Bhuvaneshwari, Lakshmi and other deities, swathed in garlands and often inlaid with small coloured electric bulbs, decorated sections of the walls.

Concentric circular patches on the ceiling betrayed the leaks in the roof through which rain seeped in. John Joseph, the union representative, told me that during the monsoons, water regularly dripped onto workers' tables. Because of the company's dire financial predicament, plans drawn up by divisional executives to relocate the entire telephone division to a newer and more centrally situated building within the factory, made no headway. With all the operations except wave soldering executed manually, none of the din, dirt and smells that could overpower a first-time visitor to a machine shop were noticeable here. Although the company had purchased a surface mounted device machine, a fully-automated process commonly used for electronic assemblies, various obstacles, including cost, prevented the telephone division from optimally exploiting its capacities to deliver tremendous gains in assembly time, higher productivity, and product reliability.

In October 2001, I returned to ITI to discover the profound toll the voluntary retirement programme had taken on the strength of the board assembly section.[26] Its effects were visible everywhere: in the half empty

---

[25] In October 2001, the telephone division as a whole employed 19 women out of a total of 596 non-officers and officers.

[26] Between December 1999 and October 2001, the strength of the entire telephone

building; in the permanently darkened spaces, the management having decided to illuminate only one section of the building in order to save on electricity; in the long rows of vacant tables and chairs; in the dust caking the pictures of those deities who are no longer being worshipped. I was also struck by just how quiet the shop floor had become. This was hardly surprising considering that the section now employed barely 75 people. From eight, the number of work groups had shrunk to three.

The wave of departures also profoundly transformed the social organization of the shop floor by sweeping away the entire complex of informal conventions and procedures that workers had devised with the objective of facilitating their daily tasks by building an orderly work environment. Not uniformly robust, the micro-regulations, in which individual operatives' activities were enmeshed, had succeeded in generating internal cohesion, solidarity of interests, and a sense of collective achievement, besides imparting a distinctive character to each group. Certain other practices, more individualistic in nature, had also ended. I no longer came across the unusual spectacle of a handful of 'stakhanovites' who systematically soldiered on after the shift ended at 2.15 pm, working an extra three or four hours with the blessings of shop bosses. Though paid no overtime, their motives for staying back were hardly disinterested. They turned over a part of their output, which they could not 'book' under their own name, for the purposes of earning incentive, to their slower colleagues and shared the proceeds with them.

With recruitment having ground to a halt after 1980, the early retirement plan, however, did not leave behind a younger workforce. The average age of the 27 men (including the supervisor and the helper) in the 09 group that I studied in 2001 was just over 54 years.[27] Four members of the group would in fact have already quit the company had it not been for a government directive in 1998 extending the retirement age from 58 to 60 years. The fatigue and weariness, engendered by decades of prolonged labour that some operatives confessed to, was manifest as

---

division (officers and non-officers) declined by 25.5 per cent. But if we count only production operatives, the decline is even steeper at 31.1 per cent. (*Source:* ITI Personnel Dept.)

[27] An aging workforce was a generalized phenomenon impinging on all departments of the factory. Of the 5216 non-officers and Grade-I officers employed by the Bangalore plant on July 2001, 58.5 per cent were aged 50 years and more. (*Source:* ITI Personnel Dept.)

Timekeeping*

Friday, 5 October 2001. 7.10 am: It is my first day on the shop floor. Though the shift got underway at 7 am, I can only see four workers in a group totalling 26 at work. The rest have clocked in, but some are reading the newspaper after having finished their breakfast. Others are still queuing in front of the tea trolley outside the main shop entrance.

7.25 am: The supervisor has just arrived.

11 am: Two of the operatives leave for a pre-lunch stroll. The official lunch timings are from 11.30 am to 12 noon. But apart from a handful of workers, all the others have quit working between 11 am and 11.15 am to go to the toilets, smoke a cigarette, and wash before proceeding to the canteen which is a five minute walk away.

12.10 pm: Barely half the 12 workers who are back in their place have resumed work. One worker is having a nap in the 'sleeping chair', so baptised because of its comfortable cane seat. He wakes up a few minutes before the break at 1.30 pm. Not everybody, though, interrupts their activity at the sight of the tea trolley. According to the shop superintendent, the pace of work slackens after lunch until the tea break and then picks up momentarily before again slackening.

2.15 pm: Music broadcast through the public address system floods all the shops. This is the signal for the overwhelming majority to put away their material and implements. A few toil on until the fag end of the shift at 2.30 pm.

Monday, 8 October. 7.15 am: Byrappa and Munniswamy alone have begun work. The tea trolley is late today so several workers are either patiently waiting in their seats or standing outside the shop. A small group is chatting huddled around Joseph, the union delegate. There is still no sign of the supervisor. Nor of Govindaraju. It is 8.20 am when the latter finally appears and slowly proceeds to assemble his first card of the day. He has been reading the newspaper in the adjoining hangar where he says a wider choice of titles is available. The appetite for information seems to be considerable. In the days to come I often caught Shah glancing at a newspaper, tucked out of sight on his knees, while inserting components. At least three of the workers in the group are also members of different newspaper and/or magazine circulation clubs operating within the hangar.
*(Field notes)

A page from the author's diary.

much on their faces and bodies as in their low productivity. Even for those not burdened by health problems, economizing their strength so as to get through the last years of their work lives was a fundamental concern.

Consequently, in the absence of any linkage between wages and individual task performance, output restriction was a common phenomenon with quite a few operatives either aiming to produce no more than the minimum quantities stipulated by the management or exceeding the figure only marginally. As Pandeyan, one of the older workers in the group, admitted, turning out an additional 100 boards every month was not beyond his reach, but he was worried of the physical costs this additional expenditure of effort would involve.

If I sit here all the time to do more production, I can get piles. I am scared of that. I already have sugar problems.[28]

Similarly, Alavandar who suffered from blood pressure said he had scaled back his monthly output from over 300 boards to between 200 and 250 partly out of a desire to protect his health condition.

Ageing, and the run of challenges associated with it, had evidently an adverse impact on productivity. Workers no longer fully possessed the two essential qualities necessary for assembly work: sharp eyes and nimble fingers in order to manipulate and insert the myriad tiny components on the printed circuit board with ease and accuracy. Nor could they easily compensate for this loss of corporeal 'plasticity' through other means such as a more rigid or alert sitting posture. The fall out from ageing was also experienced in another manner. By curtailing dexterity, it foreclosed the possibility of speed as skill maturing into an 'act of virtuosity'.[29] Like with many other forms of repetitive semi-skilled industrial activity, the only true prowess available to board assembly workers to exhibit on the shop floor was speed, albeit without compromising on quality.

Such demonstrations of ability which symbolize the mastery acquired over work, the incorporation of a perfect sense of rhythm, constitute a vital means of affirming individual identity in the context of a productive process which strives to suppress all expressions of personal initiative. If

---

[28] Field notes 2001.
[29] Nicolas Dodier, *Les hommes et les machines*, pp. 220–1.

intended to attract the attention of colleagues and superiors, self-affirmation also holds considerable personal meaning for workers, the sensation or aesthetic of an adroitly executed bodily movement helping to procure a certain degree of pleasure from one's tasks.[30] But whatever place virtuoso or distinctive forms of self-realization may once have occupied on the operatives' horizon, these had completely faded now. Stiffening finger joints coupled with visual fatigue had left no choice but to settle for more prosaic virtues such as diligence and conscientiousness.

Though of a slightly different nature, the constraints inherent in employing an aged workforce weighed equally heavily upon shop executives. With no hope of an infusion of fresh blood into the factory anywhere in the near future, they were condemned to live with this situation indefinitely. While this might not have constituted a handicap in the monopoly era, it certainly undercut the company's ability to compete effectively in a deregulated market where private companies were in a position to fully exploit the advantages derived from pressing into service a young and female workforce endowed with just the qualities the ITI operatives lacked.

WIDE RANGE OF SKILLS MOBILIZED FOR BOARD ASSEMBLY WORK

The work of assembling printed circuit boards is monotonous as well as laborious.[31] The effort required to situate minute components on the board, coupled with the glare emitted by the soldered surface of the board, places tremendous strain on operatives' eyesight, especially when they happen to be aged. Not only did the overwhelming majority of workers in the 09 group wear glasses, but quite a few complained that their vision had declined after they had joined this section. Poor eyesight, as the company itself acknowledged, was also an important cause of quality lapses. The relatively alienating character of the job was accentuated by

---

[30] Hatzfeld, *Gens d'usine*, p. 46; André Leroi Gourhan, *Le Geste et la parole* (II). *La mémoire et les rythmes*, Paris, 1991, pp. 82–3.

[31] Baldamus emphasizes the distinction between the objective and subjective aspect of monotonous work. The former refers to the repetitive nature of an activity while subjective factors consist of feelings of tedium generated by such activity. *Efficiency and Effort*, p. 52, 57.

the fact that no apparent functional logic existed between the various sequence of operations. If the process sheet prescribed the order to be followed, it shed little light on the underlying sense of that order. Besides, workers lacked all knowledge of the functions of the different types of components—a corollary of the paucity of company-sponsored training programmes. In some cases, they were even unable to identify the component, preferring instead to refer to it by its location on the board.

In principle, the task mobilized two broad categories of skills. One was of a cognitive order: memory, so as to decode the electrical values of the components from the colour bands. The second was manual: dexterity in inserting the components and in handling the manual soldering iron. Mastering these skills laid the basis for the reflexes or routines necessary to develop the third and most challenging one: speed. In addition, a host of other more general competencies, such as application in order to avoid committing mistakes, were also tapped. Because all these forms of know-how could be acquired within a few months, the management tended to be dismissive of their value. A standard reply given to non-production employees who were redeployed to the board assembly section and protested against the inadequacy of the training, on the rare occasions when they did receive any training at all, was that if 'you know abcd then you can do the job'.[32]

Workers' ignorance of the colour codes identifying the components also furnished the management with a supplementary motive to hold their task in low esteem. Given that incorrect identification of components accounted for the bulk of all operative-induced defects, nobody on the shop floor denied the utility of knowing how to read the resistance and tolerance value of components. Yet most of them did not pick up this skill. Although the company's neglect of systematic training was chiefly responsible for the situation—even the minority who were familiar with the codification learnt it for the most part, in other divisions of the factory—workers too had to shoulder their share of the blame. Because the kits already contained a slip specifying the components, memorizing the colour codes was not indispensable. Workers therefore often skipped the training sessions organized during the early years which to boot were not declared compulsory by shop executives.

[32] Interview with B. Shah (Field notes 1999).

Devdas, the repairman for 09 group, pointed out that even in the absence of formal training it was fairly easy to learn the colour codes by oneself with the aid of an elementary mnemotechnic chart. If this 'cognitive artefact' was little used, it at least appeared to be well circulated, a conclusion I arrived at after more than one worker either showed or mentioned it to me.[33] But, according to Devdas, nobody was willing to take pains to learn since they were not 'interesting in working hard'. This was definitely not true in all cases; among those who had no knowledge of component electrical values figured many high incentive earners. Nevertheless, it was clear that a certain number of structural factors significantly contributed to weakening the incentive for workers to consider expanding their skill base so as to produce more and better quality boards.

First, while the lack of knowledge of the codification system could lead to assembly errors—one worker, for example, who mixed up two types of resistors in the entire kit for 50 boards, spent over six hours replacing the components—the time lost by an operative in rectifying these errors did not in any way impinge on his wages as these were not calculated on a piece rate basis. Second, as we shall see, the shortcomings of the incentive payment scheme meant there was little motivation to raise individual output, and hence to save time by getting it right the first time every time. Third, careless workers were never sanctioned, and even if line managers wished to impose sanctions, they were not in a position to act since inspection and repair personnel systematically withheld fault information from them. Fourth, the fact that the supervisor of the 09 group himself was ignorant of the component values gave the others an added reason to imitate his example. Lastly, each work group had its own repairman who in return for a monetary compensation from the other group members, attended to some operative-induced quality lapses. Not surprisingly therefore, workers felt it was not worth their while making the personal investments necessary to memorize the colour codes. 'I am not going to do this work once I retire. So why should I learn the values of the components?'[34]

---

[33] Donald Norman, 'Les artefacts cognitifs', in B. Conein et al (eds.), *Les objets dans l'action. De la maison au laboratoire*, Raisons Pratiques, No. 4, Paris, 1993, pp. 15–34.
[34] Interview with Vishnu (Field notes 1999).

The unflattering image of board assembly work conveyed by the management was also shared by a few workers. According to Clarence, even 'uneducated workers' were capable of carrying out the job, while Mani claimed that 'assembly work does not require us to think very much'. Both of them though happened to be officers who had been recently transferred to this department against their wishes. So the negative perceptions about their current activity could well have been intended to valorize their former positions. A more nuanced appreciation was provided by Subanna, a long time operative, and it revealed the intrinsically relative nature of all judgements about what constitutes skilled or unskilled work. Board assembly work, he conceded, was not a challenging or interesting job *per se*. However, when compared with assembling telephones, a 'blind job' which merely involved 'fixing three screws', it offered far greater challenges and learning opportunities because 'we have to do different things'. As one telephone assembly operative with experience of board work himself told me, 'you can think of anything when putting on screws. But if you think of household matters when you are stuffing a board there will surely be mistakes.'[35] Indeed, as I discovered to my embarrassment on a couple of occasions, workers with whom I had engaged a conversation while they were busy inserting components invariably ended up committing errors.

The relatively variegated nature of board assembly activity was attested to by the range of operations mobilized, as much physical (inserting, bending, cutting, soldering, screwing, cleaning) as cognitive (planning, deciphering, deciding, differentiating, anticipating, memorizing, verifying) in nature.

If you stuff haphazardly . . . it will create double work and time will get wasted . . . You have to do things systematically, and before starting 'stuffing' you must think how you are going to proceed.[36]

The above remark signifies that the task was hardly as simple as the management made it out to be. As one technical manual rightly pointed out, 'if there are places in life where neatness counts, electronic assembly is one of them. A neatly-built and carefully soldered board will perform well for years; a sloppily—and hastily—assembled board will cause

---

[35] Interview with Jagannath (Field notes 1999).
[36] Interview with Govindaraju (Field notes 2001).

ongoing problems and failures'.[37] In fact, the stress both company documents and shop officials placed on high standards of workmanship amounted to an explicit recognition of the importance of workers' aptitudes and contradicted the official representation of board assembly work as child's play. While these aptitudes might perhaps have ranked quite low in a social hierarchy of skills, their contribution to ensuring good quality assembly was nevertheless decisive.

Moreover, the tactile element, an undisputed source of satisfaction for workers defining as it did the specificity of their activity, was distinctly present in board assembly tasks. Running counter to the secular trend observed by some scholars of the 'regression of the hand' in industrial work, all the operations here were either manually executed or with the assistance of small hand-held tools.[38] It was this direct and permanent contact with materials which allowed workers to literally retain in their hands the fund of tacit know-how and experience accumulated over the years, the bedrock upon which good workmanship has perforce to rest.

In his seminal contribution to the evolution of productive processes under capitalism, Harry Braverman advances the following argument. As he notes, the subordination of the workforce in order to maximize surplus extraction renders indispensable the control by employers of each step of the labour process.[39] This implies, among other things, job fragmentation or systematically separating work into its constituent elements with the objective of dispossessing workers of their knowledge and skill. This foundational principle of modern industrial work organization, common to most factory regimes dedicated to the fabrication of mass standardized goods, did not apply, curiously enough, to the assembly of printed circuit boards at the ITI telephone division. Although a strategy of extensive internal subdivision of labour was *de*

---

[37] James Young, *ELEC 201*, 2000 (*http://www.owlnet.rice.edu/~elec201/Book/assembly.html*)

[38] Leroi Gourhan, *Le Geste et la parole*, pp. 61–2.

[39] Harry Braverman, *Labour and Monopoly Capital. The Degradation of Work in the Twentieth Century*, New York, 1974, pp. 75–83. While retaining the original Marxist framework, Braverman renewed Marx's theory of the labour process by applying it to subsequent historical development, 'taking a fresh look at skills, technology and work organisation'. Paul Thompson, *The Nature of Work. An Introduction to Debates on the Labour Process*, London, 1983, p. 73.

rigueur among all its competitors, hardly surprising for such a banal, low-value product, officials at the public sector company had, on the contrary, from the outset adopted what I call a 'craft-centred' configuration, which shaped both work practices and the expenditure of effort on the shop floor in a highly distinctive fashion.

A defining characteristic of the tasks performed by board assembly operatives was their unfragmented nature with one person responsible for inserting all the components housed on a board.[40] Insofar as this practice was not followed, it was because some workers opted to create teams with their colleagues, distributing various operations amongst themselves, in order to facilitate their work, as we shall study. In other words, whatever little parcellization of work existed was paradoxically evolved from informal arrangements negotiated by workers themselves, rather than from management-sponsored initiatives.[41] The individualized nature of board assembly activity also meant that the work group played an extremely marginal role in the overall coordination of the productive process and, barring those who worked in teams, scope for effective cooperation among group members was greatly reduced.

A second particularity of the work organization was that individual production objectives were fixed on a monthly basis. These objectives had, however, undergone a slight revision. During my first visit in 1999, each worker had been required to assemble a minimum of 175 boards in a month. Later in 2001, the figure was hiked to 212 boards which corresponded to efficiency levels of 100 per cent. The conjunction of these two factors, the lack of job decomposition and monthly production targets, guaranteed a substantial measure of discretion to board assembly operatives.

They were not only free to control their work pace, but also to structure their work activity according to their interests and preferences in a manner more reminiscent of craftsmen and highly skilled workers than of semi-skilled hands engaged in routinized and atomized jobs who 'are told

[40] Female electronic operatives in the Meteor plant studied by Pun Ngai were trained to specialize in just one process. *Made In China: Women Factory Workers in a Global Workplace,* Durham, 2005, p. 82.

[41] But, as Braverman reminds us, while the worker may break the productive process down, he never voluntarily converts himself into a lifelong detail worker. *Labour and Monopoly Capital,* p. 78.

exactly what to do and how to do it' and 'are supervised closely'.[42] What we see here stands in distinct contradiction to the dynamic identified by Braverman as the overarching norm for low-value jobs (and eventually more prestigious ones too) in capitalist production: the integration of the labour process in a single operative as opposed to its dissociation. Responsible for the coordination and execution of all operations from start to finish, workers assembling a printed circuit board were also in a position to apprehend their work in its finality. They could thus derive satisfaction from having turned in a 'finished' product, a privilege systematically denied to poorly qualified hands whose work experience tended to be deeply dissatisfying because, to borrow the distinction drawn by Donald Roy, it concluded not with completion but with the 'mere summation of activity'.[43] The autonomy enjoyed by board assembly operatives necessarily implied that divisional managers retained only limited control over the labour process. Their authority was reduced to ensuring the fulfilment of monthly targets.

In general, companies adopting a strategy allowing individual workers to direct their own activity are spurred by one of the following motives. They either belong to the 'interpersonal world' of customized goods production, in which case the ability to adjust their offer to differentiated markets as well as maintain quality imperatives reposes a great deal on a craft-oriented work configuration.[44] Or they could be companies which have invested in extremely automated and sophisticated technologies, characterized by high risk levels, whose optimal performance as well as safety is contingent on workers' exercise of judgement and initiative.[45] Alternatively, they are companies operating in mass-markets which aspire

---

[42] ibid, p. 431. While certainly an exception, instances of groups of semi-skilled workers enjoying considerable discretion to structure their pace of work do exist as Bernoux et al have demonstrated. *Trois ateliers d'OS*, pp. 103–4, 108–9.

[43] Donald Roy 'Work Satisfaction and Social Reward in Quota Achievement: An Analysis of Piecework Incentive', *American Sociological Review*, Vol. 18, No. 5, October 1953, pp. 507–14 (cit. p. 511.) See also Georges Friedmann, *Le travail en miettes: spécialisation et loisirs*, Paris, 1964, p. 249.

[44] Robert Salais and Michael Storper, *Les Mondes de production. Enquête sur l'identité économique de la France*, Paris, 1993, Paris, pp. 15–16, 45.

[45] Gilbert de Terssac, *Autonomie et travail*, Paris, 1992, esp. chapters three and four; Yves Clot, *Le travail sans homme? Pour une psychologie des milieux de travail et de vie*, Paris, 1995, pp. 75–82.

to develop job enrichment programmes so as to better motivate their workforces.

Greater freedom at the workplace, the 'reappropriation of work' by its principal producers, may also in some circumstances result from successful struggles waged by workers.[46] In other cases, it can have its roots in what Jean-Daniel Reynaud calls 'autonomous regulation', a set of informal rules which workers succeed in instituting in opposition to the 'control regulation' dictated by employers and which are tolerated by the latter as it helps to correct certain of the dysfunctional aspects inherent in technico-organizational productive systems.[47] None of these considerations applied to ITI. So how then do we account for the decision to grant substantial latitude to operatives involved in assembling a product as standardized as printed circuit boards?

Actually in the late 1990s, telephone division executives had tried out a new system revolving around a more extended division of labour on a couple of occasions. The task of assembling a board was split between a group of six workers with each one called upon to insert only a few components. The management viewed this technique, known as 'line balancing' and widely followed by factories assembling printed circuit boards, as a panacea for the various ills facing the division. It claimed line balancing would help bring down operative errors, increase output, accelerate cycle times overall for telephone production, and reduce work-in-progress and inventories.[48] More significantly, it would have succeeded in regaining control over the organization of work. By affording greater transparency over the totality of the board assembly chain, the sub-division of operations would have enabled shop officials to monitor each work group's efforts on a daily basis.

---

[46] Philippe Bernoux, 'La résistance ouvrière et la rationalisation: la réappropriation du travail', *Sociologie du travail*, Vol. 21, No. 1, January-March 1979, pp. 76–90; Andrew Friedman, 'Responsible Autonomy versus Direct Control over the Labour Process', *Capital & Class*, No. 1, Spring 1977, pp. 43–57.

[47] Jean-Daniel Reynaud, *Le conflit, la négociation et la règle*, Toulouse, 1995, pp. 113–25, 229–30.

[48] According to a multi-national survey, factories assembling printed circuit cards in less developed countries use capital and labour less efficiently than their counterparts in newly industrializing economies, more responsive to organizational innovations. Ashoka Mody et al, 'Keeping Pace with Change: International Competition in Printed Circuit Card Assembly', *Industrial and Corporate Change*, Vol. 4, No. 3, 1995, pp. 583–613.

But shop floor resistance and the management's own inhibitions about forcing the issue led to the experiment being rapidly abandoned. Workers' adverse reactions owed to apprehensions that line balancing, by substituting a group-based scheme of incentive payments for a individual one, would dent their incentive earnings and give rise to mutual recriminations over the extent of each member's contribution to the group. One operative mentioned that production volumes dropped sharply after the introduction of the new process precisely because a group incentive scheme distributed rewards equally to all members. Hence fast workers scaled down their production so as to match the pace of the slower workers. The success of the experiment was further jeopardized by shop officials refusal to provide a 'reliever' to replace absent operatives. Allocating extra people as replacements, they argued, would increase overheads at a time when the company was striving to tighten its belt.

In the wake of this abortive attempt, no fresh proposals to create the 'detail worker' by atomizing board assembly jobs materialized.[49] Fears that changes could trigger protests from workers partly explained why the management was content to stay quiet. As Sharma, the divisional head, admitted,

we could take action, but there is going to be a period when production will be disrupted because of our tough stand. If the dislocation exceeds a few days and goes out of our hands to higher ups (top management), then we will face a big problem.[50]

A second reason for persisting with the existing work organization could lie in the nature of the end product. In distinct contrast to other lines of ITI's business, telephones did not represent a strategic product for the company. Haemorrhaging cash ever since the market was opened to private companies, in the year 2000, this branch accounted for less than 7 per cent of the total sales posted by the main Bangalore plant. While one consultancy firm had urged the closure of the division, top management refrained from acting on the recommendation only because telephones constituted a part of the overall equipment package supplied to DoT. Under these circumstances, shop officials perhaps felt that antagonizing the workforce by suppressing the current system of

---

[49] Braverman, *Labour and Monopoly Capital*, p. 75.
[50] Interview with B.K. Sharma.

production might have proved more onerous than maintaining the *status quo.*

Since my field work was limited to a single shop, I cannot say whether similar autonomous arrangements anchored job schedules elsewhere in the factory where printed boards were assembled, notably those divisions which turned out equipment deemed 'strategic' by the management. So in the absence of a comparative study, I shall not risk making generalizations of any kind about the nature of the labour process in ITI. This said, in the case of the operators I observed, one could also perhaps argue that they were free to structure their daily work activities just as they wished precisely because ITI's position as a public enterprise allowed them to do so. The very fact that all private telephone manufacturers adhered to strict taylorist principles of task execution throws into full relief the anomalous situation of ITI. Despite the damage wrought by competition on the fortunes of the telephone division, it faced few pressures to proceed with a radical overhaul of its existing mode of work organization.

LOGIC OF COMFORT DICTATES ORDER OF ASSEMBLY TASKS

Once or twice a week each worker received a kit containing all the material required to produce 50 boards at a time. All workers had two kits constantly in circulation so that when one batch of 50 boards was sent for wave soldering, they could immediately take up a fresh batch. Since inadequate production volumes rendered it uneconomical to run the wave soldering machine for more than half a day, delays of one to two days were common before the boards returned from wave soldering. The process sheet decomposed the assembly activity into 20 distinct steps, most of which were accomplished prior to wave soldering, and the remainder afterwards. The order of the tasks basically corresponded to the size of the components, and was dictated by a logic of comfort with the smallest ones mounted first with a view to facilitating finger movements across the surface of the board, particularly when it was densely packed.

But the process sheet did not seek to impose a one-best-way by rigorously specifying the order that was to be followed. Determining the easiest and most effective method of placing the numerous sorts of resistors or diodes was a decision left to the individual operative. Taylor's injunction to employers recommending the standardization of the 'multitude of small operations which are repeated day after day' was ignored by the methods department at ITI's telephone division either because they reckoned it was impractical or because they were simply incapable of implementing it.[51] So, in terms of its content, the process sheet represented less a 'plan-programme' than a 'plan-resource' since its objective was not to confine workers' actions within strictly defined boundaries.[52]

Once all the components had been positioned on the board, the leads were bent and the excess length cut. In principle, only ordinary wire cutters were prescribed since time standards were calculated on this basis. But quite a few operatives employed a clinch cutter, arguing that it speeded up this operation and ensured uniform trimming.

Theoretically things are very different; practically things are very different . . . If we follow the procedures of methods department, production will come down. So we follow our own techniques and work much faster.[53]

Similarly, integrated circuits have in theory to be 'stuffed' with the aid of a small suction tool in order to eliminate static charges by minimizing physical contact. But to save time all the operatives used their hands. One of the rare persons to actually have the tool on his work table jokingly remarked that if his colleagues saw him employing it they would 'call me a madman. Even officers will say that I am wasting my time. All they want is production'.[54]

After the boards returned from wave soldering and before they were sent for inspection, they had to be cleaned. Given the toxic properties of the solvent utilized for this purpose, this was a dirty, messy and risky job, and in the past, the helpers attached to each work group had been

[51] Frederick Winslow Taylor, *Shop Management* in *Scientific Management*, New York, 1947, p. 123. See also in the same volume *The Principles of Scientific Management*, pp. 24–5.

[52] On the distinction operated between a plan programme and a plan resource see Bernard Conein and Eric Jacopin, 'Les objets dans l'espace. La planification dans l'action', in Conein et al, *Les objets dans l'action*, pp. 59–84. Both terms bear the impress of Lucy Suchman's influential study of human action, though Suchman herself never directly establishes such a distinction. *Plans and Situated Actions. The Problem of Human-Machine Communication*, Cambridge, 1994.

[53] Interview with T.V. Subanna (Field notes 2001).

[54] Field notes 2001.

saddled with it. Now, though, it was the responsibility of each operative. The solvent exuded a noxious odour as well. This explained why a separate work space, situated at some distance from the workers' tables, had been set aside for this task with a view to slightly mitigating the health hazards. Not everybody, however, took the trouble of going to the cleaning area, preferring instead to attend to the boards directly in their work places. They knew full well they would be troubling their colleagues by exposing them to the unpleasant odours of the solvent, and that their behaviour, perceived as selfish, would invariably provoke angry shouts from those sitting beside them. Yet, only if the protests rose in volume did they grudgingly agree to leave their seats.

A few workers also rightly criticized the arrangements made by the management as being grossly insufficient, particularly since the cleaning area lacked special ventilation or exhaust facilities. They complained that breathing the solvent always left them with a sore throat. But although company manuals clearly stipulated the provision of protective equipment such as safety glasses, face masks and gloves, shop officials continued to ignore this instruction. They appeared to be equally indifferent to enforcing a rule prohibiting the reutilization of spent solvent to clean the boards, thus encouraging workers to keep flouting it.

Certain other violations too benefited from official complicity with shop executives themselves viewing the underlying process requirements as superfluous, cumbersome to apply, and, most importantly, as hindering production. To take the case of anti-static stations, for instance, although mandatory in the job sheets, managers argued that their non-provision had no impact whatsoever on the quality of low-cost products like telephones featuring a very limited number of integrated circuits. Insisting that operatives wear anti-static wrist straps and the like would only provoke needless tension, besides diverting attention from more pressing matters, they added. But overall, the disjunction between prescribed work and real work, a much-debated theme in industrial sociology, where workers confronted with the inefficiencies or irrationality of official rules have no choice but to transgress these rules in order to bring the product out, could not really be said to have characterized board assembly activity at ITI.[55] Apart from being restricted to a few operations and posing no

---

[55] For a discussion of the contradiction between prescribed work and real work, see *inter alia*, John Seely Brown and Paul Duguid, 'Organizational Learning and

serious threat to the integrity of the product, non-compliance with the instructions contained in the process sheet reflected less their impracticality as operatives' desire to gain time.

ISO Auditors' Visit*

Saturday, 24 November 2001. 9.30 am: Kittoor, the shop deputy works manager, conducts a final check of the shop floor to ensure everything is in order. A delegation of ISO auditors is due to arrive shortly. Their previous visit had ended in a fiasco of sorts with the shop receiving a non-conformity certificate after an operative when asked whether his tray contained defective or passed components nonchalantly shot back 'both sorts'. So this time, Kittoor is leaving nothing to chance. For the past three mornings he has personally launched a scrap hunt, peering underneath each table, prompting one wag to call for monthly checks by the auditors so that the shop remains spick and span. Supervisors have been ordered to keep workers' tables tidy and clear away all unwanted material. Trays that are ordinarily employed by no more than a couple of workers have miraculously surfaced in front of everybody. An operative who uses a bare board as a support for his soldering iron is asked to tuck it out of sight until the auditors have gone.

Kittoor returns to see if another operative, Clarence, has followed instructions to correctly label his tray and tells him to throw away the duplicate labels. Everybody is also briefed on the appropriate answer to be given in case they are quizzed on their method of inserting components. The farcical nature of the whole exercise is lost on nobody. One worker calls it a big *tamasha*. 'Tomorrow, everything will return to normal'. The visit finally passes off without a hitch. The auditors had apparently not noticed a supervisor rushing with a rack so that Clarence could comply with the official procedure and align the assembled boards on it, rather than roughly stack them one on top of the other as is the customary practice regardless of the dangers of crushing the components. *(Field notes)

From the author's diary.

Communities of Practice: Towards a Unified View of Working, Learning and Innovation', *Organization Science*, Vol. 2, No. 1, 1991, pp. 40–57; Christophe Dejours, 'Pathologie de la communication. Situation de travail et espace public: le cas du nucléaire', in A. Cottereau and P. Ladrière (ed.), *Pouvoir et légitimité. Figures de l'espace public*, Raisons Pratiques, No. 3, Paris, 1992, pp. 177–201; Donald Roy, 'Efficiency and "The Fix": Informal Intergroup Relations in a Piecework Machine Shop', *The American Journal of Sociology*, Vol. 60, No. 3, November 1954, pp. 255–66.

SHAPING A MANIPULATORY SPHERE

The autonomy enjoyed by workers consequential to the adoption of a 'craft-type' of productive system manifested itself in significant variations in the structuring and management of the immediate physical environment, in the division of labour and in work styles and practices. As recent research in the cognitive sciences has demonstrated, ensuring that a workplace is perfectly attuned to the requirements of a task entails devising a set of techniques to prepare or stabilize it.[56] Through these spatial arrangements a 'manipulatory zone', defined by Alfred Schutz, as the core strata of work reality, is created whose function is to explicitly encode the information needed to do the job in such a fashion that it can be read off without effort.[57] A mutual determination therefore operates between a given space and the activity of manipulating specific objects.[58] It is precisely this ecological dimension underpinning the exercise of work which entitles us to qualify individual actions as being situated. Not only are the actions embedded in 'particular, concrete circumstances', but the situation is fashioned by the action of normalizing the environment.[59]

Indispensable in any occupational context, intelligently configuring the contours of the 'world within my actual reach' assumes greater importance with respect to board assembly work given the preponderant role played by the hand.[60] The location of the components within the zone must be stabilized by organizing where and how they are placed so that they remain in constant proximity and view. No time must be lost searching for a component or implement. The hand must be in a position to spontaneously appropriate this world, 'inhabit' it with ease, make

[56] Kristian Hammond et al, 'The Stabilization of Environments', *Artificial Intelligence,* Vol. 72, Nos. 1–2, January 1995, pp. 305–27; David Kirsh, 'The Intelligent Use of Space', *Artificial Intelligence,* Vol. 73, Nos. 1–2, February 1995, pp. 31–68.

[57] Alfred Schutz, 'The World within My Reach and its Dimensions, Marks and Indications', in *idem, Collected Papers I. The Problem of Social Reality,* Dordrecht, 1990, pp. 223–5, 307. Schutz, of course, has adopted the term of manipulatory zone from G. H. Mead. 'The Physical Thing', in *idem, The Philosophy of the Present,* Chicago, 1980, pp. 119–23.

[58] Bernard Conein and Eric Jacopin, 'Action située et cognition. Le savoir en place', *Sociologie du travail,* Vol. 36, No. 4, 1994, pp. 475–500.

[59] Suchman, *Plans and Situated Actions,* p. viii. (cit.), 49–63.

[60] Schutz, 'The World within my Reach', p. 224.

things 'ready-to-hand'[61] by developing routines designed to transform
an 'objective space into a familiar surface of contact' tolerant of
idiosyncratic practices.[62] Indeed, the successful interaction between the
worker and his immediate spatial surroundings is a prerequisite for
achieving economic body movements, simplifying choice and perception,
smoothly coordinating actions, increasing reliability of execution,
reducing uncertainty, and lowering memory demands.[63] All these
elements ultimately combine to impart to daily work activity, a routinized
character.

The term routine is not employed here in its common sense and
pejorative acception explicitly framing an association between doing a
job machinally and deriving no satisfaction from it.[64] Instead, it signifies
actions that are dynamic and intentional but abstracted from deliberation,
actions rendered quasi-automatic and spontaneous as much by virtue of
a certain regularity as by internalizing production procedures, and where
through a long process of memorization by repetition, accumulates an
extensive stock of practical knowledge or 'contextual technical skills'.[65]
As a result, the possibilities of performing a task more rapidly are greatly
enhanced. But working quickly also means staying vigilant and
concentrated, thus once again, disproving the idea of routine as purely
machinal behaviour.

Among board assembly operatives, two modes of setting up the
workplace could be distinguished, one canonical, because enshrined in
the process sheet, and adopted by a tiny minority; the other non-canonical
and embraced by the majority.[66] In the former mode, the components

---

[61] Equipment that is 'ready-to-hand' tends to becomes 'invisible' when it is most
genuinely appropriated. The person manipulating the equipment loses awareness of it
in the course of practical activity. Hubert Dreyfus, *Being-in-the-World. A Commentary
on Heidegger's Being and Time, Division I,* The MIT Press, 1990. Cited in Suchman,
Plans and Situated Actions, pp. 53–4.

[62] Marc Breviglieri, 'Habiter l'espace de travail. Perspectives sur la routine', *Histoire
& Sociétés,* No. 9, January 2004, pp. 19–29, (cit. p. 26).

[63] Kirsh, 'The Intelligent Use of Space'.

[64] This discussion of routinized action borrows heavily from Didier Schwint, 'La
routine dans le travail de l'artisan', *Ethnologie française,* No. 3, July-September 2005,
pp. 521–9.

[65] Breviglieri, 'Habiter l'espace de travail', p. 20.

[66] The terms canonical and non-canonical practices come from Brown and Duguid.
'Organizational Learning and Communities of Practice'.

were emptied from their plastic packets into small trays measuring 24 cm by 30 cm by 2 cm. The trays were composed of around 15 compartments, three to four rows deep, each holding a specific type of component, and sorted out according to the order of their insertion on the printed circuit board.

Using the tray the first two days was difficult because I did not know in which compartment each component was located. Now I have remembered their place by heart, and my fingers automatically go to the right compartment. If I have to put R33 (resistor), I know where it is situated in the tray.

The non-canonical practice, on the other hand, consisted of aligning the components in little clusters directly on the table.[67] Typically, the number of lines never exceeded two or three. As in the case of the tray, the spatial layout adopted here corresponded to the sequence in which the components were mounted with workers' movements oriented along a left to right axis so that interpretation of the next lot to select and place was effortless. 'If all pieces are in a line, you know where to look,' while clustering highlighted their differences on the fly even as it simplified the 'visual search problem'.[68] The non-canonical mode of encoding placement order was therefore not in any way less rational or coherent than its canonical counterpart.

But this method of exploiting spatial resources constrained the worker to both repeatedly organize his work environment at the start of the day and after the lunch break, and to clear it when leaving for lunch and during shift closure by bundling all the different sorts of components back into their respective packets—a protracted task which explained why a number of 'lazy fellows', in the words of repairman Devdas, went to lunch with the components lying on their tables notwithstanding the risk of displacement. The canonical mode spared a worker of all such bother as he only needed to take the tray out from his cupboard upon arriving to work and to put it back inside when he quit.

Recourse to a work tray promoted another form of time saving. Since material shortages were common and the kitting section sometimes

---

[67] According to Kirsh, because of the way the human perceptual system functions, task execution is facilitated by laying out objects in lines rather than by estimating their area or volume. 'The Intelligent Use of Space'.

[68] ibid, p. 52, 56.

neglected to inform operatives of these shortages when distributing the kits, quite a few workers were in the habit of drawing up reminder lists or of marking on a bare printed circuit board the components that remained to be supplied. These cognitive tasks naturally took some time to accomplish as they involved cross checking the contents of the entire kit with the stock list. A worker employing a tray, however, only had to fill each compartment to immediately identify which components were unavailable. The tray then fulfilled a dual, and interconnected, representational function: in certain settings, as in tracking material supply, the surface level information embodied in it served to evaluate the situation, and thus prepares the ground for action; in others, the information directly triggered action.[69] But the external representations were not always given, and had to be constructed by the actor depending on the material and social circumstances.[70]

An equally important benefit offered by the canonical mode was that it helped to reduce the incidence of operative-induced quality defects. By physically segregating the components into distinct compartments, a tray minimized the risk of mix ups. As Devdas pointed out, when eight or nine types of resistors were spread on the table, a careless or distracted operative could easily jumble up two resistors of different values when handling or packing them. For while the 'natural meaning' linear orderings possess was a distinct virtue, they also presented dangers: the longer the line of objects, the more likely they were to be 'kicked out of order'.[71] Indeed, it was precisely the desire to avoid mistakes of this kind, inevitable when having to constantly empty and refill packets of components, that prompted most workers to go in for a piece-meal approach. As we shall study in more detail later, they preferred to 'stuff' one type of component after the other in all 50 boards rather than all types of components in one board.

Nevertheless, despite its advantages, 21 of the 24 workers in the 09 group steadfastly refused to consider adopting the official procedure. Utilizing a tray, they alleged, cramped finger movements since the compartments afforded a very narrow space to manoeuvre and hence tended to both provoke discomfort and slow down the pace of work.

---

[69] Norman, 'Les artefacts cognitifs'.
[70] Suchman, *Plans and Situated Actions*, p. 50, 54–8.
[71] Kirsh, 'The Intelligent Use of Space', p. 52.

Inversely, when arranging the components according to their guise on their tables, the visual perception of disposing a wider spatial perimeter was allied to and reinforced a tactile sensation, manifested in the freedom experienced in picking up and manipulating the components.[72] Workers also defended their system of structuring the work environment against charges of being error prone. They said the chances of mix-ups occurring were rare since most of them only assembled small batches of components at one time and therefore never emptied the totality of the kit on their tables.

PARTNERSHIPS AND INDIVIDUALIZED WORK ARRANGEMENTS

Just as dual ways of configuring the work environment existed among the operatives, duality informed the organization of work also. I have already referred to the self-directing character of the labour process in the board assembly shop. Consequently, workers were free to adopt the production arrangement best suited to their needs. The choice they disposed was between an individualized solution where one man assembled the board in its totality, and a more collective one. This entailed building a team, or partnership in shop floor jargon, with one or more colleague, on an informal basis, and parcelling out the tasks between themselves. A minority option, only three such partnerships prevailed in the 09 group. Nor had they flourished in greater numbers in the past, and even among the other work groups in the department their popularity was restricted.

For the sake of convenience, I have designated the three 09 partnerships as alpha, beta and gamma. Each comprised two people. While gamma was formed barely a year ago when I arrived, alpha and beta had been in existence for nearly a decade without any hitches. Given the shortlived nature of many collaborations, the stability achieved by alpha and beta represented a significant feat. One implicit rule governed the functioning of these micro units. Although their respective contributions might not have been strictly equal and fluctuated from time to time, each member of the team was expected to shoulder his rightful share of the workload.

---

[72] Visual perception, remarks Leroi Gourhan, operates synthetically, while touch proceeds by analysing and recreating volumes. *La memoire et les rythmes*, p. 117.

From the author's diary.

From this sketch we can visualize the seating arrangements of the assembly operatives belonging to the 09 group which I studied in detail. The positions marked vacant bore testimony to the departures caused by repeated waves of voluntary retirement. Workers sitting beside each other in order to facilitate their activity were often, but not always, those who had formed partnerships.

If one person is working hard and another is simply roaming all over the factory then things will become problematic.[73]

Subanna who belonged to the beta team added:

It is necessary to have faith and confidence in the other person that he will do his share of the work when required.[74]

Enforcing this rule was anything but simple, but the extent to which workers voluntarily complied with it determined a team's chances of survival. Allowances were, no doubt, made for those suffering from medical ailments who automatically received assistance. Two of the workers in a three-man team that I studied during my first field visit in 1999, who had undergone an operation, performed only light jobs. While one of them benefited from this measure on a permanent basis, in the case of the other the dispensation accorded was temporary in nature, and after a month or so he had again resumed his normal activities 'rather than leave everything' to the third partner.[75]

What the above example illustrates is that a spirit of give and take and mutual understanding was indispensable to guaranteeing the success of a partnership. As Mani, a member of gamma, put it, 'you must have an open mind'. In practical terms, open-mindedness signified a willingness on the part of each partner to accept certain constraints in return for the benefits yielded by a partnership. So when one went on leave, the other were ready to expend greater effort to finish both their tasks.

You should not say this is his work, this is my work, and that because he has gone on leave I have more to do today. You should think of your work . . . as both people's work. Then there won't be any heart burn.[76]

Likewise, each operative had to exhibit a degree of tolerance towards mistakes committed by the other. They had to agree to occasionally forego monetary gains in case one of them did not wish to maximize his incentive payments for a particular reason in a given month. Nor grudge the other for slackening his pace sometimes because 'each day is different for each

---

[73] Interview with Ananthanarayan (Field notes 2001).
[74] Field notes 2001.
[75] Interview with Joseph (Field notes 1999).
[76] Interview with Padmanabha (Field notes 2001).

worker and you might not feel well every day'.[77] Or refuse to accommodate personal work habits.

If I go to help the supervisor, or he goes for a small stroll now and then we should not accuse each other of wasting time and holding up our work . . . You should not say that because your partner is not working, you should also not work.[78]

Needless to say, more than one collective venture has foundered on the failure of the team members to make the necessary concessions.

While pragmatic considerations, notably the disinclination to disrupt entrenched work practices, may well have exerted a cementing influence, the exceptional longevity of the alpha and beta teams was essentially anchored in social and demographic factors. To take up the latter element first, the partners were united by generational bonds. The beta 'couple', for instance, had entered the factory the same day, and all four men (six, if we include the gamma pair as well) were practically of the same age. This is no trivial matter when working in tandem, for it means that each partner is sensitive to the other's capabilities and can keep pace with him. One worker who had joined hands with a younger colleague soon found himself constrained to end their association because he was unable to maintain the same speed.

Besides sharing similar temperaments, the two 'couples' also shared common linguistic identities, the alpha team speaking Tamil, and the beta team, Kannada. In the context of ITI, where the principal fault lines within the workforce intersected with the Kannada–Tamil divide, selecting a partner who spoke the same language was probably no accident. One could argue that for Tamil workers in particular, victims of the language agitation, a strategy predicated on primordial affinities provided an assurance that the strains and tensions of a close collaboration did not assume a linguistic colouring when it exploded. Linguistic loyalties in fact even appeared to override religious loyalties. One partnership that existed in the past brought together two Christians and one Hindu operative. But all three were Tamil speakers.

At the same time, the strong ties of friendship and mutuality binding

[77] Interview with Keshava Rao (Field notes 2001).
[78] Interview with Padmanabha (Field notes 2001).

Sociability*

Wednesday, 17 October 2001. Byrappa, one of the operatives in the 09 group, is absent today. He has taken a full day's leave to assist a colleague in the adjoining hangar who is conducting a *grihapravesha* (house warming) ceremony after having recently constructed a house. A number of workers who have been invited also go on leave after lunch while others join them after the closure of the shift. In all, almost 60 people attend the function. Some of them carry gifts from colleagues who are unable to attend for one reason or the other. The gifts essentially take a monetary form with close friends donating as much as Rs 100. For the marriage of Kalaimuthu's daughter a few months back, for instance, a sum of Rs 20,000 was collected from about 150 workers. But since the event was held in another city (Trichy), only a handful of colleagues could make the trip, each of them applying for two days of leave.

This is no negligible 'sacrifice' when measured, on one side, against the countless domestic obligations that already weigh heavily upon workers' annual leave entitlements (33 days), and, on the other, against the intense sociability that characterises shop floor life. In a year, each worker receives on average between 15–20 invitations to such rites of passage ceremonies. He attends at least half of them, often taking half a day or a couple of hour's leave for this purpose, in addition to incurring expenses on travel and gift giving.

If a genuine sense of fraternity and solidarity dictates his presence at these events, like in most social exchanges self-interest is also not entirely absent. As Marcel Mauss has reminded us in his famous essay on the gift, to receive one must give since a gift is a 'hybrid' interweaving both a principle of obligation and liberality, an act at once interested and disinterested[79]— a premise underlined by one worker in the following remark: 'If I don't go for his ceremony or even acknowledge it by sending a gift, he will also not reciprocate when I call him'.*(Field notes.)

From the author's diary.

the alpha and beta couples, and which stretched beyond the factory walls, contributed in no small measure to the longevity of the two teams. They frequently exchanged visits to each others' houses and extended financial

---

[79] Marcel Mauss, 'Essai sur le don. Forme et raison de l'echange dans les sociétés archaïques', in *idem, Sociologie et anthropologie*, Paris, 1993, pp. 145–279.

assistance 'without charging interest' in times of need.[80] Nor was this aid restricted to small sums. Munnuswamy who belonged to the alpha team had helped his partner Padmanabha, in the same grade as him, purchase a house by lending him as much as Rs 75,000 with no strings attached. But Munnuswamy's wealth and generosity did not translate into a position of dominance within the partnership. On the contrary, he unquestioningly accepted the leadership of the better-qualified and more conscientious Padmanabha with respect to practically all work related matters. As one of their colleagues in the 09 group candidly remarked, 'since Munnuswamy only knows how to execute and also often takes leave it is in his advantage to collaborate with Padmanabha'.[81]

A similar judgement could apparently be passed on Shah who formed the gamma team along with Mani. A former shop clerk, Shah was not only a very mild-mannered man in contrast to his more querulous partner, he also lacked production experience. Teaming up with Mani then obviously served his interests and he hardly seemed chagrined by his subordinate role. But for Mani too, the value of the partnership was anything but negligible. Being an officer he was ineligible to earn incentive. The sole means available to him of circumventing this rule was by joining forces with a non-officer like Shah. In the case of the beta team, both workers had the same educational qualifications. So the question of one or the other exercising leadership did not arise.

Interaction was also constant between the alpha and beta teams. Knit together firstly by spatial contiguity—they sat in parallel rows—these ties were buttressed by their social transactions. A flask of coffee circulated every morning among themselves, components in short supply kept crossing hands, shop talk was swapped, and two of them ate lunch together daily in the canteen. Beyond the 'status ritual' of exchanging salutations, neither team, however, maintained relations of any sort with their gamma counterparts.[82] This was perhaps because both Mani and Shah were newcomers to the group as well as the board assembly shop. Transferred here against their wishes, the two men made no secret either of their complete disinterest for this job, whereas the alpha and beta

---

[80] Interview with Keshava Rao (Field notes 2001).

[81] Interview with Govindaraju.

[82] Erving Goffman, *Interaction Ritual. Essays on Face-to-Face Behavior*, New York, 1982, p. 57.

partners, with the exception of Munnuswamy, ranked among the best workers in the group.

New entrants to the group, Mani and Shah were also relative strangers to each other. The warmth and complicity, born of long years of friendship and so characteristic of social intercourse within the alpha and beta teams, was therefore much less in evidence in the gamma tandem. Besides, their seating arrangement put a further brake on the free flow of communication. Unlike the other partners who sat directly beside each other, Mani and Shah sat back to back. Despite requests from the two men to Mohan Kumar who occupied the seat next to Mani, the former refused to shift. Practical considerations aside, Mohan Kumar claimed he wanted to capture the beneficial powers of the 'good spirit' that had been deposited in his seat by the previous occupant, an operative reputed for being as hardworking as sociable.[83]

From the perspective of workers and shop officials alike, a collective solution to the challenges of giving output possesses several merits. The first and biggest advantage is that by sharing work the job gets accomplished quicker. The beta team estimated it requires one-third less the time to assemble 50 boards, than an individual operative. The job which took about four and half days when done alone, the beta team claimed it could complete in three days. According to one retired operative, who was part of a three-man venture, they were able to realize in 17–18 days of 'relaxed working' the ceiling incentive target, then fixed at 300 boards, whereas an individual worker had to put in between 22 to 25 days of constant effort.[84]

Secondly, team work both helped to reduce stress and relieve monotony. This in turn created the impression of simplifying and speeding up the job.[85] The following statements highlighted these points.

---

[83] Mohan Kumar is not alone in displaying a singular sense of 'place attachment'. Like him, many other operatives are extremely sensitive to the immediate spatial environments they inhabit which come to acquire over time a strong emotional and social signification. Irwin Altman and Setha Low (eds.), *Place Attachment. Human Behavior and Environment*, New York, 1992.

[84] Interview with Joseph (Field notes 1999).

[85] As both Roy and Burawoy, based on their own experiences as a drill operator, have noted, fatigue is reduced when boredom is reduced; getting through the workday then becomes less painful. Roy, 'Work Satisfaction and Social Reward in Quota Achievement'; Burawoy, *Manufacturing Consent*, p. 78, 85, 89.

I do not like working alone. There are too many components to stock and handle. I have to do everything alone, stuffing, carrying the boards to wave soldering . . . manual soldering . . . all this is a bit of strain for me. I even feel bored because the components are very minute and handling such small components is difficult. It is also confusing when one worker has stuff all the components. If I have to stuff only five or six components, I can do it very quickly. (Joseph)

Because we are dividing the components, stuffing 50 boards does not appear to be a strain. If a worker has to work alone, it is slightly boring, there is some strain. (Subanna)

There is lesser mental tension when you work in a team. Otherwise you will be worried that you have made a mistake because you don't have time to individually check the value of each component. (Mani)

This last remark leads us to the third advantage of partnerships. Splitting up the tasks tended to decrease rejections. For not only did an operative have to insert just a few components at a time, he was also in a position to easily detect any errors committed by his partner. Finally, it afforded a certain amount of leeway to workers when going on leave.

If I am absent from the factory for a couple of hours or even a whole day, your partner will take care of your work and vice versa.[86]

So given all these benefits a collective arrangement holds, why then did the majority of workers choose to operate on an individualized basis? The principal reason for the limited spread of partnerships lay in the difficulties involved in finding the ideal partner, one who would faithfully respect his share of the effort bargain even as he was tolerant of the other person's work habits and lapses; one also who would not cause his partner to lose face before the rest of the group. As Erving Goffman has pointed out, maintaining both his or her own face, what he calls the rule of self-respect, and the face of the other participants, or the rule of considerateness, is an essential element of personal conduct in social encounters. But in work situations observing these conventions is easier said than done.[87]

If any mistakes happen the partner can shout at you. Then you feel bad. If you go out, the partner will ask, 'where have you been. There is work to be completed'.

---

[86] Interview with Mani (Field notes 2001).
[87] Goffman, *Interaction Ritual*, p. 11.

In a partnership, the person who works faster will scold the one who is slow because incentive will be less.[88]

Added another worker:

Lots of friendships get broken in partnerships. One person takes leave and the other resents it.[89]

None of these mutual recriminations and problems arose when working alone. More importantly, a worker could conserve his freedom. Being the master of his job as well as his time, he did not have to account for his actions within this 'zone of discretion' to somebody else.[90] Nor was he bound by any reciprocal ties of obligation or commitments. Despite a long experience of collective arrangements, Yesuraj, a retired operative, expressed a definite preference for assembling boards individually because

. . . I can come and go whenever I like, start work a bit late, look after my personal work. In a partnership if I go and attend to some personal matters for 10–15 minutes, the partner will do my work but he will feel a sense of resentment that I am wasting time while he is working.[91]

Much the same mixture of impulses and apprehensions fuelled Thimmana's reluctance to team up with a colleague.

If I work on my own and my mind is not good one day and I don't feel like working hard, then I need not work hard. I can make up my production the next day . . . If I am not well, I will do light work one day, and catch up the next day. I will do what I can, what I feel like. *In partnerships, there is no such liberty.* You have to pull your weight. Otherwise there will be misunderstandings and you will feel bad inside.[92]

In sum, the disadvantages attached to partnerships appeared to outweigh its advantages as a system of work organization.

Concretely accomplishing the task of assembling the printed circuit boards again threw into relief two distinct approaches or strategies which coexisted in function of individual dispositions. For want of better terms, I shall call the first mode, step-by-step and wide focussed, and the second,

[88] Interview with Jagannath (Field notes 2001).

[89] Interview with Krishnan (Field notes 2001).

[90] Robert Freeland, 'Consent and Rational Choice', *Contemporary Sociology*, Vol. 30, No. 5. September 2001, pp. 446–8 (cit. p. 448.)

[91] Interview with Yesuraj, May-June 1999.

[92] Field notes 2001. Emphasis added.

integrated and narrow focussed. The step-by-step method consisted of inserting a limited number of components at a time in all the 50 boards comprising the kit. This was the practice favoured by almost all the operatives in the 09 group, including those who had formed partnerships. In the integrated strategy, all the different varieties of components were mounted at one go in one board. Only a handful of operatives opted for this technique. In both cases therefore, overall task execution was rendered manageable by decomposing it but the underlying principles differed because the constituent elements of the task were different. The step-by-step mode works on the basis of components: a task is completed when each type of component has been inserted. The integrated mode makes the board its principal object of attention: a task is completed when each board is fully populated.

Interestingly, despite the divergences in approach, the reasons prompting workers to privilege either a step-by-step or an integrated style of working were identical. They believed that that was the best means of getting through the job easily and quickly, though neither group stressed the superiority of their method. For the practitioners of the step-by-step method, seeing the number of component clusters contract provided them with the satisfaction and sense of achievement required to persist with the job without being overwhelmed by the strain induced by repetitive activity. Inversely, for the minority who followed the alternative path, it was seeing the height of the pile of boards decline that encouraged them.

One such operative was Rao. Though reputed for his speed and the quality of his output, most of his colleagues shunned him because of his fondness for drink. Rao's monthly production rarely surpassed 250 boards. He also systematically left the factory every day a couple of hours before shift closure. So during the time he was present he tried to assemble at least eight boards from start to finish. Never short of ideas, to attain his daily quota he got his boards wave soldered not in his own shop but in an adjoining department where a former school mate ran the wave soldering machine. Apart from being assured of far superior quality soldering as this machine was an imported model, his friend also obliged him by accepting as many boards as Rao brought whereas in the assembly department there was no room for such piecemeal soldering arrangements. According to him, inserting one component after another in all 50 boards was not only extremely 'boring', it also turned the job into a never-ending sisyphean struggle.

I have the impression that there are always lots and lots of components in front of me. That their quantity never decreases.[93]

But when he took up small batches of eight to ten boards time literally flew: 'in five to six hours I can reach upto inspection stage'. Similarly, Clarence contended that if

I have to first stuff jumpers in all 50 boards and then resistors and so on, I will not have the same interest, and I will also produce less because there will be some psychological strain.[94]

On the other hand, workers who adopted the step-by-step mode of assembling found fault with the rival strategy for being time consuming.

If I have to stuff all the components at the same time, I will have to search for the holes and this takes time. Now when I am stuffing 10K resistors or ceramic capacitors, I know exactly where the holes are located and my fingers move automatically to the right place.[95]

All three remarks reflect in one manner or the other workers' temporal experience of their activity. At the same time, they implicitly point to the utility of both the step-by-step and the integrated techniques in enabling operatives to fashion the set of routines required to build a steady work rhythm, to maintain a sustained tempo of activity. For rhythm, understood as the perfect synchronization of body motions and work materials and implements, when achieved exercises a 'pull effect' or traction whose result is to make the job seem more pleasant, or less tedious and tiring, by helping time pass rapidly.[96] The 'impression of work reproducing itself indefinitely', not to mention monotony, that repetitive actions produce is partly conjured.[97] Rao's experience of time flying furnishes one illustration of how workers are carried along by the traction inherent in a particular activity. Another example comes from Mohan Raj. He mentioned that on certain mornings, once he had settled into his groove he could work without any interruptions until the lunch break. 'Sometimes when I am stuffing and trimming components I don't even notice time going by.'

[93] ibid.
[94] ibid.
[95] Interview with Ananthanarayan.
[96] For an elaboration of the notion of traction see Baldamus, *Efficiency and Effort*, pp. 59–65.
[97] Hatzfeld, *Gens d'usine*, pp. 47–8.

Rhythm does not constitute board assembly workers' sole response to the monotonous effects of repetitive work. In one of his celebrated studies, Donald Roy shows how a trio of machine tenders tamed the 'formidable beast of boredom' by instituting a series of event-based time reckoning.[98] By interrupting their schedules at fixed intervals to eat a banana, open a window, drink a coke, or share a peach they introduced some meaning to a workday that would otherwise have been punctuated only by drudgery and exhaustion. Similar informal breaks in the board assembly shop at ITI had a less varied and less formalized character; 'banana time' or 'peach time' had its equivalent in nothing more than 'cigarette time', 'stroll time', and, less commonly, in 'puja time'.

Puja Time*

Friday, 16 November 2001. 8 am: Being an auspicious day in the Hindu calendar, like on every Friday puja is being offered in the adjoining work group. The sound of the *pujari* ringing his bell can be heard throughout the shop and mingles with the odour of incense and burnt camphor. The rituals are conducted by a worker belonging to the *achari* caste. All but two people take part in the ceremony which is soon over. *Prasadam*, consisting of bags of puffed rice and rock sugar, is distributed to the participants. The material for the ceremony is paid for by the workers each of whom contributes Rs 20 every month for this purpose.

Staging the event depends largely on personal initiative. With voluntary retirement having enormously depleted the strength of the shop, the fanfare and centralized organization that distinguished the weekly celebration in the past has ceded place to a much more muted affair. In the 09 group that I studied, puja is not even performed any longer. Upset by complaints over the quantity and quality of the *prasadam* supplied, the person who acted as 'master of ceremonies' refuses to take any responsibility now, and nobody has volunteered to replace him. Once in a while, somebody or the other replaces the garlands bedecking the photos of the deities with fresh flowers.

* (Field Notes)

From the author's diary.

---

[98] Donald Roy, '"Banana Time". Job Satisfaction and Informal Interaction', *Human Organization*, Vol. 18, No. 4, Winter 1959–60, pp. 158–68.

But in sharp contrast to the experiences of Roy's own team, board operatives could paradoxically find some relief from the grind of work within their work itself. Because they simultaneously operated with two kits or two batches of 50 boards at their disposal, a change of activity was always possible. A worker who was tired of stuffing components, for instance, could switch batches and attend to touch-up work or rectify defects in the second kit. Shuffling tasks in this manner also relieved physical fatigue, for holding a board constantly can cause the fingers to go numb as well as pain in the forearm and wrists. (Both these symptoms are associated with the diagnosis of the carpal tunnel syndrome, today the most commonly reported workplace-related health disorder in several industries.) Moreover, the devolved labour process gave workers total latitude to structure the workday as they desire. So after lunch when the pace of activity appreciably declined, quite a few of them opted to clean boards or insert bigger components such as wire sockets or the keypad since these tasks demanded little concentration.[99] Likewise, some reserved manual soldering work for the morning when it was cooler. Through all these different devices then workers sought to mitigate the boredom inherent in their job.

SHIRKERS' PUNISHMENTS AND PRIDE

The craft-type of task structure that governed the productive process in the board assembly shop, doubtless, imposed definite restrictions on expanding the extraction of labour. But in the case of ITI, even less ambitious goals such as obtaining minimum output were rendered elusive by shop officials' laxity in exercising the disciplinary powers at their disposal. At least six of the 24 operatives in the 09 group consistently turned out fewer than the required number of boards every month, even as output levels for the entire group fluctuated between 175–200 boards daily as against the norm of 250 boards. (In contrast to individual production objectives, group objectives were calculated on a daily basis.) With firings, suspensions and demotions ruled out for offences like

---

[99] Workers tend to engage in more unpleasant jobs in the morning, notes Baldamus, and save operations with higher traction for the afternoon when they are more prone to weariness. *Efficiency and Effort*, p. 71.

shirking, and with career mobility assured by a system of automatic promotions, the management arguably wielded anything but a long whip over inefficient personnel. Its punitive arsenal was limited to postponing increments, delaying promotions, or, in extreme cases, cutting wages. But it hesitated to enforce any of these measures.

In principle, workers only received a warning when they failed to meet minimum production targets three months in a row. The warning could either be verbal or a written which in itself was an indication of the erratic fashion in which shop managers chose to interpret factory regulations. Moreover, on the rare occasions that charge sheets were issued either workers succeeded in getting them overturned by producing medical certificates declaring they were sick, or sanctions seldom followed. One disheartened shop superintendent told me he no longer wanted to waste his time pulling up poor workers because whenever he charge sheeted them his superiors invariably refused to hand out punishments. He also claimed to be the victim of 'emotional blackmail' on the part of workers suffering from chronic ailments whose productivity was, to say the least, negligible. Although factory standing orders permitted the dismissal of those declared medically unfit, compassionate reasons invariably militated against the application of these rules.

Another executive grumbled that the department head had dissuaded him from taking disciplinary action against a notoriously lazy and troublesome worker in his section. 'My boss asked me why I wanted to spoil the person's career'.[100] Caught in the crossfire of conflicting demands and constraints, junior-level managers were particularly frustrated by this situation of 'responsibility drift'. Under relentless pressure to raise production to satisfactory levels, they could, however, count on support from no quarter, neither from divisional officials above, nor from supervisory personnel below. The latter systematically declined to give written complaints against inefficient workers in their group when asked to do so by line officials. Interestingly, workers themselves viewed the lax disciplinary controls with a critical eye. Embarrassed by the presence of shirkers in the shop, they, however, felt the fault lay less with the shirkers for not working, than with the management for not making them work.

---

[100] Interview with V. S. Kaul (Field notes 2001).

We cannot question workers who are sitting idle. They will say when the department head is saying nothing why are we questioning them. We feel bad when management people take no action against lazy fellows. But an ordinary worker cannot go and question the management.[101]

According to Vinayagam, a senior operative, the present department head lacked the qualities of his predecessor who had combined a firm hand with an outgoing manner, and frequently visited the shop floor.

. . . If he saw somebody sitting idle, he would come and stand next to him ask why he was idling, whether he had any problems . . . But Chandrahas (the incumbent boss) is not very strict and not very free in going upto the workers to talk to them . . ..[102]

Adding to shop officials' woes, the incentive system hardly merited its name. Whereas monthly wage packets easily averaged Rs 10,000, the maximum incentive payments were pegged at barely Rs 450, and taking this sum home demanded a good deal of effort and 'sacrifice'. Given this dual dissymmetry, operatives understandably saw no sense in exerting themselves to greater lengths. Further diminishing the effectiveness of the scheme was the fact that most workers were subject to taxation. There was a marked reluctance therefore to earning higher incentive since the gains realized on one side were lost on the other by way of higher taxes. The scheme also did not cover officers, although the penury of operatives was forcing an increasing number of lower-ranking officers into assembly jobs much to their chagrin. Thus, given the relatively scant concern the management showed for enforcing production norms, it was not only surprising that the majority of operatives worked at all, but that quite a few of them worked extremely hard. Five to six members of the 09 group regularly earned maximum incentive, and took great pride in their accomplishment, even though the amount represented only a fraction of their total remuneration.[103] If quite a few operatives conformed to the stereotyped image of the public sector worker as a paid idler, an equal number, if not more, gave the lie to this stereotype.

Reaching the incentive ceiling entailed assembling 338 boards a

---

[101] Interview with Ananthanarayan, 1 December 2001.

[102] Interview with Vinayagam, 6 December 2001.

[103] In the entire telephone final assembly department which includes the board assembly shop, 27 workers out of a total of 151 earned ceiling incentive in August 2001, and 29 out of 150 in September. (*Source:* IED Tel. Divn.).

month. This was no easy goal. It could only be achieved by those who were prepared to toil continuously and renounce the pleasures of going for a stroll every now and then, returning leisurely after lunch, taking leave quite often, spending time chatting with friends, enjoying an extended tea break, or reading the newspaper. These self-disciplined souls also had to submit to the mockery, not always good humoured or charitable, of their colleagues. Those who were perceived as being particularly unsociable could even serve as explicit counter models for the others. At least three workers in the 09 group partly defended their low levels of incentive compensation by claiming they did not want to 'become like Reddy'.

A ceiling incentive worker, Reddy was the butt of much ridicule for his habit of never leaving his workspot even during tea or lunch time. As Byrappa, one of his sternest detractors told me, 'he (Reddy) has put araldite on his seat. That is why he can sit still for five or six hours'. Mockery, though, is a double-edged weapon. And Reddy himself scarcely missed an opportunity to ridicule Byrappa, the least productive operative in the group who, nevertheless, was recently promoted as a grade I officer, for failing to set an example to his colleagues by shirking less and producing more.

Since money was not the exclusive impulse, what then motivated Reddy and a few other like him to push themselves so hard to earn ceiling incentive? Reddy himself merely said he was 'interested in working' and that both the company and he stood to gain from his efforts. Ananthanarayan, another top incentive earner, provided a more illuminating answer where personal dispositions meshed with work habits and social obligations.

I simply cannot sit idle in the factory. That is *my nature*. Once I become idle, waste time chit chatting, it will not be easy to *pick up my speed again*. So I prefer to keep working continuously. It all depends on individual capacity. When we come to factory, we must work for eight hours and not waste time. *That is my duty*. Factory is paying us for eight hours and giving us a lot of benefits. I must be responsible to the company.[104]

The motivations were much the same for Padmanabha, yet another incentive maximizer.

---

[104] Interview with Ananthanarayan. Emphasis added.

Work is our life. We have to give respect to our work. I have never come late for work. If we work well and earn money, we can do anything. Our life moves well. If I have two days holidays at a stretch, I am fully bored having to sit at home. . . We can't do anything else but watch TV.[105]

Landlords, Money Lenders, and Bank Agents*

Wednesday, 31 October 2001. 10 am: Four workers belonging to other divisions have pulled up chairs around Byrappa's table and are soon engaged in a serious conversation. It is nearing lunch time when they leave. At no moment did the supervisor show any signs of intervening to break up the gathering. Byrappa later tells me that two of the workers are his relatives and had come to discuss a marriage proposal for one of their sons. The senior most worker in the group, Byrappa is also an extremely wealthy man owning six acres of prime land in the vicinity of the factory where he cultivates rice, raggi and coconuts. In the early 1970s, he wanted to quit the factory and devote his time and energy to starting a grape farm. But his father insisted he remain in ITI. Though he occasionally has to take leave, he says he finds enough time to settle all matters connected with his land on Sunday.

Byrappa is not the only person in the group with one foot in agriculture. Swamy possesses five acres of land 50 kms away from Bangalore and goes there every Saturday evening after the shift ends to supervise his crop of coconut trees. In addition, he is an arrack vendor, owns a retail shop, which is managed by an employee, one house and is building a second one. The house alone fetches him a monthly rent of Rs 5000. But he is unwilling to give up his job at ITI because business, he claims, does not offer a comparable degree of financial security. Similarly, Krishnan has opened a small petty shop in front of his house which is run by his wife. Together with the income secured from hiring out two floors of his house, his extra earnings amount to Rs 3500 every month. Indeed, rentals constitute the primary source of supplementary revenue for several workers. 19 of the 23 people in the group from whom I was able to collect this information either possess their own house or live in their in-laws' house. Of this number at least nine are enmeshed in some form of landlord-tenant relations.

contd. on next page

---

[105] Field notes 2001. These lines also illustrate the extent to which domestic work remains gendered in nature with the male wage earner leaving the burden of running the household almost exclusively to his wife. However, from the little I was able to observe of younger generation workers' families in the ITI township, a slightly more equitable division of labour seems to prevails within the reproductive sphere.

Tuesday morning, 6 November. I am sitting next to Ananthanarayan watching him assemble a board when a helper from another department approaches him for a loan of Rs 100. He curtly tells the helper to return the next day. Later, Byrappa jokingly calls Ananthu *shanbogue*, a qualifier which could mean both accountant and money lender. Ananthu himself admits to lending small sums of upto Rs 500 to colleagues, but omits to specify whether or not he charges interest. Unlike other workers in the group, he belongs to a dual-income household—his wife is employed in another public sector enterprise. So he can effectively boast of being in a much stronger financial position than his colleagues. From Swamy, who is a member, I learn too that Ananthu has been running a chit fund for a number of years to which participants contribute Rs 6000 monthly. But when I put the question to him, Ananthu flatly denies organising a chit fund, worried that an admission might land him in trouble with the management in case I tattled on him. Govindaraju also accuses Ananthu of harbouring a superiority complex and casteist sentiments. Because he is a Brahmin and a graduate to boot, he apparently interacts only with a select group of people in the shop.

Friday morning, 9 November. There is a fair deal of animation again at Byrappa's table as workers flock around it. Employed in another department, a friend moonlights as a bank agent. He has come to explain the modalities of a fixed deposit scheme offering a rebate on income tax payments. Although the company expressly prohibits anybody from engaging as an intermediary for a financial institution, the regulations are easily circumvented by workers who enrol family members as agents and act on their behalf. At least four people in the group can afford to subscribe to the scheme paying the required sum of Rs 20,000. Kittoor, the shop deputy head, passes by without even casting a backward glance. The rumour has it that he is part of a circle of brahmin and achar officers who congregate periodically at Byrappa's house for meat and alcohol, pleasures proscribed by their religious faith.
* (Field Notes)

From the author's diary.

Frequent recourse to religious metaphors of the type 'work is worship', 'work is God's gift', by certain operatives also attested to their profound sense of engagement. Notions of craftsmanship, interpreted as doing something well for its own sake, to borrow from Richard Sennett, did matter to them.[106] For radical scholars steeped in the 'hermeneutics of

---

[106] Sennett, *Culture of the New Capitalism*, p. 104.

suspicion' all such dispositions inevitably smacked of signs of false consciousness or necessity-made-virtue in much the same way that conservative theorists tend to cathect the lack of interest in industrial occupations as an innate propensity to sloth.[107] But there is no reason why discourses extolling a logic of identification with work should not be taken at face value just as are discourses fraught with a logic of denunciation because they happen to sit more comfortably with certain ideological leanings.

If expressions of attachment to work and a sense of duty *vis-à-vis* the company waxed strongest among elite operatives, they were also voiced with some nuances by their less proficient colleagues.

We have no choice but to come to work. But once you come to work, you need to take interest . . . If we work well, company and workers both will benefit. If we don't work company will run at a loss.[108]

Even the 'uncommitted' workers in the section were obliged to justify their lack of 'commitment' by pointing to their age or ill health or both. Among the board assembly operatives classified in the lowest incentive category was Rao. His monthly incentive benefits never exceeded Rs 80, but says he was more than satisfied with this amount.

I have been working for 34 years and am tired. I am at the end of my career. All I want is to give minimum efficiency, so that I am not scolded by the management.[109]

Added another worker:

I have been working 37 years, so I don't want a management officer to come and ask me why I am not giving enough production.[110]

These statements, encapsulating workers' goals and fears, are instructive for they provide us with a clue to the puzzle of why when chargesheets were seldom issued, and when the effect of sanctions, to boot, was no more than a pinprick, the majority still apprehended being 'scolded' by the management, and hence endeavoured to, as it were, spontaneously achieve production minimas.

[107] Andrew Sayer, 'Bourdieu, Smith and Disinterested Judgement', *The Sociological Review*, Vol. 47, No. 3, August 1999, pp. 403–31 (cit. p. 428).
[108] Interview with Subanna (Field notes 2001).
[109] Field notes 2001.
[110] Interview with Pandeyan (Field notes 2001).

To appreciate their attitudes, it is necessary to understand the value they placed on preserving dignity and self-respect. Following Goffman, we can argue that to maintain face on the shop floor most workers try and live up to the 'line' they are enacting of sincere or conscientious individuals who respect their part of the wage-effort bargain.[111] Determining how many hours they should work and at what pace in return for the salary paid them by the company may fluctuate from one individual to the next. But the line constrains them somewhat to satisfy the minimum production norms fixed by the management. Dropping below this threshold threatens workers with loss of face in case shop officials decide to sanction them even if the punishment meted out is essentially symbolic in nature since it inflicts no real damage to their work careers.

My promotion chances won't be affected if I get a chargesheet, but sincere workers will feel bad . . . They lose pride.[112]

Shamefacedness then ensued not so much on account of the content of the punishment, as from the act of its imposition, the stain it left on a person's record, and its public character since knowledge of somebody having received a charge sheet or a 'call upstairs' to the shop superintendent's office rarely remained confidential. This dual dimension of humiliation which erased both pride and honour emerges clearly in the following quotation:[113]

Employees do not want to see their personal record spoilt by getting a charge sheet . . . They (also) don't want to be humiliated for word is sure to spread among colleagues that they have got a banging from management.[114]

The shaming could also take a collective form with the shop superintendent occasionally summoning workers in groups of two or three and reprimanding them in front of the others. So to avoid discredit, most of them strove to reach a zone of safety which consisted of assembling the minimum required number of boards, if not every month, at least on most months. In other words, notwithstanding the management's

---

[111] Goffman, *Interaction Ritual*, pp. 5–10.

[112] Interview with Kalaimuthu (Field notes 2001).

[113] Goffman distinguishes between pride which is a sense of obligation to the self, and honour which flows from a sense of obligation to wider social units. *Interaction Ritual*, pp. 9–10.

[114] Interview with Clarence (Field notes 2001).

failure to effectively exercise its authority, disciplinary mechanisms retained their essential vitality with the fear of sanctions, and the attendant humiliation, functioning as a potent coercive force to guarantee compliance with basic production norms.[115]

RESPONSIBILITY WITHOUT AUTHORITY: PLIGHT OF SUPERVISORS

Any discussion of disciplinary matters must of necessity touch on the role and functions of the supervisor in charge of each work group. A highly influential, even dreaded, figure in the past, the ability of supervisors to extract production from the workforce and command obedience reposed chiefly on their discretionary powers to recommend promotions. But the institution of a time-bound promotion programme (TBP) in the late 1970s, coupled with the suppression of both overtime work and a system of special increments plus the increasing strength of the union, by undermining his prerogatives, brought the supervisor's empire on the shop floor crashing down. 'After TBP nobody bothered about him'.[116] A partial index of the marginal influence exercised by the supervisor, there was no personalization of the three work groups in the board assembly section. None of them were identified by the name of their heads; instead they were referred to merely by their numbers.

Under these circumstances, a role reversal of sorts occurred where it was in the supervisor's self-interest to maintain cordial relations with his subordinates rather than the other way round. Otherwise, securing their cooperation in the daily endeavour to bring the product out became an unremitting clash of wills whose outcome to boot was highly uncertain. Misdemeanours committed by workers thus generally went unreported in order to avoid antagonizing them, and if shirkers were left alone, quarrelsome individuals were requested to be transferred out of the group. The tendency for 'indulgent' behaviour on the part of supervisory personnel was further reinforced by the fact that they were often bound to workers by the strength of common ties as many had risen from the

---

[115] Sanctions, comments Jean-Daniel Reynaud, directly reinforce a given rule by punishing an infraction, and indirectly by lowering the social status of the individual. *Les règles du jeu. L'action collective et la régulation sociale*, Paris, 1997, p. 37.

[116] Interview with Sahadevan.

ranks themselves. Nor was the management in a position to turn the screws on them.

If I press supervisors for production, they will tell me, 'look sir why are you troubling us. We have only three or four more years to go before retiring. If you trouble us we will go on VRS' (voluntary retirement).[117]

Nowhere were all these difficulties reflected more acutely than in the 09 group. Nagaraj who led this entity was unanimously regarded by shop officials as totally ineffectual compared to the other supervisors in the board assembly shop. Kittoor, the deputy works manager, pinned the onus for the entire gamut of ills afflicting the 09 group, reputedly 'the least productive, the least cooperative, and the least quality conscious' of the three work groups comprising the section, squarely on Nagaraj, accused of being timorous as well as lethargic.

He (Nagaraj) does not ask workers for more production. He does not call them up when they are producing less. We have called him many times and instructed him to improve . . . He is afraid to extract work from operatives.[118]

Kittoor even hinted that the helper allocated to the 09 group displayed a greater sense of initiative and kept better track of daily output levels than the supervisor. But Kittoor acknowledged that the presence of four 'lame ducks' in the group, three grade I officers and a former shop clerk, with no previous experience of board assembly activity and completely disinterested in their job for various reasons, also redounded to the disadvantage of Nagaraj.

To do justice to Nagaraj, who was previously engaged in inspection duties, it must be said that he had not requested the job. It had been abruptly thrust upon him two years ago. Operatives belonging to his group described Nagaraj as a modest, good-natured and uncontroversial person who 'does not speak roughly', 'greets everybody when he comes in the morning', mixed freely and never failed to attend the various social ceremonies they organized—all the qualities indispensable for creating a harmonious work climate. But they candidly declared that he lacked all interest in his work and was only 'doing it out of compulsion'.[119] Once again in all fairness to Nagaraj, the job of a supervisor is anything but a

---

[117] Interview with Chandrahas (Field notes 1999).
[118] Field notes 2001.
[119] ibid.

desirable one which explains why volunteers are rare. Because he is obliged to 'listen to complaints from workers all the time', a supervisor's role is likened to that of a 'shock absorber'.[120] Indeed, one operative, although he was a grade I officer like Nagaraj, claimed he deliberately chose not to push his claims for this position in order to escape the stress and strain encumbering it.

A supervisor is answerable to the workers in the group . . . He has to do a lot of work in addition to his regular work . . . He has to run around a lot . . . After the end of the shift, he has to give details to the management about how many boards have been assembled, how many are pending with inspection . . .[121]

The function effectively carries a heavy burden of responsibility, despite being amputated of all its power and despite the meagre symbolic rewards in terms of prestige and social status linked to it. If anything, several ordinary workers found quite degrading and unpleasant the menial tasks a supervisor was quite often forced to accomplish in the course of his duties such as loading and unloading material on trolleys, pushing the trolleys and so forth. All these tasks normally fell within the province of the helper. But to speed up things the supervisor must also lend a hand and when the helper is absent as is some times the case, the former has no choice but to haul the trolley himself or lift the cartons of lacquered boards.

Moreover, in certain instances, the supervisor might even have to undertake certain jobs that a helper refuses to do. Thus, after the shop superintendent had instructed one of the supervisors, Dasappa, to tidy up the shop in honour of the arrival of an important outside delegation, I saw him personally clearing the tables and removing scrap from the gangways. He had apparently asked the helper, but the latter had categorically refused on the legitimate grounds that it was not his job but that of the sweeper. The liberty of imitating the helper's example, though, was denied to Dasappa: as an officer, factory regulations require him to perform all kinds of jobs without exception.

Indeed, the decision taken by the telephone division management in the mid-1990s to appoint officers alone to supervisory categories was intended precisely to overcome the difficulties caused by the refusal of worker-supervisors to assist helpers or to substitute for them. These

[120] Interview with V.S. Kaul.
[121] Interview with Clarence (Field notes 2001).

worker-supervisors also knew they could count on the intervention of the union in the eventuality of the company charge sheeting them. Officer-supervisors, however, enjoyed no such protection since the union was not entitled to represent their interests and the officer's association is 'only a dummy association', powerless to defend them.

When we were workers we were safe, but as grade I officers we have to do everything including a labourer's job. Top management questions us and says they don't want to know how we get things done, but they want production.[122]

Since the supervisor had no voice whatsoever in the way operatives belonging to his group organized their day-to-day activities, his principal production responsibility, together with that of watching over his group and persuading it to work, entailed maintaining a smooth flow of material from one area to another so that the printed circuit boards arrived at the final phase of telephone assembly with minimal delay. Consequently, three distinct functions were rolled into one in his person: those of feeder, chaser and checker. Each was equally important, generated its own pressures, and keeps him constantly on the move. While Nagaraj himself jokingly qualified his work as 'wandering here and there', along with the shop superintendent to whom they reported, supervisory staff were the busiest people on the shop floor, literally running from pillar to post throughout the shift.

Until the late 1980s, each group comprised a feeder. But after the management abolished this post in order to prune the number of auxiliary staff, the supervisor was constrained to shoulder this burden. (On my first trip I had noticed a feeder officiating informally in one work group. He had been selected by his colleagues to assist the supervisor. Subsequently the group disappeared.) The first, and most important, job of the supervisor *qua* feeder was to distribute kits to all his operatives after having procured them from the kitting section. Then, once the boards were assembled, he had to send them for inspection. Any defective boards had to be returned by him to the operatives or the repairman. The task of both dispatching the boards for lacquering and submitting boards that had come back from this operation for further inspection controls, was also his. Finally, after inspection clearance, he had to deliver the boards to quality control.

---

[122] Interview with Natesan (Field notes 1999).

Performing the job of a chaser would absorb only a limited portion of the supervisor's time and also be considerably facilitated if the kits were complete. It would also expose him to less criticism from operatives. Unfortunately, this was not the case. A combination of material shortages plus kitting errors meant that he had to devote considerable energy to following up on components that remained to be supplied, besides having to endure the complaints and sardonic remarks of workers who invariably blamed him for the disruptions provoked by a missing or undelivered item. Some more enterprising operatives or those having friends in kitting went directly to this section to sort things out, but the majority believed that taking such pains was not incumbent upon them. At the same time, the supervisor was required to clear bottlenecks by chasing any material held up at the inspection or the lacquering stage.

Nagaraj had no hesitations in defining his job as 'tense' and his own situation as 'weak and difficult'. He blamed workers for 'mak(ing) the supervisor tense', but was lucid enough to trace his predicament back to the front-line position that supervisors occupied in the factory hierarchy.

They (workers) ask the supervisor for solutions which lie in the management's hands and when the management does not find a solution, the supervisor's position *vis-à-vis* workers becomes weak and difficult. The supervisors also lack knowledge to find alternative solutions and this creates difficulties.[123]

So when one sharp-tongued operative, after patiently hearing out Nagaraj that one had to be more tolerant of the kitting section's lapses 'because all workers are brothers', retorted that this was no excuse for carelessness, all that Nagaraj could do was give a sheepish grin and leave the scene. Fed up of drawing attention to the sub-standard quality of moulded items such as key buttons, another operative, Balu, compared the supervisor to a football 'who goes up to the management when workers kick him and comes down to workers when management kicks him'. Balu, however, reiterated his determination to continue complaining even though he knew that Nagaraj 'can take no action' and might not even have been relaying workers' problems back to his superiors because 'he has so many other things to attend to'.[124]

Yet powerless though he might have been to improve the situation on the shop floor, the friendly rapport Nagaraj had succeeded in building

[123] Field notes 2001.
[124] ibid.

with the operatives in his group meant that he could count on their cooperation, a fair deal, in acquitting his daily functions. For instance, Padmanabha acted as his unofficial assistant, providing kits to workers when the supervisor was absent from the workspot, and helped him sort out and distribute certain non-kit components. Padmanabha undertook this task on a purely voluntary basis and drew no particular benefit from it. Similarly, when the supervisor asked workers to attend to some minor repair work in order to spare the repairman, these requests were never turned down. When I commented on this fact, Nagaraj replied: 'Everybody obliges. Otherwise production will not move. This is a chain-link job'.

Nagaraj was also extremely fortunate in another respect. In sharp contrast to the other work groups, the helper attached to his group, Muniappa, was hardworking, in relatively good health, and dependable, rarely taking leave. In return, Nagaraj, a caste Hindu, went out of his way to treat the helper with respect and consideration, regardless of the fact that the latter was a Dalit. As Muniappa told me, 'if I am absent one day, the supervisor will find it really hard. He has to do the work that I do, so when I come things are more easy for him'.[125] Both Nagaraj's attitude towards Muniappa and the latter's statement furnish a useful indication of one fundamental aspect of their relationship to which I have already alluded earlier. Notwithstanding the yawning hierarchical gulf separating the two, it was not so much the supervisor as the helper who held the upper hand in this relationship since work imperatives placed the former in a situation of strong dependency *vis-à-vis* the latter. Indeed, stating that no worker played a more important role in contributing to the efficient performance of the supervisor than the helper would hardly amount to an exaggeration in view of the extent to which the jobs of the two categories, standing, ironically, at opposite ends of the chain of command, were interlinked.

HELPERS' POSITION IN WORK HIERARCHY

The functional dependency of supervisors on helpers was accentuated by a couple of structural factors. Not only did the telephone assembly shop in its totality suffer from an acute shortage of helpers, many of

[125] ibid.

those available had been declared medically unfit to accomplish the heavy manual tasks that behoves to this category of personnel. Thus the minority who were actually in a position to do their job commanded substantial bargaining power. This reality was reflected as much in the uphill battle the management faced whenever it tried to transfer them to other sections, not to speak of its failure to consolidate all the helpers into a common pool, as in the highly restrictive demarcation of occupational territories that the helpers had succeeded in enforcing of their own initiative. Helpers in the board assembly shop, for instance, systematically refused to carry out the tasks of their counterparts in the final assembly and lacquering shops. As a result, when a helper went on leave in the lacquering shop, Kittoor, the shop deputy head, had to coax an operative to temporarily replace him failing which production would have been held up. Issuing charge sheets against the helpers was also pointless and could only serve to further poison the climate on the shop floor, because, as Kittoor pointed out, sanctions were seldom imposed.

At the same time, the unyielding line adopted by the helpers must be traced back to the frustrations engendered by the nature of their work. Helpers' jobs were dead-end jobs in the fullest sense of the term. Leaving aside the physical exertion expended in carrying, lifting and fetching all day every day, their near-total lack of formal educational and technical capital automatically disqualified them from laying claim to any other kind of activity. While the time-bound promotion scheme assured them of regular promotions upto a point, it did not entitle them to more rewarding or less demanding forms of occupation.

As Muniappa lamented, he was performing the same set of tasks as he had been when he first entered the factory 31 years ago. 'There has been absolutely no change in my work'. Nor did he expect any changes in the remaining years of his career. Deeply embittered with both the union and the management for having failed to envisage measures to improve the condition of helpers, he added that he was no less competent to 'fix a couple of screws' than any of the operatives assigned to telephone final assembly work. With no windows of opportunity for bettering their work prospects helpers believed therefore they stood to gain little from cooperating with shop management by agreeing to its demands for greater flexibility. In sum, the case of the helpers underlines the disjunction that can some times exist between a formalized system of job classifications and the bargaining strength diverse professional categories actually wield.

Or the risks attendant upon attempting to read shop floor production relations directly from occupational designations. However lowly ranked it might be, even the most subordinate group is never so fettered as to find itself always at the receiving end of the power equilibrium.[126] On the contrary, depending on the situational logic of its interactions with other groups, it has the possibility of leveraging the resources at its disposal to momentarily place its relations with its superiors on an equal footing, and even reverse the direction of power flows.

Yet, paradoxically while helpers were in a position to extract respect and dignity from supervisors and shop officials, they struggled to obtain similar treatment at the hands of workers, who were often guilty of arrogant behaviour and verbal aggression. According to Muniappa, operatives spoke to him rudely. 'They say I am an uneducated fellow. So I have to shut my mouth and do my job.'[127] Indeed, the resentment generated among helpers *vis-à-vis* the company at the impossibility of securing alternative work was not simply confined to the fact that it condemned them to a lifetime of toil at strenuous and unpleasant tasks. Equally painfully, it eliminated their chances of getting a respectable job, one that bestowed a more gratifying self-image. The negative status connotations overlaying a helper's job was unambiguously articulated by Muniappa when he compared himself, first, to a '*dhobi* carrying bundles of clothes on our back', and then to a non-person whose presence on the shop floor was not even spatially materialized by such basic markers as a 'table or chair that I can call my own. Wherever I find a vacant seat, I sit . . .'.

But the inferior status of the helper was not merely linked to the menial character of his occupation, perceived as inferior, a point underlined by the low levels of literacy of those doing it. It was also inescapably connected to the fact that most of the arms and backs that executed the labouring chores belonged to Dalits. Helpers therefore carried a double stigma, occupational and ascriptive, the mutually reinforcing tendency of which had the effect of projecting and amplifying the stereotypic idea that the generally uneducated Dalit worker was best suited for the position of a helper.

As Everett Hughes has so justly observed, a striking paradox of modern

---

[126] This argument has, of course, received its fullest expression in Crozier. *Le phénomène bureaucratique*, p. 202.

[127] Field notes 2001.

industry is that even as it plays the role of 'grand mixer of peoples', it is 'almost universally an agent of racial and ethnic discrimination'. By generating among managers, foremen and workers a 'body of opinion and lore concerning the work capacities and habits of various ethnic groups', which may often not correspond to verifiable fact, industry engenders discriminatory practices.[128] All this, in turn, accounted for the high-handed and disparaging attitudes of board assembly operatives, most of whom were educated and/or technically qualified caste Hindus, and who wished to entertain no friendly relations with helpers. The only operatives in his group with whom Muniappa mixed were Clarence, a Christian, and Byrappa, an extremely sociable person. He even kept his distance from the other two Dalit workers in the group (whose caste identity I came to learn from Clarence).

Operatives' inconsiderate treatment of helpers might have also stemmed from the knowledge that the latter's incentive payments were contingent on total group output. If the group produced more, the helper earned more money, and inversely. One could therefore advance the hypothesis that operatives saw helpers as being obligated to them, for without their efforts the latter would be ineligible for incentive. This in turn provided the justification for their behaviour, especially if they believed these efforts had not been adequately recompensed by acts or expressions of 'gratitude' on the part of helpers.

The barrier separating operatives from helpers had also widened for another reason. A feature of shop floor life that had captured my attention during my first visit in 1999 was the informal work practices instituted by a certain number of groups. One such practice consisted of workers 'farming' out the task of cleaning the printed circuit boards to helpers once all soldering operations were completed. In return, helpers received a sum varying from Rs 7 to 10 from each worker in the group every month. If this arrangement gave the appearance of being equitable for both sides—workers gained time since they could concentrate on assembling the boards while helpers gained additional income—in reality operatives emerged as the principal beneficiaries. They were spared the inconvenience of doing a dirty and hazardous task, given the toxic

---

[128] Everett Hughes, 'Queries Concerning Industry and Society Growing Out of Study of Ethnic Relations in Industry', in *idem, The Sociological Eye: Selected Papers,* Chicago, 1971, pp. 74–5.

properties of the chemical utilized for rinsing the boards. Nevertheless, one consequence of this internal division of labour was that by creating a context of mutual dependency it helped to forge closer bonds between operatives and helpers.

On my second visit two years later, I found this arrangement no longer existed. In each of the three work groups still standing, workers personally attended to cleansing operations. If a few members of the 09 group were reluctant to pay the helper, the principal explanation for this changed situation lies in Muniappa's own refusal to perform this task. While his decision could be attributed partially to health and monetary factors—apart from the odour of the solvent making him nauseous, he said, he did not need the extra money—status considerations predominated.

. . . I don't want to go with a begging bowl in my hand on payday to ask operatives for money if I clean their cards.[129]

The upshot of Muniappa's decision, however, was to reduce interactions between him and the operatives to minimal levels since the latter were no longer reliant on him to carry out their 'dirty' work.

REPAIRMEN CONFRONTED WITH DILEMMA

No such sentiments of status deprivation afflicted the repairman. Together with the helper, he constituted the second auxiliary worker in the group. On the contrary, by virtue of his technical knowledge his prestige within the group was unequalled by anybody else, least of all the supervisor. The fact that his work table, like those of other repairmen, was placed at a slight distance from those of the operatives was not only because he required more room to dispose the hundreds of boards surrounding him. The physical separation also functioned as a spatial index of his distinctive position on the shop floor.

Yet, curiously, for over a decade the function of the repairman had ceased to officially exist. In 1989, as part of the drive to reduce overheads by pruning the size of auxiliary personnel, telephone division officials had eliminated this job throughout the division. Operatives had to individually attend to repair tasks with some allowances being made in time standards for this purpose. But incapable of even identifying

[129] Field notes 2001.

component values, leave alone checking the circuitry or transmission parameters, workers in each group responded to this measure by designating one repairman of their own. This was invariably the same person who had officiated as a repairman in the past. For his labour, the latter received a certain number of assembled boards from each group member on the basis of which he claimed incentive. In the 09 group, for instance, for every hundred boards workers produced they turned over eight to the repairman, Devdas. This informal arrangement encountered no objections from the management, fully aware that it was impossible for a group to function without a repairman given the operatives' limited technical qualifications.

Shop managers, however, conceded that the decision to formally abolish the occupation of repairman, while yielding a few benefits, had caused a major, and unanticipated, problem. It deprived them of the possibility of obtaining vital feedback on human-induced errors. Despite pressure from quality control personnel, repairmen were reticent about divulging the identities of persons guilty of negligent work. Exposures of this kind not only risked provoking conflicts with the operative; more importantly, the operative could legitimately object that if he gave the repairman a share of his monthly output it was precisely in order to ensure that mistakes were rectified by the latter, and could therefore, threaten to stop rewarding the repairman.

Devdas himself admitted that he was placed in a delicate position, and his discourse amply reflected the pulls and tugs of contradictory impulses. On the one hand, there was no dearth of careless workers in the group who 'work fast to gain incentive, but do not concentrate'. According to him, at least half the group fell into this category. As he repeatedly pointed out, repairmen would, by and large, be superfluous if workers exercised greater vigilance. He was also scathing in his judgement of the work ethic of inspection personnel, several of whom showed 'no interest in their work' and just 'roam about for three or four hours'. Doing his job correctly, as he put it, would mean reporting all these people to the management! But he found it morally repugnant to even consider taking this step in view of the implicit code of solidarity binding all the workers in the shop.[130]

---

[130] According to Hatzfeld, quality inspectors face more or less similar dilemmas at Peugeot. *Gens d'usine*, p. 90

I cannot give their names to the management . . . They are all my colleagues. We have all been working together for many years. If a worker is suspended his life his spoilt . . . All that I can do is advise operators who make faults to be more careful and point out their mistakes . . . The same way I try and tell inspection, 'look there have been lots of mistakes this week, so please try and reduce them'.[131]

On the other hand, by declining to identify negligent workers and inspectors Devdas added to his own difficulties. Since sanctions were never enforced against them, they continued to shirk their responsibilities with the result that his workload only increased. 'Nobody makes an effort to improve'. Thus while repairmen were in principle only supposed to correct electrical flaws, slack mechanical inspection obliged him to attend to both types of defects. Torn between the desire to see work practices change and a sense of obligation towards his colleagues, he was resigned to the *status quo* prevailing, as he recognized the immutable logic of functioning of a public sector company.

This is a government factory. So you cannot take action against anybody. Nobody is properly responsible.[132]

---

[131] Interview with Devdas (Field notes 2001).
[132] ibid.

chapter seven

Workers and Independent Unionism

Writing in 1977, the sociologist N.R. Sheth bemoaned that 'very little material of real contemporary value' on the sociology of Indian industrial workers is available.[1] Our knowledge, even today, of the demographic profiles and socio-economic origins of wage earners in both the organized sector and the informal sector has not advanced greatly. The qualitative turn, the dominant explanatory paradigm today in the social sciences has arguably rendered survey data, questionnaires, formal interviews and the like totally *démodé*, at least in the field of labour research. The ahistoricism inherent in most formal social sciences methodologies has also not contributed to popularizing these techniques among historians.[2]

Nevertheless, both the necessity and utility of integrating a quantitative dimension into historical research is undeniable. Possessing 'hard' data on workers' birthplaces, their educational qualifications, entry strategies

[1] N.R. Sheth, 'Sociological Studies of Indian Industrial Workers', *Sociological Bulletin*, Vol. 26, No. 1, March 1977, pp. 76–90 (cit. p. 76).

[2] Larry Griffin and Marcel van der Linden, 'Introduction. New Methods for Social History', *International Review of Social History*, Vol. 43, Supplement 6, 1998, pp. 3–8.

into the labour market, modes of recruitment and so forth can only render more fruitful, coherent and convincing qualitative analyses of forms of collective action or cultural practices where the temptation to advance implicitly quantitative statements without definite quantitative evidence is often all too strong. Existing sociological surveys of factory operatives are unfortunately only of limited value. By restricting their views to cross-sectional snapshots, they present static images. Burdened by a marked synchronic bias, what emerges from these studies is a composite picture of a 'typical' worker, defined on a once-and-for-all basis by a cluster of fixed, even immutable, traits or attributes which while useful is inadequate. The emphasis on generalization and the search for patterns of regularities means that evolutions in the structural composition of the workforce receive short shrift.

To avoid the same pitfalls, we have deployed a conventional statistical tool, multivariate procedures, but one put to decidedly historical uses, thereby distinguishing our approach from that commonly embraced by sociologists. The population of 1129 employees from the Bangalore plant of ITI that our sample survey covered makes it the largest of its kind to be conducted so far of the organized sector workforce in the country.[3] In compiling our database, we have adopted an inter-generational perspective as opposed to an intra-generational one so as to stress the significance of temporal factors in our findings.[4] This solution which combines two levels of analysis offers us the dual advantage of weaving into our examination of the aggregate results a more dynamic reading,

---

[3] Richard Lambert's survey of five factories in Poona covered a population of 821 people; the research piloted by Vaid in Kota (Rajasthan) had a sample of 462 people; the multi-city survey conducted by Goyal in Gujarat included a sample of 298 people; Sharma selected 262 workers in his study of a Bombay automobile plant; and the multi-unit sample of Holmström in Bangalore took in 1134 people. Holmström's survey features two private sector and two public sector firms, among them ITI which is not named but only designated as 'Factory A'. All the sample size figures are drawn from the studies of their respective authors, and Baldev R. Sharma, 'The Industrial Worker: Some Myths and Realities', *EPW*, Vol. V, No. 22, 30 May 1970, pp. 875–8. Prior to Holmström's study, another comparative survey also featuring ITI was conducted by Arya. The sample consisted of 181 workers. P.P. Arya, *Labour Management Relations in Public Sector Undertakings*, New Delhi, 1982.

[4] The totality of the conclusions of the survey is available in our doctoral dissertation, *Usine Indienne. Travail, firme et société dans une entreprise d'État, Indian Telephone Industries. Bangalore (1948–2002)*, EHESS, Paris, 2007.

attentive to the variations and contrasts that manifested themselves as the factory absorbed each new wave of workers. For while transversal tendencies cutting across the generations were not absent, the structural features of the workforce remained anything but constant from one period to the next.

Our sample population is drawn from five successive cohorts of workers who entered the factory over a period of five decades starting from the foundation of the company in 1948. Between 1950–80, the workforce expanded at an explosive pace reaching its apogee in 1980 when the plant counted almost 19,500 people on its rolls (Table 7.1).

Table 7.1: Workforce Strength, ITI Bangalore (1949–2002)

Year	Officers	Non Officers	Total
1949	na	na	80
1950	29	529	558
1951	42	1084	1126
1952	56	1466	1522
1953	66	1984	2050
1954	66	2316	2382
1955	81	2872	2953
1956	93	3559	3652
1957	99	4206	4305
1958	135	5024	5159
1959	158	5593	5751
1960	186	6589	6775
1961	254	7498	7752
1962	274	8128	8402
1963	339	8926	9265
1964	377	9695	10,072
1965	417	10,354	10,771
1966	441	11,143	11,584
1967	491	12,048	12,539
1968	527	12,378	12,905
1969	548	12,879	13,427
1970	658	13,211	13,869
1971	701	13,641	14,342

Table 7.1: *Contd./-*

Year	Officers	Non Officers	Total
1972	726	14,090	14,816
1973	838	15,035	15,873
1974	948	15,623	16,571
1975	1127	15,951	17,078
1976	1174	16,651	17,825
1977	1318	17,035	18,353
1978	1440	17,615	19,055
1979	1611	17,767	19,378
1980	1744	17,752	19,496
1981	1697	16,921	18,618
1982	1849	16,526	18,375
1983	2156	16,009	18,165
1984	2227	16,018	18,245
1985	2259	15,816	18,075
1986	2447	15,614	18,061
1987	2712	15,299	18,011
1988	2703	14,603	17,306
1989	2766	14,047	16,813
1990	2712	13,782	16,494
1991	2883	13,037	15,920
1992	2886	11,153	14,039
1993	3129	10,280	13,409
1994	3055	9472	12,527
1995	2761	8662	11,423
1996	2532	7826	10,358
1997	2921	6635	9556
1998	2842	6038	8880
1999	2799	5451	8250
2000	2723	5174	7897
2001	2554	4668	7222
2002	1942	3743	5685
2003	1522	3023	4545

Source: ITI Personnel Department.

Throughout this period of three decades, the workforce registered a growth every year without exception. Only from 1981 onwards when the first wave of retirements got underway and restrictions imposed on recruitment, did the numbers proceed to decline, before shrinking drastically during the 1990s under the impact of a voluntary retirement scheme.[5] While about a quarter of the sample population arrived in the 1950s, another 28 per cent joined in the 1960s, close to 37 per cent in the 1970s, 6 per cent in the 1980s and under 1 per cent in the 1990s (Table 7.2). These figures bear a rough equivalence with the evolutions in the strength of the workforce at the Bangalore plant.

Table 7.2: Sample Population by Entry Year

Entry Year	Frequency
1948–58	281
	(24.89)
1959–68	323
	(28.61)
1969–78	433
	(38.35)
1979–88	84
	(7.44)
1989–98	8
	(0.71)
Total	1129
	(100)

Note: Figures in brackets are percentages.

It is worth record here that in distinct contrast to certain other public sector plants, notably in the steel sector (Bhilai, Rourkela, etc.) where cheap, un-unionized and insecure contract workers have been increasingly replacing regular employees, ITI has refrained from adopting such low road labour practices.[6] The shop floor has by and large remained the

[5] Whereas the recruitment of non-officers totalled 4064 people between 1975–79 alone, the numbers plummeted to 1209 employees between 1980-89, and then to 179 between 1991-2001. (*Source:* ITI Personnel Dept.)

[6] In the case of Bhilai see Parry, 'Proletarian Vanguard?'; for Rourkela see Christian Strümpell, 'Industrial Restructuring and Tribal Resistance in Contemporary Rourkela,

preserve of permanent operatives partly because, backed by union representatives, they fought to keep this space their own with an eye to protecting incentive payment levels.[7] Partly because with the introduction of capital-intensive electronic exchanges in the second half of the 1980s, the management struggled to ensure adequate work loads even for regular workers, let alone think of bringing in temporary ones.

This said, the company did rely on a cost-saving stratagem. For a period of two decades from the mid-1960s to the mid-1980s, to smoothen out work flows, shop bosses in some departments tended to farm out low-skilled labour intensive assembly operations to what were euphemistically called 'cooperatives'. Three such entities were established in close proximity to the factory and placed directly under company control with its personnel manning all supervisory and managerial posts. Staffed exclusively by women who in most cases were dependents (wives, daughters, widows, and even mothers) of ITI employees, they obviously enjoyed none of the advantages available to their male kin by way of good wages, welfare provisions, virtual lifetime tenure, union representation and the like. On a few occasions to meet rush orders for products like telephones, some of the women also worked inside the factory but apparently not alongside regular staff. Opposition from the latter aside, top management too disapproved of these practices due to its 'unwanted consequences, labour laws etc.'.[8] Hence under the guise of disinterested benevolence the cooperatives provided the company access to a pool of cheap, reliable and docile labour.[9] However, by the end of

Orissa', paper presented at the conference, 'Neoliberal Crises in Post-Reform India: Ethnographic Perspectives on Agrarian and Industrial Distress', Max Planck Institute for Social Anthropology, Hälle, 24-25 September 2009. A similar dynamic of informalization with respect to the private sector is discussed in Andrew Sanchez's interesting study of Tata Motors. 'Deadwood and Paternalism: Rationalising Casual Labour in an Indian Company Town', paper presented at the conference, 'Neoliberal Crises in Post-Reform India'.

[7] Shop officials I interviewed at the telephone division, for example, openly acknowledged that fear of worker and union protest was what dissuaded them from deploying cheaper and more conscientious contract workers in particular for tasks requiring stringent quality standards.

[8] Note from Chief Financial Manager, 22 December 1989.

[9] Labour charges for assembling a telephone inhouse amounted to Rs 9.79, whereas the same task could be done for as little as Rs 2.80 by the cooperatives. This gives us an idea of the significant cost economies the company could realize. Tel. Divn. note, Ref. PPC-T/18, 23 April 1986.

the 1980s, an empty order book meant that only one of the three cooperatives continued to function and that too at half pace. Further, going by the sources on hand, it would appear that even when their capacities were utilized optimally, their total strength seldom exceeded 400 women. Once again resistance from factory operatives to soft incentive jobs going out is likely to have dissuaded the management from expanding the scale of the cooperatives' activities.

In the case of non-production operations too, the company adhered to a fairly identical strategy. Recourse to the services of peripheral workers to undertake construction work and other manual tasks within the factory premises and the township was not uncommon. According to the management, on average they obtained between 20–25 days of employment every month—an assertion contested by the union—and were entitled to coverage under the Provident Fund Scheme. The figures are incomplete, but ITI does not seem to have pressed vast armies of casuals into service. Despite doubling in size over a period of six years, in January 1972, there were no more than 644 such workers as against a regular workforce approaching 15,000 people.[10] Prodded both by union pressure and persistent individual demands, the management also embarked at periodic intervals on 'decasualization' drives destined to induct some of the more long-serving casual hands onto the permanent rolls of the factory. Thus in 1978 alone, 300 of them received standard contacts.[11]

Casualization progressively morphed into contractualization from the early 1990 onwards, once voluntary retirement began depleting the strength of certain indirect departments such as the canteen, hospital and security. To fill these posts, the company turned to labour contractors. Both central and state government regulations proscribed the use of contract labour in sweeping, cleaning, nursing and security jobs.[12] Similarly, in 1996, the Supreme Court made it mandatory for companies deploying contract workers in prohibited areas to absorb them. Although, ITI refused to comply with these injunctions, they nevertheless had a dissuasive effect with the size of the contract pool being scaled down.

[10] Personnel Department note. Hereafter PD note.
[11] Minutes management-union meeting, 18 November 1978.
[12] The notification issued by the central government forbidding central public sector enterprises to hire contract labour in certain areas dated back to December 1976 itself. In April 1997, the Karnataka government issued a ruling quite similar in nature.

From roughly 600 in 1997, the number contracted by half in the year 2000.

Our analysis of the morphology of the ITI labour force also diverges from the sociological surveys in that it depends exclusively on information gathered from individual personnel files maintained by the company rather than on questionnaires and/or formal interview schedules.[13] A proverbial treasure trove for scholars, shedding light on the entire career of a worker from the time of entering the factory to the date of retirement, these records contain two types of information which we may broadly designate as sociological and professional in content. These details such as birth dates, educational qualifications, caste and job experience contained in the personnel files require to be supported by officially certified documents, which are cross-checked by the management. One could state, therefore, that they constitute a relatively more reliable source of information in comparison with the formal interview and questionnaire techniques where the risk of observer bias influencing respondents' answers can hardly be discounted.[14]

Geographical origins: One striking feature about the origins of our sample population is that 40 per cent of the employees could claim local and urban roots, having been born in Bangalore (Table 7.3).[15] Further reinforcing this local hue, not only did three out of four employees come from within Karnataka for the period as a whole, albeit significant variations from one decade to the next, the majority of them were born

[13] Our survey relies on an unstratified systematic random sample where every fifth personnel file for a given year was selected.

[14] The example of Kannan backs our contention about the relative reliability of our source material. An electrician in the machine maintenance shop, he was asked by the personnel department to furnish an education certificate. After several reminders, he replied that he had returned to his home town to try and get the document from his school only to discover that it had closed down. A few weeks later, the company informed Kannan that after verification it had learnt the school continued to exist, and since he had failed to produce formal proof of his qualifications he was being classified as 'uneducated'. Personnel File 3019.

[15] Rejecting as 'myth' the notion of the rural origins of Indian factory workers, Sharma has argued, on the basis of five studies conducted between 1957–69, that 47 to 73 per cent of the workforces surveyed are drawn from an urban milieu. 'Myths and Realities'. A similar opinion was voiced by the National Commission on Labour which affirmed that 'industrial work had ceased to be the monopoly of migrants from villages'. *Report of the National Commission on Labour*, New Delhi, 1969, pp. 31–4 (cit. p. 31). (Hereafter *NCL Report*.)

in what could be called the natural hinterland of Bangalore, the southern maidans. The six districts constituting the maidans (Bangalore district, Chitradurga, Kolar, Mandya, Mysore and Tumkur), and situated within a radius of 200 kms from Bangalore, accounted for over 80 per cent of the sample which while originating from the state were not 'natives' of the capital city (Table 7.3). So whatever intra-state migration that occurred to tap the job openings in ITI was essentially short distance in character.[16]

Even the remaining quarter of the sample whose birthplaces were located outside Karnataka did not have to travel from very far afield. All but 1 per cent of the employees belonged to the three neighbouring southern states with Tamil Nadu heading the list (12 per cent), followed by Andhra and Kerala (6 per cent each) (Table 7.3). This confirms the findings of an important study conducted in the early 1970s which contended that Bangalore's attraction as a metropolitan growth pole did not exceed a macro-regional perimeter.[17]

Moreover, residents from Tamil Nadu and, to a smaller extent, Andhra Pradesh, migrated in the main from districts contiguous to Karnataka and which had a long tradition of sending unemployed youth to Bangalore in search of work.[18] In the case of Tamil Nadu, one out of three people in the sample was born in North Arcot district. The salience of the premise, commonly advanced by social scientists, that the pull factors propelling migratory projects 'do not operate randomly but rather apply only to specific destinations', distinguished by the presence of kin or friendship networks and access to information about potential employment

[16] This point has already been highlighted with reference to the colonial era: even in the absence of long-distance migration of the kind that distinguished other major industrial centres like Bombay and Calcutta, employers in Bangalore encountered few problems in securing cheap and plentiful supplies of labour. *Report of the Labour Investigation Committee*, New Delhi, 1958, pp. 68–9; Nair, *Miners and Millhands*, pp. 192–3.

[17] In Rao and Tiwari's ambitious survey, conducted in 1973–74, of 1000 family heads residing in Bangalore, 58 per cent of the immigrants came from Karnataka, 21 per cent from Tamil Nadu, 8 per cent each from Andhra and Kerala, and only 4 per cent from the rest of the country. V.L.S. Prakasa Rao and V.K. Tiwari, *The Structure of an Indian Metropolis. A Study of Bangalore*, New Delhi, pp. 245–54.

[18] According to Simmons, migrants from North Arcot, Salem and Chittoor also constituted a significant proportion of the labour force at the Kolar gold mines. Colin Simmons, 'The Creation and Organization of a Proletarian Mining Labour Force in India. The Case of the Kolar Gold Fields, 1883–1955', in M. Holmström (ed.), *Work for Wages in South Asia*, New Delhi, 1990, p. 76.

Table 7.3: Birthplace by Entry Year

Entry Year	Un-known	B'lore	B'lore District	Southern Maidans	Other Karnataka	Andhra	Tamil Nadu	Kerala	Other	Total
1948–58	0	128 (45.55)	19 (6.76)	54 (19.22)	7 (2.49)	8 (2.85)	47 (16.73)	13 (4.63)	5 (1.78)	281 (100)
1959–68	3 (0.93)	112 (34.67)	21 (6.50)	54 (16.72)	21 (6.50)	17 (5.26)	54 (16.72)	37 (11.46)	4 (1.24)	323 (100)
1969–78	0	173 (39.95)	42 (9.70)	106 (24.48)	26 (6.00)	37 (8.55)	31 (7.16)	15 (3.46)	3 (0.69)	433 (100)
1979–88	0	41 (48.81)	9 (10.71)	12 (14.29)	7 (8.33)	6 (7.14)	5 (5.95)	4 (4.76)	0	84 (100)
1989–98	0	2 (25)	0	3 (37.5)	1 (12.5)	1 (12.5)	1 (12.5)	0	0	8 (100)
Total	3 (0.27)	456 (40.39)	91 (8.06)	229 (20.28)	62 (5.49)	69 (6.11)	138 (12.22)	69 (6.11)	12 (1.06)	1129 (100)

Notes: Figures in brackets are percentages.
All tables presenting the results of the multivariate analysis have been conduced with the SAS programme.

opportunities and other such crucial life issues, is fully borne out by the following quotation.[19] Born in Jolarpet, an important railway town in North Arcot district, Krishnan who joined ITI in 1963 explains that

most of the Tamil workers in ITI are from North Arcot. So through friends I knew there was a job opening in ITI and that an advertisement (released by the company) had appeared in *Deccan Herald*. Over 20 of my classmates from Jolarpet had joined ITI. At that time the passenger train from Jolarpet to Bangalore used to take about five hours and we could get down at KR Puram station (very close to where ITI is located).[20]

In other words, migration was not merely a function of economic distress at home, but also the awareness of outside job opportunities which was much stronger in North Arcot than in South Arcot for various reasons.[21]

In the case of migrants from Andhra, the influence of specific labour catchment areas was even more pronounced: two out of three employees in our sample came from the districts of Nellore (49 per cent) and Chittoor (19 per cent). Equally significant, this spatial clustering or segmentation intersected with a caste and occupational clustering. All but two of the 34 workers born in Nellore district belonged to 'Untouchable'[22] communities (Adi Andhra), and all but one of them were hired by ITI for menial tasks such as sweeping and cleaning or as labourers.[23] If the practice of reserving dirty work for 'outcastes' is hardly

[19] D.W. Anthony, 'Migration in Archeology: The Baby and the Bathwater', Vol. 92, No. 4, *American Anthropologist*, 1990, pp. 895–914 (cit. p. 899).

[20] Interview with Krishnan.

[21] Joseph Schwartzberg, 'Occupational Structure and level of Economic Development in India: A Regional Analysis', Monograph No. 4, Census of India 1961, New Delhi, pp. 141–2.

[22] Although a bureaucratic coinage, we have preferred to employ the term of Scheduled Caste, and/or 'Untouchable', more neutral 'but not value free while evocative of the conditions' of these groups, instead of that of Dalit given its strong political colouring. Oliver Mendelsohn and Marika Vicziany, *The Untouchables. Subordination, Poverty, and the State*, Cambridge, 1998, p. 2.

[23] Exclusive practices leading to the concentration of certain factory occupations in the hands of a particular caste or ethnic or religious grouping is not an uncommon occurrence. For details, see Chitra Joshi, 'Kanpur Textile Labour. Some Structural Features', *EPW*, Vol. XVI, Nos. 44–46, November 1981, pp. 1823–38; Arjan de Haan, 'Unsettled Settlers, Migrant Workers and Industrial Capitalism in Calcutta', *Modern Asian Studies*, Vol. 31, No. 4, 1997, pp. 919–49; Heuzé, *Ouvriers d'un autre monde*, pp. 237–8. Nor is such clustering the appanage of 'backward' countries like India, as Tamara Hareven and Randolph Langenbach have documented in their study of a New England

surprising, the fact that these occupations were monopolized to a large extent by one ethnic grouping attests to the important role played by kinship or friendship connections in providing information about job openings in the company.

What does a correlation of the data pertaining to workers' birthplaces with their year of entry into ITI tell us about evolutions in the morphology of the workforce and company hiring policies? Focussing first on the structure of the workforce, we find that Bangalore-born workers constituted the single largest group in all years (Table 7.3). Barring the 1990s, a non-representative period anyway, their share consistently stood above 34 per cent, though inter-decade fluctuations can be observed. A similar uneven movement is visible as far as workers from the southern maidans are concerned. The upshot of these shifts and swings was that employees originating from Karnataka, after having made up almost three-fourth of the total sample workforce during the 1950s, saw their share drop to around 64 per cent during the 1960s and then grow to 80 per cent in the next decade for reasons shall we examine.

Other inter-generational variations also emerge. Employees in our sample from the maidan areas recruited in the 1950s and 1960s came in the main either from the neighbouring Bangalore district, or from cities which had an industrial base like Mysore or KGF, or from agriculturally depressed districts like Kolar (Table 7.4). Migrants from the other, and more advanced, agrarian districts such as Mandya, Tumkur and Hassan were distinctly in the minority to begin with. The trend reversed somewhat in the 1970s.

Even as the flow from the traditional catchment areas such as Bangalore, Kolar and Mysore districts did not slacken, equally there was a significant increase in intake from the other districts. One could speculate that many of these employees were the children of peasants, beneficiaries of the green revolution that areas like Mandya and Tumkur witnessed. Indeed, leaving aside Bangalore district, more members of the maidan population who entered ITI in 1970s cited agriculture as their father's occupation, more than for any other section of our sample.

The completion of the construction of the Krishnarajasagar Dam over the Cauvery river by 1956, by introducing canal irrigation facilities

---

textile mill. *Amoskeag. Life and Work in an American Factory City*, New York, 1978, p. 127, 229–31.

Table 7.4: Birthplace Southern Maidans

Birthplace	cohort 1950s	cohort 1960s	cohort 1970s	cohort 1980–90s	Total population
Bangalore district	19	21	42	9	91 (28.4)
Chitradurga	3	3	5	1	12 (3.7)
Hassan	2	3	11	1	17 (5.3)
Kolar dist.+KGF	23	24	42	6	95 (29.7)
Mandya	1	2	15	1	19 (5.9)
Mysore	19	20	16	1	56 (17.5)
Tumkur	7	2	17	4	30 (9.4)
Total	73	75	148	24	320 (100)

Note: Figures in brackets are percentages.

indispensable for the cultivation of cash crops such as sugar cane and paddy, had contributed in no small measure to the prosperity of the land-owning sections of the rural population. Included in 1962 in the all-India Intensive Agricultural District Programme, aimed at maximizing agricultural production, Mandya also witnessed a tremendous expansion in both public and privately-funded educational institutions at all levels.[24]

These macro-level developments are clearly reflected in the improved educational standards of our cohort. The number of employees from these areas equipped with technical qualifications rose almost three fold from about 22 per cent in the 1960s to 60 per cent in the following decade. In fact, individuals in our sample who came from a rural

[24] For details, see T.S. Epstein, *South India: Yesterday, Today and Tomorrow. Mysore Villages Revisited*, London, 1973, pp. 72–5. On the economic and social impact of the advent of canal irrigation in the Mandya region, see Epstein's earlier study, *Economic Development and Social Change in South India*, Manchester, 1962; and Frédéric Landy, *Paysans de l'Inde du sud. Le choix et la contrainte*, Paris, 1994.

background possessed better educational and technical credential than those born in worker households. Having invested in the education of at least one of their male offspring as part of the overall family life course strategy, better-off farmers now aspired to fructify this capital by sending their sons to the cities to find employment, preferably in the government or in state-owned companies where the promise of exclusive job rights and the attached prestige could redound to the advantage of the employee on the matrimonial market.[25]

In this quest for upward mobility, contingency too played a decisive role, such as events on the political landscape. For as we shall study in depth in chapter nine, the increase in the proportion of employees recruited from the maidan districts in the 1970s can be attributed to the upshot of the linguistic agitation that gripped Bangalore from the late 1960s onwards. This in turn led to state government authorities exerting pressure upon public sector managements to privilege 'sons of the soil' when filling up vacancies for unskilled and semi-skilled jobs Thus, four out of five workers recruited during the 1970s in our sample were born in Karnataka (Table 7.3).

Further confirmation of the nativist orientation to hiring policies is provided when we study the evolution in the strength of our non-local population. Two contrary movements emerge. On the one hand, there is a significant diminution in the proportion of employees originating from Tamil Nadu and Kerala, the two main outside linguistic groupings accused of depriving local Kannada youth of employment opportunities and against whom much of the hostility crystallized, though Keralites were generally less subject to vilification than Tamilians. Whereas 17 per cent of the workforce recruited in the 1950s and 1960s was from Tamil Nadu, this figure was cut by more than two in the 1970s and again fell in the following decade (Table 7.3). Likewise, in the case of employees from Kerala, their numbers while growing almost three-fold to 11 per

[25] As Landy has shown in his stimulating study of rural migratory strategies in three Mandya villages, one 'wet', two 'dry', investment in educational capital held the strongest appeal for groups situated at polar ends of the caste and class hierarchy, dominant Vokkaliga farmers and landless 'Untouchable' families, though not for quite the same reasons. Frédéric Landy, 'Migration et enracinement dans le Maidan', in J.L. Racine (ed.), *Les attaches de l'homme. Enracinement paysan et logiques migratoires en Inde du sud*, Paris, 1994, pp. 79–141.

cent between 1959–68 dropped to less than 4 per cent a decade later before rising marginally by one point in the 1980s (Table 7.3).

On the other hand, no such shrinkage affected those in our sample born in Andhra. Not regarded as outsiders by the local Kannada population, given the cultural affinities between the two communities, the share of Andhra employees registered a progressive increase and crossed the eight per cent mark in the 1970s. Even in the 1980s, they comprised about 7 per cent of our sample workforce (Table 7.3). What we then witness over time is a narrowing down rather than a diversification of the principal migratory areas from where our non-local population originated. In sum, the fact that the numerical strength of employees recruited either from Bangalore itself or from within Karnataka increased rather than decreased over time for political and other reasons, clearly demonstrated their success in controlling access to the most prized industrial occupations on the labour market.

Linguistic orgins: Given the sharp cleavages running through the workforce in the aftermath of the clashes pitting Kannada workers against Tamil workers (cf. chap. nine), the linguistic background of the labour force represents a determining variable. Given the numerical weight of Karnataka-born employees in our survey, native Kannada speakers predictably enough were the largest linguistic entity, making up 45 per cent of the population (Table 7.5).[26] Tamil speakers came next (31 per cent), followed by Telegu speakers (11 per cent) and then Malayalis (6 per cent). Moreover, with the exception of the 1950s when a slightly higher proportion of Tamilians could be found, the hegemony of the Kannadigas went unchallenged in the later periods. In the 1970s, for instance, they outnumbered Tamil employees more than two to one.

At the same time, the non-negligible presence of Kannada speakers, originating from different parts of the state, from the very inception of ITI challenges the popular essentialist representation portraying the local Kannadiga as bound to his peasant moorings and loath to take up industrial occupation. This interpretation may have been valid for the colonial epoch. By alleviating the pressure on rural resources, the broad-based patterns of land distribution prevalent in the old princely state of Mysore translated into fewer landless labourers and in turn reduced the

---

[26] In Holmström's random sample, Kannada speakers accounted for 42 per cent of the population. *South Indian Factory Workers*, p. 25.

Table 7.5: Entry Year by Mother Tongue

Entry Year	Unknown	Kannada	Tamil	Telegu	Malayalam	Other	Total
1948–58	7	106	113	33	10	12	281
	(2.49)	(37.72)	(40.21)	(11.74)	(3.56)	(4.27)	(100)
1959–68	4	119	106	33	40	21	323
	(1.24)	(36.84)	(32.82)	(10.22)	(12.38)	(6.50)	(100)
1969–78	3	234	106	55	16	19	433
	(0.69)	(54.04)	(24.48)	(12.70)	(3.70)	(4.39)	(100)
1979–88	0	42	30	8	3	1	84
		(50)	(35.71)	(9.52)	(3.57)	(1.19)	(7.44)
1989–98	0	4	2	1	1	0	8
		(50)	(25)	(12.5)	(12.5)		(100)
Total	14	505	357	130	70	53	1129
	(1.24)	(44.73)	(31.62)	(11.51)	(6.20)	(4.69)	(100)

Note: Figures in brackets are percentages.

necessity for local inhabitants to migrate to urban centres in search of work. But the situation definitely appears to have evolved in the wake of Independence. Far from being allegedly incapable of enduring the hardships and disciplinary constraints imposed by the factory regime, Kannada speaking employees were no less enthusiastic than any other group in seizing valued opportunities for economic and social advancement that a permanent job in the newly created public sector enterprises offered them. As we shall see, they were also the best educated group, boasting the highest proportion of college graduates, the technically most qualified group, the best placed group in the occupational hierarchy, and, if house ownership is an index of wealth, the most affluent group. In other words, more than any other section of the workforce, it was the local Kannadigas who exemplified a labour aristocracy.

The fact that the preponderant majority of our sample came from Karnataka did not, however, imply that all were Kannada speakers. On the contrary, more than a third of all those born in Bangalore were Tamil speakers. Or to put it differently, a greater number of Tamil speaking employees were born within the frontiers of Karnataka than in Tamil Nadu, clearly underscoring their right to be designated as insiders. Likewise, over one in three Telegu speakers mentioned Bangalore as their birthplace. Inversely, testifying as much to the linguistic heterogeneity of Bangalore as to the relatively 'subordinate' status of Kannada in the state capital, only 40 per cent of our total Kannadiga population originated from the city. Indeed, Kannada speaking employees born in Bangalore outnumbered their Tamil speaking counterparts only during the 1960s and 1970s. In the other periods, they were in the minority.

Gender composition: We have already commented on the relative incongruity of ITI's position where it relied on an essentially masculine labour force to manufacture products sexually stereotyped as female work by most of its competitors. Although statistics for the previous years are unavailable, in 1976, the company counted barely 687 women, or under 4 per cent of the total factory strength of 17,929 employees. Of these just over a third worked directly as operatives. By the year 2000, not only had the overall number of women declined to 530, but less than 90 women could be found on the shop floor.[27]

Moreover, a petition signed collectively by 42 women operatives in November 1986 sheds light on the discrimination they suffered. Although most of them had been doing assembly jobs for several years, following a measure enacted by the company at the bidding of the union, they were redeployed virtually overnight as labourers, and their posts occupied by male labourers who enjoyed greater seniority. Complaining bitterly that they lacked the strength of their male counterparts to load and transport materials on trolleys from one department to another, the women added that, since many were widows and hence obliged to singlehandedly assume the burden of child caring, performing extra manual work in the factory will now only 'make our life (at home) more miserable'.[28] But the management does not appear to have reversed its decision.

Why did ITI carry so few women on its rolls, although at least one senior executive acknowledged that a bigger female contingent would have considerably facilitated the task of enforcing disciplinary controls?[29] As in the case of the textile and jute industry, the factory legislation

[27] PD files.

[28] PD files, petition dated 11 November 1986.

[29] Interview with D. Subramanyam. Anecdotal evidence suggests that notwithstanding the regulatory constraints, BEL, another Bangalore-based public sector unit also specializing in electronic products, employed a bigger female contingent than ITI. This is even more true for private firms like BPL which directly competed with ITI in areas such as telephone manufacture in the post-liberalization era.

restricting the hours of work for women seems to have functioned as the principal deterrent.[30] In addition, women were also perceived as unreliable and costly on account of their reproductive roles, being frequently absent and taking maternity leave 'without any limitations as to the number of times it can be avail of (sic)' during which period the company had to pay their wages even as it had to find and train replacements.[31] Indeed, in order to avoid having to concede maternity benefits at all, company standing orders initially stipulated that only unmarried women and widows 'without encumbrances' would be eligible for employment.[32] Bowing to union pressure, the company later expunged this clause. However, when replying to the National Commission of Labour enquiry in 1967, it put forth two recommendations: greater flexibility with respect to working hours of women, and restricting maternity benefits to 'not more than 2 or 3 times upto superannuation'.[33] One could also advance the hypothesis that this policy of restricting women's participation in the labour force was congruent with the 'ideology of the single male earner'.[34] Public sector workers, after all, comprised a labour aristocracy in the fullest sense of the term. Paid good wages in return for moderate effort levels, endowed with generous welfare measures, promised virtually a lifetime tenure, benefiting from the prestige associated with employment in a government firm—all these status-enhancing attributes which could be parlayed outside the factory sphere into supplementary monetary and symbolic rewards went to make a job in an enterprise such as ITI one of

[30] For details, see, *inter alia*, Leela Fernandes, *Producing Workers. The Politics of Gender, Class, and Culture in the Calcutta Jute Mills*, Philadelphia, 1997, pp. 52–3; Joshi, 'Kanpur Textile Labour'; Arjan de Haan, 'Towards a Single Male Earner: The Decline of Child and Female Employment in an Indian Industry', *Economic and Social History in the Netherlands*, Vol. 6, 1994, pp. 145–67; Morris, *Emergence of an Industrial Labor Force*, pp. 65–8; Uma Ramaswamy, *Work, Union and Community*, p. 25.

[31] Replies to National Commission on Labour questionnaire, 1967 (PD files). See also interview with Y. Munnuswamy.

[32] PD circular no. 107, 10 February 1954.

[33] Reply to National Commission on Labour questionnaire.

[34] de Haan, 'Towards a Single Male Earner'. The salience of this ideology in other socio-historical contexts too has been ably demonstrated by several women historians. See, for example, Kathleen Canning, 'Gender and the Politics of Class Formation: Rethinking German Labor History', *The American Historical Review*, Vol. 97, No. 3, June 1992, pp. 736–68; and Sonya Rose, 'Gender at Work. Sex, Class and Industrial Capitalism', *History Workshop Journal*, No. 21, Spring 1986, pp. 113–31. I am grateful to Samita Sen for urging me to pursue this point.

the most coveted positions on the labour market. Employees' reluctance to leave this 'citadel of security and relative prosperity' once they had secured a foothold is reflected both in the extremely low turnover rates and the longevity of service recorded in our survey.[35] Not only did most persons remain on the company rolls until retirement or death, but two out of three members of our population who quit had put in a service of 20 years or more, and close to one out of two could boast of a presence in excess of 30 years.[36]

The concept of a labour aristocracy has at all times and places been anything but gender neutral. On the contrary, at its core stood the adult male worker whose trade and skills generated the material resources required to provide for the entire family's needs. If men backed by their unions took the intiative in preventing women from competing for these highly-valued occupations, employer complicity was also indispensable in facilitating exclusionary strategies of this kind from achieving their ends. That such occupations came to be earmarked as a male preserve in the public sector too is a possibility scholars can afford to overlook only at their own risk. Nevertheless, going by the example of ITI this appears to have been accomplished less at the behest of workers and their representatives than of company officials whose habitus is likely to have persuaded them to subscribe to the upper-caste and middle class ideology restricting women's mobility to the household. References to the sexual immorality of female factory hands, and the importance, consequently, of insulating women from such social perils by placing industrial work beyond their purview, regularly dotted official reports.[37] The power of this moralizing discourse in shaping managerial mindsets and, in turn, corporate policies, must not be under-estimated.

By promoting the ideal of a male-dominated labour force, managements then sought to simultaneously realize two interlinked objectives, both of which embodied a resolutely paternalistic logic. On the one hand, it helped to preserve patriarchal authority by reinforcing the distribution of traditional gender roles within the working class

---

[35] Holmström, *South Indian Factory Workers*, p. 137.

[36] Over half the respondents (56.9 per cent) in Arya's survey expressed no desire to shift to another company, least of all to a private firm, while four out of five persons said they would advise their friends and relatives to join ITI because of the job security and welfare benefits it offered. *Labour Management Relations*, p. 54, 65.

[37] Samita Sen, 'Gender and Class: Women in Indian Industry, 1890–1990'.

household. There was no possibility of contesting the male worker's preeminent position as sole breadwinner. On the other, it allowed the paterfamilias, guaranteed as he was of a 'family' wage, to discharge his responsibilities of upholding the honour of women members by discharging them from the obligation of having to seek outside wage employment. Since they eschewed all contact with other men, their honour would not be compromised.[38] 'Dependent domesticity' which signified confining women to the home in their sexually stereotyped roles of wife and mother thus was the condition upon which rested the family's claims to respectability.[39]

The notions of honour and respectability as articulated in this context, it must be stressed, were a wholly masculine construction with women being reduced to passive subjects in need of male protection from the threat of sexual abuse. Indeed, our sources reveal that several of the women who entered ITI's ranks were widows. Wives of employees who had died in service, they had been recruited on what the company termed compassionate grounds. In other words, they belonged precisely to that category wherein the male breadwinner was no longer present to safeguard their honour.[40]

The gender bias defining the composition of the ITI workforce finds an eloquent echo in our sample. Women employees made up barely 3 per cent of our population. Their demographic and social characteristics, however, betray few divergences from those of their male counterparts. Of local origin for the most part, over a third of them were born in Bangalore, while another third came from the rest of Karnataka (Table 7.6). The majority (45 per cent) were also Kannada speakers. Can we

---

[38] Skilled Hindu and Muslim textile workers in Bombay, Chandavarkar affirms, prided themselves on the fact that their womenfolk were not constrained to work, female employment in the mills connoting low status. Rajnarayan Chandavarkar, *Origins of Industrial Capitalism in India, Business Strategies and the Working Classes in Bombay, 1900–1940*, New Delhi, 1994, p. 99, 225. A similar argument is advanced by Samita Sen with respect to the Bengal jute mills. 'At the Margins: Women Workers in the Bengal Jute Industry', in *Worlds of Indian Industrial Labour*, pp. 239–69. See also Gyan Pandey, 'Rallying Around the Cow. Sectarian Strife in the Bhojpuri Region, c. 1888–1917', *Subaltern Studies*, Vol. II, New Delhi, 1986, pp. 60–129.

[39] Sen, 'Gender and Class', p. 84.

[40] Widows also appear to have represented a non-negligible proportion of the female workforce in the Kanpur textile mills as well as the Bengal jute mills. For Kanpur, see Joshi, *Lost Worlds*, pp. 112–13; for Bengal, see Sen, 'At the Margins'.

Table 7.6: Women Workers' Birthplace, Mother Tongue

Birthplace	Female pop.	Mother Tongue	Female pop.
Bangalore	13 (36.11)	Kannadiga	16 (44.45)
Other Karnataka	12 (33.33)	Tamil	10 (27.77)
Other	11 (30.55)	Other	10 (27.77)
Total	36 (100)	Total	36 (100)

Note: Figures in brackets are percentages.

conclude from these details that no stigma was attached to Kannadiga women enrolling for factory jobs, even during the early years of ITI's existence? It would fly in the face of the notion, commonly articulated by Kannadiga men in particular, that to start with, all the women workers were Tamilians and Anglo-Indians, i.e., 'outsiders' and of a lower social status, and hence fit to take up industrial work where they had perforce to mingle with men?[41]

Caste composition: Statistics pertaining to the caste identities of employees is, predictably enough, restricted to the SC and ST. Even this information was not systematically collected until the mid-1950s with the job application forms carrying no mention of this issue. From the early 1990s, classification of employees belonging to the other backward castes also became obligatory. The SC and ST employees are slightly over represented in our sample comprising just under 22 per cent of the population. Their strength in the factory proportionate to the total workforce started exceeding 20 per cent only from the early 1980s onwards when recruitment had decreased. In 1988, for instance, the ratio of SC-STs to caste Hindus stood at 1:4.

The geographic origins of our SC population shows no divergence from the other sections of the workforce. While nearly three out of four SC-STs mentioned Karnataka as their birthplace, over 40 per cent came from Bangalore. Of those originating from outside the state, the overwhelming majority belonged to Andhra Pradesh (Table 7.7). But

[41] Interviews with S. Krishna, 12 February 1999; and Srinivasa Rao.

Table 7.7: SC-ST Workers' Birthplace, Mother Tongue

Birthplace	SC-ST pop.	Mother Tongue	SC-ST pop.
Bangalore	107 (43.67)	Tamil	104 (42.45)
Other Karnataka	70 (28.57)	Kannada	77 (31.43)
Andhra	49 (20)	Telegu	63 (25.71)
Other	19 (7.75)	Other	1 (0.41)
Total	245 (100)	Total	245 (100)

Note: Figures in brackets are percentages

contrary to the dominant trend, Tamil speakers (42 per cent) constituted by far the single biggest linguistic grouping, followed by Kannadigas (31 per cent), and then Telegus (26 per cent). The prominence of Tamil SC in our sample reflects in all likelihood the heritage of the colonial period when Adi-Dravidas from the former Madras Presidency, attracted by the employment opportunities, flocked to Bangalore and the KGF mines.[42] Of the 49 employees in our sample born in KGF, no doubt in mining families, 23 were Tamil SC-STs.

The group with the lowest levels of educational and technical qualification, as we shall see later, SC-ST persons predictably enough were heavily over-represented in the bottom-most strata of the occupational hierarchy—a conclusion also arrived at by all the sociological surveys conducted in the past on industrial workers. The inferior status of the jobs performed by them is thrown into full relief when we examine the occupations they filled in our sample. Not only were most of the sweepers SC-STs, and of Adi Andhra origin, the lowest community in the caste hierarchy in Karnataka, but one out of five SC-STs worked as a sweeper (Table 7.8).

Another 30 per cent provided portable muscle power on the shop floor and in the shipping department, or executed menial jobs in-non

[42] Nair, *Millhands and Miners*, p. 25; Simmons, 'Creation and Organisation of a Proletarian Mining Labour Force', p. 82.

Table 7.8: Occupations by Caste

Occupation	Non SC-ST	SC-ST
Learner–Apprentice	216 (24.43)	28 (11.43)
Labourer, Helper, Attender, Packer	139 (15.72)	72 (29.39)
Sweeper	20 (2.26)	52 (21.22)
In Machine Trades	117 (13.24)	26 (10.61)
Toolmaker	78 (8.82)	16 (6.53)
In Electrical Assemby	56 (6.33)	3 (1.22)
Inspector	72 (8.14)	17 (6.94)
Store-keeper, Planner, D-man	92 (10.41)	9 (3.67)
Clerk	92 (10.41)	22 (8.98)
Total	884 (100)	245 (100)

Note: Figures in brackets are percentages.

production areas like the canteen and hospital. Though they accounted for less than 4 per cent of the total in auxiliary occupations such as production planning, store keeping, and draughtsmanship, in inspection and white collar clerical jobs, where a college degree was often mandatory, the share of the SC was more or less comparable with that of the caste Hindus. This suggests that they might have successfully exploited reservation quotas in the field of higher education.

Overall, our findings confirm the position of 'Untouchable' employees as the most disadvantaged group in the factory on all counts. They carried over intact into the realm of work all the enduring deprivations and disabilities afflicting them in the broader societal context. Even though a permanent place within the ranks of organized labour in the public sector citadel represented a non-negligible achievement, and by itself, stood out as an index of upward mobility, their condition inside the factory hardly differed from their condition outside, especially in terms of their stigmatization as 'outcastes' by caste Hindu employees because of the kinds of jobs they performed. While they were no doubt the objects of envy of the vast armies standing outside the walls of the citadel, the lack of educational and technical qualifications condemned them typically to menial and dirty work, and contributed to reinforce their inferior status. Since most SC-ST employees remained rooted in and identified by traditional caste functions, social inequalities tended to be reproduced within the factory setting.[43] The brooms they carried, or the trolleys laden with material or dirty plates they pushed continue to serve as physical markers of their degradation. Employment in a large state-owned enterprise like ITI therefore had the paradoxical effect of simultaneously empowering and disempowering the 'Untouchables', neutralizing their quest for dignity and respectability even as it helped to promote their social and economic uplift.[44]

Educational and technical qualifications: A cross-sectional snapshot of the educational levels of our population presents a picture of a relatively unqualified workforce. Barely 10 per cent of our sample had gone to college and while over a third had passed SSLC, close to 30 per cent had not passed the school leaving exam. In addition, 23 per cent either possessed no formal education or had only studied up to primary school (Table 7.9). Adopting a temporal dimension also does not substantially modify the above image, and belies any simplistic assumptions of an unilinear progression in educational standards from one generation of workers to the next, paralleling the introduction of more sophisticated technological systems by the company.

True, the proportion of employees in our sample without any education posted a dramatic decline, falling from over 30 per cent in the 1950s to under 5 per cent three decades later. Nevertheless, 12 per cent of those recruited in the 1970s still lacked a qualification of any sort. Employees with no more than a primary education certificate also became a rarity by the 1980s. Likewise, the proportion of employees having a PUC degree climbed more than four-fold between the 1950s and 1970s.

---

[43] On the continuity in the occupations performed by 'Untouchables' in urban contexts, see also Robert Deliège, *The Untouchables of India*, Oxford, 1999, pp. 140–45.

[44] A similar argument is posited by Galanter with respect to 'Untouchable' employees in government administrative jobs. Marc Galanter, *Competing Equalities. Law and the Backward Classes in India*, New Delhi, 1984, p. 110.

Table 7.9: Educational Qualifications by Entry Year

Entry Year	No education	Primary	upto SSLC	SSLC	PUC	Degree	Total
1948–58	88	21	62	91	8	11	281
	(31.32)	(7.47)	(22.06)	(32.38)	(2.85)	(3.91)	(100)
1959–68	39	11	108	139	25	1	323
	(12.07)	(3.41)	(33.44)	(43.03)	(7.74)	(0.31)	(100)
1969–78	54	34	135	158	37	15	433
	(12.47)	(7.85)	(31.18)	(36.49)	(8.55)	(3.46)	(100)
1979–88	4	3	31	28	13	5	84
	(4.76)	(3.57)	(36.9)	(33.33)	(15.48)	(5.95)	(100)
1989–98	1	1	1	0	4	1	8
	(12.5)	(12.5)	(12.5)		(50)	(12.5)	(100)
Total	186	70	337	416	87	33	1129
	(16.47)	(6.2)	(29.85)	(36.85)	(7.71)	(2.92)	(100)

Note: Figures in brackets are percentages.

Still, quite surprisingly, the cohort hired in the 1970s turned out to be less qualified than the one that immediately preceded it (Table 7.9). Offsetting this decline, a distinct improvement in the levels of technical qualifications can be observed, as shall be discussed. The management had apparently arrived at the conclusion that as long as employees had studied up to or passed SSLC, the threshold fixed for production operatives, and possessed an industrial trade certificate, higher skills were in no way essential to operate the technologies introduced by the company.

Which linguistic groups did the poorest and best-educated sections of our sample come from? The Telegu speaking population held the lowest credentials. Given the high literacy rates prevailing in Kerala, high school education was also more widespread among Malayalam (90 per cent) and Tamil speaking (73 per cent) employees than among Kannadigas (66 per cent). But this last group contained a much higher proportion of college graduates (16 per cent) as compared to the other linguistic communities. What this implies is that compared with the other groups, more Kannada speakers came from relatively better-off households which could afford to invest in college education.

Matching data concerning educational levels with caste identities produces more or less the expected conclusions (Table 7.10). One out of

Table 7.10: Educational Qualifications by Caste

Educ. Qualif	non SC-ST	SC-ST
No education	104	81
	(11.78)	(33.06)
Primary	56	14
	(6.34)	(5.71)
upto SSLC	249	88
	(28.2)	(35.92)
SSLC	372	44
	(42.13)	(17.96)
PUC	74	13
	(8.38)	(5.31)
Degree	28	5
	(3.17)	(2.04)
Total	883	245
	(100)	(100)

Note: Figures in brackets are percentages.

three SC-ST persons was uneducated as against under 12 per cent for caste Hindus, and if a larger proportion of SC-STs had studied up to SSLC, the proportion of caste Hindus who had graduated from high school (42 per cent) was more than double the figure for SC-STs (18 per cent). But when it came to college education, the disparities between the two groups was slightly less pronounced, suggesting that SC-STs may have been able to benefit somewhat from reservations.

In yet another indication of the ITI workforce's relative lack of qualifications, two out of three people in our population had no technical training. Behind this broad-brush picture, a gradual improvement in standards from one generation to the next, though, can be detected, paralleling the spread of public and privately-funded vocational education institutions throughout the country. While barely 20 per cent of the cohort recruited in the 1950s and 1960s had some sort of technical qualification, the figure climbed to 50 per cent in the following decade before descending to 40 per cent in the 1980s (Table 7.11).

Technical education was most widespread in our sample among the Kannada speakers. They accounted for more than half the total of trained employees with Tamil speakers making up another quarter. In contrast,

Table 7.11: Technical Qualifications by Entry Year

	Nil qualif	*Trade certificate*	*Apprentice*	*Diploma*	*Typing*	*Other*	*Total*
1948–58	222	6	2	15	21	13	279
	(79.57)	(2.15)	(0.72)	(5.38)	(7.53)	(4.66)	(100)
1959–68	267	22	2	15	11	6	323
	(82.66)	(6.81)	(0.62)	(4.64)	(3.41)	(1.86)	(100)
1969–78	217	127	42	19	11	17	433
	(50.12)	(29.33)	(9.7)	(4.39)	(2.54)	(3.93)	(100)
1979–88	52	5	17	2	5	3	84
	(61.9)	(5.95)	(20.24)	(2.38)	(5.95)	(3.57)	(100)
1989–98	4	0	2	0	2	0	8
	(50)		(25)		(25)		(100)
Total	762	160	65	51	50	39	1129
	(67.61)	(14.2)	(5.77)	(4.53)	(4.44)	(3.46)	(100)

Note: Figures in brackets are percentages.

barely 7 per cent of Malayali speakers were equipped with vocational skills, although this group counted the maximum number of high school-educated employees. This tends to corroborate our earlier remarks suggesting that sections of Kannadiga employees belonged to families which commanded greater financial resources than the other linguistic communities to be able to sustain their offspring throughout the duration of the training period which in some cases could extend to four years. Disadvantaged with respect to general education, the SC-ST people received an equally raw deal when it came to technical training (Table 7.12). Of all those in our sample who possessed a specialization, 85 per cent were caste Hindus and barely 15 per cent SCs and STs. Expressed in overall terms, more than one out of three caste Hindus were equipped with vocational skills as opposed to one out of five SC-STs.

Recruitment: In distinct contrast to the findings reported by virtually all sociological studies of industrial workforces in the post-Independence period, the evidence from our sample emphatically shows that the system of recruitment in ITI relied exclusively on formal bureaucratic mechanisms. To ensure fairness and transparency, well-codified selection procedures were instituted by the personnel department almost from the very inception of the company. These procedural norms took the

Table 7.12: Technical Qualifications by Caste

	non SC-ST	SC-ST
Trade Certificate	125 (34.25)	35 (9.59)
Apprentice	60 (19.23)	5 (9.43)
Diploma	48 (15.38)	3 (5.66)
Typing	44 (14.1)	6 (11.32)
Other	35 (11.22)	4 (7.55)
Total	312 (100)	53 (100)

Note: Figures in brackets are percentages.

form of minimum educational qualifications, trade tests, medical examinations, the delivery of a conduct certificate by a gazetted government officer, character verification, and probationary periods. From the early 1960s onwards, even for the lowest ranked production jobs, the management required candidates to have studied upto high school at least and to undergo an aptitude test.[45] Formal educational credentials were dispensed with only for purely menial occupations.

The various steps adopted to vet the character and antecedents of new entrants best illustrated the bureaucratic character of the entire process. Apart from seeking confirmation of past career records from the concerned employer(s) in the case of those claiming previous job experience, the company sent the recruitment file in its totality for verification to the additional district magistrate of the area from where the employee originated, the district police authorities, the police intelligence department in Bangalore, and the local police station in Bangalore where the employee resided. Only after clearing this barrage of checks could the employee hope to be issued with a definitive appointment order.

Thus Gopalan, a machine tender from Kerala, was sacked even before

[45] Note on Recruitment and Promotion in Indian Telephone Industries, 9 April 1963.

completing his probationary period. Police officials from the state had sent a report warning the management that as an active member of the Communist Party, Gopalan was 'likely to be disloyal and abuse the confidence placed in him by virtue of his appointment and hence he is not suitable for appointment in Government service'.[46] Likewise, information supplied about Kondaiah that he had been dismissed for theft by his former employer, the army, put a hasty end to his services in ITI.[47] It is worth noting that in the wake of the outbreak of the Naxalite agitation in the late 1960s these controls were reinforced with respect to candidates born in Kerala and who had resided there for more than twelve months during the past five years. In addition to the usual investigations, the company was ordered to send their application forms to the Ministry of Home Affairs in Delhi for scrutiny.[48]

As a result of all these formalized measures, not only was recruitment direct and unmediated with groups such as jobbers, *sirdars*, *mistris* and the like which had fulfilled the functional role of intermediaries in the hiring process during the colonial epoch being conspicuously absent.[49] More significantly, even informal social channels, articulated via kinfolk, castefolk, fellow villagers, friends and the like working in the factory, played a very marginal role in securing employment for prospective candidates. While the effectiveness of these networks in relaying information about job openings was undeniable, personal connections

[46] Personnel File 12151, CID report dated 12 March 1963.
[47] Personnel File 13125.
[48] OM No. 3/8(S)/67-Ests (B), 6 September 1968.
[49] A voluminous literature exists on the centrality of different categories of intermediaries utilized by employers in pre-Independent India to mobilize labour. See, *inter alia*, Rajnarayan Chandavarkar, 'The Decline and Fall of the Jobber System in the Bombay Cotton Textile Industry', *Modern Asian Studies*, Vol. 42, No. 1, 2008, pp. 117–210; Ranajit Das Gupta, 'Structure of the Labour Market in Colonial India', *EPW*, Vol. XVI. Nos. 44–46, November 1981, pp. 1781–1806; R.K. Newman, 'Social Factors in the Recruitment of the Bombay Millhands', in K.N. Chaudhuri and C.J. Dewey (eds.), *Economy and Society. Essays in Indian Economic and Social History*, New Delhi, 1979, pp. 277–95. For an opposing thesis contesting the importance of the *sirdar* in recruiting labour to the Bengal jute mills, see Arjan de Haan, 'Migrant Labour in Calcutta Jute Mills: Class, Instability and Control', in P. Robb (ed.), *Dalit Movements and the Meanings of Labour in India*, New Delhi, 1993, pp. 186–224. That such intermediaries were indispensable to employers even in advanced capitalist economies is highlighted by David Montgomery's analysis of the *padrone* system with reference to immigrant Italian labourers in the US. *The Fall of the House of Labor. The Workplace, the State and American Labor Activism, 1865–1925*, Cambridge-Paris, 1989, pp. 75–8.

were of little direct utility in helping to land a job in distinction to the observations reported by most sociological research.[50]

Nor was the union in any position to exert influence and act as patrons by promising jobs in return for influence and bribes.[51] A demand formulated by the union in 1971 calling for the presence of one elected representative on all selection committees as well as the right to inspect all recruitment-related records was rejected out of hand by the management.[52] For certain, the children of ITI employees aspiring to join the company received 'special consideration' or 'out of turn' employment, but our sample contains no more than 20 such cases. Besides, the management argued that accepting the union's demand to systematically give preference to employees' dependents in recruitment would amount to a violation of constitutional provisions.[53]

We can discern at least three plausible reasons as to why ITI set up such a tightly-regulated and impersonal hiring policy. First, it ensured that the management retained control over a key corporate function, namely the selection of individuals deemed suitable to perform a set of tasks, monitored by a personnel department worthy of its name as opposed to many of the more archaic branches of industry which 'externalized' this function to intermediary agencies. Next, it is quite likely that company officials consciously sought to discourage particularistic tendencies and favour instead the formation of as broad-based a labour force as possible. In step with the secularistic tenets of the Nehruvian nation-building project of which the public sector was a crucial component, managements, doubtless, were required to ensure that opportunities for access to all categories and types of occupations prevailed equally for all social groups. There could be no room for stratification along caste, religious or linguistic lines. Achieving this goal called for

[50] According to Sheth, for example, recruitment in the factory he studied was made exclusively through networks of kin and friends. *Social Framework of an Indian Factory*, pp. 75–7. An identical point is posited by Panjwani, 'Living with Capitalism'.

[51] The intervention of union leaders was as important as the recommendations made by kinfolk and friendly officers in gaining access to employment opportunities in a large mechanized public sector plant in W. Bengal. Gaurang Chattopadhyay and Anil Sengupta, 'Growth of a Disciplined Labour Force. A Case Study of Social Impediments', *EPW*, Vol. 4, Nos. 28–30, July 1969, pp. 1209–16.

[52] PD note, 26 May 1971. See also union letter to the management, 9 January 1971.

[53] Minutes management-union meeting, 26 February 1972.

getting rid of labour contractors who by definition operated by leveraging primordial attachments.

Finally, the establishment of formalized selection procedures corresponded to ITI's status as a publicly-owned company.[54] Accountable to a host of watchdog bodies, the top management might have been concerned to preempt accusations of nepotism and favouritism in all areas, especially one as sensitive as recruitment in a labour-surplus economy where job security, something that a government-owned undertaking alone could provide, remains all-important.[55] As the very official Report of the National Labour Commission remarked in 1969, in the newer establishments and particularly the public sector, employers have 'adopted practices which give to employment seekers a feeling that their just claims will not be disregarded'.[56] One must be cautious, though, not to exaggerate the sense of probity exhibited by state-owned undertakings: bureaucratic hiring mechanisms hardly constituted an infallible anti-corruption device.

Moreover, unlike enterprises run by the state governments as well as in certain sectors such as mining where a plethora of clientelist networks translated into constant political interference in recruitment issues, the managements in firms such as ITI appear to have been generally insulated from these kinds of pressures.[57] In the words of a former head of the Bangalore plant,

apart from the choice of factory site, there was no other political interference in the Bangalore unit at least. When I was executive director, I did not get any phone calls from state or national level politicians asking me to oblige them in any way.[58]

---

[54] Recruitment to non-executive posts at the state-run Bhilai steel plant too followed a formalized path, being mediated by local employment exchanges. Parry, 'Two Cheers for Reservation: The Satnamis and the Steel Plant'.

[55] Official reports regularly drew attention to the connection between the prevalence of corruption and high levels of labour turnover, on the one hand, and recourse to jobbers, on the other. Chandavarkar, 'Decline and Fall of the Jobber System'.

[56] *NCL Report*, pp. 72–3. Holmström confirms the NCL's observations, noting that recruitment policies in the public sector, while more bureaucratic and formal, and inclined to accord considerable weight to paper qualifications, are also more fair than in the private sector. *South Indian Factory Workers*, p. 49.

[57] For details of political meddling in recruitment policies in the Dhanbad collieries, see Heuzé, *Ouvriers d'un autre monde*, p. 198, 306, 354–5.

[58] Interview with Srinivasa Rao.

Though instances of politicians and government officials interceding on behalf of workers who having resigned sought reinstatement were not unknown, the management apparently did not have to unduly struggle to adhere to its prescription that 'all cases of persons recommended (for recruitment) by high personages should be considered on their merits only'.[59]

Probing our recruitment data reveals that nearly 28 per cent of our sample found work by answering newspaper advertisements. Such advertisements were placed by the management both in English language and in certain vernacular dailies. A quarter of the employees had directly submitted written applications to the company. Another 18 per cent had first worked as casual employees before being appointed on a permanent basis on the company's rolls. Those selected through the channel of the employment exchange comprised 17 per cent of our population. Finally, 4 per cent of the recruitments consisted of dependents, both widows and sons, of employees who had died in service.

Integrating a temporal perspective, and the variations that emerge allows us to underline three points. First, the principal mode of recruitment in the decade 1948–58, petitioning the company directly for jobs remained a well established practice in later years as well (Table 7.13). Second, if advertisements accounted for almost a third of all hirings in our sample in the years 1948–58, the figure rose to over a half in the next decade. This increase is quite paradoxical for it occurred precisely at a time when the government introduced the Compulsory Notification of Vacancies Act (1959). As its name indicated, the legislation rendered it obligatory for public and private sector companies alike to list all job openings with local employment exchanges.

But dissatisfied with the quality of candidates recommended by the exchanges, ITI continued to simultaneously advertise vacant posts despite repeated objections raised by exchange officials.[60] The number of new entrants who came through the employment exchanges in the 1960s also seem to have been marginal.[61] Nevertheless in the context of growing

---

[59] Minutes staff selection committee, 27 February 1950.

[60] See letter from ITI to Ministry of Transport and Communication, Ref. W/RCT(19), 27 March 1963; Ref. W/R-118(32), 11 January 1965; letter to Dept. of Employment and Training, Ref. W/R 118, 5 May 1965.

[61] Of the 1088 appointments made by the Bangalore plant in 1964–65, barely 158,

Table 7.13: Recruitment Mode by Entry Year

Recruitment Mode	1948–58	1959–68	1969–78	1979–88	1989–98	Total
Unknown	22	19	42	3	0	86
	(25.88)	(22.35)	(48.83)	(3.53)		(100)
Casual	31	43	91	38	5	208
	(14.9)	(20.67)	(43.75)	(18.27)	(2.4)	(100)
Advertisements	102	166	44	1	0	313
	(32.59)	(53.04)	(14.06)	(0.32)		(100)
Direct	121	79	78	2	0	280
	(43.21)	(28.21)	(27.86)	(0.71)		(100)
Employ. Exchange	3	13	162	16	1	195
	(1.54)	(6.67)	(83.08)	(8.21)	(0.51)	(100)
Dependents	2	3	16	24	2	47
	(4.26)	(6.38)	(34.04)	(51.06)	(4.26)	(100)

Note: Figures in brackets are percentages.

pressure from the state government to tilt recruitment policies expressly in the direction of 'sons of the soil', from the early 1970s onwards the company relied very sparingly on newspaper advertisements.

This brings us to our final point. The overwhelming majority (83 per cent) of the recruitments made via the official employment agencies in our sample occurred during the decade 1969–78 (Table 7.13). Moreover, since people wanting to register with the employment exchange in Bangalore or in other parts of Karnataka had to furnish proof of residence, it naturally follows that the overwhelming majority of our population selected through the exchanges had either been born in the state or been living here for several years. This detail squares with our earlier findings pointing, on the one hand, to a sharp contraction in the flow of migrants arriving from Tamil Nadu and Kerala during the 1970s, and, on the other, to an equally steep hike in the number of employees of local origin in the same period. In other words, a clear cause-effect equation prevailed between the mode of recruitment privileged by the management and the ethnic composition of the workforce at a specific moment.

---

or 14.5 percent, were exchange-sponsored candidates. Letter from industrial relations manager, ITI Bangalore to Ministry of Communications, 8 January 1968.

Job experience: From an initial examination of our aggregate data, one could quite easily conclude that the ITI workforce was a relatively experienced workforce. More than one out of two employees in our sample had worked elsewhere before joining the company (Table 7.14). The duration of these jobs as indicated in the personnel files varied from six months to over five years. Over half these persons had also stayed on for four years or more with the same employer, testifying to a considerable degree of stability.

But the above statistics do not reveal the movements from one decade to the next. If the first generation of recruits could boast of the maximum experience with three fourths of our population having been employed earlier, the generation that followed in the 1960s counted the highest proportion of new entrants to the labour market (Table 7.14). Just one out of three people had worked prior to being recruited by ITI. Thereafter the situation took an upward turn. In the 1970s, 55 per cent of the cohort had previous job experience with the figure mounting to 65 per cent in the next decade.

While details of previous employment experience are not available in their entirety, our findings show that for the majority of the population this experience was relatively diversified in scope. If roughly

Table 7.14: Job Experience by Entry Year

Entry Year	Nil Experience	Job Experience	Total Population
1948–58	72	209	281
	(25.62)	(74.37)	(100)
1959–68	221	102	323
	(68.42)	(31.57)	(100)
1969–78	189	244	433
	(43.65)	(56.35)	(100)
1979–88	28	56	84
	(33.33)	(66.33)	(100)
1989–98	0	8	8
		(100)	(100)
Total	510	616	1129*
	(45.17)	(54.56)	(100)

Notes: (*Three unknown cases)
Figures in brackets are percentages.

one out four people in our sample had been employed as casual labourers in the company, one out of two had held jobs similar to those they occupied on joining ITI. The management therefore clearly preferred to hire people who brought to their current employment direct experience in the job they performed and hence were of much greater utility to the company. Given that the majority of those with prior experience were assigned relatively qualified jobs in ITI (machine tenders, tool makers, inspectors, etc.), this would also tend to prove that their previous employment had required them to dispose some amount of skill.

From our data, we also learn that in over three-quarters of the cases, the former employer(s) was situated in Bangalore, stressing both the spatially circumscribed character of workers' experience and the economically strategic position exercised by the capital city as a regional node of employment. Even those workers not born in Bangalore had for the greater part found work here first before being recruited by ITI. Among the previous employers, the army emerged as a major player with about 9 per cent of our sample identifying themselves as ex-servicemen. A handful also came from P&T as well as from big local engineering companies like HAL and Kirloskar and textile companies like Binny's.

Did previous employment experience carry with it the rewards of greater occupational mobility? The answer is yes if we compare the careers of these employees with those entering the labour market for the first time. But the beneficiaries tended to be clustered more at the lower and upper reaches of the mobility scale than in the middle. Nearly 39 per cent of our population without any previous experience fell into the very low or low mobility category, 27 per cent enjoyed median mobility, and roughly 34 per cent high or very high mobility. The equivalent figures for employees possessing job experience were respectively 32 per cent, 29 per cent and 39 per cent (Table 7.15).

Entry age: An examination of our sample shows that two out of three workers were aged no more than 25 years at the time of recruitment (Table 7.16). The majority (45 per cent) fell within the age bracket 21 to 25 years. Inversely, the fact that one worker out of three was aged 26 years and above suggests that the company's endeavours to build a young workforce were not entirely crowned with success. Our data also shows important inter-generational variations. If we consider the successive

Table 7.15: Job Experience by Mobility

Mobility	Nil Experience	Job Experience
Very Low	25 (8.56)	32 (9.11)
Low	90 (30.82)	79 (22.5)
Median	78 (26.71)	103 (29.34)
High	70 (23.97)	102 (29.05)
Very High	29 (9.93)	35 (9.97)
Total	292 (100)	351 (100)

Note: Figures in brackets are percentages.

generations first, the cohort recruited in the 1960s was by far the youngest with 83 per cent of the sample aged 25 years and below (Table 7.16). While the cohort recruited in the 1980s enjoyed the dubious distinction of being the oldest with barely 37 per cent of its members aged 25 years

Table 7.16: Entry Age by Entry Year

Entry Year	15–20 yrs	21–25 yrs	26–30 yrs	31–35 yrs	36–40 yrs	>41 yrs	Total
1948–58	63 (22.42)	115 (40.93)	69 (24.56)	25 (8.9)	7 (2.49)	2 (0.71)	281 (100)
1959–68	130 (40.25)	138 (42.72)	39 (12.07)	10 (3.1)	2 (0.62)	4 (1.24)	323 (100)
1969–78	44 (10.16)	236 (54.5)	131 (30.25)	20 (4.62)	1 (0.23)	0	433 (100)
1979–88	8 (9.52)	23 (27.38)	37 (44.05)	13 (15.48)	3 (3.57)	0	84 (100)
1989–98	0	2 (25)	1 (12.5)	3 (37.5)	2 (25)	0	8 (100)
Total	245 (21.7)	514 (45.53)	277 (24.53)	71 (6.29)	15 (1.33)	6 (0.53)	1129 (100)

Note: Figures in brackets are percentages.

and below, the corresponding figures for the 1950s and 1970s stood respectively at 63 and 65 per cent.

The marked divergences in demographic profiles, setting apart the 1960s generation from all the others, can in all probability be traced back to managerial policy decisions advocating the infusion of young blood to take up the production of the more modern crossbar exchanges which commenced towards the end of this decade. One might also argue that notwithstanding the infancy of the company, the slightly higher age levels of the 1950s generation as compared to the 1970s generation bore a relation to the nature of the labour market in the immediate aftermath of Independence. Because of the dearth of skilled personnel in the engineering trades—the first industrial training institutes came up only in the mid-1950s—and because the company had still not devised its own in-house training programmes, workers equipped with many of the skills required by the company were quite likely to have acquired these in the course of previous employment opportunities. Therefore by the time they joined ITI they must have been relatively old.

BIRTH AND GROWTH OF THE UNION

Tracing the history of the growth of the union at the Bangalore plant in any detail is rendered problematical by the fragmentary character of the sources accessible to us. What we do know for sure is that the union was born in July 1950, barely two years after the plant went on stream, and was registered in October 1950.[62] Interestingly, the driving force behind the formation of the union were not blue collar but white collar employees, led by a typist in the sales department apparently reputed for his Gandhian beliefs, earning for him the nickname of 'Telephone Gandhi'.

Being a public sector company, and therefore expected to conform to the role of a 'model employer', the management promptly gave its blessings to the initiative and recognized the union.[63] It is worthwhile noting the

---

[62] R. Sundaram, 'The Union is Born', ITI Employees Union, Bangalore, nd (1963); Julian Reindorp, *Leaders and Leadership in the Trade Unions in Bangalore*, Bangalore, 1971, p. 27.

[63] Starting with the First Plan, various official reports had stressed the need for state-owned companies to serve as an example for the rest of the country by paying acceptable wages, providing satisfactory working conditions and welfare amenities, and

speed and ease, not to mention the various facilities subsequently accorded to them, with which unions in the public sector secured recognition from managements. This was in stark contrast with the protracted uphill, and often bloody struggles unions in the private sector invariably had to wage to earn recognition.[64] Indeed, in ITI, the first general body meeting which followed the election of the leadership was presided over by the managing director in person who also conceded to certain demands on the spot. Certain senior executives too initially joined the union and even held key posts in the hierarchy. Neither company regulations nor the union constitution imposed any restrictions on individual officers either enrolling as members in the union or from holding office. What the management did, however, veto was the union representing officers' interests either individually or on a collective basis. This situation would remain unchanged until 2001 when, as we shall study, the rules were unilaterally amended and officers prohibited from contesting or voting in union elections, a measure effectively designed to undercut their interest in belonging to the union.[65]

Calling itself an association rather than a union to start with, the union's efforts to win employees' confidence enjoyed only modest success during the early years: membership declined from 756 in 1952 to just over 600 the following year despite the increase in total worker strength from 1466 to 1984.[66] Until 1953 the leadership also remained in employees' hands. But at this date dissatisfaction with the performance of the insiders, perceived both as not being tough enough *vis-à-vis* the management and lacking experience, prompted the rank-and-file to bring in two outsiders, K. Kannan and A.N. Singh; they were elected respectively to the top posts of president and general secretary. Both

---

respecting trade union rights. *First Plan*, pp. 580–1; *Report of the Administrative Reforms Commission on Public Sector Undertakings*, Simla, 1967, p. 80.

[64] Even a company as renowned for modern managerial practices as TISCO agreed to concede demands for representation by its workforce only in the aftermath of a strike. Datta, *Capital Accumulation and Workers' Struggle*, pp. 155–60; Blair Kling, 'Paternalism in Indian Labor: The Tata Iron and Steel Company of Jamshedpur', *International Labour and Working Class History*, No. 53, Spring 1998, pp. 69–87. For a good example of big private firms' hostility to unionization, see Eamon Murphy, *Unions in Conflict. A Comparative Study of Four South Indian Textile Centres 1918–1939*, New Delhi, 1981.

[65] Ref. P&A/IR&I/EU-07, 14 September 2001.

[66] 'The Union Marches On', ITI Employees Union, Bangalore, nd (1963).

men were connected to central trade union federations. A participant in the nationalist struggle and one of the most powerful trade unionists in Bangalore during the 1960s in particular, Kannan belonged to the socialist-linked Hind Mazdoor Sabha (HMS) union, whereas Singh had close ties with the All India Trade Union Congress (AITUC).[67]

The presence of outside leaders with relations to political parties has often been blamed, and rightly so, for the proliferation of unions at all levels (plant, company, and industry), resulting in the disunity of the workforce, a major cause of the endemic weakness of the trade union movement in India.[68] Moves by one central federation to establish a foothold inside a plant invariably triggered a process of chain reaction with other organizations encouraged to follow suit.[69] The competition between unions for hegemony being essentially a competition to acquire numerical strength, either by increasing the size of their constituencies within the working class or by carving out fresh ones, no federation was prepared to concede, at least not without putting up a fight, the right to speak for workers' interests to a rival entity. To put it slightly differently, since all collective action takes the form of projects geared to definite objectives, and hence strive to delimit an exclusive territory whose sense

[67] For details of Kannan's career, see Reindorp, *Leaders and Leadership,* pp. 123–34.

[68] However, Murphy is right to state that the relationship between outside leaders and the rank-and-file is far more complex than has generally been portrayed in most studies. Workers, he argues, play an active role in organizing and running outsider-led unions which is hardly likely to have been the case had they remained passive or gullible pawns manipulated by the leadership to serve its political interests. *Unions in Conflict,* pp. 215–16, 221–2. See also Dilip Simeon, *The Politics of Labour under Late Colonialism. Workers, Unions and the State in Chota Nagpur 1928–1939,* New Delhi, 1995, pp. 336–7. For unionists' own perceptions of the pros and cons of insider-outsider leadership, see Reindorp, *Leaders and Leadership,* pp. 37–8. Links between political parties and trade unions have proved problematic not just in India. The politicization of the union movement in France has not only been blamed for intensifying competition between rival organizations, but more importantly, as one of the factors responsible for the decline in levels of union membership since the mid-1970s. Gérard Adam, *Le pouvoir syndical,* Paris, 1983, p. 51; Michel Lallement, *Sociologie des relations professionnelles,* Paris, 1996, p. 51.

[69] Interestingly, the Mysore Labour Act which predated Independence sought to curb both the multiplicity of unions and external leadership. It allowed only one trade union in each factory and no more than two outside leaders in any union, but the first provision restricting the number of unions received short shrift after 1947 from successive Congress governments intent on implanting the INTUC.

424 *Telecommunications Industry in India*

is not purely geographic, territorial conflicts between rival projects are only in the order of things.[70]

Further exacerbating this dynamic was the fact that most outsiders nurtured political ambitions of their own, typically utilizing their bases in the labour movement as a springboard to enter the electoral arena. The political advantages accruing from an involvement in union activities were hardly negligible: it enabled leaders to raise funds for their election campaigns, enrol union activists to participate in these campaigns, and, above all, try to gain members' votes.[71] But each successive formation of a new union only further fragmented and weakened the workforce, ultimately leaving employers to arbitrate between the different competing representative claims. As Michael Fernandes, the veteran head of the ITI union in Bangalore pointed out,

> where ever there is an union affiliated to a central organization, in the majority of cases there will be multiplicity of unions. All workers will not accept a single ideological bent . . . And when there is multiplicity of unions, workers invariably tend to suffer, they have no peace of mind and there is industrial unrest.[72]

Surprisingly, in the case of ITI, the induction of outside leadership produced no divisive effects on the workforce. One reason for this lay in the decision of workers to select two representatives, Kannan and Singh, who stood at polar ends of the ideological and political spectrum. Conscious or not, this decision turned out to be an extremely farsighted one whose benefits employees as well as the management would reap. For short of dislodging the other from his position, something the base would probably not have countenanced, Kannan and Singh were now

[70] Jean-Daniel Reynaud, *Les règles du jeu*, pp. 104–5. In his work on unionism in the Coimbatore textile industry, E.A. Ramaswamy notes that inter-union rivalry expressed itself with particular intensity in newly established mills, as each union pushed hard to capture the maximum number of members. *The Worker and his Union. A Study in South India*, New Delhi, 1977, pp. 113–16, 121–6.

[71] An undated flyer put out by five supporters of Fernandes, for example, read as follows: 'Many workers have expressed their keen desire to support Shri M.B. FERNANDES in the Assembly Election on 5–1–83, so that he may win and support the cause of workers and the downtrodden in the Assembly and outside . . . Since his financial condition is hopelessly bad it is necessary to provide him with publicity materials etc. Therefore a Election Campaign Committee has been set up. The Committee appeals to all workers to contribute liberally by purchasing immediately coupons of Rs. 2, or Rs 5, or Rs 10 . . . .'

[72] Interview with Michael Fernandes.

effectively prevented from attempting to affiliate the ITI union with either of their own national federations.

In other words, the divergent political sympathies of the leadership, while giving rise to a constant tug-of-war at the helm insulated workers from the risks of multiple unionism. At the same time, it contributed to creating the foundations for a robust tradition of plant-level unionism which guaranteed the independence of the organization, an essential determinant of its ability to negotiate with the management from a position of strength and stability. A review of labour conditions in the Bangalore factory, conducted by the Ministry of Labour in the early 1960s, after commenting on the 'good and cordial' state of industrial relations, implicitly credited this to the union's policy of autonomy. Notwithstanding Kannan's association with the HMS, the report underlined the vigilance of the other representatives.

. . . Due care is taken by the Executive Committee as well as by the General Council of the Union to steer clear of all political affiliations and to ensure that outside political influences do not affect its working within the ITI (sic).[73]

Hence, the outside representatives were well aware that workers had selected them first and foremost for their trade union competencies, and only secondarily for their ideological convictions.[74] They also knew that any attempts on their parts to forge bonds of a more enduring or definitive character between the union and a national federation would alienate the support of the rank-and-file. But independence also carried a price. It eliminated the possibility of leveraging the resources of the central organizations as well as the connections binding them to political parties to exert pressure upon the company and the government especially in conflict situations. The efforts of the ITI union leadership to mobilize

---

[73] *Industrial Relations and Implementation of Labour Enactments in Indian Telephone Industries, Bangalore: A Case Study* (1963–65), New Delhi, 1966, p. 3.

[74] Though referring to a different socio-political context, Flanders notes that the vast majority of workers in the UK belong to unions because of the latter's industrial activities and not its political activities. Elsewhere he writes, 'trade unions are singularly pragmatic bodies, deeply distrusting theories and ideologies.' Allan Flanders, *Management and Unions: The Theory and Reform of Industrial Relations*, London, 1975, pp. 27–8, 39, 280–1 (cit. p. 280). This distrust of ideology no doubt explains the vanguard role Leninism assigns to the party, i.e., intellectuals, in spearheading revolutionary change. See also Van Dusen Kennedy, *Unions, Employers and Government: Essays on Indian Labour Questions*, Bombay, pp. 202–03.

support for their cause both during and after the stay-in strikes staged in 1964 and 1966, for instance, attracted little response from the national federations.

A distinctive feature of the workers' movement in Bangalore in general, plant-level unionism would remain an unshakeable article of faith with ITI employees throughout the history of the union, a faith dictated more by pragmatic strategic considerations, though, than by ideological ones.[75] Preserving the autonomy of the union translated into safeguarding its unity. Refusing to adhere to the political line laid down by a central bureaucracy, or accept its definition of 'legitimate' union behaviour, workers understood, constituted one of the best means of checking inter-union rivalry, ensuring in the process that their cause was not weakened. With a single organization defending their interests there were no divisions which the company could exploit. Deprived of the possibility of playing one union off against the other, it was obliged to recognize the legitimacy of the union as the sole representative of the employees, empowered to express the aspirations of the workforce in its totality rather than any one particular section.

Workers own 'home-grown ideology',[76] this culture of trade union autonomy that ITI workers embraced (whether it was done self-consciously or not is besides the point) has been described by one French historian as the dominated culture of the labour movement as opposed to the dominant Leninist culture.[77] At its core resided a certain notion of pluralism. The diverse and conflicting political allegiances of workers were not considered to be an obstacle to their cooperating on issues of

---

[75] Of the five central government–controlled public sector firms in Bangalore, in BEL and HMT alone would unions continue to function under an external leadership. Moreover, in both HAL and BEML, internal leadership was the norm from the very outset which also explained why like in ITI a single union flourished. Inversely, the presence of outsiders affiliated to national federations in BEL and HMT was synonymous with multiple unionism, though in certain units of HMT, only one union existed later. For a more exhaustive analysis of unionism in the Bangalore public sector, see Dilip Subramanian, 'La convention brisée. Les relations professionnelles dans le secteur public industriel de Bangalore et la grève de 1980–1981', Paris, 1995, chap. 2 (mimeo).

[76] Perlman, *Theory of the Labor Movement*, p. 6, 272–9. In his classic study, Perlman contrasted this home grown ideology to the ideology imported into the labour movement by intellectuals.

[77] Jacques Julliard, *Autonomie ouvrière, Etudes sur le syndicalisme d'action directe*, Paris, 1988, pp. 267–8.

common concern to them. Echoing the reformist doctrines of Eduard Bernstein, in their eyes, trade unionism was synonymous with unity while 'politics', or more precisely partisan politics, bred disunity. Hence it was imperative to exclude all such trace of 'politics' from the trade union sphere.

The strength of ITI workers' attachment to the principle of trade union independence together with their appreciation of the advantages of single union representation was brought out in unmistakable terms by one study. Less than 3 per cent of the interviewees came out in support of multiple unions. On the contrary, they attributed the success of their organization in securing benefits for the workers not so much to the capabilities of the leadership as to their unity. Inversely, the leadership claimed their bargaining power was high because the rank-and-file backed the union en masse.[78] Similarly, in October 1980 when the Indian National Trade Union Congress (INTUC) announced its intention of setting up a rival union in the Bangalore factory, the leadership of the main union volunteered to resign and organize fresh elections in a bid to preserve the unity of the organization. Strikingly, this decision was endorsed by all the officials, including the general secretary, a well-known Congress supporter, but one who wanted to keep his political loyalties distinct from his trade union activities.[79]

But to conclude from the foregoing that the conflicting political allegiances of the union delegates did not represent a source of tensions would be incorrect.[80] Moves by one group of officials to issue a resolution

---

[78] Arya, *Labour Management Relations*, p. 16. The author also interviewed union leaders and workers in Heavy Electricals (India) where no less than seven unions functioned. The leaders were unanimous that only the management had benefited from the multiplicity of unions, while the majority of workers said they wanted not more than two unions. Of course, E.A. Ramaswamy has pointed to the positive effects of competition in the union market place for both leaders and the 'led', arguing that it forced the former to remain attentive to the needs of the base, while stimulating higher levels of involvement in organizational activities on the part of the membership. But one might seriously ask whether workers would not have willingly foregone these benefits for the more substantive gains a solidary bargaining front constituted. *The Worker and his Union*, pp. 116–17.

[79] ITI Union circular no. 50/80, 24 October 1980. Though the INTUC went ahead and formed a separate union, it declined to test its strength in an open electoral contest. But with a membership barely in excess of 30 employees and the company refusing to accord recognition, it rapidly disappeared from the scene.

[80] In the mid 1960s, the political affiliations of ITI union officials were as follows:

in September 1974 condemning the ruling Congress-I party for reducing workers' bonus payments, for example, encountered tremendous resistance from another faction which supported the Congress-I.[81] Relations between the pro- and anti-Congress-I representatives also worsened in the wake of the imposition of Emergency in June 1975. Spearheading the opposition to the Emergency rule within the ITI union was Fernandes.

An insider, having joined the company as a management apprentice in 1955, his total integrity and commitment to the union (he remained a bachelor until 1983); his competence as well as his social and linguistic capital (he came from a middle class background, possessed a science degree, and was extremely articulate in English); freedom from caste attachments (he was a non-practising Catholic); and political neutrality (though a socialist sympathizer, he had no party links until 1977); all these factors had earned Fernandes a substantial and loyal following among the rank-and-file. Known initially through his work for an association dedicated to improving the technical skills of factory supervisory personnel, he had decided to actively participate in the affairs of the union after a financial scam had discredited the organization in the eyes of the management and employees alike. But family circumstances too partly influenced his decision: besides Fernandes, another of his brothers was intimately connected with the trade union movement elsewhere in the country. First chosen as a union representative in 1961, Fernandes had held the all-important post of general secretary since 1965, being elected unopposed on two occasions. In 1970, he was also elected to the Bangalore municipal council as an independent candidate from a constituency, Ashok Nagar, with a relatively large worker population.

In December 1975, Fernandes came out openly against the government when, along with a few other public and private sector trade unionists, he addressed a memorandum to Indira Gandhi threatening to launch a major agitation if the Bonus Ordinance was not repealed.[82]

---

ten of them belonged to the Congress (R), three to the Jan Sangh, one to the Praja Socialist Party and one to the Congress (O). Arya, *Labour Management Relations*, p. 109. Similar information for later periods is not available.

[81] Interview with Fernandes.

[82] Promulgated in September 1974, the Payment of Bonus Ordinance dispensed companies who failed to post or show profits from the obligation of having to grant bonus.

Arrested immediately, he was imprisoned for a year and dismissed from ITI at the government's instigation. Profiting from his absence, the Congress-I group within the union proceeded to capture the post of general secretary during the 1976 union elections. It is also alleged to have willingly acquiesced in the state labour authorities' decision to prohibit Fernandes from contesting the elections.[83] However, after the Janata Party assumed power in April 1977, he was not only reinstated by the company, but allowed to stand for union elections too, being triumphantly elected as president.

Elected twice subsequently to the Karnataka State Assembly as a Janata Party member, Fernandes retained the presidency of the union until the 1980s. This was despite the pro-Congress union members' efforts to thwart his chances by fielding a former ITI worker and local Congress politician, A. Krishnappa, for the top post on more than one occasion. However, the rank-and-file judged the merits of the two contesting candidates, Fernandes and Krishnappa, exclusively on the basis of their trade union competencies, thus demonstrating anew their determination to insulate union activities from the influence of party politics.

In addition to worker opposition, a second explanation for the absence of multiple unionism in ITI was that external leadership never struck very deep roots here.[84] Kannan stayed on as president until 1976, but thereafter workers preferred to only elect factory employees to this post. But even prior to this date, insiders had always occupied the key operational post in the union, that of general secretary who controlled the communication and administrative resources of the organization, ever since Singh stepped down in 1963. Once he quit the union in the wake of an embezzlement scandal, the membership decided to entrust this post to an insider.

At the same time, the choice of an insider for the all-important post of general secretary was suggestive of an important shift in the thinking and attitudes of the membership. Workers, no doubt, felt that the skills and experience needed for the job were available within the factory, though until 1976, college-educated, white collar employees, proficient

---

[83] Interview with Fernandes.

[84] Workers in the Kolar gold mines, comments Nair, also entertained considerable reservations about the formation of unions under outside leadership, even when they were independent. *Miners and Millhands*, pp. 163–71.

in English, alone held this post. If anything, an insider stood at a distinct advantage over an outside leader, by virtue of the fact that he was more familiar with the functioning of the company, the way company executives reacted to different problems, the styles and dispositions of individual managers, and the grievances of employees both as a collective and as individuals, all of which greatly facilitated his task, and in turn ensured his ability to deliver results.

Workers had also perhaps come to realize that in public sector undertakings where the state as the owner was the ultimate decision-making authority on all issues, outside leaders were not going to prove very much more effective than insiders in securing improvements in working conditions and remunerations. For once the state had resolved to take a firm stand against conceding to the employees' demands, no amount of union pressure was likely to succeed in 'coercing' it to back down, so pronounced was the power differential between the two sides and in all situations.[85] Both the staying powers and the repressive might of the government were forcefully driven home during the long drawn out 1980–81 parity strike, involving ITI and the other Bangalore-based public sector enterprises. Despite the repercussions of huge production losses on the economy, the government remained intransigent right until the end grinding down the strikers' resistance.

A third factor that helped to safeguard the unity of the ITI union had to do with the ingenuity of the internal leadership. In 1974, the union formed a credit cooperative society whose principal objective was to assist employees in times of financial hardship by dispensing soft loans. A brainchild of Fernandes, the cooperative would grow into an immensely successful organization, its influence and utility to the workforce perhaps outstripping that of the union. By the early 1980s, its membership encompassed almost two-thirds of the total workforce. In principle, any worker who purchased at least one share worth Rs 101, in addition to paying a sum of Rs 21, was entitled to join the cooperative. But the rules also clearly stipulated that admission was open only to those who belonged to the official union.

---

[85] To give just one example, Datta Samant, who was reputed for wresting sizeable bonus awards from private sector employers, failed to obtain more than the statutory minimum bonus of 8.33 per cent at the state-owned Mazagaon Docks in Bombay. Ramaswamy, *Worker Consciousness and Trade Union Response,* p. 77.

As Fernandes explained, he had deliberately included this clause in view of the overall context where rising antagonisms, generated by linguistic and political rivalries, risked endangering the cohesiveness of the union. Tying the membership of the cooperative with that of the union, however, made it easier to defeat divisive manoeuvres: potential dissidents would be unwilling to forego the financial benefits the cooperative offered. This carrot and stick policy thus went a long way towards preserving the unity of the union. In other words, by stabilizing the articulation of the stakes as well as the rewards of membership and the penalties of non-membership, the creation of the cooperative society served to stabilize workers' collective identity as embodied in the union.[86]

Thanks to this clause (restricting membership in the cooperative to union members) no worker would want to hurt ITI union and defect with the idea of starting a rival union, and risk losing membership in the cooperative society. The clause was even stricter than the anti-defection law (introduced by the Indian government in 1985 to prevent venal politicians from swapping parties).[87]

In fact, Fernandes believes this policy of a 'closed shop' cooperative was instrumental in foiling the plans of national federations such as the INTUC and the Bharatiya Mazdoor Sangh (BMS) to establish a base in the Bangalore factory. Even those sections of the rank-and-file which expressed sympathy with the political view of these two bodies refused to leave the main union and join them. Placing the size of BMS's potential following among ITI workers at over 3000, one such supporter complained bitterly that but for the dual membership conditionality, linking the union and the cooperative, the union 'would have collapsed long ago'.[88]

The creation of the cooperative society by the union as well as the clause restricting membership to union members could thus be interpreted as furnishing an illustration of Mancur Olson's celebrated thesis. The provision of selective private incentives, in the form of financial benefits, was intended to reward 'rational, self-interested individuals' to remain within the union in order 'to achieve their common or group

---

[86] I am paraphrasing an argument elaborated by Catherine Paradeise with respect to a different context. 'Acteurs et institutions. La dynamique des marchés du travail', *Sociologie du travail*, No. 1, 1988, pp. 79–105.

[87] Interview with Fernandes.

[88] Interview with Panduranga Rao, 5 January 1998.

interests', while dissidents, or 'free riders' to employ Olson's terminology, would be punished by excluding them from the same incentives.[89] But Fernandes' attempts to introduce a similar clause in another unit of ITI (Palakkad) as well as in other plants were systematically thwarted by the authorities who felt it curtailed workers' freedom to form trade unions.[90]

TOP MANAGEMENT ENCOURAGES PRINCIPLE OF JOINT REGULATION

One final factor operating to check the proliferation of rival unions at ITI Bangalore was corporate policy. Although no predetermined or explicit policy options defining its overall industrial relations strategy appears to have been drawn up, the management certainly had a vested interest in ensuring that outside leaders did not seek to affiliate the ITI union with a national federation. Like the workforce, it had witnessed the enormously disruptive impact of multiple unionism on production and industrial peace in BEL and HMT. In both these Bangalore public enterprises, violent clashes frequently erupted both inside and outside the factory between AITUC and INTUC loyalists as the two federations muscularly competed for employees' support from the late 1960s onwards. ITI executives therefore had every reason to promote the principle of independent unionism and internal leadership in order to maintain the unity of the union which in turn paved the way for a stable industrial relations environment.

Towards this end, it decided to recognize only one union, the biggest, which was granted the legitimate monopoly to both represent the interests of the entire workforce and negotiate on its behalf on all issues bearing upon the wage contract. This engendered a process of 'representative bureaucracy'[91] or joint regulation where the union, with the objective of protecting workers' industrial rights, actively participated in the production of rules in the sphere of employment, work conditions and industrial relations, thereby assuring the legitimacy of these rules.[92]

---

[89] Mancur Olson, *The Logic of Collective Action: Public Goods and the Theory of Groups*, Cambridge (Mass.), 1971, p. 2.

[90] Even at the Bangalore plant, the rules of the cooperative had to be amended in December 1986, and provisions made to admit officers who were not union members.

[91] The term comes from Gouldner, *Patterns of Industrial Bureaucracy*, p. 24.

[92] Flanders, *Management and Unions*, pp. 41–2; J.D. Reynaud, *Le conflit, la*

We (the management) made it very clearly from the beginning that we only wanted a single union, irrespective of who was heading it. We made it known that we would not recognize a second union.[93]

To its credit, the company faithfully stuck to its word. In 1964, drivers of ITI buses, transporting workers to and from their residences, launched a separate union, alleging that the main union was not fighting for their interests, and submitted a memorandum of demands to the company. The management flatly refused to negotiate with their representatives, as 'the management recognises only the ITI Employees' Union and they (the drivers) may continue as hitherto to represent their grievances through the . . . union or through their Department'.[94] In the face of this rigid stance, the drivers' union lapsed into dormancy until 1979 when all its members chose to re-enter the fold of the mother organization.[95]

Describing the state of industrial relations as 'generally cordial' and 'fairly stable', an official report issued in the early 1980s attributed this to the existence of a single union. Unitary representation, it added, had made it 'possible for both the management and workmen to have a better understanding of each other's view points'.[96] Earlier, workers' representatives had depicted an equally upbeat scenario. Celebrating the

---

négociation et la règle, pp. 24–5, 53–5 and *passim.* But as Reynaud rightly cautions, such legitimacy is always partial and relative, never absolute. Nor should joint regulation, often a compromise between control regulation, dictated by managements, and autonomous regulation, produced by workers, be understood as eliminating the confrontation between the two sides given its inability to cover all aspects of factory life. See also Alan Fox, 'Industrial Relations: A Social Critique of Pluralist Ideology', in J. Child (ed.), *Man and Organisation: The Search for Explanation and Social Relevance,* London, 1973, pp. 186–221. On the costs and benefits of jointly determined rules for employers, see Batstone et al, *Consent and Efficiency,* pp. 292–4.

[93] Interview with Srinivasa Rao. Interestingly, the architect of this policy, the personnel chief, had held a similar position in a leading Bangalore private firm, MICO. In some of ITI's other units, however, it was less successful in countering the growth of rival unions.

[94] PD circular no. 1048, 6 September 1965.

[95] Note to ITI board, 160th meeting, item no. B 12, March 1978; ITI Union circular no. 50/80, 24 October 1980.

[96] The fact finding team also blamed the protracted 1980–81 parity strike more on 'faulty policy on formulation and implementation of agreements rather than bad industrial relations at the shop floor (sic)'. 'Report of the Expert Committee on Public Enterprises', in *Reports/Recommendations of Various Committees on Public Enterprises,* New Delhi, 1990, p. 7.

union's thirteenth birthday in 1963, Kannan wrote that relations between the union and the company 'has always been cordial and good', since it rested on 'the community of common interests rather than differences'. He also heaped generous praise on the management for never having interfered 'with the affairs of the Union or to dominate its activities (sic)'.[97]

The principle of joint regulation gained further legitimacy with the drawing up of a well-codified and formalized grievance dispute procedure. This measure also marked a supplementary step towards creating a stable industrial relations climate, devised as it was to institutionalize conflict as much by enshrining the idea of 'industrial justice' which guaranteed employees equality of treatment as by operating as a safety valve for the expression of shop floor discontent.[98] Of course, one could argue that by channelling conflict into tightly-contained avenues, the grievance procedure 'turns struggles between classes into struggles between the individual and the company', and, consequently, guarantees the reproduction of the capital-labour relationship in its current form.[99] Inversely, there could be no gainsaying the protection it afforded to workers from managerial arbitrariness, and therefore constituted a pivotal element of the regulatory framework governing workplace relations.[100]

Put into place in September 1961, apparently at the initiative of the company, the dispute settlement machinery in ITI, in common with similar systems elsewhere, specified a certain number of successive steps or stages, in this case three, for processing employee complaints.[101] The blanket definition given by the management to the term meant that grievances could be raised with respect to practically all aspects of work: wages, overtime, leave, transfer, promotion, seniority, work assignment,

[97] K. Kannan, 'An Unique Union', ITI Employees' Union, Bangalore, nd (1963).

[98] The term is borrowed from Burawoy, *Manufacturing Consent*, p. 114.

[99] Michael Burawoy, 'The Anthropology of Industrial Work', *Annual Review of Anthropology*, VIII, 1979, pp. 231–66 (cit. p. 255).

[100] The web of rules, including grievance procedures, devised in large unionized workplaces upheld the rights of employees, contends one scholar, but at the cost of fostering a low trust syndrome. A. Fox, *Beyond Contract: Work, Power and Trust Relations*, London, 1973, chap 2, cited in Sanford Jacoby, *Modern Manors: Welfare Capitalism since the New Deal*, Princeton, 1997, p. 240.

[101] An excellent study of the workings of grievance procedures can be found in James Kuhn, *Bargaining in Grievance Settlement*.

working conditions, interpretations of rules, suspensions, and dismissals. To enable supervisors and shop floor executives handle the entire process smoothly so as to 'keep morale high', ensure that the employee did not lose face or dignity, and that the management did not forego its rights, the personnel department mapped out a detailed set of guidelines.[102]

Pointing out that they would have to continue working with the employee who filed the grievance, shop bosses were therefore advised, among other things, to 'listen patiently' to the aggrieved worker even if they believed him to be wrong, not to 'get upset or resort to threats' in case no agreement was reached, and to avoid 'personal consideration' for 'what counts is not who is right, but *what* is right'.[103] But recommendations urging managers to attend to grievances within the prescribed time limits generally went unheeded. Delays of one to two years were common before workers obtained redress.[104]

Statistical data concerning the number of grievances recorded and settled by the company is very patchy. So we are unable to state with any certitude whether or not employees made extensive use of these procedures to ventilate their discontent, and hence adhered to a 'legitimate' framework. From the information on hand, we find that the company arbitrated 468 grievances from 1967–76, or on average 52 grievances annually. Of these the crushing majority (356) were connected to the highly sensitive question of promotions and seniority. Interestingly, complaints directly bearing upon work are conspicuously absent, a manifest sign that the performance demands imposed upon the workforce by the company were anything but stringent. Since the problem of occupational mobility was successfully resolved in 1979, following the introduction of a seniority-based promotion scheme, we may presume that the subsequent years witnessed an appreciable decline in the total number of grievances filed.

Consistent with its role as a 'model employer', ITI also contributed to solidly entrenching the union and facilitating its functioning by granting it an extensive array of facilities, whether to everyday organizational affairs of the union or to the holding of union elections. Regardless of whether company officials acted with purposive self-consciousness or not, such a

---

[102] Ref. ASJ.4, 30 December 1978.

[103] ibid. Emphasis in original.

[104] Arya, *Labour Management Relations*, pp. 149–50.

strategy clearly had the effect of making the union an essential component of the 'mechanism of social control', able to discipline the workforce whenever and wherever the management could not.[105] Quite a few of the concessions involved little direct cost for the management as well which could in return depend on the conciliatory and accommodative attitude of the union. Furthermore, coopting the union as a subordinate partner in the exercise of social control implied, as Pierre Bourdieu has pointed out, entrusting it with the responsibility of spelling out what was 'just' or 'correct' when organizing a struggle, notions which normally encapsulated dominant class definitions of what is legitimate or illegitimate with respect to both the nature of the demands raised and the tactics deployed.[106]

Of the different measures agreed to by the company, the establishment of a system of 'check-off', whereby union subscription dues were directly deducted from workers' pay packets, was by far of the utmost importance and utility to the union.[107] It enabled the latter to seal its hegemonic position, and gain complete control over the workforce.[108] Like most of its counterparts, the ITI union had consistently struggled to persuade the rank-and-file to pay its dues, to 'convert temporary movement into permanent organization', and the low levels of membership bore

[105] Richard Hyman, *Industrial Relations: A Marxist Introduction*, London, 1975, p. 68. Interestingly, the non-Marxist perspective is hardly at odds with the radical analysis. Flanders and Fox state that when trade unions cannot effectively play their role as 'managers of conflict, then an essential part of the mechanism of social control on which we rely for order in industry, breaks down'. A. Flanders and A. Fox, 'Collective Bargaining: From Donovan to Durkheim', in *Management and Unions*, pp. 241–76 (cit. p. 246). However, as Burawoy warns, employers must also take care to preserve the legitimacy and autonomy of the union if the latter is to maintain its grip over the workforce. *Manufacturing Consent*, p. 112.

[106] Pierre Bourdieu, *Questions de sociologie*, Paris, 1984, pp. 254–63.

[107] Few Indian employers were as 'enlightened' as ITI to consent to providing check-off; at best, they allowed their unions to collect subscriptions inside the factory after working hours, or on pay days. Kennedy, *Unions, Employers and Government*, p. 156.

[108] Only by exercising power over its members, is the union able to exert power for them, asserts Hyman. *Industrial Relations*, pp. 64–5. According to Reynaud, the 'rules of the game' underpinning the industrial relations system subsist only when trade unions succeed in commanding the loyalty of their membership. This also explains why situations characterized by frequent 'spontaneous' worker protests are invariably those where the union leadership has lost legitimacy *vis-à-vis* the rank-and-file. *Le conflit, la négociation et la règle*, pp. 94–5.

testimony to this difficulty.[109] Although the numbers had shown a rise from 1960 onwards, the union still counted no more than 4060 members in 1963, or less than half the entire workforce. In April 1964, check-off was introduced for the first time. But while the union claimed that nearly three-fourths of the workers had signed in favour of the measure, its effects on membership figures are impossible to assess because the company arbitrarily withdrew it a few months later to punish the union for having gone on strike.

Arguing that the decision threatened not only to penalize the union but the management as well since the physical collection of subscriptions would inevitably entail some waste of production time, the union called for the reintroduction of check-off on at least two instances.[110] However, according to company officials, the system possessed several disadvantages: it gave an 'artificial boost to the strength of the union', deprived employees of the possibility of withholding their dues in case of dissatisfaction with the union's performance, and, by reducing the scope for top-down interactions, rendered the leadership less sensitive and responsive to the needs of the base. Only in 1972, apparently at the urging of the then Communications Minister H.N. Bahuguna, did ITI accept to reestablish this facility. The following year, the union's strength more than doubled with 13,509 workers registered on its rolls out of a total of 15,035.[111] Thereafter, membership levels as a percentage of the overall workforce would systematically cross 95 per cent. The practice of check-off also helped to massively swell the union's coffers, making it among the richest in Bangalore. In December 1994, the union's cash assets amounted to Rs 2.14 million, apart from which it possessed prime property in the city valued at Rs 30 million.[112]

In addition to the various 'infrastructural' facilities, union officials directly enjoyed a number of privileges. They were granted free time to permit them to transact union business during factory hours as well as special leave with pay for the purpose of attending union meetings, court proceedings and the like.[113] In addition, they worked only morning shifts

[109] Flanders, *Management and Unions*, p. 43.

[110] Minutes management-union meeting, 8 July 1966; 10 November 1970.

[111] 'Profile of ITI Employees Union', Personnel Dept., nd.

[112] ITI Employees Union, Bangalore, General Secretary's Report for 1991–95, April 1996, p. 24, 75.

[113] The company allotted a total of 1,100 hours of special leave, adjustable over a

given that the bulk of the employees came to the factory during these hours, could move relatively freely from one department to another and out of the factory, and were allowed as a matter of custom to travel free of cost on company buses.

Over time, some of these perks also came to be extended to officials of the numerous bodies existing alongside the union both within and outside the factory premises. These not only included bipartite statutory institutions, intervening either in workplace related issues (Works Committee, Safety Committee, Incentive Committee, etc.), or in the provision of social benefits (Canteen Committee, Provident Fund Committee, Death Relief Fund Committee, etc.). They also covered other associations devoted to welfare, cultural and sports activities which in several cases had originated from the independent initiatives of employees.

During the 1960s, some department heads, at least apparently, exercised a fair measure of vigilance to ensure these facilities were not put to misuse. From one document, we learn of a union representative being obliged to conform to the regulations and 'maintain a movement register indicating the duration and time of day . . . taken (sic)' for discussions with employees and the management.[114] The register was also carefully scrutinized since the representative's union responsibilities were thought to be interfering unduly with his ability to carry out day-to-day factory tasks. But it is fairly clear that starting from the 1970s these controls progressively slackened, in parallel with the erosion in discipline noticeable in all areas of factory life, encouraging union officials as well as those belonging to the other organizations to ride roughshod over the facilities they had been accorded. There were, no doubt, sporadic attempts by the company to reimpose order, but, by and large, it appeared to have resigned itself to accepting this state of affairs.

At the same time, the hail of protest encountered by officials who

---

six-month period. Replies to Ministry of Labour questionnaire, 1976. Union officials at TISCO were also allowed to attend union meetings during working hours, but as the author points out this was a rare privilege in the Indian context. K. Mamkootam, 'Industrial Relations in a Steel Plant', in E.A. Ramaswamy (ed.), *Industrial Relations in India*, New Delhi, 1978, pp. 41–62.

[114] Note from deputy engineer Engineering Dept., 24 February 1964. First elected to a union post in 1961, Fernandes claimed that he continued to attend to factory work until 1967 after which he was compelled to dedicate all his time to union activities. Interview with Fernandes.

sought to adopt a tough line could hardly have encouraged their counterparts to imitate their example. Accused of 'uncivilized behaviour', and of subjecting union activists under his charge to 'ill-treatment, harassment and humiliation', one of the section heads in the shipping department found himself 'gheraoed' (literally, surrounded) by about 60 representatives, led by the union general secretary and the vice president. Abused and called a 'dictator' and a 'coward', he was given eight days by the protestors to mend his ways. Otherwise, they threatened to not only put up posters throughout the factory denouncing his misdeeds, but also to take 'direct action' against him.[115] Subsequently, the department head reported that the officer had committed no fault other than trying to get shop delegates to comply with factory rules.[116]

In effect, union officials were often found guilty of 'unauthorized movement' within the factory. When caught, they tended more often than not to react by 'picking up a quarrel' with security personnel or 'creating a big scene'.[117] According to the management, misuse of the special leave facility had become a widespread phenomenon, leave being 'recommended indiscriminately' for union delegates who were absenting themselves from the factory to run their own business ventures and for other personal ends.[118]

Nor did they conscientiously go about their jobs when present. If anything, the majority of representatives saw a post in the union hierarchy as providing them with unlimited licence to shirk. This certainly constituted one of the 'attractions' of a union career.[119] Company rules stipulated that all union officials, regardless of their function, must work a certain

---

[115] Security Dept. note, 19 July 1985. (Hereafter SD note). Expressing regret, the union later stated that the incident was not premeditated and had only occurred because the officer had refused a dialogue with shop delegates. See letter 27 July 1985.

[116] Note 20 July 1985.

[117] See SD notes, Ref. SY/FD/10, 16 December 1977; 10 March 1983; 7 April 1983; 19 March 1985.

[118] Minutes management-union meeting, 1 May 1982; Interview with Shankar Prasad, 1 December 2001.

[119] Uma Ramaswamy underlines a similar phenomenon in the Coimbatore textile mills. *Work, Union and Community,* p. 64, 72, 84–5. It is worthwhile contrasting these attitudes with those described by Huw Beynon, albeit with reference to another context, where shop stewards at one of Ford's UK plant were often obliged to work much harder than the rank-and-file because supervisors kept a constant watch over them. *Working for Ford,* Wakefield, 1975, p. 220.

number of hours daily.[120] But as the size of the workforce steadily expanded, the time devoted to productive labour, not just by top union leaders, but even by shop delegates, had decreased to a point where, by a tacit accord with department heads, both groups stopped working altogether. The overall breakdown in discipline, and the periods of idleness stemming from the management's inability to schedule work loads uniformly throughout the year, further enabled shop delegates to evade factory chores.

The company responded to all these infractions by submitting a proposal to the union, in January 1977, amending the guidelines laid down to regulate the activities of union representatives.[121] Three years later, not even the slightest progress had been made, although 'discipline was deteriorating day by day'.[122] Finally, in July 1982, or five years after it had first raised the issue, the management succeeded in wrenching the union's approval and issued a revised code of conduct. In addition to maintaining the existing curbs on their movements, henceforth top union officials were required to work for at least one hour daily and the lower echelons, four hours. Yet, barely a few months later, we hear the management complaining that the movements of union representatives 'beyond the prescribed hours', far from being 'curtailed despite requests', were in fact on the increase.[123] It went on to add that discipline would be strictly enforced from then onwards. Once again, reality appears to have trumped intentions with little being concretely achieved.

As a confidential memo sent by the personnel manager in September 1991 to all division and department heads at the Bangalore plant admitted, guidelines to regulate the activities of representatives of the different organizations had been issued '*time and again*'.[124] Nevertheless, they continued to 'move without any valid reasons or authority.[125] Mincing no words, another internal document, after noting that union

---

[120] To attend to union activities, the president and general secretary were dispensed from regular factory work for four hours daily, other officials for four hours every alternate day, and executive committee members for four hours twice a week. 'Machinery for Dealing with Union Problems and to Regulate the Union Activities', ITI Personnel Dept., nd.

[121] Minutes management-union meeting, 25 March 1977.

[122] Minutes management-union meeting, 7 and 16 January 1980.

[123] Minutes management-union meeting, 5 November 1982.

[124] Ref. WLU-16, 11 September 1991. Emphasis added.

[125] ibid.

representatives, right from shop delegates upwards, did no work at all, pointed out that

there is no control over their movements after punching their attendance card . . . This is because of *inadequacy of Administrative enforcements* (sic).[126]

What is doubly striking is that in August 1993, a fresh company directive reduced the number of hours shop delegates needed to work from four to two.[127] Even this scaled-down objective proved elusive in the production shop where I spent close to eight weeks in 1999 and 2001 observing work practices, despite renewed declarations by the management that it would no longer tolerate any misuse of their position by delegates.

Following the union elections in 2001, personnel department officials, drawing attention to the fact that over half the new representatives were direct production workers (59 out of a total of 116), clearly stated that they would not be permitted to stay idle at a time when the factory faced a shortage of operatives. Already, one divisional head had suggested downsizing the number of delegates in line with the overall decline in manpower strength.[128] The management also announced plans to crack down on middle and low ranking union leaders who had unauthorizedly appropriated factory space and other company facilities to set up their offices. Whether or not it carried out its threat remains unknown, but delegates promised to resist any attack on what they claimed were their 'traditional privileges'.[129]

Instrumental in helping to firmly anchor the union within the social fabric of the factory environment, the management also sought to promote the democratic functioning of the union through the provision of various facilities intended to facilitate the organization of free and fair elections on a regular basis. One could again argue that the management was only acting out of pure self-interest. Entitling employees to exercise their rights at frequent intervals and without fear meant that union representatives had no choice but to stay tuned to the aspirations of the base.

This is turn lessened the likelihood of the management, not to mention the union, being caught off-guard by any sudden explosion of discontent.

---

[126] PD note, 28 March 1996. Emphasis added.

[127] PD circular no. WLU/16, 9 August 1993.

[128] Ref. DGMT/64, 31 July 1999.

[129] Interview with Kovi Ramu, Assistant Secretary ITI Employees Union, 3 November 2001.

With their credibility and, eventually, chances of reelection at stake, representatives could, in effect, be relied upon to bring to the company's attention problems as and when they arose, allowing for solutions to be explored, if not found, before things got out of hand. At the same time, elections guaranteed the legitimacy of the leadership, a key ingredient in the preservation of industrial peace, for only if the leaders commanded the loyalty of the workforce could they also be expected to maintain control in moments of crisis.

Such an interest based interpretation of the management's actions, while it may be discounted only at the risk of considerable naiveté, however, does only limited justice to reality, especially in the context of the public sector. For there is no reason to believe that the ITI management did not take seriously its obligations of a 'model employer' as laid down in several official reports. In contradistinction to the practices of private firms, the role of a 'model employer' placed the onus of upholding and protecting workers' basic rights squarely upon public sector managements. Respecting workers' rights then entailed enabling them to freely choose their representatives.

Moreover, the idealism generated by the nationalist movement continued to suffuse the early years of Independence, and for a number of high ranking public sector executives, regardless of whether they believed in Gandhian humanism or in Nehruvian egalitarianism, the task of nation building called for the fair and just treatment of workers, though such sentiments often also smacked of a paternalistic attitude to labour issues. As Gérard Heuzé has remarked, the public sector represented the arena *par excellence* where a paternalist compromise was elaborated, defined both by the integration of a certain measure of conflict and regulation associating the Indian state and its employees who acceded to the status of protected subjects.[130]

So, while perhaps conducive to securing the company's long term objective of forging a consensual industrial relations climate, the provision of facilities for the organization of union elections must also be viewed as a step in the direction towards fulfilling its broader social responsibilities. To borrow from Luc Boltanski and Laurent Thévenot,

---

[130] Gérard Heuzé, 'Le monde du travail indien et les organisations de salariés. Les grandes transformations des années 1980', in R. Cabanes et al (eds.), *Salariés et entreprises dans les pays du Sud. Contribution à une anthropologie politique*, Paris, 1995, p. 237.

we may say that ITI management's actions combined principles deriving from two orders of worth, an industrial order based on efficiency, and a civic order which laid emphasis on values of equity and solidarity.[131]

The assistance extended by the management with respect to the holding of union elections took two forms: all employees were granted up to four hours of free time, those involved in organizing the election and the counting of votes were also eligible for a day's paid leave. By 1991, the number of persons who benefited from this measure had risen to 543. In addition, a personnel department officer was delegated to oversee the entire electoral process and ensure there were no irregularities.

Curiously, this practice was instituted not at the company's behest, but at the request of the union, intent on avoiding all charges of fraud or foul play that were likely to be levelled as much from within its ranks as from outside. Second, the management made available a variety of material facilities: hiring out the company auditorium at a nominal cost for the general body meeting and permitting the elections to take place within the factory premises.

Needless to say, the management struggled just as hard to prevent these facilities from being abused as it did all the other benefits it provided the union and the other organizations with. The hurly-burly generated in the course of the run-up to the different elections not only disrupted production schedules, but also provoked other problems. Canvassing during working hours was a routine phenomenon, as candidates fighting the elections and accompanied by a retinue of supporters, the size of which was proportionate to the status of the individual, moved freely from department to department distributing pamphlets and exhorting employees to vote for them.

Generous use was also made of company material to fabricate handbills, posters, and the like which then adorned shop and factory walls as well as the company's fleet of buses. Indeed, virtually no election went by without the personnel department complaining of candidates repeatedly absenting themselves from their workspots in order to solicit votes,[132] of paper, cardboard sheets and packing materials being wasted,

[131] Boltanski and Thévenot, *De la justification.*
[132] See, for instance, a personnel department note (9 November 1993) stating than an employee standing for elections to the work committee had been missing from his workspot for three consecutive days because he was busy canvassing.

photocopying machines misused, and the expenses the company had to incur to remove 'pamphlets strewn around' and clean walls 'disfigured by writing, painting and pasting . . . posters'.[133] Yet, by the management's own admission, the very fact that it was compelled to issue circulars 'time and again' warning against such practices, disclosed its singular lack of success in persuading employees to adhere to the rules.[134]

In one instance, a group of 300 employees started shouting slogans and stopped factory buses from leaving. They were upset that a couple of their colleagues had been caught painting the name of a candidate on the sides of a bus and handed over to the security department. However, 'since the employees were in an aggressive mood', security officials promptly released the two offenders so as 'to avoid further problems'.[135] Whether or not similar motives dissuaded the management from pursuing its plan to both discontinue the staging of union elections inside the factory and during working hours because it 'is causing considerable disturbance to production activity' is not known.[136] But after the idea was initially mooted in 1978, we hear nothing more about it until 2001 when for the first time, union elections were held outside the factory premises.[137]

OFFICERS BARRED FROM PARTICIPATING IN UNION

The 2001 elections were also noteworthy on account of the tough stand adopted by the management on two other matters. For one thing, it threatened to seek the disqualification of any candidate caught violating company regulations.[138] This declaration apparently did not go unheeded: the repeated references to candidates and their supporters canvassing during factory hours that we read of in the past were conspicuously absent from company records on this occasion. For another, in a move

---

[133] See PD circular no. 2740, 3 December 1986; no. 2989, 15 September 1987; no. 3223, 26 June 1989; no. 4022, 9 May 1996; letter to ITI Employees Union, Bangalore and ITI Credit Cooperative Society, 13 September 1995.

[134] PD circular no. 3945, 4 August 1995.

[135] SD note, Ref. SY/FD/10, 23 and 24 November 1984.

[136] Minutes management-union meeting, 18 November 1978.

[137] In 1995, however, the company informed the union that barring elections to statutory bodies (works committee, safety committee, etc.), in future no other elections would be allowed inside the factory or in its vicinity. Letter to ITI Employees Union, Bangalore and ITI Credit Cooperative Society, 13 September 1995.

[138] PD circular no. 4406, 21 September 2001.

deliberately designed to weaken the union's numerical strength and finances, the rules were arbitrarily modified in July 2001 to bar officers from participating in any manner in union elections.[139]

In parallel, the system of deducting union dues directly from employees' pay packets was withdrawn with respect to officers. With the union already prohibited from defending officers' rights, individually and collectively, the combined effect of both these decisions was to further deprive officers of any objective reason for wanting to stay on in the union. As company executives pointedly argued, the 'interests of the officer community' were represented by the officers' association, not the union, and all issues concerning officers were discussed and settled with the former.[140] Common membership in the union was also viewed as weakening officers' ability to exercise effective control over non-officers. Conscious that the union would not embark on any forms of agitations which risked interrupting production at a time when ITI was already struggling to replenish its order books, the management clearly capitalized on this context to railroad long envisaged measures.

Consequently, the 2001 elections marked a watershed in the history of the ITI union at the Bangalore plant. The fact that participation in the elections was restricted to non-officers alone inaugurated the transformation of the union from an inclusive body, to which both officers and non-officers could belong, to an exclusive one. What must not be forgotten is that a significant proportion of officers in Bangalore were officers only in name, having risen from the ranks thanks to a seniority-based promotion scheme.[141] Given the symbolic rewards associated with this category, if not within the plant at least in the wider social sphere, becoming an officer definitely constituted the crowning moment of their working lives.

Still, many of these worker-officers remained extremely attached to the union, and were fully aware that but for its efforts to implement of

---

[139] This directive did not apply to Fernandes who, though an officer, had already retired from the company in August 1992. According to him, at the time of his promotion to the officer category in 1966, he had asked the union committee to statute on whether his union responsibilities conflicted with his changed status, and the committee had said no. Interview with Fernandes.

[140] Ref. P&A/IR&I/EU-07, 14 September 2001.

[141] Roughly 70 per cent of the 2698 officers listed on the rolls of the Bangalore plant in March 2000 had joined the company as non-officers. Ref. P&A/MP/ST/215, 3 January 2001.

the promotion scheme they would have never reached their current positions. So retaining their union membership represented a way of demonstrating their continued loyalty to the union, something which the company's decision now rendered next to impossible. To put it slightly differently, by driving a wedge between officers and the union, the union was also being isolated from a non-negligible section of its 'organic' base.

Bitterly opposed by the union leadership, the management's actions effectively excluding officers from playing any role inside the union did not, however, leave all workers dissatisfied. Even though it might not have reflected the general sentiment of the workforce, a handbill put out by one candidate during the 2001 elections celebrated the birth of the 'first ever union without officers' as the realization of a 'long standing dream'.[142] Officers filling posts in the union hierarchy naturally meant fewer opportunities for non-officers, and this no doubt explained in part why some employees now welcomed a union *sans* officers.[143]

Workers also felt that officers who contested elections often did so for purely personal considerations with an eye to enjoying the best of both worlds, the honours and privileges of a union charge together with the status and prestige of an officer. More importantly, the ability of officer-union representatives to successfully defend employees' interests when dealing with company executives was doubted. This was because *qua* officers these representatives could not count on the union to protect them. Therefore, they had to carefully weigh the risks of exhibiting an overly combative or militant stance against the likelihood of antagonising the management and even exposing themselves to sanctions.

. . . after becoming officers, union officials are ineffective in solving workers' problems since officers are scared that the company might take action against them and transfer them elsewhere . . . as workers we don't have the same fear in fighting the management as officers.[144]

---

[142] PD files, nd. Demands by certain workers that non-officers promoted as officers should not be allowed to continue in the union had in December 1990 led the union leadership to organize a referendum on this issue. In the referendum, employees voted overwhelmingly in favour of officers retaining their union membership.

[143] Officers accounted for only 7 of the 115 elected union representatives in 1990. This figure is unlikely to have increased substantially in later years. See ITI Union circular, 8 December 1990.

[144] Interview with Kovi Ramu. Apart from not having the same legal standing as a trade union, the ITI Officers' Association which represented officers' interests, lacked

As Gérard Adam has pointed out, the organizational choices made by a union should be interpreted neither as an extension of its ideology, nor as a technical support system for action. Instead, such choices articulate the union's conception of worker democracy and the objectives it intends to pursue.[145] In the case of the ITI union, although the general assembly of workers was constitutionally the sovereign body of the union, real power rested in the hands of the executive committee. Meeting every month and sometimes more frequently, it was this body which determined and executed the ends and means of all union action.

In comparison, the general assembly whose primary function was to ratify the union budget and approve the various policy measures and programmes decided by the executive committee, was convoked only once a year when not at longer intervals. No meeting of the general body was called between 1990–95, or between 1996–2001, for instance, although the rules stipulated that it should meet annually. Defending this 'subversion' of democratic procedures, Fernandes argued that

. . . in practice, in a union of 16 or 17,000 members like ours it is just not possible . . . to satisfy this particular bylaw of the constitution of a yearly general body meeting . . . (The union) is too big and all kinds of problems crop up. It is such a heterogeneous group, language problems, political problems, all kinds of problems can flare up, and can cause undesirable situations . . . The whole meeting can collapse on a frivolous matter . . . Of late, some workers have started making some noise about the delay in holding the meeting.[146]

As per its constitution, the union had to organize elections once every two years. But for a variety of reasons, it often struggled to conform to this obligation, especially during the 1990s. Richard Hyman has asserted that because unions normally operate in a hostile social environment, broader structural determinants cannot be ignored when analysing the question of internal democracy. Undoubtedly valid in certain

---

the strength to bail out its members when they got into trouble with the management. Whereas the union often succeeded in overturning or indefinitely stalling transfer orders and other such 'punitive' measures in the case of non-officers, the officers' association was powerless in similar situations.

[145] Adam, *Le pouvoir syndical*, pp. 3–4, 35–6.

[146] Interview with Fernandes, 17 December 1995. Given these difficulties, Fernandes had suggested replacing the annual assembly with a delegates' conference, each delegate representing roughly 25 workers. The proposal, however, was rejected by the membership.

circumstances, this argument cannot be stretched too far. Factors internal to the functioning of the union and the style of leadership also often act as obstacles to the achievement of meaningful worker governance.[147]

In the earlier decades, strikes, lockouts, protracted litigations, the imposition of Emergency had all caused elections to be delayed at the Bangalore plant, but the delays rarely exceeded more than a year.[148] However, between 1991–2001, despite the absence of pressing internal or external circumstances, employees were given the opportunity to exercise their industrial rights on just three occasions (1991, 1996, and 2001), essentially because of personal rivalries at the helm of the union.[149] We managed to locate only one mention in the company records concerning the reactions of the rank-and-file to the frequent denial of its rights. In June 1995, about 250 employees gathered inside the factory during the lunch break to demonstrate against the leadership's sequestration of power beyond its mandated term. All the speakers denounced the 'dictatorial ways' of the top officials and urged them to call elections promptly; there was also talk of seeking legal redress.[150] Interestingly, though the security files claim that the meeting had been organized without official permission, three policemen were present on the scene at the request of the company which feared a 'clash between two groups'.[151] This reference to the possibility of trouble erupting seems to indicate that supporters of one of the two rival factions within the union stood at the forefront of this show of protest.

[147] Hyman, *Industrial Relations*, pp. 68–9, 73–7. Elections as a rule are infrequent if not rare in companies where the union leadership relies on the management and government support for its survival. TISCO was one such example. Mamkootam, 'Industrial Relations in a Steel Plant'.

[148] However, no elections were organized between 1955–61 because of litigation over the embezzlement of union funds. Interview with Fernandes.

[149] See ITI Union circular, 6 September 2001; 12 September 2001. Prior to this, the management had already complained about elections being much overdue at the Bangalore plant whereas they were being held regularly at the other units. Minutes management-union meeting, 19 June 2000. A cartoon in a flyer brought out by one candidate, lampooning the union leadership, depicted Fernandes and V. Ramaswamy, the union general secretary, standing in the dock before a judge pleading: 'My Lord we have broken the law, but please do not order the conduct of elections. We are ready to pay any penalty in cash. After all the employees' union money is with us (sic)'. PD files.

[150] Ref. SY/FD/10, 17 June 1995.

[151] ibid.

At the same time, elections generally injected little fresh blood into the union hierarchy. Quasi-permanency of tenure is hardly a feature exclusive to the ITI union; still, the longevity of certain union careers was, by any standards, impressive.[152] As one senior representative conceded, there had been no efforts to 'develop a second-line leadership'.[153] Adds one worker:

There is not much choice between J.B. Nagaraj and Ramaswamy (the leaders of the two opposing groups each of whom contested for the post of general secretary). If workers are unhappy with Ramaswamy, they will vote for JB regardless of his errors and vice versa. There are no other candidates, partly because nobody comes forward to contest elections.[154]

In the 2001 elections newcomers finally succeeded in toppling the old guard, filling 83 posts out of a total of 116.[155] Still, even on this occasion, immobility ruled at the top. Reinstated as president, Fernandes remained in this post for 24 years, after having served earlier as general secretary for 12 years. The incumbent general secretary, V. Ramaswamy, who was also reelected had officiated in one capacity or the other in the union for almost 30 years. Even though both men had retired from the company nearly a decade ago, they obviously believed that the union should not be deprived of their experience.

---

[152] Underlining the oligarchic nature of the leadership in French unions, Adam remarks that trade union organizations everywhere are closed societies which one quits with difficulty once one has reached a level of high responsibility. *Le pouvoir syndical*, pp. 30–2. Similarly, Hyman notes that until 1958 only 12 per cent of British union bosses left office after defeat in a ballot. *Industrial Relations*, pp. 78–80. Beynon strikes a different note stating that while shop stewards at the Ford plant invariably carried on unopposed in elections, such continuity did not signify any sort of despotism. In case an opponent emerged with support from a large enough section of workers, the incumbent stepped down before the elections. *Working for Ford*, p. 198. In the US, 20 to 60 per cent of local union officials were replaced every three years when elections were held, while at the national level turnover rates of union presidents ranged from 9 to 12 per cent a year. Richard Freeman and James Medoff, *What do Unions Do?* New York, 1984, pp. 210–11. More generally, on the difficulties involved in giving up public action, see Albert Hirschman, *Shifting Involvements. Private Interest and Public Action*, Princeton, 1981, p. 94.

[153] Interview with N. Venugopalan.

[154] Interview with Yesuraj, May–June 1999. Ramaswamy comments on the indifference of Coimbatore textile workers to union elections with the result that leaders could retain their positions for as long as they wished. *The Worker and his Union*, p. 164.

[155] PD files, nd.

Veteran union officials also figured among the losing candidates in the last elections. One of the contestants for the post of general secretary had held this post for a total of 16 years, including nearly 11 years in a stretch. The organizing secretary had served in the union for almost 15 years, albeit with interruptions. Until his defeat in the 2001 elections, the union vice president had been unseated from this post on only one other occasion in three decades. As the careers of these three individuals themselves showed, union officials could not afford to take the loyalty of the membership for granted, and some measure of change did occur, though only fitfully. Much like professional politicians, union representatives were extremely reluctant to rejoin the ranks once they had tasted the perks of office.[156] Moreover, defeat quite often represented but a temporary setback, and some officials were prompt to revive their public careers in other spheres of factory social life. Thus those who had been 'punished' by the rank-and-file in the union elections were sometimes able to regain its favour in the elections to the union credit cooperative society, and then utilized this post as a springboard to bounce back into the union hierarchy. As one representative declared,

I did good work in the credit cooperative society as treasurer. I introduced new loans . . . improved the situation of society staff in terms of salary and benefits. Later they worked for me during the union elections.[157]

Long tenures were apparently common at the lower rungs of the union chain-of-command as well. While we do not dispose sufficient data, several executive committee and general council members seem to have conserved their posts for upwards of 15 years. None, though, could surpass the record of one GC member who was elected for seven consecutive terms before finally opting for voluntary retirement.

As far as members were concerned, the immobility at all echelons of the union hierarchy did not constitute a wholly negative phenomenon. By virtue of their longevity, delegates had the advantage of being extremely familiar with the functioning of the company, the way the management reacted to different problems, and the grievances of workers both as a

---

[156]After his defeat in the 2001 elections, the former organizing secretary of the union requested the company for a transfer outside the Bangalore plant in order to escape the humiliation of having to be seen working in his old department by employees. The company was expected to agree to his request.

[157] Interview with Venugopalan.

collective and in individual cases. Hence they were well armed to defend employees' interests. Besides, since the majority of officers in the personnel department also rarely changed posts, the leadership developed close relationships with them which often proved useful in resolving quotidian issues. Interestingly, union officials attributed the deterioration in labour-management ties, particularly at the Bangalore unit from the mid-1990s onwards, to the arrival of new executives alien to the company's culture and style of functioning.

There were no IR problems in the past, but today senior officers are coming from outside. Vasudevan (corporate head of personnel) has come from Kudremukh, a state-owned mining company, and Chatterjee (head of personnel at the Bangalore plant) from NTPC (National Thermal Power Corporation). They do not know the ITI culture. They are trying to force changes rapidly, impose their will.[158]

The low turnover rates probably suggested that limited competition prevailed for union jobs. Despite the benefits and prestige these positions carried, it is quite possible that a union career exercised very little appeal for the mass of ordinary workers. In the 2001 elections, for example, there were just 290 candidates contesting the 116 posts that were available, or 2.5 candidates per post. Of these, only one was a woman.[159] For, needless to say, union office remained an exclusively male preserve. In the nearly five decades of the organization's existence, the first time that a woman candidate managed to get elected was in 2001. Given the totally skewed gender balance of the factory workforce, the leadership never thought it necessary or worthwhile to promote greater female representation, among other things by encouraging women employees to stand for elections. Unfortunately we lack similar information for elections held prior to 2001, so we cannot say if contestants for union jobs faced stiffer levels of competition in the past.

ORDINARY WORKERS RELUCTANT TO CONTEST FOR UNION OFFICE

In the interviews we conducted with employees, barring a handful who at one point or the other had been actively involved in the union, none

---

[158] ibid.
[159] PD files, nd.

of the others expressed any interest in running for union office.[160] This was true even of employees whose life histories, personal stature, and combativeness in day-to-day work issues could well have predisposed them towards a more serious engagement in the affairs of the union. These employees cited a variety of reasons to justify their indifference, reasons which in more than one instance were dictated by the logic of self-preservation and corresponded to a strong desire to maintain their integrity.

First, quite a few of them claimed they were ill-equipped to become union representatives. This had less to do with the question of personal abilities than of being temperamentally unsuited.[161] Employees argued that they lacked the 'thick skins' the function demanded and without which it would be impossible to endure the constant carping and criticisms the base subjected the leadership to.[162]

We also have to face unnecessary complaints from workers when we are in the union. They will unnecessarily blame the union whether you do a good job or bad. That I cannot tolerate. Union people who are doing good work still get a bad name (sic).[163]

Added another worker:

I am not interested in being active in the union because in public life you must accept being scolded and criticized by all and sundry. I am a sensitive person.[164]

---

[160] Our knowledge of the machinery of union governance and the dialectics of the relationship between the leadership and the rank-and-file in India continues to be grossly inadequate for want of in-depth ethnographic enquiries. The only full-length study available, and an invaluable contribution to the topic notwithstanding its shortcomings, dates back to 1977, namely E.A. Ramaswamy's pioneering work, *The Worker and his Union*. Concentrating on the Coimbatore textile industry like E.A. Ramaswamy, the section devoted by Uma Ramaswamy in her book, *Work, Union and Community*, to workers' interactions with the union also provides useful insights.

[161] In the case study conducted by Beynon and Blackburn, workers at a food producing plant in the UK justified their reluctance to hold union office on two grounds: they did not possess the skills required for the role; the job of a shop steward was deemed to be unattractive. Huw Beynon and R.M. Blackburn, *Perceptions of Work. Variations within a Factory*, Cambridge, 1972, pp. 133–4. See also Beynon's own later study at Ford where workers, if they raised the issue of personal aptitude, also underlined the high levels of commitment the job of a shop steward demanded as a reason for not wanting to assume this responsibility. *Working for Ford*, pp. 200–1.

[162] The shop stewards interviewed by Beynon all described their job as a 'thankless one' where they 'get stick' from all sides. *Working for Ford*, p. 196, 219–24.

[163] Interview with Anantha Padmanabha, 1 December 2001.

[164] Interview with Krishnan.

In other words, the constraints of the public sphere where one had to face humiliation, mask one's true sentiments, and 'beg for votes' far outweighed its rewards.[165]

Closely connected to this conception of the public figure as somebody basically 'unfree' were apprehensions centring on conflicting definitions of justice or dueness. Taking on a union job, employees feared, would, by definition, entail having to compromise on the elementary notion of justice they upheld where belief in the idea of just deserts was capital. In their eyes, this belief contradicted with the abstract, collective principles of justice guiding the union's actions where regardless of considerations of right and wrong it was duty-bound to protect the interests of all employees. The following statement unambiguously brings out this perceived disjunction:

Because of my popularity, my friends were pushing me to contest union elections, but I did not wish to do so. I am for justice in all matters, so I won't defend workers who don't work, but as a union official I will be forced to take up their cause with the management.[166]

Failing to defend a worker even when the union knew he or she was guilty of some offence would have undermined the very *raison d'être* of the union's function and damaged its credibility in the eyes of the workforce. Besides, it risked creating a dangerous precedent which the management could be tempted to subsequently exploit.

Third, and most significantly, union responsibilities and its attendant burdens were viewed as being fundamentally incompatible with doing a fair day's work. What employees valued most was to be regarded, particularly by their colleagues, as 'sincere workers', a term that meant conscientious, worthy of the wages the company paid them. This positive self-image that they sought to project, in their discourse, if not in practice, was entwined with its reverse, the negative representation of the union official, widely-perceived to be lazy, self-serving, and corrupt, who utilized his position to shirk work and feather his own nest at the expense of the rank-and-file.

. . . union officials do not work, but get salary. I don't like this . . . after working hours only, we must go for union activity (sic).[167]

---

[165] Interview with Govindaraju.
[166] Interview with Vinayagam, 22 November 2001.
[167] Interview with Sahadevan.

Even more brutal was the following assessment:

Union officials get elected not to serve workers, but to go out of the factory to do their personal business.[168]

There were also complaints of pressure, not always subtle, being sometimes being brought upon operatives to turn over a part of their daily output to shop delegates after the management wanted all delegates to work a certain number of hours.

The worker cannot go against the union officials. In case of any problem he has to approach the union only.[169]

Representatives' reputations suffered an additional grievous blow from the knowledge that the sons of the bosses heading the two main factions within the union had succeeded in securing jobs in the company at a time when recruitments had virtually ceased. Of the top officials, only Fernandes and a couple of others conserved the unanimous respect of the rank-and-file.

Workers also reproached certain union representatives of abusing their positions to extort bribes from members. For certain, corrupt practices were far less embedded or institutionalized in the ITI union relative to other workers' organizations present in the public sector.[170] Nevertheless, in the overall context of deference that characterized the relationship of the base with the leadership, the obligation of having to pay for services they were entitled to receive as a matter of course further emphasized

[168] Interview with Thomas Mathew, 24 November 2001.

[169] Interview with Sahadevan.

[170] If the endemic corruption that pervaded virtually all aspects of the unions' functioning in the Dhanbad collieries had few equivalents elsewhere, unions in the nationalized jute mills in Calcutta were also regularly suspected of selling jobs. For details of the Dhanbad unions, see Heuzé, *Ouvriers d'un autre monde*, pp. 298–300, 347. On the jute mill unions, see de Haan, 'Migrant Labour in Calcutta Jute Mills'. More generally, Bardhan observes that it is not uncommon for certain union leaderships in the public sector to try and trade-off managerial corruption, nepotism and other irregularities with fake payrolls, overstaffing, absenteeism and overtime payments for normal working hours. Bardhan, *The Political Economy of Development in India*, pp. 69–70. Bribing union officials to obtain jobs and promotion was also an established practice in the privately-owned Coimbatore textile mills, states Uma Ramaswamy. *Work, Union and Community*, pp. 81–4.

employees' sense of vulnerability and subordination *vis-à-vis* union officialdom.[171]

Employees most directly affected by corruption were those whom the company had charge sheeted for misconduct. They were therefore dependent upon union representatives to defend them, sometimes before an enquiry committee, a dependence generally accentuated by employees' total ignorance of the procedures and mode of functioning of the disciplinary machinery.[172] To make sure that the representatives showed up at the grievance hearing and defended the case to the best of their ability, employees frequently had no choice but to offer a bribe. This could either take the form of an outright monetary payment, or a loan that would never be acquitted, both financial transactions being accompanied by a 'dinner party' at a restaurant where the worker footed the bill.

Employees seeking help from union officials to solve their personal demands were the other victims of the latter's venality. Thus paying a bribe considerably facilitated matters for those who wanted to be transferred from the Bangalore plant to other ITI units or regional offices located in or near their place of origin. Similarly, workers applying for loans from banks or other financial institutions could hope to get the process expedited if influential union officials, in return for monetary compensation, agreed to endorse their applications. Union representatives were also sometimes accused of misappropriating funds. In a petition to the head of the Bangalore plant, three workers who had filed a complaint against a general council member for allegedly pocketing a sum of Rs 7000 allocated for worker education tours, wrote that he was now threatening them and wanted them to withdraw their complaint.[173]

WORKERS INSTRUMENTAL ATTITUDE TOWARDS UNION

Coexisting alongside this unflattering portrait of the union representative that employees painted were their ambivalent attitudes towards the

---

[171] Contrary to what Kennedy writes, it is not the 'western observer' alone who 'is struck by the social differences between leaders and members' of trade unions. Indigenous scholars are equally struck by this phenomenon. *Unions, Employers and Government*, p. 87.

[172] Discrimination by union officials in the handling of grievances was also a common topic of complaint among workers in the Chicago engineering plant studied by Burawoy. *Manufacturing Consent*, p. 114.

[173] Ref. SY/FD/10, 5 November 1986.

organization.[174] It was the combination of these two factors that to a large extent determined ordinary employees' refusal to embark upon a union career. The utility of the union in imposing definite limits on the exercise of managerial authority, safeguarding their existing interests, and obtaining supplementary benefits in future was definitely something none of the employees had to be prompted into recalling. Having a union that was not subservient to the management, they understood, was consubstantial with their condition of being wage earners. Nor were they in anyway sparing in their praise of the achievements of the ITI union. Conscious that the advent of deregulation by transforming the company into a pale shadow of its former self had irrevocably shattered the foundations of the union's strength, workers, nonetheless, highlighted, among other things, its success in securing the establishment of the seniority-based promotion scheme. Most of them knew that but for this scheme, they would have stagnated at the bottom of the occupational ladder.

Yet while prompt in recognizing the value and necessity of the union's existence at a collective level, albeit from a purely instrumental perspective, workers expressed an unwillingness to do so at an individual level.[175] The bulk of the workers we interviewed said they had never approached the union with work-related grievances, let alone personal ones, throughout their career. They were persuaded of possessing the resources to manage their everyday working lives without any recourse to union assistance or protection.

Paradoxically, it was the very achievement of the union which had brought about the biggest improvement in the economic well-being and social status of employees, namely the instituting of the promotion scheme, which had served, in no small measure, to attenuate its importance in the eyes of the ordinary worker. For with promotions now automatically adjusted to a rigorously codified time scale, the scope for managerial arbitrariness evaporated with the result that workers had

[174] According to Burawoy, complaints voiced by workers against the union are directed more at individual representatives than at the union as an institution. *Manufacturing Consent*, p. 113.

[175] In his study of factory workers in Bangalore, Holmström describes most workers' relation to the union as 'transactional'. The union provided a service when needed (promotion, grievances, disciplinary action, etc.); in return it occasionally asked for sacrifice, solidarity and enthusiasm. *South Indian Factory Workers*, pp. 71–2.

far less need to turn to the union. In addition to the elaborate complex of impersonal regulations that governed practically all aspects of the wage contract, a bureaucratized system of career advancement did more than just put an end to the management's power to 'reward by intuition', to borrow from Richard Sennett.[176] It also seriously curtailed an essential function played by the union, and one that defined its legitimacy, the redressal of work injustices.

Reinforcing employees' impressions of autonomy was the failure of shop delegates to satisfactorily tackle certain collective problems such as poor quality raw materials or inadequate tools. These problems proved to be a constant irritant because they kept recurring, interfering with the swing of work and the flow of output, and in so doing, sparked further doubts about the effectiveness of the union. That the union had made various attempts to raise the matter with the management and that it lacked the means to pressure the latter into finding a definitive solution, especially in the post-deregulation phase when the company was badly stretched for cash, were details not lost on most workers. Still, as I noticed during the time I spent on the shopfloor, seldom was an occasion missed to mock the delegates, openly as well as behind their backs, and call into question their competence and utility. Mostly good natured in spirit, such shows of verbal aggression must be understood as forming part of the customary banter that endowed a shop with a distinctive character, ordinary employees being only too content to get an opportunity to cut the delegates down to size.

Workers also felt they could personally do without the union for another reason: being 'sincere workers' who executed their tasks diligently and conformed to factory regulations, they always managed to stay clear of trouble. As they pointed out, it was only a small section of employees against whom the company regularly pressed disciplinary charges who were the principal 'clientele' of the union, relying on its interventions to escape punishment.

. . . Union is only meant for frauds and third class people; those who are long absentees, chargesheeted for theft, etc . . . Decent employees will never approach union officials. What work do we have with them?[177]

---

[176] Richard Sennett and Jonathan Cobb, *The Hidden Injuries of Class*, New York, 1993, p. 157.

[177] Interview with B. Narayana Murthy, 19 October 1997. A fairly similar view is

Excessive as the point of view articulated in these lines might appear to an outside observer, it was one shared by a number of ordinary employees and dovetailed with the abiding lack of esteem in which they held the majority of the union representatives. Workers seemed to establish an automatic homology between the leadership and those sections of the membership most dependent on the union; it was as though only 'insincere' employees would call upon the services of unscrupulous delegates.

The situation described above of minimal contact between the leaders and the 'led', no doubt, reflected by and large, the prevailing reality of worker-union relations in many firms, and not just in India.[178] Frantz, for example, speaks of the traditional gap that exists in every political party or trade union between the rank-and-file and the leaders.[179] Nevertheless, variables exclusive to ITI also probably explained why workers here took a certain pride in their ability to stay aloof from the union. The market structure which guaranteed the company a monopoly position allied to its status as a state-owned enterprise operating under soft budget constraints, signified that the drive for higher rates of labour productivity and cost economies, in principle the keystone of managerial action in a capitalist system of industrial production, ranked at the bottom of ITI management's priorities.

This in turn radically conditioned the nature of authority exercised over the workforce. Executives at the telecommunications manufacturer were guilty not so much of abusing their prerogatives to intensify work loads so as to extract surplus value, as of failing to utilize their extensive powers to enforce even standard effort norms, as we demonstrated in an earlier chapter. Indeed, describing the order of employment relationships in the factory as indulgent would be no misnomer. Skirmishes at the frontier of control over the pace of work were non-existent. Time

---

expressed by workers in the engineering company interviewed by Sheth, *Social Framework of an Indian Factory*, p. 166.

[178] See, for instance, Beynon and Blackburn, pp. 126–8, 130–1; Alf Lüdtke, 'What happened to the "Fiery Red Glow"? Workers' Experiences and German Fascism', in *idem* (ed.), *The History of Everyday Life. Reconstructing Historical Experiences and Ways of Life*, Princeton, 1995, pp. 198–251; Panjwani, 'Living with Capitalism'; Michèle Perrot, *Les ouvriers en grève, 1871–1890*, Paris, 1974, p. 311 (Vol. 1); Sheth, *Social Framework of an Indian Factory*, pp. 159–60, 163–8, 201. According to Heuzé, ordinary workers' disinterest in unions derives in part from the shallow roots of craft consciousness among Indian workers. 'Le monde du travail indien et les organisations de salariés'.

[179] Frantz Fanon, *The Wretched of the Earth*, Harmondsworth, 1974, p. 85.

standards once established were seldom subject to cuts. Nor did workers have much occasion to complain of close supervision or, for that matter, of other forms of supervisory harassment. No managerial category had seen its power and importance shrink as dramatically and rapidly as had foremen following the implementation of the time-bound promotion plan; they were given responsibility but could not exercise authority. So with antagonisms thoroughly muffled at the point of production, workers understandably enough had few reasons to seek assistance from the union.

On the shopfloor in a private sector, officers are scared. They may be asked to quit if they do not deliver the goods. That generally does not happen in the public sector. So there is a more relaxed atmosphere in the shop floor.[180]

This statement by Michael Fernandes is readily corroborated by senior ITI executives. Their comments also illuminated another fundamental reason for the arms-length relation many ordinary workers maintained with the union: the guarantee of job security undergirding a job in a state-run undertaking. Workers knew full well that unless they committed a serious offence such as assaulting a manager or stealing company property, they were assured of retaining their jobs until retirement.

Compared to the private sector the pressure on the workforce is much less in the public sector. We do not want to push a worker beyond his capacities, to do one and a half times more than what he is capable of doing . . . Moreover, workers had no fear of getting sacked in the public sector. There are more rules and regulations here and less arbitrariness. You cannot be sacked overnight as in the private sector.[181]

Adds another executive:

Because we worked on a cost-plus basis, there was no incentive for the management to put pressure on workers to give more production like in the private sector. In private sector there is always tension between the management and workers. Shop bosses have to show targets daily. But we were not facing competition.[182]

---

[180] Interview with Fernandes.

[181] Interview with C.R. Datta Gupta.

[182] Interview with L.G. Varadharajan. E.A. Ramaswamy writes: '. . . features common to the private sector such as constant rationalization of methods and revision of work norms, running down of the labour force . . . are . . . absent in the government-owned concerns'. He goes on to add that 'the fact certainly is that coping with work (in the public sector) has not been a problem'. *Worker Consciousness and Trade Union Response*, p. 144.

Hence, informed by their own deeply-held notions of self-dignity, personal morality and justice, employees' negative appreciation of the leadership served to dissuade them from standing for union office. These attitudes were further buttressed by the sentiment that the union was relatively unimportant to them and had little meaning at a personal or individual level.

COSTS OF FINANCING UNION ELECTIONS

At the same time, financing an election campaign called for some means, and the employees whom we spoke to were either unwilling or unable to assume the expenditure involved.[183] For low ranking functions such as executive committee or general council posts a minimum amount of Rs 500 was required in order to print flyers and other electioneering publicity material. This figure could easily rise two- or three-fold or even more if candidates wished to woo employees more vigorously by plying them with tea, coffee, and snacks, buying them cigarettes, inviting them to restaurants, and even hosting 'parties' where alcohol and non-vegetarian food were served.

If the desire to exploit the prestige associated with a union job accounted in part for the conspicuous spending candidates indulged in, they were also frequently motivated by less symbolic reasons. Employees contesting from the hospital, transport and canteen departments, for instance, spent liberally to guarantee their victory because

union officials movements in this constituency are very free. There are no security checks here. So they can go and attend to their personal work easily . . . The man who stood for GC post from transport (in the 2001 elections) has a side activity. He is a partner in a school in a village near the factory.[184]

Candidates vying for the higher level union jobs obviously needed deeper pockets commensurate with the larger audiences they addressed. Deploying much the same vote-pulling stratagems, albeit on a much

[183] Elections to other worker bodies such as the House Building Society and the Credit Cooperative Society were even costlier affairs in view of the infinitely greater opportunities for personal enrichment a post here offered. Candidates intent on participating in the share of the spoils had therefore perforce to spend substantial sums of money to win votes.

[184] Interview with Krishna Kumar, ITI Personnel Manager, 13 December 2001.

larger scale, as those resorted to by contestants for the less strategic posts, they had to incur considerable sums of money as well on taking care of their 'followers', namely employees who latched on to one or the other union leader so as to avoid working.

> Only five per cent of the workers sitting in my union office all day have real problems. The rest are followers, they sit from morning with us, drink tea and coffee, and don't work. It is difficult for me to tell them not to come to my office.[185]

The utility of the 'followers' to their patrons was never more evident than during union elections when they canvassed actively on behalf of the latter and attended to the nitty-gritty. In return, they had to be fed as well as kept provided with numerous cups of tea and coffee, packets of cigarettes, and, as election day neared, with alcohol to ensure that their efforts did not flag. Funds for the campaigns of the better known candidates sometimes came from wealthy sympathizers inside the factory who offered to print handbills and posters, put up banners, buy food for the followers, or even organize a party to boost the candidate's chances. Asked why these sympathizers exhibited such generosity, one union representative declared:

> If I win they in turn have a chance of being elected to other bodies because of the influence I wield as an union official . . . They can (also) be part of your group, move with you during campaigning and *they do not have to work*.[186]

Political parties to which the candidates belonged also occasionally lent a helping hand. In addition to cash, certain candidates also parlayed advantages in kind. Thus one of the officials of the ITI Consumer Cooperative Society, with an eye on a union job acquired the nickname of 'kerosene Appanna', because of his practice of supplying employees with domestic supplies of extra sugar and kerosene, besides helping them obtain ration cards.

A final element that contributed to restricting the rank-and-file's participation in the activities of the union was linguistic chauvinism. In the wake of the assertion of Kannada nativism in Bangalore from the late 1960s onwards and the concomitant cycle of violence directed at Tamil employees inside ITI, Kannadigas dominated the union since Tamil

---

[185] Interview with Venugopalan.
[186] ibid. Emphasis added.

candidates seldom came forward to contest union elections. Not only could the risk of physical attacks on them not be excluded, but, as many of them soon realized, their chances of winning were minimal given that few Kannada workers were likely to vote for them. Indeed, after 1969, Tamil presence in the union could be described as no more than token. One of the rare Tamil employees who did succeed in getting elected, including twice to the upper echelons of the organization, was N. Venugopalan.

Born in neighbouring Tamil Nadu, he had migrated to Bangalore in his youth to avoid being arrested for his participation in the anti-Hindi linguistic agitation that rocked Tamil Nadu during much of the 1960s. Hired as a learner in the telephone division of ITI in 1964, his work as a volunteer during the 1964 and 1966 stay-in strikes had enabled him to be first elected to the central incentive committee, progressing from there to the works committee and finally to the union.

To catch workers' eye, incentive committee is a good post because of the financial gains it brings to them. Later I went to works committee. Union was not taking care of problems like cloak room, cleanliness of the hangar, providing water coolers, so I got a chance to be active here.[187]

Asked why he subsequently wanted to become a union representative, his answer was striking for its candour: while ideals of service were not absent, self-interested behaviour seemed to be the prime motivation.

I preferred the union to other bodies because more work can be done by attending to day-to-day problems. More knowledge can be gained of the factory. *It is possible to stand for other elections later like MLA. Privilege of union post is that you don't have to work.* Once you are elected you remain a leader, even if you are defeated. Union officials' movements in factory is also not controlled. Prestige also of being an union official. You can talk to chairman any time or any management officer.[188]

Other worker discourses contained the same mix of opportunism and service centredness

If linguistic loyalties dictated employees' voting preferences in no small way, so too apparently did caste loyalties. Indeed, in the opinion of the management and employees alike, caste superseded all other criteria when

---

[187] ibid.
[188] ibid. Emphasis added.

it came to selecting a candidate, particularly with respect to executive committee and general council posts.

> Workers do not think whether a candidate is suited for a post, his capacities, etc. They think only whether he belongs to same caste, or is a relative or his religion.[189]

According to Fernandes, the union president,

> given that politics, caste, language and money play a big role in all kinds of elections, there is no way that we can prevent its influence in union elections . . . In the assembly or parliamentary elections, we see the newspapers full of caste analyses of the candidate or the constituency. No government cabinet is formed without reference to caste. Workers are involved in politics and get attracted to political parties. All this has its reflection in the shop floor and in union election results and in the union's actions.[190]

Employees running for elections were also often accused of requesting the caste associations to which they belonged, and which were present inside the factory, to endorse their candidatures. Furthermore, Fernandes complained that the weight exerted by caste identities in shaping the outcome of union elections was having a spill-over effect in certain areas of union activity, thus hampering its smooth functioning. Workers were often reluctant, he claimed, to report grievances to the union representative responsible for their shop or department, and instead sought out a representative from their own caste to take up their problems.

> The employee does not believe that the union man is somebody neutral and will look on the case on its merits and fight for him.[191]

Not all representatives though ceded to the siren calls of their caste brethren. But when they did intercede, and in so doing undermined the influence of other representatives by encroaching on their territory, it inevitably generated tensions within the union hierarchy, besides heightening the awareness of caste distinctions.

Given the paucity of reliable evidence, reading off the influence of caste from the actual results of the elections is a risky proposition for an outsider. The task is further complicated by the absence of verifiable

---

[189] Interview with Surappa, 9 January 1998.
[190] Interview with Fernandes, June 2000.
[191] ibid.

data on the caste composition of the workforce with the exception of
SC-ST employees. Though the dominant caste in Karnataka, Lingayats
were thought to be a relative minority in the factory, counting fewer
than 750 employees even in the mid-1970s.[192] In comparison, Vokalligas,
the other big caste grouping in the state, were much better represented
with their strength estimated at close to 2000 prior to the introduction
of the voluntary retirement programme.[193] Still, they are believed to
have been outnumbered by the Brahmin contingent whose size varied
between 2500 and 3000 employees.[194] Counterbalancing their numerical
superiority was the anti-Brahmin sentiment that existed at a broader
social level, the pro-management tag that stuck to Brahmin representatives
given that many senior executives were Brahmins, and the limited presence
of Brahmins in production areas.[195] Only for those posts where the entire
workforce voted did Brahmin candidates stand a reasonable chance of
winning.

To the extent that the shadow of caste fell over union politics, there is
no doubt that it was a direct consequence, one among numerous, of the
language agitation. Once language had become the basis for identification
and differentiation, the affirmation of other primordial markers could
only have been a short step away. One could also legitimately ask whether
the creation of the ITI SC-ST association in 1976 did not provide a
further impetus to this process of cementing caste identities and, its
logical corollary, the instrumentalization of caste for electoral gains.
Though the association never issued a formal call to its members
instructing them to vote for a particular candidate, it is commonly
believed that the backing of SC-ST employees was decisive in assuring
the election of a backward caste to the key post of general secretary in
1996 ousting the incumbent, a Brahmin.

But caste considerations told only a part of the story. As shall be
shown in chapter nine, relations between the SC-ST association and the

---

[192] Interview with Shivanna, Secretary ITI Lingayat Association, 27 March 1999.

[193] Interview with B.V. Rajan, Secretary ITI Hombe Gowda Association, 7 May 1999.

[194] Interview withY. Krishnamurthy, Secretary ITI Brahmin Sabha, 31 March 1999.

[195] In distinct contrast to Tamil Nadu, for several reasons the non-Brahmin movement
in Karnataka developed without displaying the same potency and cohesiveness. For a
broader exposition of the theme, see James Manor, *Political Change in an Indian State.
Mysore 1917–1955*, New Delhi, 1978, pp. 31–3, 58–72 ff.

union turned from mutual suspicion during the 1980s into outright hostility in the early 1990s. The former insistently denounced the union for allegedly pursuing discriminatory policies against the interests of SC employees, particularly on the vexatious question of promotions. Thus in the 1996 elections, a candidate enjoying the blessings of the SC-ST association, Hanumanthaiah, ran for the post of president against Michael Fernandes, and seriously challenged him. Already on one occasion in the mid-1980s, a female SC-ST candidate called Dommu Kondamma who worked as a sweeper had opposed Fernandes. But despite SC-ST employees accounting for slightly more than 21 per cent of the factory workforce, Kondamma apparently failed to pick up more than 12 per cent of the total vote.[196]

Now, Hanumanthaiah's share of the vote climbed to a little under 30 per cent, a definite sign that he had succeeded in rallying much of the SC-ST community (24 per cent of the factory strength) behind his banner.[197] Through this display of unity it wished to loudly register its discontent *vis-à-vis* the union and its top officials, accused of having overturned the advantages SC-ST employees enjoyed earlier. Thus if the attempt to mobilize caste ties for electoral ends paid off this time, it was essentially because it served to articulate employees' grievances. As the contrasting results of the two elections underlined, SC-ST employees did not blindly support candidates belonging to their community; caste loyalties crystallized and surfaced in full only when material interests were also thought to be at stake.

More strikingly, the fact that caste identities and linguistic identities ran along contradictory tracks not only scotched the facile assumption of SC-ST employees forming a homogenous bloc, it even gave rise to quite bizarre situations. The enduring antagonisms between Kannadigas and Telegus, on the one hand, and Tamilians, on the other, that vertically bisected the ITI workforce, translated into the signal paradox where Tamil SC-ST workers could countenance the idea of voting for a Brahmin candidate like Venugopalan on grounds of linguistic affinity.

[196] Interview with Fernandes.
[197] ITI Union circular, 18 May 1996.

UNION REPRESENTATIVES PROVIDE WIDE RANGE OF SERVICES

All this is not to suppress, or minimize, the force of caste in capturing the imaginations of the workforce. But critical as these subjective attachments may have been in determining the choice of a representative, other, more material, factors also entered into the picture. Employees weighed a candidate's previous record, compared notes on his competency, scrutinized his integrity, checked his accessibility to the membership, examined his overall style and approach to problems, and assessed his readiness to confront the management. As Bourdieu has noted, the task of a delegate or spokesperson is to employ a language which enables individuals to universalize their experiences without, however, depriving them of the possibility of articulating their experiences. He goes on to add that what is operational in the act of delegation is less a delegate's discourse than other criteria, often impalpable, such as 'style', accent, corporal bearing and so forth, all of which facilitate a sense of identification.[198] The following quotes all illustrate in varying ways and degrees this analysis:

To win elections, you must build confidence in workers. Confidence is built by your work, your way of talking to them, your ability to explain things clearly and in-depth to workers. Results matters less some times than the way you approach the workers' problems, be attentive to them, be a good listener, show that you are making efforts, inform them of your efforts. Yours hands should also be clean.[199]

Voicing a near-identical opinion, one worker declared:

I vote in union elections depending on the candidate's personal character, and his union service and track record. Both aspects are equally important. A candidate must be friendly, listen patiently to workers' problems, have an obliging nature.[200]

Considerable emphasis was placed on candidates being of an 'obliging nature', a term which denoted at once being helpful and demonstrating concern for employees' needs, and which had the non-negligible merit

[198] Bourdieu, *Questions de sociologie*, pp. 63–4, 248–9, 261–2.
[199] Interview with Venugopalan.
[200] Interview with Sahadevan.

of drawing attention to the fact that if caste probably mattered so did the ethos of service.

If one worker repeats to others that an union official has helped him to solve a problem or not helped him, it can decide the fate of the official.[201]

The politics of reputation then determined whether workers exercised positive or negative material and symbolic sanctions, such as voting or not voting for a representative, diffusing a favourable or unfavourable image of him, which in turn contributed to placing the relations between leaders and 'led' on a less unequal plane.[202] The value of a good name, and the cost of a bad name, was something evident to union officials who understood the importance of being seen to affirm their sense of obligation through a bodily engagement in the problems of the rank-and-file, as opposed to mere verbal displays of solidarity. So when irate second shift operatives called Venugopalan to the factory, to complain about canteen personnel not serving food properly, he promptly went along with them although he had gone home for the day.

Workers know that I live close to the factory. So if I don't go they will grumble and say that I have become too big for my boots.[203]

Likewise, John Joseph, the executive committee member in charge of the telephone printed circuit board shop, mentioned that whenever workers from his shop were hospitalized he visited them.

I check if they have any financial problems, and sometimes try and collect money from colleagues . . .[204]

A worker from the SC-ST community in the printed circuit board shop said that he had voted not for his caste fellow who contested against Joseph in the 2001 elections, but for the latter because

---

[201] ibid.

[202] James C. Scott, *Weapons of the Weak. Everyday Forms of Peasant Resistance*, New Haven, 1985, pp. 24–5. Nevertheless, Scott claims the rich suffer from the costs of a bad name only through the symbolic sanctions levied by the poor (slander, gossip, and character assassination), whereas the powerful are in a position to impose both economic as well as social sanctions on 'disreputable' subordinates.

[203] Interview with Venugopalan.

[204] Interview with John Joseph, 19 November 2001.

he does good work. He doesn't suck up to the management, or act hyprocitely taking one stand with the management and another with workers, nor does he speak badly to workers.[205]

Indeed, despite the presence of an estimated 60 SC-ST employees in this shop, the SC-ST candidate managed to picked up a total of only 40 votes.[206] According to Joseph,

workers have faith that I am not prone to caste or language feelings. I am very social. I mix with all. I go wherever workers ask me to go, wherever they have problems . . . to the ITI hospital, outside the factory . . . Sometimes, I have to solve traffic problems or household problems as a friendly service. I have to intervene in quarrels between a father and the children.[207]

What the above lines revealed was that a 'good' union representative was not only judged by his ability to remedy shop floor-related grievances and to do so speedily. Equally importantly, he was judged by the resourcefulness he displayed in assisting members who faced difficulties outside the factory.[208] Indeed, representatives devoted most of their time and energy attending to non-production concerns. While workers did come to them with complaints about incentive payment computations, harassment by the management officers and so forth, the problems representatives were expected to solve pertained in the main to what Venugopalan qualified as 'welfare issues'.

These fell into two categories. The first related to internal factory matters. Workers relied on the representatives to perform the function of intermediaries. The latter were either expected to take up workers' problems with a bureaucratic and obstructive factory administration, or to accelerate the process of securing loans for them from the different equally bureaucratic welfare institutions (provident fund trust, death relief fund, etc.) that operated within the plant. Pointing out that 'if you go on your own to admin block, your case will not be dealt with quickly', one worker remarked,

---

[205] Interview with Vinayagam.

[206] Interview with John Joseph.

[207] ibid.

[208] Stating that shop stewards acted as watchdogs and counsellors, Beynon remarks that because of their 'overwhelming sense of obligation' towards union members, they also dealt with members' family difficulties along with other personal problems such as tax, law and order matters and the like. *Working for Ford*, p. 217, 222.

the main problem for most workers is to get a PF (Provident Fund) loan or Rafi Welfare loan quickly. To get a PF loan, you have to leave your work spot, lose incentive, obtain a movement badge which is not easy, then you lose a lot of time waiting in the PF section. So to avoid all this, workers prefer approaching union officials to help them out.[209]

Workers, especially those who living within a five km radius from the factory were obligatorily covered by the ITI hospital, also sought the representatives' aid in order to avoid having to receive medical treatment at the hospital. Both the union and workers were scathing in their criticism of company health personnel. In meetings with the management, union officials repeatedly complained of the doctors whom they accused of being callous, non-cooperative, and often absent from their work spots.[210] Given the poor levels and standards of care provided by the ITI hospital, workers then obviously preferred to consult outside establishments and specialists. To be able to do so, though, required the authorization of ITI doctors, and they could be persuaded to refer the case elsewhere only if requested by union representatives.

The second set of 'welfare issues' that representatives had to address, focussed on extra-factory issues. These ranged from trying to obtain government jobs and emergency bank loans and college admissions (for employees' children and other family members) through to helping clear employees' house building projects with municipal authorities, getting a defective street light repaired, arranging for a ration card, patching up family quarrels, and intervening in local law and order matters. Many of these social functions performed by the union representative used, in fact, to be customarily discharged by the jobber (*sardar* or *mistri*), in the early stages of industrialization, especially in the textile mills, and just as it enabled the jobber to sustain submission and respect, it helped the representative to boost his personal standing and gain workers' loyalty.

Finding a solution to the extra-work problems faced by workers invariably necessitated the intervention of local politicians as well as police officials. Well-connected union officials, therefore, held a distinct edge over those who could not leverage similar resources for the benefit of employees. This detail also partly accounted for the care taken by higher

[209] Interview with Irudayaraj.

[210] Minutes management-union meeting, 17 October 1986; 8–15 February 1988; 8 May 2000.

470 Telecommunications Industry in India

ranking union leaders in particular to both cultivate ties with political parties and publicize these connections among the rank-and-file. Workers in the printed circuit board shop knew, for instance, that Joseph had *entrées* to at least two ministers in a former Congress government. Joseph himself informed me that his circle of friends included no less than nine police inspectors in the city.

If workers have problems with rowdies in their locality who are harassing them, or their family members they come and tell me.[211]

Similarly, Venugopalan boasted that because of his close links with the local Congress assembly member, the Bangalore Development Authority had lowered the cost of the 'no-objection' certificates it issued to employees wishing to build a house from Rs 5000 to Rs 800.

These workers are indebted to me. They say that they built their house because of my help. They will then spread word amongst others during election time that Venugopalan is capable of doing good work, he keeps his word.[212]

That the services extended by the leadership to employees allowed for the creation of ties penetrated by the logic of clientelism is undeniable. The provision of a broad array of services paved the way for union representatives to attract to and maintain in their fold a loyal group of supporters who in turn constituted the fulcrum of the representative's power. The mechanics of the entire process is succinctly captured in the following quotation.

Once you become a union official, you gain a small group of supporters who are obliged to you. The official might have helped them personally in administration side or in PF section or in getting the right medicines from ITI hospital . . . Once a group of supporters forms around an official he keeps getting elected.[213]

Equally undeniable, this clientelist nexus was totally free of the coercion and physical violence normally attendant upon such relations.[214] Workers were in no way captive clients of one or the other union representative. They could openly express their discontent by voting for another

---

[211] Interview with John Joseph.

[212] Interview with Venugopalan.

[213] Interview with Irudayaraj.

[214] As Heuzé mentions, violence served as the solvent for the clientelist practices of the union leadership in the Dhanbad collieries. *Ouvriers d'un autre monde*, pp. 295–300.

candidate without fear of inviting reprisals. This was possible largely because the union was not a creation of the company and operated on an independent basis, its legitimacy contingent at all times on the electoral support of the base.

Union officials who lose do so because they have become arrogant, think themselves as a boss, and do not oblige workers . . . Keshava Murthy (an EC member in the crossbar division) lost the elections because of this. He would tell workers who came to him with a problem to come the next day. He could have solved the problem easily that same day, but by putting off workers permanently and asking them to come the next day he was trying to show to others that he had lot of workers grouped around him permanently. Workers got irritated by the delay, that they had to keep requesting him continuously to solve their problems.[215]

Commenting on the defeat of Venugopalan in the 1987 union elections, one worker said that employees had been disappointed with his 'misleading ways' and so wanted to 'teach him a lesson', before deciding to 'give him a chance again' in the subsequent elections where he won.[216] Union representatives thus could ill-afford to rest on their laurels. The support of the rank-and-file was not given once for all, something union officials could presume for granted. On the contrary, it had to be continuously earned and nourished by proving a tangible commitment to workers' interests. Besides, getting re-elected generally tended to be a far more difficult task than getting elected since dissatisfied workers were more prone to cast their vote against a representative than satisfied workers to vote for him. To put it in another way, clientelism stood on relatively strong democratic foundations, manifest in employees' freedom to revoke their representatives' mandate.

This point is also corroborated by the seeming orderliness which characterized the union elections. On the whole, their organization was marred neither by violence nor by irregularities of any kind.[217] This could, however, perhaps be attributed as much to company surveillance as to the presence of police forces. The records available with us speak of

[215] Interview with Irudayaraj.

[216] Interview with Sahadevan.

[217] The use of physical violence to ensure the victory of incumbents, writes Mamkootam, was a routine feature of union elections at TISCO. 'Industrial Relations in a Steel Plant'.

only two incidents of trouble. In the first, Venkataswamy, a canteen worker, was assaulted by his colleague Ramaiah and one of his friends after the latter had lost the elections. Ramaiah is reported to have threatened four other canteen workers as well.[218] In the second case, a security department note commended the local police for controlling an 'unruly mob who were trying to surge into the counting area in a drunken state to create chaos while counting of Votes was on'. Police reinforcements had been called up, the note added, because security personnel had apprehended 'very hot forceful contest for various Office bearer's posts (sic)'.[219]

[218] Ref. SY/FD/10, 11 November 1986.
[219] Ref. SY/FD/10, 20 February 1991.

chapter eight

Rank-and-File Challenge to Union and Management Authority

A review of the industrial relations climate over five decades at the flagship Bangalore plant of ITI discloses a mixed picture where periods of relative consent and stability coexisted along with periods of intense conflictuality. Chronologically speaking, it is possible to identify three distinct temporal cycles: the 1950s–60s followed by the 1980s–90s where the company experienced a fair to high degree of industrial peace. Sandwiched between these two longer time bands were the short 1970s, a stormy decade of unbroken turbulence and agitation as workers repeatedly vented their discontent, sometimes violently.

Between 1948–68, barring two strikes, the Bangalore factory witnessed very little labour trouble. The first strike occurred in 1964 or over a decade and a half after the birth of the company. The second strike broke out two years later and like the first turned out to be a rather brief affair. But from the closing years of the 1960s onwards, the factory would be rocked by a series of explosive and protracted conflicts: linguistic antagonisms engendered by the rivalries between Kannada and Tamil workers, disputes over work practices, agitations to reform company promotion policies, and struggles against the government's efforts to enforce wage restraint culminating in the defeat of the massive, united strike by workers in all five Bangalore public sector companies in March 1981. The strategy employed by the management to promote a harmonious work environment, through a system of joint regulation, after having yielded the solicited dividends during the 1950s and 1960s thus stood in shambles by the end of the 1970s.

A number of factors—demographic, social, economic and organizational—specific to this period combined to explain why during the years stretching from around 1968–81 contractual relations attained the extreme volatility that they did.[1] This situation was by no means unique to ITI. In the history of the post-colonial state, the seventies will arguably go down as a decade of unprecedented labour strife; while the threat of imprisonment and worse during the Emergency years imposed a momentary lull, the temperature in the various industrial centres rapidly rose again with the return to democratic rule.[2] For certain, some of the same underlying causes that stoked workers' anger elsewhere in the country also propelled events at ITI. Nevertheless, local determinants played a predominant role.

First, the creation of the crossbar division had resulted in the recruitment of a fresh workforce which being younger also tended to be more contentious. Second, there was growing frustration among older workers over the lack of adequate career advancement opportunities, and the discriminatory attitude exhibited by the company towards these groups added to their sense of alienation. Third, at a time when runaway food prices were stretching worker family budgets to the limits, the anti-inflationary wage-fixation measures of the government generated deep

[1] Commenting in 1969 on employers' remarks that workers were capitalizing on the security afforded to them by favourable legislation to display a greater degree of defiance towards their superiors, the National Commission on Labour, hardly a bastion of radical thinking, wrote that such reasoning ignores the fact that '. . . (a) worker today is more politically conscious than before, more articulate in his criticism of the existing order and more sensitive to his conditions and hardships. He has participated in the political and constitutional processes of elections'. *Report of the National Commission on Labour*, pp. 34–5.

[2] The number of worker days lost on account of strikes and lockouts after contracting from 36.37 million in 1974–75 to 12.37 million two years later, rose more than three-fold to reach 39.26 million in 1978–79 before falling to 29.82 million the following year. *Economic Survey*, various years.

resentment.[3] The authorities' obduracy on the question of the volume of annual bonus payments which was quite meagre for non-competing public sector enterprises like ITI also served as a permanent incitement to protest. Fourth, the emergence of a nativist Kannada movement in Bangalore, committed to the advancement of autochthonous economic and cultural interests, had a substantial fallout on the city's lower classes. It polarized the ITI workforce far more deeply than the workforces of other centrally-owned public enterprises. Fifth, the erosion of disciplinary mechanisms in the wake of the upheavals provoked by the language conflict facilitated the crystallization of shop floor grievances into collective action. Last, instability and changes within the union hierarchy had ended up weakening the leadership's grip over the rank-and-file.

Indeed, many of the agitations that erupted during these years stood out on account of their spontaneous character, and it was precisely this inability of the union to prevent its members from forcefully asserting their autonomy that regularly earned it the reproval of company officials. One further point must be stressed. Whereas labour disputes during both the 1960s and from the 1980s onwards revolved chiefly around bread and butter issues, the 1970s stood out because workers simultaneously fought to satisfy their aspirations for greater occupational mobility and to win higher monetary benefits. In addition, there were periodic challenges to managerial prerogatives to organize work in the crossbar division. It was the prevalence of these diverse types of struggles— economic, non-economic, work-related—which helped to define this decade as the high watermark of labour militancy in ITI.

This cycle of strife and ferment was supplanted by a much longer cycle of quiescence, even passivity, that, starting in the early 1980s, continued for close to two decades. The unchallenged domination of Kannada workers over the social structures of the factory, the establishment of an automatic promotion scheme, and a compromise of sorts over the distribution of annual bonus payments, all played a significant role in alleviating tensions and rendered possible the restoration of industrial relations to a more 'normal' state. At the same time, collective

---

[3] Inflation jumped from 5.6 per cent in 1971–72 to 25.2 per cent in 1974–75, and while the middle and late 1970s saw a stabilization of the wholesale price index, the situation once again began to worsen from February 1979 onwards. Joshi and Little, *Macroeconomics and Political Economy*, pp. 105–10, 123–5, 143–6.

memories of the failed wage parity strike which convulsed all five Bangalore-based public sector companies in 1980–81, exercised a suitably chastening influence on the combativeness of the rank-and-file. The dispute which dragged on for close to three months had brought far more hardship than gains, underlining in the process the powerlessness of the strikers and the unions in the face of government intransigence. As a result, workers as well as their representatives could not be blamed for entertaining few illusions about the chances of success of a smaller struggle at the level of a single company.

But acknowledgement of the invincibility of state power did not constitute the only constraining force on workers' actions. From 1991 onwards, economic imperatives in the form of deregulation, or to be more precise, its consequences on the competitive position of ITI, also contributed to the meltdown in protest activity. For workers knew full well that the rollback of the company's monopoly privileges had undermined its financial basis to a point where its existence stood in peril. As such, the management lacked the means to satisfy any demand of importance, and any attempt to realize these by paralysing production could prove suicidal by inflicting a further blow on the company's fortunes and threatening their own jobs in the bargain.

Not surprisingly, under these circumstances of the nine strikes that took place between 1982–2003 at the Bangalore plant, one lasted three days while the remaining eight were token one-day strikes. An accurate barometer of the resigned mood shrouding the base, none of these strikes were specific to the company either. Workers merely participated in country-wide work stoppages launched in conjunction with other trade union organizations.[4] Other agitational activities conducted by the union leadership also betrayed the same exclusively symbolic tonality: shouting slogans, wearing protest badges, boycotting meals, burning effigies, public processions and rallies and relay hunger strikes—ritualized activities all, whose effect neither deceived the leaders nor the 'led'. On two instances alone (1995 and 1999) did labour troubles directly bearing upon problems internal to ITI cause a disruption to production. Interestingly enough, the initiative behind both these demonstrations, which fizzled

---

[4] Some of these national strikes also entailed no financial losses for ITI workers since the company used to allow them subsequently to work on holidays to make up for the loss of wages and production.

out as rapidly as they had erupted, came from within the ranks of workers themselves, the object of their anger being as much the union leadership as the management. It is also worth record that the decline in labour militancy observed in ITI during the 1980s and 1990s mirrored a more general phenomenon cutting across all sectors of Indian industry.[5] So pronounced was the retreat of unions in the organized sector, as the state increasingly and openly rallied to the side of employers in the aftermath of economic liberalization, that more man-days came to be lost on account of lockouts than strikes.[6]

Of the three broad categories of demands that underpinned the various struggles waged by ITI workers, we will first examine those relating to the redressal of perceived economic grievances. Then, we will take up the issue of occupational mobility together with the step-by-step formation of an internal labour market, the institutional mechanism devised to secure workers' social status. Finally, we will look at demands focussed on questions of work and the exercise of managerial authority at the point of production which will also include a discussion of the contradictory dimensions of shop floor culture. Each type of demand imparted to the ensuing struggles a specificity, a dynamic and intensity of its own which was reflected most clearly in the extent of workers' mobilization and in their attitudes to the union leadership as well as the management.

---

[5] Between 1982–97, the number of strikes, the number of workers involved in strikes, and the number of man days lost on account of strikes, all recorded decreases. The number of man-days lost due to strikes, for instance, dropped from a high of 52.1 million in 1982 to 10.6 million in 1990 to 6.29 million in 1997. *Indian Labour Year Book*, New Delhi, 1995, p. 13; Annual Report (2001–02), Ministry of Labour, p. 9. Much the same story of ebbing strike activity could also be told for the advanced economies. For details, see Reynald Bourque, 'Les nouvelles tendances de la négociation collective en Amérique du Nord', in G. Murray et al (ed.), *L'état des relations professionnelles*, Toulouse, 1996, pp. 329–350; Guido Baglioni, 'Industrial Relations in Europe in the 1980s', in G. Baglioni and C. Crouch (eds.), *European Industrial Relations. The Challenge of Flexibility*, London, 1991, pp. 1–41.

[6] Annual Report (2001–02), Ministry of Labour, p. 9. A recent study of union response to privatization from 1991 to 2003, covering a dozen states, and which supplements official strike statistics with print sources, however, disproves the assumption of labour quiesence in the post-reforms era. Katrin Uba, 'Labor Union Resistance to Economic Liberalization in India. What can National and State Level Patterns of Protests against Privatization Tell Us?' *Asian Survey*, Vol. XLVIII, No. 5, September-October 2008, pp. 860–84. For the shift in government attitudes, see Jenkins, *Democratic Politics and Economic Reform in India*, pp. 249–52.

THE FIGHT FOR MONETARY GAINS

The first strike in the history of ITI which occurred in December 1964 turned out, quite astonishingly, to be a stay-in strike. Prior to this date, underlying currents of tension had periodically surfaced without, however, impinging on production activities. The 1964 strike flared up after the company rejected the charter of demands submitted by the union. Among the demands figured wage increases ranging from Rs 40 to 60, the payment of house rent allowance, and the linkage of dearness allowance (DA) to the consumer price index. Shortlived, the conflict ended after four days with the management and workers' representatives agreeing to refer some of the issues for arbitration to the communications minister.

Four features of this struggle deserve attention. First, it was workers and not the union representatives who dictated the course of events. Although the union had instigated the agitation, it quickly found itself outflanked by a more militant base, leaving it with no choice but to play 'catch-up' and back the former's actions. It was this inability of the leadership to impose its definition of the situation which explained why the dispute took the form of a stay-in strike—a relatively rare occurrence in the Indian context as well as a rather audacious decision on the part of the union leadership. It had no previous experience of conducting a strike of any kind, let alone one as logistically challenging as an occupation of the factory, a form of action defined as a 'counter-possession' or social re-appropriation of space by workers.[7]

Signs of the union's difficulty in controlling things were already evident in early November. To exert pressure on the company, a one day go-slow protest had been launched towards the end of October. Not only did it drag on for several days, but the management even complained that the protest was being intensified.[8] Workers were apparently acting on their own initiative: a company circular reproduced a letter written by the union president Kannan expressing '. . . surpris(e) to learn . . . that there is a go-slow strike in the factory'.[9] That the rank-and-file was in a highly combative mood was conclusively demonstrated in a strike ballot where

[7] Gustave-Nicolas Fischer, 'L'espace comme nouvelle lecture du travail', *Sociologie du travail*, No. 4, October-December 1978, pp. 397–422.

[8] PD circular no. 989, 2 November 1964.

[9] PD circular no. 990, 4 November 1964.

8017 workers out of 8133 voted in favour of a strike.[10] Following this, the union staged a one-day work stoppage towards the end of November. However, as in the case of the go-slow, 'an atmosphere of strike continued in the factory'.[11] On 12 December, workers in certain shops started slowing down production without consulting their representatives. Faced with this *fait accompli*, the union now formally declared a stay-in strike. When the afternoon shift employees reported for work at 2 pm, they were allowed to enter the plant. In the management's calculations, once these workers went in, the morning shift personnel would automatically leave the premises thus draining the strike of its momentum and energy. These plans badly backfired when the first shift workers refused to quit their work spots.[12]

The second noteworthy aspect of the 1964 strike was the cooperation extended by the management, but for which sustaining the conflict beyond the first day would have been practically untenable. In the words of one high ranking executive, 'there was no confrontation between the management and workers. It was almost a picnic'.[13] Initially, some of the more hawkish officers wanted the canteen to be shut down in a bid to coerce the union and the workers into submission. Fortunately for the strikers, the then managing director N.V. Shenoi turned down the suggestion and instructed the canteen authorities to keep supplying food to the 8000 odd people present within the factory.

Shenoi was an intelligent and humane officer. He said that the canteen would be kept open since the management would have to keep talking to the union, and that the strike did not turn the union into an enemy whereas shutting down the canteen would antagonize workers and the union and would have adverse long term effects.[14]

The company also placed no restrictions on the movements of union activists who were allowed to go out and re-enter the factory as they wished. The union reciprocated these friendly gestures by agreeing subsequently to work on certain holidays in order to make up for the loss of production.

[10] Arya, *Labour Management Relations,* p. 146.
[11] ibid.
[12] Interview with Venugopalan.
[13] Interview with Srinivasa Rao.
[14] Interview with Fernandes.

Third, the strike threw into relief a commendable capacity for self-organization on the part of workers and their representatives alike. Despite its inexperience in organizing a struggle, the union promptly set up 'vigilance committees' in all shops to ensure the strike remained orderly and peaceful. Acts of sabotage and theft had to be prevented at all costs, so that 'the management would have no cause to declare a lock-out'.[15] Each vigilance committee comprised ten activists. Besides serving as an information conduit for the leadership, the task of the activists consisted of monitoring the activities of workers in each shop, relaying messages from workers to their families and vice-versa, and purchasing cigarettes, *beedis, paan*, newspapers, and other such small needs of the strikers. Care was exercised to see that nobody consumed alcohol inside the plant.

We also had to reassure workers that the company would not take action and dismiss strikers, that the union would take care of everything.[16]

The efforts of the union to maintain discipline and harmony proved extremely effective with the management corroborating Fernandes' statement that

not a pin was shifted from its place. There was not a scratch on any machine or material nor on any person.[17]

Lastly, given that the conflict was above all, an affair of the rank-and-file, the union leadership experienced considerable difficulties in bringing it to a close.[18] Whereas the union had persuaded the top management to agree to arbitration and both sides had also settled on the choice of an arbitrator, certain sections of the workforce were apprehensive that a mediated arrangement would go against workers' interests. (Announced

---

[15] ibid.

[16] Interview with Venugopalan. The function of strike committees, observes Michèle Perrot in her outstanding study on strikes in late-19th century France, is not merely to govern but also to mobilize energies and ensure worker participation. *Les ouvriers en grève, 1871–1890,* Paris, 1974, p. 428 (vol. 2).

[17] Interviews with Fernandes and Srinivasa Rao. Underlining the demise of luddite practices among French strikers, reflected in the insignificant number of attacks on machinery, Perrot attributes this sense of restraint to a complex of factors: fear, respect for private property, a desire to protect their instruments of work, and the integration of the logic of industrial capitalism. *Les ouvriers en grève,* pp. 513–14, 576–80 (vol. 2).

[18] All the information in this paragraph is drawn from interviews with Fernandes and Venugopalan.

shortly afterwards, the arbitration award actually upheld employees' claims.) Opposed to this solution, they therefore insisted on pursuing the strike until all their demands had been conceded. To add to the union's woes, certain shop floor representatives also began lending their voices to this chorus of contestation. Others, feeling the strain of three days of intense activity, aspired to call off the strike, but were worried about the negative reactions such a decision could provoke among the base. Finally, after long hours of discussion, the union leadership succeeded in winning over the mass of strikers to its position.

In December 1966, the Bangalore factory was once again the scene of a fresh and even longer conflict. Angered by the company's decision to unilaterally withhold paying higher DA to employees on the grounds that a wage board appointed by the government for the engineering industry was reviewing the entire DA question, the union and workers were now fighting to overturn this decision. In addition, their protest was also aimed at wresting bigger annual bonus payments.

Bonus was a very emotional issue, but DA was an even more volatile issue since it surfaced every month whereas bonus was a yearly affair. One issue reinforced the other and increased the anger of workers.[19]

Claims for bonus represented a permanent source of tension both in the public and the private sector. Its size determined, in theory, by a company's profitability levels, bonus had, however, over time come to be regarded as a deferred wage given the low purchasing power of the Indian worker. It was seen as customary payment which enabled him to acquire certain 'luxuries' (clothes, household articles, etc.) during the festival season, which he could never have afforded on the regular salary. It had therefore 'acquired a status of right that had to be met', and a significant proportion of industrial disputes in the country touched upon employers' refusal to satisfy this right.[20]

The 1966 conflict shared certain common traits with the one that had broken out two years earlier. Not only was it a stay-in strike, but it too escaped from the control of the leadership. Indeed, Kannan, the then union president, described the agitation as perhaps the most trying

---

[19] Interview with Fernandes.

[20] C.K. Johri, 'Industrial Relations in India: The Critical Phase', *Bulletin of Comparative Labour Relations*, No. 7, 1976, pp. 31–53; Charles Myers and Subbiah Kannappan, *Industrial Relations in India*, London, 1970, pp. 350–7.

event in his whole union career.[21] In the leadership's scheme of things, the strike was intended to be no more than a short, one-day affair: the factory would come to a standstill during working hours. This would 'give the management a blow', and then, having registered its protest, the union would order a return to normalcy the following day.[22] The union had failed, however, to reckon with the depth of workers' resentment and its carefully scripted scenario of moderation soon gave way to a more radical one. A sizeable proportion of workers along with several shop floor delegates refused to return home in the evening, and expressed their determination to continue the strike. Suggestions by top union officials to fight the issue through legal channels to start with, since the government had referred the bonus demand for arbitration, but not DA, were shouted down, constraining the union to once again follow, rather than lead, the rank-and-file. Subsequently, both Kannan and Fernandes would blame the intensification of the dispute on pro-communist sympathizers intent on embarrassing the existing leadership— an accusation impossible for us to verify. The vigilance committees were again reactivated and they played much the same role as in the past.

Where the similarities between this strike and its predecessor ended was in terms of the attitude of the management. If workers had counted on it to act benevolently when deciding to press on with their agitation they would be badly mistaken. In distinct contrast to the earlier stay-in strike, on this occasion, the top management declared a lockout on the second day of the dispute, and, then, instructed canteen officials to stop providing food to the strikers. In itself, the lockout decision carried little weight; apart from putting a stop to workers entering the plant, the company adopted no concrete steps to evict the strikers from within the factory premises. What the lockout did was have an adverse effect on the morale of workers, who viewed it as a foretaste of tougher measures to come such as police intervention inside the factory with its cortege of beatings and arrests, and victimization by the management.

Similarly, the move to shut down the canteen had no immediate impact. Workers promptly took over its running, setting up a committee for this purpose. Nevertheless, shortages in food supplies became increasingly noticeable over time. A negotiated solution to workers'

[21] Reindorp, *Leaders and Leadership in the Trade Unions in Bangalore*, p. 127.
[22] Interview with Fernandes.

grievances was rendered particularly problematic by the variegated nature of their demands: if the claim for DA payments could to some extent be regarded as a bilateral matter falling within the resort of ITI management, this was hardly the case for bonus. An inter-industry issue with repercussions for state-owned enterprises throughout the country, only the government had the power to shape a satisfactory compromise.

So, given the combination of managerial belligerence, the reservations of the union leadership, and dissensions among the representatives, it was not surprising that workers' enthusiasm and commitment rapidly flagged. From the third day of the conflict, growing numbers began slipping out of the factory. This in turn created considerable tension as union activists sought to persuade them, sometimes forcibly, to remain inside.

The union would not allow us to come out. Volunteers were posted near the main gate to stop us, but some workers who had an adjustment with security managed to leave.[23]

Adds another worker:

Many workers under the pretext of union activities would leave the factory and return later.[24]

Initially, except women employees who had been free to return home from the first day itself, the only ones permitted to leave by the union were sick workers or those whose presence was urgently required by their families. But as the strike lengthened and the demoralization and exhaustion of workers proportionally rose, the union would find itself powerless to stem the flow of desertions. By the tenth day, when it was formally lifted, the strike had completely petered out. The financial and other sacrifices made by the workers would not go entirely in vain; the management would be more or less obliged later to grant both the demands which had occasioned the conflict. But for the moment, the sole concession it offered consisted of an engagement not to enforce disciplinary sanctions against any of the strikers.[25]

What memories did workers themselves retain of the strike? All those whom we interviewed confessed to an overwhelming sensation of

[23] Interview with Sahadevan.
[24] Interview with Krishnan.
[25] Reindorp, *Leaders and Leadership in the Trade Unions in Bangalore*, p. 128.

boredom[26] which heightened as the strike progressed and which they sought to mitigate by playing cards and dice, chatting with friends, strolling around the factory, taking turns to clean the factory space, reading books and newspapers, or resting.[27]

It was a bit like being inside jail since our liberties were curbed. But we had to make some sacrifice to achieve our goals.[28]

Another representation of the event to etch itself strongly on their minds was the material discomfort they had to endure from having to spend ten continuous days inside the plant. Workers 'used to eat, change clothes and sleep inside as if they were living in a big concentration camp'.[29] Although their families had sent sheets and blankets, they complained of suffering from the December cold, forced as they were to sleep on packing material on the floor or on work tables. Sanitary conditions too sharply deteriorated with each passing day since only a limited number of toilets were available for use. Others recalled the dwindling quantities of food distributed towards the end of the strike. Yet quite a few workers accommodated themselves to these privations and stayed inside until the end as a 'matter of principle'.[30]

BONUS CONFLICTS RISE TO THE FORE

Following the 1966 strike, conflicts related to monetary demands receded into the background. The reason for this lay in part on employees spontaneously channelling their energies into non-economic protests as collective action to improve their career prospects came to be viewed as the overriding priority throughout the first half of the 1970s. But starting from 1976, economic struggles again vigorously dominated the industrial

[26] It was precisely to keep workers in good spirits, dispel sentiments of fear, and prevent any untoward incidents that an entertainment committee was formed during the 1936 stay-in strike at Renault's giant Paris plant. Bertrand Badie, 'Les grèves du Front Populaire aux usines Renault', *Le Mouvement Social*, No. 81, octobre-décembre 1972, pp. 69–109.

[27] Stay-in strikes, as Fischer has justly remarked, offered workers an opportunity, often for the first time to visit the entire factory and to move around the premises freely. 'L'espace comme nouvelle lecture du travail'.

[28] Interview with Cyril D'Souza, 23 November 2001.

[29] Arya, *Labour Management Relations*, p. 147.

[30] Interview with Krishnan.

relations horizon for the next five years. The government and P&T refused to grant ITI workers the statutorily mandated maximum annual profit sharing bonus of 20 per cent on a regular basis, in sharp contrast to most of the other Bangalore public enterprises. As a result, the issue turned out to be the principal bone of contention and reached a point where disputes over the levels of bonus payments became a hardy annual fixture.[31]

Persistent delays in the finalization and distribution of these payments due to procedural and other reasons added more fuel to the fire. Indeed, bonus claims informed either entirely or partly four of the five mass agitations that broke out between 1976–81 at the Bangalore plant. As the union underlined in a letter addressed to the Ministry of Communications in 1976, workers were

> frustrated, agitated and much worried about the fluid situation and the frequent change of Management's policy regarding the percentage eligibility of profit sharing bonus and also of the delay in the payment always after other comparable Public Sector Industries in Bangalore had paid 20 per cent bonus to their workmen . . . (T)he repetition every year of negligence of workers' legitimate right and request to receive 20 per cent bonus is not a good sign of even an iota of healthy industrial relations (sic).[32]

Four years later, the union would employ stronger language to reiterate much the same grievance.

> Will the government open its eyes only if frustrated and exasperated workers resort to violence and destruction of the factory? Representations and express telegrams and peaceful actions during the last two months have not brought bonus to 20,000 workers . . . Quick delivery of cabinet approval is required before the situation gets out of control (sic).[33]

---

[31] Of the five central government-owned units located in Bangalore, three (HMT, BEL and BEML) were entitled to pay the maximum bonus amount of 20 per cent, being classified as competitive companies, i.e., companies which realized at least a fifth of their sales on the open market, unlike ITI and HAL which fell into the non-competing category. After the 1966 strike, however, when the question of bonus payments figured prominently, the ITI union moved the courts prompting the management to progressively increase its offer while awaiting the conclusions of the judiciary. On two occasions in the early 1970s, workers in ITI even received the full 20 per cent. But as part of the ongoing repression of the working classes following the imposition of Emergency, the maximum bonus (or *ex gratia*, as it was called) for non-competing state-owned firms was pegged at 10 per cent.

[32] Letter 16 September 1976.

[33] ITI Union circular no. 41/80, 29 September 1980. See also circular no. 43/83,

What is more, the union and the rank-and-file's conviction that the government, by denying them of their rightful share of company profits, was treating them unjustly, and hence contributing to both poisoning the work environment and demotivating employees, found favourable echoes within the ranks of company officials as well. For the latter, ITI workers had a 'reasonable case' for demanding 20 per cent bonus since their efficiency and skills were 'certainly comparable' to those of their counterparts in the other Bangalore public companies which regularly awarded the maximum amount.[34] Top executives also denounced the pricing formula finalized between P&T and ITI, arguing that the prices fixed for the company's products were 'not at all reasonable and fair', and prevented it from realizing adequate profits which in turn impacted negatively on the size of the bonus package.[35]

Of the four bonus disputes that intervened during the late 1970s, only one, strictly speaking, was a strike; besides, it involved other issues such as the introduction of an automatic promotions scheme. The remaining incidents corresponded to collective demonstrations which were seldom officially organized by the union. Even on those instances when the union did take the initiative it tended to be upstaged by more militant elements within the workforce. Two of the demonstrations, one occurring in September 1976 and the other in September 1980, witnessed a fair amount of material and bodily violence and culminated in the imposition of a lockout. It is on them that we have chosen to focus our attention for while sharing certain common features they also differed in a number of respects.

Significant because of its timing, the 1976 agitation flared up against the backdrop of the Emergency and represented an open defiance of the government directive banning all forms of protest activity. It was preceded by major changes at the helm of the union, the implications of which would be decisive for the future course of events. Neither of the two organizational stalwarts, Kannan, the longstanding union president, and

---

27 August 1983 where the union would once again complain that the bonus agitation had become something of an annual ritual because of the failure of the management to 'realize its legal and moral responsibility' to pay bonus on time.

[34] Letter from C.S.S. Rao, ITI Chairman, to Thomas Kora, Additional Secretary, Ministry of Communications, 13 August 1979.

[35] PD note, 20 September 1976.

Fernandes, the general secretary, both reputed for their moderation, participated in the August 1976 elections. Imprisoned by the government shortly after the promulgation of the Emergency and dismissed from the company, Fernandes had been barred by the state labour department from contesting the elections, while Kannan had decided to quit the union. A Tamilian by origin, Kannan had increasingly become a figurehead president. As the language conflict gained in intensity, his influence was marginalized by Kannada representatives who now numerically dominated the union hierarchy. Further, in the absence of Fernandes, Kannan was allegedly 'finding it very difficult to keep (the union officials and executive members) under control', and had 'expressed dissatisfaction with the violent, aggressive, non-cooperative and intemperate attitude' of some representatives.[36] So with neither man present on the scene to mediate between and rein in the rival factions, the union was in complete disarray, according to a company document.

Different members are pulling in different directions. Essentially, one group feels that the Union had been very weak in the past and they must now adopt strong and violent methods to achieve their objectives. The other group is more sober, responsive and responsible.[37]

Snapshots established by the security department identifying the members of this 'violent group' together with the other 'ringleaders' allow us to better discern the backgrounds and trajectories of the activists thought to be instrumental in igniting the agitation. Of the 30 individuals blacklisted by security, all of whom by and large faithfully corresponded to the stereotypical representation of the labour agitator privileged by official discourse ('he is a very vocal and rebellious type of worker', 'he is a habitual absentee', etc.), only a small minority (six) could be described as relatively junior workers with less than a decade's tenure to their credit. The overwhelming majority (27) were involved either directly or indirectly in production-related tasks, and belonged to semi-skilled and unskilled categories.

While the preponderance of activists from strowger, the biggest of the four product divisions in the Bangalore plant, was predictable, the records mention only one activist belonging to the transmission division as opposed to six in crossbar, despite both divisions being roughly

[36] ibid.
[37] ibid.

equivalent in size.[38] The greater levels of involvement noticeable among crossbar employees was in all likelihood the consequence of the division's emergence as the bastion of the chauvinist Kannada Chaluvali movement within the factory. Indeed over a third of the 'ringleaders' (12) were presented as staunch backers of this movement who had taken the lead in threatening and beating Tamil workers both within and outside the factory, persuading the police to file assault charges against some of them.

But interestingly, the security list also contained the names of a few Tamil 'trouble makers' whose allegiances to the Dravida Munnetra Kazagham (DMK) had singled them out for particularly rough treatment at the hands of Chaluvali supporters. The enduring bitterness and cleavages produced by these events precluded in all likelihood the possibility of concerted action between Kannada and Tamil activists at the time of the bonus dispute. Still, the active implication of these Tamil workers in the dispute, influenced, to some extent, perhaps by the DMK's opposition to the Emergency, suggested that the victimization to which they had been subjected during the course of the linguistic clashes had not squeezed the spirit of fight out of them.

The agitation got underway early in the morning of 20 September 1976. No sooner had the first and general shift workers reported for duty by 7.30 am than they quit their workspots and marched towards the factory administration building. There they shouted slogans demanding their legitimate share of 20 per cent bonus as well as castigating the company's failure to grant bonus on time. Custom dictated the timing of bonus payments, so that workers received this amount by the end of August or early September prior to Ganesha Chathurthi so as to enable them to meet the different expenses the festivities necessitated. That the tradition had been violated on this occasion accentuated their resentment.

Dismissive of the capacity of employees to act independently, one company report pinned the responsibility for the outbreak of the disturbances exclusively on some union officials. By virtue of their privileges, under normal circumstances these representatives showed up for work only after the mass of the workforce did. But that day they apparently came to the factory much earlier and 'tried to incite the workers

[38] In 1978, crossbar counted 2831 workers on its rolls and transmission 2807 workers.

in various hangars/workshops to come out and take part in the agitational demands . . . These people were being instigated and pulled out of the workspots to collect in a mob . . .'[39] Other testimonies from ITI executives recorded by the police claimed that union delegates 'threatened the workers with dire consequences' if they did not join them.[40] Corporate narratives framing the conflict thus tended to reproduce the familiar tropes of union 'instigators' coercing workers into action and transforming them into a 'mob'. In the process, they stressed the distinction between an unruly, dissatisfied leadership and a contented and obedient rank-and-file in an attempt to legitimize the exercise of managerial authority.[41]

By 9 am, large numbers of workers—the company estimated the figure at 10,000—had gathered behind the building housing the factory administrative offices. They soon began throwing stones and smashing scores of window panes. Anti-government slogans whose political overtones were clearly manifest in the repeated calls urging Indira Gandhi to quit power and for the withdrawal of the state of Emergency were also raised. For memories of the repressive anti-inflationary measures enacted by the ruling Congress regime over the last two years remained fresh in their minds. Like other public sector workforces, ITI employees had also suffered from the government's decision to partially impound the increases in dearness allowance payments organized labour was entitled to receive. They had also been affected by a directive issued in October 1975 to all non-competing public enterprises restricting the maximum bonus to 10 per cent, whereas by the management's own computations, they were expected to earn close to 16 per cent.[42] All of this now lent an added edge to the demonstrators' anger.

[39] PD note, nd (September 1976).

[40] See, *inter alia*, statements by U.V. Nayak, Divisional Manager, Transmission Division, ITI Bangalore; C.R. Datta Gupta, Divisional Manager, Crossbar Division; K.M. Shanbhogue, Divisional Manager, Telephone Division. Ref. Crime No. 256/76 Krishnarajpuram Police Station, 22 September 1976.

[41] The 'instigator' theory in industrial conflict finds its counterpart and precedent in what one author has called the 'riffraff' thesis, used to explain pre-industrial urban violence. Mark Traugott, 'The Mobile Guard in the French Revolution', *Theory and Society*, Vol. 9, No. 5, September 1980, pp. 683–720.

[42] Letter from ITI Union to the Minister of Communications, 16 September 1976. A few months after the declaration of Emergency, the management wanted the union to publish an appeal urging workers to donate a day's wages to the Prime Minister's Relief Fund for the benefit of flood victims. The union, though, refused to do so on the

Two hours later, following a meeting between senior executives and the union leadership, the latter informed the assembled mass that the company's highest offer could not exceed 10 per cent since its hands were tied by government orders. Workers were therefore requested to end their agitation. Like the earlier announcements, this one too went unheeded. Instead, the agitation took a far more violent turn. A small contingent of policemen which had moved inside the factory premises in a bid to hold back the crowd were pelted with brickbats and metal components such as coils and relays. This led the management to ask for troop reinforcements and the city police commissioner himself arrived on the scene.

With passions showing no signs of cooling down even after the end of shift working hours at 2.15 pm, police responded to fresh attacks on them by firing tear gas, prompting the workers to rush back inside the hangars. Barricades assembled out of packing cases and drums were hastily thrown up along the main factory arteries. To further obstruct the passage of the police, three company lorries were doused with oil and set on fire. Small groups of protestors also sought to prevent the fire fighting staff from putting out the flames by hurling stones and other objects in their direction. This display of resistance would, however, turn out to be shortlived. After an ultimatum delivered by the police commissioner warning everybody to leave the premises before 4 pm, failing which not only would the hangars be forcibly evacuated, but the company would no longer provide buses to transport everybody home, workers quietly streamed out of the plant.

Nevertheless, the fact that there was no let up in the intensity of the protests for several hours on end was significant if only because it highlighted the patent failure of the union leadership to fulfil its social control functions. Immediately afterwards, the management declared a lockout. According to it, factory property worth around Rs 300,000 had been destroyed. But not even a single machine had been touched attesting to the formidable capacity of the 'mob' for self-restraint. The lockout continued for six days. It would only be lifted after workers signed individual undertakings agreeing to accept the 10 per cent bonus

---

grounds that the harsh policy measures enacted by the government with respect to bonus had created an 'uncongenial climate'. Minutes of management-union meeting, 29 October 1975.

amount as final, a wage deduction of Rs 20 intended to defray the costs of the damages caused to factory property, and to make good the loss of production by working on holidays.[43]

Due to lacunae in our sources, a certain amount of confusion surrounds the events underlying the 1980 bonus agitation. Like the 1976 agitation, this conflict was once again triggered by delays on the part of the government in announcing the size of bonus payments for non-competing public enterprises such as ITI. But unlike the previous occasion, in 1980 protests were initiated by the union, even though it would be completely marginalized later, helpless in preventing the rank-and-file from wresting control of events and imprinting a violent pattern on them. Yet if the violence definitely expressed workers' sense of exasperation at the refusal of the authorities to find a timely and permanent solution to a recurrent problem, its principal victims paradoxically happened to be union officials, some of whom were severely assaulted by workers for reasons that remain unclear.

Determined to preempt trouble of the kind that had afflicted the 1976 agitation, the union leadership proceeded with extreme caution when launching the protests this time, placing definite limits initially on the scope of its actions. Wedded as it was to legalistic principles of functioning given its commitment to ensuring the survival of the organization, violence undermined its legitimacy and questioned the limits of its disciplining powers.[44] So as a first step, it was decided to only stage a *dharna* before the office of the head of the Bangalore plant. By way of a supplementary precaution, top union officials and executive committee members alone were authorized to participate in the event. The tempo was to be stepped up the next day, 30 September, with general council members entering the fray as well. Unfortunately for the union this strategy of prudence or limited confrontation where the objective was to progressively build up pressure on the management came unstuck in no time. On 30 September, even before the leadership could resume the *dharna*, the rank-and-file spontaneously chose to make its voice heard, as this report from the telephone division revealed.

---

[43] After repeated requests from the union, the management subsequently refunded this amount of Rs 20 to workers. PD note, 30 March 1977.

[44] A trade union official's 'first instinct is to preserve the organisation', writes J.D. Reynaud. 'Preface', in Gérard Adam, *Le pouvoir syndical*, Paris, 1983, p. vi. See also Richard Hyman, *Strikes*, London, 1978, p. 50, 79–81.

Around 8.30 am, it is reported that two of the union officials entered F92 (a machine shop) and some operative staff surrounded them. In spite of the officials stating that *any agitation elsewhere was not due to any call from the Union*, some of the operative staff started shouting slogans and inciting the others to stop work and go out of the hangar along with them. A crowd collected and started moving out of the unit. However, all the ladies and many operators remained behind, but did not start their work.[45]

In the strowger division, the locus of the protests was the rack wiring department, a perennial 'hotspot' in view of the strategic position its workers occupied in the production chain. Shortly after clocking in, operatives here began shouting and thumping tables even as others moved from one shop to the next mobilizing colleagues to 'leave the job and join them in the demonstration'. Glass partitions inside some the hangars were shattered as were window panes in managers' offices.[46] No equipment or machinery suffered damage, though, speaking once again for the protestors' ability to resist 'luddite' impulses. In the plant mechanical department, foremen complained to line managers that a big group of people neither 'allowed (them) to carry on with their work' nor to 'stay in their respective hangars', compelling them instead to go to the administration building.[47] So within a couple of hours of the start of work in the morning, production had ceased in most shops and large numbers of slogan-shouting workers, estimated at 13,000 by the management, had congregated behind the administration building.

In previous demonstrations, workers had always stopped at the metal gate, a physical marker symbolizing the separation between the production areas and the factory administration. But this time, some of them entered the administration building after prising open the chain locking the 'justice gate', as it was commonly known. There, they forced employees who were still working to step out, and hurled stones, broken flower pots and components, smashing several window panes. A handful of workers even broke into the office of the director of the Bangalore plant, causing minor material damage and injuring the chief security officer on the head in the process. The protestors' defiant mood was in clear evidence when they challenged the investigating police officials

---

[45] Tel. Divn. note, 1 October 1980. Emphasis added.

[46] Strowger Divn. note, 1 October 1980.

[47] Plant Mechanical Dept. note, 3 October 1980.

brought in by the management, to leave the room where they were seated, and then proceeded to stone the room. Workers also warned the chief security officer against authorizing police forces to set foot inside the factory.

At the same time, sections of the rank-and-file appear to have been greatly angered by the attitude of few union leaders, in particular the general secretary, V.S. Ramaswamy. Not only did they raise slogans demanding his resignation, but one worker also struck him with an iron rod. In all, three union leaders had to be hospitalized with injuries while a few others received blows. It is quite possible that the violent treatment meted out to these representatives reflected political cleavages within the union hierarchy which may have been exacerbated by the return to power of the Congress (I) earlier in 1980 after the implosion of the Janata government.[48] Indeed, prior to the outbreak of the agitation, a union circular had denounced as 'mischievous, dangerous and foul' rumours of divisions among the top leadership over the question of bonus.[49] Did this very public denial of divergences actually amount to a confirmation of the existence of internal tensions which exploded into the open in the heat of the conflict? Lacking clearcut evidence we have no means of substantiating our statement.

We are also handicapped by the paucity of information on how the protests subsided. According to the management, the demonstrators were totally impervious to appeals made by the personnel department head urging them to disperse. But in contrast to the 1976 agitation, no police troops entered the factory. This could perhaps be attributed in part, to the prevailing political circumstances which placed greater constraints on the deployment of state repressive power in contrast to the past, when Emergency rule was in full force; in part, by company officials realizing that summoning the police might further inflame passions and inflict incalculable harm to industrial relations.

So in the absence of coercive measures what persuaded the crowd to break up? For by the company's own admission the majority of the workforce had returned home by the time the first shift ended at 2.15 pm. One plausible answer is that even though law and order forces did

---

[48] Ramaswamy was known for his Congress sympathies which could possibly have placed him at odds with the pro-Janata faction headed by Fernandes.

[49] PD files, nd.

not intervene, employees apprehended such a possibility after seeing police officials arrive at the factory. Unwilling to risk a reprise of the events of four years ago, they therefore decided to voluntarily leave the scene before it was too late. Besides, while production appeared to have ground to a halt in most departments, not all workers directly took part in the agitation. This is borne out by a closer reading of the company documents themselves. We have already cited the case of the telephone assembly shop where male and female operatives stopped working, but several of them refused to quit their workspot. Similarly, their colleagues in the injection moulding department 'did not go out or start shouting slogans', even as they shut down their machines. Workers behaved no differently in the telephone machine shop.

. . . the crowd entered shouting slogans . . . Machines were stopped and a few people followed the crowd . . . Many stayed behind, but did not start working.[50]

In some departments such as inward goods inspection and the plating shop, the report even stated that 'normal work went on till late in the afternoon'.[51]

Similar evidence is unavailable for the other divisions. Hence we must be careful not to draw sweeping conclusions about the extent of the involvement of the work force in the agitation. Yet the management also acknowledged that from about 10 am 'large numbers of workers' from all divisions went on leave. No doubt wary of remaining inside the factory premises in case the protests turned violent, they slipped out of the factory through a rear gate.[52] According to a memo submitted by the superintendent of the plant mechanical department, 'attendance was very thin after 12 noon' since many workers did not return following the lunch break.[53] These different fragments of information when pulled together casts some doubt on the company's assertion that 'all the employees of the factory working in the (morning) shifts struck work . . . and assembled before the administration building'.[54] Did the number of demonstrators truly correspond to the figure of 13,000 mentioned in the official sources? Or had their strength been deliberately inflated in

[50] Tel. Divn. note, 1 October 1980.
[51] ibid.
[52] ibid.
[53] Plant Mechanical Dept. note, 3 October 1980.
[54] PD note, nd.

order to exaggerate the threat of 'serious damage to life and property' that the crowd represented, and thereby justify the decision to enforce a lockout?[55]

A punitive measure, the lockout was clearly perceived by top executives as a means of reaffirming their authority over a disorderly workforce. Accusing the union of stalling the company's efforts to curb the unregulated movements of employees and shop floor representatives for several months, one report categorically declared that the bonus agitation was a 'culmination of growing indiscipline in the factory'.[56] In a move therefore to restore discipline, the management not only refused to lift the lockout for 10 days. It also backed up this collective sanction with individual punishments, suspending 23 workers for almost a month. Of these, two would later be dismissed and three others demoted one grade.

THE 1980–81 WAGE PARITY STRIKE

Nevertheless, the workers seem to have erased memories of the management's heavy handed actions from their minds extremely rapidly. For in December 1980, or less than three months after the bonus dispute ended, they again struck work. On this occasion, workers in ITI were acting in concert with their colleagues in the other four Bangalore state-owned companies to compel the authorities to respect the terms of the collective agreement guaranteeing wage parity with workers in BHEL. The issue then directly pitted the unions and the workers against the central government which would not hesitate to harness its full might—repressive, propaganda and judicial—of state power to smash the strikers' resistance.

Lest it be forgotten, it was the government itself which in the early seventies had taken the initiative to link remuneration packages in the Bangalore enterprises with that of BHEL with a view to imposing wage restraint. It had exerted considerable pressure on the Bangalore unions in order to achieve this goal, before brusquely deciding a few years later to severe this linkage. Conceding parity, feared the Indira Gandhi-led Congress (I) Party, which had returned to power, would create a dangerous precedent. Not only would it yield equal rewards to all Bangalore plants

---

[55] ibid.
[56] PD files, nd.

defined by unequal standards of performance; it also threatened to encourage less profitable and less productive companies elsewhere to raise similar demands. Disappointed by the purportedly mediocre resource mobilization record of the public sector, the government aimed to substitute the integrated framework of wage bargaining that had hitherto governed the process of compensation fixation in units such as ITI with a more individualized system stressing company performance. So to categorize the parity strike as just another wage strike would only be half true. For both sides, the fundamental procedural issue of rules—imposing new rules for the government and defending existing ones for the unions—was just as vital as that of their substantive material interests.

The struggle was unprecedented in the history of the public sector in terms of its length, the number of participants, and its financial consequences.[57] It brought together under the banner of the Joint Action Front (JAF), a platform federating the principal unions in all five plants, a total of 125,000 workers across the country, of whom 80,000 were situated in Bangalore alone.[58] It was the first time too that a collective leadership coming from different political horizons was piloting such a large strike and for such a long duration. The strikers stayed out for 77 days before returning to work in the middle of March 1981 empty handed. It is tempting to interpret the handling of both this conflict and the epic Bombay textile strike, which erupted at around the same time and which also ended in a resounding defeat, as a continuation of the hardline stance towards labour pursued by Indira Gandhi ever since the repression of the railway strike in 1974. But her post-Emergency reign was also noteworthy for the shift in official policy priorities in favour of the private sector.[59] To ensure this new rapprochement between state

---

[57] The strike, post-strike disturbances and the lock-out resulted in a total loss of 71.7 million man days in BEL, BEML, HAL, HMT and ITI, while production losses amounted to a massive Rs 180.15 million. *Public Enterprises Survey*, 1980–81, 1981–82.

[58] Besides Bangalore, the other major strike centre was Hyderabad where close to 16,000 workers in HMT, HAL, ECIL, Bharat Dynamics, Hindustan Cables and Mishra Dhatu Nigam stopped work. In addition, units of ITI in Rae Bareli, Naini, Palakkad also went on strike for varying periods as did units of HAL in Lucknow, Nasik, Koreput and Barrackpore, and HMT in Cochin.

[59] Kohli, 'Politics of Economic Growth, Part I: The 1980s'.

and capital realized its goals of boosting levels of economic growth required the state to keep its side of the bargain of taming organized labour.

The withdrawal of the strike by the JAF did not, however, succeed in normalizing the industrial relations climate. On the contrary, the resumption of work merely had the effect of displacing the spatial location of the conflict from outside the factory walls to the point of production. The highly vindictive attitude pursued by the Congress (I) government towards the strikers, characterized notably by the recourse to blacklegs, the failure of the authorities and the JAF to arrive at a satisfactory compromise, and the indignation animating the workforce which had endured considerable deprivation and humiliation during the course of the dispute, all of this contributed to embitter shop floor relations. As a result, ITI and some of the other plants experienced a fairly extended period of turbulence lasting for about ten weeks until June 1981. The unrest reached its dénouement in a 26-day long lockout after a hunger-strike staged by the JAF leaders was forcibly interrupted by the Karnataka government and the hunger strikers arrested, provoking riotous scenes in the heart of Bangalore as irate workers went on the rampage.

Significantly, it was not the union but the rank-and-file that proved to be the driving force behind the work stoppages, the attacks against strike breakers, the manhandling of supervisory and production personnel and other such incidents which rocked the various plants in the weeks following the repeal of the strike. Whereas the strike had been an institutionalized affair featuring the union leadership and the state, with workers (and managements) being reduced to the role of passive spectators, the subsequent conflict assumed the traits of a spontaneous confrontation between managements and workers, largely unmediated by the formal union structure.[60] To put it in another way, the strike gave way to the 'unofficial strike'. The spontaneous dimension framing the protests of the post-strike period also accounted for their attendant violence relative to the actual strike which remained by and large peaceful. In terms of its substance, dynamics and dénouement (a lockout), the

---

[60] For a detailed enquiry of both the strike and the unofficial strike see Dilip Subramanian, 'Bangalore Public Sector Strike, 1980–1981. A Critical Appraisal', *EPW*, Vol. XXXII, No. 16, 19 April 1997, pp. 843–53; and 'Bangalore Public Sector: The Unofficial Strike 1981'.

events of the unofficial strike then bore a pronounced resemblance to the collective protests conducted in the past in ITI.

Two aspects of the parity strike merit attention. First, because the JAF had expected the government to rapidly concede its demands, it had given no thought to collecting strike funds. Workers were therefore subjected to a great deal of financial distress. Their survival hinged on their ingenuity, their success in tapping traditional networks of family and community solidarity, and the neighbourhood moneylender. A number of workers sent their families back to their home towns and villages, and in certain cases, they too left Bangalore. Those who stayed behind had to resist the strong arm methods of the police and hoodlums linked to the Congress Party as well as the siren calls of managements to resume work.

Yet neither the stick nor the carrot proved of much help to the government in its repeated endeavours to break the strike. Until the very end, the overwhelming majority of the strikers remained united behind the leadership, returning to work only when the JAF called on them to do so. What enabled them to withstand the hardships caused by over two months of lost wages was essentially the sick-leave benefits distributed by local medical authorities. The Employees State Insurance (ESI) scheme assured organized sector workers of up to 50 per cent of their monthly wages in the eventuality of any sickness. The strikers now availed of this compensation often with the complicity of the ESI staff or factory medical personnel who in return for a bribe furnished them with false medical certificates.[61] Hence, in an ironic twist, state largesse in the form of social security benefits enabled workers to sustain their struggle even as the government tried its best to starve them into submission.

Second, notwithstanding its generalized and massive character, the strike was above all an affair of the leadership. There were no serious efforts to draw the mass of workers into the struggle. Workers were encouraged to passively support the strike by staying away from work,

---

[61] From an examination of sickness benefit compensations disbursed by the ESI Centre in Dooravani Nagar where ITI is located, we find that between January and July 1981 the lowest amount paid in a given month stood at Rs 710,000. In comparison, the highest amount paid during the same period in the previous year never exceeded more than Rs 180,000. Cash Book Account No. 2, Employees State Insurance Scheme, Bangalore 16. Predictably, the ESI Act was amended to bar striking workers from claiming sickness or disablement benefits.

but not to actively participate in it.[62] This should not be taken to suggest
that they would necessarily have rallied behind the agitational programme
of the JAF *en masse* had the latter sought to drum up support. Preoccupied
as workers were in securing the necessary wherewithal to last out the
struggle in the absence of any material assistance from the unions, it is
more than likely that their involvement would have been at best minimal.
We only wish to imply that the legalism of the leadership—a legalism
shaped as much by the institutional arrangements of the overall industrial
relations system as by elements specific to the public sector—categorically
ruled out a strategy providing for sustained collective action due to its
violence-generating potential.

With the example of earlier labour conflicts in ITI in particular serving
as a salutary reminder of the dangers presented by independent worker
initiatives, the JAF was understandably determined to prevent a repetition
of these events, especially since the presence of a far greater number of
strikers on this occasion multiplied the risks of the strike spinning out of
'control'. It also feared that any outbreak of violence, apart from hurting
workers the most, would also inevitably deflect attention away from their
demands, disqualify them from occupying the moral high ground and
add grist to the official propaganda mill in portraying the strikers as
'anti-national' elements. So from the outset, the JAF sought to restrict
the engagement of the rank-and-file in order to ensure that its objective
of a peaceful and orderly strike was not subverted under the pressure of
mass action.[63]

These concerns also accounted for the contradiction between the
rhetoric of mobilization and militancy which framed the discourse of
the JAF convenors and the reality of their actions—a contradiction which
more generally throws into relief the unresolved tension inherent in the
role of the trade union leader where the imperatives of legitimacy often
tend to collide head on with that of respectability. For if the need to

[62] One worker told me that he and his friends had spent most of the time during the
strike playing cricket in the day and cards in the evening 'without stakes because we had
no money'. He also claimed that a disproportionately large number of babies were born
in the year following the launch of the strike. Interview with Bhaskar Rao, 4 January
1998.
[63] *Deccan Herald* and *Prajavani*, the two biggest circulating daily newspapers in
Karnataka, held the government squarely responsible for the strike, accusing it of having
violated its contractual obligations. It is doubtful whether they would have stuck to
this worker-friendly editorial line had the conflict strayed from its pacific course.

uphold their image as a strong leader totally committed to the workers' cause compels them to employ a resolutely combative language when addressing the base, they are pulled in the contrary direction of accommodation and compromise by the obligation to project an image of responsibility and reasonableness. Only by demonstrating that they are capable of exercising their judgement to rise above the immediate expectations of workers can they hope to retain their credibility as a reliable interlocutor in the eyes of the authorities and employers, and in turn, secure their own positions and the stability of their organizations.[64]

Thus on the one hand, the JAF instructed activists to set up area committees in various parts of the city for the purpose of mobilizing workers for public meetings and agitations. On the other hand, it took no steps to either inject a sense of purpose into these committees or to provide them with the means required to function effectively. As a consequence, many of them existed only in name. In a way, this was hardly surprising: given the reluctance of the leadership to broaden the base of the struggle, a dynamic and tightly knit network of area committees, well positioned to galvanize collective solidarities, was totally superfluous to its requirements. One could even argue that the interests of the leadership militated against the emergence of a powerful grass roots structure as it could have contested the path of order and moderation to which the JAF continued to remain faithful even as the position of the government progressively hardened.

Yet another example of the disjunction between the rhetoric of the leadership and its actions pertained to the choice of its agitational activities. On the one hand, it adopted fairly militant forms of protest like *rail roko* and *jail bharo* which in principle threatened to disrupt the functioning of the city and cause severe law and order problems. On the other, it contented itself with conducting these protests in an extremely symbolic fashion with barely a few hundred strikers taking part as though it had intended these actions to be no more than a token, theatrical gesture of dissent as opposed to a genuine show of anger. Transgressing

---

[64] Joshi spotlights the important role played by unions in legitimizing industrial discipline where they simultaneously expressed worker grievances and ratified disciplinary codes instituted by employers. *Lost Worlds*, pp. 174–6. See also Arthur Ross who draws a distinction between the 'agitational motive' of unions and their 'organizational motive' in order to underline the contradictory nature of their functions. 'The Natural History of the Strike', in A. Kornhauser et al (eds.), *Industrial Conflict*, New York, 1954, p. 35.

the self-imposed line distinguishing 'permissible and subversive industrial disorder', the JAF believed, perhaps not wrongly, would invite severe repression from a government notorious for its hostility towards organized labour.[65] Other agitations, equally militant in terms of their content, announced with much fanfare by the JAF as part of its plans to intensify the conflict never saw the light of day. The overall approach of the leadership to the strike was best captured by a news caption in a Bangalore daily where the self-restraint exhibited by the strikers during the course of one demonstration won them the encomium of 'Gentlemen Agitators'.[66] A photograph of the event published by the newspaper also showed more police forces present at the scene than protestors.

In sum, the parity strike represented a turning point in the history of ITI and would have a profound influence in shaping the contours of the future industrial relations landscape. The bitter defeat experienced by the strikers served to drive home the message that no amount of pressure exerted in isolation by one section of organized labour, however large in size, could inflect the position of an adversary endowed with resources as inexhaustible as the state, once it had resolved not to concede workers' demands. Thoroughly demoralized, the union leadership both in ITI and the other Bangalore companies would abstain from staging any strikes of significance after 1981.

THE FIGHT FOR SOCIAL STATUS

Economic grievances aside, another major source of labour discontent was the vexatious issue of occupational mobility and seniority. Prior to the introduction of the time-bound promotion scheme at the end of the 1970s, mandating the principle of automatic promotions, establishing steady advancement paths had ranked at the bottom of ITI's priorities. Opportunities for moving up the job ladder were limited and depended on the unrestricted discretion of foremen and shop superintendents. With the labour force composed of young workers and turnover rates insignificant, mobility hinged essentially on the creation of new posts which in turn was contingent on increased production volumes.

---

[65] Robert Dubin, 'Constructive Aspects of Industrial Conflict', in *Industrial Conflict*, p. 45.

[66] *Deccan Herald*, 15 February 1980.

At the same time, an extremely constricting classificatory grid disposed workers in the two biggest divisions, strowger and transmission, in terms of their trade and grade-wise seniority on a shop or departmental basis. This gave rise to narrow lines of progression. For instance, a category-6 driller or turner in the strowger relay machine shop or wireman in the relay assembly shop could only expect to move to a category-5 job in the relay machine or the relay assembly shop, and not in any other strowger department, leave alone another division such as transmission or crossbar.

Supervisors were not encouraging movement from one shop to another . . . If we lost one worker, we would not get a replacement. So workers would grow in the same shop or hangar and given that the factory was growing there was no question of workers being surplus.[67]

As Peter Doeringer and Michael Piore remark in their influential book on internal labour markets, the scope of lines of progression or mobility clusters typically opposes the interests of managements and the labour force.[68] While the labour force favours broad lines of progression with extensive geographical and occupational coverage so as to further advancement opportunities, employers seek to restrict mobility clusters to individual departments.

The biggest drawback associated with the departmental seniority system in ITI was that it discriminated against long service workers. Despite performing the same kind of job, senior workers in shops characterized by comparatively low levels of mobility, sometimes lagged behind their juniors who worked in shops offering more promising promotion prospects. Not surprisingly, this kept alive a permanent source of tension inside the plant. The justification provided by company officials for persisting with this arrangement embraced putatively social as well as efficiency considerations. First, they claimed that employees transferred on promotions encountered a frosty reception in the new department and were unpopular because they were perceived as having encroached on the preserve of 'insiders'. Second, while say a miller or an adjuster executed more or less the same task regardless of his location in the factory, owing to variations in the nature of work from one department to another,

---

[67] Interview with Srinivasa Rao.

[68] Peter Doeringer and Michael Piore, *Internal Labor Markets and Manpower Analysis*, Lexington, 1971, p. 59.

a newcomer would take time to develop job-specific skill sets and knowledge, and hence lead to a loss of production.[69]

Departmental promotion committees, comprising the personnel manager, the administration officer and the concerned department head, and blessed with considerable powers, conducted the screening process. While according due weight to seniority, they also emphasized merit and suitability as operative criteria, the interpretation of which rested upon the committee members' evaluation of a worker's disciplinary record and other reports.[70] Although the union waged a constant fight to prioritize length of service, excluding the other two factors, the company contended, would undercut efficiency by elevating individuals regardless of their ability. Not that the departmental committees distinguished themselves as paragons of allocative efficiency. Exploiting their latitude to reward undeserving candidates more often than they might have wished to recognize, some of the committee's decisions only went to prove that the rubbery gauge of 'ability' as a measure of fitness could mean anything the management wanted it to mean.

Promoted twice in consecutive years, Ramaswamy, an accounting clerk, got a fresh promotion the very same year his superiors issued him with a couple of warnings for negligent work.[71] The case of Achar furnished an even more damning indictment of the twin norms of merit and suitability championed by the company. A clerk in the shipping department, he was reprimanded on no less than ten different occasions for various offences, suspended for one day, and saw his increment postponed for several months. Yet none of this deterred the departmental committee from appointing him to higher ranking posts twice in the span of a decade.[72]

Small wonder then that the entire selection process came in for scathing criticism from union and employees alike who accused especially foremen of playing favourites. Over 40 per cent of the individuals surveyed in one study harboured the conviction that 'no honest man could make progress in the factory'.[73] Asked to rank the most important criteria in

[69] Minutes of management-union meeting, 12 October 1963; 4 March 1964.

[70] PD note, 23 March 1976.

[71] Personnel File no. 137.

[72] Personnel File no. 597.

[73] Arya, *Labour Management Relations*, pp. 27–8. See also Holmstrom, *South Indian Factory Workers*, p. 55.

determining mobility, they first cited seniority, followed by favouritism, better training, and, lastly, merit. Voicing a wide-spread sentiment, one operative said,

I am a good worker, but the one who used to get promotion is the worker who sucks up to the management.[74]

A retired shop boss acknowledged that

before TBP (time bound promotion), there were some cases of partiality in promoting workers. Some officers were getting personal and domestic work done by workers, taking bribes and gifts from them in the form of unpaid loans. Workers understood that these loans would never be repaid.[75]

Discrimination was also sometimes seen as wearing the garb of caste. After noting that little distinguished the quality of his workmanship from that of his colleagues, a charge hand in the rack wiring department openly accused the management of turning down his repeated representations for promotions because he belonged to an 'Untouchable' caste.[76] According to another worker,

when DPCs (departmental promotion committees) existed, caste feelings came in the way of workers getting promotion. Brahmins were getting priority because lots of officers were Brahmins. Anti-Dalit feelings were very strong at one time . . .[77]

Mobility data drawn from a statistical sample survey conducted by us also reveals the levels of discrimination faced by 'Untouchables'. While one out of three caste Hindus in the sample got zero or just one promotion in a span of ten years, in the case of 'Untouchable' employees this figure totalled 45 per cent.

Workers and their representatives highlighted other shortcomings as well in the company's promotion policies. According to the company, although the wage scales for each of the seven categories across which the totality of the labour force was distributed were designed to cover a maximum tenure of ten years before the worker arrived at the end of the scale, most people progressed to the next level well before then. During

---

[74] Interview with Vinayagam.
[75] Interview with S. Mukherjee.
[76] Letter from David Chandra Paul to ITI general manager, 24 August 1960.
[77] Interview with Govindaraju.

the first half of the 1960s, shop floor operatives obtained on average a promotion at an interval of four years and seven months, though the delay for clerical staff extended to six years, and for other groups such as drivers, to six years and three months.[78]

Nevertheless, there were several instances of workers stagnating in each category as they had attained the topmost limit of the wage scale and found all avenues for upward advancement blocked. Unskilled groups among the workforce, such as helpers, labourers and sweepers, or those lacking formally certified qualifications, in particular, were trapped in these dead end jobs. For instance, Muthiah who joined as a sweeper in 1949 earned his first promotion 16 years later.[79] Similarly, in a career spanning over two decades, Perumal, an uneducated labourer, not only advanced just twice, but the second promotion took 18 years in coming.[80] Many other lowly qualified employees shared these two individuals' plight. The company, though, described their condition as 'inevitable' since higher category jobs could not be created artificially to accommodate employees.[81] As a palliative measure, shop bosses occasionally recommended workers for special increments. But while permitting worthy candidates to be rewarded, such discretionary incentives, symbolic markers of managerial authority, also inevitably lent themselves to abuse.

Complaints from machine tenders about facing discrimination *vis-à-vis* their counterparts in assembly shops could also be frequently heard. Because they were responsible for bringing out the final product, and hence were strategically better positioned to disrupt delivery schedules, assembly hands could effectively count on more promising career prospects. So even as the factory kept expanding numerically, the lack of occupational mobility grew even more pronounced. Between October 1966 and September 1969, barely 3 per cent of the total labour force at the Bangalore plant succeeded in qualifying for promotions, although the management felt this figure to be 'satisfactory'.[82] As a result, workers were condemned to even longer periods of wait: if it had taken under five years in 1964 to climb from one category to the next, in 1969 it

---

[78] Minutes of management-union meeting, 7 July 1964.
[79] Personnel File no. 478.
[80] Personnel File no. 451.
[81] Minutes of management-union meeting, 3 September 1965.
[82] Minutes of management-union meeting, 19 January 1970.

took on average seven years and three months to climb from category-6 to 5, and six years from category-5 to 4.[83] Attempts by the union to try and revise the company's promotion policies by fighting it in the labour courts also proved abortive.[84]

WORKERS SEEK REDRESS THROUGH PETITIONS

Because the question of an orderly career progression was intimately entwined with notions of self-adequacy, personal legitimacy and justice, the denial of promotion opportunities, by contesting workers' ability, was bound to provoke cracks in what Richard Sennett has called 'the badge of individual worth'.[85] As one employee declared after having been superseded by a junior colleague, '. . . *such incident pulls me down and make me sick due to mental agony.*'[86] Another worker who received a warning for 'unruly behaviour' after coming to the factory in an inebriated state, much to the surprise of his superiors who had never seen him exhibit such 'strange behaviour' before, spoke of his disappointment at not having been promoted.[87] Still another submitted his resignation in a pique of anger before withdrawing it.[88] All these and other employees understood their careers in terms of what Everett Hughes has defined as a 'moving perspective in which the person sees his life as a whole and interprets the meaning of his various attributes, actions and the things which happen to him'.[89]

But workers did not bow passively to these perceived injustices, symptomatic in their eyes of managerial arbitrariness and partiality. In addition to the weapon of union pressure, they also deployed individual strategies to articulate their grievances and seek redress. Some sought the intercession of influential outside patrons such as politicians or government officials who wrote to the company to endorse the requests of their clients, 'a genuine hard worker but unfortunately . . . he is allowed

[83] ibid.

[84] Industrial Dispute between the Workmen and the Management of ITI, Ref. No. 265/65–66, 31 May 1965.

[85] Sennett, *The Hidden Injuries of Class*, p. 62, 153–5.

[86] Personnel File no. 1869. Citation as in original.

[87] Personnel File no. 4838.

[88] Personnel File no. 1151.

[89] Hughes, 'Institutional Office and the Person', in *The Sociological Eye*, p. 137.

to be superseded (sic)'.[90] Others threatened to take the exit route and regularly applied for jobs elsewhere. But in their quest for justice the technique most widely utilised by ordinary workers was the petition. Instances of individuals writing five or six times to the company were hardly rare, and their perseverance sometimes paid off.

We have been able to assemble a small corpus of these petitions which, by recording first-hand the grievances and argumentative codes employed by workers to vindicate their claims, provides us with precious insights into their feelings and aspirations.[91] Indeed, these supplications constitute the sole formal archival traces directly left by ITI workers—traces from where their voices emerge undistorted and unmediated by the management and the union, even if we allow for the formulaic quality of the appeals. That their veritable authors may sometimes have been friends, colleagues or professional scribes, equipped with the requisite expressive conventions to plead the petitioner's cause, must not be ignored either.

Of the 30 petitions that make up our sample, 13 were submitted by auxiliary workers (store keepers, planners, inspectors, etc.), seven each by clerical staff and production workers, and three by service personnel (drivers, sweepers, etc.). The group comprised only men. Barring eight of the petitioners, all the others possessed fairly high levels of technical skill or educational qualifications. An analysis of the form and content of these texts uncovers a number of common characteristics. Written in English and typed, both details implying that certain employees probably enlisted the services of more literate persons to help them frame their representations, these varied in length from one to three pages, though the majority did not extend beyond a page. In line with factory procedures, individuals appealed in most cases directly to the highest authority in the plant, the managing director or the general manager.

Well aware that 'posing as humble supplicants (was) a necessary aspect

[90] Letter 18 June 1955.

[91] On the importance of petitions as a medium for historians to reconstitute the lives of ordinary people, see, *inter alia*, Lex Heerma Van Voss, 'Introduction. Petitions in Social History', *International Review of Social History*, Vol. 46, Supplement 9, 2001, pp. 1–10 (hereafter *IRSH*); Andreas Würgler, 'Voices from Among the "Silent Masses": Humble Petitions and Social Conflicts in Early Modern Central Europe', *IRSH*, Vol. 46, 2001, pp. 11–34; David Zaret, 'Petitions and the "Invention" of Public Opinion in the English Revolution', *American Journal of Sociology* , Vol. 101, No. 6, May 1996, pp. 1497–555.

of petitioning', the idiom of deference pervaded the requests.[92] But synonymous as deference may have been of the weakness of the petitioner's position, it could not conceal their resentment. The aggrieved tone which ran through the texts left no one in doubt as to whom employees blamed for their status woes. While leaving unchallenged the company's right to decide labour mobility, the supplicants did not hesitate to challenge the soundness of its decisions. In terms of their construction, the petitions adhered, by and large, to an identical narrative format where the telling of each 'work history' unfolded in three successive moments or acts. The first moment foregrounded what could be called the rhetoric of demonstration. Here petitioners sought to demonstrate their ability and value to the company, thereby implicitly contrasting their loyalty with the management's 'disloyalty', in order to justify, to make self-evident their demand for promotion. The repertory of arguments developed for this purpose illuminated the plurality of interpretations each person attached to the significance of his work.

They highlighted their faithfulness to the company: 'I am aged 37 years and fifty per cent of my age has already been devoted in rendering my service to ITI', (Dhanraj, attendant); 'I have put up a total service of 22 years in our esteemed organisation without any bad remarks', (Zacharias, charge hand). They stressed their diligence: 'I have neither availed a single day's leave on loss of pay or punched my card late on any occasion during my ten years service in this factory . . .' (Nair, machine tender); 'I have not only allowed the innumerable mental worries not to disturb my quality of work, but also I have tried my level best to put in the maximum zeal possible', (Ranganathan, planner).

They drew attention to their skill and efficiency: 'I know my work . . . I know the nook and corner of factory, and how to keep such places tidy and clean . . . what to do during the time of heavy rains, etc.', (Abbiah, sweeper); '. . . the recent celebrations for bringing out the 1000th Rack must give you an insight into the amount of work put in by me all through and the amount of technical knowledge derived thereby', (Subbiah, planner). They emphasized the importance of valorizing practical experience over formal qualifications: '. . . kindly give due

---

[92] Potukuchi Swarnalatha, 'Revolt, Testimony, Petition: Artisanal Protests in Colonial India', *IRSH*, Vol. 46, 2001, pp. 107–29 (cit. p. 114).

consideration to the qualities required for day to day production than for any such qualifications through certificates which may not very help a progressive industry like ours' (Masilamani, inspector).

They pointed to the heavy responsibilities shouldered by them: 'In this kind of work . . . important and far reaching decisions have to be taken on the spur of the moment . . . This requires my unceasing vigilance and alertness at all times . . .' (Dharmalingam, senior shop clerk); 'It may not be out of the way if I mention that I have actually become very indispensable in the big, huge highly transacted telephone stores since the present senior Store Keeper is quite new to his job', (Gopal, store keeper) They referred to their willingness to assume additional tasks: 'From March 1952, I was acting as a Supervisor in the Joining-up Section. After a few months I was asked to look after Bank-Multiple Section too. From that time onwards, I was looking after both the sections without any promotion or increments', (Chandra Paul, charge hand). They underlined their contributions and achievements: 'I played my part in successfully bringing out in an attractive manner the booklet entitled *Six Years of Progress*. Considerable ingenuity had to be employed in giving the final touches to this publication . . .' (Vedavyasa Rao, senior clerk); 'The production which was far below the schedule was brought up to schedule by me. Further . . . I have been awarded two awards for the suggestions made by me . . .' (Ananthu, charge hand).

Petitioners supplemented these work-related claims with one important extra-work argument to legitimize their claims for upward advancement. This centred on the financial hardships involved in supporting a large family on a small salary. In the words of Nagabhushan, a typist in the engineering department,

My present basic salary is Rs 95 per month . . . My family consists of six souls and the monthly minimum maintenance comes to approximately Rs 200. I leave this to your sweet discretion to see how much I am disabled every month even to meet the very essential needs of a growing family particularly in these hard days.[93]

Adds Papaiah, a semi-skilled worker:

As I am having a large family to support and I being the only earning member,

---

[93] Letter to ITI personnel manager, 18 June 1955.

I am finding it very hard to maintain my family in these hard days as the income I get by way of salary . . . is not at all sufficient to meet both ends.[94]

In addition to functioning as a testimonial to their individual capabilities, the petitions then also conveyed an explicit reminder to the company of its obligations to sustain the material well being of petitioners and their families. In sum, the principles of justification mobilized by employees in their contention with the management, if they were to some extent grounded in a domestic order of worth which focussed on values such as loyalty to superordinates and reciprocal duties, drew their inspiration primarily from the same industrial order of worth upheld by the management where the yardsticks of productivity and efficiency served to measure individual worth.[95] It was because both employees and the management belonged to the same 'moral world' that the claims of the petitioners could appear as sensible and legitimate.[96] The contention between the two sides did not correspond to a confrontation between two rival regimes of justification or generality, thus facilitating the possibility of arriving at a compromise.

The second moment in the narrative process was informed by the rhetoric of denunciation. The act of denunciation actually encapsulated two forms of injustice. First, individuals reproached the management for denying them promotion. In the majority of instances, grievances had to do with the marginalization of seniority claims because promotion rules often enabled junior workers to vault over the heads of senior colleagues. The following lines exemplified the reactions of several petitioners.

I was anxiously waiting for my next promotion in the near future. But to my surprise I came to know that some of my juniors were promoted . . . Even I can't dream of such a thing to be happened (sic).[97]

---

[94] Letter to ITI works manager, 1 August 1955.

[95] Boltanski and Thévenot, *De la justification,* pp. 206–16, 253–9.

[96] Analysing complaints addressed by workers to the authorities in post-reforms China, Thireau and Hua also underscore the importance of elaborating a set of normative referents. By appealing to common notions of equity and justice held by the powerful and the weak alike, this discourse places the former under a moral obligation to intervene in favour of the petitioners. Isabelle Thireau and Linshan Hua, 'Le sens du juste en Chine. En quête d'un nouveau droit du travail', *Annales HSS,* No. 6, November-December 2001, pp. 1283–312.

[97] Letter from Palainiswamy to ITI managing director, 13 October 1963.

Supplicants sometimes backed their complaints with detailed comparisons of career trajectories to prove that they had effectively been superseded by their juniors. Workers with poor disciplinary records but who had been promoted, were singled out. Overall, the petitions bore witness to the attentiveness with which promotion movements across the factory were surveilled. The task was rendered relatively easy by the classificatory system adopted by the company where all employees were identified by a serial number, the higher the number the more junior the worker and vice-versa. Paradoxically, even as the arbitrariness of the management in giving promotions turned the factory into an arena of competing claims, the bureaucratization inherent in all industrial organizations by creating what could be called 'enumerated communities' greatly facilitated the process whereby persons could stake out their claims.[98]

At the same time, petitioners continued to pitch their demands exclusively in the language of seniority, the 'keystone of their moral economy' as it were, even though company officials religiously informed disappointed candidates that other criteria also determined promotion decisions.[99] From the point of view of workers, instituting seniority provisions to regulate occupational mobility not only provided a bulwark against arbitrary management control. It represented a moral claim for preference over newer entrants by those who had devoted long years of their lives to the company. In a work context defined by scarce opportunities for progression and which pitted one group of workers against another in the fight for these opportunities, no other principle could appear more equitable to them than this one.[100] Having said this, the divisive potential inherent in the establishment of seniority rights can hardly be denied. Even as this mechanism protected the interests of certain categories of employees it also sanctified profound gender, racial

---

[98] I have borrowed the term, 'enumerated communities' from Sudipta Kaviraj. He has, however, used it in the context of a modern nation state which by deploying various techniques of objectification creates such a community. 'The Imaginary Institutions of India', in P. Chatterjee and G. Pandey (eds.), *Subaltern Studies VII*, New Delhi, 1995, pp. 1–39.

[99] Carl Gersuny and Gladis Kaufman, 'Seniority and the Moral Economy of U.S. Automobile Workers, 1934–46', *Journal of Social History*, No. 18, Spring 1985, pp. 463–75 (cit. p. 464).

[100] No scientific answer exists, remark Freeman and Medoff, as to whether seniority rights are socially desirable or undesirable. But depending on the perspective, privileging length of tenure has both costs and benefits. *What do Unions Do?* p. 15, 133–5.

and generational biases at workplaces, and acted as a brake on labour unity.[101]

The second form of injustice petitioners denounced related to the management's failure to respect its engagements. Quite a few of them spoke of having received oral assurances of promotion from their superiors in case they performed satisfactorily. But while they had laboured hard to keep their part of the bargain, company officials had not done so and therefore let them down. One act of injustice—unrewarded effort—was thus compounded by another—the betrayal of a promise. Pointing out that he had 'joined the factory on the assurance that I will be promoted if found efficient in about six months', Gangaraju, an inspector in the test set department complained bitterly of having to wait '4 long years' before being promoted and even then he was still earning less than what his previous employer used to pay him.[102] Equally resentful, Sundar, an inspector in the relay adjustment department wrote that he had

been promised orally by the Works Manager before the S.S.S (senior shop superintendent) and some of my co-workers that I would be posted to a place where cat. (category) 4 was done and if I were to pick up that job, I would be considered for promotion to cat. 4.[103]

But five years later the company had still not fully honoured its 'oral assurance'.

The third and final moment in the narrative structuring of the petitions was underpinned by the rhetoric of affect. Here the injustice experienced by the petitioners found expression in the language of feeling and emotions. Here we can hear them voicing their hurt and anger, their disappointed hopes, the injuries inflicted upon their dignity by the denial of what they judged to be their due rights to mobility as well as the lack of adequate rewards for their efforts and loyalty. A clerical employee

---

[101] On this point see Crozier, *Le phénomène bureaucratique*, pp. 81–4; David Montgomery and Ronald Schatz, 'Facing Layoffs', in D. Montgomery, *Workers Control in America. Studies in the History of Work, Technology and Labor Struggles*, Cambridge, pp. 139–52; Ronald Schatz, *The Electrical Worker. A History of Labour at General Electric and Westinghouse 1923–1960*, Urbana, 1983, chap. 5. Interestingly, Hareven argues that the union in the New England textile factory studied by her attached greater weight to the issue of seniority than did mill hands who felt it clashed with traditional patronage networks. *Family Time and Industrial Time*, pp. 304–05.

[102] Letter to ITI managing director, 19 January 1955.

[103] ibid.

with a 'fine record of loyal and efficient service' felt abased at having to request the management for promotion because

> I never thought that I would have to fight out my case for recognition, as due recognition of services rendered by me should have automatically come off long ago from the righteous management of this reputed concern.[104]

Prahlada Rao, a factory guide, complained that he had been 'relegated to a very pathetic level' after 12 years of service, thus totally belying his expectations of 'a fairly good career in ITI'.[105] Blaming the company for having neglected to give 'due consideration either to service or experience', a store keeper declared that the

> ultimate result of my strenuous and long service of 7 years has landed me into lowest grade where far junior are better placed . . .[106]

Resentment at the failure to provide adequate positive incentives also surfaced in other petitions.

> I join(ed) this First National Industry (ITI) in the formative stages in the earnest and sincere hopes of bettering my prospects in life, but I regret to mention here that despite my more than 10 years of exemplary service, I have not been properly encouraged in the present position.[107]

Despite 'spar(ing) no pains in putting my knowledge into my daily work', Muthe Gowda, a technical assistant in the production planning department claimed that 'his progress in the Deptt. (department) has not been in relation to the important projects entrusted to me and their progress and expansion day by day . . .'[108] Dhanraj, an attender, said that he had obtained a post-graduate degree after joining the factory. But

> I have not derived any advantage and material benefit for suffering and hardships I have undergone to acquire this qualification.[109]

All of this was bound to have exercised an adverse effect on the performances of workers. Indeed, so discouraged was one 'diligent, sincere

---

[104] Letter from D. Dharmalingam to ITI personnel manager, 22 June 1955.
[105] Letter to ITI joint general manager, 13 June 1964.
[106] Letter from Srinivasa Murthy to ITI general manager, nd.
[107] Letter from Shashidharan to ITI general manager, 1 April 1963.
[108] Letter to ITI general manager, 18 November 1956.
[109] Letter to ITI administrative manager, 9 July 1976.

and enthusiastic' draughtsman by the fact that his promotions claims had been overlooked 'in preference to those who had similar qualifications and less experience' than him, that he believed this 'invidious distinction' was 'bound to dampen the enthusiasm of an official like me entrusted with work of a responsible nature in an important department like Industrial Engineering . . .'[110]

Other employees, who possessed the requisite resources, such as sportsmen representing the company, threatened even more explicitly to withhold their services. Thus a cricket player whose talents had propelled ITI to distinction in local tournaments warned that he would leave for a rival public enterprise because his juniors had received promotion but not him. The threat did not go unheeded: the following year the employee advanced to a higher category post.[111] Such cases where petitioners commanded sufficient individual bargaining power to deliver an ultimatum and extract concessions from the management were, however, exceptional. For the overwhelming majority of persons, their best chances of obtaining their requests for promotion rested on showing the maximum of on-stage deference. Besides, as 'demands for a favour, or for the redressing of an injustice', the very nature of the petition itself excluded the usage of a belligerent tone.[112] All that employees could do then was 'pray for a sympathetic consideration' of their demands, 'solicit the favour' of and seek 'acts of kindness' from the company.

WORKERS RESORT TO COLLECTIVE ACTION TO GAIN PROMOTION

But these demonstrations of humility did not in any way connote passivity or submissiveness on the part of the workforce. Alongside such individual mechanisms as the petition, workers also resorted to collective forms of protest to press their grievances. The first recorded traces of concerted action over the question of promotion opportunities dated back to October 1965. Officials in the strowger switch wiring shop complained

---

[110] Letter from Ramaswamy to ITI general manager, 22 January 1959. ITI workers cited 'quicker promotions' as the measure most conducive to stimulating higher individual work effort. Arya, *Labour Management Relations*, p. 66.

[111] Letter to ITI general manager, 12 June 1957.

[112] van Voss, 'Introduction. Petitions in Social History', p. 1.

that a small group of inspection staff had launched a go-slow. From 50 switches daily, they were now checking only 30–32 switches, thereby affecting production both in the shop and in other departments. According to the union, the go-slow reflected the inspectors' unhappiness at the absence of established perspectives of career progression.[113]

Unrest once again spontaneously flared up in June 1971, but on a much broader scale this time. Concentrated in the main strowger division, the immediate cause of the trouble had to do with the management's hasty and imprudent decision to implement the recommendations of the job evaluation committee in the crossbar and transmission divisions. The creation of the crossbar division in 1965 coupled with changes in the nature of manufacturing processes for strowger equipment in particular, due to the increasing integration of indigenous material as well as the consolidation of various operations, had led to the institution of a plant-wide job evaluation scheme in the mid-1960s. Priority was given to the crossbar division, a new product line and where delays in conducting the evaluation had produced 'a lot of dissatisfaction', since no promotions could be granted so long as the various occupations had not been 'objectively' codified and distributed hierarchically.[114]

In January 1971, the committee submitted its report with respect to crossbar and suggested upgrading virtually all lower category jobs. In the case of strowger, because of the 'complexity and the large number of jobs involved', the committee still remained many months away from finishing its task.[115] But instead of waiting for the entire evaluation process to be over, the top management, influenced, no doubt, by the status of crossbar as the showcase of the company, announced at the end of May 1971 promotions for as many as 460 crossbar operatives and for 300 transmission division operatives.[116] Predictably enough, the news unleashed a surge of anger amongst the strowger labour force.

Demanding that their loyalty to ITI be rewarded by the same treatment extended to crossbar and transmission workers, around 3700 strowger machine and assembly hands now went on a two-day long wildcat strike

---

[113] Minutes of management-union meeting, 15 October 1965.

[114] Note on Promotion Procedure and Present Position, ITI Personnel Dept., 7 July 1972.

[115] ibid.

[116] Reply to Ministry of Labour questionnaire, 1972.

in early June.[117] Only after the management promised to ensure the rapid completion of the job evaluation programme did the union representatives succeed in restoring order. Still, sporadic work stoppages continued to interrupt the flow of production throughout the month in the relay, switch and telephone machine and assembly shops, notwithstanding warnings from the management that such illegal work practices would invite punishments.[118] Nor did partially meeting a long standing demand of the union and the workers to modify the seniority rules, with a view to better facilitating the movement of personnel from one shop or department to the other, pave the way for a return to normalcy.

More worryingly for company officials, the agitation also began progressively spreading to other areas of the factory. Already in March 1972, nearly 600 clerical staff 'came out of their offices at about 11 am and were standing silently in the veranda', to protest against the delays in completing job evaluation of non-production activities.[119] The walkout ended quite quickly after union representatives intervened and persuaded the employees to return to their workspots. But the fact that the union was 'neither a party nor supported this demonstration' far from reassuring the management, was on the contrary, a disturbing indication that the former did not fully control the situation.[120]

This was further borne out by another event. Towards the end of April, between 300 and 400 strowger operatives assembled near the main canteen in anticipation of a meeting with top union officials. Irked by their failure to appear after a while, the demonstrators then converged upon the administration gate, or 'justice gate' in worker parlance, which separated the factory premises from the administrative offices, and raised slogans crying 'We Want Justice', 'We Want Fernandes'. When the union president came out, accompanied by other delegates, workers reiterated their demand for equal opportunities with crossbar. The union vice president, V. S. Ramaswamy, a crossbar employee, was accused of 'being favourably disposed towards Crossbar', and hence unworthy of their trust.

---

[117] ibid. Minutes of management-union meeting 2 June 1971.

[118] Position regarding Labour Situation at ITI Bangalore, ITI Personnel Dept., nd (1972).

[119] ibid.

[120] Reply to Ministry of Labour questionnaire.

They also urged for further changes in the seniority rules since the fundamental question of the protection of long service workers' rights remained unresolved.

Immediately after this incident, the head of personnel wrote to the union to air the management's concern over the difficulties experienced by the union leadership in imposing its authority over an increasingly recalcitrant workforce. Stating that instances of 'large number of workers leaving their places of work and collecting around some Union Office Bearer or the other to demonstrate or voice their protest . . .' were growing in frequency, he expressed surprise that '. . . such abandonment of work, demonstrations, etc. have been happening . . . in the absence of a specific . . . and important dispute between the Union and the Management . . .'. After pointing out that the ITI chairman had personally discussed all these problems with the top union leaders, the letter ended by brandishing the threat of a lock-out in case the various acts of 'mass indiscipline' remained unchecked.[121]

A few days later at a meeting between the two sides, the management again underscored the role of the union in preventing 'indiscipline . . . and loss of production'.[122] None of these admonitions delivered the anticipated results. From an internal note dated May 10 we learn that setters and operatives in the key automatic machine shop who previously attended to five machines were now refusing to attend to more than four machines and that too only if they were placed in the same row; in the strowger switch adjustment shop, operators were only willing to adjust the switches and not repair them, despite being required to do both jobs and despite being promoted; similarly in the strowger plating shop, recently promoted workers were executing only a portion of their tasks; in the coil winding department, though a number of lower category jobs had been upgraded, efficiency levels had dropped from 120 to 80 per cent.[123]

Another note dated 12 May revealed that the unrest had enveloped a number of crossbar shops as well. For reasons of flexibility as well as labour control, shop bosses commonly followed the practice of assigning

---

[121] Letter from personnel manager to ITI Employees Union, Bangalore, 29 April 1972.

[122] Minutes of management-union meeting, 10 May 1972.

[123] PD files, 10 May 1972.

higher category jobs to lower category operatives. They were promised promotions within a year or so if they accepted to do the job in the interval and met the required targets. Now, crossbar operatives in four assembly shops plus the testing department refused to continue performing higher category work after learning their promotions would be delayed. Ironically, it was not the management but the union which was responsible for the delay. Pointing out that it was on the verge of finalizing its proposals to amend the existing seniority rules and introduce a system common to the whole factory, the union leadership had requested for a temporary postponement of all promotion decisions in order to 'avoid the discontent among some sections of workers from assuming larger proportions'.[124] When crossbar line authorities asked the shop delegate to communicate this information to the operatives and instruct them not to slow down work, the delegate 'expressed his inability to speak to them and advised us to speak to the (union) Secretary or Vice President'.[125] To add to the management's woes, it could also not enforce disciplinary sanctions against workers for declining to undertake higher category tasks as these were 'clearly beyond the purview of their legitimate work'.[126] Soon afterwards, overtime work ground to a halt as attendance had dropped by 10 to 12 per cent, thus further hampering production. Output levels were not even expected to cross those recorded the previous year, let alone meet the target fixed for 1972–73.

In early June, angered at not having obtained their promotions, between 100 and 150 crossbar workers marched to the administration building where they staged a sit-down demonstration. Chanting slogans attacking both the management and the union, they dispersed after about 30 minutes.[127] The following month it was the turn of strowger workers in the selector shop to down tools for almost three hours 'for no justified cause or reason'.[128] Another document, though, claimed they had shouted slogans demanding the same promotion benefits as those granted to crossbar operatives.[129] A few days later an even longer work stoppage

[124] Letter from ITI union to management, 28 April 1972.
[125] PD note, 12 May 1972.
[126] PD note, 17 May 1972.
[127] Reply to Ministry of Labour questionnaire.
[128] PD circular, 5 July 1972.
[129] Reply to Ministry of Labour questionnaire.

occurred, lasting six hours and involving employees from the plant mechanical department in all divisions. The department head reported that everybody had gathered outside the main hangar to discuss their 'grievances regarding promotion and seniority'.[130] Apparently frustrated by the attitude of the union too, they had insisted on convoking union representatives to the spot; only after the latter intervened was a semblance of normalcy restored.

Subsequently, shop officials suspended nine mechanics on charges of refusing to work and instigating their colleagues to stop working. The entire department then promptly walked out causing disruptions to 'essential services like compressors and boilers'.[131] To ensure these could not be operated, switch fuses were removed and thrown away, and supervisory staff forcibly prevented from attending to the equipment. Interestingly, an official document claims that the mechanics had expressed their hostility to the principle of a combined factory seniority being debated by the union; they preferred the prevailing division-wise configuration, viewed as far more conducive to their career advancement chances.

From the foregoing account, the wholly spontaneous character of the agitation is self-evident with the union intervening at various moments only in its disciplinary or social control capacity to try and restore order. Acting on their own initiative from start to finish, workers' anger in certain instances appeared to be directed as much at the management as at the union, their protests being designed to keep up the pressure on both parties. Aware of the mutually incompatible nature of their respective interests, each group of workers pinned its faith on its own strength, seeing direct action as the most effective means of making its voice heard. At the same time, the agitation proved to be a protracted affair, dragging on for almost a year, even though the tremors that shook the plant with the greatest frequency, if not intensity, were concentrated during a six-month period stretching from March to August 1972. But, paradoxically, the actual demonstrations, the work stoppages, walkouts and so forth, rarely lasted for very long; whether these forms of protest could not be sustained beyond a short period because of workers' inability or reluctance to organize themselves more effectively is a moot question.

[130] PD files, 9 August 1972.
[131] ibid.

That the confrontation persisted for several months can be explained by the highly charged nature of the underlying issue of contention. Occupational mobility not only fused together material and symbolic rewards, money and status, in one indissoluble whole. It not only constituted the principal arena where questions of justice and equity emerged to the fore with sharp focus, given the importance accorded by workers to the question of seniority rights, the conviction that career progression stood in direct proportional relation to service tenure occupying a central place in their worldview. In the context of industrial work where *pace* Sennett the injuries of class are not always hidden, it also played a fundamental role in validating and reinforcing the self-image of workers by operating as a tangible marker of recognition of their individual abilities and contributions to the enterprise.[132] The struggle for improved promotion opportunities was thus also undeniably a struggle for dignity and respect, one that workers waged in order to carve out a meaningful place for themselves in a hierarchical factory 'community'.

Yet, notwithstanding its exceptional duration and its impact on production, the conflict remained small scale and localized in form. Of the three production divisions, one, transmission, experienced no disturbances whatsoever. Even in the other two divisions, going by the official documents, participation in collective action tended to be rather restricted. In strowger, the epicentre of the agitation, barring the wildcat strike at the start, the overwhelming majority of workers stayed quiescent. This was also true in the case of crossbar where the protests to boot did not spread beyond the walls of the assembly shops to suck in the machine shops. More significantly, as we saw, workers in the two divisions were not bound by a common set of demands. Whereas delays in granting promotions occupied centre stage in crossbar, strowger workers wanted the same promotion entitlements as those bestowed on crossbar personnel. It was this disjunction in the nature of the demands which essentially accounted for the fragmented, uncoordinated, and sporadic character of the agitation. The succession of local disputes that punctually flared up

---

[132] As Sennett again pertinently observes, rewards for blue collar workers are earned collectively, through contractual bargaining which distinguishes categories and not individuals, whereas white collar rewards flow from the recognition of individual achievements. *The Hidden Injuries of Class*, pp. 35-6.

never threatened to have a snowball effect and coalesce into a factory-wide 'general' strike. To put it slightly differently, instead of a battle of full-blown proportions, organized and directed from the top, which united the mass of workers in a common cause and simultaneously erupted on all fronts, the company witnessed a series of individualized, short-lived, spatially circumscribed skirmishes 'led' from below and staggered in time.

NEW SENIORITY RULES INSTITUTED

What ultimately brought the wave of protests to a close was an agreement signed by the company and the union in August 1972 enshrining a new set of seniority norms to govern promotion decisions. The principle of divisional seniority adopted in most production areas now gave way to a trade-based segmentation encompassing the factory in its entirety. All operatives were segregated, first, vertically in terms of their designated trades, and, then, horizontally in terms of their category within each trade. This highly bureaucratic exercise entailed identifying all the different machine and assembly trades available within the factory (45 and 57 respectively) after which trades sharing fairly similar levels of skill and responsibility had to be consolidated into a single group. So welders formed one group, wiremen another group, moulders still another, and so forth. In all, 14 such broad groupings existed for the machine trades and four with regard to the assembly trades. In short, by further subjecting promotion policies to administratively located rules and procedures, the new agreement marked an important step forward towards the creation of a full-fledged internal labour market, albeit the management clinging on to criteria such as suitability and merit.

Viewed through the optic of workers' interests, a seniority grid applicable right across the factory presented at least two significant advantages. First, with the axis of mobility being extended from an intra-divisional plane to an inter-divisional one, a far more extensive range of opportunities automatically opened up for the workforce. Not only was a strowger press operator or adjuster now entitled to seek promotion within his trade in the crossbar or transmission division. In order to facilitate optimum career progression, workers also had the right to change trades, even being authorized to cross over from the machine shop to the assembly shop and vice-versa, though in all such cases the candidate was required to demonstrate his aptitude for the job by passing a 'trade test'.

Second, and intimately connected to the above, the modified seniority rules eliminated a major source of friction among older and younger workers by making sure that the claims of long-service workers were no longer ignored. The removal of all restrictions on the lateral mobility of the workforce meant that the earlier practice of a crossbar or transmission division tool setter with fewer years of service than a strowger tool setter superseding him, simply because the latter was barred from applying for a post in crossbar or transmission, could not repeat itself in future. As the management itself agreed, the new dispensation by redressing the 'main and justified grievance' of senior workmen was 'logical and fair both to the employees and to the Industry'.[133] Notwithstanding company officials' persistent opposition in the past to the introduction of common plant-wide seniority rankings for fear of the disruptive impact this could have on production plus the higher retraining costs involved, they had come to realize that only a solution of this nature could help to restore industrial peace.

Ironically, in the search for a mutually acceptable compromise, overcoming the resistance of the management might have been a less strenuous task for the union than winning over elements within the union executive and its own membership. By the union's own admission, the dispute over seniority and promotions represented the 'most complex and difficult major problem ever faced by (it)', given the divergent interests of different sections of the workforce. In fact, company officials blamed the divisions within the union executive for the leadership's failure to 'carry the workers by persuasion (sic)' and urge them to maintain 'normal production' while it finalized a fresh seniority protocol.[134] As one union circular lamented, not only did 'each large group (of) . . . workers look at the problem from the angle of its own interests'; the interests of each group also often tended to collide with the 'interests of another group', therefore considerably complicating things for the union leadership.[135] A few weeks before the conclusion of the agreement, an official document categorically stated that no initiative tabled by the union with respect to seniority 'can give complete satisfaction to all the

[133] Minutes of management-union meeting, 19 June 1972.
[134] Minutes of 130th board meeting, 9 June 1972.
[135] ITI Union circular, 18 May 1972.

workers in the different divisions . . . in view of (their) conflicting aspirations . . .'[136]

The cleavages criss-crossing employees' ranks separated them as much along generational lines as along divisional and trade ones. Junior workers by and large preferred to maintain the principle of divisional seniority as it prevented more senior colleagues from other divisions from pressing their claims for promotion. Much the same applied to crossbar and, to a slightly lesser extent, transmission workers who benefited from the fact that production volumes in these divisions were expanding at a brisker pace than in strowger, resulting in the creation of more and higher ranking jobs. Likewise, qualified workers in departments such as machine and plant maintenance and the tool room where the possibilities for progression were comparatively greater perceived little advantage in switching over to a classificatory scheme embracing the entire factory. Infighting on the subject of seniority rights then could only have served to further strain the internal cohesion of the union at a time when the wounds inflicted by the linguistic clashes between Kannada and Tamil workers were yet to heal.

The implementation of the revised seniority norms notwithstanding, mobility continued to remain a highly contentious issue. After a lull of about five years, signs of unrest once again became visible. In June 1977, declaring that it was under pressure from the rank-and-file and shop delegates to 'take a more forceful stand', the union issued the management with an 'ultimatum' to rapidly introduce a routinized time-bound promotion scheme (TBP).[137] Under the scheme, workers would automatically progress from one category to the next upon completion of a stipulated number of years of service without reference to any of the hitherto operative criteria such as seniority, merit or suitability. Shortly after this ultimatum, company officials complained that despite extensive recourse to overtime work, production and efficiency levels had declined over the previous year in strowger, crossbar and telephone divisions. Operatives in these divisions, it declared, had adopted an 'agitational approach' and several cases of unauthorized work stoppages had been reported.[138]

---

[136] Promotion Policy for Factory Operatives, ITI Personnel Dept., nd (June 1972).

[137] Minutes of management-union meeting, 14 June 1977.

[138] Minutes of management-union meeting, 28 July 1977.

In December 1977, trouble broke out anew. The protagonists this time were unskilled workers, a group which had derived no benefits at all from the changes effectuated to the company's promotion policies. These workers had typically entered ITI as casual hands before being made permanent, and since they possessed no formal qualifications their chances of progressing up the job ladder were nonexistent.[139] In what had become by now a hardy ritual, nearly 300 sweepers, helpers, attenders, gardeners, labourers and the like congregated behind the administration building and began shouting slogans. Denouncing the fact that most of them had not received a single promotion even after working for 12 or 14 years, the demonstrators raised slogans strongly critical of the union leadership, accusing it of neglecting those situated at the bottom-most layer of the occupational hierarchy.

Meanwhile, the union renewed its demand for the implementation of a time bound promotion programme. Warning the company that growing dissatisfaction over the lack of mobility would impinge on production volumes, union officials urged it to follow the lead of other state-owned enterprises such as BHEL and BEL which had already devised structured career paths for their workforces.[140] In a strike ballot held in mid-August 1979, 84 per cent of the workers voted in favour of going on strike, an eloquent statement of the rank-and-file's support for the course of action advocated by the leadership. Exactly a month later the strike got underway and ended nine days later in an emphatic victory for the workers. The management conceded all the demands put forward by the union. As it later admitted, 'very negligible' promotion opportunities had 'created hardships to a large number of employees (sic)'.[141] Even though implementational and other difficulties continued to fuel unrest in certain pockets for some time, over 3300 promotions were granted in the very first year itself of the institution of the time bound promotion scheme, and an additional 2057 in 1980 which went to prove just how beneficial this measure was to the workforce.[142]

---

[139] A confidential note acknowledged that unskilled sections of the workforce in ITI stagnated in dead end jobs for much longer periods than in any other Bangalore public enterprise. PD note, 31 December 1977.

[140] Minutes of management-union meeting, 22 November 1978.

[141] Salient Features of TBP Scheme, nd.

[142] PD files.

So with the new promotion system in place, the transition to a full-fledged internal labour market whose defining trait was the articulation of careers to a fixed temporal horizon was finally complete. Where managerial discretion and arbitrariness had conditioned mobility, formally administered mechanisms, enforced by collective agreements, now regulated the entire process. 'Under TBP, even the chairman can't recommend somebody for a promotion'.[143] Where some workers could earn two promotions in as many years and others none in ten years, a precisely codified time scale was now elaborated to determine the movement from one category to the next. Depending upon the promotion channel into which a worker was slotted, which in turn was related to the content of his/her work task and level of education, the wait period for advancement varied from six to eight years.[144] Subsequently, this qualifying span would be reduced by one year for all employees.[145] Only a poor disciplinary record could retard, though not halt, the climb up the job ladder. Employees punished for serious infractions saw their promotions delayed by two years, and those punished for minor infractions by one year; these conditions too were relaxed later.[146]

To be sure, by bestowing rewards on 'sincere and lazy' workers alike, the new procedures attracted criticism especially from those sections of the workforce disappointed at having failed to realize higher dividends from their educational capital.[147] As one disgruntled computer technician declared,

---

[143] Interview with Govindaraju.

[144] Two classificatory exercises underpinned the time bound promotion scheme. First, employees were distributed under three broad categories: technical operative, technical non-operative, and non-technical. The first category covered all blue collar occupations both within and outside the shop floor, the second category merged personnel such as planners, draughtsmen, and technicians, and the third mainly clerical jobs. Then, on the basis of their jobs and formal qualifications, employees in each category were accommodated into one of the ten promotion channels that had been created. Thus while channels one to three regrouped all technical operative personnel, channel one consisted exclusively of unskilled or low skilled workers, channel two of semi-skilled workers, and channel three of skilled workers.

[145] Memorandum of Settlement (Modifications to the Time Bound Promotion Scheme for Non-Officers), 4 November 1985.

[146] PD note, DMT/32 A, 9 October 1985.

[147] Interview with Vadiraj Hatwar.

when I see a lazy employee being automatically promoted I get frustrated . . . if you are good, you should get promotions based on merit.[148]

Echoing a similar view, another qualified worker lamented that he had

lost all opportunity to show my skills, improve my status and build a career because of TBP . . . There are no incentives for or recognition of the skills of qualified workers like diploma holders . . . TBP has brought an end to the differences between non-qualified and qualified workers.[149]

Such sentiments were confined to a small minority, however; without losing sight of its shortcomings most of the persons whom we interviewed enthusiastically endorsed the TBP as a positive achievement. What they most appreciated about the scheme was the freedom from managerial caprice and, its logical corollary, the fairness that it ensured, as the following quotations underscore.

—Everybody now has a chance to get promotions regularly. Otherwise, if you join as a operator, you will continue as a operator until the end.[150]

—Educated and uneducated workers, good and bad workers, all now have a chance of getting regular promotion. This is good because there is no partiality now, no chance of jealousy. Before the management used to show a lot of discrimination and favouritism . . .[151]

—You can't help the fact that good and bad workers get promotion under TBP. Before we were never getting promotions. It is true that there is no reward now for good workers. That is an anomaly in the scheme which the management and the union should solve.[152]

—TBP is good in one way, because it removes the chances of stagnation. The bad aspect is that workers become lazy. As long as their attendance is regular, everybody is sure to get promotion whether he works or not.[153]

Thus, the impulse for establishing a complex of impersonal, systematic rules, embedded in the social matrix of the firm, came entirely from the ITI union and the rank-and-file. Few objective compulsions weighed

---

[148] ibid. Some of the workers interviewed by Holmström voiced an identical grievance. *South Indian Factory Workers*, pp. 101–11

[149] Interview with R. Paneerselvam, 27 October 1997.

[150] Interview with Anantha Padmanabha, 1 December 2001.

[151] Interview with Vinayagam.

[152] Interview with Krishnan.

[153] Interview with Sahadevan.

upon the company to secure employee loyalty through the creation of internal job systems. What constrained it to embark on this road was worker militancy alone which often developed autonomously of the union. Both orthodox and radical theses of internal labour markets tend to conceptualize this institution as arising from or being moulded by the unilateral action of employers aspiring for greater technical efficiency, totally minimizing the agentic role played by workers in this process.[154] But as Paul Osterman has justly pointed out, '. . . while it is true that internal labour markets can be imposed from above as part of an anti-labour strategy, they can also result from a struggle from below by workers for whom the system of job rights and regulation is a desired improvement'.[155] To put it slightly differently, even assuming that bureaucratic forms of control contributed to organizing the workplace more efficiently and to obtaining the desired work behaviour from workers, neither of which was necessarily true always, employers were hardly the sole beneficiaries. Workers also derive appreciable advantages from routinized structures of labour control given the constraints they placed on managerial freedom as various studies have illustrated.[156]

Indeed, following Michael Burawoy, internal labour markets must be

---

[154] For certain, a radical historian like Richard Edwards takes care to present the workplace as a 'contested terrain', analyzing the evolution in the various types of control systems governing the social relations of production as a response in part to endemic conflict between capital and labour. Nevertheless, the rise of internal labour markets is viewed exclusively from the standpoint of managerial efficiency and the imperatives of profitability, leading him to conclude that they constitute a highly effective instrument in forging a compliant and individualized workforce. That workers could be the *agens movens* in building such regulatory institutions, and that they stood to gain as well from the existence of these institutions is something he totally glosses over. *Contested Terrain*, especially chap. 8. See also David Gordon, Richard Edwards, and Michael Reich, *Segmented Work, Divided Workers. The Historical Transformation of Labor in the United States*, Cambridge, 1982, pp. 186–90

[155] Paul Osterman, 'Introduction: The Nature and Importance of Internal Labor Markets', in *idem* (ed.), *Internal Labor Markets*, Cambridge (Mass.), 1984, pp. 1–22 (cit. p. 11). A similar argument is also posited by Batstone et al, *Consent and Effeciency*, pp. 290–03.

[156] See, *inter alia*, Lenard R. Berlanstein, *Big Business and Industrial Conflict in Nineteenth Century France. A Social History of the Parisian Gas Company*, Berkeley, 1991, pp. 317–18; Bernard Elbaum, 'The Making and Shaping of Job and Pay Structures in the Iron and Steel Industry', in *Internal Labor Markets*, pp. 71–107; Jonathan Zeitlin, 'From Labour History to Industrial Relations', *Economic History Review*, Vol. XL, No. 2, 1987, pp. 159–84.

seen as forming one of the three foundational pillars, the other two being collective bargaining and the grievance dispute machinery, upon which rests the edifice of the 'internal state' which coordinates the interests of the management and labour in most big enterprises.[157] One can plausibly argue that the operations of these three 'political or ideological apparatuses of production' create the objective preconditions for 'manufacturing consent' to the existing social relations of production.[158] But this is to forget that they are also instrumental in imposing constraints on managerial discretion and in empowering workers as industrial citizens, endowed with a series of clearly defined rights and obligations. The institutional arrangements underpinning the internal state subordinate employers and workers alike to the rule of law which can only be changed through joint regulation and therefore possessed relative autonomy.

If the principle of automatic promotions assured ITI workers of steady upward advancement, for the company it held out the possibility of greater flexibility in the deployment of labour. Though the top management had initially dragged its feet about overhauling the company's promotion policies, it soon understood that conceding this specific demand of the union could also serve its own ends. In a note to the ITI board of directors justifying its decision to implement the TBP, which in effect amounted to relinquishing an essential managerial prerogative, that of evaluating selected individuals and conferring scarce rewards on them, it cited reasons of technical efficiency. At a time when ITI faced 'drastic technological changes', occasioned by the phasing out of the old electro-mechanical exchanges, the new arrangements, the management contended, would allow it to better adjust to these changes by facilitating the rotation of personnel and the allocation of multiple tasks, and removing restrictions on internal transfers.[159] To enable a

---

[157] Burawoy, *Manufacturing Consent*, pp. 110–20, 198. He defines the internal state as a set of relations that organize, transform or repress struggles at the point of production.

[158] Burawoy, *Politics of Production*, p. 11, 87. See also *Manufacturing Consent*, p. 92, 96, 104–07, 186–8, 231. However, in common with other radical scholars, Burawoy tends to both downplay the active involvement of workers in the formation of internal labour markets as well as to undervalue those features which advance the interests of the workforce, preferring instead to concentrate on the negative, i.e., divisive, individualizing, class collaborative dimensions of promotion and seniority rules.

[159] Note to ITI board, 180th meeting, item no. B10, August 1981.

person to perform a range of jobs calling for different skills, the company also agreed to provide on-the-job or specialised training. But no such initiatives materialized, foiling plans to foster functional flexibility and worker polyvalence. As one internal memo dated 1985 observed, frustration was growing among lower level employees because the nature of their jobs remained identical even after moving to a higher grade, thus depriving them of opportunities to acquire fresh skills.[160] This statement clearly attested to the failure of the company to develop the right kinds of training programmes.

Low ranking employees were not the only groups to find themselves bound in an occupational straitjacket. Notwithstanding the official rhetoric about TBP 'provid(ing) scope for job enrichment', a combination of minimal turnover, insufficient work loads, and the absence of training meant that semi-skilled and skilled workers too were condemned to continue doing the same job despite receiving promotions.[161] To quote one machine tender who rose to become an officer,

though I am an assistant engineer today, I am not in charge of any group or department. There is no change in my job with TBP, only monetary benefits . . . Before TBP, an assistant engineer was a very powerful man.[162]

In other words, a pronounced disjunction existed between the nominal and the real, between the title and the function or the job.[163] By emptying the job of most of its signification, the material rewards attached to the title bore minimal correspondence with its symbolic rewards. So to the extent that the internal labour market in ITI offered individuals very little prospects of occupational change and upgradation of their skill base and responsibilities, it represented a significant deviation from the textbook model which stressed the importance of these aspects in ensuring the efficient functioning of this institution.[164] In such a context, the

---

[160] Ref. DMT/32 A, 9 October 1985.

[161] Memorandum of Settlement.

[162] Interview with Ravindranath, 7 January 1998.

[163] Pierre Bourdieu and Luc Boltanski, 'Le titre et le poste, rapports entre le système de production et le système de reproduction', *Actes de la recherche en sciences sociales*, No. 2, 1975, pp. 95–107. As they point out, the holder of the title has the right to feel entitled to the rights normally associated with the title.

[164] Doeringer and Piore, *Internal Labor Markets and Manpower Analysis*, pp. 18–22, 39; Olivier Favereau, 'Marchés internes, marchés externes', *Revue économique*, Vol. 40, No. 2, March 1989, pp. 273–328.

definition of professional mobility took on a highly restrictive meaning. It merely signified higher money wages, while excluding the possibility of expanding proficiency, qualifications and experiences.

Nevertheless, during the 1980s the operational difficulties associated with the working of this system of guaranteed promotions did not prove insurmountable. One friction point concerned the tool room where workers who had been elevated to supervisory posts refused 'do the basic tool making job' entailing the loss of valuable skills to the company.[165] Stating that the number of workers left to be supervised in the tool room had sharply dwindled, the management pointed out that the TBP had engendered a situation where there were more officers and supervisors now than operatives. By the early 1990s, this 'cancerous phenomenon' had spread to other departments too with the result that the shortage of operatives threatened to throw production schedules off course.[166] So skewed had the composition of the labour force become that the ratio of officers to non-officers now stood at 1:3, and was forecast to further drop to 1:2 by the end of the decade.[167] Company officials also apprehended the impact of these changes on the structure of the officer categories. They believed that as more and more individuals came up the ranks thanks to automatic promotions, disciplinary controls would further slacken as these worker-officers would be unable to exercise sufficient authority over workers given their shared social origins and ties of mutuality.[168]

Every time a worker is promoted as an officer, we lose a good worker and get a bad supervisor.[169]

---

[165] Ref. DMT/32 A, 9 October 1985. See also minutes of management-union meeting, 1 May 1982, 26 June 1982, 27 September 1983.

[166] Interview with S.K. Chatterjee, 7 November 2001. Prior to 1985, the company employed various filtering techniques to ensure that only 'merit worthy' workers were selected as officers. However, in the wake of a judicial ruling automatic promotions became the norm all the way through to grade I, the lowest officer category.

[167] PD note, nd. Prior to the introduction of the TBP in 1980, the ratio of officers to non-officers was of the order of 1:10, before falling to 1:7 in 1985 and then to 1:5 in 1990. PD note, 10 August 2000.

[168] In 2000, over half the 2696 officers on the rolls of ITI Bangalore had joined the plant as workers. Ref. P&A/MP/ST/215, 3 Jan 2001.

[169] Interview with S.K. Chatterjee.

Totally repudiating the utility of the TBP to the point of labelling it a 'tragic mistake', the top management vented its criticism at various aspects of the scheme in December 1993 at a joint meeting with unions from all units of ITI.[170] It claimed that automatic promotions nurtured complacency since mobility was delinked from performance; that even employees deemed as surplus obtained promotions; and that most of the promotions were 'unrelated to organisational requirements'.[171] All these anomalies would seem to bear out Doeringer and Piore's contention that the allocative efficiency of internal labour markets proportionately decreases as rules designed to guarantee job security and the equitable treatment of the labour force are strengthened in response to pressure from workers and unions as well as under the weight of customary practices.[172]

Yet strangely enough not only did the management decline to take prompt steps to address any of the problems caused by the TBP. It also compounded its difficulties by agreeing, not once but on two separate occasions, to satisfy a union demand for a reduction in the promotion time span for different groups of workers, not all of whom could claim high qualifications.[173] In May 2000, a proposal to withdraw the TBP and replace it with a vacancy-based promotion formula as in the past was finally submitted. Not unsurprisingly, the union turned down the proposal as it did alternate suggestions to reform the existing arrangements. Nor did the top management demonstrate very much 'enthusias(m) about forcing the issue, since it has not realised that TBP is hurting the company'.[174]

---

[170] ibid.

[171] Minutes of 11th ITI Joint Committee meeting, 30 December 1993.

[172] Doeringer and Piore, *Internal Labor Markets and Manpower Analysis*, p. 192. For a contrary view, see Emmanuelle and Jean-Daniel Reynaud, 'La regulation des marchés internes du travail', *Revue française de sociologie*, Vol. XXXVII, No. 3, July-September 1996, pp. 337–68.

[173] Note to Board, 273rd meeting, item no. C1, July 1994; PD note 20 March 1998. Thus apart from diploma holders and trade certificate holders, even SSLC graduates benefited from these measures. Angered by the dilatoriness of the union in finalizing its proposals with regard to the relaxation of promotion time limits, these workers were also at the forefront of the sudden explosion of discontent the Bangalore plant witnessed in September 1995.

[174] Interview with P. A. Vasudevan, 16 December 2001.

WORK CONFLICTS

In addition to the agitations conducted in favour of higher bonus payments and greater promotion opportunities, the turbulence witnessed by ITI during the 1970s also had its source in conflicts bearing on questions of work organization. Though circumscribed to a few small pockets, these conflicts kept recurring intermittently much to the dismay of the management. What is also worth noting is that the grounds for discontent had essentially to do with problems such as supervisory arbitrariness, disciplinary controls, and overtime and incentive claims. Protests against increased work loads were conspicuous by their absence. This was hardly surprising. Since company profitability levels were not contingent upon a reduction of labour costs and/or higher labour productivity, shop bosses faced no pressure whatsoever to enforce more stringent effort norms, especially in the pre-reforms era. The combination of soft-budget constraints plus ITI's monopolistic privileges meant that workers here never experienced the harsh constraints of surplus extraction.

Prior to the 1970s, our sources contain only scattered references connecting shop floor disturbances to work-related grievances. One such incident dated back to June 1960. Kalaimuthu, a drilling machine operator in the telephone machine shop, was charge sheeted by the foreman for having assaulted his colleague, Dasan, outside the factory main gate. Dasan had earlier complained to the charge hand that Kalaimuthu was wasting time in the toilet, an accusation that had angered the latter. Protesting against the foreman's decision, all the operatives in the shop downed tools after the lunch break and gathered outside his office. Insisting that they wanted to talk to the factory general manager, they resumed work only 45 minutes later after the official personally came to the scene and heard them out. A security report subsequently attributed workers' reaction to the fact that the foreman had refused to charge sheet Dasan as well and so was showing favouritism. In their view, the foreman should not even have interfered in the first place since the fight occurred outside the factory walls. Although Kalaimuthu and two of his colleagues would be accused of 'inciting their colleagues to disrupt work', the security report underlined the spontaneous character of the demonstration, stating that 'all the operators joined together and walked out'.[175]

---

[175] Security Dept. note, 8 July 1960.

Evanescent and isolated though this contestation of authority may have been, it had the merit of illuminating the normative values that went to forge a specific shop floor culture. It demonstrated the importance workers, at least here, attached to notions of equity and fair play in regulating their everyday relations with the management. In general, the willingness to comply with factory discipline is premised on the expectation that supervisory and other personnel will conform to certain basic standards of justice, the violation of which tends to produce considerable resentment. For it was not the foreman's right to punish that the machine tenders had called into question, but his partiality in awarding punishment; or to utilise a distinction established by Bénédicte Reynaud, it was less the rule than the decision which proved problematic.[176] The failure to act even-handedly entailed the arbitrary exercise of power. This proved unacceptable to workers as it left them totally at the mercy of the foreman's whims.

Playing favourites also threatened to drive a wedge into their ranks and nourish suspicions about where each person's loyalties ultimately lay. Discontent with the unjust behaviour of the foreman was reinforced by the fact that Kalaimuthu had, strictly speaking, broken no factory rules: his fight with Dasan had taken place outside the factory walls. Besides, the sentiment voiced by the workers that the foreman should have stayed aloof from what was essentially a private matter seemed to indicate that they implicitly sympathized with Kalaimuthu in taking Dasan to task for having reported him to his superior. After all, informers and tale-bearers were no more popular on the shop floor than in any other social configuration predicated on power relations. They compromised the fundamental unity of the group, breached the 'us' versus 'them' cleavage workers tried to erect in order to preserve an autonomous space for action, and gave the management an unfair advantage in the quotidian conflict of wills that presided over the negotiation of order on the shop floor.

---

[176] Rules are characterized by their abstract, hypothetical and permanent quality. They refer neither to events, facts, or persons, but to a type of situation. In contrast, decisions are concrete, categorical and impermanent. They designate a person or a group of persons by name. Because the justification for the decision is never explicitly contained in its enunciation, it can often appear as arbitrary. Bénédicte Reynaud, *Le salaire, la règle et le marché*, Paris, 1992, pp. 49–52.

The story of Kalaimuthu's dealings with the foreman did not end here. Transferred to another department, he continued to return to his old shop in what seemed to be a calculated design to provoke and mock the authority of his ex-boss. On one such occasion, after he was told not to waste time and to return to his workspot, he is said to have behaved rudely with the foreman, shouting 'at the top of his voice' that the latter had no business to issue him with any orders.[177] But with no witnesses available to back the foreman's complaint, the company was compelled to drop the misconduct charges it had pressed against Kalaimuthu. Whether this was because the incident occurred when other workers and managers were absent from the scene, or whether it was because workers' sense of collective solidarity enjoined them from giving evidence against one of their colleagues, is something we cannot tell. But the incident attested to the everyday forms of 'resistance' individual workers were capable of devising so as to make life difficult for foremen they disliked.

Not all workers enjoyed the same luck as Kalaimuthu. The example of Palainiappan reveals just how problematic sustaining generalizations about shared moralities and the substance of shop floor cultural norms can be. A qualified tool maker and union activist with a long disciplinary record to his name, he was sacked from ITI after being accused as the main instigator of a two-hour long work stoppage in August 1965 in the strowger tool room. The exact cause of the disturbance remains unknown. But a flyer brought out later by Palainiappan spoke of the 'nasty and bad treatment' meted out since many years to workers in the tool room, 'a citadel of slavery (where) any initiative taken to remedy the suppressive activities was nipped in the bud'.[178]

True or false this assertion may have been, it is the proceedings of the disciplinary committee, whose conclusions led to the dismissal of Palainiappan, which are of immediate interest to us. From a reading of the committee's report, we find that three of his colleagues testified against him. According to them, he was responsible for switching off their machines and preventing them from continuing with their tasks. One of the workers, Naidu, further implicated Palainiappan by declaring that the latter had told him in advance of the plans to disrupt production.

[177] Personnel File no. 4035.
[178] PD files, nd (1966).

Naidu added that he had passed on the information to the supervisory staff—a damning confession of 'betrayal' by all counts. Furthermore, by Palainiappan's own admission there was no enmity or prejudice clouding his ties with Naidu or the other two workers who deposed against him, though he would later claim otherwise.[179]

The possibility of company officials having brought pressure of some kind on these three key witnesses to furnish false evidence against Palainiappan cannot be dismissed. Nor can we ignore the fact that their primary motivation may have been to clear themselves of trouble. But equally, we must not allow romanticized notions of worker mutuality to obstruct our judgement. It is quite possible that for multiple reasons all workers did not necessarily subscribe, or at all times, to a monolithic 'us' versus 'them' perception of productive relations as constituting the immutable bedrock of shop floor culture. Hence, they did not consider themselves morally bound to keep their lips sealed irrespective of the nature of their colleagues' actions. Values other than automatic worker solidarity underpinned their definition and understanding of ideal behaviour in the workplace—values such as diligence, good work (in the sense of its execution), regular attendance, respect of factory regulations.

This is all the more true when we accept that shop floor dispositions reflect the interplay of internal and external references whose combinatory logic and importance depend on personal and contextual factors. These dispositions owe as much to the experience of the reality of work as to the beliefs, prejudices and outlooks formed outside the productive domain in the web of social interactions knitting workers to other universes, and which were inevitably carried over to the factory. Workers' interpretative frameworks are seldom anchored in an exclusive register, be it the factory or the outside social world. Considerable scope therefore exists for the expression of rival conceptions of desirable and undesirable standards of conduct at work.

The records of the ITI security department substantiate our point. They contain several anonymous letters written by employees condemning colleagues and the management personnel alike for shirking their work responsibilities in one way or the other. Indeed, but for these

---

[179] Enquiry Committee Report, Ref. ASP 2308 (48), 6 January 1966; Letter from Palainiappan to Jagjivan Ram, Minister for Labour and Employment, 6 August 1966.

tip-offs, the company would have struggled to apprehend many of the offenders. For certain, the assimilation by many ordinary workers of normative precepts central to the managerial representation of the 'committed' worker signified the triumph of this discourse, but this did not necessarily transform them into 'class collaborators'. The anonymous denunciations of individuals who transgressed factory disciplinary codes were in all likelihood inspired by the same notions of justice and probity that on other occasions oriented the fight against highhanded supervisors and other officials. Workers might have judged as unfair and dishonest the actions of those who capitalized on the obedience of the majority as well as managerial laxity to abuse regulations and avoid work especially when the company was paying them their wages in full every month. So they denounced these offenders.

Much the same ethical compulsions could perhaps be said to have determined the attitude of Naidu and the other two witnesses towards Palainiappan. We have already referred to his troubled disciplinary record. Repeatedly warned for a string of offences (loitering, insubordination, irregular attendance, shoddy work, etc.), line officials claimed that 'due to his indiscipline, the morale of the shop is impaired'.[180] While everybody may not have endorsed this opinion, Palainiappan's failure to work conscientiously, his disdain for rules to which the others had no choice but to adhere, could well have antagonized a few of his colleagues to a point where they were willing to testify against him. His dismissal could therefore have been viewed, if not as deserved, at least as inevitable, a fateful end to a turbulent career. Yet even as some took sides against Palainiappan, others chose to publicly defend him. A joint petition signed by as many as 61 workers in the tool room declared that he was 'neither the leader nor the instigator' of the wildcat strike and urged the company to reinstate him without delay.[181] Shows of solidarity with the victimized worker then went in hand with acts of 'unsolidarity'. Workers were neither unanimously hostile to nor supportive of him.

Thus, the example of Palainiappan throws into relief the pitfalls involved in what could be designated a populist conceptualization of shop floor cultural codes. In this perspective, work culture is posited as forming a compact and coherent whole whose normative commitments

---

[180] Note FWS/1, 7 September 1963.
[181] Personnel File no. 4035.

are embraced by all members of the group which in turn creates the conditions for united action. The possibility of individuals asserting alternative, rival convictions is evacuated or downplayed.[182] But a 'miserabilist' reading tends to be equally reductive of workers' experiences. By giving weight to the fissured and differentiated nature of worker practices, attributed to their diverse origins, habitus and interests, it often implicitly denies the possibility of collective activism.[183]

To put it in other words, a populist explanation generally stresses the weight of factors internal to the world of work, showing how the position occupied by workers in the productive apparatus and their experience of the social relations of production moulds their orientations, and, more generally, their identity. A miserabilist explanation, on the other hand, is likely to privilege the influence of external coordinates, pointing to how meaning systems imported from outside the productive space penetrate and mediate attitudes on the shop floor towards colleagues and the management alike. Our understanding of worker culture therefore often gets pigeon holed into one or the other of these polar compartments.

A way out of this impasse could be to view the populist and the miserabilist narratives[184] not as antinomic but as complementary, and

---

[182] For a forceful exposition of such an interpretation of shopfloor culture in the context of France, see Beaud and Pialoux, *Retour sur la condition ouvrière*, pp. 32–6, 326, 337–8. The tendency to overemphasize the cohesion and unity of dominated groups in their confrontation with elites can even be observed in an author of the stature of E.P. Thompson in his studies of the village community and the moral economy. For a critique of Thompson's position, see, among others, Maxine Berg, 'Women's Work, Mechanisation and the Early Phases of Industrialisation in England', in *The Historical Meanings of Work*, pp. 64–98; and Suzanne Desan, 'Crowds, Community and Ritual in the Work of E.P. Thompson and Natalie Davis', in L. Hunt (ed.), *The New Cultural History*, Berkeley, 1989, pp. 57–61.

[183] Less commonly developed than the populist thesis, echoes of the miserabilist thesis can be found in the writings of Alf Lüdtke. Explaining the term *eigensinn*, a core concept in his work, he asserts: '*Eigensinn* meant distance not just *vis-à-vis* expectations "from above" but also towards expectations originating with one's workmates'. 'What happened to the "Fiery Red Glow"? Workers' Experiences and German Fascism', p. 227. Likewise, the title of one of his essays, 'Polymorphous Synchrony. German Industrial Workers and the Politics of Everyday Life', (*IRSH*, No. 38, 1993, pp. 39–84), is revelatory of the way he sees working class culture.

[184] Claude Grignon and Jean-Claude Passeron have employed the binary populism versus miserabilism to analyse a spectrum of approaches, literary and academic, to popular culture in general. *Le savant et le populaire. Misérabilisme et populisme en sociologie et en littérature*, Paris, 1989.

538 *Telecommunications Industry in India*

to accommodate them within a single analytical framework.[185] This way we can conserve the strengths of each explanatory mode while eliminating their weaknesses, one acting as a necessary corrective to the other. In sum, adopting a dialectical approach offers the potential of yielding a more dynamic and nuanced decoding of work culture, one which neither feels obliged to privilege the expression of a common meaning, nor to overstate the implications of the existence of divergent worldviews. Instead, we would obtain a picture of shop floor culture that is more heterogeneous than homogenous in its composition, more polyphonic than symphonic in tonality. But this sensitivity to the internal tensions of group dynamics marches in step with a recognition of the generative power shared values and motivations can have in fostering a sense of collective purpose and identity depending on the operative context. A commitment to these values means that their violation can produce a high degree of consensus with workers prepared to join forces to defend them even at the risk of inviting sanctions.

RECURRENT LABOUR TROUBLES IN CROSSBAR DIVISION

The overwhelming majority of the conflicts surrounding issues of work organization that erupted during the 1970s at the Bangalore plant were concentrated in the crossbar division. One explanation for this 'exceptionalism' could lie in the central position occupied by this division in the Kannada–Tamil linguistic violence (see chapter nine). Since local Kannadigas numerically dominated the crossbar workforce, the Chaluvali movement had drawn its staunchest sympathizers from among the rougher elements here. Many of the worst acts of intimidation and violence committed within the factory as well as in the neighbouring areas during the course of the language conflict were, in fact, the handiwork of pro-Kannada crossbar agitators. Emboldened by their success in silencing the Tamil workers, they would take the lead in fighting shop officials once the focus of contention switched from questions of

---

[185] Discussing the critical question of explanatory paradigms, Lynn Hunt writes that 'historians of culture really do not have to choose (or really cannot choose)...between unity and difference, between meaning and working, between interpretation and deconstruction'. 'Introduction: History, Culture and Text', in *The New Cultural History*, pp. 1–22 (cit. p. 16).

identity to those of work. The dismissal in 1973 of a group of Chaluvali loyalists, accused of being involved in an assassination attempt on a top ITI executive, would enable the management to partly reaffirm its authority. But even afterwards there were periodic reports of output restriction.

In addition to the presence of a large number of native Kannada speakers on its rolls, the crossbar division also distinguished itself from the other divisions by employing younger and better qualified hands. These two variables, demographic and educational, the company believed, would help to cultivate greater compliance with the strict standards of productive efficiency and work discipline it aspired to enforce in crossbar. What it did not apparently bargain for, however, was that the addition of lower age levels plus higher skill levels could also give rise to a more 'autonomous' and assertive workforce which would rapidly chafe at the disciplinary strategies the company tried to impose.

. . . the workers joining crossbar were better educated, many were diploma holders. So they knew their rights and Labour Act very well, what welfare measures they were entitled to.[186]

As one senior manager declared, the crossbar workers 'proved very vocal and vitiated the ITI atmosphere'.[187]

Moreover, generational differences in both perceptions and self-perceptions, moulded in part by differences in educational entitlements, also probably meant that compared with the first generation of ITI workers who joined the company during the first 15 years of its existence, the crossbar workers identified themselves less fully with the company. Nor were they likely to have shared the *ma-baap* attitude of their seniors, their sense of obligation and loyalty towards the company which expressed itself in terms of filial gratitude for having made them a 'respectable member of society' by giving them a job when they often did not even possess a high school degree.[188]

On holidays when I . . . pass in front of the company sometimes, I automatically bow my head in gratitude . . . If I had not got a job in ITI . . . I don't know what would have happened to me with only a SSLC failed degree. What I could have

---

[186] Interview with Surappa.
[187] Interview with A.V. Krishnamurthy.
[188] Interview with Govindaraju.

expected from life? There are degree holders who struggle to get a job and don't get the same salary as I do today . . . I might have some complaints against ITI, but it is equal to my mother.[189]

Much the same feelings of gratitude, the same metaphorical linkage equating the company to one's parents, run through the following lines:

By joining the factory I have been able to marry, have children, bring them up, build my own house, gain status and dignity in society . . . ITI is more than my parents. My father and mother only gave me birth, but ITI gave me life.[190]

The first generation worker who spoke these words, however, contrasted his sentiments with those of his juniors, hired after the mid-1960s. According to him, these workers' relationship with the company tended to be more distant because 'they might feel they could have got higher salaries if they had joined elsewhere'.[191] Of course, such claims may also have been designed to underscore the distinction between loyal and disloyal workers, disciplined strowger workers and unruly crossbar workers. Still, they suggested the variations in attitudes towards the company that could prevail from one generation to the next and/or between groups of workers possessing greater or lesser amounts of educational capital.

To start with, crossbar executives made a fair amount of headway towards achieving their objective of establishing the division as a 'model of excellence' for the rest of the company to follow. Despite the myriad technical problems that plagued the fabrication of the new exchanges, crossbar enjoyed an enviable reputation for order and discipline. Close vigilance was maintained over operatives' movements on the shop floor, the permission of the supervisor had to be obtained in order to go to the toilet, and adherence to punctual time-keeping insisted upon. Deviations from manning levels specified by BTM, the Belgian technology partner, were restricted to a minimum. Nor was the clutter and disorder characteristic of workplaces in strowger tolerated here. But faced with a

---

[189] Interview with Joseph.

[190] Interview with Govindraju. The precedence given to the 'foster parent', the employer, over the natural parents in this discourse perhaps betrayed the vicissitudes of the worker's own biography—virtually disowned by his father after the early death of his mother. But this does not in any way detract from the overall import and authenticity of the statement.

[191] ibid.

groundswell of protest in the early 1970s, the company reverted to the traditional indulgent pattern of labour relations in a bid to appease the workforce. The arrival of a new management team, less 'tough on discipline' than its predecessor, to oversee the division sealed the change in orientation.[192]

. . . Had crossbar been a separate entity, these tough measures might have succeeded. But since it was located alongside strowger, crossbar workers were able to compare the situation in their division and in strowger.[193]

While the struggles waged over questions of work organization shared some similarities with monetary and mobility struggles with respect to the forms of collective action that gave them meaning, variations dominated. If work stoppages were a common feature of all three types of struggles, go-slows were by far the preferred weapon of workers when it came to voicing work-related grievances. The resulting protests therefore lacked the explosive dimension that suffused the fight for higher bonus or equal promotion opportunities where wildcat strikes went hand in hand with noisy demonstrations and whose disruptive impact was both more manifest and immediate. We do not know why crossbar workers opted in the main for go-slows. Did they think it was more appropriate to the kinds of demands they were raising? Or more effective than other forms of agitation for being less public, more anonymous in its overall articulation—characteristics that perhaps frustrated the company's manoeuvres to break shop floor resistance by singling out the 'ringleaders' for punishment?[194]

Accurately dating the labour unrest that affected the crossbar division at various intervals during the 1970s, and even later, is rendered problematic by the lacunae in our sources. But, notwithstanding its sporadic character, the first wave of protests appears to have been the

---

[192] Interview with S.K. Ramanna. Assistant Works Manager of the crossbar division from 1964–71, before being removed overnight when labour troubles erupted, Ramanna sharply criticized top management for failing to extend adequate support to him and his colleagues. Its weakness, he claimed, led to the worsening of the unrest.

[193] Interview with Srinivasa Rao.

[194] Kuhn remarks that US tyre workers may have shifted their protests from wildcat strikes to production slowdowns in response to management sanctions against those participating in the former. James Kuhn, *Bargaining in Grievance Settlement. The Power of Industrial Work Groups*, Columbia, 1961, pp. 176–7.

strongest, lasting for a prolonged period of almost three years before dying out finally in 1973. Overall output levels are thought to have declined by 30 to 40 per cent while labour efficiencies, according to a document dated October 1973, stood below 50 per cent compared to 90 per cent in the strowger and transmission divisions.[195] The conflict had its epicentre in the platine wiring department from where it progressively spread to other assembly shops such as frame wrapping and cable wiring and then to the machine shops where the scale of workers' involvement was less extensive.

Two factors accounted for the vanguard role played by the platine department. First, supervisory highhandedness exercised itself forcefully here.

Labour problems in platine wrapping group was because of supervisors. One of them used to treat workers like bonded labour, speak to them disrespectfully, never call workers by their name but refer to them impersonally 'Hey you fellow, come here'. Workers demanded an apology from him.[196]

Second, platine workers occupied a strategic position in the division of labour. As the penultimate operation in the fabrication of the crossbar switch, platine wiring constituted a vital link in the production chain. All the sub-assemblies were put together in this department. So any disruptions at this stage inevitably tended to have an impact on the next and final stage and retarded deliveries to the customer.

Moreover, conjunctural developments further encouraged these workers to try and exploit their bargaining power to reorder work regulations to their advantage. Because technical and other complications had already thrown crossbar production schedules into complete disarray (see chapter two), the management faced tremendous pressure from P&T to hand over equipment on time. Otherwise, supplementary imports would have become indispensable in order to ensure the commissioning of the new electro-mechanical exchanges did not suffer from further delays. Appeals urging ITI workers to make a 'very dedicated and earnest

[195] Minutes of management-union meeting, 26 October 1973.

[196] Interview with Irudayaraj. Alf Lüdtke also draws attention to workers' resentment at being addressed familiarly or familialy by foremen. 'Cash, Coffee-Breaks, Horseplay: *Eigensinn* and Politics among Factory Workers in Germany *circa* 1900', in M. Hanagan and C. Stephenson (eds.), *Confrontation, Class Consciousness and the Labour Process. Studies in Proletarian Class Formation*, New York, 1986, pp. 65–95.

effort' to step up output, however, seem to have left them unmoved.[197] During the first nine months of the year 1972–73, the Bangalore plant produced barely half its total target of 110,000 crossbar lines. As one senior official confessed,

we could not break the go-slow in platines and in frame wrapping . . . (these) were final operations, with one following the other. So workers were able to strangle us here. If platines were not produced, frames would not move. We could not offload frames to the ancils . . . We charge sheeted some workers, held enquiries. But we could not charge sheet the entire division . . . *We had to admit defeat.*[198]

The company's 'defeat' in the platine and frame wrapping departments entailed conceding several of the workers demands. Some of these were relatively minor such as improving lighting arrangements and distributing better quality screw drivers and pencils.[199] Others had more weighty implications. ITI not only had to relax time standards for a wide range of jobs to 'values well below Bell Telephone standards'.[200] It was also constrained to allocate overtime work to a larger number of workers than planned initially, notwithstanding tough talk to the contrary. The issue of overtime, in fact, motivated the go-slow organized in several crossbar assembly shops towards the end of 1972.

A system of two-shift working (morning and afternoon) had been well established, if not well accepted, in both the strowger and transmission divisions. In crossbar too, shop officials had successfully tested it out for a short period in July 1972. Six months later, when the measure was reintroduced in a bid to both increase output levels and reduce overtime payments workers reacted with extreme hostility. Within the space of a few weeks, labour efficiency shrunk by half to 35 per cent. According to the management, the go-slow represented a 'deliberate attempt . . . to force the withdrawal of the second shift' so as to 'pressurise

---

[197] PD circular no. 1545, 24 January 1973.

[198] Interview with Srinivasa Rao. Emphasis added. Distinguishing between police and military strategies of control, William Reddy notes that employers follow the former strategy. Punishment is applied only to selected individuals, 'conspicuous opponents' and not to the entire group both because of the lack of resources and the sheer impracticality of resorting to coercion on a large scale. *Money and Liberty in Modern Europe. A Critique of Historical Understanding*, Cambridge, 1994, p. 161.

[199] Minutes of management-union meeting, 26 October 1973.

[200] ibid.

(it) to grant overtime' and thus compensate for the eventual loss of production.[201] The 'blackmail' paid off to some extent: the company held firm to the principle of operating two shifts, but it had to readjust upwards the proportion of employees eligible for overtime work.

Incentive payments stood at the heart of the fresh wave of labour unrest the crossbar division experienced for much of 1976. Once again, the principal sites of contestation were the platine wiring and frame wrapping departments with the plating shop subsequently entering the fray.[202] Once again the management was required to make significant concessions in order to restore industrial peace. Unhappy with the performance of a new incentive scheme, introduced in January 1976, workers in these two shops had been systematically holding back output for several months.

Under the scheme, base efficiencies had been marginally raised from 72 to 80 per cent. This had translated, complained workers, into reduced incentive earnings, especially with respect to jobs where time rates were already tight. When the union intervened, it was accused of being partly responsible for the problem, having given its agreement to the revised incentive formula. The management then responded in October 1976 by charge sheeting a few persons.[203] Still, the go-slow persisted. Tensions finally eased a few months later after line officials agreed to cut time standards for different operations by as much as 20 per cent. But whether workers satisfied the latter's expectations and reciprocated these conciliatory gestures with higher production volumes is doubtful.[204]

The issue of incentive claims would remain a source of tension even during the following decade. Pointing to the low output levels prevailing in the crossbar plating shop over a period of several months, an internal note dated February 1985 blamed this situation primarily on discontent with incentive earnings. It also stated that the previous month operatives had 'reacted rather violently', shouting and demanding explanations from the department head after receiving their pay slips. A few days later, a register used for the purposes of calculating incentive and other related

---

[201] PD circular no. 1545; Minutes, 26 October 1973.

[202] Minutes of management-union meeting, 24 August 1977.

[203] Minutes of management-union meeting, 27 October 1976.

[204] IED note, 14 February 1977. See also minutes of management-union meeting, 15 February 1977.

documents were found in a 'very damaged condition'.[205] The note added that workers had wanted to destroy records containing evidence of their poor performance. The unrest appears to have persisted for some time, as suggested by the management's readiness to take disciplinary action, deferring its plans of suspending some workers only at the request of the union which promised to rapidly restore normalcy.[206]

Leaving aside this incident, there are no other references in our sources to work-related protests in the crossbar division throughout the 1980s. This was perhaps understandable. If conjunctural factors had helped bolster workers' bargaining power a decade earlier, these same factors explained their diminished clout a decade later. Demand for the type of crossbar switches manufactured by ITI at the Bangalore plant was not only slowing down. More significantly, the product line in its totality was condemned to be phased out by the second half of the 1980s in line with P&T's plans to modernize the national network by shifting from electro-mechanical to fully electronic telephone exchanges. Under these circumstances, the management was totally immune to pressure of any kind workers might have chosen to exert.

To conclude, a common thread running through all three types of struggles discussed above, namely those waged over monetary, mobility and work-related issues, was the vigour with which workers affirmed their agency, their capacity for autonomous action. They either directly spearheaded protest activity, or on those occasions when the initiative came from the union, often succeeded in wresting control from the leadership and imposed their own definition of the situation, one which tended to stress confrontation over moderation. How do we account for this marginalization of the union, its repeated failure to perform its disciplinary role of imposing restraint on the workforce? Explanations must necessarily vary in function of the type of struggle under review, although it cannot be denied that their spontaneous character often stemmed from the fact that workers' discontent was as much targeted at the union as at the management.

In the dispute over incentive claims, for instance, crossbar workers blamed the union for having ratified the increase in efficiency levels which served as the basis for calculating monthly incentive earnings. At the

---

[205] IED memo, 2 February 1985; 21 February 1985.
[206] PD note, 21 February 1985.

same time, workers knew the union would have considered as unjustified, even illegitimate, some of their demands, such as cancelling the second shift so that they could obtain additional overtime work, especially since the company was already allocating overtime. So they had no choice but to press this demand independently. Similarly, on more than one occasion during the course of the agitations for enhanced advancement opportunities, we saw employees vigorously taking the union hierarchy to task for its failure to act in conformity with their expectations. But this element alone did not suffice to explain why these agitations flared up more often than not at the instigation of the rank-and-file rather than the union.

As we have demonstrated, sharp cleavages existed within the ranks of the workforce over the question of seniority norms and promotions, a reflection as much of the effects of corporate policies as of the inherently stratified nature of the workplace. Because of the paradoxical character of occupational mobility, it is a force at once capable of unifying and dividing the workforce. A highly evocative symbol of self-dignity and equity and hence universal in its appeal, it nevertheless allows for a gamut of conflicting interpretations in function of the specific interests and aspirations of different generational and professional groups. These competing claims meant that no group at the Bangalore plant could entrust or count on the union to defend its own demands. Doing so would have compromised the very *raison d'être* of the union which was to uphold the interests of the workforce in its entirety. To justify its representative status in the eyes of the management and its members alike, and preserve the unity of the organization, not to mention the positions of its officials, it had by definition to transcend all sectional obligations. Considerations of greater good had to take precedence over minority preferences. Under these circumstances, resorting to spontaneous action represented the sole means for each section of the workforce to make its voice heard.

What distinguished the struggles over monetary demands from the other two types of collective struggle was that employees did not so much as take the lead as they captured the initiative from the union's hands once the protests had got underway. We find this pattern of a dovish leadership capitulating to a hawkish base repeating itself during both the stay-in strikes and the 1980 bonus demonstrations. In each instance the strategy of moderation chosen by the union rapidly crumbled under pressure from the workers who either obliged it to harden its position or sidelined it altogether as they radically altered the course of the conflict. Dismissive of the effectiveness of the union's approach, they no doubt felt that alternative, more combative tactics were indispensable, one which unambiguously translated the depth of their resentment *vis-à-vis* the government and the company into action, if the latter was to be persuaded to concede their demands. From the standpoint of the base, the institutional concerns motivating the leadership's behaviour meant little. While the union unsuccessfully sought to exercise restraint by opting for token demonstrations as opposed to genuine trials of strength so as to protect its long term bargaining relationship with the management from suffering undue damage, workers had probably learned from experience that the only language the latter was capable of understanding was the language of force.

Simultaneous with the expression of workers' dissatisfaction with the leadership's performance, the spontaneous dimension present in many of these struggles also served to spotlight certain aspects of the relations between the union hierarchy and the rank-and-file which rose to the surface only during times of crisis. Under normal circumstances notions of deference may well have dominated the attitudes of ordinary workers towards union officials (but not shop floor delegates), and the authority of the officials subjected to few challenges. But this was hardly the case once quotidian routines were swept aside by conflict. In such moments of rupture, relations between leaders and 'led' underwent a transformation with the roles of the two sides being inverted.

As the driving force often behind the agitations, workers now felt empowered to hold union officials accountable for their decisions and actions. As we saw on a couple of instances, they insisted on summoning their representatives to the scene of the protests and demanding explanations from the latter. They were required to publicly justify their line of action, defend various measures to which they had given their accord, answer their detractors—obligations all to which they seldom had to submit in times of normalcy. If workers perceived the leadership as being unresponsive to their aspirations, these occasions allowed them to both vehemently signal their dissatisfaction as well as to issue a categorical warning that the continued neglect of their aspirations would trigger further such contestatory practices embarrassing to the authority and prestige of the union.

Thus, spontaneous struggles provided workers with the opportunity of carving out a space, perhaps temporary, to question established structures of power within the union. In these moments of crisis a modicum of internal democracy seeped into the functioning of the organization, and underlined the importance the base attached to the principle of accountability *vis-à-vis* the leadership. It is quite likely, however, that neither internal democracy nor accountability flourished for very long once conditions returned to a state of normalcy. Evidence would suggest that the combination of deeply ingrained styles of exercising power, the force of hierarchical values in what remained a highly stratified social system, worker indifference and inertia rapidly diluted the impact of whatever changes may have intervened during periods of conflict.

While interactions between union representatives and the rank-and-file at the Bangalore plant of ITI may not have resembled the *babu-coolie* relations, shot through with the 'semiotics of domination and subordination', depicted by Dipesh Chakrabarty, patronage and deference nevertheless remained the operative terms framing these everyday interactions.[207] Yet the display of worker agency in the form of go-slows, wildcatting, and demonstrations served to remind the leadership that it could not take its authority for granted, that passivity on the part of the 'led' could just as soon be supplanted by rebellious militancy. Retaining power and legitimacy hence enjoined the union bureaucracy to stay at least minimally attuned to the wishes of the membership.

---

[207] Dipesh Chakrabarty, *Rethinking Working-Class History. Bengal 1890–1940*, New Delhi, 1989 pp. 143–54 (cit. p. 144). For a critique of such a reified reading of union-worker relations, see Joshi, *Lost Worlds*, p. 205.

chapter nine

Passions of Language and Caste

Well before our own postmodern condition and new academic disciplinary trends in the shape of post-structuralism and feminist theory pushed the question of the plural character of human identities on to the centre stage, social scientists have grappled with the problematic nature of the continuity in time and the unity in space of an individual. As Philippe Corcuff has pointed out, G.H. Mead in his enquiry into the social construction of the self, undertaken as early as the 1930s, had underscored the tremendous diversity of selves existing in each person and which corresponded to different social situations.[1] This theme would also be developed in considerable detail subsequently by Erving Goffman. In *Frame Analysis* he draws attention to the multiplicity of frames within which individual experiences are anchored and understood, and in so doing portrays a highly fragmented picture of a person.[2] Indeed, much of Goffman's work addressing the identity of the self permanently oscillates between a position of unity

---

[1] Philippe Corcuff, *Les nouvelles sociologies*, Paris, 2002, pp. 96–7.
[2] Erving Goffman, *Frame Analysis*, Harmondsworth, 1975.

and one of disintegration.[3] Neither plurality nor unity are given on a once-and-for-all basis, nor do they stand in opposition to each other. Instead, they must be viewed as complementary and operating in osmosis in the course of everyday interactions.

In labour history, engagement with the issue of identity has taken slightly different forms. From the early 1980 onwards, scholars have been increasingly obliged to confront the inadequacies of their core organizing category of class. The reasons had as much to do with shifting intellectual paradigms and the emergence of new sites of historical research as with sweeping geopolitical transformations.[4] That class identity did not and could not exhaust the total explanatory space of social action, and that other competing forms of identity rooted in race, gender, religion and the like equally structured workers' dispositions and relations became part of conventional wisdom. Striving to explain all social phenomenon within the procrustean framework of class which also signified ignoring or dismissing as 'false consciousness' all attachments and practices that failed to conform to class-political agency was thus rightly viewed as reductive of workers' experiences even when the consequences of their loyalties to ethnic or religious ties resulted in an objective weakening of their position by creating divisions which in turn tended to reinforce the power of employers and state authorities alike.

In the Indian context, the problematic of non-class axes of identity rose to the fore as historians turned their attention to outbreaks of communal riots during the colonial period in which workers often played a prominent role. While they may have sometimes been enrolled as foot soldiers by Hindu and Muslim elites, workers also did not hesitate to take the initiative in attacking one another both within the factory sphere and in urban neighbourhoods.[5] In the process, their demonstrations of agency exposed the shortcomings of explanations which endeavoured to

[3] Albert Ogien, 'La décomposition du sujet', in R. Castel et al, *Le Parler frais d'Erving Goffman*, Paris, 1989, pp. 100–09.

[4] Lenard Berlanstein, 'Introduction', in *idem* (ed.), *Rethinking Labour History: Essays on Discourse and Class Analysis*, Urbana-Chicago, 1993, pp. 1–12; Geoff Eley and Keith Nield, 'Farewell to the Working Class?' *International Labor and Working Class History*, No. 57, Spring 2000, pp. 1–30.

[5] Nandini Gooptu, 'The Urban Poor and Militant Hinduism in Early Twentieth-Century Uttar Pradesh', *Modern Asian Studies*, Vol. 31, No. 4, 1997, pp. 879–918; Joshi, *Lost Worlds*, pp. 261–5.

preserve an unsullied image of the working class by ascribing such 'unproletarian' actions either to the manipulatory stratagems of communal leaders or to the competition for jobs in a labour surplus economy.[6] The unpalatable fact that workers assaulted and some times killed other workers only because they were Hindus or Muslims, and hence perceived as being different from them, and for no other apparent cause, was something that many Marxist historians found hard to countenance.

Scholarly attempts to comprehend the grip exercised by ethnic affinities in shaping workers' worldviews at certain historical moments, and inversely, the displacement of class dispositions, have schematically speaking taken two directions. The first may be called the culturalist conceptualization of identity.[7] Framed in opposition to the productivist or social structuralist interpretations hitherto dominant in the field, it offered an important corrective to the argument that the various traditional features of Indian society operating as a drag on working class consciousness owed their existence essentially to the incomplete transition to capitalist development in India, a process hindered by the economic imperatives of colonial rule.

In the culturalist analysis, the persistence of caste and community ties is seen as a legacy of a hierarchical and inegalitarian culture, the strength of these ties being so binding, permanent and all encompassing that they are incapable of transformation by workers' own practices. Regardless of the forms of expressions of class identity that could periodically emerge, these are deemed as marginal in that they could have no enduring impact on the complex of primordial values and norms that shaped the individual habitus. Such an essentialist reading of cultural influences on the process of identity formation, as the historian Chitra Joshi has justly remarked, tends to reify culture even as it leaves people with no real hope of reordering the matrix of relationships into which they are born.[8]

---

[6] In the case of US labour historiography, David Roediger has brilliantly demonstrated the limitations of materialist accounts of race riots in antebellum America which tend to situate them exclusively in factors such as labour market competition. *The Wages of Whiteness*, London, 1995, chap. 5.

[7] The most forceful proponent of this view is of course Dipesh Chakrabarty, *Rethinking Working-Class History*.

[8] Joshi, *Lost Worlds*, p. 7. See also by the same author, 'Labour History and the Question of Culture', (*http://www.indialabourarchives.org/publications/c_joshi.htm*).

The second direction taken by Indian labour historiography as it grapples with the significance of issues such as caste and religion in structuring practices at both an individual and collective level arrives at a recognition of the plural or heterogeneous character of workers' identities.[9] In this perspective, depending on the contextual logic of the situation, workers are just as capable of assertions of class consciousness as of caste or communal consciousness, moving from one contending identity to the other. None of these different forms of social identity are considered to be exclusive or inherently in conflict and thus liable to negate each other. Unities forged in the crucible of a struggle against employers or the state did not eliminate sectional differences inspired by caste or religion. Conversely, the potential for future class-based protests is hardly ruled out by workers redrawing boundaries to express communal or regional solidarities which lead them to temporarily joining forces with the upper classes even as it pitted them against other groups of workers.

In other words, just as it is false to oppose class dispositions and community dispositions (regardless of the fact that for the ideologically inclined observer the former might seem a more desirable outcome than the latter) nor are class loyalties and sectarian divergences inherent in the condition of workers.[10] Emphasis on the multiplicity of identities enables us to escape the trap of binary oppositions where one or the other element invariably tends to be over determined.[11] It also presents

[9] Rajnarayan Chandavarkar, 'Questions of Class: The General Strikes in Bombay', in *Worlds of Indian Industrial Labour*, pp. 205–37; Joshi, *Lost Worlds*, pp. 10–11, 275–6; Nair, *Miners and Millhands*, pp. 28–31. Though I have grouped the first two authors together for the sake of convenience, their approaches also diverge in important respects. For a radical post-structuralist conceptualization which stresses the inherently heterogeneous and permeable nature of all collective identities, see Kian Tajbaksh, 'History of a Subject or the Subjects of History? (Or: Is a Labour History Possible?)', *Studies in History*, Vol. 11, No. 1, January-June 1995, pp. 143–62.

[10] Scholars have commented on the heuristic benefits of replacing the term 'class consciousness' with that of 'class dispositions' as proposed by Katznelson in his influential essay on working class formation. Not the least of these gains has been to liberate empirical research from the pursuit of the holy grail of 'true' consciousness. Ira Katznelson, 'Working Class Formation: Constructing Cases and Comparisons', in I. Katznelson and A. Zolberg (eds.), *Working Class Formation. Nineteenth Century Patterns in Western Europe and the United States*, Princeton, 1986, pp. 3–41.

[11] van der Linden and van Voss speak of the 'indeterminacy problem' haunting labour historiography, i.e., the difficulty in reconciling class categories with those of non-class ones (gender, race, ethnicity, etc.). According to them, scholars will have

the advantage of retaining class as more than just a descriptive concept, but without endowing it with the analytical primacy it enjoyed previously. Instead we can envision it as a site where unities are realized, transiently but nevertheless decisively, resting on new networks of relations and new ways of ordering the social world. The task at hand then for the historian becomes not so much to measure 'class consciousness' amidst much hand wringings as to its frequent absences as to identify the specific conjunctures and causal determinants that render possible the articulation of one or the other form of identity.[12]

Our own standpoint accords with the position presented above. A defining characteristic of all social beings is the plural identities they embody. To successfully engage with and make sense of the diverse and contradictory life worlds in which individuals are enmeshed entails affirming parts of their selves while silencing others, a unified self being constructed through a process of 'narrative identity'.[13] In much the same way, only by recognizing the multiform subjectivities of worker can we come to terms with the contending nature of their actions without it appearing to be schizophrenic as well as understand the co-existence of class and non-class forms of identity. This is what allows them in certain circumstances to transcend the boundaries of religion or language to fight for their common interests while in others their behaviour is tightly circumscribed within these boundaries giving rise to sectionalism. Both the unity of workers and their divisions therefore must be perceived as two faces of the same coin, neither condition being exclusive or

---

perforce to privilege one over the other, a contention which appears to again fall prey to the habit of perceiving workers' practices in either/or terms. Marcel van der Linden and Lex Heerma van Voss, 'Introduction', in L. Voss and M. Linden (eds.), *Class and Other Identities: Gender, Religion And Ethnicity in the Writing of European Labor History*, New York, 2002, pp. 1–39.

[12] Studies of working class formation, as Margaret Somers observes, are rooted in an 'epistemology of absence': explanatory energies have been concentrated essentially in deciphering why the working class has failed to realize its revolutionary mission. 'Workers of the World, Compare!' *Contemporary Sociology*, Vol. 18, No. 3, May 1989, pp. 325–9 (cit. p. 325).

[13] Paul Ricœur, *Soi-même comme un autre*, Paris, 1990, cited in Corcuff, *Les nouvelles sociologies*, p. 101. Following Ricœur and other scholars, Margaret Somers has also argued that social identities are constituted through narratives. 'Narrativity, Narrative Identity, and Social Action: Rethinking English Working-Class Formation', *Social Science History*, Vol. 16, No. 4, Winter 1992, pp. 591–630.

irreversible. It is the contingency of the social which gives rise to both the class conscious and the communally conscious worker.

Framing the problematic in this manner, however, still begs the question how the movement between contending social identities is actually negotiated, how workers who at one historical juncture were engaged in bloody clashes against one another in the name of religion or language, chose at another not very distant juncture to bury, 'magically transcend' their differences and forge a common front against employers and the state.[14] Did not memories of communal hatred and violence impede, even foreclose the possibilities for collective action?[15] One could arguably attribute this passage from sectionalism to class solidarity to the heroic efforts of political and trade union leaders to mobilize and reconstitute the rank-and-file along class lines. But what place does this then leave for the affirmation of worker agency?[16]

In this chapter, our focus will be on studying first the language conflict that rocked the Bangalore plant of ITI for several years in the late 1960s and early 1970s as Kannada speaking workers challenged the domination Tamil workers had exercised within the productive space as well as the company-controlled township. Then, we shall consider the antagonisms marking relations between caste Hindu and Scheduled Caste workers, provoked in part, by the compensatory discrimination programme instituted by the state to promote the social and economic uplift of the 'Untouchables'. The notions of 'us' and 'them' articulated during the course of both these confrontations thus diverged sharply from those generated in times of strikes and other forms of collective action where

---

[14] Joshi, 'Hope and Despair', p. 174. According to her, it is the 'erasures of memory' which allows for the transcending of sectarian loyalties. If this is so, then one must ask how these 'erasures' are actually accomplished.

[15] I am grateful to Jonathan Parry for pointing out this problem to me.

[16] In attempting to delineate what is culturally specific to the worlds of Indian labour, caution is required not to essentialise attributes such as linguistic or caste loyalties and view them as unique to the Indian context. Exclusionary strategies and politics derived from race, gender, region or nation also marked, and continue to do so, the experiences of workers in the West. For a discussion, see Roediger, *The Wages of Whiteness*; *idem*, 'Race and the Working Class Past in the United States. Multiple Identities and the Future of Labour History', *IRSH*, Vol. 38, 1993, pp. 127–43. On the emergence of a race-stratified workforce in Britain during the inter-World War years, see Laura Tabili, '*We Ask for British Justice': Workers and Racial Difference in Late Imperial Britain*, Ithaca, 1994.

other subjectivities, predicated on an awareness of common interests and common mutuality, triumphed. Given the nature of the composition of the ITI workforce where Muslims constituted a very tiny minority, the principal lines of differentiation ran not along the axis of religion, but along the axes of language and caste. As a result, barring one incident, communal hostilities were conspicuous by their absence.

LANGUAGE AND WORKERS' POLITICS

The deepening economic crisis in the country from the mid-1960s onwards provided a fertile terrain for the emergence of sons of the soil movement in different states. Demands for barring outsiders, differentiated as such either on the basis of linguistic or spatial coordinates, from the labour market particularly with respect to highly valued employment in government services, had already been echoed in the pre-Independence period and during the 1950s.[17] Still, it was only during the turbulent post-Nehruvian era that nativist aspirations expressed themselves with full vigour. An acutely competitive job market combined with rising and massive levels of unemployment among the urban educated youth paved the way for a wave of protests in various parts of the country. Frustrated by constricted mobility avenues, local youth directed their anger at migrant communities and called for a halt to inter-state migration even as they insisted on their 'birth right' to preferential treatment.

Scholarly attention has focussed in the main on the role played by the Shiv Sena in Bombay in championing autochthonous interests.[18] The campaign of violence orchestrated by the Shiv Sena against migrants from the southern states, especially Tamilians, perceived as having

---

[17] See, for instance, the report of Rajendra Prasad on the Bengali–Bihari question. *All India Congress Committee Papers*, New Delhi, 1939; *Main Report of the Labour Investigation Committee*, New Delhi, 1958, p. 34, 120. For the 1950s, see Jonathan Parry and Christian Strümpell, 'On the Desecration of Nehru's "Temples": Bhilai and Rourkela compared', *EPW*, Vol. 43, No. 19, 10 May 2008, pp. 47–57.

[18] See, *inter alia*, Dipankar Gupta, *Nativism in a Metropolis: The Shiv Sena in Bombay*, New Delhi, 1982; Mary Katzenstein, *Ethnicity and Equality: The Shiv Sena Party and Preferential Policies in Bombay*, Ithaca, 1977; Jayant Lele, 'Saffronization of the Shiv Sena: The Political Economy of City, State, and Nation', in S. Patel and A. Thorner (eds.), *Bombay. Metaphor for Modern India,* Bombay, pp. 185–212.

cornered a disproportionate share of jobs in all areas, forced many of them to flee the city. But much the same violent and xenophobic colouring tainted agitations elsewhere too.[19] Ironically the strident denunciations of Kannada nativist groups, accusing Tamilians and Malayalis of depriving local language speakers of their rightful employment benefits, coincided with similar denunciations voiced by the Shiv Sena against migrants from Karnataka, assimilated as Tamilians.[20]

In Bangalore, the driving force behind the campaign for jobs for sons of the soil were the Kannada Chaluvaligars, the latter word meaning agitators. Formed in 1966 by Vatal Nagaraj, the son of a farmer-cum-small shop keeper, the movement drew its supporters not so much from the labouring classes as from the lower middle classes. A Chaluvali activist was typically male, young, a high school graduate, and either jobless or employed in the service sector. The choice of a bicycle as election symbol graphically underscored both the social base of the organization and the groups most likely to be seduced by its appeals.[21] Committed to protecting the cultural as well as economic interests of Kannada speakers in the city, on the economic front, the Chaluvaligars focussed their attention on job entitlements in the five Bangalore-based public sector companies. This was a perfectly logical strategy. The biggest employers of labour in the city, the jobs these companies offered constituted one of the most coveted prizes on the employment market. For more than providing relatively good wages for leisurely work rhythms, they guaranteed security of contract combined with a generous array of social measures all of which contributed to elevate the social status of the incumbent.

During the 1950s, finding work in one of these companies as a production operative or even in a white collar position with no more than a secondary school certificate was hardly unimaginable. But competition for these jobs progressively intensified as managements tightened selection criteria in consonance with the steady expansion in educational and vocational training facilities. By 1966 as many as 15

---

[19] Myron Weiner, *Sons of the Soil. Migration and Ethnic Conflicts in India*, New Delhi, 1988.

[20] Even as late as the early 1990s, several potential migrants from the Mandya village studied by Fréderic Landy were reluctant to search for work in Bombay because of the risk of discrimination against south Indians. 'Migration et enracinement dans le Maidan'.

[21] Weiner, *Sons of the Soil*, pp. 292–3.

government-run industrial training institutes operated in the state.[22] As a result, more and more applicants now boasted a trade certificate, and local Kannadigas, particularly those belonging to the peasant castes, appear to have been in the forefront of this race to acquire technical proficiency. Ensuring they were able to fructify this capital by obtaining positions commensurate to their ambitions hinged on keeping out rivals from within and outside the state.

It is in this context of a growing scramble for employment among aspiring candidates armed with improved credentials, but uncertain about finding an outlet for them, that we must situate the actions of the nativist organizations. For an enduring grievance of the Chaluvaligars concerned what they considered to be the under-representation of Kannada speakers in the labour force of public sector companies because of the purportedly discriminatory practices of managements which preferred migrants from Tamil Nadu and Kerala. Hence the benefits of industrialization in the city accrued not to 'local' people but to outsiders. The refrain of under representation would continue to punctuate the discourse of all nativist organizations all the way through to the mid-1980s, even though it had become abundantly clear by this point that the public sector had evolved into a stronghold of Kannada presence in the city from where support for other agitations could be readily mobilized.

The Chaluvaligars represented only one facet, and one moment in the development of Kannada nationalism whose roots stretched back to the early twentieth century. What, however, distinguished Vatal Nagaraj's movement from other Kannada associations, past and contemporary, was both the content of its activities—a preoccupation with employment—and its style—a propensity for violence to ensure compliance with its demands. Mapping the broader socio-historic contours of Kannada nationalism also enables us to understand how economic considerations while an essential component were not the sole determinant in forging the perceptions of Chaluvaligars and Kannada

---

[22] During the Second Five Year Plan (1956–61), the capacities of the industrial training institutes in the erstwhile Mysore state were expanded to accommodate 448 additional seats for fitters, 176 additional seats for turners, and 224 seats for mechanical draughtsmen. The Third Five Year Plan (1961–66) witnessed the creation of another 848 additional seats for fitters, 400 seats for electricians, 364 seats for welders, and 312 seats for turners. *Report of the Study Group on Employment and Training*, New Delhi, 1969, p. 151.

protagonists in general, and in contributing to cast the local language speaker as a victim of discrimination in his/her own state. The role played by political, cultural, historical, and demographic forces in framing the Kannada imaginary was no less critical.

For lest we forget, the theme of Tamil outsiders depriving 'local' people of their rightful opportunities for economic and social mobility had a long heritage and was hardly confined to the subaltern classes. The British policy of importing dewans from Madras presidency to administer the affairs of princely Mysore provoked tremendous resentment among the indigenous elite, the first to raise the slogan of 'Mysore for Mysoreans'. This has prompted Bjorn Hettne to describe the struggle for power between the Madras and Mysore palace elites as the underlying cleavage running through all political controversies in the state from the late nineteenth century until at least 1910.[23] But to read off the demands of the Chaluvaligars as little more than a re-enacting of age-old tensions, this time among wage earners, would be fallacious.

In a series of extremely perceptive essays, the historian Janaki Nair has analysed the social construction and distinctive features of the Kannada movement both during colonial rule and in the aftermath of Independence.[24] First, Kannada nationalism compared unfavourably with the more important linguistic nationalisms (Tamil, Bengali, Marathi etc.) that sprang up under British paramountcy. It both lacked and envied their creative vitality and self confidence. An object of particular desire and resentment was Tamil nationalism whose cultural influence radiated powerfully across Bangalore.[25] Shaking off this dependency would in fact constitute one the first acts of self-assertion by Kannada artistes

[23] Bjorn Hettne, *The Political Economy of Indirect Rule. Mysore 1881–1947*, London, 1978, pp. 72–4, 253–5. As Tamil speaking Brahmins, the two rival factions, though, shared common caste and linguistic affinities.

[24] Janaki Nair, 'Kannada and Politics of State Protection', *EPW,* Vol. XXIX, No. 44, 29 October 1994, pp. 2853–4; *idem,* '"Memories of Underdevelopment". Language and its Identities in Contemporary Karnataka', *EPW,* Vol. XXXI, Nos. 41–42, 12–19 October 1996, pp. 2809–16; *idem,* 'Language and Right to the City', *EPW,* Vol. XXXV, No. 47, 18 November 2000, pp. 4141–6. See also by the same author, *The Promise of the Metropolis. Bangalore's Twentieth Century,* New Delhi, 2005, chap. 6.

[25] On the complex nature of relations between Kannadigas and Tamilians, see V.K Nataraj, 'Kannadiga-Tamilian Nexus in Bangalore', *EPW,* Vol. XXXVI, Nos. 5–6, 3 February 2001, pp. 503–04.

once they had realized their objective of securing a linguistically unified state.

Second, prior to the linguistic reorganization of Indian states in 1956 which paved the way for the emergence of Mysore (or Karnataka after its renaming in 1973) as it exists in its current physical configuration, Kannada speakers were dispersed across five different administrative entities.[26] The absence of clearly defined territorial frontiers unified by a common political administration within which the Kannada 'nation' could imagine itself as a single community further accentuated sentiments of inadequacy.[27]

Third, in the post-Independence period, Kannada nationalism has had to increasingly operate within a segmented linguistic market. In the hierarchical division of labour between languages produced by capitalist industrial development, Kannada had no choice but to accept the hegemonic sway of English over the economic and technological fields and settle for dominance within the highly restricted sphere of culture and politics. Yet even here its ascendancy has been far from uncontested, facing challenges from Hindi and Tamil cultural products circulated in particular through the medium of cinema and television. Strenuous efforts to impose Kannada as the language of official communication have also not delivered the solicited results. The confluence of all these factors have contributed to make contemporary Kannada nationalism a

---

[26] The upshot of the whims and fancies of colonial administrators, Kannada speakers could be found in Hyderabad, Coorg, the presidencies of Madras and Bombay, as well as the princely state of Mysore which would form the nucleus of the new state in 1956. For a discussion of the struggle to merge the different Kannada speaking territories under a common administration, see, *inter alia*, P.B. Desai, *A History of Karnataka. From Pre-history to Unification*, Dharwar, 1970, pp. 434–6; Manor, *Political Change*, pp. 184–7; H.V. Sreenivasa Murthy and R. Ramakrishnan, *History of Karnataka*, New Delhi, 1978, pp. 334–8.

[27] In the words of Desai, 'outsiders looked at a Kannada man either as a Madrasi, a Marathi, a Hyderabadi or a Mysorean, but never as a Kannadiga'. *History of Karnataka. From Pre-history to Unification*, p. 434. Another author writes that before the creation of Mysore, Kannada people felt 'almost like depressed classes'. I.M. Muthanna, *History of Karnataka. History, Administration and Culture*, Mysore, 1962, p. 355. But as we know enthusiasm for the idea of a united linguistic state waxed less than strongly among important caste groups such as Vokalligas who feared the attendant political domination of Lingayats. James Manor, 'Language, Religion and Political Identity in Karnataka', in D. Taylor and M. Yapp (eds.), *Political Identity in South Asia*, London, 1979, pp. 170–90.

'beleaguered nationalism', so racked by a sense of inferiority and insecurity that it perceives itself as 'unoriginal, weak, even imitative . . .'.[28]

Equally importantly and interestingly, Nair has argued that the crisis of Kannada nationalism bears no relation to the demographic and spatial specificities of Bangalore. The capital city effectively exemplifies linguistic heterogeneity and 'cosmopolitanism' in sharp contrast to all other south Indian state capitals.[29] Though Kannada speakers constitute the largest single group, they accounted for no more than 35 per cent of the city's population in 1981 with Tamil speakers following next (24 per cent) and then Urdu (19 per cent) and Telegu speakers (17 per cent).[30] This linguistic diversity is as much a legacy of colonial rule when the city was divided into a polyglot east and a relatively monolingual west as a product of Bangalore's unique geographic position. Located within close proximity to the borders of Tamil Nadu and Andhra Pradesh, it has always attracted large numbers of migrants from both states—people who flocked to the metropolis to take advantage of the greater and more diverse employment opportunities available here. From the mid-1950s, onwards, though, intra-state migratory flows seem to have overtaken inter-state flows.[31] But if Bangalore has come to symbolize the dominated status of Kannada, the roots of this subordination, emphasizes Nair, do not lie in a demographic deficit as the champions of Kannada nationalism insist, but in the cultural and economic domains. This, more than anything else, explains the course of linguistic politics in the state from the mid-1980s onward with Kannada identity increasingly manifesting itself in acts of violence, and linguistic and religious minorities being singled out for attack.

[28] Nair, 'Memories of Underdevelopment', pp. 2809–10.

[29] In Trivandrum (capital of Kerala), 86 per cent of the population speak the main language of the state, while in Madras (capital of Tamil Nadu), this figure stands at 76 per cent, and in Hyderabad (capital of Andhra Pradesh), it is 51 per cent. Samuel Johnson and M. Lingaraju, 'Inter State Migration and Linguistic Reorganisation of States: An Analysis of Census Data', Working Paper, ISEC, 1991, p. 27.

[30] *Census of India 1981. Portrait of Population of Karnataka*, New Delhi, 1989, p. 76.

[31] Bangalore's distinctive status *vis-à-vis* the other south Indian capital cities also stands out on another register. According to the 1981 census, in-migration rates from other states to Bangalore is 151 per thousand (of which 78 were from Tamil Nadu) whereas it is 75 in Madras and 52 in Hyderabad. In 1961, in-migration rates to Bangalore were 201 per thousand with the figure falling to 162 in 1971, unmistakable evidence of slackening inter-state migratory flows to the city. Johnson and Lingaraju, 'Inter State Migration and Linguistic Reorganisation of States', p. 20.

JOBS FOR SONS OF THE SOIL IN THE PUBLIC SECTOR

Because the nativist movements often crystallized into formal political structures, epitomized by the example of the Shiv Sena, mainstream political parties were also obliged to rally to the cause of the sons of the soils, if only with an eye to the ballot box, and recognize their claims to territorial exclusiveness.[32] Restrictions were imposed on outsiders through a system of preferences for local people in employment, education and housing. Notwithstanding constitutional provisions guaranteeing equal opportunities for all citizens regardless of their ethnic origins, these were subverted in one manner or the other by state governments as they proceeded to enact domicile rules geared to denying 'aliens' access to highly valued scarce resources.[33] Given the limitations on their own capacities to sponsor employment generating initiatives with the potential to absorb large numbers of the urban jobless, state authorities also exerted pressure on private and public sector employers to adopt hiring policies which gave pride of place to the indigenous population.

Such pressure bore down far more strongly on public enterprises both because they generally tended to be bigger employers of labour, and because they came under the control of the government, albeit in many cases the centre and not the state, and hence were viewed as more tractable (and perhaps being less efficient and cost conscious were also more willing to enrol surplus personnel) than private companies. Pronouncements from parliamentary committees and other agencies urging the selection of local people for unskilled and semi-skilled positions in public sector companies only added grist to the political mill.[34] Thus in its report

[32] Vatal Nagaraj himself was elected to the Karnataka state assembly on three occasions (1967, 1972, 1989), while the political party which he formed won six seats in the 1971 Bangalore municipal elections. Weiner, *Sons of the Soil*, p. 292; T.M. Joseph, 'Politics of Recruitment in Public Sector Undertakings. A Study of the Nativist Movement in Bangalore', Unpublished Phd dissertation, University of Bangalore, 1994, p. 68.

[33] In the wake of the Telengana student agitation in the late 1960s, the constitution itself was amended so as to authorize the principle of residential qualification as a condition for public employment and for admission to educational institutions. The scope of the amendment, though, was restricted to the Telengana region. Weiner, *Sons of the Soil*, pp. 253–4.

[34] COPU (1969–70), *Production Management in Public Undertakings*, 76th Report, Fourth Lok Sabha, New Delhi, 1970, p. 71; COPU (1971–72), *Personnel Policies and Labour Management Relations in Public Undertakings*, 17th Report, Fifth Lok Sabha, New Delhi, April 1972, p. 23.

submitted in 1969, the National Commission of Labour admitted that protectionist demands in the sphere of job entitlements had acquired political overtones in many states because of the failure of economic developments to match rising local expectations. Endorsing declarations by the central government that sons of the soil be given preference, the Commission went on to express its reservations at the latitude enjoyed by public sector top managements in recruitment. State governments, it felt, should also be allowed a voice in these matters to ensure an equitable distribution of the fruits of industrialization.[35] But it is important to note that the definition of 'local' advanced in official documents sharply diverged from the essentialist conceptions, based on ascriptive status, defended by the nativists.

Official bodies were also unanimous in recommending local employment exchanges as the exclusive channel of recruitment for lower echelon posts requiring standard educational and technical qualifications. Compliance with this recommendation by the central public sector companies, in particular the big steel plants whose workforces were quite heterogeneous in their ethnic composition, appears to have been fitful, though. This was partly because managements feared it would impair productive efficiency and foster the 'evils of provincialism'.[36] Still, the purpose of such a measure was definitely to privilege the local population since exchange registration rules enforced residential qualifications as the basic criterion.

In the case of Karnataka, applicants whose parents were neither residents of the state nor could claim Kannada as their mother tongue had to produce a certificate showing they had been living in the state for at least five years. But even credentials of this kind were inadequate as the authorities had apparently taken a decision to authorize only individuals who had studied in educational institutions within the state to register with the employment exchanges.[37] A leader of a Tamil cultural

---

[35] *Report of the National Commission on Labour*, pp. 77–8. One of the study groups set up by the Commission, however, believed that recognizing the exclusive rights to employment of local people in public sector companies is 'harmful from the national point of view'. *Report of the Study Group on Sociological Aspects of Labour-Management Relations*, New Delhi, 1968, pp. 48–9.

[36] Nigel Crook, *India's Industrial Cities: Essays in Economy and Demographics*, New Delhi, 1993, pp. 35–6; Tulpule, 'Management and Workers'.

[37] Weiner, *Sons of the Soil*, p. 341.

organization in one Bangalore public sector company complained of wilful linguistic bias on the part of employment exchanges. According to him, even when Tamilian and Malayali candidates had been born and educated in the state, the exchanges were refusing to sponsor their names to prospective employers.[38] This sentiment is shared by a number of other Tamil workers as well who belonged to the state.

Even though you might have been born here, if you have a Tamil name you cannot get employment in Karnataka in any government service. Only in the private sector can you hope to find a job.[39]

At the same time, the Karnataka government's move to utilize education and/or length of residence as the legitimate yardstick by which to classify a 'local' person hardly satisfied the nativist organizations. Attached to a strictly essentialist definition of identity, one where *jus sanguinis* took precedence over *jus solis*, for them only somebody who had inherited Kannada as his/her mother tongue could stake an authentic claim to being a son of the soil. Thus even second or third generation migrants who spoke a language other than Kannada were branded as outsiders. Subsequently, one of the nativist organizations would accept the definition of a Kannadiga proposed by an official committee as someone who had lived in the state for at least 15 years and knew to read and write Kannada.[40]

This question of selecting the appropriate identity markers to characterize a 'local' person, one that was either inclusive or exclusive in its coverage, was hardly a banal one given the implications it could have on the employment front. Privileging language as the determining criteria as the nativists desired would, for instance, have resulted in disqualifying a substantial number of potential candidates from competing for various kinds of jobs for which they would otherwise have been eligible. The divergent stances held by the government and the nativists regarding who qualified or not as a local person came to the fore during the course of a discussion in the Karnataka Legislative Assembly over the number of sons of the soil employed in the five Bangalore-based public sector companies.

---

[38] Joseph, 'Politics of Recruitment', pp. 207–08.
[39] Interview with Balamurali (Field notes 2001).
[40] Joseph, 'Politics of Recruitment', p. 136.

When questioned on this issue in 1969, the figures produced by the state labour minister reveal a mixed picture. With the exception of BEL where local people were definitely in the minority, accounting for barely 39 per cent of the total workforce, in the other four plants, the reverse was true. While Mysoreans (the marker Kannadiga emerged consequent to the renaming of the state in 1973) occupied 82 per cent of all posts in HMT and 71 per cent in BEML, their share stood at 67 per cent and 63 per cent respectively in ITI and HAL.[41] A detailed occupational breakdown with respect to ITI also showed that for no category of posts did the share of Mysoreans fall below 57 per cent.[42] The minister left unspecified who exactly the term 'Mysorean' referred to, but it is more than likely that it designated all those born in the state rather than just Kannada speakers.

This is borne out by an ITI document. Replying to an enquiry from the labour commissioner on the number of Mysoreans and non-Mysoreans employed by the company, it notes that he had defined the former as 'persons born in Mysore'.[43] What this signified is that while the political discourse of the government may well have chosen to conflate sons of the soil with Kannada speakers—and the fact that this discourse quite literally found expression through the agency of Kannada could only have contributed to consolidate the association between the two elements—in its official pronouncements it struck a different chord. It unambiguously enunciated an extensive definition of citizenship, emphasizing territorial over linguistic identity, conscious that a restrictive definition could impact negatively on Kannada migrants settled in other states as well as violate constitutional provisions on the subject.[44]

Subsequently, the government appears to have revised its position. In addition to either having been born or lived in the state for a certain number of years, it ruled that a Kannadiga was somebody capable of

[41] Reindorp, *Leaders and Leadership in the Trade Unions in Bangalore*, p. 84.

[42] Note to Board, 115th meeting, item no. B7, 8 May 1970. Mysoreans held 57 per cent of officer posts, 74 per cent of administrative posts, 76 per cent of technical posts, 67 per cent of production posts, 73 per cent of Class IV menial posts (attendants, sweepers, helpers, etc.), and 72 per cent of learner and apprentice posts.

[43] ibid.

[44] A circular issued by the Indian Engineering Association noted that attempts to define local people other than by territorial markers 'is likely to have serious constitutional and legal implications'. Circular no. 231-I.E., 28 August 1969.

speaking, reading and writing Kannada.[45] But in the context of our present discussion, adopting the official conception of a Mysorean (or Kannadiga) exposed the accusations of the Chaluvaligars as nothing more than empty rhetoric calculated to whip up anti-outsider sentiments. With the exception of BEL, the levels of representation of the local population in the public sector companies could be judged quite satisfactory since they made up more than 60 per cent of the workforce.

Another set of figures further disproves the nativist charges. Over a span of two decades from 1948, when ITI was founded, to 1969, a little over two-thirds of the 13,669 people it had recruited originated from within the state.[46] Just how many of them were Kannada speakers and thus conformed to the nativist criteria of a local person, is something we cannot determine. Still, it would be quite safe to assume that a significant proportion of these employees were full blooded sons of the soil: as we have seen from the findings of our own statistical sample (see chapter seven), with the exception of the 1950s, Kannada speakers enjoyed a numerical superiority in ITI during all other periods. Besides, the production of the new crossbar exchanges from the early 1960s onwards saw a fresh generation of workers enter the factory who for the most part, were better qualified Kannadigas.

There is no reason to suppose why the situation should have differed in the other public sector companies leaving aside BEL. Nor why Kannada speakers should not have comprised the majority of local employees, and as such the single largest element within the workforce, even prior to the eruption of the nativist agitation. For while land holding patterns obtaining in the state may have initially attenuated the need to leave the countryside, migration to the cities appears to have gathered pace from the mid-1950s onwards in the wake of the linguistic reorganization of Mysore. Peasant castes enriched by the green revolution and having seized the benefits of an expanding educational system to endow their male offspring with the qualifications required to compete on the urban labour market were unlikely to have allowed the city population to indefinitely monopolize the dividends of industrial development.

---

[45] PD note, 1 March 1993. In a way, instituting such distinctions on the basis of language made little sense since bilingualism and even multilingualism was a widespread phenomenon among workers and other subaltern groups.

[46] Note to Board, 115th meeting.

In HMT, which counted the highest number of 'Mysoreans', selection procedures favouring Kannada speakers preceded the Chaluvilagars' rise to prominence. These had been consciously devised by the head of personnel, who later became a union leader, in an endeavour to smash the AITUC-affiliated union.[47] The manipulative gambit of the management had the effect of infusing strong linguistic overtones into the bloody rivalry between the INTUC union, which had the backing of the company and drew into its fold the Kannada recruits, and the AITUC union which disintegrated in the face of concerted attacks by its opponents. Even in BEL, the management resorted to much the same divisive manoeuvres. To undermine the strength of the AITUC union, it propped up a rival structure whose members consisted essentially of new Kannada migrants.[48] Organizational conflicts between opposing unions aimed at defending or securing representative rights therefore also turned into pitched battles between 'local' Kannadigas and Tamil and Malayali 'outsiders' because of corporate interference. What this suggests is that if for no better reason than to check the influence and militancy of the communist unions, some public sector companies at least had realized the advantages to be gained by absorbing sizeable numbers of Kannadigas.[49]

Given the initial reluctance of the indigenous Kannada population to become industrial 'proletarians', it is possible that state-owned enterprises during the formative phase of their growth until around the end of the 1950s included more Tamil employees. Many of them, however, were likely to have been born within the state. Yet, even during these years, as we have observed with respect to our ITI sample population, Kannada speakers formed a non-negligible component of the workforce, though we must be cautious about extrapolating from the case of ITI to draw similar conclusions with respect to the other plants. To affirm therefore,

---

[47] Interview with M.S.C. Rao, April-May 1981.

[48] ibid.

[49] As labour historians have shown, leveraging primordial loyalties to divide workers, weaken unions and break strikes was a strategem commonly resorted to by employers during the colonial period. Chandavarkar, *The Origins of Industrial Capitalism in India*, pp. 422–3; *idem*, 'Questions of Class'; Murphy, *Unions in Conflict*, p. 4, 63, 74–5 and *passim*.

as Nair has done, that the period from the late 1960s onwards witnessed a dramatic reordering of recruitment patterns in the public sector with one linguistic group (Kannadigas) replacing others (Tamilians and Malayalis) might not be entirely accurate.[50] For not only did the example of ITI evince to the presence at all times of Kannada speaking employees in more than token strength; reliable and comprehensive information on the linguistic composition of the workforces for all public companies, allowing us to trace eventual shifts and try to connect them to managerial decisions, is also unavailable.[51]

What does seem plausible is that starting from the mid to late 1960s, a combination of official pressure conjoined with the fear of agitations by the Chaluvaligars, company executives' own sympathies for the nativist cause, and the adoption of new modes of recruitment triggered a mutually reinforcing phenomenon. On the one hand, there was a decline in the recruitment of migrants from Tamil Nadu and Kerala, and, on the other, an increase in the induction of Kannada speakers in all five plants, thus sealing their position of dominance. Measuring the precise magnitude of these changes, however, will require both more and better quality data and comparative studies of the other public sector companies. Just how perilous the task of accurately assessing the size of the different linguistic groups can be is confirmed by this example: in 1984, statistics published in the press, and supplied, no doubt, by the company itself on the findings of an official committee, placed the number of Kannada speaking employees in HAL at a staggering 90 per cent.[52] In an academic study conducted six years later, this figure had shrunk by half, although in the intervening period, the total size of the workforce had decreased by no more than 19 per cent.[53]

In November 1968, the state authorities first raised the question of the Bangalore-based public sector units granting special treatment for sons of the soil in appointments. With the Chaluvaligar leaders, who by

---

[50] Nair, 'Memories of Underdevelopment'.

[51] Even a study explicitly devoted to hiring policies in two Bangalore public sector undertakings (HAL and BEL) is unable to shed much light on the subject of the linguistic composition of the workforce. Joseph, 'Politics of Recruitment'.

[52] Nair, *Promise of Metropolis*, p. 256. Kannada organizations, however, claimed the statistics over-estimated the number of local language speakers in public sector companies.

[53] Joseph, 'Politics of Recruitment', pp. 92–4.

now had succeeded in penetrating the institutional political arena, accusing the government of inaction, it was obliged to prove the contrary. As Veerendra Patil, the chief minister, would later declare, 'can you name any state which does not prefer its own people?'[54] At a meeting convoked by Patil, he expressly instructed the heads of the five companies to reorient their recruitment policies and ensure that as long as qualified Kannadigas were available, non-Kannadigas would not be considered. Embracing the rhetoric as well as the grievances of the nativists, he added that managements were inclined to favour 'persons coming from outside the state to the exclusion of Mysoreans'—a statement clearly identifying Mysoreans with Kannada speakers given that local people, understood as having declared the state as their birthplace, suffered in no way from under-representation in four of the five plants.[55]

In turn, the executives assured Patil that regardless of 'whatever might have happened in the past', from now onwards, they would give special consideration to local people.[56] But while agreeing to rely on the local employment exchanges for this purpose, they expressed considerable dissatisfaction with the functioning of this mechanism. Interestingly, barely a fortnight before their meeting with the chief minister, all five executives had unanimously objected to demands from state officials calling on the public sector companies to discontinue their practice of simultaneously notifying vacancies to the employment exchanges and releasing advertisements in the English and local language press. They were asked to stop advertising job openings since this allowed everybody to apply, including migrants from neighbouring states. The companies, however, complained that restricting their methods of recruitment would hamper their autonomy and frustrate efforts to attract the best candidates since none of the government's instructions applied to the private sector.[57] A year later, Patil again pressed the issue of preferential treatment. In a

---

[54] Weiner, *Sons of the Soil*, pp. 292–3.

[55] Note to Board, 115th meeting.

[56] ibid.

[57] Meeting of Coordination Committee of Union Industries, 4 November 1968. After underlining the inherent contradiction that prevailed between the idea of preferential treatment and that of equal opportunity enshrined in the Constitution, the five Bangalore public enterprises also pointed out the impossibility of determining what would constitute a just or fair share of jobs that should rightfully go to local people.

letter to the five companies, he communicated a resolution of the state advisory board on technical education urging all public enterprises in Bangalore to appoint only diploma and graduate holders from the state to supervisory and technical posts.[58] In other words, state officials even aspired to place certain types of skilled occupations beyond the reach of migrant candidates.

Meanwhile, the ITI management wrote to the Ministry of Communications seeking advice on whether it should modify its recruitment procedures in the light of its meeting with the chief minister. Pointing out that Patil's injunctions carried important policy implications, the company feared that employing local people on a preferential basis could contravene constitutional principles relating to equality of opportunities. The ministry's reply highlighted two points. First, no directive issued by the state government endowing sons of the soil with a first claim to all jobs would be applicable to ITI in view of its legal status as a private limited company as opposed to a statutory body. Second, the company stood on strong ground to contest any such directive in the courts as a possible violation of the constitution.

Encouraged by these remarks, ITI executives, after noting the satisfactory levels of representation of Mysoreans on its pay rolls, decided it would be unwise to circumscribe the 'recruitment of personnel . . . to any particular state . . .'[59] Otherwise, not only would its image as a national public sector company suffer, but so would operational efficiencies given the 'complicated nature of technical work' undertaken by the factory.[60] Consequently, they also ruled out any changes to its selection procedures, declaring that the company would continue to fill vacant posts both by releasing advertisements and via employment exchanges.

To what extent did the management's actions match its words? Once again the absence of sources hampers us from answering this question to our satisfaction. But the information we dispose for a brief period uncovers no dramatic transformation in personnel policies. In 1968, local people constituted nearly 69 per cent of the total workforce. Five years later,

---

[58] Letter no. CMI 2639/69, 11 December 1969.
[59] Note to Board, 115th meeting.
[60] ibid.

this figure had risen to 72 per cent (see table).[61] Whether or not this upward movement persisted, we do not know. A roughly identical trend is visible on the recruitment front. Over a period of six years from 1968-74, the proportion of fresh entrants originating from within the state averaged 71 per cent.[62] It is also very probable that the vast majority were Kannada speakers whose names had been forwarded by local employment exchanges and who were then selected by personnel department officials identified with the nativist cause. Being Kannadigas themselves, one could have expected the latter to ensure that employment opportunities in the company went, as far as possible, to 'true' sons of the soil.[63] As one former Chaluvali activist remarked, despite his antecedents as a 'trouble maker', as testified by his known links with the nativist movement as well as the BMS trade union prior to joining ITI, he was still able to get a job here because 'we had a Kannada sympathiser . . . in the personnel department who was the recruitment officer'.[64]

It is also worth noting that the ITI union, which, as we shall study, had passed into the hands of Kannada loyalists, had urged the management to favour the recruitment of local people. For this purpose, it recommended setting all examination papers in Kannada too so as to improve the chances of Kannada speaking candidates. The suggestion was turned down by the company. Besides noting that all business

[61] Size of local population in ITI workforce

Year	Locals as % of total workforce
1968	68.9
1970	70.1
1971	70.4
1972	70.6
1973	72.3

Source: ITI Personnel Dept.

[62] Arya, *Labour Management Relations in Public Sector Undertakings*, pp. 25–6.

[63] According to Joseph, the majority of Kannadiga personnel officers he interviewed in HAL and BEL felt Kannadigas should receive preferential treatment in recruitment for all positions. Interestingly, Tamil officers born and brought up in the state also endorsed this point of view, though one presumes that their definition of 'Kannadigas' did not only encapsulate native language speakers. 'Politics of Recruitment', pp. 221–2.

[64] Interview with Basavarajappa, 12 February 1999.

transactions were conducted in English, it feared setting a precedent and encouraging other linguistic groups to ask for similar facilities.[65] Subsequently, a member of the ITI board of directors representing the Karnataka government declared that the personnel department head at the flagship Bangalore factory should preferably be somebody from the state or at least be

conversant with Kannada so that he could deal with Personnel & Industrial Relations problems in the language of the administration of the state (sic).[66]

Disagreeing with this view, the ITI chairman, who himself was a Kannada speaker, felt that the job only required an experienced person. In reality, however, most people chosen to run the personnel department fitted one or the other of the above criteria.

That the state authorities had no wish to be upstaged on an issue as sensitive as employment by the nativist groups, which were attentively monitoring the recruitment policies of various public institutions, is also evident from the admonitions addressed at periodic intervals to the five public sector units reproaching them for not doing enough to promote local representation. Thus in 1976, the Department of Employment and Training pointed out that the problem of qualified persons not obtaining work in companies located in Karnataka had 'attracted severe criticism' in the legislative assembly. It then went on to write:

There is a growing feeling among the people of the State, as also in Government that the employment potential generated by the industrialization in the State has not accrued to the benefit of the local population to the extent desirable and necessary . . . The existence of such a feeling has a detrimental effect on the industrial climate in the State.[67]

Much the same message was reiterated in the early 1980s by the secretary, Department of Commerce and Industry. Even though by now, the numerical dominance of local language speakers in the labour force of public sector companies hardly remained in doubt, he still found it necessary to convene a meeting of the five chairmen because

. . . of widespread feeling among the public that local persons are not being

---

[65] PD note, 26 May 1971.
[66] Minutes of 186th Board meeting, 6 April 1982.
[67] No. EEX/CR-98/76-77, 24 June 1976.

appointed in the Bangalore-based central PSUs even to posts of lower cadres of administration.[68]

The government's efforts to prevent the nativists from re-appropriating the slogan of jobs for sons of the soil and transforming it into a subject of heated public debate did not, however, fully succeed. In 1984, Kannada organizations took to the streets claiming that 'local' people had been denied their rightful share of employment opportunities in the new Wheel and Axle plant set up by the central government on the periphery of Bangalore. The authorities immediately announced the formation of a committee whose terms were to determine job entitlements for Kannadigas in the central public sector industries. Known as the Sarojini Mahishi Committee, it recommended that in function of the category 65 to 100 per cent of all posts should be reserved for local people. Apart from the likelihood of these targets already having been achieved for certain categories, the recommendations also came at a time when manning levels in all five companies had started to peak.

Indeed, with quite a few of them soon destined to experience a sharp fall in fortunes as they tumbled from the 'commanding heights' of the economy it was downscaling not recruitment that would become their principal preoccupation in the years ahead as they desperately sought to shed surplus manpower and pare down their wage bill in order to stay afloat in the new deregulated market environment. Nevertheless, the non-implementation of the Mahishi committee's proposals should not obscure the achievements of the nativist organizations in successfully imposing the claims of Kannada speakers to privileged blue collar jobs. While the linguistic composition of the public sector workforces might not have acquired the fully homogenous texture desired by some of the more extreme-minded nationalists, Kannadigas had clearly established themselves as the dominant group—a good measure of their numerical superiority being the status enjoyed by Kannada as the undisputed lingua franca of communication at the work environment in all but the upper most echelons of the factory hierarchy. The right of the sons of the soil to the city had become 'materialized in its most important sense as a right to jobs in the city'.[69]

---

[68] Minutes of meeting between secretary, Commerce and Industries Department, Government of Karnataka and PSU representatives, 3 July 1981.

[69] Nair, *Promise of Metropolis*, p. 254.

LINGUISTIC TENSIONS SURFACE IN ITI

The emergence of the Chaluvali movement on the political scene of the city recast the public face of Kannada nationalism. From being an essentially peaceful movement, it now took on a more violent colouring where resorting to intimidation and physical attacks against linguistic and religious minorities was considered both legitimate and necessary in order to uphold the interests of Kannada speakers. The full blast of this violence would only be experienced in the 1990s, but the seeds of this muscular brand of nationalism had been planted in the late 1960s itself and one of the terrains where it first germinated was ITI.

Kannada intellectuals are fond of vaunting the tolerant, pacific, and open minded impulses of the local people, defining these traits as somehow inherent to the persona of the Kannadiga.[70] Constructing and propagating representations of this kind offer important advantages especially in moments of conflict. If somebody fails to conform to the stereotype, the burden of responsibility for the transformation in behaviour can be conveniently shifted onto the actions of the other. Indeed, it is precisely this justificatory logic that informed the attempts of certain Kannada intellectuals to condone and brush aside the excesses committed in the name of language. It is the 'cunning' and 'scheming' Tamilian (or Muslim, as would subsequently be the case) who by abusing the civility of the Kannadiga is guilty of forcing him to act contrary to his true nature.[71] In other words, the Tamil is a victim of his own misdeeds, somebody who fully deserved the rough 'justice' meted out to him by the Kannadiga whose patience had finally run out. Much the same tropes would frame the interpretation of the language agitation in

[70] According to Desai, Karnataka with her liberal outlook and broad sympathies has always been tolerant and generous in religious and other matters. *History of Karnataka. From Pre-history to Unification*, p. 437. Similarly, a poem by K.V. Puttappa praises 'Mother Karnataka' as a 'peace resort of all people . . . Garden for Hindus, Christians, Muslims, Parsis, Jains as well'. Cited in K.S. Singh, 'Introduction', in *idem* (ed.), *People of India. Karnataka*, New Delhi, 2003, p. xx.

[71] All these motifs abounded in the discourse of the local media as well as in the various cultural products (audio cassettes, tabloids, etc.) that circulated in Bangalore following the kidnapping in July 2000 of Rajkumar, the cultural icon of the Kannadigas, by the Tamil forest brigand, Veerapan. Tejaswini Niranjana, 'Reworking Masculinities. Rajkumar and the Kannada Public Sphere', *EPW*, Vol. XXXV, No. 47, 18 November 2000, pp. 4147–50.

ITI. Not only would Kannadiga union leaders and employees pin the cause of the troubles essentially on the arrogance, parochialism and overt disdain exhibited by the Tamilians for the local language.[72] More interestingly, Tamil workers too, motivated perhaps by the desire to seem at once impartial and different from the mass of their linguistic brethren, would in part introject and articulate an identical discourse.

With some nuances, the theme of the tolerant Kannadiga has also crept into scholarly accounts of the nativist movement. Thus speaking of the Chaluvaligars, James Manor writes that the 'raucous bands' who rode around Bangalore in 'open trucks shrieking outrage at the pathetic fate of the mother tongue' were greeted with 'smirks and hoots of laughter in Kannada neighbourhoods'.[73] Just which neighbourhoods these were and which sections of the population reacted in this manner is something he chooses not to tell us. In much the same vein, Mark Holmström, clearly referring to ITI though the company is not named in his study, states that the language clashes inside the factory were 'trivial' and that most workers attributed it to 'demagogues and loafers'.[74]

The evidence at our disposal, albeit its fragmentary character, totally contradicts the findings of both authors. The disturbances witnessed in ITI were anything but 'trivial'. They dragged on for almost five years during which period linguistic minority groups, namely Tamil, and to a lesser measure, Malayali workers, both being designated as 'outsiders' unlike their Telegu counterparts, lived in a state of considerable fear. Although the systematic campaign of intimidation and physical aggression claimed no lives, it left profound scars on the social fabric of the plant, not to mention its victims, and irrevocably cleaved workers along linguistic lines. Moreover, while the instigators of this violence may well have been 'demagogues and loafers', their actions far from encountering 'smirks and hoots of laughter' enjoyed, on the contrary, the support, tacit as well as open, of many Kannada speaking workers, union representatives and executives. This meant that Tamil employees could

---

[72] Notwithstanding the communist ideology of the organization he represented, a Kannadiga leader of the AITUC union in the city had no qualms in employing much the same essentialist tropes as the nativists, describing Tamilians as 'arrogant by nature'. Joseph, 'Politics of Recruitment', p. 214.

[73] Manor, 'Language, Religion and Political Identity', pp. 172–3.

[74] Holmström, *South Indian Factory Workers*, p. 37.

neither count on the management nor the union to take firm measures to bring the situation under control.

Linguistic tensions in ITI appear to have been activated some time around 1968, coinciding with the twin phenomenon of the growth of the Chaluvali movement in the city and the influx of large numbers of fresh Kannada hands into the factory. The mushrooming Kannada presence both inside the factory and in Krishnarajapuram, the adjoining neighbourhood where several employees lived, associated with the preponderance of local language speakers on the payrolls of the New Government Electrical Factory, a big state government-owned plant situated just a few kilometres away from ITI, would contribute to make the area a major Chaluvali stronghold.

Indicative of these new dynamics, prior to the municipal corporation elections in 1971, it was loyalists in ITI who took the initiative in organizing several processions and meetings in the vicinity of the factory which were addressed by Vatal Nagaraj, the Chaluvaligar leader.[75] These workers also formed the backbone of the Kannada Aikya Sadhaka Sangha, an association professing allegiance to the Chaluvaligars but nominally independent, which had come up in the Krishnarajapuram area and could in times of need enlist the muscle power of Kannada and Telegu youth from nearby villages. The geographic location of ITI, embedded as it was in an industrial and semi-rural milieu receptive to ideas championing the primacy of the sons of the soil, was thus one of the reasons why linguistic exclusiveness succeeded in the first place in striking roots in ITI, and then in cutting such a wide swath in contrast to the other Bangalore-based public sector units. Anecdotal evidence appears to suggest that the nativist discourse did not grip imaginations so intensely in these plants for reasons that remain to be elucidated.

The fact that the reach of the Kannada protagonists in ITI extended well beyond the factory walls given their ability to both mobilize local villagers and workers from neighbouring factories as well as Chaluvali activists throughout the city had important implications. The flow of violence was exclusively unidirectional with Tamil workers remaining passive all through. Despite being a relatively sizeable force within the company as well as in the township, and belying their stereotypical image of belligerence promoted by Kannadigas, Tamil workers eschewed all

---

[75] SD notes 9 December 1970; 20 February 1971; 28 February 1971; 7 April 1971.

acts of physical resistance fearful that it would invite severe reprisals against their families.

Tamilians could not organise themselves and fight back because the township was ringed by villages where Kannadigas and Telegus were in the majority.[76]

As one Kannada worker living in a village close to the township told me,

We used to go in a big group to the colony (township) and go to people's houses and give them a good beating.[77]

Adds another employee:

. . . if one Tamil worker was attacked, none of the others came to his support because they were scared . . . He had to face the music himself.[78]

Although plans to form a Tamil Sena were mooted by a group of young Tamil workers in order to defend community members from attacks, nothing concrete materialized.[79] So to describe these events as 'clashes', as Holmström has done, amounts to a misnomer since one group was perpetually at the receiving end of the violence. At the same time, there was a widespread perception among the victims, and perhaps Kannada workers too, that the state government headed by Veerendra Patil, by echoing the demands of the Chaluvaligars on the employment front, identified with the overall aspirations of the nativist cause and would therefore not intervene to protect minority groups. The refusal of local police officials to register complaints of Tamil workers on the rare occasions when they mustered courage to bring charges against their aggressors, furnished first hand evidence of a partisan state machinery.

When we used to go the police station, they would say who asked you to leave Tamil Nadu and come here, forgetting that many of us were born here.[80]

Why did Tamil workers become the principal target of attacks and not Malayalis? True, in terms of their numerical strength the latter did not represent the same threat as the former; nonetheless, like Tamilians, Malayalis too had been stigmatized as 'outsiders' by the nativist

---

[76] Interview with Paneer Selvam.
[77] Interview with Byrappa (Field notes 2001).
[78] Interview with Iruyadaraj.
[79] Interview with Venugopalan.
[80] Interview with Paneer Selvam.

organizations, accused of depriving local people of their rightful job entitlements. Yet while Malayali employees in ITI clearly apprehended being the next victims of the Kannadigas once Tamilians had been reduced to silence, these grim predictions did not come to pass: not even a single Malayali was subjected to rough treatment. Understanding the reasons behind this phenomenon will enable us to draw attention to the limitations of a purely essentialist interpretation of the agitation. For while the source of much of the violence incontestably lay in the linguistic identities of individuals and the desire to restore Kannadiga pride, perceived as having been trampled underfoot by Tamilians, material interests and calculations, both economic as well as non-economic in nature, played an equally important role in deciding why some escaped unscathed but not others, even among Tamil workers.

We have already referred to the influence exerted by spatial determinants in shaping the course of events in ITI, namely its proximity to pockets of strong Kannada presence where to boot the nativist message had considerable resonance. But the significance of factors internal to the company, in particular the specific manner in which the field of forces was configured can hardly be discounted. In effect, the principal explanation for the patterns of violence, its selective character, can be traced back to the prevailing structures of representation and authority. The issues at stake were plainly those of power relations touching on the right to determine who could legitimately speak in the name of the workforce and who could direct work tasks on the shop floor. Both these privileges, Kannada workers believed, should as a matter of right automatically go to them; both until the late 1960s were chiefly the preserve of Tamil workers.

As mentioned in chapter seven, during the first decade or so of the company's existence, Tamil workers enjoyed a slight numerical edge over their Kannada counterparts. Like the nativist organizations, Michael Fernandes, the ITI union leader, a 'Kannadiga' though not a native Kannada speaker (his mother tongue was Konkani), blamed this phenomenon on the discriminatory practices of Tamil recruitment officials, guilty of 'favouring their people against an equally suitable Kannadiga'.[81] On the other hand, Tamilian interpretations accord with the standard stereotypes popular among them, counterpoising the

[81] Interview with Fernandes.

naturally hard working and manly Tamilian to the weak Kannadiga as manifested in his putative aversion for industrial occupations.

Tamilians because they had come from outside, especially from drought prone areas, would make efforts to find work wherever they could and so a number of them joined factories. Local Kannadigas because they had their own land, own houses, own businesses took less interest in factory work. Working in a factory meant for them that like slaves you had to be inside for 8 hours for just Rs 10. So they preferred staying outside.[82]

Even more caricatural is this opinion voiced by another Tamilian worker:

In the early years, Kannadigas would not come for factory work or any hard work. They would not come out of their house before 10 am saying that it was cold.[83]

Such interpretations while perhaps true during colonial rule certainly did not hold good after Independence as the findings of our sample study underlined. Nevertheless, the greater presence of Tamilians on the company's pay rolls during the 1950s translated into their monopolizing virtually all the positions within the union hierarchy.[84] An identical scenario obtained in other bodies such as the works committee, the fine arts society, the death relief fund and the like. As Fernandes pointed out,

Players in the sports club would all be Tamils, control of these bodies were all in the hands of Tamils . . . there used to be very few Kannada items in a fine arts performance . . . All this was resented by the Kannada population . . . Tamils should have had the foresight to try and accommodate the Kannadigas and be friendly. They (Tamilians) were rubbing it in their own way and had their own sense of importance and would look down upon these people (Kannadigas). This was also a cause for tension developing.[85]

Likewise, the overwhelming majority of supervisory personnel were drawn from Tamil ranks.

Once again statistical data is unavailable, but until 1974, a Tamilian held the post of union president and with the exception of a handful of

---

[82] Interview with Vinayagam.

[83] Interview with Venugopalan.

[84] A prosopographic study of trade union leaders in Bangalore, published in 1971, showed that of the eight men who came from Karnataka, only two were Kannada speakers. The others were in the main Tamilians. Reindorp, *Leaders and Leadership in the Trade Unions in Bangalore.*

[85] Interview with Fernandes.

Kannadigas, all the other upper echelon union officials until the late 1960s belonged to the Tamil community. Moreover, while English officiated as the written language of the union, though even here circulars and pamphlets were printed in both English and Tamil, quotidian activities of the union were conducted almost exclusively in the latter language. 'Union gate meetings, general body meetings were all in Tamil, and partly in English', recalls Fernandes.[86] So even as the linguistic balance was increasingly tilting in favour of Kannada employees, making them the biggest group within the factory, they found themselves in a paradoxical situation of being dominated within the power structures of the plant.

Not only were they constrained to take orders from Tamil supervisors and foremen who typically did not speak to them in Kannada; not only were they dependent on Tamil delegates to defend their interests; but so long as Tamilians continued to rule over the union their own hopes of acceding to these posts, sources of social status and patronage, and satisfying their ambitions of becoming 'big men' in the factory community were virtually nil. In other words, ITI was a microcosm of the overall predicament of the Kannadiga in Karnataka to which we have referred earlier, the dominated status of the language and culture in the broader public sphere being refracted in the dominated position of Kannada workers in authority and decision-making structures. But while reversing the condition of Kannada in the outside world called for a phenomenal imaginative leap, reordering the social institutions of the factory to ensure the primacy of Kannadigas, especially at a representational level, was a task well within reach.

KANNADA WORKERS SEIZE CONTROL OF UNION

Pointing to the underlying power dimensions of the language agitation also furnishes an answer as to why ironically some of its key and most violent leaders were not Kannada workers but Tamilians who, however, had lived all along in exclusively Kannada neighbourhoods. It also explains why a large number of Telegu workers wholeheartedly embraced the nativist cause as their own. For while they may have shared cultural and emotional affinities with Kannada workers, this factor alone hardly

[86] ibid.

sufficed to justify their active involvement in the agitation. Indeed, several Tamil workers reserved their harshest denunciations for the Telegus, accusing them of having incited the Kannadigas to resort to violence so as to further their own ends of becoming union leaders. While an interpretation of this kind once again squares with Tamil representations of the 'weak' and 'lethargic' Kannadiga who needed to be prodded into action, it, nevertheless, conveys Tamil workers' own reading of the situation.

A lot of Reddys (Telegus) started acting as great Kannada champions and they used to come and threaten Tamil workers also. Telegus joined hands with Kannadigas because they felt they could gain some benefits as well . . . Some Tamilians were also involved in the anti-Tamil agitation so that they could get leadership posts (in the union).[87]

Striking an identical note, Venugopalan, one of the rare Tamil representatives who continued to hold union office even after the language conflict, claimed that

the problem was really created by Telegus because they want to come to the forefront. Also some Thigalas . . . who usually speak Tamil joined in as well as a few Tamilians . . . All wanted to come to leadership positions (in the union).[88]

However, the groundswell of anti-Tamil passions scything through the factory deterred Venugopalan from running again for office in the 1969 union elections. In fact with the exception of Kannan, the union president who anyway wielded far less power compared to the general secretary, and was not an ITI employee, no Tamilian participated in the elections that year, persuaded that they risked being severely beaten if they did so. From this point onwards, Kannada employees took over all the levers of command in the union never to relinquish it again.[89] The iron grip maintained by them is illustrated by the fact that in all the

[87] Interview with Vinayagam.

[88] Interview with Venugopalan. According to him, his own friendly equations with a group of Telegu workers coupled with his political connections were what allowed him to escape physical assault at the hands of Kannada activists even at the height of the agitation.

[89] At around the same time as Kannadigas were dislodging Tamilian employees from positions of power in the ITI union, a similar tussle for union leadership occurred at a big Bangalore private sector firm, MICO. Reindorp, *Leaders and Leadership in the Trade Unions in Bangalore*, p. 111.

elections from 1969 onwards, at least 10 of the 12 upper echelon posts went systematically to them. Indeed, the number of Tamil union representatives seldom exceeded more than five out of a total of 115, and barring one or two of them none of the others were able to rise above the level of shop delegates. Even those like Venugopalan who did manage to accede to more important functions in the union hierarchy, having been elected twice as organizing secretary, faced restraints.

I could not contest for a higher post like general secretary because of language problems. I did not want to stir controversy.[90]

One Tamil worker recalled how his father, also employed in the company and extremely active in the union prior to the linguistic troubles, had stood for elections on a later occasion and was trounced.

My father was identified as a Tamilian and so he lost. He was very disillusioned because he had devoted himself to the union cause all his life. He said that he had not worked for Tamilians, but for workers as a whole.[91]

Following their triumph in the 1969 elections, Kannada speaking employees also succeeded in eliminating Tamil and enforcing Kannada as the sole official language of the union alongside English. For a brief while circulars and pamphlets were distributed in Tamil as well in addition to the other two languages. But mounting pressure from Kannada activists brought this practice to an end despite warnings from Fernandes. Removing Tamil, he argued, would impair the mobilizational capacities of the union by further discouraging the mass of Tamil workers, and preventing those who could neither read English nor Kannada from keeping abreast of union activities.[92] That the more radical Kannada protagonists had no hesitations about coercing even union representatives comes to light in the following statement of Fernandes.

There was a group of very vociferous Chaluvali supporters who would see any decision from a Chaluvali angle and if it was not acceptable to them, they would bring pressure on individual (union) committee members and come to the meeting place in a big group and insist on decisions being taken the way

---

[90] Interview with Venugopalan.

[91] Interview with Paneer Selvam.

[92] On the impact of the language agitation on union solidarity, see also Arya, *Labour Management Relations in Public Sector Undertakings*, p. 110.

they wanted . . . Before one committee meeting, they prevented me from going inside until I had agreed to their point of view (about stopping Tamil circulars). *They physically held me back.* I was the general secretary of the union. *There used to be physical pressure.*[93]

As one top executive put it, the 'Chaluvali group within the factory had almost became a parallel union'.[94] Thus, the conflict over linguistic identities between the two communities must be viewed first and foremost as a concerted drive on the part of Kannada workers to stamp their hegemony over the factory public sphere by capturing control of representative institutions such as the union. A decisive moment in the agitation, the takeover of the union by the sons of the soil also signified that the victims of the campaign of violence could expect to obtain no assistance from it.

Most office bearers were Kannadigas so they used to support the Chaluvalis by defending them in enquiries when they were charge sheeted, or pressuring shop supervisors to withdraw complaints against them. Also to get the votes of Chaluvalis, union officials supported them.[95]

Indeed, as Fernandes confessed, 'I knew Tamil workers felt that I was not protecting them enough'.[96] Ironically, Kannada militants' opinion of him did not differ very greatly. Most of them suspected him of lacking genuine commitment to the nativist cause.

But it was not the union alone which declined to rein in the activities of the Kannada militants. Company officials were even more culpable of inaction and if the troubles persisted for as long as they did, the responsibility lay squarely with the former for failing to exercise their vast arsenal of disciplinary powers in time. This in turn further worsened the plight of Tamil workers, virtually extinguishing their possibilities of seeking redress from any quarter, even as it encouraged their Kannada counterparts to act with impunity. In fairness to the management, their ability to press charges against the instigators of the violence was often hampered by the fact that the victims invariably declined to submit written complaints apprehending stronger reprisals from their aggressors in case they did so.

[93] Interview with Fernandes. Emphasis added.
[94] Interview with Srinivasa Rao.
[95] ibid.
[96] Interview with Fernandes.

There were lots of instances of workers being beaten and bleeding, but when questioned by us (the management) they would say they fell down and hurt themselves.[97]

A security report, after confirming that a Tamil machine tender had been assaulted on the shop floor, noted that although the incident had occurred in full view of other workers, supervisors and the charge hand only two persons had initially agreed to come forward as witnesses. But even they had later retracted their statements because of fears that

Venkataswamy (the aggressor) being a member of Kannada Aiykya Sadhaka Sangha might mobilise the whole gang of his party or engage some *goondas* to threaten their life.[98]

The report also added that the shop superintendent, a Kannadiga, despite having been informed of the incident had failed to take any action.[99] So even on the rare instances when Tamil employees gave a formal complaint it proved to be of little use.

It is important to specify here that while Tamilians accounted for the majority of supervisors and charge hands, Kannada speakers dominated executive positions at all levels. Among them the sons of the soil theme is thought to have enjoyed considerable popularity. We have already referred to the important role played by Kannada personnel officials in favouring the recruitment of local language speakers from the mid-1960s onwards. But the support did not stop here. At the prompting of Kannada employees, the company agreed to stop the screening of all Tamil films in the ITI township, authorized the celebration of the Rajyotsava festivities in a big way, introduced Kannada signboards and so forth.[100] More crucially, certain high ranking officials, both Kannada and non-Kannada speakers, strove to harness the nativist cause to production imperatives. In an attempt to solve recurrent labour problems in some shops and improve output levels, they actively patronized the leaders of the agitation, heard out their grievances, and propped them up as *de facto* representatives of the workforce.

[97] Interview with Srinivasa Rao.

[98] Ref. SY/R-19, 27 October 1971.

[99] The worker himself claimed that the shop superintendent had sought to destroy all traces of evidence connected with the incident. Letter to ITI chairman, 7 November 1971.

[100] Celebrated on 1 November, Rajyotsava day commemorates the birth of Karnataka in its present territorial configuration.

The management thought that by appealing to workers' Kannada sentiments, go-slows and production disruptions could be overcome. So Chaluvali activists would be called rather than union people when the management wanted to get higher output. Activists would be called for meetings, thus giving them importance . . .[101]

Shop bosses' motivations for cultivating the Kannada activists thus underlined the imbrication between linguistic and material interests. Executives (not all of whom were Kannada speakers in the first place) backed Kannada employees not just because they shared common linguistic affinities. They did so also with an eye to realizing their own immediate objectives. Pragmatic considerations therefore meshed tightly with affective bonds. This strategy would, however, eventually badly backfire on the management, forcing it to adopt drastic measures against some of the Kannada militants. Still, in the meanwhile it had the effect of unambiguously demonstrating to all sections of the workforce on whose side company officials' sympathies lay.

The principal loci of the troubles within the factory were the two divisions which contained the biggest concentration of local language speakers and where inversely, Tamilians constituted a minority, crossbar and telephone. These were also the two divisions where shop managers had elevated Kannada activists to the status of unofficial spokesmen for the workforce. Directed against all material manifestations of Tamil linguistic identity, the acts of aggression took a verbal as well as a physical form. Tamil workers caught reading a vernacular newspaper or magazine or speaking their language within the factory premises were threatened and in some cases beaten. A good measure of the climate of fear prevailing in the factory, workers, ever ready to accept overtime in normal conditions, began partially declining these opportunities to earn additional income. Instead of working a full extra eight-hour shift late into the night, Tamil operatives now stayed back for only a few hours 'so that we could return home safely before it got too late'.[102] But Tamil workers who had been raised in the state and were therefore proficient in the local language said they had less concern for worry than migrants who knew little or no Kannada.

---

[101] Interview with Srinivasa Rao.
[102] Interview with Yesuraj.

Once two Kannadigas who heard me speak Tamil and came and threatened me, saying that I should speak only Kannada. I retorted that I knew both languages perfectly well.[103]

Another 'local' Tamilian adds:

If you did your work properly and behaved courteously there would be no problems. I would speak to Kannadigas in Kannadiga.[104]

In addition to Tamil workers, Tamil speaking supervisors were equally exposed to threats and beatings. That the majority of supervisory personnel came from the ranks of Tamilians was deeply resented by Kannada workers who believed there was no reason why 'outsiders' should command them in their own state. Many supervisors' insistence on issuing instructions in Tamil instead of Kannada heightened the feelings of resentment and humiliation. All of this created a strong backlash, and if conquering the union was an easier and more realistic goal than occupying supervisory positions by force, the next best alternative consisted in defying the authority of its incumbents. This resulted in a sharp erosion in disciplinary controls as supervisors turned a blind eye to infractions of all kinds, convinced that discretion was the better part of valour. Indeed, the twin problems of poor work ethics and lax time keeping that plagued ITI, assuming massive proportions over time, had its origins to a large extent in the breakdown of supervisory power witnessed during the language disturbances. As one top executive confessed,

insubordination clearly increased with the Chaluvali agitation since a number of supervisors were Tamilians . . . Chaluvali people from one division would go to another division and threaten supervisors and first level managers there so that it would be difficult to identify these worker later and take disciplinary action.[105]

More generally, even when there were no attempts to intimidate Tamil supervisors, Kannada workers, capitalizing on the situation, would refuse to comply with instructions issued by the former, declaring that officers alone were entitled to direct their tasks. While no Tamil middle management or senior executive suffered bodily harm, they too felt the force of intimidatory tactics. A Tamilian who ran the crossbar plant maintenance department, for instance, was shown an organizational chart

[103] Interview with Vinayagam.
[104] Interview with Iruyadaraj.
[105] Interview with Srinivasa Rao.

by a group of Kannada activists. The names of all the Tamil officers contained on the chart had been underlined and the plant maintenance head informed in categorical terms that they would be beaten up in case they sought to take disciplinary action against Kannadigas.[106]

What all this suggested is that overlaying linguistic rivalries also figured the dynamics of everyday shop floor production relations at whose core lay issues connected with the exercise of authority, the allocation of tough and easy jobs, and the distribution of incentives. Indeed, one of the most vicious assault cases involved a supervisor, Palani. He was singled out just as much because he was a Tamilian as because of the partiality he showed in reserving high incentive earning jobs for good workers as well as his chums. Envy at the sizeable incentive gains certain operatives regularly took home also partly explained why they were roughed up. Likewise, Tamil IED men received threats because it was they who fixed job timings while fast workers were warned to reduce their pace in order to forestall the risk of the management tightening time standards. So while the linguistic identities of the victims incontestably provided the impulse for the violence directed against them, to attribute all instances of aggression exclusively to this factor would be incorrect. Economic interests also often loomed large.

RESENTMENT OF TAMIL CULTURAL PRODUCTIONS

Similar incidents of violence also occurred in the township. A group of Kannadigas forcibly entered the house of a Tamil employee and smashed a record player because he was listening to Tamil music on a festive occasion.[107] Noisy scenes used to be created and abusive language shouted outside certain houses, especially those belonging to union representatives. Tamil medium students enrolled in the ITI school saw their books snatched and torn. Highlighting the sense of fear that had come to grip the Tamil population, the son of a worker living in the township, who subsequently joined the company, remarked that people were obliged to lower their voices when speaking Tamil in public.[108] According to another longtime resident of the township,

[106] ibid.
[107] SD note, 23 September 1970.
[108] Interview with Anthony Raj.

We kept a low profile during the language agitation. We would return home directly from work and would not go to the circle (where the shops were located) because we were scared that Kannadigas would throw stones at us.[109]

Not all the violence that occurred in the township, though, was the work of factory employees alone; Chaluvali members from outside also often entered the fray. Nor must one overlook the possibility that acts of aggression committed in the name of language both inside the factory and in the township could sometimes conceal disputes involving monetary transactions. Using force to recover a long overdue amount, to persuade a co-worker to write off a loan, or to settle scores over the distribution of chit fund dividends—all these objectives were much easier to achieve in exceptional moments when violence was fairly widespread and had the sanction of several groups than under normal circumstances. This is borne out by a management letter which claimed that the most brutal elements involved in the agitation lent their muscle power to money lenders charging 'huge rates of interests' and organizers of unauthorized chit funds 'who need a strong arm' to pursue their activities.[110] Similarly, given that Tamil youth had tended to rule the streets of the township until now, the agitation furnished rival Kannada factions with an ideal occasion to dethrone them and take their place. Spatial contentions thus lent an added edge to linguistic animosities.

Before if anybody in the township opposed Tamils, they would be threatened and beaten up. Tamil youth controlled the township. They would not stand in the queue in the movie theatre. This was resented by Kannadigas who started assaulting Tamil youth leaders, went to their houses . . .[111]

Indicative too of how the overall atmosphere of violence could provide the stimulus for acts of violence against other minority groups, on at least two occasions Muslims were also set upon. In one instance, Kannada activists sought to set fire to a room in the ITI hostel, situated in the township, where two Muslim employees were sleeping. 'Outsiders' by virtue of their religion, the two men were also 'outsiders' in the territorial sense: they happened to be Kashmiris employed at the Srinagar unit of the company and who had come to Bangalore to receive training.[112]

[109] Interview with V. P. Raju, 1 November 1997.
[110] Ref. GM(P)/CM-1, 5 November 1973.
[111] Interview with Anthony Raj.
[112] Ref. SY/R/19, 14 February 1972.

The second attack followed on the heels of communal rioting in 1972 in one area of the city, Munireddypalyam. Despite making up a very tiny fraction of the workforce, quite a few Muslim employees, including a senior personnel department officer, were assaulted by Kannada militants.[113] But while this incident could be interpreted as a Hindu-Muslim clash, the religious overtones should not blind us to the underlying linguistic dimensions, less plainly visible but equally important. For while they may have been Muslims, these employees were also Urdu speakers, a language generally perceived by many Kannadigas as no less threatening than Tamil, though for different reasons, and one which would incur the future wrath of nativists in Bangalore.[114]

Nevertheless, the group that suffered the maximum remained Tamilians, and in addition to attacks against individuals, their institutions were also targeted. Thus the premises of the Tamil Mandram were completely vandalized. Of the four cultural associations organized along linguistic lines that existed in the township (the others being the Kannada Sangha, the Telegu Mithrulu and the Kerala Samajam), the Mandram was by far the most active, best funded, most united, and most efficiently managed of them (all four distinctions being acquired later by the Kerala Samajam). Apart from hosting regular cultural events where it is true Tamil artistes, some of whom came from Madras, held exclusive centre stage, a great deal of the organizational energies of the Mandram went into conducting Pongal, the Tamil New Year.[115]

The festivities often lasted up to a fortnight, and the final programme was characterized by considerable pomp and fanfare. The presence of Karunanidhi, the Tamil Nadu chief minister as the chief guest one year, only enhanced the reputation of the event as the most attractive of all the Pongal celebrations held in the public sector even as it redounded to the prestige of Mandram officials. Kannada employees, though, eyed

[113] Ref. GM(P)/CM-1, 5 November 1973.

[114] In October 1994, protesting against the telecast of an Urdu news bulletin on a state-owned channel, riots erupted in Bangalore leaving 25 people dead and property losses of unprecedented magnitude. On the perceived threat posed by Urdu to Kannada, see Nair, 'Memories of Underdevelopment'.

[115] As Nair has pointed out, following the linguistic reorganization of the state, Kannada artistes in Bangalore demanded pride of place in the Ramotsava celebrations which had hitherto been largely monopolised by Tamil performers. *Promise of Metropolis*, pp. 248–9.

the resounding popularity Pongal enjoyed year after year in the township with a mixture of both envy and resentment. Even as they were obliged to recognize the organizational talents of the Mandram in tapping a range of resources, and its ability to instil a sense of cohesion and common purpose among its members, the very qualities displayed by Tamilians also cruelly highlighted their own lacks and inadequacies thus stoking a high degree of resentment. Despite living in their own state, the fact that their celebrations often failed to match the appeal of Pongal was something Kannadigas found galling, an uncomfortable reminder that on the cultural front too they were being upstaged by 'outsiders'. This was perhaps one of the reasons why those who ransacked the premises of the Mandram, besides manhandling its secretary, took care to systematically destroy all the photographs of Tamil artistes covering the walls of the meeting hall.[116] Following the attack, the premises of the association remained locked for five years.

We have already alluded to the company's decision at the behest of Kannada militants to prohibit the screening of Tamil movies in the township. Linguistic exclusivism, as articulated in the belief that in Karnataka only Kannada films should be shown, no doubt partly motivated the demands of local language speakers. But coexisting alongside these sentiments can also be discerned the same patterns of envy and resentment noted above as well as economic considerations. Tamil movies were without comparison bigger crowd pullers and hence bigger money spinners than their Kannada counterparts. This meant that exhibitors not just in the township but in the city as well definitely preferred to run Tamil films.[117] Banning them therefore eliminated the principal source of competition for Kannada films. While this measure guaranteed them a longer screen life, it hardly promised larger audiences.

Interestingly, one Kannada militant, who himself later sought to reconcile his job in ITI with a career in the movie business, acknowledged the technical superiority and sophistication of Tamil cinema in comparison with Kannada films. Yet, it was not fear, he claimed, that had led the nativists to say 'we don't want Tamil films in our area'.[118]

[116] Interview with Balaji, Secretary ITI Tamil Mandram, 23 June 1999.

[117] Responding to various protectionist demands raised by Kannada associations, exhibitors in Bangalore complained that after two or three weeks Kannada films invariably ran to near empty audiences. Nair, 'Memories of Underdevelopment'.

[118] Interview with Basavarajappa.

Nevertheless, he and other Kannada employees are unlikely to have found very palatable the spectacle of larger-than-life cardboard cut-outs of MGR and Sivaji Ganesan adorning the front of the ITI cinema theatre. Or the sight of huge crowds of Tamilians thronging outside the theatre when films starring these heroes were released even as Kannada films struggled to draw audiences.

The high degree of intolerance manifested by Kannada employees as reflected in their endeavours to forcibly expel all traces of Tamil from the public space, to literally reduce the language to silence both inside the factory and in the township, must be seen as a response to what one Chaluvaligar denounced as the 'linguistic fanaticism' of Tamils.[119] In other words, Kannadigas took objection to what they felt was an all-consuming and exclusive devotion on the part of the latter towards their language and culture which in turn led to the belief that other languages and cultures were inferior in status and hence unworthy of consideration.[120] Indeed, the trope of the 'ungrateful' or 'treacherous' Tamilian who had lived in Karnataka for several decades, 'ate its rice and drank its water', but still refused to learn or speak the local language, recurred constantly in the discourse of Kannadigas we interviewed.

One Tamilian living in the township proudly told me that since 30 years he had not learnt a word of Kannada. This irritated me and I went to hit him and abused him.[121]

For more than one Kannada employee, the excessive pride Tamilians took in their own language, and inversely the low esteem in which they held the local language, expressed itself most eloquently in certain Tamilians insisting that the former address them only in Tamil on the shop floor.

[119] ibid.

[120] Describing the modern Tamil subject as suffused with the language, Ramaswamy writes that devotion to Tamil in its most radical articulation demands that individuals transcend attachment to their bodies and lives, i.e., be prepared to sacrifice themselves for the language. Sumathi Ramaswamy, *Passions of the Tongue. Language Devotion in Tamil India, 1891–1970*, Berkeley, 1997, p. 66, 255–6. See also Norman Cutler, 'The Fish-eyed Goddess Meets the Movie Star: An Eyewitness Account of the Fifth International Tamil Conference', *Pacific Affairs*, Vol. 56, No. 2, Summer 1983, pp. 270–87.

[121] Interview with Vadiraj Hatwar.

Tamils think their own language is great and do not give importance to other languages. This is a universal problem . . . If they did not wish to speak Kannada, they should at least have kept quiet instead of showing disrespect to our language.[122]

Quite strikingly, some Tamil workers, both locally born and migrants, do not dispute these accusations. 'Even when they knew Kannada, some of our fellows would talk only in Tamil', admits Venugopalan.[123]

Exclusivist in their linguistic consciousness, Tamil workers were judged to be no less exclusivist in their social interactions.

Tamilians are a bit like Chinese. They don't mingle with locals when they go out of their state. They pursue their own traditions outside, celebrate their own festivals, live differently . . .[124]

The same worker who had grown up in the ITI township contrasted the attitude of Telegu and Malayali residents with that of Tamilians. Whereas the other two groups freely donated to youth who went from house to house collecting funds for the Kannada Rajyotsava celebrations, Tamilians on the contrary not only paid up with great reluctance; some even refused to contribute on the grounds that the celebrations did not concern them. In much the same vein, a Kannada machine tender, charged with assaulting a Tamil co-worker a couple of years before the language agitation broke out, bitterly complained in a letter to the personnel department that two years after having been posted to the shop he had still not succeeded in making friends with any of the Tamilians in his group 'who form a gang and do not like a Kannadiga in their midst'.[125] He went on to add that the Tamil worker who claimed to have been assaulted had 'regularly cut jokes and teased him'.[126]

This last statement effectively touched another raw nerve of the Kannadigas. Almost all those to whom I spoke complained of how the Kannada worker was the object of frequent Tamil mockery and ridicule, implicitly hinting that the sentiments of linguistic superiority harboured by Tamil workers translated into convictions of mental superiority (not to mention physical superiority given their putative propensity to do

---

[122] Interview with Basavarajappa.
[123] Interview with Venugopalan.
[124] Interview with Vadiraj Hatwar.
[125] Personnel File No. 3195.
[126] ibid.

hard work). One important ingredient of this 'superiority complex' resided in the differences in the staple diets of the two communities since Tamilians ate rice and Kannadigas, ragi. In other words, it was not just what they spoke that supposedly nourished the 'higher' intellect of the Tamilians, but also what they consumed. As Arjun Appadurai observes, food has always fulfilled two diametrically opposed functions in India. It can serve to indicate and construct social relations characterized by equality, intimacy or solidarity; or it can sustain relations informed by rank, distance or segmentation.[127]

Thus Tamilians associated rice with a sophisticated food, at once mentally and physically stimulating, in contrast to ragi regarded as a coarse food, one that produced sluggish minds and weak bodies.[128] Through these opposing representations of rice and ragi which the Tamilians successfully imposed given their numerical superiority during the early years, and which valorized one linguistic community even as it devalorized the other, cultural differences became converted into status distinctions.[129] Herein lay the source of numerous taunts Tamil workers tended to direct against their Kannada colleagues. The following quotations from two Kannada workers bespeak the depth of the sentiments of injured pride and self-esteem even as they make clear the idea that Tamil workers received their just deserts.

They (Tamilians) used to say that because we ate ragi *mudde* (balls) we had no sense, that we were ignorant fellows, village bumpkins. *We taught them a nice lesson* . . . Now, those who are suffering from sugar problems (diabetes) come and ask us for our good ragi. (Byrappa).[130]

Tamil workers themselves were responsible for the language troubles . . . They were extremely arrogant, used to make fun of Kannadigas as ignorant bumpkins. They felt that Kannada was nothing compared to Tamil language and literature. They always had a superiority complex. (Govindaraju).[131]

---

[127] Arjun Appadurai, 'Gastro Politics in Hindu South Asia', *American Ethnologist*, Vol. 8, No. 3, 1981, pp. 494–511.

[128] According to Epstein, the prestige attached to cultivating paddy as well as eating rice led many farmers in the 'wet' Mandya village, studied by her, to prefer rice to ragi. *Economic Development and Social Change*, p. 50. Ironically, nutritional discourse has consistently underlined the dietary deficiencies of rice eaters compared to wheat eaters.

[129] Pierre Bourdieu, *La Distinction*, Paris, 1979. See especially pp. 435–48.

[130] Interview with Byrappa. Emphasis added.

[131] Interview with Govindaraju. Emphasis added.

Krishnan, a migrant from North Arcot, who has been living in Bangalore for almost four decades now, acknowledges the provocative behaviour of some of his fellow Tamil workers. Strikingly, in his comments too surface the familiar stereotype of the tolerant and good natured Kannadiga driven to violence after his legendary patience had been exhausted.

> . . . some Tamilians were also responsible for the agitation because *Kannadigas were very calm and non-violent* at first. Tamilians would tease them, say Kannadigas had no brains, no civilization, treat them as lower class, criticize their work . . .[132]

Paneerselvam, a Tamil worker who was brought up in the ITI township, also admits that Tamilians 'committed mistakes'.

> Arrogance was shown by some of our people . . . Workers from North Arcot who joined *en masse* would not mix with non-Tamilians. They would mock Kannadigas saying they were illiterate . . .[133]

Vinayagam, a locally born Tamil worker, voices much the same viewpoint where again we hear the theme of Kannadiga patience running out.

> In some Tamil workers minds, rice eating is higher status whereas ragi is lower class. This is wrong . . . They would tell jokingly that because Kannadigas ate ragi, they had less brains. Such jokes would lead to disputes. *How long will you keep quiet if somebody constantly teases you?*[134]

Exemplifying the 'ungrateful', 'fanatical', and 'overbearing' Tamilian were supporters of the DMK, the Tamil regional party. Not only had these workers sworn loyalty to a party known to be the most fervent champion of the Tamil language, but also to one implanted in the neighbouring state of Tamil Nadu, thereby doubly signalling their extra-territorial allegiances. Besides, a number of these DMK backers had been

---

[132] Interview with Krishnan. Emphasis added.

[133] Interview with Paneer Selvam.

[134] Interview with Vinayagam. Emphasis added. Revealing just how profoundly ingrained cultural prejudices and representations are in individual mentalities, he, nevertheless, adds: 'It is true that ragi eaters are a bit lazy, because it is not easy to digest it (ragi) easily'. See also Chattopadhyay and Sengupta, 'Growth of a Disciplined Labour Force. A Case Study of Social Impediments'. According to them, jibes pertaining to dialect differences and personal habits between East and West Bengali workers in a public sector plant in West Bengal often ended in fights.

elected as union representatives. So it is plausible that they were viewed as competitors occupying positions coveted by but denied to Kannada speakers. It was the combination of all these factors which explained why these workers were singled out for particularly harsh treatment during the course of the language agitation. Quite a few of them would be taken to the toilets and assaulted and their clothes torn.

The open and vigorous assertions of sympathy in favour of the Tamil party inside the plant only served to add fuel to the fire. Electoral victories of the party both in Tamil Nadu and in Bangalore would be greeted by pro-DMK workers with much acclaim and the distribution of sweets. Such actions had the effect of inflaming Kannadiga passions, already angered by the DMK's success, albeit modest, in carving out a space for itself on the city's political landscape. Having opened local units of the party in Bangalore, in 1971 it won seven seats in the City Corporation Council.[135] In the eyes of nativist organizations, Tamilians living in Bangalore therefore had access not just to economic power via jobs in the public sector but to political power as well. Support for the DMK on the shop floor also took more symbolic forms. Thus the plastic sleeves of pliers and wire cutters which conformed to a specific colour code, say, white or blue, depending on the nature of the task to be performed, tended to be replaced with the red and black colours of the Tamil party. Similarly, the edges of work tables were covered with red and black tape in a bid to establish the political identity of the occupants by visually demarcating their territory.

Kannada activists' reaction to all these practices was no different from their attitude towards Tamil: red and black became proscribed colours especially with respect to dress codes. People seen wearing any combination of these two colours were promptly warned to give them up.

When I first joined the factory and had not yet received my uniform, I came to work one day in a reddish pink shirt and a pair of black trousers. A Chaluvali advised me to wear something different the next day. I obeyed him.[136]

Similarly, after being alerted by a friend, Sahadevan, a Malayali machine tender, decided against wearing a new pair of red socks with his black

---

[135] Joseph, 'Politics of Recruitment', pp. 101–02.
[136] Interview with Mohan Kumar (Field notes 2001).

shoes. Michael Fernandes recalled the dramatic case of a lady worker who fainted after a group of Kannada workers surrounded her and insisted that she remove her red and black striped sweater. The efforts of the Kannada protagonists to impose their own visual markers, however, failed to deliver the expected results. After having been persuaded to adopt the red and yellow colours of the Chaluvaligars, the ITI football team staged an inglorious first round exit from a premier tournament which to boot was being held in Bangalore that year. The following year the team reverted back to its traditional colours.[137]

If the Tamil employee crystallized all the attributes of the 'bad' outsider in the eyes of Kannadigas in ITI, the Malayali employee on the contrary incarnated the 'good' outsider. Since their numerical presence was much weaker, and since they neither directly competed with the Kannada speakers for influence within the union hierarchy, nor exercised authority over them on the shop floor in supervisory roles, one could argue that Malayali employees had objectively greater chances of being tolerated than Tamilians. But there were also other important reasons why Malayalis in their totality escaped unharmed during the language agitation.

First, virtually all of them had made the effort to learn the local language and spoke to Kannada employees in their mother tongue. As one Kannadiga pointed out,

Malayalis are not like Tamilians. They learn to speak Kannada fluently and in a very short time.

For the sons of the soil, this testified to the absence of an exclusivist linguistic consciousness, and in turn, a willingness to accept Kannada as the dominant language in the public sphere. The logical corollary of such a posture was a voluntary acquiescence by Malayali workers of their status as a minority or subordinate group in the fullest sense of the word, one which constituted no threat to Kannada since it did not strive to publicly or aggressively affirm its identity, and hence one which did not need to be coerced into silence.

We (Malayalis) were not affected by agitation because we are not adamant about speaking our own language.[138]

---

[137] ibid.
[138] Interview with Sahadevan.

Second, and interlinked to the above point, they were seen as being more ready to freely mix with Kannadigas and integrate into local society. Asked why Kannadigas voiced no opposition to Malayalam films being screened in the township, one Chaluvali backer explained,

we have no problem with Malayalam films because Kerala people mix with us. They adjust with everybody wherever they go. They are not fanatics like Tamilians.[139]

Moreover, in distinct contrast to the Tamil Mandram, the Kerala Samajam displayed much greater sensitivity to Kannadiga sensibilities. It took good care when organizing its festivities and cultural programmes to give prominence both to the local language and local personalities. Kannada artistes were systematically included, Malayali employees made it a point to perform a play in Kannada or sing Kannada songs, and Kannada public figures, including politicians, were feted on occasions like Onam.[140]

A complex picture of the language agitation thus unfolds from the foregoing narrative where we can identify four interlinked and mutually reinforcing strands, each contributing in distinct ways to fuelling Kannadiga animosities. First, and most critically, local language speakers found themselves excluded from positions of authority and patronage in the union and other representative organizations. Second, they believed that Kannada was neither being given pride of place in the public sphere nor being accorded due respect by Tamil supervisory personnel and workers. Third, derogatory references to their supposedly inferior mental capabilities left Kannada employees feeling deeply humiliated and accentuated their sentiments of being dominated inside the factory. Four, even as Tamil linguistic nationalism was denounced for its exclusivist worldview, this very same quality, an eloquent testimony to the passion and devotional zeal it succeeded in inspiring among its followers, was also avidly coveted by Kannada protagonists. Thus the acts of violence that punctuated the language agitation must be understood just as much as an attempt to avenge injured pride and dignity and enforce the primacy of Kannada as a struggle for institutional power, demonstrating in the

[139] Interview with Basavarajappa.
[140] In 1989, for instance, the female Kannada novelist, Pankaja, was invited as the guest of honour for the Onam celebrations. On another occasion, it was the turn of the Kannada Sahitya Parishad President, G.S. Siddalingaiah.

process that Kannada nationalism was no less lacking in the muscular attributes that Tamil nationalism possessed.

MANAGEMENT SACKS INSTIGATORS OF AGITATION AFTER ATTACK ON EXECUTIVE

In September 1973, the management finally decided to crack down. It dismissed one of the principal leaders of the agitation, Thyagaraja Iyer, for assaulting a canteen official. A notoriously undisciplined worker, he conspicuously figured in all the worst cases of violence that had occurred both in the factory and the township. Employed in the crossbar division, he was also one of the 'Kannada' militants (he himself was a Tamil speaker by birth) whom shop bosses had initially courted and sought to promote as an unofficial representative of the workmen. Just how short-sighted and misguided this strategy proved to be was borne out when Iyer and his gang began utilizing their influence to coerce workers in various crossbar shops to restrict individual output in an attempt to compel the management to both liberalize time standards and grant additional overtime. To try and overcome this problem, the latter initially transferred a few of the leaders to non-production shops, a decision which it later admitted was a 'mistake' since the go-slows persisted.[141] By manhandling the canteen supervisor, Iyer now furnished company executives who had at last realized the need for sterner steps, with a convenient pretext to sack him.

Kannada activists responded to this action by obliging the union to declare a one day protest in October which saw all workers taking mass leave.[142] But thereafter the top union leadership refused to stage any further collective shows of solidarity with Iyer, despite confronting tremendous pressure from Kannada protagonists as well as Vatal Nagaraj. The Chaluvaligar leader had plunged into the fray after having been solicited by Iyer and his associates. They, no doubt, believed that the involvement of the Chaluvaligar leader would persuade both the company and the union to settle the problem rapidly.

But once Nagaraj realized that the mass of the workforce would not lend their support to any protest actions in favour of Iyer's reinstatement,

[141] Ref. GM(P)/CM-1, 5 November 1973.
[142] ITI Union circular, 11 October 1973.

he abandoned interest. Iyer and some of his friends then resorted to a final desperate step. They hired a local criminal to attack Ajit Dutt, the head of the crossbar division and the person instrumental in instituting the disciplinary proceedings that led to Iyer's dismissal. On 6 December, Dutt was stabbed several times by a group of assailants outside his house in the township, but managed to survive.[143] Attacks on other crossbar executives as well as union leaders were also feared, obliging the company to request for police protection.

Roughly ten days after the stabbing incident, the company summarily dismissed 13 workers, all close associates of Iyer and like him, key figures in the language agitation. It contended that their continued presence in the factory threatened to endanger the lives of non-officers and officers alike, besides further impairing production and productivity. It also defended its expeditive action, the decision to sack the 13 persons without holding a formal disciplinary enquiry because the climate of insecurity and fear prevailing in the factory made it impossible to adhere by the procedures mandated by the company grievance system. According to an internal document, people were 'mortally afraid of these employees' to even consider submitting written complaints let alone give evidence against them before a disciplinary committee.[144] So in the end, it required an attack on an executive for company officials to wake up to the gravity of the situation and take much overdue measures to restore order, despite knowing that ordinary workers were being intimidated and assaulted on a regular basis for the past five years without any hope of receiving assistance from the management. Interestingly, after planning to organize a strike ballot to protest against the dismissals, the union later announced that it would press the issue through legal channels.[145] Workers were apparently strongly opposed to going on strike, obliging the leadership to back track from its earlier decision.

The company's forceful actions had the desired effect in bringing back stability to the workplace. The language agitation petered out, Kannada

---

[143] Police First Information Report No. 173497, K.R. Puram Police Station, 6 December 1973.

[144] PD note, nd. Clause 17.1 of the standing orders authorized the management to terminate the services of any permanent employee 'if it is no longer required in the interest of the company'.

[145] ITI Union circular, 20 December 1973; Letter from ITI personnel department to assistant labour commissioner, Bangalore, Ref. WPT.27, 30 March 1974.

protagonists clearly worried that they risked the same fate as Iyer and his gang if they continued to resort to violence. On the other hand, the use of force was by now superfluous given that they had achieved their principal objective of wresting control of the union as well as all the other representative institutions and literally reducing Tamilian workers to silence. The domination of Kannadigas and Kannada over all spheres of factory life was assured. From this point onwards linguistic rivalries between the two communities would cease to be a source of overt antagonism.

The ITI Kannada Sangha and several Kannada militants would play an active role in the 1982 Gokak language movement which convulsed Karnataka. But apart from one stray incident where Tamil newspapers and magazines were seized from a shop in the township and destroyed, the demonstrations sparked no other acts of violence in ITI.[146] More significantly, the factory remained by and large peaceful during the 1991 anti-Cauvery riots which resulted in substantial loss of life and property in certain areas of Bangalore. Nor did the abduction in July 2000 of the Kannada movie star Rajkumar by the Tamil brigand, Veerapan, give rise to any disturbances.

Yet, notwithstanding the absence of conflicts in ITI after the 1970s, the language agitation engendered a situation where the Kannada-Tamil divide came to operate as the fundamental line of fracture within the workforce, determining and explaining, to a large measure, workers' dispositions and actions *vis-à-vis* their colleagues. A sign of the power of linguistic consciousness to subsume all other loyalties, including caste and religion, was the cleavage between Tamil speaking workers on one side and Kannadiga and Telegu workers on the other within the Scheduled Caste Employees Association. This fissure has effectively prevented the SC from leveraging their numerical strength to influence union elections by voting as a single, united group. Much the same polarization along linguistic lines has undermined the functioning of the ITI Christian Association which regroups Protestant employees.

---

[146] SD note, 23 February 1982. What is worth noting is that Fernandes publicly opposed the Gokak's movement's demands to make Kannada the sole medium of school instruction throughout the state, his position earning him the wrath of Chaluvaligars across the city. See the two articles written by him, 'Gokak Report and the Minorities', in *Deccan Herald*, 16 and 17 April 1982.

It was through the overarching prism of language then that workers viewed and decoded everything that happened to them and around them not just in the factory but in the township as well. In the words of one recently retired Tamil operative,

even though outwardly we are polite to each other and say hello, inwardly everybody is identified according to their linguistic background. The intimacy and cooperation that existed in the past among workers has been lost ever since the language agitation.[147]

Similarly, Fernandes observes that the conflict put an end to the 'camaraderie, the free social intercourse' that characterized relations in the past.[148] We must be careful not to overlook the sentiments of nostalgia which quite often tends to permeate such statements, the desire to project an idealized and consensual vision of the past among workers and their representatives alike obscuring certain realities. For lest we forget if everyday relations between members of the two linguistic communities consequent to the language agitation was distorted by the domination exercised by the Kannadigas, earlier these relations had borne the imprint of Tamilian domination. If Tamil employees found themselves adopting a decidedly defensive and guarded posture in their quotidian relations with Kannada employees after 1973, something akin to the inverse was likely to have obtained up to the late 1960s.

This is not to deny the depth of the wounds inflicted by the traumatic events of the language conflict which continues to provoke feelings of resentment among Tamilians, clearly embittered at having been reduced to a powerless minority, lacking adequate representation in the union and other factory institutions. The fact that nearly three decades later the screening of Tamil films in the ITI township is still prohibited, despite repeated appeals from the Mandram, is seen by many Tamilians as symbolizing their subordinate status in the company. An even starker effacement of Tamil is its absence from the board identifying the Mandram office in the township with only English and Kannada markings being utilised. As Fernandes noted,

The pendulum had been taken too far to one end by one group (Tamilians), now it went too far to the other end. In the past there would have been Tamil

---

[147] Interview with Yesuraj.
[148] Interview with Fernandes.

songs in ITI cultural activities. Now it is only Kannada ... The language problem did cause a lot of sadness.[149]

However, according to Fernandes, the conflict did not harm the functioning of the union or weaken its bargaining strength in subsequent years, implicitly suggesting that Tamil workers continued to extend support to union activities. Gauging the levels and intensity of rank-and-file engagement is a task fraught with difficulties, all the more so in the context of ITI where not only did no rival organization exist, but where union membership conditioned membership in the credit cooperative society and in turn access to the soft loans and other welfare benefits that it distributed. So we have no means of discerning whether or not the arrival of an exclusively Kannada leadership at the helm of the organization had a negative impact on Tamil employees and resulted in alienating them from the union.

Having said this, it must be remembered that the mass of individual workers regardless of their linguistic identities claimed to have little or no contact with the union, in part because of the nature of production relations in a public sector company like ITI. Kannadiga control of the union is therefore unlikely to have caused a shift in behaviour on the part of Tamil members. On the other hand, at a collective level there are no indications of Tamil workers having stayed away from the various protests and strikes that marked the industrial relations horizon of the company throughout the mid-1970s and early 1980s. The famous wage parity dispute of 1980–81 was a totally united affair, although one could argue that any overt signs of refusing to participate in this or any other collective struggle could have revived accusations of 'treacherous' and 'disloyal' Tamilians and exposed them to acts of violence.[150] In sum, despite the profound schism the language agitation created within the ranks of the workforce, the union's position does not appear to have been fragilized. It continued to function as the principal site where worker solidarities expressed themselves in times of conflict against the company and the government alike.

[149] ibid.
[150] Charges of treachery and disloyalty did surface during the 1980–81 strike. In a bid to break the strike, supporters of the ruling Congress party sought to fan linguistic animosities by accusing Tamilian and Malayali workers of preventing their Kannada colleagues from rejoining work. See Subramanian, 'Bangalore Public Sector Strike'.

CASTE AND WORKER POLITICS

While provisions for the reservations of jobs in the central government for the so called backward classes dated to the last years of British rule, these measures, which formed part of the larger programme of what Marc Galanter has termed compensatory discrimination, received their 'constitutional anchorage' after Independence.[151] In the case of public sector firms, some variations obtain in the percentage of reserved jobs both from one enterprise to the other, and from the quotas fixed by the central government—variations related as much to their specific geographic location as to the category of posts in question. In ITI, all executive posts which are filled on an all-India basis are earmarked to the order of $16^{2/3}$ per cent for the SCs and $7^{1/2}$ per cent for the STs. These figures correspond to their share of the country's total population. As far as non-executive posts are concerned where applicants normally, but not always, come from within the state, quotas for the SC stand at 13 per cent (later hiked to 15 per cent) and for the ST at 5 per cent. This roughly approximates the size of these two groups in the population of Karnataka.[152]

The decision to extend reservations from the administrative services to the public companies was endorsed in 1954 itself. But in a telling commentary on the lack of urgency and concern manifested by policy makers, it became totally mandatory only two decades later.[153] Expressing concern at the restraints protective discrimination were likely to impose on managements on account of the non-availability of suitable SC and

---

[151] Marc Galanter, *Competing Equalities. Law and the Backward Classes in India*, New Delhi, 1984, p. 1, 41. For quota details, see Galanter's monumental work which continues to remain the most comprehensive and perspicacious account of the entire clutch of constitutional policies promulgated by the Indian state to promote the equalization of life chances for the 'Untouchable' castes and the supposedly aboriginal tribes.

[152] The hike in quotas for SC candidates occurred in 1985 in accordance with the census results published in 1981. According to the 1981 census, SCs accounted for 15.07 per cent of the total Karnataka population and STs 4.91 per cent. *Census of India 1981. Portrait of Population of Karnataka*, 1989, pp. 87–8.

[153] It was only after a working group headed by M.R. Yardi, Additional Secretary in the Ministry of Home Affairs had submitted its recommendations that all public sector undertakings should follow the same rules and procedures as government departments with respect to job reservations for SC and ST that presidential directives to this effect were issued.

ST candidates, in particular in technical, financial and higher administration areas, the Ministry of Home Affairs declared that it '. . . would not like to fetter altogether the discretion of the management . . . in the matter of staff recruitment'.[154] What is also worth recording is that even though from the late 1960s onwards reasons of political expediency prompted the government to exert pressure on public sector top managements to provide the SC and ST with their rightful share of employment opportunities, they paid little heed to this issue.[155] Consequently, although the total strength of the public sector workforce in the mid-1960s was roughly equivalent to that of the entire central government, the former carried on its rolls only one-eight the number of SCs that the central government did.[156]

In 1971, the Bureau of Public Enterprises warned managements that the prime minister was unhappy that the representation of SC and ST employees continues to be 'most inadequate' and urged them to take 'vigorous steps' to resolve the problem.[157] But its admonitions appear to have been in vain; a few years later a ministerial document acknowledged that 'the implementation of the reservation orders was not quite satisfactory'.[158] Even after the presidential directive enforcing reservations went into effect in 1974, the BPE wrote:

There is a feeling that the employing authorities do not always observe the Directive in the true spirit and consequently there is delay in extending . . . protection to these communities.[159]

Nevertheless, the effectiveness of statutory reservations in putting a halt to years of exclusion is borne out by the employment statistics registered

[154] O.M. No. 5/13/56-SCT, 14 November 1956.

[155] From 1967–71, the Congress government headed by Indira Gandhi was dependent for its majority on support from SC and ST members of parliament. Lelah Dushkin, 'Backward Class Benefits and Social Class in India, 1920–1970', *EPW*, Vol. XIV, No. 14, 7 April 1979, pp. 661–7.

[156] While SC employees accounted for just under 9 per cent of all central government jobs in 1966, the share of their counterparts in the public sector did not even cross 1 per cent. Galanter, *Competing Equalities*, p. 102. According to Dushkin, once these disparities became public, pressure began mounting on the government to compel public sector managements to speedily implement reservations. 'Backward Class Benefits'.

[157] D.O. No.6 (1)/71-BPE (IC), 8 December 1971.

[158] Letter from under-secretary, Ministry of Communications to ITI chairman, Ref. U. 49022/3/73-FAC, 6 February 1974.

[159] D.O. No. F.6 (24)/73-BPE (IC), 22 March 1974.

in 1975. Though in comparison to the government not as many lower caste members could be found in the upper echelons of state-owned enterprises (Class I and II posts), not only had their presence ceased to be token as was the case previously, but in the lower grades (Class III and IV posts) the reverse was true.[160] More of these jobs went to the SC and ST in the public sector than in the government.[161]

Interestingly, these trends repeated themselves in the following decade. The data available for 1987 shows that while only a portion of the upper bracket administrative posts reserved for the SC and ST were filled in the central government as well as in the public sector, obtaining a high ranking job continued to pose greater challenges for these candidates in the latter than in government departments.[162] Whether this was because the more specialized technical skills needed to run an industrial organization prompted managements to set entry level qualifications that the lower castes could not hope to fulfil for obvious reasons, or because of the existence of more entrenched, albeit covert, forms of discrimination

---

[160] Under the four-tier classificatory system established by the central government, Class I corresponds to senior administrative posts, Class II to other administrative posts, Class III to clerical posts, and Class IV posts covered attendants, peons and the like. This nomenclature was adopted by all the state governments and public sector undertakings as well, despite its lack of pertinence for classifying industrial occupations. Thus in ITI, virtually all production and non-production jobs performed by non-officers were listed as Class III jobs.

[161] SC-ST Employment 1975

	Govt. (%)	Public Sector (%)
Class I	4	1.7
Class II	5.6	3.4
Class III	13	19.7
Class IV	22.6	38.1

Source: Galanter, *Competing Equalities*, p. 103.

[162] SC-ST Employment, 1987

	Govt. (%)	Public Sector (%)
Class I	8.23	4.86
Class II	10.1	6.17

Source: *Twenty-Eight Report of the Commissioner for Scheduled Castes and Scheduled Tribes*, 1986–1987, New Delhi, pp. 107–08.

is a moot question.[163] However, in the case of subordinate posts, not only did the share of these groups surpass the stipulated norm in both the central government and in the enterprises under its control, but their numbers were once again much higher in the public sector than in the government services.[164]

Table 9.1: SC-ST Proportional Strength at ITI Bangalore (1966–96)

	1966°	*1971°*	*1974°*	*1980**	*1986**	*1990**	*1996#*
Class I	1.2%	1.6%	1.7%	5.1%	7.1%	11.7%	11.6%
Class II	1.9%	2.1%	3.9%	5.2%	5.5%	7.7%	15.4%
Class III	11%	12.7%	15.6%	19.6%	21.8%	24.1%	26.4%
Class IV	24.9%	34.6%	40.6%	54.5%	53.8%	53%	75%
Sweepers	93.2%	99.2%	90.3%	87.2%	77.2%	100%	63.8%
Total	14.1%	15.8%	17.9%	20.9%	22%	23.3%	24.4%
Total workforce growth	—	23.8%	15.5%	17.6%	(7.4%)	(8.7%)	(37.2%)

Notes: °as of January 1; *as of March 31; #as of July 1.
Figures in brackets indicate negative growth.
Source: ITI Personnel Dept.

In ITI, the management claimed that it had not waited for the preferential schemes to be officially enforced to enrol the beneficiary groups in fairly large numbers. In the mid-1960s, SC and ST employees

---

[163] An official survey conducted in the early 1960s not only showed that no more than a third of the SC-ST persons enrolled in employment exchanges had passed SSLC or a higher level examination, but they had very poor academic records to boot. Those holding technical trade certificates also numbered under 4 per cent. *Report of the Seminar on Employment of Scheduled Castes and Scheduled Tribes*, New Delhi, 1965, pp. 238–47.

[164] SC-ST Employment, 1987

	Govt. (%)	*Public Sector (%)*
Class III	14.4	18.5
Class IV*	20.1	30.8

Note: *(excludes sweepers.) In the public sector, 77.5 per cent of all sweepers came from the 'Untouchable' communities.
Source: *Report of the Commissioner for Scheduled Castes and Scheduled Tribes*, 1986–87.

already comprised 14 per cent of the overall workforce (see Table 9.1). Given that the equivalent figure for the public sector as a whole barely reached 1 per cent, this was a signal achievement on the part of the company. Its efforts to build a more balanced workforce was also reflected in its hiring policies: if nearly one out of five new recruits between 1965–73 came from the SC and ST community, this figure rose to one out of two between 1974–84.[165] For non-officer jobs, apart from according supplementary weightage to the results obtained by SC and ST candidates in SSLC examinations, threshold entry standards do not seem to have been lowered.[166] But this was not true with respect to executive grade posts. Opposed initially to a dilution in minimum requirements, the management was obliged to revise its stance over time in order to accelerate the induction of the SCs into Classes I and II.[167]

Laudable as all these measures taken by ITI were, they should not blind us to the chronic under-representation of the SC and the ST at the upper reaches of the occupational pyramid (see Table 9.1). The company certainly succeeded in ensuring that these historically disadvantaged groups cornered their share of what one scholar has described as 'middle class benefits' and 'lower class benefits' in the form of access to Class III and Class IV jobs. But when it came to the distribution of 'elite benefits', namely Class I and II posts, the failure to make significant headway was evident.[168] In this respect, the overall pattern of representation at ITI hardly differed from that of the other public sector companies.

This is not to say that the situation registered no improvement. On the contrary, over a period of two and a half decades from 1966–90, SC and ST presence in Class I rose nearly ten fold and in Class II four fold. Still, at no point of time were the statutory targets attained in the case of officer category posts. In 1990, for instance, by when recruitment in

---

[165] Replies submitted to Study Group I of Parliamentary Committee on Welfare of SC-STs, 30 July 1981 (ITI Personnel Dept. files); PD circular no. 3, 12 July 1984.

[166] Identical entry standards also applied to SC and ST applicants and to caste Hindus alike with respect to non-officer posts at the Bhilai steel plant. Parry, 'Two Cheers for Reservation'.

[167] Replies to Parliamentary Study Group (1981). Such a measure had already been recommended by the BPE in 1971 which also wanted special pre-entry training to be provided if necessary.

[168] Job reservations in the administration and public sector represented only one facet of lower class, middle class or elite benefits. These benefits also often contained a political, educational and financial component. Dushkin, 'Backward Class Benefits'.

ITI had more or less ceased, SC and ST persons held less than 12 per cent of all Class I jobs and under 8 per cent of Class II jobs. That a greater proportion had made it to Class I rather than to Class II also implies that upward mobility was a less formidable obstacle for those who had already penetrated the top echelons, namely officers, than for those who were striving to progress to the higher grades from the lower ones, namely workers, because of the siphoning effect.[169]

Table 9.2: SC-ST Employee Occupational Strength

	1966°	1971°	1974°	1980*	1986*	1990*	1996#
Class I	0.06%	0.09%	0.13%	1.42%	1.51%	2.38%	4.95%
Class II	0.43%	0.58%	0.88%	2.36%	2.22%	2.99%	9.98%
Class III	63.94%	67.4%	74.1%	70.5%	79.9%	85.8%	78%
Class IV	22.6%	20.2%	17%	19.4%	9.91%	3.69%	0.35%
Sweepers	12.9%	11.7%	7.87%	6.26%	6.38%	5.07%	6.69%
Total	100	100	100	100	100	100	100

Note:　°as of 1 January; *as of 31 March; #as of 1 July.
Source:　ITI Personnel Dept.

What Table 9.2 clearly underscores is that the backbone of the SC-ST workforce in the plant was formed by Class III employees who contributed to at least three-fourths of the total strength. Even after the introduction of the time-bound promotion programme, no more than a very small fraction could hope to advance to Class II partly because of the limited number of posts available, partly because they did not possess the requisite educational credentials. As the results of our statistical sample demonstrate, (see chapter seven) SC-ST workers constituted the least qualified sections of the workforce. Not only were one out of three persons from these communities uneducated as against under 12 percent in the case of caste Hindus, but the proportion of those who had graduated from high school (18 percent) was less than half the figure for the latter (42 percent).[170] When it came to college education, the disparity between

---

[169] Galanter points to a similar phenomenon in the administrative services. *Competing Equalities*, p. 95, 105.

[170] For a more general discussion of the disparities in educational levels between the SCs and other households, see Geetha Nambisan, 'Equity in Education? The Schooling

the two groups was slightly less pronounced: a little more than 11 per cent of caste Hindus were either PUCs or degree holders as against 7 percent of SC-STs who had, no doubt, benefited from reservations. Very few of them, however, possessed technical training of any sort. Just one out of five SC-STs in our sample was equipped with vocational skills as opposed to more than one out of three caste Hindus.

We must also keep in mind that for certain high ranking positions SC and ST employees enjoyed no preferential treatment. Regulations exempting a range of scientific and technical functions from reservations in government departments and in higher education institutions on grounds of efficiency equally applied to the R&D departments of public sector firms.[171] Thus in ITI, posts of R&D engineers above a certain grade were placed outside the scope of reservations. Attempts to challenge this dispensation by a representative of the SC-ST welfare cell, sceptical of whether all the incumbents of these posts were really 'conducting, directing and guiding research work', encountered a firm riposte from the management.[172]

What is more, notwithstanding the stronger presence of SC and ST employees at the higher echelons of the occupational hierarchy, their overall numbers still remained extremely small. Even as late as 1990, less than 6 per cent of the total SC-ST workforce occupied officer positions (see Table 9.2).[173] Once again this represents a significant accomplishment compared to earlier periods when the figure failed to cross even 1 per cent. Still, it not only shows just how few persons from the lower castes were being directly hired in officer grades. It equally highlights the limits of internal vertical mobility. For most SC and ST employees, the lack of educational qualifications foreclosed the possibility of acceding to the rank of an officer. SC and ST officers who had been able to rise to the

---

of Untouchable Children in India', in G. Shah (ed.), *Untouchables and the State*, New Delhi, 2002, pp. 79–128.

[171] On the wisdom of exempting certain positions in public employment, but not others, from reservation, see A.M. Shah, 'Job Reservations and Efficiency', *EPW*, Vol. XXVI, No. 29, 20 July 1991, pp. 1732–4.

[172] Note to Board, 179th meeting, June 1981; PD note, 19 February 1983.

[173] In the late 1990s, the company throughout its different units counted between two to three SC general managers, six to seven assistant general managers, and around 15 deputy general managers. Interview with Prabhakara, President SC-ST Employees Association, ITI Bangalore, 15 May 1999 and 7 July 2000.

apex also struggled to make or influence policy decisions favourable to their community members at large. As Prabhakara, President of the SC-ST Employees Association at the Bangalore plant, stated

in bodies like the staff selection committee, our people are marginalized by non SC-ST officers who are always in the majority.[174]

More dishearteningly, other high ranking SC-ST officers, he added, had turned their backs entirely on the mass of their fellow employees. This partly corroborates the thesis of a 'Harijan elite'[175] afflicted by a 'phenomenon of wilful amnesia' in the pursuit of individual upward mobility.[176]

Many SC officers do not even talk to SC non-officers or subordinate officers . . . Those who have improved their situation have forgotten the lot of the others. They think they are different from the others . . . These officers do not bother about anything, they just come do their work and go. They are happy with their salary and their status.[177]

According to company officials, their inability to fill the designated quotas in Classes I and II stemmed primarily from the paucity of suitable candidates.[178] We dispose no means of checking the validity of this statement. Similar arguments with reference to government departments at both the central and state levels have been contested by some authors.[179]

---

[174] ibid.

[175] The notion of the Harijan elite was popularized by T. Sachchidananda, *The Harijan Elite: A Study of their Status, Networks, Mobility and Role in Social Transformation*, Faridabad, 1976. Similar arguments about the 'vivisection' of the 'Untouchables' into a 'bourgeoisie' and an 'underprivileged mass'; or of the 'widening gap' between an educated urban fringe and the uneducated rural population have been posited by other authors. For the first viewpoint, see T.K. Oomen, 'Sources of Deprivation and Styles of Protest: The Case of the Dalits in India', *Contributions to Indian Sociology*, Vol. 18, No. 1, January-June 1984, pp. 45–61. The second viewpoint is articulated by Harold Issacs, 'The Ex-Untouchables', in J.M. Mahar (ed.), *The Untouchables in Contemporary India*, Tucson, 1972, pp. 375–410. A contrary argument can be found in Mendelsohn and Vicziany, *The Untouchables*, pp. 252–7.

[176] D.R. Nagaraj, *The Flaming Feet. A Study of the Dalit Movement*, Bangalore, 1993, p. 7.

[177] Interview with Prabhakara.

[178] According to one survey, of the 24,163 vacancies notified to the employment exchanges as being reserved for SC and ST candidates, only 9767, or just 40 per cent, could be filled up. *Report of the Seminar on SC-ST Employment*, pp. 8, 238–40.

[179] Galanter, *Competing Equalities*, p. 97; Barbara Joshi, *Democracy in Search of*

Replying to a letter from the Ministry of Communications in July 1972, expressing dissatisfaction at the large number of posts remaining unfilled, the management declared that despite being given preferential treatment many SC and ST persons failed to meet the minimum standards in tests and interviews.[180] Moreover, very few candidates were being sponsored either by the department of social welfare or the local employment exchanges. Nor was the company receiving sufficient responses to advertisements even when they were marked 'special advertisement for SC/ST only'.[181]

A couple of years later, ITI announced its intention to award special scholarships to SC and ST students in engineering colleges situated near the different units of the company. Once these students had graduated they would be immediately absorbed into the company. This grassroots initiative, however, does not seem to have yielded the expected fruits.[182] Poorly endowed in comparison to government awards, over a period of six years from 1980–86 not even one of the four annual scholarships instituted by the company found takers.[183] Nevertheless, the growth in the intake of SC and ST officers, discernible from the 1980s onwards, seems to suggest that the management of the Bangalore plant took quite seriously the injunctions urging it make 'concerted efforts' in this direction.[184] That it was obliged to justify the limited presence of SC and ST employees in Classes I and II at regular intervals also indicates that the government was monitoring the situation quite carefully and exerting pressure on the company to ensure compliance with the policy guidelines.

Besides, the practice of 'dereservations' was stopped. In the past, if a post earmarked for a SC and ST candidate remained vacant for three

---

Equality: Untouchable Politics and Indian Social Change, New Delhi, 1982, p. 17; M.A. Khan, *Reservation for Scheduled Castes. Gaps between Policy and Implementation*, New Delhi, 1994, pp. 165–6.

[180] The upshot of discriminatory practices, Galanter writes of 'very severe attrition' among SC and ST candidates at the interview stage, though not for highly qualified posts. *Competing Equalities*, p. 99.

[181] Ref. D.O. No. A-14011/3/72-Fac, 11 July 1972; 15 July 1972.

[182] Ref. W/R-SCT/130A, 12 March 1978.

[183] Note to Board, 172nd meeting, item no. B4, August 1980; and 220th meeting, item no. B7, July 1986. The discouraging response persuaded the management to raise the scholarship amount from Rs 4000 to Rs 6000 annually as well as relax certain other conditions. Our sources do not tell us whether these measures produced better results.

[184] D.O. No. COR-H-007, 30 June 1981.

years, the company invited applications from everybody with the result that it invariably went to a non-SC person.[185] But in 1979, the company's board of directors ruled that a reserved position was so to speak 'inalienable' and had to be 'carried forward' regardless of the time it took for it to be filled by a member of the beneficiary group.[186] So while the overall administration of the compensatory discrimination scheme by the government has attracted justified criticism, the dysfunctional aspects of the scheme being attributed to a lack of commitment and political will on the part of politicians and bureaucrats alike to redress recurrent problems, it would be misleading to accuse it of complete indifference.

Under-representation in the upper rungs intersected with over-representation at the bottom. Here again developments at ITI conformed to the larger picture.[187] What we notice is that the reserved quotas particularly in Class IV were exceeded even before the preferential schemes became formally *de rigueur* in the public sector. Between 1966–90, the share of SCs and STs more than doubled, rising from 25 per cent to 53 per cent (Table 9.1). The figure would have been even higher had we included sweepers in this category. A similar growth is visible with regard to Class III appointments: 24 per cent of these jobs went to them in 1990 as against 11 per cent in the mid-1960s.[188]

Another point deserving of attention is the extremely weak representation of the Scheduled Tribes even at the foot of the job ladder,

[185] The statistics are patchy, but the company 'dereserved' 484 posts between 1968–70 of which only a fraction (2.3 per cent) fell into Classes I and II. Between 1976–80, an additional 16 Class I and II positions were thrown open to all candidates. Replies submitted to Study Group I of Parliamentary Committee on Welfare of SC-STs, 17 September 1971.

[186] Note to Board, 165st meeting, 1 May 1979. Dereservations also aroused deep resentment among the respondents of the survey conducted by Khan. *Reservation for Scheduled Castes*, pp. 132–4.

[187] A study of reservations in government departments in Karnataka shows that quotas were reached and exceeded only in Class IV (17.5 per cent). Yet even for these jobs some individual departments failed to meet the minimum norm. For Class III posts, the share of SC and ST employees stood at 8 per cent, while for class II and I posts the figure was even lower at respectively 6.1 per cent and 6.9 per cent. Khan, *Reservation for Scheduled Castes*, pp. 84–98, 165–8.

[188] The massive concentration of SC and ST employees in Class III posts seems to imply (i) a gradual improvement in the educational levels of new recruits, allowing them to directly join in Class III; (ii) the effectiveness of the company's time bound promotion programme in enabling Class IV workers to advance up the job ladder.

not to mention the summit. For while we have spoken all along of SC and ST employees as though they represented a solidary bloc, pronounced disparities marked their respective situations: the lion's share of all reserved jobs went in fact to the SCs. The company complained that local employment exchanges and other public agencies were struggling to send enough ST candidates even for Class III and IV jobs, thus preventing it from filling the quotas for these groups.[189] In this respect too, developments at ITI dovetailed with the broader scenario obtaining both in the government services and other public sector firms where as a rule the 'Scheduled Tribes lag behind the Scheduled Castes' in availing of the benefits of protective discrimination due to historical circumstances.[190] Thus, throughout the period 1966–90, ST employees failed to account for even 1 per cent of the total workforce (see table below).[191] If anything, we notice a decline in their share towards the end, notwithstanding the higher representation in Class I posts.

In a survey conducted in Karnataka in the early 1990s, respondents belonging to SC and ST categories contended that the clustering widely prevalent in the lower categories represented a calculated ploy by government departments and other public institutions to preserve the dominance of the clean castes over the top bracket posts. For by hiring more and more SC-ST persons to fill inferior status occupations, their aggregate share in the workforce would rise and progressively conform to the statutory prescriptions thus enabling these employers to avoid

---

[189] Replies to list of points for discussion with representatives of the Ministry of Communications regarding reservations and employment for SCs and STs in ITI, 1981.

[190] Virginius Xaxa, 'Protective Discrimination: Why Scheduled Tribes Lag Behind Scheduled Castes', *EPW*, Vol. XXXVI, No. 29, 21 July 2001, pp. 2765–72.

[191] Scheduled Tribes Proportional Strength of ITI Workforce

	1966°	1971°	1974°	1980*	1986*	1990*
Class I	—	—	—	0.45%	0.59%	1.36%
Class II	—	0.18%	0.45%	0.27%	0.43%	0.42%
Class III	—	0.12%	0.22%	0.80%	0.86%	0.67%
Class IV	1%	0.75%	0.40%	1%	1.36%	1.19%
Sweepers	—	0.38%	0.38%	0.70%	0.60%	—
Total	na	0.18%	0.24%	0.74%	0.83%	0.68%

Note: °as of 1 January; *as of 31 March.
Source: ITI Personnel Dept.

censure.[192] It is quite unlikely that the ITI management deliberately opted for such a discriminatory strategy. We have already seen that it faced considerable pressure from the government to show results in increasing the number of lower caste officers. This together with the collective show of assertion by SC and ST employees, who had formed themselves into an association to defend their interests, as we shall study, meant that the management's actions were subject to constant scrutiny.

Having said this, it is clear that over-representation in Classes III and IV explained, more than anything else, the unbroken progression in the size of the SC and ST contingent at the Bangalore plant. Comprising around 14 per cent of the total workforce in the mid-1960s, their share crossed the 20 per cent mark in 1980 and rose further to 23 per cent a decade later (see Table 9.1). Even thereafter their numbers continued to grow—in 2001, a little more than one out of four workers belonged to the SC-ST community—despite the significant contraction recorded in overall manning levels, a consequence of the impact of the voluntary retirement scheme. This showed that early retirement, and its attendant financial incentives, held no appeal for SC and ST employees. As the weakest section of the workforce, they clearly preferred the long term advantages of job security and the benefits and status public sector employment procured, to short term monetary rewards.

At the same time, exceeding the official quotas in Classes III and IV could be regarded as a partial compensation or reparation for the large numbers of Class I and II posts that systematically remained vacant. On the other hand, it laid the management open to charges of 'discriminating' against non-SC and ST aspirants, irrespective of their 'merit', by depriving them of the possibility of competing for these lower echelon jobs. Additional concessions granted to SC and ST persons by way of a relaxation of educational standards and examination performances only served to compound this 'discrimination'. In a labour market characterized by conditions of extreme imbalance between demand and supply, and where government employment represented the greatest imaginable good, however marginal the extra gains netted by one group, it still meant fewer opportunities for others.[193] This is to say that although the

---

[192] Khan, *Reservation for Scheduled Castes*, p. 134.

[193] According to Mendelsohn and Vicziany, the share of the SCs and STs in all public sector employment (central, state and local governments) did not exceed 1.5

company's actions were essential and just, from the standpoint of social equity, in helping to ensure the redistribution of scarce resources and opportunities to historically disprivileged groups, they were not cost-free. By enabling SC and ST candidates to garner a greater proportion of lower category jobs than what they were legally entitled to, the management is very likely to have intensified sentiments of resentment among caste Hindu workers already smarting from the effects of the job reservation policy, and hardened the lines of cleavage running through the workforce.

To cite just one example, after it became known that the company was launching a special recruitment drive to make up the shortfall in SC candidates in the higher categories, a pamphlet opposing this measure was distributed in a couple of departments, leading to tensions between SC employees and the rest of the workforce.[194] Even in a factory defined by relatively low levels of skills such as ITI, many caste Hindu workers appeared to be convinced that the operation of a fully 'meritocratic' system would have disqualified most SC workers who were not employed in menial positions from holding the jobs they now did.

RESENTMENT AGAINST RESERVATIONS IN PROMOTIONS

Reservations in government and public sector employment did not merely cover entry-level recruitments. They also encompassed promotions. Simultaneously with the presidential directive of 1974 mandating job quotas in the public sector undertakings, a compulsory quota for promotions came into effect.[195] Thus in ITI, 15 per cent of promotions in all categories were earmarked for the SCs and 7.5 per cent for the STs. In the wake of the introduction of an automatic seniority-based promotion programme in the late 1970s, reservations in promotions ended, but not without provoking an extremely hostile response from the SC-ST Employees Association, as we shall see.

The necessity for reservations was experienced just as intensely at the

---

million people—a figure that represented 1. 25 per cent of the total SC-ST population in the country. *The Untouchables*, pp. 137-8.

[194] Minutes of SC-ST Cell, 6 September 1989.

[195] For details of government policy on reservations in promotions, see Galanter, *Competing Equalities*, pp. 99–101.

promotion stage as in initial recruitment, and for much the same reasons. It constituted an important mechanism for ensuring a greater proportion of SC and ST persons at higher levels who might otherwise have struggled to climb up the job ladder. For notwithstanding the weight accorded to seniority, career advancement in a public sector company like ITI largely hinged on favourable evaluation by foremen and department officers. In quite a few instances, workers were required to undergo an 'aptitude' test, designed apparently to measure their skills. The scope for particularistic prejudices determining decisions was therefore considerable, and the SC-ST Association certainly believed this to be the case.

Claiming that the annual confidential reports where employees' ratings were consigned did not favour the SCs, the association wanted the reports to be discontinued with respect to its members. The evaluations, in its opinion, 'do not always reflect the factual position, but personal prejudices, malice and bias are allowed to come into play . . .'[196] Company officials argued that 'reasonable weightage' was given to SC employees when considering their promotions claims.[197] But this meant nothing in a context where they risked a *priori* being subjected to discrimination. The fact that 27 of the 35 grievances settled by the company between 1978–80 alone pertained to promotions clearly illustrated the depth of SC and ST employees' preoccupations over this question.[198]

While it is job quotas that have attracted maximum public attention, debate and controversy, it is promotion quotas that have stirred the maximum resentment within administrative departments,[199] and probably in public sector undertakings as well, judging by the events at ITI.[200] Caste Hindu workers were extremely angered by the SCs receiving fast track promotions especially when it allowed them to vault over the

[196] Letter from SC-ST Association to Parliamentary Committee on Welfare of SC-STs, nd.

[197] Replies to Parliamentary Committee (1971).

[198] PD files.

[199] Khan writes of a determined attack against promotions through reservations in government departments, universities and state corporations in Karnataka. *Reservation for Scheduled Castes*, p. 173.

[200] Promotion quotas stoked strong passions at the Bhilai steel plant too, observes Parry. 'Two Cheers for Reservation'.

heads of more senior and experienced colleagues. If as the union president Michael Fernandes noted, 'nobody likes it under own's caste if by favouritism or nepotism a junior is promoted', there was every chance of indignation waxing even stronger when 'Untouchables' become bosses of seniors.[201]

This is unmistakably borne out by a petition submitted by a group of caste Hindu workers sometime in the late 1970s, accusing the management of misinterpreting the presidential directives and showing 'undue advantage' to SC and ST employees with the result that other sections of the workforce were being discriminated against.[202] A pamphlet issued shortly afterwards reiterated these charges in even more strident language. Titled 'For Justice', it bitterly protested against junior employees superseding senior

. . . competent persons, not because of any higher qualification, or any extra-ordinary performance, but because they belong to a particular caste. They belong to SC/ST. The policy very much affects the feelings of the seniors . . . whose future will be in dark (sic).[203]

The signatories of the pamphlet, whose numbers and identities remain unknown, warned of the divisive impact of these preferential policies which

. . . will definitely cause disparity and divides unity among the workers . . . (w)hen everybody are striving for the workers unity with a slogan "ONE-UNION ONE INDUSTRY" . . . No person with a good conscience can appreciate and accept the policy which ignores the senior persons, their sincere and efficient work . . . on the other hand the consideration is only for caste and for nothing else (sic).[204]

Interestingly, the signatories added that they had 'never raised any objections' to reservations at the recruitment stage. They only wanted to eliminate 'disparity among workers during promotion'.[205]

Similarly, an important reason motivating the formation of the Non-

---

[201] Interview with Fernandes. Similar fears of having to work under junior SC persons, contends Khan, haunt caste Hindu government employees too. *Reservation for Scheduled Castes*, pp. 70–1.

[202] PD files, nd.

[203] PD files, 8 August 1977.

[204] ibid.

[205] ibid.

SC and ST Employees Welfare Association at the Bangalore plant was the resentment generated by the attempts of the SC-ST Association to fight for the continuation of preferments in promotions. Affiliated to a larger state-wide movement, the Non-SC and ST Association emerged in 1985 to oppose what it called the 'special privileges' the SC-ST Association was trying to obtain as well as to warn both the union and the management from succumbing to the pressure exerted by the Scheduled Caste representatives.[206] The SC-ST Association immediately called for a ban on this rival body—an action the company stated only the government could take since the formation of such bodies did not violate company rules, although it agreed that the existence of the Non-SC and ST Association was a source of tension inside the factory.[207] Ultimately, there was no need for government intervention; after an initial spurt of activity the Non-SC and ST Association ceased to exist but on paper. Nevertheless, its very emergence, its success in mobilizing several employees to publicly identify with its cause all bespoke the powerful sentiments of discontent and 'injustice' promotion quotas aroused among caste Hindu employees.

Moreover, the fact that litigations over reservations touched in the main on promotions rather than on initial recruitment also reflected the sensitive nature of this question. Of the 27 cases reviewed by Galanter between 1950–77, whose focus is restricted to the central government, at least 19 involved reservations in promotions.[208] Based on this evidence, he rightly concludes that the legal wrangles over job quotas 'may be viewed less as communities fighting over entrance into government service than as government servants . . . fighting over opportunities for advancement'.[209] In ITI too, it was reservations at the promotion stage that provoked the most serious legal confrontation, one that produced an unusual coalition of forces to boot, where the management and the union locked hands to counter the challenge launched by the SC-ST Association. The latter's decision to drag the time-bound promotion programme before the courts in fact served as the detonator for the creation of the Non-SC and ST Association.

---

[206] PD files, nd (1986).
[207] PD note, 10 November 1985.
[208] Galanter, *Competing Equalities,* p. 104, 503–04.
[209] ibid, p. 504, 512.

Before chronicling this legal battle, we need to first examine the rise of the SC-ST Association and its endeavours to evolve into an alternative locus of power to the ITI union in defending the interests of SC employees. As it explicitly affirmed, 'the interests of SC/ST cannot be protected unless we as a body are recognized for the purpose of exclusively serving the cause of SC/ST employees, since there is no one to protect our interests'.[210] The ITI union had effectively not considered it necessary to adopt special measures to facilitate greater SC representation particularly in the upper echelons of the organization.[211] Never in the history of the union had even one of the 12 key organizational posts ever gone to an SC person. At best they could aspire to be elected as an executive committee member, but more often than not they languished at the bottom of the union hierarchy as members of the general council, a post which as the SC-ST Association bluntly remarked was hardly one to be reckoned with. Thus in the 1996 elections, if 17 of the 78 general council members belonged to the SC and ST community, only three of the 25 executive committee representatives did so.

Nor could they boast of a stronger presence in any of the other elected factory bodies with the exception of the death relief fund. To give one example, only one of the 18 elected directors of the union credit cooperative society, an extremely influential organization, was an SC-ST person. It is open to question whether even he would have won had this post not been specifically reserved for the SCs.[212] All this went to

[210] Letter from SC-ST Association to Minister of Communications, 29 December 1982.

[211] Complaining of greater discrimination in the union than on the shopfloor, SC workers in the Coimbatore textile mills stated that they were kept out of leadership positions within the union. Uma Ramaswamy, *Work, Union and Community*, p. 106, 108, 111–13. Similarly, as Ghanshyam Shah notes, even in left-dominated trade unions Brahmin and 'Untouchable' workers did not enjoy equal social relationships. 'Caste, Class and Reservation', *EPW*, Vol. XX, No. 3, 19 January 1985, pp. 132–6. See also E.A. Ramaswamy, 'Trade Unionism and Caste in South India', *Modern Asian Studies*, Vol. 10, No. 3, 1976, pp. 361–73. Intent on demonstrating that a well organized labour movement can transcend caste and other primordial loyalties, some of the evidence the author offers, however, tends to run counter to his thesis.

[212] In 1996, not even a single of the eight office bearers of the fine arts society came from the SCs, nor did any of the five representatives of the canteen committee while only one of the eight works committee member did so. But an SC employee who was also the head of the SC-ST Association, occupied the post of president of the ITI officers' association.

highlight the measure of SC and ST employees' alienation from the public sphere of the factory, their divorce from its 'civic life' and the institutions which nourished it.

The SC-ST Association in ITI was founded in 1975 in the wake of the presidential directives instituting job reservations in the public sector. Its birth participated as well in the broader awakening of 'Untouchables' across Karnataka. In response to the upsurge in atrocities committed by the upper castes throughout the state,[213] moves to bring together the different social and cultural groups active among the 'Untouchables' under the banner of one state-level organization gained pace and would culminate in the formation of the Dalit Sangarsh Samiti (DSS) in 1977.[214]

Membership details relating to the association are unavailable. Still, most SC and ST employees at the Bangalore plant appear to have joined the organization at some point or the other, though it is doubtful whether they regularly paid their monthly subscription of one rupee.[215] The principal objective of the association was to oversee the correct implementation of the government's reservation policies by ensuring management compliance. But it also aspired to more lofty ambitions geared to the social amelioration of its members and their dependants. Among other things, it entertained plans to run a school, open a library and reading room, and launch a mutual insurance society to encourage habits of thrift and temperance. None of these plans saw the light of the day.

Nor did it succeed in realizing its goal of usurping the hegemony of the union and securing for itself the status of the sole representative of

---

[213] According to Mendelsohn and Vicziany, Karnataka reports a far higher incidence of caste atrocities than the neighbouring southern states of Tamil Nadu or Andhra. They believe this phenomenon could be related to the influence traditionally exercised in the northern part of Karnataka by Maharashtrian culture, a state which ranked high on the national list for atrocities committed against 'Untouchables'. *The Untouchables*, p. 75.

[214] Simon Charsley, 'Caste, Cultural Resources and Social Mobility', in S. Charsley and G.K. Karanth (eds.), *Challenging Untouchability. Dalit Initiative and Experience from Karnataka*, New Delhi, 1998, pp. 44–71; Ambrose Pinto, 'Karnataka: Atrocities on Dalits; Dalit Sangarshan Samithi's Response', in W. Fernandes, *The Emerging Dalit Identity. The Reassertion of the Subalterns*, New Delhi, 1996, pp. 109–21.

[215] In the mid-1990s, the association claimed a nominal membership of around 2100 employees, or between 85 to 90 per cent of the total SC and ST strength at the Bangalore plant. Interview with Prabhakara.

SC and ST employees. Despite repeatedly renewing its demands for recognition, these were all turned down by the management. According to the latter, the government had issued strict orders prohibiting the recognition of all employees' organizations based on caste or religion. To buttress its demand, the association cited the pronouncements of the commissioner for ST-ST disapproving the government's decision and pointing out that the SC and ST employees had 'distinctive interests' which did not receive adequate attention from the general unions.[216]

Company officials, however, remained inflexible. Sharing the government's views, they feared that legitimizing the SC-ST Association by granting it formal representative status could cause discord within the factory, create an unhealthy precedent prompting the formation of other particularistic bodies, and undermine the authority of the union. Emphasizing the monopoly over bargaining rights exercised by the union, it made clear to the association that 'whatever problems they have should come through the union'.[217] Thus instead of seeking to fragilize the established union by propping up a rival faction, a path that many companies would all too cheerfully have embarked upon, the management, on the contrary, strove to uphold the stability of the union perhaps because it felt that its own interests would be best preserved this way.

Attempts by the association to acquire the other trappings of institutional power available to the union such as the right to check-off and office accommodation also ended in failure. Nevertheless, following a *dharna* staged outside the ITI corporate office in 1984 which attracted a fair deal of media attention, it was able to obtain a two-room building in the township to house its office. Another of its long standing demands to restructure the SC-ST Cell was settled as well, and the number of SC delegates hiked from one to two to sit alongside the three company nominated officials, all caste Hindus. A by-product of the presidential directives which stipulated the creation of a cell in all public sector companies, the function of this body was notably to monitor the progress of the implementation of reservations and to record and settle individual

---

[216] ITI SC-ST Welfare Association memorandum to Parliamentary Committee on SC-ST Welfare, 28 June 1986. According to the SC-ST commissioner in 1975, not even one instance of a general union raising the issue of implementation of job reservations had come to his notice. Cited in Galanter, *Competing Equalities*, p. 508.

[217] P&A/IR/G-20, 30 January 1978; PD circular no. 2363, 4 March 1983.

grievances of SC and ST employees. But wrangling over the size of SC representation persisted just as did complaints about the incapacity of the cell to tackle anything other than minor problems.[218]

At the same time, the association pressed for an increase in the quota of houses earmarked for SC and ST employees in the township from 10 per cent to 22.5 per cent.[219] As it stated, its members not only often lived in sordid conditions for want of sufficient means. Even when they could afford to pay for better quality accommodation, caste Hindu landlords refused to rent it to them once their identities became known.[220] Worried perhaps about the protests conceding this demand could elicit from caste Hindu workers, the personnel department declined. But in the early 1990s, imitating the example of a few other Bangalore-based public sector companies, it decided to grant scholarships to the children of SC and ST employees enrolled in professional courses like engineering, medicine and dentistry. The company's financial woes, though, meant that the scholarships were quite poorly endowed: in some years, each student barely received Rs 100 a month.

Another demand, more symbolic in nature but no less significant, raised by the association called for declaring the birthday of Bhimrao Ambedkar, 14 April, a holiday. Here again the response of the management reflected the same blend of ambivalence and half heartedness that characterized some of its other decisions. While agreeing in principle to the suggestion, it declined to make the holiday a permanent fixture thus obliging the association to fight for it every year. Besides, the commemoration was combined with the Tamil New Year. So once in every four years, when the Tamil New Year preceded Ambedkar's birthday by a day, the latter event was only declared a 'restricted' holiday (i.e., the company would remain open but employees who wished to absent themselves were free to do so). Since the union also did not think it worthwhile to push the issue, the management faced no pressure to celebrate what was after all the birthday of a key national figure on a more befitting scale.

[218] PD notes, 9 May 1988; 2 February 1994.

[219] SC-ST Association memorandum to ITI managing director, 7 March 1983; Memorandum to Parliamentary Committee (1986).

[220] The maximum discrimination Scheduled Caste millhands in Coimbatore complained of facing was on the residential front. Ramaswamy, *Work, Union and Community*, p. 108, 111, 113.

In 1979, ITI introduced the Time Bound Promotion programme (TBP) with a view to terminating years of intermittent conflict entailed by the progressive constriction of mobility opportunities as production operations stabilized. Since the programme guaranteed the principle of automatic career advancements for everybody regardless of vacancies, the management announced the abrogation of reservation in promotions. The decision immediately saw the SC-ST Association filing a writ petition challenging the constitutional validity of the TBP. Without reservations, it argued quite legitimately, opportunities for SC workers to become officers, or to even move to the top worker grades would sharply diminish given the modalities of the new scheme.

The top management, however, informed the SC-ST Association that the government had endorsed its stand that automatic promotions rendered quotas superfluous.[221] It also subsequently pointed out that the TBP had procured substantially greater benefits for the SCs, and workers in general, than would have been the case had the scheme not existed. Going by the company's calculations, between 1979–87 SC and ST employees had received over 4000 promotions or 20 per cent of the total, whereas under the earlier dispensation, the figure would not have exceeded 500.[222] But it omitted to mention that barely 3 per cent of all non-officers who had risen to officer ranks were SCs, and that their share of promotions to the highest worker grades failed to exceed 11 per cent.[223] In other words, SC beneficiaries of the TBP consisted in the main of lower category employees, thus confirming the association's misgivings about the new scheme.

Nevertheless, as a concessionary gesture, attendance norms for SC and ST employees were relaxed by 20 per cent in order to improve their progression prospects. Firm data proving absenteeism levels to be much higher among these groups, particularly on account of alcoholism, is unavailable. But impressionistic evidence, and information relating to salary attachments, does suggest this is the case among sweepers and

[221] Ref. No.6(7)/80-BPE (GM-I) SC-ST Cell, 8 March 1983; OM No.6/27/85-BPE (SC/ST-Cell), 29 June 1987.
[222] Barring 1982 when 15.2 per cent of all promotions went to SC and ST employees, in no other year did their share drop below 18.5 per cent. PD files.
[223] Karnataka High Court ruling on writ petition No. 5700/1980 and writ petitions Nos. 4916–4918/1980, 12 January 1990. The figures are for the period 1979–89.

others performing menial tasks.[224] At the same time, a confidential circular put out by the corporate office advised executives in the different plants that '. . . before declaring the employee belonging to SC/ST community "unfit" for promotion, due consideration should be given to the fact that they belong to those communities (sic)'.[225] Paternalist and condescending as the tone of this advice certainly was, it at least had the merit of warning individual officers from too zealous an application of the promotion regulations.

More crucially, in 1981, after discussions with the union, the management wrote to the government asking for permission to reduce by one year, the promotion span for SC and ST employees. Thus an SC labourer in the lowest grade would have had to wait six years and not seven like the rest of his colleagues before climbing to the next grade. A concession of this order, the management argued would contribute substantially to allaying the apprehensions of SC employees that the TBP was detrimental to their interests.[226] But after a three year-long delay, the authorities finally vetoed the proposal for unspecified reasons.[227]

In 1990, a full decade after the SC-ST Association had submitted its first writ petition, the Karnataka High Court passed a judgment in its favour. The court ruling not only ordered the company to restore the principle of reservations in promotions. It also wanted the reservations to be applied with retrospective effect—a decision which if implemented would have seen a virtual newcomer leapfrogging over a worker 10 or 15 years his senior. In the words of Fernandes,

there would have been a real upheaval in the factory. Other workers would have stopped doing work.[228]

Alarmed at the repercussions the judgment was bound to have on the industrial relations climate, the management promptly filed a counter appeal in the Supreme Court. It also persuaded the union to be a party

[224] Parry claims that overall SC workers at Bhilai possessed attendance records no worse than those of caste Hindus and in some instances were even more conscientious. 'Two Cheers for Reservation'.

[225] Note to Board, 202nd meeting, item no. C4, April 1984.

[226] Minutes of 180th meeting of Board, 26 August 1981; Letter from ITI chairman to Ministry of Communications, 30 September 1981.

[227] Ref. DM No.6/7/80-BPE (SC-ST Cell), 18 October 1984.

[228] Interview with Fernandes.

to the legal action on the grounds that a failure to involve itself would be interpreted by the Court as a sign of lack of interest and incite the former to 'freeze' the TBP. Valid as this contention was, the union's appearance as a litigant alongside the company would, however, have the effect of heightening antagonisms between it and the SC-ST Association.

Already on one occasion in the past, association representatives had *gheraoed* a top union official. A meeting between the union executive committee and the SC-ST Association where the latter's demand to be associated in all meetings with the management was rejected, had also ended in a 'lot of shouting, noisy scenes, etc'.[229] Nor had union leaders reacted kindly to periodic rhetorical blasts branding them as 'exploitative feudal caste Hindu lords' who in collusion with the management were determined to deprive the SCs of their rightful gains.[230] Association officials in turn would blame the union for 'spreading propaganda that we are corrupt. This is believed by our members since they are not very educated'.[231]

At the same time, the High Court verdict rekindled animosities among caste Hindu workers. A section of employees organized themselves into what they called the 'Save TBP Committee'. An appeal was launched to collect funds to meet the costs of a writ petition they planned to file in the Supreme Court to try and get the High Court judgment overturned. Another petition titled 'Equality and Opportunity' alleged that implementing the High Court orders would not only defeat the very idea of equality enshrined in the constitution. It would also result in the company falling 'sick' for

... if SC/ST are promoted after two years of service while other workers have to wait five to seven years, the question of efficiency of the administration of this industry will become a laughing stock (sic).[232]

Warning that the 'silence of a volcano should not be taken for granted', the petition urged all caste Hindu employees to sign it and send it to the chairman.[233] In the end, the volcano never erupted as charge sheets issued by the management quelled the activism of the 'Save TBP Committee'

---

[229] SD report, 24 July 1984.
[230] PD files.
[231] Interview with Prabhakara.
[232] PD files, nd (1990).
[233] ibid.

militants. Still, all these activities once again testified as much to the tide of resentment flowing through caste Hindu workers as to the deeply divisive impact of promotion quotas on the labour force.

In 1993, the Supreme Court quashed the High Court settlement. The judges upheld the arguments of both the company and the union that reservations were not necessary since the TBP assured all workers of automatic promotions. They also concurred that but for the scheme opportunities for upward mobility for SC workers and the others alike would have been severely curtailed.[234] But the court verdict neither succeeded in pulling the curtain down on the controversy nor precluded other legal battles.

A few years later, the SC-ST Association again raised the matter before the industrial tribunal. The decision of the tribunal prohibiting the management from promoting certain categories of employees until a final ruling had been delivered saw tensions mounting anew within the factory. Ultimately, a high court order staying the award of the industrial tribunal helped to temporarily resolve the impasse.[235] But attempts to improve relations between the SC-ST Association and the union by arriving at a durable compromise over the entire vexatious subject of reservations in promotions failed to make much headway. A proposal by the former recommending a reduction of one to two years in promotion spans for SC and ST employees is thought to have secured the backing of the top union leadership. But the executive committee, perhaps angered as much by the association's litigational activism as by what it considered, not always wrongly, to be intemperate attacks on the union, flatly rejected the proposal.

Nor have the fortunes of the SC-ST Association itself shown signs of flourishing with any great vigour. By Prabhakara's own admission, in the wake of the Supreme Court judgment its activities have declined paralleling the flagging interest of the membership. Since 1993 no elections have been held, and the association is strapped for cash with the majority of the members rarely paying their subscription, though

they always ask us to provide accounts . . . We tell our people that they are paying the union which is not fighting for their cause, but not paying the association.[236]

---

[234] Supreme Court ruling on civil appeal Nos. 4672–75 of 1990, 21 September 1993.

[235] Karnataka High Court order on Industrial Dispute No.7/94, 3 March 1999.

[236] Interview with Prabhakara.

Symbolizing its condition, the association's office in the township which it fought so hard to obtain remains permanently locked now. Aware that transforming itself into a rival union, and a minority one at that with no bargaining rights, rather than yielding advantages would only succeed in intensifying the hostility of the union and caste Hindu employees, the association has decided against embracing this course of action. It is equally aware that the totality of SC and ST employees in the plant will not join a Scheduled Caste union. For this would mean quitting the main union and in turn losing the monetary benefits they derive as members of the union-controlled credit cooperative society.

Our members have a personal loyalty to union officials who as credit cooperative society directors sanction loans for them. I can talk of self respect and constitutional rights, but a worker is more bothered whether his loan is sanctioned quickly or some other material help he requires is tended to . . .[237]

Much the same reasons also militated against the Scheduled Castes developing into a real force to be reckoned with during the union elections. In principle, by voting as a cohesive, solidary bloc they could expect to exert pressure on caste Hindu candidates to consider their interests more favourably. But at these crucial moments

. . . we are seldom united . . . We can act as a minority union . . . but this requires awareness of the membership a willingness to sacrifice.[238]

For the moment the 'sacrifice' is disproportionately shared among a small group of hard pressed volunteers who devote considerable time and energy as well as financial resources in order to ensure the survival of the association. As Prabhakara points out, being formally endowed with the status of an association as opposed to that of an union operates as a handicap since 'members' psychological commitment is limited'.

. . . Because our fight does not give continuous results, members lose interest. They are only interested in short term gains. When the problems are solved, they stop coming to the association. This is particularly true of high level officers . . .[239]

---

[237] ibid.
[238] ibid.
[239] ibid.

ANTAGONISTIC RELATIONS BETWEEN CASTE HINDU AND SC WORKERS

Reservations undeniably contributed to the economic and social betterment of SC-ST employees by providing them with good salaries, perquisites, job security, prestige and patronage. But did it guarantee them acceptance and genuine integration into the institutional culture of the factory? Relations between the SCs and caste Hindus, irrespective of whether they were officers or non-officers, both inside the factory and in the township were characterized by a diffuse but persistent undercurrent of conflictuality. Both groups seem to have drawn clear lines of separation signifying a complete absence of social interactions between them. Graphically symbolizing the rejection and stigmatization they continued to encounter, SC workers invariably dined alone in the factory canteen as did quite a few officers.[240] The story was no more encouraging in the township. As Prabhakara sadly admitted,

there are no occasions when our people and Hindus are invited to the same function . . . To change the attitude of caste workers is a very time consuming process.[241]

Scheduled Caste employees complained of being subject to discriminatory practices at the hands of both the management and other workers. Company officials in turn accused them of 'crying wolf' in order to escape punishment for acts of indiscipline, while caste Hindu workers alleged they were invariably victims of false charges foisted by the SCs who abused the civil rights legislation specifically enacted by the government in their favour. The number of cases of discrimination reported by SC employees do not seem to be very high: exact statistics are unavailable, but from our sources, we have been able to identify no more than a total of 20 complaints over a period of two decades.[242] So

[240] On the permanent sense of devaluation and alienation experienced by various categories of SC employees in work environments, see the poignant testimonies in Issacs, 'The Ex-Untouchables'; and Ramesh Kamble, 'Untouchability in Urban Setting. Everyday Social Experience of Ex-Untouchables in Bombay', in *Untouchables and the State*, pp. 171–204.

[241] Interview with Prabhakara. Social segregation based on caste ties does not, however, seem to have to been exclusive to the ITI township. See Chattopadhyay and Sengupta, 'Growth of a Disciplined Labour Force'; and Joshi, *Democracy in Search of Equality*, pp. 95–6.

[242] Of the 16 grievances registered by the SC-ST Cell from 1993-95, just two pertained to charges of discrimination.

we must be careful against overemphasizing the prevalence of overt caste prejudices, just as we must not underestimate how deep the roots of particularistic prejudice ran among caste Hindu employees, even when they did not always push their way to the surface. Yet, overall a pervasive sentiment of mutual suspicion and sullen hostility, each group rancorous for different reasons of the other's position and 'privileges', definitely clouded relations between caste Hindus and the SCs in ITI.

If reservation policies at both the initial recruitment and the promotion stage, conjoined with the protracted legal tug-of-war involving the union and the SC-ST Association, contributed in no small manner to permanently fuelling tensions, another factor played an equally decisive role. This was the new found sense of assertion manifested by the 'Untouchables', not just in ITI, but throughout the country, determined to demand and fight for what D.R. Nagaraj has described as 'their structural rights as well as their right to social and cultural space'.[243] This assertiveness was deeply resented and resisted by the clean castes; the modest empowerment of these historically disadvantaged groups, through a combination of compensatory discrimination programmes and anti-disability laws, plus the vigilance exercised by various 'Untouchable' organizations posed a challenge to their own power and self-image of superiority.[244] Indeed, a couple of authors have equated the increasing tide of violence experienced by the 'Untouchables' in several Indian states partly to a caste Hindu backlash against preferment policies and the rising economic and status levels enjoyed by certain sections of the lower caste.[245]

Within the workplace, reaffirmations of upper caste authority may no longer have assumed the form of openly abusing an SC sweeper or labourer as a '*chandala*', a '*holeya*' or a '*madiga*', because of fear of the stiff penalties this offence could attract (even though the law did not always deter the use of such invectives). [246] Still, other affronts to their dignity

---

[243] Nagaraj, *The Flaming Feet*, p. 36.

[244] A telling illustration of clean caste indignation, one author claims that 'Untouchables' in Karnataka have 'developed an offensive/belligerent attitude towards all castes in public life and this has created a negative public image'. The term 'public' as defined here, no doubt, excludes the 'Untouchables'. G. Thimmaiah, *Power Politics and Social Justice. Backward Castes in Karnataka*, New Delhi, 1993, p. 155.

[245] Mendelsohn and Vicziany, *The Untouchables*, chapter 2; P.S. Krishnan, 'Untouchability and Atrocities', in *Untouchables and the State*, pp. 272–89.

[246] A highly opprobrious term, designed to emphasize the ritual impurity of the

persisted. Citing one such example, the SC-ST Association alleged that the head of the sanitation department, incensed by the reservation policy, had sworn to work the sweepers so hard that he would

> take out your (the sweepers') life for the salary that is paid here . . . My son is working in a Private Sector and earning Rs 700, though I am upper caste, but you Scheduled Caste fellows join as Sweepers in Public Sector and earn more than my son's salary.[247]

Even if we assume for the sake of argument that the allegation was fabricated, it nevertheless offered an illuminating insight into SC perceptions of caste Hindu perceptions of how compensatory discrimination had impinged on the latter group's interests. In much the same vein, the head of the security department is reported to have rebuked an SC guard who had complained against a caste Hindu colleague that

> you SC people staying in a slum area come with a begging bowl to secure a job and after getting a job you become great (sic).[248]

Here again we notice that it is resentment at the status mobility employment in the public sector is viewed as having provided to the SCs which lay at the heart of the offensive remarks made by the security officer. It was as though these disprivileged categories would have continued to accept their traditional place at the bottom of the social order and grant customary deference and respect to their 'superiors' but for the greater upward mobility they now derived from official policy prescriptions.

Such behaviour, however, was not confined to junior level managers. The imprint of deeply ingrained caste values found equally strong expression in the prejudices articulated by caste Hindu employees towards

---

'Untouchables', Chandalas are the lowest of the 'Untouchable' castes, being assigned the task of handling corpses. The term literally means 'eaters of dogs'. Louis Frédéric, *Dictionnaire de la civilisation indienne*, Paris, 1987, p. 269. Holeyas and Madigas are the two principal 'Untouchable' castes found in Karnataka. Derived from *hola*, a Kannada word for a dry crop field, holeya designates a man working on such a field. Despite the putative higher status of the Holeyas since they belong to the right hand castes, unlike the Madigas, part of the left hand castes, scholars claim that far stronger pejorative connotations attach to the term Holeya than to Madiga. Simon Charsley and G.K. Karanth, 'Dalits and State Action: The SCs', in *Challenging Untouchability*, pp. 19–43.

[247] Memorandum to Parliamentary Committee (1986).

[248] Minutes of SC-SC Cell, 17 June 1987.

their SC colleagues and the harassment they occasionally visited upon the latter. Thus Chikanna, an SC labourer in the moulding shop suffering from periodic mental disorders, was the object of repeated insults and taunts. Workers were in the habit of calling him 'Andhra *Thothi*'; although he had orally complained on several occasions, the supervisor as well as higher officers declined to take action against these workers.[249] Transferred later to another department, he was charge sheeted for getting into a fight with two caste Hindu co-workers. A disciplinary committee, however, cleared him of all wrongdoing and laid the blame squarely on the other two men. Besides harassing him regularly, they were found to have abused and assaulted Chikanna after he had refused to go and call one of them to the telephone, saying he was not their 'domestic servant'.[250] Once more, it is an act of assertion by an SC person, an attempt to transcend the position of subordination 'ritually' assigned to him, that had stung the ire of upper caste workers, unaccustomed and unwilling to countenance such forms of 'defiance'.

Our second example of caste prejudice is of a different and more complex nature. Manohar, a qualified SC worker, filed a complaint against Ramu, a security guard, who is reported to have addressed a caste Hindu worker within Manohar's earshot as a '*holeya*' and a '*madiga*' bastard in a deliberate attempt to provoke and insult him. The caste Hindu worker, assured of his 'twice born' status, treated the matter as a joke. But when Manohar cautioned Ramu against referring to the SCs in such a demeaning manner in public, the latter 'left in a huff'.[251] He also subsequently denied having uttered any such remarks. After an internal enquiry, the security department, however, confirmed Manohar's version of the event and expressed regret that 'such words have come out from the mouth of security staff who is supposed to give protection to the oppressed Class (sic)'.[252]

It is quite possible that the incident had no other significance apart from furnishing a supplementary illustration of prejudicial attitudes inside the factory, and involved nobody else but the two men. Yet another

---

[249] *Thothi* is a variation of a caste name given to 'Untouchable' scavengers whose job consisted of removing human excreta and carrying it in baskets on their heads.

[250] SD files case No. 7/87, 9 and 20 January 1987.

[251] SD files, 27 September 1985.

[252] SD files, 8 October 1985.

reading of the facts suggests that what appeared on the surface as essentially a personal dispute might in fact also have been a refraction of the larger ongoing institutional conflict between the union and the SC-ST Association with Manohar and Ramu being engaged in a proxy war of sorts. For if the former was an active member of the association, the latter happened to be a union executive committee member. Besides, the two men had enjoyed friendly relations for the last couple of years, but according to Manohar, they had become progressively estranged.

He (Ramu) has been behaving indifferently with me as if I am his enemy. As days passed I understood that it was due to his inherent dislike for SC/STs of which association I am an Office Bearer (sic).[253]

Lacking other evidence, we have no option but to accept Manohar's statement at face value. But given that the security department, not always reputed for being sympathetic towards the SCs, had corroborated Manohar's story, there is no reason not to believe the motives ascribed by him for Ramu's actions.

It goes without saying that whatever ill treatment, humiliation and stigmatization the SCs faced, it was those situated at the bottom of the occupational hierarchy who bore the brunt of it. The fact that many of them were illiterate, indebted, given to heavy drinking and sanctioned regularly by the management for various offences made them all the more easy objects of rejection, scorn, and mockery.[254] Particularly vulnerable were sweepers. Although there had been a progressive decrease in the intake of sweepers from the SCs, the majority of sweepers in ITI still continued to come from these communities to a point where they even exercised a complete monopoly over this occupation by default in certain periods.[255] The mechanics of an invidious and enduring social equation, linking the 'Untouchables' to scavenging inevitably meant that at least some of them would be slotted by the company into the same ritually 'defiling' tasks that they had traditionally performed in the caste

---

[253] SD files, 27 September 1985.

[254] In our statistical survey, the SCs and STs included two times more debtors (27 per cent) than caste Hindus.

[255] While 13 per cent of all SC employees worked as sweepers in 1966, no more than 5 per cent did so in 1990 (see Table 9.2). This phenomenon stemmed perhaps from the higher educational proficiency of subsequent generations of SC applicants who had acquired the resources indispensable to opening up alternative occupational avenues.

hierarchy.[256] Indeed, in a petition submitted to a parliamentary fact finding body in 1986, the SC-ST Association claimed that the head of the sanitation department had expressly demanded for 'Untouchables' alone to be assigned to this department since caste Hindu workers, appointed as sweepers, did not perform their tasks conscientiously.[257]

This is indirectly borne out by a quarrel featuring two women sweepers employed in the ITI hospital, one an SC, Narasamma, the other a 'clean' caste belonging to the Balajiga caste, Jayalakshmi. Extremely resentful and frustrated at having to continue working as a sweeper, despite her repeated requests for a change of job more 'befitting' her caste status, Jayalakshmi is reported to have declared aloud on one occasion that 'such cleaning jobs are only fit for Mala and Madiga people and not for a Balajiga lady like her'.[258] When questioned by Narasamma, she abused Narasamma:

you Madiga women. I know you are eating dirty things and your people are cleaning the roads and carrying night soil.[259]

A little later, Jayalakshmi pushed Narasamma from the stool on which she was sitting and shouted at her:

You are not a queen to sit on the stool and if you sit on the stool how can I sit on that. You belong to Mala Madiga and you have to sit on the floor and not on the stool.[260]

Subsequently, the inquiry committee concluded that Jayalakshmi had indeed spoken and acted in this manner. A particularly virulent example of caste prejudices, it not only illuminated the strength of the stereotype entertained by caste Hindus identifying sweeping exclusively with the 'Untouchables'. It also demonstrated the linkages operated by the upper castes on the basis of a purely ascriptive logic between various notions of

---

[256] Robert Deliège comments on the paradoxical nature of Indian untouchability where the very tasks the 'Untouchables' perform, rendering them indispensable to the social order, also simultaneously contribute to their exclusion from this order. *The Untouchables of India*, p. 120.

[257] Memorandum to Parliamentary Committee (1986). Moreover, managerial complicity enabled clean caste sweepers in some instances to obtain transfers to less 'degrading' jobs.

[258] Minutes of SC-ST Cell, 25 July 1996.

[259] ibid.

[260] ibid.

dirt that extended all the way from the work the 'Untouchables' did to the food they ate right to their very being, all of which in turn defined their inferior social status even as it exercised a deeply polluting or defiling effect on the upper castes who entered into contact with them. But for this ascriptive belief, Jayalakshmi by virtue of the task she performed should have been just as polluting as Narasamma.

Still, stigmatized as his/her job may have been by caste Hindus, an SC sweeper on the permanent rolls of a public sector company like ITI enjoyed a far greater degree of financial and job security and respectability than an SC domestic sweeper or a casual labourer, and was greatly envied by them for these reasons.[261] Moreover, to the extent that some persons from these groups at least had escaped immiserization, and all its attendant humiliations, by finding work in the public sector, even if it entailed cleaning toilets and sweeping floors, optimistic assumptions about the transformative power of industrial development to function as the engine of social mobility did not prove totally utopian. Having said this, sweepers in ITI were often condemned to remain in this job for long years, some times even throughout their working lives, even though in a cosmetic gesture they were formally redesignated as sanitary service cleaners.[262] A policy of job rotations, providing for their transfer after a minimum of five years service to other departments as trolley men, helpers, and attenders, was implemented for about a decade before being abandoned from 1990 onwards. Nor were special training programmes for the SCs pursued in earnest; repeated appeals from the SC-ST Association that a quarter of all training seats be mandated for its members never found favour with the company.[263]

What must also be noted is that job changes while entitling some

[261] According to Deliège, municipal sweepers living in the Tamil Nadu village studied by him were regarded as a privileged group by 'Untouchable' coolies. *Untouchables of India*, p. 138. For a stimulating essay on the meaning of work for 'Untouchable' sweepers in Benares and the sense of self-assertiveness manifested by them, see Mary Searle-Chatterjee, 'The Polluted Identity of Work: A Study of Benares Sweepers', in S. Wallman (ed.), *Social Anthropology of Work*, London, 1979, pp. 269–86.

[262] PD circular no. 2298, 30 August 1982.

[263] Minutes of meeting between SC-ST Association and general manager, ITI Bangalore, 30 April 1978; Memorandum from SC-ST Association to ITI managing director, 7 March 1983. Data for the earlier years are unavailable, but 16 per cent of SC and ST employees attended training programmes in 1993–94, 14.9 per cent in 1994–95, and 10.6 per cent in 1995–96. (*Source:* ITI Personnel Dept.)

sweepers to 'a qualitative change in their status' had disqualified others from enjoying the same benefits on gender grounds.[264] In a petition submitted by SC women sweepers, they complained of discrimination, pointing out that despite having toiled for ten years in some cases none of them had succeeded in obtaining a transfer.[265] The company justified the lack of horizontal mobility by arguing that male sweepers had greater seniority and could be easily redeployed throughout the factory unlike women because of the restrictive clauses contained in the factory legislation.

Besides, since only female sweepers could be used to clean women's toilets (no restrictions, though, were placed on their attending to men's toilets), they could not expect to receive the same treatment as their male counterparts—an argument that effectively dashed whatever hopes these women might have entertained of moving some day to a better job even as it emphasized the gendered nature of sweepers' tasks. Thus even transfer requests motivated by ageing disabilities were turned down.[266] A list drawn up by the SC-ST Association showed that seven women sweepers had performed the same job for 20 years, prompting it to lament that 'the SC/ST are born to do sweeping jobs life long . . .'.[267]

In addition to the sanitation department, the plating shop, the shipping department and the canteen also contained fairly large pockets of SC and ST workers. According to one estimate, they comprised between 25 to 30 per cent of the shipping workforce, and, quite ironically, nearly 40 per cent of canteen personnel.[268] Despite their supposedly ritually 'impure' status, like their caste Hindu counterparts in the canteen they too were engaged in preparing, cooking and serving food. Work in all these departments shared certain common attributes: it was invariably dirty, often physically demanding, and sometimes posed health hazards. Alleging that SC labourers in the plating shop were 'treated almost like slaves', the SC-ST Association claimed on one instance that two of its members had sustained severe burns because they had been forced to handle chemicals though their job did not require them to do so.[269]

---

[264] Letter from SC-ST Association to director, ITI Bangalore, 2 January 1997.
[265] Minutes of SC-ST Cell meeting, 17 November 1986.
[266] Minutes of SC-ST Cell meeting, 7 November 1995.
[267] Letter from SC-ST Association to director, ITI Bangalore, December 1993.
[268] Interview with Prabhakara.
[269] Letter from SC-ST Association to director, ITI Bangalore, 18 February 1985.

Predictably, the management refuted all charges of prejudice, claiming that the 'placement of personnel in various departments is not based on caste'.[270] Nevertheless, the findings of the factory health and safety inspector on the state of working conditions in the ITI canteen, though they did not specifically refer to SC and ST employees, spotlighted the company's indifference to the welfare of those toiling here.

Intervening at the behest of the SC-ST Association, after the management had proved unresponsive to its complaints and the union had displayed no interest in raising the issue, the factory inspector exposed in unambiguous terms the harsh rigours of work that prevailed in the canteen. Workers were denied the benefits of fixed rest intervals. Because of the absence of lifts, they were obliged to carry extremely large vessels, containing between 70 and 80 kgs of food up several flights of steps. There was a constant risk therefore of accidents occurring, especially of workers being burnt by hot liquid preparations. Poor flooring in the kitchen further accentuated this risk. No effective exhaust systems had been installed to clear smoke. Nor were workers being sent for regular medical checks. In 1985, two years after the factory inspector had submitted his report, ITI had still not acted on even a single of the recommendations contained in it. In the end, it required the chief factory inspector to issue a warning notice before the company reluctantly sanctioned the amounts required to modernize the kitchen and improve working conditions.

Nevertheless, the canteen continued to remain a permanent trouble spot, marked by the expression of strong tensions between SC workers and canteen officials on one side, and between the former and the rest of the workforce on the other. A banal dispute over the cleaning of plates between one SC worker and two non-SC workers ended with the former apparently being insulted and called an 'Untouchable'.[271] On another occasion, 'heated arguments' erupted between SC workers and the others after the security department, acting on a tip-off that three SC persons had unauthorizedly quit the factory, arrived at the canteen to conduct a check.[272] Complaints and collective representations by the association

---

[270] Memorandum to Parliamentary Committee (1986).

[271] Letter from SC-ST Association to director, ITI Bangalore, Ref. EDR/BB/8/85, 29 July 1985.

[272] SD files, case no. 72/91, 31 August 1991.

and SC-ST workers accusing canteen supervisors of discriminatory practices, harassment and instigating communal rifts were also common occurrences. Supervisors were charged with favouring the 'elite class' who because of the violation of job rotation procedures systematically got light tasks to the detriment of SC workers.[273]

Establishing the authenticity of these claims is, to say the least, extremely problematic. There were certainly instances of conflicts unconnected to caste prejudices being twisted to give them a caste colouring. Investigations by the management into a complaint of harassment received from an SC canteen worker against his caste Hindu colleague revealed that the contention between the two men arose from their business transactions outside the factory.[274] Similarly, dismissing all allegations of harassment, the canteen manager on one occasion stated that nobody worked for more than '3.30 or 4 hours per day'.[275] Hence the question of extracting more effort from SC workers just did not arise. Illustrative certainly of the staunch determination of SC and ST employees as well as their representatives to defend their rights, a justified reaction to long years of subordination, ill treatment, and forced silence, one cannot also exclude or overlook the possibility that accusations of discrimination could serve a purely instrumentalist function. That they might be designed to exert pressure on department officers to drop legitimate disciplinary proceedings against SC workers.[276] As the ITI chairman pointed out in a reply to the head of a parliamentary committee on SC-ST welfare,

. . . there has been a rigid and fixed attitude on the part of a few members (of the SC-ST association) that they are being discriminated. Even an action taken against an employee who happens to belong to SC/ST in the interest of maintaining discipline and general welfare . . . has been viewed by some as if the action has been initiated merely for the reason that the employee belongs to SC/ST community . . .[277]

---

[273] Letter from SC-ST Association to director, ITI Bangalore, 18 February 1992.

[274] Minutes of SC-ST Cell, 24 August 1988.

[275] PD note, 13 December 1993.

[276] White supervisors in the US, especially in the southern states, fearing accusations of discrimination are often wary of disciplining Afro-American workers, remarks Peter Vallas. 'Burawoy's Legacy', *Contemporary Sociology*, Vol. 30, No. 5, September 2001, pp. 442–4.

[277] D.O. No. COR-20 (SCT), 8 September 1985.

The case of Sampath also bears out how some SC employees could be tempted to exploit their caste status in order to wriggle out of trouble, though we must be cautious not to generalize on the basis of a single, even extreme, example. A notoriously undisciplined worker as well as a 'tough' who boasted close links to the Karnataka Sangha and the Rajkumar Fans Association, two organizations committed to a muscular defence of Kannada culture, he had been sanctioned by shop officials on numerous occasions for a range of offences. Claiming that he 'takes support from the SC-ST Association and the ITI union as and when it suits him', one note added that both these bodies had intervened in the past to 'close many cases of misconduct by the employee'.[278]

In 1989, after the management decided to reduce his salary as punishment for repeated violations of factory regulations, Sampath wrote to the chairman: 'since I am a Scheduled Caste person, some officers have treated me like a slave and I am being mentally tortured . . .'[279] He subsequently filed a law suit, demanding damages from ITI for suffering discrimination and followed it up with a petition to Rajiv Gandhi where he mentioned that the company was dominated by Brahmins who were harassing him because of his origins. Interestingly, he also accused the SC-ST Association of being mired in corruption. The next year, he submitted an appeal to the Karnataka chief minister as well as the new prime minister, V.P. Singh. All these efforts did not go in vain. Not only had the management to justify on two separate occasions to a central SC-ST oversight body why it punished Sampath and prove that his allegations were false. It also had to submit to questioning by the police civil rights enforcement cell.

It is worth recording here that like the management, caste Hindu workers were invariably of the opinion that the victimization SC employees complained of was a red herring to escape disciplinary sanctions. Deeply embedded caste prejudices played themselves out in the refusal to acknowledge that not all these complaints were baseless. Just as these prejudices explained the selective memories which led upper caste employees to conveniently forget that a Vokalliga machine tender or wireman was the first to shout discrimination when charge sheeted by a Lingayat supervisor, and vice versa, and for much the same reasons

---

[278] Personnel File No. 10434Q.
[279] ibid.

that a SC worker might do so. Even the more liberal-minded clean caste personnel whose sense of even handedness allowed them to concede that SC labourers may have suffered ill treatment at the hands of some upper caste officers firmly believed such behaviour was a vestige of the past.

If an SC-ST worker is penalized for absenteeism and issued a charge sheet, he immediately contacts his association. The association is very strong and capable of pressurizing the management to withdraw the charges. Otherwise, the association will create problems. It will say that the department head who issued the charge sheet is harassing the worker for many months and therefore the worker is not reporting for duty. The management is scared of taking the risk and punishing the SC-ST worker. But non SC-ST workers are treated differently by the management which goes ahead with disciplinary charges. SC-ST workers are a privileged section today. *Comparatively a Brahmin is a Dalit.*[280]

These lines make for interesting reading in terms of the contrast they draw between the position of the SC and his non-SC counterpart. It emphasizes what has become a standard feature in the rhetoric of caste Hindu workers where a reversal of roles is discursively constructed to demonstrate that it is no longer the SC worker who faces discrimination but the caste Hindu; that it is no longer the SC worker who is defenceless, in need of protection and whose plight is to be pitied, but the caste Hindu.[281]

SCHEDULED CASTE EMPLOYEES ACCUSED OF ABUSING LEGAL RIGHTS

It is necessary to specify at this juncture that the anti-disabilities legislation enacted since the mid-1970s afforded in principle a far greater degree of protection to 'Untouchables'. The Protection of Civil Rights Act (1976), not only broadened the definition of 'public place' where untouchability could not be practised, it also imposed stiffer penalties on offenders and strengthened enforcement provisions. Subsequently, in an attempt to control the growing incidence of atrocities against 'Untouchables' across

[280] Interview with Vadiraj Hatwar. Emphasis added

[281] Strong parallels can be traced between the discourse of caste Hindu workers *vis-à-vis* SC workers and Hindu nationalists *vis-à-vis* Muslims, defined not as 'outcastes' but as 'outsiders' who illegitimately enjoy the special dispensations granted by a 'soft' state seen as pandering to their interests for reasons of electoral expediency.

the country, the government promulgated an even more stringent and comprehensive statute in 1989, the Scheduled Castes and Scheduled Tribes (Protection of Atrocities) Act. Scholars have argued that due to implementational failures neither piece of legislation has proved very successful, in particular in the countryside, in either reducing untouchability or levels of violence against 'Untouchables'.[282]

Nevertheless, in the context of an urban industrial workplace, the law appears to have been fairly effective in curbing certain public acts of shaming and indignity, designed to affirm the superiority of the upper castes, such as the use of abusive language. The licence that caste Hindu officials, and workers, had granted themselves in the past to call an 'Untouchable' an untouchable to his/her face carried with it definite risks now, as SC workers, having realized the protection the legislation offered them took increasing recourse to it. So to the extent that the law fulfilled its regulatory function of exercising a restraining influence on individual behaviour, it could be credited in however modest a way with fashioning a 'new civic culture'.[283] To quote the president of the SC-ST Association,

before it was customary for our people to be abused under their caste name, to be called a *holleya*, son of a *holleya* or *madiga*. To fight such harassments, the association started lodging complaints in the police station under the SC-ST Atrocities Act. We also kept the Civil Rights Enforcement Cell informed and when the police came inside the factory and wanted to arrest some offenders, there was a big commotion . . . It created fear . . . Today harassments of our people have sharply declined because of the protection of the law. Caste Hindu workers are restraining themselves. Insults using caste names have come down (sic).[284]

If the legislative measures operated as a potent weapon in the fight against various forms of discrimination, it could equally be subject to misuse and pressed into use with an eye to settling personal scores that had no bearing on caste discrimination. Indeed, this was what caste Hindu workers generally contended. They accused the SCs of taking advantage

---

[282] Marc Galanter, *Law and Society in Modern India*, New Delhi, 1997, pp. 208–21; Harsh Mander, 'Status of Dalits and Agenda for State Intervention', in *Untouchables and the State*, pp. 147–70; Krishnan, 'Untouchability and Atrocities'.

[283] Mendelsohn and Vicziany, *The Untouchables*, pp. 125–7, 266–8.

[284] Interview with Prabhakara.

of the law to foist false charges and declare they had been subjected to public humiliation (a punishable offence) whenever a quarrel occurred—an accusation that the SC-ST Association conceded was sometimes true. As a result, caste Hindu workers were interrogated by the police and even briefly arrested on occasions. Not surprisingly, all of this had the effect of driving an even deeper wedge between SC workers and the others.[285] The following statements eloquently capture the sentiments of a few caste Hindu employees.

. . . SC-ST employees are misusing the legal provisions. In the name of caste, they are threatening others. Quarrels are given a caste dimension by them . . . In the township if a neighbour has refused some request of a SC-ST worker, he will put him (the neighbour) into trouble by complaining to the police.[286]

Claiming that the government was supporting the SCs, another worker ruled out the possibility of amicably resolving any problem that arose with an SC worker.

You cannot talk things over with them (SC workers). It can immediately become a big issue. If any SC-ST worker gives a complaint against you, the police can arrest you straight away.[287]

Likewise, a longtime resident of the ITI township who was frank enough to admit that interactions between SC workers and the others had always been minimal, declared that the distance between the two groups was now widening. According to him, this situation had arisen only because the former were 'wrongly utilizing the privileges' they had got from the state and fabricating 'all kinds of charges against us'.[288]

The Non-SC and ST Association in fact advanced the 'increasing number of false complaints' brought against caste Hindu employees as one of the reasons motivating its formation. Claiming that it was 'alarmed' by such a development and wanted to tackle the 'problem in a legally

---

[285] After three caste Hindu canteen workers had been reported to the police for allegedy entering the house of an SC person at night, they addressed a petition to the director of the Bangalore plant in 1988 claiming that the accusation was groundless. The petition went on to add that SC workers were 'spoil(ing) cordial atmosphere in the Canteen bringing division amongst . . . employees under the name of Schedule Caste (sic)'. PD files, 15 February 1988.

[286] Interview with Anthony Raj.

[287] Interview with Narayana Murthy.

[288] Interview with Bhaskar Rao.

organized manner' via the association, it noted that the union's efforts to resolve the problem had failed to yield results because of the non-cooperative attitude of the SCs.[289] The union had effectively set up a fact finding committee in 1985 to conduct an independent enquiry after two caste Hindu workers facing prosecution for having allegedly insulted an SC worker denied any wrongdoing. But with the latter refusing to talk to the committee, it soon had to wind up its activities. Interestingly, the Non-SC and ST Association sought to defend not just the interests of caste Hindu employees but executives as well. Speaking in their name, it declared that false complaints would have a deleterious effect on ITI as a whole since officials, feeling threatened, would 'lose interest' and no longer strive to 'extract even the expected normal work' from SC and ST workers. This in turn would cause other workers to 'lose their personal interest in their work (sic)', leading to the ruin of the company.[290]

Another site of recurrent tension was the security department. Relations between SC employees and their superiors, between the former and their other colleagues, and between caste Hindu security personnel and SC employees in other factory departments were all often fraught with suspicion and conflict. Collective representations targeting certain security officials for 'not treating them as human beings and harassing every time (sic)' emanated at regular intervals from SC security guards.[291] They complained of receiving warning orders on flimsy grounds, of leave requests being sanctioned with great difficulty, and of transfer demands being stalled. Employees singled out the senior security officer, a Lingayat 'bent on harassing SC-ST employees' ever since one of his caste brethren in the company was charged for a civil rights offence.[292]

Once again disentangling 'fact' from 'fiction' poses considerable problems, and the management's own statements have a contradictory

---

[289] Non SC-ST Welfare Association circular, 8 December 1985.

[290] PD files, nd (1986). When asked how they stood up to over zealous officers in the absence of union representation, following the dissolution of the organization by the judiciary a few years ago, a group of Bhilai workers blithely replied that this posed no problems: 'We just threaten to report the officer to the Harijan *thana* for calling us Chamars'. (Personal communication from Jonathan Parry.)

[291] Memorandum to Parliamentary Committee (1986); Letter from SC-ST Association to director, ITI Bangalore, 13 August 1991; Minutes of SC-ST Cell 5 August 1992.

[292] Memorandum to Parliamentary Committee (1986).

character. In one instance, after justifying the disciplinary action taken by the Lingayat officer in question against an SC worker, we see it pompously declaring that 'it is not correct to attribute motives for an act done by an officer in the bonafide exercise of his official responsibilities . . .'[293] But on another, it was compelled to declare that it had 'advised' the same officer against referring to the caste names of SC employees when talking to them—a clear admission that he was in the habit of doing so.[294]

On the other hand, a complaint filed by Mastanappa, a security supervisor, that a caste Hindu colleague, Jaganathan, had publicly abused him as an 'Untouchable' was found to be false. Mastanappa had apparently granted compensatory leave to another security guard so that he could attend to the former's personal business. When the department head came to know of the matter, Mastanappa blamed Jaganathan for having reported him resulting in an angry exchange of words between the two men.[295] There is no means of ascertaining whether or not Jaganathan did blow the whistle. But the very fact that he was singled out as the prime suspect by Mastanappa spoke volumes for the nature of their relations.

That not all claims of discrimination were genuine is thrown into relief by the following incident. It involved an SC worker in the ITI hospital, Anjaiah, and a caste Hindu security guard, Reddy. In a petition submitted to the director of the Bangalore plant, Anjaiah accused the latter of harassing him for several months. In addition to being insulted, he also had to submit to the humiliation of repeated body checks in front his colleagues since Reddy suspected him of stealing medicines. The affair would probably have taken a less serious turn but for the police arresting Reddy in response to a complaint lodged by Anjaiah. After securing Reddy's release on bail, the security department at once formed an enquiry committee for as it pointed out, the 'entire functioning of the department is in question'.[296] The committee which comprised an SC officer heard 12 witnesses in all, including the two protagonists, before concluding that Reddy had not misused his position to harass

---

[293] ibid.
[294] PD note, 18 December 1989.
[295] SD files, 23 September 1991.
[296] SD files, case No. 33/93, 22 and 28 April 1993.

Anjaiah. Both men lived in the township and a quarrel over a banal issue apparently explained the entire chain of events.

Disputes over false caste certificates also sharpened antagonisms between SC and caste Hindu workers, on the one hand, and the SC-ST Association and the union, on the other. This time, though, the roles were reversed with the SCs accusing the upper castes of submitting misleading claims. Given the value placed on government employment, and given also 'the equivocal and ambiguous, fluid and shifting' nature of the nomenclature of caste groups enumerated in the official schedule, it is not surprising that quite a few caste Hindus tried to pass off as a member of this or that SC or ST community by obtaining a false caste certificate in order to enter the administrative services or the public sector.[297] In Karnataka, attempts to manipulate equivocal nomenclature related in particular to ST because positions reserved for them remained largely unfilled. Indeed, in the words of the director of SC and ST, the problem of false certificates had reached 'epidemic proportions' in the state towards the end of the 1970s.[298] Various clean caste groupings with names resembling those of ST communities tried and succeeded in acquiring ST status.[299]

In ITI, the controversy over false caste certificates spilled into the open in 1983. This followed the SC-ST Association forwarding a list with the names of 30 employees who had either obtained a job or secured promotion benefits by pretending to belong to the STs. As the state SC-ST directorate, mincing no words, underlined, despite being aware of the problem, the management 'appear to have been *careless to the point of irresponsibility*' in not properly scrutinizing the claims presented by employees.[300] Driving home the management's negligence, it went on to add that some of the so-called ST employees had originally not declared themselves as belonging to these communities, i.e., they had produced certificates after having joined the company once they realized all the advantages that could be gained by changing their caste status.

---

[297] Galanter, *Competing Equalities*, p. 283.

[298] Letter from Director Scheduled Castes and Scheduled Tribes, Govt. of Karnataka to ITI chairman, D.O.No. 14/1/88-RU, 17 October 1988.

[299] For example, Kurubas, a low caste Hindu group, claimed their names were synonyms of Jenu Kurubas and Kadu Kurubas, two ST groups; likewise, Naiks and Nayaks passed themselves off as Nayakas.

[300] Letter from Director SC-ST. Emphasis added.

For the SC-ST Association, the question of false certificates was no trivial matter: the beneficiaries had, through fraudulent means, appropriated entitlements that should rightfully have gone to authentic ST persons. The company also appears to have responded positively to the association's concerns, at least in the initial stages, by taking prompt disciplinary action against the offenders. Despite protests from the union, it suspended around 20 workers, some of whom were later dismissed and others demoted to the lowest category. The union contended, not wrongly but not ethically either, that in view of the penury of ST candidates which prevented the company from filling the quotas reserved for them, the false certificate holders had not deprived members of these communities of employment opportunities or obstructed their promotion prospects.[301] However, more than a decade and a half after the problem first came to light it had yet to be fully resolved. Confirming the charges of the SC-ST Association that several impostors continued to remain on the company's pay rolls, a confidential management note admitted in 1997 to 'inordinate delays' even in punishing employees proved to have submitted counterfeit certificates.[302]

A few concluding remarks are necessary. First, teleological arguments inspired in one way or the other by modernization theory predicting the diminishing influence of caste consciousness as industrial development makes inroads into traditional Indian society have clearly proved unfounded. Far from evaporating, caste sentiments have on the contrary redoubled in vigour in a public sector company like ITI mainly under the impact of the compensatory discrimination programme, the repercussions of which have been to split the workforce along caste lines and create two distinct groups, beneficiaries of the programme and non-beneficiaries.

Second, the vigorous assertion of primordial loyalties in the form of language and caste, and the strife they generated, highlighted the extent to which a state-run enterprise like ITI had failed to conform to the vision of nationalism inherent in the Nehruvian modernizing project. In this scheme of things, the role of the public sector in the nation-

---

[301] Letter ITI union to Chief Personnel Manager, ITI Bangalore, 3 September 1995.

[302] PD note, 19 June 1997. Khan notes a similar lack of enthusiasm on the part of the state government in tackling the problem of false caste certificates. *Reservation for Scheduled Castes*, p. 175.

building process extended beyond its manifest economic objective to a civic cum pedagogical mission where it would help fashion a worker who defined him/herself first of all as an 'Indian' rather than as a Kannadiga, a Hindu or a Lingayat. As we have seen, developments at ITI ran in the opposite direction. Instead of functioning as the crucible from which emerged the new secular-minded worker, the scramble for benefits, material and symbolic, that the company made available transformed it into a cockpit of ethnic rivalries where the perception of differences was accentuated as each group strove to secure what it esteemed to be its rightful share at the expense of others. The idea of the national in so far as it existed in this conceptualization was thus one of proportional representation based on regional and sub-nationalisms as opposed to a national at whose core stood the unified citizen subject.[303]

At the same time, the linguistic and caste antagonisms brought to the fore contrasting sets of dynamics. The Kannadiga–Tamil clash for hegemony threw up pressures that were essentially local/regional in character. How and to what extent these particularisms could be accommodated within the framework of a national policy that governed the operations of a public sector company was the challenge confronting the management. It had to tread a fine line between showing sensitivity to the demands raised by the various regional actors and refusing to compromise on constitutional principles guaranteeing equal opportunities for everybody. In the case of reservations, the company was following policy prescriptions whose spatial validity embraced the country at large. Unlike in the case of linguistic rights where national norms had to take into consideration local/regional interests to a significant degree, when it came to preferment for the SCs and STs the terms of reference of the nationally-mandated norms were totally binding. Legitimizing opposition to them by invoking the safeguard of regional or local rights was not possible since no distinction could be made here between the local, regional and national spheres. Successive rulings by the judiciary had had the effect of defining reservations exclusively from the vantage point of the national leaving no space for competing interpretations.

Our third point concerns the sharp differences in the nature of relations between caste Hindu and SC workers at ITI and in another public sector company, the Bhilai steel plant. Reading Jonathan Parry's highly

---

[303] I am indebted to Janaki Nair for this insight.

stimulating account of what he describes as a 'cost-benefit analysis' of the effect of reservations in Bhilai, we find little of the tensions and conflicts observed by us in Bangalore.[304] A good measure of harmony and sociability underpinned the ties binding the clean castes and the 'Untouchables', belonging mainly to the Satnami caste, both on the shop floor and beyond the perimeter walls too, though these interactions were limited to the permanent workforce. To give just one example, not only did workers from the two groups eat together, but they also shared food brought from home.[305] (Parry also contrasts the prevalence of commensality in Bhilai with the commensal distance maintained by caste Hindu workers from Satnamis in a private sector plant.) Indeed, according to Parry it is less caste than regional ethnicity that operates as a source of discord in Bhilai.

How then are we to account for the fact that while job reservations generated a powerful sense of resentment among caste Hindu workers at ITI and further distanced them from the SCs, they barely scratched the surface of social relations at Bhilai?[306] The answer is provided in part by Parry himself. According to him, a variety of factors, not the least being the specific character of the labour process in a steel plant which demands a high degree of cooperation and trust between all members of the work group combined to create a distinctive institutional ethos, a 'melting pot' in his words where caste distinctions progressively dissolved.[307] One could argue that an institutional culture is shaped not just by elements internal to the institution but also external to it, a detail that Parry perhaps

---

[304] Parry, 'Two Cheers for Reservation'. (cit. p. 130).

[305] Uma Ramaswamy also highlights the breakdown of commensal restrictions in relations between male caste Hindu and 'Untouchable' workers in the Coimbatore textile mills. This was rendered possible by the necessity of close interaction on the shop floor. *Work, Union and Community*, pp. 105–07.

[306] More than Bhilai it is with another public sector steel mill, Rourkela, that the pattern of social interactions in ITI bears close resemblance. Like the latter, Rourkela witnessed considerable internal strife on account of linguistic, regional and religious cleavages. Like ITI, but unlike Bhilai, Rourkela also had a relatively homogenous labour force where one ethnic group enjoyed a distinct numerical advantage. Indeed, in their comparative study of Bhilai and Rourkela, Parry and Strümpell posit a definite cause-effect link between the heterogenous composition of the workforce in the former plant and the relatively muted expression of sectarian identity visible there. 'On the Desecration of Nehru's "Temples" '.

[307] Parry, 'Two Cheers for Reservation', p. 149. See also by the same author, 'Working and Shirking in Bhilai'.

tends to underestimate since he concentrates exclusively on attributes specific to Bhilai.

Nevertheless, by drawing attention to the system of work organization and the solidarities that aggregated around it (though, of course, there is no reason why working together should only produce cohesive collectivities), he points to the principal reason behind the contrasting patterns of social relations between caste Hindu and SC workers at the two companies. For components identified by Parry as constitutive of the institutional culture of Bhilai, such as the ambition to forge a modern Indian worker emancipated from all primordial allegiances plus the paternalist social reformism of the management, were also in a way common to ITI and possibly to all public sector companies founded in the Nehruvian heyday. Where ITI diverged from Bhilai, however, was in terms of its labour process and the levels of qualification of its workforce, both of which in turn gave rise to a different set of production relations.

For one thing, in contrast to the more collective dimension of steel making operations, the detailed division of labour underlying the fabrication of telecommunications equipment imparted to work an extremely individualized or parcellized character. The scope for mutual assistance on the shop floor was thus limited; performing their respective tasks seldom required operatives to cooperate closely with each other in machine shops as in assembly shops. Nor did they need to demonstrate in the course of their daily routines the sense of togetherness and solidarity that was almost indispensable for steel mill workers given the often quite hazardous nature of their job where each person's physical safety depended on the vigilance exercised by the other. All of this meant that interdependence in the workplace was the exception rather than the norm at ITI.

Moreover, even on those occasions when their tasks necessitated mutual interaction, it practically never brought together caste Hindu and SC workers for the simple reason that the latter were confined in the main to menial positions. In Bhilai, Satnamis seem to have acquired the educational and technical qualifications that opened the doors to even fairly skilled production jobs with the result that work groups contained both caste Hindu and Untouchable workers, fostering in turn ties of affinity between members of the two communities. In ITI, however, access to semi-skilled and skilled jobs was to a large measure foreclosed to SC workers as they lacked the requisite educational and technical capital. This point returns us to the structural features of the labour process in ITI. Because assembling switching equipment did not call for the same levels of skill and competencies as making steel, the company could be satisfied with a less qualified workforce, the upshot of which was that far more SCs who joined ITI did so at the very bottom of the occupational hierarchy than did caste Hindus for obvious reasons.

Our final remark touches on one aspect of the compensatory discrimination programme. On the one hand, by guaranteeing SC workers protection against public acts of shaming and humiliation, the civil rights legislations enacted by the government have effectively succeeded in laying the foundations of 'a new civic culture'.[308] Frequent recourse to the law by SC workers drove home the message to their clean caste colleagues that they had to modify their modes of outward behaviour. Otherwise, they ran the risk of facing punitive legal sanctions. In other words, the increasing affirmation of their rights by the 'Untouchables', and, its corollary, their refusal to grant customary deference to the upper castes did occasionally spark a backlash on the part of caste Hindus both within the factory space and outside. But, more significantly, it also had the effect of exercising a restraining influence on the latter and curbing certain highly visible discriminatory practices, notably the habit of abusing 'Untouchables' by referring to their caste names.

On the other, this new civicism has failed to ensure their integration within the common institutional culture of the factory. It has neither created the conditions of possibility for SC workers to accede to positions of influence within various representational bodies like the union, nor managed to guarantee their acceptance by caste Hindu employees in everyday life. Latent forms of discrimination continue to remain profoundly entrenched in the work environment, the total absence of all bonds of sociability between members of the two groups a warrant to the unchanging attitudes of the clean castes, convinced at heart of the inferior status of the 'Untouchables'. In sum, while empowering 'Untouchables' by safeguarding their citizenship rights, the new civic culture has yet to make them first class citizens at work.[309]

---

[308] Mendelsohn and Vicziany, *The Untouchables*, pp. 125–7.

[309] Referring to the overall Indian social context, Mendelsohn and Vicziany state that the new civic culture has been 'pragmatic and superficial rather than transformational' in its scope. While this assessment may not be very far off the mark, in the case of ITI we must be careful not to minimize the impact of this culture via the law in recasting upper caste public behaviour. ibid, p. 266.

Conclusion

Throughout the course of this book, I have endeavoured to analytically highlight different aspects of the functioning of what I have called a bureaucratic regime of production. I have sought to demonstrate the manner in which this regime shaped the dispositions and strategies of the four principal actors implicated in this organizational space: state, management, union and workers. An examination of their respective actions has also thrown into relief the long and unflattering catalogue of ills bedevilling ITI: political interference in corporate strategy formulation and official neglect, chronic managerial inefficiencies and low levels of motivation, lack of cost consciousness and a culture of unaccountability, substandard products and poor work ethics, indiscipline and overmanning.

At the heart of the various deficiencies constitutive of the company's functioning we find the same causal patterns or mechanisms at play, and which by repeating themselves tend to lend a systemic character to these deficiencies. On the one hand, as in the case of discipline, work effort, or quality, employees systematically capitalized on managerial laxity to roll back the lines of authority and carve out large spaces of discretion and autonomy for themselves which over time threatened to jeopardize the efficient working of the company. On the other, inflexible administrative controls flowing from state policy interventions interlocked with corporate inefficiencies of all kinds to aggravate the difficulties confronting the enterprise. Fused together, these two partly distinct strands could be viewed as the common determinate factor that illuminated and accounted for several aspects of ITI's operations. At the same time, I have pointed to the deep seated incapability or unwillingness of the company to take corrective steps. Resistance to change, we know, is ingrained in all organizations, especially large ones.[1] Few companies can conceive of transforming themselves unless galvanized by the threat of a serious crisis compelling them to break with past dispositions, norms, and practices. Nevertheless, in the case of ITI notwithstanding the magnitude of the crisis it faced, effecting structural change has proved particularly intractable.[2] As management theorists are fond of repeating, developing 'correct' policies for restructuring is not sufficient; an organizational capacity or 'will' to restructure is also necessary.

An explanation for both the problems facing the company, and the failure to remedy them, must lead us back to the three foundational attributes on which a bureaucratic production regime rests: state ownership, soft budgetary constraints, and the lack of competitive pressures. It should be emphasized here that in order to seize the distinctive character of such a regime, it is indispensable to consider in unison all three determining attributes. An exclusive focus on any one of these elements without relating them to the other two can furnish only a partial clarification: it is their mutually reinforcing effect that spotlights in its entirety the specificity of this regime. As comparative studies of state-socialist and capitalist firms have shown, neither ownership patterns *per se* nor the type of budgetary constraints in vigour *per se* can help account for the contrasting performances of enterprises. What made the difference in each instance was exposure to competition.

[1] Midler has argued that it is the extreme coherence of the technico-institutional devices put into place by large corporations which inhibits localized or decentralized attempts at change since such initiatives threaten to progressively undermine the foundations of the entire edifice. This, in turn, explains the 'fantastic inertia' these companies exhibit, their inability to continuously adapt to the environment culminating in a 'succession of major traumatisms . . .' 'Les concepts au concret', in *Le Travail: marchés, règles, conventions*, p. 47.

[2] Andrew Pettigrew et al, *Shaping Strategic Change. Making Change in Large Organizations: The Case of the National Health Service*, London, 1992, p. 6.

Conclusion 651

As the sociologist Michael Burawoy has shown based on his own shopfloor experiences as a blue collar operative both in the US and in state-socialist Hungary of the two engineering plants where he worked in Hungary, the first utilized its capital and human resources far more optimally than the second; the first plant also functioned more efficiently and strove more purposefully to rationalize its operations and innovate than the Chicago company where Burawoy had previously been engaged as a machine tender. The critical variable determining organizational performance in each case was the level of competitive pressure. As a subsidiary of a vertically integrated multinational corporation, producing essentially for other divisions of the corporation, the Chicago firm was removed from the market circuit unlike the Hungarian firm which exported a large part of its output to the West.[3]

In the Indian context, the operation of soft budget constraints and monopoly privileges when conjoined had a decisive impact on the operations of state owned firms: they contributed to eliminate all incentives for managements to remedy organizational shortcomings, let alone aim for higher standards of performance. Because the people running monopolies know, first, that alternative options for satisfying customers' needs are non-existent, and, second, that in case of financial difficulties the exchequer will come to their rescue, they can afford to tolerate a high degree of slack in their mode of functioning. Dysfunctional or unprofitable departments do not in any way compromise the survival of the firm, and while irate customers (organizations as well as individuals) might resort to voice to communicate their complaints and grievances, the exit option is foreclosed to them. Under such circumstances, voice becomes relatively ineffective. Exclusive market power and soft budget constraints thus have a mutually consolidating effect in removing all compulsions for change. Only in moment of political crisis when the state threatens to withdraw its paternalistic shield by cutting subsidies and other forms of financial assistance, and decides to deregulate markets are managements of monopoly companies motivated to improve efficiency.

[3] Burawoy and Luckacs, *The Radiant Past*, pp. 9–12, 71–2, 79–80. Similarly, Bardhan and Roemer argue that inefficiencies of public firms stem less from their ownership status than from their monopoly position. 'Market Socialism. A Case for Rejuvenation'.

It is a well known fact that inertia plays an important role in the persistence of institutional anomalies of all manner.[4] Inertial drag tends to be further reinforced in those instances where policy officials accord limited importance to the industrial sector in question; and the public firm is enmeshed both in a vertically integrated structure and in monopoly-monopsony relations, i.e., where the end user of its products also enjoys unrestricted market power and therefore itself faces no competitive pressures which could persuade it to demand increased levels of efficiency from its supplier. ITI exemplified this predicament. Not only did politicians treat telecommunications as a non-priority area, a 'luxury' good and hence undeserving of adequate budgetary support from Plan outlays. The status of P&T/DoT as a monopoly provider of telephone services in the country would also remain unchallenged until the mid-1990s. Because telecommunications was absent from the government's list of developmental priorities, it did not consider it worthwhile until the early 1980s to even investigate, let alone eliminate, the causes of the abysmal performance of this sector.[5]

Similarly, being a monopoly entity itself, P&T/DoT could safely tolerate its own inefficiencies and those of ITI, absorbing them without incurring any risks to its own position or finances. It would hardly be an exaggeration to state that until the mid-1980s, the provision of new telephones connections was dictated not by considerations of customer service, but by the logic of patronage. Once P&T/DoT had satisfied the needs of the politico-bureaucratic establishment (and those of the families of politicians), it had to answer no further questions about how effectively

---

[4] Organizational inertia is generated by both internal and external factors. Among the internal causes figure sunk costs in plant, equipment and personnel, the dynamics of political coalitions, and a tendency for precedents to become normative standards. Entry and exit barriers dominate external factors. Michael Hannan and John Freeman, 'Structural Inertia and Organizational Change', *American Sociological Review*, Vol. 49, No. 2, April 1984, pp. 149–64. See also R.C.O. Matthews, 'The Economics of Institutions and the Sources of Growth', *The Economic Journal*, No. 96, December 1986, pp. 903–18.

[5] The failure, more generally, of policy makers to impose a regime of disciplinary planning on the Indian capitalist class, an indispensable condition for achieving satisfactory rates of economic growth, and the reasons for this failure, have been explored at length by Chibber. *Locked in Place*, especially chapters 2 and 6.

it acquitted its responsibilities as a provider of public goods.[6] Nor was it unduly pressured by the government to try and improve standards of telephone communications. This also explained why, notwithstanding the flood of complaints from users, it neither took firm measures to make sure ITI conformed consistently to the prescribed quality standards, nor did it penalize its manufacturing arm when it supplied defective equipment.

This cosy single buyer-single vendor market structure binding P&T/DoT and ITI then enabled each to turn a blind eye to the inefficiencies of the other, even as it meant that the latter would be run along the lines of a government department rather than according to the imperatives of a business enterprise. The cost-plus pricing method adopted to govern commercial transactions between state authorities and public companies, while easy to calculate and administer since it required minimal amounts of information, granted further latitude to ITI escape 'orthodox' financial controls. Both ITI and P&T/DoT could cheerfully accommodate their mutual dysfunctionalities. In fact, the chronic inefficiencies that characterized the functioning of both parties tended to get inbuilt into the working of the system through a process of mutual reinforcement, setting a fixed pattern to the interactions between each party. In doing so, it gave rise to a vicious cycle, the consequences of which were equally negative for the two organizations as for all service users barring the elite.

It is true that in certain situations where ownership is completely delinked from management, giving rise to an agency-information problem, the efforts of state authorities to compel productive efficiency from managements can be hindered by the lack of adequate information about the causes of poor performance. Such constraints, however, hardly applied to ITI: given the interventionist style of P&T/DoT's administrative practices, state officials had first hand knowledge of the company's inner workings. Sealing off the domestic market from all but very limited telecommunication equipment imports, by erecting a supplementary protective barrier, further eroded the motivation for ITI to raise performance levels.

Consequently, neither spurred by competitive pressures nor by

[6] 'Politicians took very little interest in telecommunications—other than procuring connections for family and friends', notes Mody. 'State Consolidation through Liberalization of Telecommunications', p. 115.

externally or internally devised control mechanisms, which may have generated greater accountability and organizational discipline, there was nothing to prevent the two organizations from behaving as 'lazy monopolists', setting a high price for low quality products not so much in order to amass super profits but because they were unable to contain costs.[7] In such a context, the phenomenon of 'rent seeking' behaviour by all concerned parties (politicians, bureaucrats, managements, unions, workers) was bound to flourish as well.[8] It was this conjunction of elements, i.e., a monopoly producer of equipment catering to the needs of a monopoly supplier of services (at least until the end of the 1990s), that imparted to the bureaucratic regime of production prevailing in ITI its distinctive character.

But state ownership signified more than captive home markets. It was also synonymous with the loss of managerial autonomy, and, its corollary, government intervention in corporate strategy formulation. The advantages accruing to ITI from its status as a public sector enterprise were therefore offset by the numerous constraints attached to that very same status, and the sum total of constraints perhaps outweighed the advantages. A weighty corpus of literature is available to demonstrate that the 'genetically inherited ills' of the public sector in India had their origins in the government discharging its ownership duties in an 'indecisive and unbusinesslike' manner.[9]

This book has already identified several of those 'unbusinesslike' decisions. It has described how the technology choices of P&T/DoT functionaries combined with the political choices of the government with respect to the siting of new units severely harmed the long-run interests of ITI. It has also discussed at length how a number of the company's operational difficulties owed as much to government policy options, notably the stringent restrictions on imports, as to the inefficiencies of P&T/DoT. If curbs on the purchase of foreign

---

[7] The term is borrowed from Albert Hirschman who contrasts maximizing monopolists to a little noticed type of monopoly tyranny, one exercised by 'lazy' monopolists, and marked by the oppression of the weak by the incompetent. *Exit, Voice, and Loyalty. Responses to Decline in Firms, Organizations, and States*, Cambridge (Mass.), 1970, p. 59.

[8] Anne Krueger, 'The Political Economy of Rent Seeking', *American Economic Review*, Vol. 64, No. 3, June 1974, pp. 291–303.

[9] Bhaya, 'Colossus with Feet of Clay', p. M58.

technology, by restricting its access to the latest process innovations, left the company saddled with outdated manufacturing techniques, an important cause of poor quality, the financial indiscipline manifested by the parent administration meant that an already under-capitalized ITI constantly faced a liquidity crunch.

At the same time, the problems of organizational slack besetting ITI, associated with the management's response to these problems, provide a pardigmatic example of the workings of the soft budget constraint. By constituting an impregnable safety barrier, the combination of a totally protected domestic market which in turn gave company officials permanent latitude under a regime of administered prices to revise upwards production costs and still post profits, as well as the assurance of job security, freed them from all compulsions of increasing efficiency levels. To quote Harvey Leibenstein, one of the few neo-classical micro-economists who has attached more weight to 'X-efficiency' factors than to allocative efficiency, 'where the motivation is weak, firm managers will permit a considerable degree of slack in their operations and will not seek cost-improving methods'.[10]

Thus, quite paradoxically, far from being a positive enabling element, the twin guarantees of monopoly access to the domestic market coupled with the certitude of generating profits perpetuated a chain of inefficiencies that ultimately threatened to endanger the very existence of ITI once it lost its privileges in the aftermath of deregulation. Instead of encouraging the company to aim for higher performance standards, its dominant market position, on the contrary, created a pervasive sense of complacency from top to bottom where, on the one hand, change was either shunned or resisted, and, on the other, work ethics were allowed to steadily decline. In this respect, ITI's experience bears close parallels with that of British state-owned firms, notably British Leyland.[11]

What this case study also reveals is that within the specific structure of the Indian telecommunications market whose defining feature was a vertically integrated monopsony-monopoly relationship between P&T/

[10] Harvey Leibenstein, 'Allocative Efficiency vs. "X-Efficiency"', *The American Economic Review*, Vol. 56, No. 3, June 1966, pp. 392–415 (cit. p. 408). I am grateful to Bernard D'Mello for the reference.

[11] For an elaboration of this point, see Owen, *From Empire to Europe*, chap. 9; and Whisler, *British Motor Industry*, esp. Introduction and chaps. 4 and 6.

DoT and ITI, neither of the 'mechanisms of recuperation' described by Albert Hirschman could accomplish their stated function of keeping the company 'on its toes'.[12] Indeed, his overall argument that a situation of tight or complete monopoly could be preferable to the existence of competition in galvanizing flabby public enterprises to correct glaring inefficiencies, reaches its limits here. According to Hirschman, customers who cannot exit or withdraw will be more vocal in pressing complaints than those who have other alternatives, thus inducing firms to act.[13] In other words, one 'lazy monopolist' providing public goods might occasionally be forced to adopt a more responsive attitude when confronted with a growing volume of complaints from customers. But in a market structure where two 'lazy monopolists' operating in tandem exercise a total stranglehold over the choice and quality of goods and services available to users, voice tends to be totally silenced while exit is ruled out. The end result is apathy and resignation among customers.

In this context, it is essential to stress that while I have chronicled at great length the disastrous repercussions of the advent of deregulation for ITI, we must not lose sight of just how beneficial this policy measure has proved to be for long suffering subscribers. Opening the telecommunications equipment market to competitive forces has helped to bring down the interminable waiting lists for new connections, ensured access to cheaper and better quality equipment, and improved the overall functioning of the national network and vastly extended its footprint, especially in rural areas, through the introduction of new technological inputs, all factors indispensable for stimulating economic growth.

Underlining the negative consequences of a 'lazy monopolist' mindset as I have done with respect to ITI does not in any way imply an endorsement of the neo-liberal thesis arguing that public sector companies are programmed for failure. As I have stated right at the start of this book, I do not believe that public enterprises, because of the presumed original sin of state ownership, are pathologically predisposed to turning out costly and shoddy goods with the complicity of an apathetic management, a lazy workforce and self-interested union officials. Or that they are as a rule ineptly and wastefully managed in contrast to

---

[12] *Exit, Voice, and Loyalty*, p. 3, 55, 82–3. Voice, he writes, is handicapped when exit is not possible.

[13] ibid, pp. 45–51, 56, 58, 70–1.

private firms. There are enough well-run and profitable public enterprises, even in India, to disprove the contentions of its detractors. The corporate fiascos of the last few years have also unambiguously exposed the pretensions of privately owned companies to staking the moral and economic high ground of organizational efficiency for themselves. Nevertheless, the safety belt furnished by soft budgetary constraints does tend to skew the calculations and practices of state sector executives. When this factor concatenates with other referents such as secure job tenures, the absence of a credible system of rewards and penalties and loose monitoring by the political review authorities it is clear there is insufficient incentive to achieve higher performance standards. Furthermore, in the specific case of ITI, it was the particular institutional and regulatory configuration put into place by policy makers from its inception, notably the decision to subject both the production and distribution of telecommunications equipment to tight vertical integration, which provoked all manner of distortions and accounted for many dysfunctional features of its operations. Since the supervisory ministry purchased the quasi-totality of ITI's output and undertook responsibility for its distribution, the company was completely cut off from customers and final markets. One could contend that a greater degree of contact with end users might have been more conducive to fostering organizational behaviour which valorized cost and quality consciousness and customer-responsiveness.

This is say that other 'worlds of possibilities' which contained the potential of engendering a different, and perhaps more satisfactory outcome for the company, the government and the public at large, existed.[14] For these potentialities to have materialized, though, it required the articulation of a different institutional, normative and competitive mix. Lest it be forgotten, on at least two separate occasions, proposals had been tabled to detach ITI from the Ministry of Communications and place it under the wings of either the Ministry of Industries or the Department of Electronics so as to secure greater autonomy for the management as well as ensure better growth prospects for the company (see chap. one). On both occasions, P&T officials succeeded in persuading the government to veto these proposals. In the light of the current vogue

---

[14] Charles Sabel and Jonathan Zeitlin (eds.), *Worlds of Possibilities. Flexibility and Mass Production in Western Industrialization*, Cambridge, 1997.

for counter-factual history, one could well ask: 'What *if* the government had acted on these recommendations'.[15] Had it done so, it is possible that this present narrative might have carried an altogether happier ending.

Indifferent to the wants of customers, a bureaucratic factory regime in the Indian configuration, however, created the conditions which allowed its workforce to establish itself as a labour aristocracy. From the standpoint of employees, such a regime signified an elevation in social status by providing them with important material and symbolic advantages. The most coveted positions on the labour market, employment in state owned companies entitled job holders to more than just decent wages for relaxed work rhythms. It also promised them security of contract and a generous array of welfare benefits, thereby conferring tremendous prestige on the employee of the state, 'beneficiary of the aura that surrounds this institution'.[16]

Enjoined by the state to act as 'model employers' solicitous of the well being of their workforces, public enterprises could not only afford to concede demands for regular salary hikes and enhanced welfare measures more easily than private companies. Being cushioned by soft budget constraints and the lack of competition, they could also afford to do so without insisting on a reciprocal obligation on the part of employees and unions to step up productivity and maintain tighter standards of discipline. The fact that certain welfare provisions were unilateral concessions on the part of managements further underscored the above point, just as it demonstrated that not all the gains enjoyed by employees were the fruit of successful collective protest actions. To formulate the point differently, in the context of a state sector firm, managerial decisions advancing the interests of the workforce do not necessarily have to reflect the true bargaining power of unions.

For much the same reasons, managements could also readily agree to coopt the union as a subordinate partner in administering the workforce, sharing some of its command prerogatives with the latter by instituting a policy of joint regulation. Norms pertaining to promotions, discipline,

[15] Andrew Roberts (ed.), *What Might Have Been: Imaginary History from 12 Leading Historians*, London, 2004.

[16] Gérard Heuzé, 'Les deux classes ouvrières du pays d'entre les deux rivières', *Annales ESC*, No. 2, March–April 1987, pp. 265–81 (cit. p. 268).

conflict resolution, work conditions, collective bargaining were all determined in collaboration with workers' representatives, giving rise to an elaborate framework of impersonal, tightly codified rules, the 'investments of form' associated with their elaboration infusing them with temporal stability, spatial validity and relative autonomy.[17] By ensuring protection from arbitrary managerial domination, these rules, together with the institutional arrangements undergirding them, empowered employees as industrial citizens possessing clearly defined rights and obligations.

While formalized norms designed to regulate the workplace by coordinating the interests of employers and employees are equally characteristic of large private corporations, having in fact originated within these organizations, two points distinguish public from private 'bureaucratic controls'.[18] First, in public firms the ambit of these norms tends to be much more extensive, leaving very few spheres of activity uncovered; it is difficult, for example, to find in private companies the equivalent of the automatic seniority based promotion schemes that several state sector undertakings had introduced. Second, the role devolved to public sector unions as much in the production of these norms as in their administration generally exceeds in importance that of their private sector counterparts.

Employment security was then intimately connected with wage security in the bureaucratic regime of production. This stood in contra-distinction to state-socialist firms in the former Soviet bloc where employment security marched in step with wage insecurity. Workers here received no minimum wages, being paid on the basis of a straight piece rate system, forcing them to expend considerable effort as Miklos Haraszti's incisive account of his experiences as a miller in a Hungarian factory illustrates.[19] What this suggests is that the foundations of the social pact tying managements, unions and employees in public companies does not rest on a fordist trade off between higher wages and higher levels of labour productivity. Instead wage and non-wage concessions granted to the workforce are designed to secure their cooperation in

---

[17] Laurent Thévenot, 'Les investissements de forme', *Cahiers du centre d'études de l'emploi*, No. 29, 1985, pp. 21–71.

[18] The term, of course, comes from Edwards, *Contested Terrain*.

[19] Miklos Haraszti, *A Worker in a Worker's State. Piece-Rates in Hungary*, Harmondsworth, 1981.

fulfilling annual production targets set by the supervisory ministries and on the basis of which managements' performances are evaluated.

Any increase in targets from one year to the next is achieved not by extracting greater surplus from workers, but typically by offering them supplementary amounts of overtime expenditure. In sum, public firms must be seen as the privileged site of a social compromise where state involvement ensures the direct producers of labour an equitable share of the gains of industrialization. Master of the general interest, the direct implication of the state in the industrial sphere is designed just as much to fulfil a social (and political) function upon which its legitimacy partly rests as an economic function. Put in other words, economic planning, employment relations and social welfare are often (but not systematically) closely integrated through the rule of law in state enterprises.[20]

One other feature of the bureaucratic production regime must be noted. Because the influence state officials exercise over the affairs of public firms is so all pervasive, struggles launched by workers invariably acquire a political dimension and come to be directly targeted at the authority of the state itself. This has enormous consequences on the eventual outcome of a struggle given the extent of power disparities separating the two sides, with workers and unions obviously lacking the range of institutional resources that the state can promptly mobilise to overcome all forms of protest. Thus once the state has decided to stand firm, employees and unions' chances of successfully imposing their collective strength to secure their demands, however legitimate these may be, are virtually nil.

If a bureaucratic factory regime guarantees its workforce social and economic uplift, can we conclude from the example of ITI that such a configuration is synonymous with the heteronomy of managements, dispossessed of their command prerogatives by the administrative ministry? Moreover, given that several of the dysfunctional traits identified in the operations of ITI are hardly exclusive to the telecommunications supplier, or more generally to Indian public sector companies, but can just as easily be found in state-owned undertakings in the developed economies of the West, not to speak of other parts of the developing

---

[20] Noel Whiteside and Robert Salais, 'Introduction', in *idem* (eds.), *Governance, Industry and Labour Markets. The Modernizing State in the Mid-Twentieth Century*, London, 1998, pp. 1–22.

world, can the validity of the paradigm of the bureaucratic regime be extended beyond the Indian context? Framing the question in this manner, leads us directly to a discussion of the role of the state and the nature of its relations with the public sector in general. Establishing comparisons is rendered difficult by the dearth of monographic studies, and not just in India, devoted to state-run industrial enterprises. Nevertheless, we can advance a few tentative hypotheses.

Far from being undifferentiated, state intervention falls into various categories, and for schematic purposes can be located on a continuum ranging from maximum to minimal intervention. Thus if a *dirigiste* state stands at one extreme, at the other extreme we find the liberal state. Hemmed between these two polar opposites are the planning state which leans closer to the *dirigiste* model of action and the instigator state tilting in the direction of the liberal model.[21] (Needless to say, denationalizations and the rollback of the state, attendant upon the triumph of neo-liberal economic thought, in both the advanced North and the developing South have considerably attenuated the scope for active state involvement in the economy.) Depending upon the temporal context and the industrial sector in question, and consonant with its overall policy objectives, state interventionism can oscillate from *dirigisme* to liberalism.

Such a typology presents the dual advantage of bringing a wide range of national contexts and practices within a single analytical framework. It also helps to demonstrate that the same government, regardless of its ideological affiliations, can adopt different strategies towards different industries.[22] Thus to take the example of France, if the state embarked upon the *dirigiste* road with respect to the steel and telecommunication sectors, structured by monopoly conditions, it played a planning role in

[21] Claude Durand et al, 'Dirigisme et libéralisme: L'État dans l'industrie', *Sociologie du Travail*, No. 3, 1985, pp. 251–72. According to him, the dirigiste state besides defining specific guidelines as well as resource mobilization actively participates in their implementation. The liberal state, on the other hand, is satisfied with the role of a shareholder, extending financial backing and monitoring performance. In the planning state, policy makers, keeping in mind the larger political implications, formulate the industrial objectives, corporate alliances and the product mix, but do not intervene in their realization. Finally, the instigator state sketches out the broad goals for an industrial sector and allows managements total autonomy to translate them into action.

[22] Not one state, but many possible 'states' can be found in Britain and France, comment Whiteside and Salais, whose principles of action vary by area and over different periods of time. 'Introduction'.

the aeronautics and space industry, an instigatory role in the electronics industry, while privileging liberal policy orientations in automobiles and textiles, two highly competitive areas.[23]

In the Indian situation, one could argue that state interventionism in public sector companies essentially ran along *dirigiste* lines.[24] Given the authority vested in the hands of the state through the instrumentality of planning to secure the process of capital accumulation by laying the foundations of a modern industrial economy, policy makers invariably saw their command functions as extending to cover the operations of public undertakings as well. That these bureaucratic controls persisted much longer than may have been really necessary can to some extent be attributed to the phenomenon of 'rent seeking', where politicians and policy makers came to have a vested interest in maintaining state sector companies firmly within their orbit of jurisdiction.[25] But I believe the direct hands-on involvement witnessed in ITI–an involvement that could be qualified as 'authoritarian'–represented an extreme version of *dirigisme* since it had the effect of practically stripping the management of all autonomy, and was the exception rather than the rule.[26] An explanation for this phenomenon can be traced back to the particular status of P&T/ DoT, at once owner and sole client of the company. The regulatory controls exercised by the state were direct rather than indirect in nature.

Similar direct controls prevailed in certain sectors such as steel. So it is possible that other Indian public companies too found themselves in a similar predicament as ITI. But they were not locked in vertically integrated relations with their tutelary authority to whom they sold the totality of their products and services. Consequently, one could speculate that milder forms of *dirigisme* prevailed in these companies. While investment decisions pertaining to the location of new plants and capacity expansion definitely remained a prerogative of the state, as well as perhaps

[23] Claude and Michelle Durand, 'L'État dans l'entreprise. Le systeme de décision', in C. Durand (ed.), *De l'économie planifiée à l'économie de marché, l'intervention de l'Etat dans l'industrie*, Paris, 1991, pp. 42–64.

[24] Kornai distinguishes between four degrees of paternalism, the most extreme being where central authorities dictate input allocation without taking into consideration the firm's wishes. ITI would fall into this last category. *Economics of Shortage*, pp. 562–8.

[25] Krueger, 'The Political Economy of Rent Seeking'.

[26] The term is borrowed from Durand, though he uses it in a slightly different sense. 'Dirigisme et libéralisme'.

the selection of technology partners, it may not have interfered in operational matters.

Bagaram Tulpule, the trade union leader who headed the Durgapur Steel Plant for a short while in the early 1970s, however, has a different story to tell. According to him, officials from the Steel Authority of India (SAIL), the giant holding company formed to oversee the operations of Durgapur and its sister plants, constantly meddled in plant-level personnel issues even as they offered 'little practical guidance and support'.[27] He goes on to add that following the launch of SAIL in 1973, the Durgapur management was completely eliminated from the process of policy elaboration. That Durgapur was no isolated or eccentric case is borne out by the conclusions of the numerous official committees established at periodic intervals to investigate the workings of state enterprises. Highly critical of excessive bureaucratic interference, and warning of its adverse impact on the efficient running of these enterprises, all these bodies repeatedly urged the government to adequately empower public sector executives so that the reality of their functions corresponded to their titles.[28] All of this would then suggest that regardless of the industrial segment the situation of ITI did not qualitatively differ much from that of the majority of state-controlled companies.

So if the *dirigiste* paradigm of action is hardly exclusive to India can we conclude that nothing sets apart Indian public firms from other such companies elsewhere? Based on his study of the state-owned coal mining industry in Bihar, the anthropologist Gérard Heuzé speaks of an Indian 'mode of production'.[29] He defines this productive organization, on the one hand, as a difficult accommodation between contradictory realities where economic rationality–augmenting production and productivity– clashes with social considerations–providing jobs for the vast army of unemployed–and, on the other, as a judicious arrangement between these same realities and the complex interests of local elite groupings and the needs of the state.

This equation might well be true for a relatively backward sector such as mining, located that too in one of the most underdeveloped regions of the country. But to what extent can the argument be generalized to

---

[27] Tulpule, 'Managing Durgapur', (Part II), p. 24.

[28] See chapter one, fn 20.

[29] Heuzé, *Ouvriers d'un autre monde,* p. 328.

the more modern branches of the public sector owned by the central government? Jonathan Parry and Christian Strümpell's instructive comparative study of the Bhilai and Rourkela steel plants reveal considerable differences in the nature of interactions between managements and the political establishment.[30] While the former was relatively insulated from political pressure emanating from local clientelist networks, in Rourkela the opposite was true. The weight of political compulsions in influencing managerial decisions with respect to recruitment was clearly visible in the ethnically homogenous composition of the Rourkela workforce where the claims of the local Oriya population were systematically privileged. Bhilai on the other hand, remained far more faithful to Nehru's founding vision of the public sector as the proverbial melting pot where the myriad regional, linguistic and religious identities merged to create the secular modern nation.

So although overmanning was widespread at both plants, in one, it stemmed less from employment-generating considerations than from managerial inefficiencies and low effort norms, while at the other the reasons lay in satisfying demands of local politicians for jobs for sons-of-the soil. The consequences of political intervention also proved far reaching. In distinct contrast to Bhilai which on the whole experienced minimal communal violence by Indian standards, the ethnically diversified structure of its workforce serving to buffer antagonisms, Rourkela has been periodically convulsed by savage riots marked by killings of Muslims and other 'outsiders'. Political arm-twisting seems to have been a standard phenomenon at the Durgapur steel plant as well. But reading Tulpule's account, one gathers the impression that the demands for job provision levied upon company executives were mediated through the trade unions affiliated to the various parties rather than emanating directly from local politicians.[31]

Trends at ITI followed more the Rourkela pattern than the Durgapur or Bhilai schema. Unlike in Durgapur, none of the top executives at the Bangalore plant whom I interviewed said they had been approached either directly or indirectly by local political leaders to appoint kinfolk and supporters. The personnel department therefore had never been obliged to bend formal recruitment procedures in order to favour certain

---

[30] Parry and Strümpell, 'On the Desecration of Nehru's "Temples"'.
[31] Tulpule 'Managing Durgapur', (Part I).

candidates. But like in Rourkela, the management faced tremendous pressure to reserve the lion's share of jobs for the indigenous people. As I have shown in the final chapter, during the language agitation that rocked Bangalore in the late-1960s, the Congress-I chief minister Veerendra Patil himself took the lead in insisting on increased representation for native-born Kannada speakers in the workforce of ITI and the other city-based public enterprises. The official injunctions also yielded the requisite dividends, notwithstanding the management's initial attempts at resistance on the grounds that employing local people on a preferential basis threatened to violate constitutional principles relating to equality of opportunities. As a result, whatever progress the company might have made during the 1950s towards achieving the Nehruvian ideal of regrouping an ethnically diversified workforce in a shared space had melted into air a couple of decades later.

Thus, the case of Bhilai aside, and despite some degree of variation in their situational dynamics, in the other three plants managements had to make allowances for local political compulsions. Owned by the central government and hence unaccountable to state governments, most aspects of corporate strategy may well have been determined directly in consultation with the supervisory ministry unmediated by local politicians. On the question of recruitments, though, a crucial source of patronage dispensation in a job-hungry nation, state leaders were determined to have a voice and, to the extent possible, their share of the spoils. The degree to which public sector executives are insulated from or exposed to political pressures is therefore context-specific and depends on complex sets of contingencies, both variables excluding the possibility of facile generalizations. From these isolated examples it would also appear that Heuzé's characterization of the public sector company as an unstable and shifting compromise between economic and social goals brokered by a medley of political forces is not entirely without justification. But once again only a much needed accretion of knowledge through research into the inner fabric of these enterprises can enable us to fruitfully explore the relations between what is specific and universal to their organizational systems. The urgency of pursuing such a task cannot be over stressed at a time when it is legitimate to entertain doubts about the future of state-owned companies both in India and elsewhere.

Epilogue

In August 2007, I returned to the main Bangalore plant after a lapse of over three years for a short visit. From media and other sources I knew ITI had recorded no improvement whatsoever in its position. Losses had continued to steadily pile up year after year, crossing the Rs 4000 million mark in 2005–06. Nevertheless, I was still taken aback by what I saw and learnt in the course of my conversations with employees and the management. The abstractions of the balance sheet were sorely inadequate preparation for coming to terms with practical ground realities.

Already during my first visit in the mid-1990s, the spatial fabric of the factory bore ample testimony to the decline in ITI's fortunes. I remember having been struck by the phantom hangars I crossed, stripped of all activity and human presence but still replete with material traces of past vitality. The rows of unused machines, exhortatory posters of all manner hanging limply from the walls alongside the images of Hindu divinities silently looking down, the dust-clogged furniture, all these lifeless objects merely appeared to be awaiting a sign to regain their former utility. Some of these derelict spaces predated the advent of economic reforms and the rollback of ITI's monopoly privileges. The technological mutation materialized in the transition from electro-mechanical to electronic systems during the mid-1980s had already spelt the doom of a range of manufacturing processes. As the hardware content of the exchanges decreased and metal parts gave way to electronic components, all the machine shops had progressively disappeared and with them the different trades they had long sustained. Other abandoned or partially abandoned hangars, however, directly reflected the disastrous effects of deregulation.

Each successive field trip that I undertook thereafter only served to furnish supplementary evidence of the plant's steady and apparently unstoppable downward journey. The vacant spaces kept extending while the levels of production activity kept shrinking paralleling the constant outflow of operatives who had quit the plant, in most cases after opting for voluntary retirement (VR). Still, there were sufficient number of workers milling around the factory premises, enough movement and noise, and even a bustle of sorts emanating from a few shops to preserve the fiction of a functioning organization.

This fiction had more or less completely evaporated when I revisited the plant in 2007. The Oxford Dictionary refers to a factory as a building or a group of buildings where goods are manufactured or assembled chiefly by machine. Going by this definition, the Bangalore plant had ceased to be a factory in all but name. Barring a couple of shops attending to repair work, production had virtually ceased everywhere else. Lacking technology or funds to purchase material or orders from its principal client, BSNL, shop managers were unable to allocate jobs to their personnel who consequently stayed idle the entire workday.[1] Far from being an engaging prospect, this enforced idleness proved oppressive for most workers. As Ramu, a qualified toolmaker told me, 'you cannot imagine how painful and tiring it is to sit doing nothing for eight hours day after day. Once you have finished reading the paper and chatting with your colleagues there is nothing else to do'.

The network services division, responsible for undertaking the installation and maintenance of communications equipment on a turnkey

---

[1] For reasons best known to itself, from April to August 2006, BSNL arbitrarily discontinued the reservation quota which guaranteed ITI a 30 per cent share of the service provider's total equipment requirements. Brief to Parliamentary Standing Committee on Information Technology, 14 October 2006.

basis, notably for the army, alone exhibited a semblance of activity. But even here an employee claimed that his tasks occupied him for no more than three or four hours. 'The rest of the time I look after union matters'. Only the monkey colonies noisily trapezing across their tree-top homes seemed to show no signs of being affected by the plant's moribund state. Walking from one half-lit and forlorn hangar to the next, I was also surprised to see just how few people remained in the factory. Not only had the strength of the overall work force in Bangalore contracted by more than half between 2002–03 and 2006–07, falling from 4545 employees (officers and non-officers) to 2151, but of this number, barely 450 comprised direct production operatives.[2]

Of course, top officials continued to rail against the persistent ineffectiveness of the voluntary retirement scheme in persuading employees to exit, particularly those located in some of the company's northern units.[3] Despite the scheme having been in operation for a decade and a half, one official estimate still placed at close to 3000 employees the number deemed as surplus to the company's requirements out of a total labour force of 13, 415 people. Nevertheless, the Bangalore plant accounted for almost 39 per cent of the 4967 employees who had opted for the 'golden handshake' since 2002–03.[4] The scare tactics pursued by the management, congruent with the recommendations of consultancy firm PwC, of delaying the payment of salaries, in some cases by several months, had apparently yielded the requisite dividends. Interpreting this action as an indicator of the company's worsening difficulties, many workers had chosen to leave before it was too late.

[2] *Source*: ITI Personnel Department.

[3] See minutes of unit heads meeting, 11–12 April 2006 where the plants were advised to combat the 'lukewarm response' to voluntary retirement through 'aggressive campaigning' and the establishment of counselling cells.

[4] VR Departures (officers and non-officers)

	2003–04	2004–05	2005–06	2006–07
Bangalore	1315	179	164	265
Rae Bareli	1142	1	3	13
Naini	727	65	196	150
Mankapur	78	5	1	20
Total	3726	299	410	532

Source: ITI Corporate Office.

As some of my worker and union friends pointed out to me, but for the company's incapacity to assure the timely payment of VR amounts– delays ranging from one to two months were not uncommon–because of its hopeless financial predicament, employee response would have been even stronger, something that the management itself recognized.[5] Quite a few potential candidates, especially those with dependent children, feared the company would not honour its monetary commitments towards them once they had taken VR and left. The consequential wave of departures meant that from being the biggest of ITI's six operations, the mother Bangalore outfit now ranked behind the other three major units (Rae Bareli, Mankapur and Naini).[6]

Moving around the various administration offices, I found much the same gloom and sense of inutility, the surreal waiting-for-Godot mood that I had in the factory premises. Normally impervious to shop floor developments, neither the tall cement wall that demarcated the administrative block from the factory, nor the massive granite blocks utilized for the former's construction, earning for it the name of 'stone building', seemed to serve as a buffer on this occasion. The manpower cell which occupied a long, cavernous room and where even as late as 2001 sat 30 employees, now contained just five people, distinctly outnumbered by the empty desks and chairs surrounding them. Next door, Unchalli, the head of the Industrial Relations section, declared point blank that the section 'had almost become redundant'. After 23 years of service, Unchalli himself was leaving ITI at the end of the month to join a private firm. 'Remuneration in the private sector is three times higher. In ITI they are not even paying our salaries in time'. Though the company had agreed to distribute non-officers' salaries by the tenth day of the month, officers often had to wait until the 20th day.[7]

From another personnel department officer, I learnt that the company was 'headless' for several months now. Thought to be acting directly on the orders of Sonia Gandhi, the Communications Ministry had

[5] PD note, 2 September 2006.

[6] In 2006–07, the Rae Bareli plant had 4093 employees on its pay rolls, Naini 2452 employees and Mankapur 2284 employees.

[7] management-union Apex Meeting, June 2005. Notwithstanding this engagement, in 2006 employees received their salaries for the month of March in the third week of May. As an official note bluntly stated, the reasons for delays in the disbursement of salaries are 'well ingrained in minds of employees.'

summarily sacked the incumbent chairman Y.K. Pandey. Appointed in 2003, Pandey had straight away been confronted by a crucial problem– the refusal of the banks to extend adequate credit to ITI given its mounting losses.[8] In the light of its dismal internal resource mobilization record (see chapter three for details), the banks' decision was fraught with consequences. It restricted access to much-needed working capital to execute even the limited orders on hand which in turn threatened to trigger a vicious cycle where the company sank even deeper into the red and, not being able deliver equipment on time to BSNL, further compromised its credibility.[9]

To tackle the fund shortage, Pandey began momentarily diverting employees' wages to meet working capital requirements. This manoeuvre, however, backfired when workers in Rae Bareli together with their families, capitalizing on Sonia Gandhi's visit to her constituency, blocked her motorcade to protest against the non-payment of salaries for several months. Lending a sharper edge to these grievances were the complaints of numerous VR beneficiaries of not having received their compensation on time either. Pandey had already alienated Rae Bareli employees as well as Congress-I politicians when shortly after taking over as chairman he had announced the closure of the plant before backing down in the face of widespread public outcry.

Official displeasure with the ITI chairman also stemmed from the larger question of its corporate performance. The government faulted him for having failed to turn around the company despite the provision in 2004–05 of an aid package worth Rs 9240 million. In return, Pandey is believed to have promised to cut the wage bill by 25 per cent and to divest cash-draining welfare facilities like the hospital, but succeeded in achieving neither goal. In his defence, it must be stressed that the aid allocated by the government represented only a fraction of the company's original demand, it had come almost two years after the demand had gone to the supervisory ministry and that too in several tranches, and finally most of it had been utilized not for productive investment purposes

---

[8] By March 2007, total accumulated losses stood at a massive Rs 15,500 million.

[9] The management claimed it could increase annual sales volume three fold on the condition it secured a regular flow of working capital. ITI Revival and Funding Plan, June 2007.

but to settle voluntary retirement disbursements and statutory obligations such as gratuity.[10]

Pandey was not the only high-profile figure to have abruptly quit the company. The Bangalore union too had witnessed a significant leadership change, a change which would leave an undeniable impact on the nature of union-management relationships. Shortly before the union elections in March 2007, Michael Fernandes, the veteran leader announced he would be not be recontesting the post of president—a post which he had held uninterruptedly for close to three decades. Fernandes had apparently seen the 'writing on the wall', as one executive put it. Increasingly accused of adopting pro-management positions, in 2006 workers had overturned a proposal to reappoint him as an honorary official of the credit cooperative society, a satellite union organization, notwithstanding his central role in the creation of the cooperative and its subsequent successful growth. In the wake of this incident, Fernandes had judged it wiser to relinquish the presidency of the union at the end of his term rather than risk the ignominy of defeat. The support publicly extended by Fernandes to the management's practice of not paying salaries on time on the grounds that the company lacked the means to do so had particularly angered workers. They also reproached him for having failed to leverage his family connections during the years of the BJP government, when his brother George Fernandes held the important defence portfolio, to try and obtain orders from the army for the company on a permanent basis.

Fernandes' decision to withdraw from the union was not cost free for the new leadership. In addition to his stature, vast experience and good rapport with high level executives, aided in this by their common middle class habitus, another significant status marker distinguished Fernandes from his successors in the union: his command over the 'language of command'.[11] Always essential when dealing with the upper echelons of management, fluency in English had assumed even greater weight in the present setting where barring one exception all the top corporate posts

---

[10] As evidenced by the example of the public sector banks, restructuring could succeed provided the government was prepared to inject the sums of money required for this purpose. T.T. Ram Mohan, 'Deregulation and Performance of Public Sector Banks', *EPW*, Vol. 37, No. 5, 2 February 2002, pp. 393–7.

[11] Cohn, 'The Command of Language'.

at the Bangalore plant were occupied by North Indians who spoke no Kannada at all. This linguistic equation placed the freshly elected union representatives at a tremendous disadvantage given their lack of proficiency in English which in turn had the effect of straining communications between the two sides. As one personnel department officer remarked, 'the union people are familiar with the difficulties confronting the plant, but they are unable to present their point of view correctly'. Fernandes' standing with top management had also helped to partially check the eroding influence of the Bangalore plant in the face of the ascendancy of the Rae Bareli unit thanks to the 'Sonia factor'. (Rumour had it that the Congress-I party boss stayed at the ITI guesthouse during her periodic constituency visits.) His departure now definitively sealed the shift in the power axis to the latter plant.

The same day that I visited the factory, I dropped in to see a friend in the township. Vadiraj was a second-generation ITI employee. In his early forties, he had spent his entire life in the township where he had met his wife, Asha, the daughter of an ITI employee too. Following the death of his father in 1986, he had been recruited on 'compassionate grounds' as a data entry operator in the computer department. Vadi was deeply attached to the township, taking pride in the well-planned and spacious layout, the unpolluted and garbage-free environment, the safe and uncongested streets where children could happily play, the uninterrupted supplies of water and electricity, and more generally, the quiet and laid back atmosphere that prevailed—in a nutshell, the antithesis of a modern Indian city. And during one of our conversations he had jokingly remarked that like his father and mother who had died in the township, 'I too might die here'.

When I reminded him now of his statement in the light of ITI's crippling financial woes, he brushed it aside with a laugh. While maintaining a façade of optimism about the company's future prospects, a natural reaction given his role as the sole bread winner in a family of three, he admitted that the township had changed beyond recognition. 'I don't know my neighbours anymore because many of them are not ITI people'. In effect, with company personnel occupying only a third or so of the township's 1700 houses, the management had decided to cut its losses and begun renting out the vacant houses to employees from other public service organizations as well as the government and the army. Much the same process of 'de-exclusivizing' was also taking place with regard to some of the company's other welfare facilities. Once the exclusive preserve of employees' children, the ITI school located within the township had lifted this entry barrier so much so that the overwhelming majority of students now were outsiders. Similarly, the ITI hospital had opened its doors and beds to general patients.

A few days later I went to talk to S.K. Chatterjee, the company's personnel chief and most likely future chairman. (The government effectively appointed him to this post at the end of 2007.) Together with other head office personnel, Chatterjee had relocated from the corporate building situated in the heart of Bangalore and which had now been rented out for cost-saving reasons, to more modest premises within proximity of the factory.[12] He had just returned from a pilgrimage to Sabarimala in Kerala, having climbed right to the top of the steep hill with his belongings on his head where the celebrated temple housing the deity Ayappan stood. As he readily acknowledged, the ardours of this trek would in all likelihood pale away besides the task awaiting him of running ITI.

The root cause of the company's problem continued to remain technology and for much the same reasons as in the past. Firstly, it lacked proprietary know-how in the all important domain of wireless telephony, a substantive handicap now that demand for fixed line connections, its staple revenue-earner in the past, had almost totally dried up. Between March 2005 and March 2007, the national subscriber base of fixed line services had fallen from 47.7 million to 40.7 million.[13] The impact of this fall found a direct echo in the company's balance sheet: in 2006, it derived less than 9 per cent of its turnover from switching equipment compared to around 60 per cent a few years ago. Secondly, official policy choices imposed considerable restrictions on the management's room for manoeuvre.

In September 2003, ITI had signed an agreement with the Chinese equipment vendor Shenzhen Zhongxing Telephones (ZTE) authorizing it to take up the manufacture of infrastructure for cellular networks based

[12] Another important economy measure had entailed the removal of Central Industrial Security Force personnel charged with protecting the Mankapur, Naini, Palakkad and Rae Bareli factories. This move, the management claimed, had yielded annual savings of Rs 480 million.

[13] *Source*: Telecom Regulatory Authority of India. In 2002–03, for instance, the rapid growth of BSNL's cellular services had translated into the service provider losing 1.6 million fixed line subscribers. *Business Line*, 10 April 2003.

on the Code Division Multiple Access (CDMA) standard (see chapter four).[14] Four years on, the public sector enterprise had yet to commence production for the simple reason that it was still waiting to obtain the official green light. The government apparently saw no contradiction in its decision to concurrently import large quantities of fully assembled systems from none other than ZTE itself even as it prohibited indigenous production, claiming it represented a security threat to the nation at large. As a result, ITI's role was confined to merely installing the equipment for client BSNL, and even here certain advanced technical operations were directly handled by the Chinese company.

As Chatterjee lamented, 'we are only traders, middlemen, and the value addition done by us is very limited'.[15] At the same time, with equipment prices in free fall, doubts had also surfaced about the economic viability of turning out CDMA infrastructure locally even if the government happened to reverse its options. Minimum investments of the order of Rs 1200–1500 million in testing equipment and new facilities at the Bangalore plant needed to be made before production could get underway, and the company feared this expenditure could prove unprofitable in the long run. Furthermore, from the standpoint of BSNL, its preferred technology choice was not CDMA but the rival GSM standard which had successfully established itself as the dominant standard in the Indian market.[16] Although the public sector service provider had equipped its network in certain regions with CDMA, it accounted for under 12 per cent of its total mobile subscriber base.[17]

---

[14] Two main competing network technologies exist in cellular services: CDMA and Global System for Mobile Communications (GSM). While CDMA, a relatively new commercial technology dating to the early 1990s has been the dominant network standard for North America and parts of Asia, GSM has established its supremacy across western Europe. The main disadvantage with CDMA-equipped phones is that it cannot offer international roaming.

[15] The fact that ITI was only involved in trading and not manufacturing with respect to CDMA equipment disqualified it in principle from the ambit of BSNL's preferential purchase policy. The operator, however, closed its eyes to this anomaly.

[16] GSM's share of the overall Indian mobile market stood at 73.1 per cent with the remainder being held by CDMA. Barring BSNL, the only other major operators to have adopted CDMA were Tata Tele and Reliance. *Source:* ITI Corporate Office.

[17] As of March 2007, the breakdown of BSNL's total subscriber base read as follows: wireline 36.4 million, wireless 30.57 which further divided into GSM (27.02 million) and CDMA (3.55 million). *Source:* ITI Corporate Office.

Unlike in the case of CDMA systems, the government had raised no objection to ITI manufacturing GSM infrastructural equipment locally. So relying on know-how supplied by Alcatel (or Lucent as it is now called), the management had allocated these products to the Mankapur and Rae Bareli factories. This decision, though, foreclosed the possibility of the Bangalore plant picking up a slice of the business. Moreover, the relatively modest size of the Indian market for mobile handsets together with the rapid pace of product obsolescence, in addition to ITI's own structural deficiencies—technological backwardness, lack of competivity, bureaucratic procedures, and regulatory constraints—meant the plant could also not consider leveraging its manufacturing facilities to turn out handsets.

Nor could it count on the R&D department to come to its rescue with new products. Although the brain drain sustained in the immediate aftermath of deregulation had badly destabilized the company's research efforts (see chap five), it had still managed to retain pockets of expertise in areas such as equipment encryption where it was engaged in several projects for the army in particular. Responsibility for coordinating these projects had been entrusted to Ashok Anand, a well-recognized specialist in this field. Anand had built a strong working relationship with the army and was reputedly capable of pulling in annual orders of Rs 500–1000 million on the strength of his name. But hopes of further breakthroughs collapsed when he and his entire team of 60 people defected. A clash of wills with Pandey who himself boasted of a research background, ended with Anand leaving to join another public sector company, ECIL.

If technology remained a perennial bug bear for ITI, so did the dispersion of its production facilities. Indeed, the principal reason for its financial haemorrhage lay in the high levels of fixed expenditure incurred in running six units most of whose order books were empty. Although the company continued to suffer from overmanning, given the chronic paucity of funds, the management lacked both the discretion to implement the voluntary retirement programme on a systematic basis and to make it financially more attractive in order to induce reluctant employees to consider availing of this incentive.[18] Chatterjee himself

---

[18] Company officials wanted to hike the voluntary retirement compensation amount from 45 days salary for every year worked to 60 days. Management-union Apex Meeting, 7–8 December 2006.

believed that in the present context, operating two plants more than sufficed, but declared he was powerless to shut down the others. 'We are victims of the situation. The government is maintaining six units for political reasons. Closures will create difficulties for politicians'. Lucid about what he could expect to achieve in case he became chairman, Chatterjee added: 'I can only try and keep the situation going as it is and prevent a down turn or things from worsening'. ITI's condition also sharply contrasted with that of some of its counterparts located in Bangalore such as BEL, HAL and BEML. While a large and regular flow of defence contracts kept the growth wheels turning at the first two companies, demand for metro rail coaches stimulated by the development of suburban transport networks assured BEML of adequate work.

Nevertheless, even the task of maintaining ITI afloat promised to be a formidably intimidating one in the absence of an experienced executive cadre whom Chatterjee could call upon to tackle ITI's intractable problems. Not only had there been a steady stream of desertions at the middle management level, the organizational backbone, to other city-based state enterprises, the fallout, to some extent, of a decision taken by Pandey to freeze all promotions for officers as part of the overall cost-cutting drive. The company also stood on the verge of losing almost its entire leadership at one stroke. Of the 12 general managers occupying key corporate positions, 10 were scheduled to retire between 2007–09. By common consensus, the candidates tipped to replace them lacked both their knowledge and competencies. 'The shortage of good personnel at the top will be felt', remarked one official.

After my meeting with Chatterjee, I returned to the factory to see B.K. Sharma, the former head of the telephone division who now oversaw the newly established installation and commission division (IC), charged with setting up wireless infrastructure for BSNL in different parts of the country. Sharma had been associated with ITI and more specifically the Bangalore plant since childhood. His father Bhagram Sharma had joined the plant shortly after its creation in 1948 as a chargehand in the tool room. From there he had risen to the rank of a manager before retiring in 1979. For a good part of his career he had also lived in the ITI township. So his son had literally grown up under the shadow of the factory walls. Trained as a mechanical engineer, after completing his studies B.K. Sharma had received three job offers, including one from ITI, but aware that he would not escape comparisons with his father he was reluctant to come here. 'I wanted to go to BEL before changing my mind because ITI had a better image then'. Recruited in 1973 during the factory's heyday, Sharma had had ample time to observe and, no doubt, reflect on the reasons behind its progressive downhill tumble.

The problems confronting him now in his present post furnished a classic illustration of the recurrent dysfunctionalities bedevilling the company. Although the Bangalore plant counted a sizeable contingent of idle workers, one of Sharma's main grouses was that his division paradoxically lacked adequate personnel. As against its manpower requirements of between 600–700 employees, it had secured just one-fifth of this number. The reasons had to do in the main with the parochial agendas pursued by other division heads, apprehensive that surrendering their personnel to the IC division would create shortages in case their own divisions received orders in the near future. At the same time, Sharma expressed considerable scepticism about the effectiveness of the training programmes conducted by the company to familiarize employees with CDMA technology. Irregular, restricted in duration, haphazard in the selection of candidates with interested employees not being chosen even as others were forced to attend, these programmes also failed to achieve their stated objective. Barely 5 per cent of all those who received training are believed to have subsequently integrated the IC division. And many of those who did volunteer to join the division found the requirements associated with the job overly demanding.

Setting up cellular infrastructural facilities effectively necessitated employees having to leave Bangalore and going to the installation site where conditions generally tended to be less comfortable than on the shopfloor. To ensure continuity, they also had to spend some amount of time in the field away from their families. This, employees were extremely reluctant to do.[19] 'Some say they have aged parents to look after, others that they have school and college-going children, still others that they have to get their daughters married'. With employees unwilling to remain in the field for more than a couple of weeks, the work teams were subject to constant disruption much to the chagrin of BSNL. The operator is

---

[19] According to one executive, employees at the Mankapur and Rae Bareli factories tended to be less home-bound than their Bangalore counterparts. He attributed this, interestingly enough, to the greater mobility of their children who invariably had to migrate in search of jobs.

known to have complained on more than one instance at what it saw as the inadequate commitment and engagement of ITI field staff, blaming delays in the commissioning of the equipment on the poor service provided by ITI.[20] It was precisely to resolve this issue that the head of a Bangalore plant issued a directive in February 2007 insisting that all personnel sent to the field should spend a minimum period of two months.[21] The measure, however, only succeeded in stirring employee resentment which culminated in some of the team heads relinquishing their responsibilities.

To satisfy BSNL's demands for better quality service, the management had also progressively taken recourse to contract personnel. Between 2004–06, close to 720 contract engineers and technicians were hired on the back of three-year long job guarantees, a clear indication that the company did not consider this to be either a short term or a stop-gap step.[22] No doubt, resistance on the part of permanent employees to going to the field explained why the company had been obliged to recruit contract staff. But this decision was also related to the skill imbalance impinging on the composition of the regular labour force. For apart from the large numbers of unqualified personnel still present on the company's rolls, even those possessing technical credentials did so mainly in the obsolete mechanical and electrical trades and not in electronics where the needs were greatest.[23] The intake of contract engineers and technicians with competencies in electronics thus allowed ITI to dispose a skill base better calibrated to the changed technological imperatives.

Before leaving, I asked Sharma how he envisaged the future of the Bangalore plant. His answer minced no words: 'it is waiting time for everybody. All are looking at the real estate value of the plant'. In effect,

[20] In his Republic Day address in January 2007, the head of the Bangalore plant, implicitly acknowledging BSNL's criticisms, exhorted employees to 'rise to the occasion to complete the job (of installing and commissioning CDMA systems) in the stipulated time'.

[21] Ref. GMB/Cors/CDMA-WLL, 14 February 2007.

[22] Contract engineers received a consolidated monthly wage ranging from Rs 12,000-14,000 and technicians, diploma holders for the most part, Rs 6000. Both categories were also beneficiaries of the company medical scheme.

[23] In 2006, 24 per cent of the total workforce possessed at best a high school degree while the proportion of engineering degree and diploma holders was only a couple of points higher. *Source*: ITI Personnel Dept.

ITI's principal assets now were the sprawling tracts of land it owned in the city whose estimated worth was of the order of a staggering Rs 16,700 million. Following the closure in 2002–03 of the small Electronic City plant (EC) located on the outskirts of Bangalore, half the land had already been divested. Several empty buildings standing beyond the perimeter of the main factory walls had also been leased out. As the ITI Revival and Funding Plan which was being drawn up in the summer of 2007 for submission to the government noted, 'real estate could be a significant factor'.[24] Towards this end, the management had identified some 50 acres of surplus land at the Bangalore factory, the sale of which together with the remainder of the EC plant land would enable the company to wipe off a portion of its losses.[25] While the ITI Board had endorsed this proposal, the union had raised strong objections, worried, perhaps not wrongly, that this process of piecemeal asset disposal marked the beginning of the end, the prelude to the shut-down of the plant.

* * * *

Post scriptum: In October 2009, ITI announced that it was inviting bids from Indian and global corporations to establish three joint venture units in Bangalore, Rae Bareli and Naini. They would operate as independent entities with ownership rights being vested not in the hands of the government but the domestic or foreign partner which would be entitled to acquire a maximum shareholding of 74 per cent. In other words, the government had resolved to surrender both its ownership and managerial prerogatives over these three plants, retaining at best a minority stake in them. Thus, nearly a decade after the Public Sector Disinvestment Commission had urged the privatisation of ITI (see chap. five), policy makers had finally decided to implement its recommendations. The chain of events that had first been set in motion with the progressive elimination of ITI's monopoly privileges in 1984 had reached its penultimate stage. All that remained now for the final curtain-call was to find buyers for the three plants.

[24] ITI Revival and Funding Plan.
[25] Ref. ITI/COHR/PL.76, 29 July 2006.

Index